THE COMPLETE AIR FRYER COOKBOOK FOR BEGINNERS

1000+ QUICK & EASY AIR FRYER RECIPES FOR SMART PEOPLE ON A BUDGET. FRY, BAKE, GRILL & ROAST YOUR FAVORITE FOODS

Olivia Chambers

TABLE OF CONTENTS

AIR FRYER FUNCTIONS AND COOKING TIPS

Air Fryers have many perks to offer when it comes to improving quality of life. It helps in maintaining your wellness and fitness.

Versatile Options

Air Fryer allows you to cook a diverse range of foods, be it chicken tenders, mushrooms, crispy fries, fried shrimp, mozzarella sticks, or grilled vegetables. You want to grill, fry, roast, or bake your foods? Air Fryers are there to prepare them in real quick time. A specific ultra-modern range of Air Fryers also allows you to make many recipes in a single cooking session.

Superfast Heating

Unlike the traditional frying method, Air Fryers takes only a few minutes to heat and prepare foods. They are always ready to make meals whenever you crave fried foods. Most Air Fryer models get ready in only 3 minutes to heat up properly, and they can also go as high as 400 degrees F to make you crispy meals.

Natural Food Taste

It's quite common for anyone to worry about their food's ability to delight them with their mouthwatering flavors. When it comes to Air Fryers, things are no different. Air Fryers prepare meals without compromising on their taste profile. As far as the taste is concerned, they can easily be compared with deep-fried foods.

Time Saving

With only 24 hours to complete everyday routine tasks, time has become a genuinely luxury in our fast-paced lifestyle. Air Fryers are designed to save your precious cooking time by serving you crunchy snacks and fried cuisines in a matter of minutes. If you are always on a tight schedule, Air Fryer is no less than a time savior.

Space Saver and Ease of Cleaning

Cleaning after cooking foods is also very easy as they are designed for effortless cleaning. On top of that, they don't take up much of your counter space and require quite less space to store.

Cooking Tips

◆ Vegetables are one of the easiest foods to cook in an Air Fryer. A wide variety of plants can be cooked, be it delicate beans to root vegetables. For the best cooking experience, firstly, soak the vegetables, especially the harder ones, in cold water for 15-20 minutes. Then, dry them using a clean kitchen towel.

◆ Keep in mind that you should always aim to cook your food to the desired doneness because the recipes are flexible, and they are designed for all Air Fryer models. If you feel that the food needs more cooking time, then adjust it and cook for a few more minutes. It is not a thumb rule to stick to recipe time only as certain ingredients can vary in their size and firmness from one country to another.

◆ Roasting with air is a new cooking trend you have to try because you can finally prepare your winter favorites.

◆ You can bake your favorite recipes in your Air Fryer but always check with the machine's manual before using new baking ware with Air Fryer.

◆ When it comes to the cooking time, it changes depending on the particular Air Fryer model, the size of food, food pre-preparation, and so on. For shorter cooking cycles, you should preheat Air Fryer for about 3-4 minutes; otherwise, if you put the ingredients into the cold cooking basket, the cooking time needs to be increased to 3 additional minutes.

◆ Use a good quality oil spray to brush food and cooking basket; it is also helpful for easy cleanup.

BREAKFAST

1. Radish Hash Browns

Preparation Time: 10 minutes
Cooking Time: 13 minutes
Servings: 4

Ingredients:

- 1 lb. radishes, washed and cut off roots
- 1 tbsp olive oil
- 1/2 tsp paprika
- 1/2 tsp onion powder
- 1/2 tsp garlic powder
- 1 medium onion
- 1/4 tsp pepper
- 3/4 tsp sea salt

Directions:

- Slice onion and radishes using a mandolin slicer.
- Add sliced onion and radishes in a large mixing bowl and toss with olive oil.
- Transfer onion and radish slices in air fryer basket and cook at 360 F for 8 minutes Shake basket twice.
- Return onion and radish slices in a mixing bowl and toss with seasonings.
- Again, cook onion and radish slices in air fryer basket for 5 minutes at 400 F. Shake the basket halfway through.
- Serve and enjoy.

2. Vegetable Egg Cups

Preparation Time: 10 minutes
Cooking Time: 20 minutes
Servings: 4

Ingredients:

- 4 eggs
- 1 tbsp cilantro, chopped
- 4 tbsp half and half
- 1 cup cheddar cheese, shredded
- 1 cup vegetables, diced
- Pepper
- Salt

Directions:

- Sprinkle four ramekins with cooking spray and set aside.
- In a mixing bowl, whisk eggs with cilantro, half and half, vegetables, 1/2 cup cheese, pepper, and salt.
- Pour egg mixture into the four ramekins.
- Place ramekins in air fryer basket and cook at 300 F for 12 minutes
- Top with remaining 1/2 cup cheese and cook for 2 minutes more at 400 F.
- Serve and enjoy.

3. Spinach Frittata

Preparation Time: 5 minutes
Cooking Time: 8 minutes
Servings: 1

Ingredients:

- 3 eggs
- 1 cup spinach, chopped
- 1 small onion, minced
- 2 tbsp mozzarella cheese, grated
- Pepper
- Salt

Directions:

- Preheat the air fryer to 350 F. Spray air fryer pan with cooking spray.
- In a bowl, whisk eggs with remaining ingredients until well combined.
- Pour egg mixture into the prepared pan and place pan in the air fryer basket.
- Cook frittata for 8 minutes or until set. Serve and enjoy.

4. Omelet Frittata

Preparation Time: 10 minutes
Cooking Time: 6 minutes
Servings: 2

Ingredients:

- ♦ 3 eggs, lightly beaten
- ♦ 2 tbsp cheddar cheese, shredded
- ♦ 2 tbsp heavy cream
- ♦ 2 mushrooms, sliced
- ♦ 1/4 small onion, chopped
- ♦ 1/4 bell pepper, diced
- ♦ Pepper
- ♦ Salt

Directions:

- In a bowl, whisk eggs with cream, vegetables, pepper, and salt.
- Preheat the air fryer to 400 F.
- Pour egg mixture into the air fryer pan. Place pan in air fryer basket and cook for 5 minutes
- Add shredded cheese on top of the frittata and cook for 1 minute more.
- Serve and enjoy.

5. Cheese Soufflés

Preparation Time: 10 minutes
Cooking Time: 6 minutes
Servings: 8

Ingredients:

- ♦ 6 large eggs, separated
- ♦ 3/4 cup heavy cream
- ♦ 1/4 tsp cayenne pepper
- ♦ 1/2 tsp xanthan gum
- ♦ 1/2 tsp pepper
- ♦ 1/4 tsp cream of tartar
- ♦ 2 tbsp chives, chopped
- ♦ 2 cups cheddar cheese, shredded
- ♦ 1 tsp salt

Directions:

- Preheat the air fryer to 325 F.
- Spray eight ramekins with cooking spray. Set aside.
- In a bowl, whisk together almond flour, cayenne pepper, pepper, salt, and xanthan gum.
- Slowly add heavy cream and mix to combine.

- Whisk in egg yolks, chives, and cheese until well combined.
- In a large bowl, add egg whites and cream of tartar and beat until stiff peaks form.
- Fold egg white mixture into the almond flour mixture until combined.
- Pour mixture into the prepared ramekins. Divide ramekins in batches.
- Place the first batch of ramekins into the air fryer basket.
- Cook soufflé for 20 minutes
- Serve and enjoy.

6. Simple Egg Soufflé

Preparation Time: 5 minutes
Cooking Time: 8 minutes
Servings: 2

Ingredients:

- ♦ 2 eggs
- ♦ 1/4 tsp chili pepper
- ♦ 2 tbsp heavy cream
- ♦ 1/4 tsp pepper
- ♦ 1 tbsp parsley, chopped
- ♦ Salt

Directions:

- In a bowl, whisk eggs with remaining gradients.
- Spray two ramekins with cooking spray.
- Pour egg mixture into the prepared ramekins and place into the air fryer basket.
- Cook soufflé at 390 F for 8 minutes
- Serve and enjoy.

7. Vegetable Egg Soufflé

Preparation Time: 10 minutes
Cooking Time: 20 minutes
Servings: 4

Ingredients:

- ♦ 4 large eggs
- ♦ 1 tsp onion powder
- ♦ 1 tsp garlic powder
- ♦ 1 tsp red pepper, crushed

- 1/2 cup broccoli florets, chopped
- 1/2 cup mushrooms, chopped

Directions:

- Sprinkle four ramekins with cooking spray and set aside.
- In a bowl, whisk eggs with onion powder, garlic powder, and red pepper.
- Add mushrooms and broccoli and stir well.
- Pour egg mixture into the prepared ramekins and place ramekins into the air fryer basket.
- Cook at 350 F for 15 minutes Make sure soufflé is cooked if soufflé is not cooked then cook for 5 minutes more.
- Serve and enjoy.

8. Asparagus Frittata

Preparation Time: 10 minutes
Cooking Time: 10 minutes
Servings: 4

Ingredients:

- 6 eggs
- 3 mushrooms, sliced
- 10 asparagus, chopped
- 1/4 cup half and half
- 2 tsp butter, melted
- 1 cup mozzarella cheese, shredded
- 1 tsp pepper
- 1 tsp salt

Directions:

- Toss mushrooms and asparagus with melted butter and add into the air fryer basket. Cook mushrooms and asparagus at 350 F for 5 minutes Shake basket twice.
- Meanwhile, in a bowl, whisk together eggs, half and half, pepper, and salt. Transfer cook mushrooms and asparagus into the air fryer baking dish. Pour egg mixture over mushrooms and asparagus.
- Place dish in the air fryer and cook at 350 F for 5 minutes or until eggs are set. Slice and serve.

9. Spicy Cauliflower Rice

Preparation Time: 10 minutes
Cooking Time: 22 minutes
Servings: 2

Ingredients:

- 1 cauliflower head, cut into florets
- 1/2 tsp cumin
- 1/2 tsp chili powder
- 6 onion spring, chopped
- 2 jalapenos, chopped
- 4 tbsp olive oil
- 1 zucchini, trimmed and cut into cubes
- 1/2 tsp paprika
- 1/2 tsp garlic powder
- 1/2 tsp cayenne pepper
- 1/2 tsp pepper
- 1/2 tsp salt

Directions:

- Preheat the air fryer to 370 F.
- Add cauliflower florets into the food processor and process until it looks like rice.
- Transfer cauliflower rice into the air fryer baking pan and Drizzle with half oil.
- Place pan in the air fryer and cook for 12 minutes, stir halfway through.
- Heat the remaining oil in a small pan over medium heat.
- Add zucchini and cook for 5-8 minutes
- Add onion and jalapenos and cook for 5 minutes
- Add spices and stir well. Set aside.
- Add cauliflower rice in the zucchini mixture and stir well.
- Serve and enjoy.

10. Broccoli Stuffed Peppers

Preparation Time: 10 minutes
Cooking Time: 40 minutes
Servings: 2

Ingredients:

- 4 eggs

- 1/2 cup cheddar cheese, grated
- 2 bell peppers cut in half and remove seeds
- 1/2 tsp garlic powder
- 1 tsp dried thyme
- 1/4 cup feta cheese, crumbled
- 1/2 cup broccoli, cooked
- 1/4 tsp pepper
- 1/2 tsp salt

Directions:

- Preheat the air fryer to 325 F.
- Stuff feta and broccoli into the bell peppers halved.
- Beat egg in a bowl with seasoning and pour egg mixture into the pepper halved over feta and broccoli.
- Place bell pepper halved into the air fryer basket and cook for 35-40 minutes
- Top with grated cheddar cheese and cook until cheese melted.
- Serve and enjoy.

11. Zucchini Muffins

Preparation Time: 10 minutes
Cooking Time: 20 minutes
Servings: 8

Ingredients:

- 6 eggs
- 4 drops stevia
- 1/4 cup Swerve
- 1/3 cup coconut oil, melted
- 1 cup zucchini, grated
- 3/4 cup coconut flour
- 1/4 tsp ground nutmeg
- 1 tsp ground cinnamon
- 1/2 tsp baking soda

Directions:

- Preheat the air fryer to 325 F.
- Add all ingredients except zucchini in a bowl and mix well.
- Add zucchini and stir well.

- Pour batter into the silicone muffin molds and place into the air fryer basket.
- Cook muffins for 20 minutes
- Serve and enjoy.

12. Jalapeno Breakfast Muffins

Preparation Time: 10 minutes
Cooking Time: 15 minutes
Servings: 8

Ingredients:

- 5 eggs
- 1/3 cup coconut oil, melted
- 2 tsp baking powder
- 3 tbsp erythritol
- 3 tbsp jalapenos, sliced
- 1/4 cup unsweetened coconut milk
- 2/3 cup coconut flour
- 3/4 tsp sea salt

Directions:

- Preheat the air fryer to 325 F.
- In a large bowl, mix together coconut flour, baking powder, erythritol, and sea salt.
- Stir in eggs, jalapenos, coconut milk, and coconut oil until well combined.
- Pour batter into the silicone muffin molds and place into the air fryer basket.
- Cook muffins for 15 minutes
- Serve and enjoy.

13. Zucchini Noodles

Preparation Time: 10 minutes
Cooking Time: 44 minutes
Servings: 3

Ingredients:

- 1 egg
- 1/2 cup parmesan cheese, grated
- 1/2 cup feta cheese, crumbled
- 1 tbsp thyme
- 1 garlic clove, chopped
- 1 onion, chopped
- 2 medium zucchinis, trimmed and spiralized
- 2 tbsp olive oil

- 1 cup mozzarella cheese, grated
- 1/2 tsp pepper
- 1/2 tsp salt

Directions:

- Preheat the air fryer to 350 F.
- Add spiralized zucchini and salt in a colander and set aside for 10 minutes. Wash zucchini noodles and pat dry with a paper towel.
- Heat the oil in a pan over medium heat. Add garlic and onion and sauté for 3-4 minutes
- Add zucchini noodles and cook for 4-5 minutes or until softened.
- Add zucchini mixture into the air fryer baking pan. Add egg, thyme, cheeses. Mix well and season.
- Place pan in the air fryer and cook for 30-35 minutes
- Serve and enjoy.

14. Mushroom Frittata

Preparation Time: 10 minutes
Cooking Time: 13 minutes
Servings: 1

Ingredients:

- 1 cup egg whites
- 1 cup spinach, chopped
- 2 mushrooms, sliced
- 2 tbsp parmesan cheese, grated
- Salt

Directions:

- Sprinkle pan with cooking spray and heat over medium heat. Add mushrooms and sauté for 2-3 minutes Add spinach and cook for 1-2 minutes or until wilted.
- Transfer mushroom spinach mixture into the air fryer pan. Beat egg whites in a mixing bowl until frothy. Season it with a pinch of salt.
- Pour egg white mixture into the spinach and mushroom mixture and sprinkle with parmesan cheese. Place pan in air fryer

basket and cook frittata at 350 F for 8 minutes
- Slice and serve.

15. Egg Muffins

Preparation Time: 10 minutes
Cooking Time: 15 minutes
Servings: 12

Ingredients:

- 9 eggs
- 1/2 cup onion, sliced
- 1 tbsp olive oil
- 8 oz ground sausage
- 1/4 cup coconut milk
- 1/2 tsp oregano
- 1 1/2 cups spinach
- 3/4 cup bell peppers, chopped
- Pepper
- Salt

Directions:

- Preheat the air fryer to 325 F.
- Add ground sausage in a pan and sauté over medium heat for 5 minutes
- Add olive oil, oregano, bell pepper, and onion and sauté until onion is translucent.
- Put spinach to the pan and cook for 30 seconds.
- Remove pan from heat and set aside.
- In a mixing bowl, whisk together eggs, coconut milk, pepper, and salt until well beaten.
- Add sausage and vegetable mixture into the egg mixture and mix well.
- Pour egg mixture into the silicone muffin molds and place into the air fryer basket. (Cook in batches)
- Cook muffins for 15 minutes
- Serve and enjoy.

16. Blueberry Breakfast Cobbler

Preparation Time: 5 minutes
Cooking Time: 15 minutes
Servings: 4

Ingredients:

- 1/3 cup whole-wheat pastry flour
- ¾ teaspoon baking powder
- Dash sea salt
- ½ cup 2% milk
- 2 tablespoons pure maple syrup
- ½ teaspoon vanilla extract
- Cooking oil spray
- ½ cup fresh blueberries
- ¼ cup Granola, or plain store-bought granola

Directions:

- In a medium bowl, whisk the flour, baking powder, and salt. Add the milk, maple syrup, and vanilla and gently whisk, just until thoroughly combined.

- Preheat the unit by selecting BAKE, setting the temperature to 350°F, and setting the time to 3 minutes Select START/STOP to start.

- Spray a 6-by-2-inch round baking pan with cooking oil and pour the batter into the pan. Top evenly with the blueberries and granola.

- Once the unit is preheated, place the pan into the basket.

- Select BAKE, set the temperature to 350°F, and set the time to 15 minutes Select START/STOP to begin.

- When the cooking is complete, the cobbler should be nicely browned and a knife inserted into the middle should come out clean. Enjoy plain or topped with a little vanilla yogurt.

17. Granola

Preparation Time: 5 minutes
Cooking Time: 40 minutes
Servings: 2

Ingredients:

- 1 cup rolled oats
- 3 tablespoons pure maple syrup
- 1 tablespoon sugar
- 1 tablespoon neutral-flavored oil, such as refined coconut, sunflower, or safflower

- ¼ teaspoon sea salt
- ¼ teaspoon ground cinnamon
- ¼ teaspoon vanilla extract

Directions:

- Insert the crisper plate into the basket and the basket into the unit. Preheat the unit by selecting BAKE, setting the temperature to 250°F, and setting the time to 3 minutes Select START/STOP to start.

- In a medium bowl, stir together the oats, maple syrup, sugar, oil, salt, cinnamon, and vanilla until thoroughly combined. Transfer the granola to a 6-by-2-inch round baking pan.

- Once the unit is preheated, place the pan into the basket.

- Select BAKE, set the temperature to 250°F and set the time to 40 minutes Select START/STOP to begin. After 10 minutes, stir the granola well. Resume cooking, stirring the granola every 10 minutes, for a total of 40 minutes, or until the granola is lightly browned and mostly dry.

- Place the granola on a plate to cool, when the cooking is complete. It will become crisp as it cools. Store the completely cooled granola in an airtight container in a cool, dry place for 1 to 2 weeks.

Variation Tip: You can change this recipe to include some of your favorite granola ingredients, such as dried fruits, different types of nuts, and even goodies such as chocolate chips. Stir them in after the granola is done, but before it's completely cool.

18. Mixed Berry Muffins

Preparation Time: 15 minutes
Cooking Time: 15 minutes
Servings: 8

Ingredients:

- 1 1/3 cups plus 1 tablespoon all-purpose flour, divided
- ¼ cup granulated sugar
- 2 tablespoons light brown sugar
- 2 teaspoons baking powder

- ♦ 2 eggs
- ♦ 2/3 Cup whole milk
- ♦ 1/3 Cup safflower oil
- ♦ 1 cup mixed fresh berries

Directions:

- In a medium bowl, stir together 1 1/3 cups of flour, the granulated sugar, brown sugar, and baking powder until mixed well.

- In a small bowl, whisk the eggs, milk, and oil until combined. Mix the egg mixture into the dry ingredients just until combined.

- In another small bowl, toss the mixed berries with the left over 1 tablespoon of flour until coated. Gently stir the berries into the batter.

- Two times the 16 foil muffin cups to make 8 cups.

- Insert the crisper plate into the basket and the basket into the unit. Preheat the unit by selecting BAKE, setting the temperature to 315°F, and setting the time to 3 minutes Select START/STOP to start.

- Once the unit is preheated, place 4 cups into the basket and fill each three-quarter full with the batter.

- Select BAKE, set the temperature to 315°F, and set the time for 17 minutes Select START/STOP to begin.

- After about 12 minutes, check the muffins. If they spring back when lightly touched with your finger, they are done. If not, resume cooking. When the cooking is done, transfer the muffins to a wire rack to cool. Repeat steps 6, 7, and 8 with the remaining muffin cups and batter. Let the muffins cool for 10 minutes before serving.

19. Homemade Strawberry Breakfast Tarts

Preparation Time: 15 minutes
Cooking Time: 20 minutes
Servings: 6

Ingredients:

- ♦ 2 refrigerated piecrusts
- ♦ ½ cup strawberry preserves
- ♦ 1 teaspoon cornstarch
- ♦ Cooking oil spray
- ♦ ½ cup low-fat vanilla yogurt
- ♦ 1-ounce cream cheese, at room temperature
- ♦ 3 tablespoons confectioners' sugar
- ♦ Rainbow sprinkles, for decorating

Directions:

- Place the piecrusts on a flat surface. Cut each piecrust into 3 rectangles using a knife or pizza cutter, for 6 in total. Discard any unused dough from the piecrust edges.

- In a small bowl, stir together the preserves and cornstarch. Mix well, ensuring there are no lumps of cornstarch remaining.

- Scoop 1 tablespoon of the strawberry mixture onto the top half of each piece of piecrust.

- Fold the bottom of each piece up to enclose the filling. Press along the edges of each tart to seal using the back of a fork.

- Insert the crisper plate into the basket and the basket into the unit. Preheat the unit by selecting bake, setting the temperature to 375°F, and setting the time to 3 minutes Select start/stop to start.

- Once the unit is preheated, spray the crisper plate with cooking oil. Work in batches, spray the breakfast tarts with cooking oil and place them into the basket in a single layer. Do not stack the tarts.

- Select bake, set the temperature to 375°F, and set the time to 10 minutes Select start/stop to begin.

- When the cooking is complete, the tarts should be light golden brown. Let the breakfast tarts cool fully before removing them from the basket.

- Repeat steps 5, 6, 7, and 8 for the remaining breakfast tarts.

- In a small bowl, stir together the yogurt, cream cheese, and confectioners' sugar. Spread the breakfast tarts with the frosting and top with sprinkles.

20. Everything Bagels

Preparation Time: 10 minutes
Cooking Time: 10 minutes
Servings: 2

Ingredients:

- ½ cup self-rising flour, plus more for dusting
- ½ cup plain Greek yogurt
- 1 egg
- 1 tablespoon water
- 4 teaspoons everything bagel spice mix
- Cooking oil spray
- 1 tablespoon butter, melted

Directions:

- In a large bowl, using a wooden spoon, stir together the flour and yogurt until a tacky dough forms. Transfer the dough to a lightly floured work surface and roll the dough into a ball.

- Cut the dough into 2 pieces and roll each piece into a log. Form each log into a bagel shape, pinching the ends together.

- In a small bowl, whisk the egg and water. Brush the egg wash on the bagels.

- Sprinkle 2 teaspoons of the spice mix on each bagel and gently press it into the dough.

- Insert the crisper plate into the basket and the basket into the unit. Preheat the unit by selecting bake, setting the temperature to 330°F, and setting the time to 3 minutes Select start/stop to begin.

- Once the unit is preheated, spray the crisper plate with cooking spray. Drizzle with the bagels with the butter and place them into the basket.

- Select BAKE, set the temperature to 330°F, and set the time to 10 minutes Select START/STOP to begin.

- When the cooking is complete, the bagels should be lightly golden on the outside. Serve warm.

21. Easy Maple-Glazed Doughnuts

Preparation Time: 10 minutes
Cooking Time: 14 minutes
Servings: 8

Ingredients:

- 1 (8-count) can jumbo flaky refrigerator biscuits
- Cooking oil spray
- ½ cup light brown sugar
- ¼ cup butter
- 3 tablespoons milk
- 2 cups confectioners' sugar, plus more for dusting (optional)
- 2 teaspoons pure maple syrup

Directions:

- Insert the crisper plate into the basket and the basket into the unit. Preheat the unit by selecting air fry, setting the temperature to 350°F, and setting the time to 3 minutes Select start/stop to begin.

- Remove the biscuits from the tube and cut out the center of each biscuit with a small, round cookie cutter.

- Once the unit is preheated, spray the crisper plate with cooking oil. Work it in batches, place 4 doughnuts into the basket.

- Select air fry, set the temperature to 350°F, and set the time to 5 minutes Select start/stop to begin.

- When the cooking is complete, place the doughnuts on a plate. Repeat steps 3 and 4 with the remaining doughnuts.

- In a small saucepan over medium heat, combine the brown sugar, butter, and milk. Heat until the butter is melted and the sugar is dissolved, about 4 minutes

- Remove the pan from the heat and whisk in the confectioners' sugar and maple syrup until smooth.

- Dip the slightly cooled doughnuts into the maple glaze. Place them on a wire rack and dust with confectioners' sugar (if using). Let rest just until the glaze sets. Enjoy the doughnuts warm.

22. Chocolate-Filled Doughnut Holes

Preparation Time: 10 minutes
Cooking Time: 30 minutes

Servings: 12

Ingredients:

- 1 (8-count) can refrigerated biscuits
- Cooking oil spray
- 48 semisweet chocolate chips
- 3 tablespoons melted unsalted butter
- ¼ cup confectioners' sugar

Directions:

- Separate the biscuits and cut each biscuit into thirds, for 24 pieces.

- Flatten each biscuit piece slightly and put 2 chocolate chips in the center. Wrap the dough around the chocolate and seal the edges well.

- Insert the crisper plate into the basket and the basket into the unit. Preheat the unit by selecting air fry, setting the temperature to 330°F, and setting the time to 3 minutes Select start/stop to begin.

- Once the unit is preheated, spray the crisper plate with cooking oil. Brush each doughnut hole with a bit of the butter and place it into the basket. Select air fry, set the temperature to 330°F, and set the time between 8 and 12 minutes Select start/stop to begin.

- The doughnuts are done when they are golden brown. When the cooking is complete, place the doughnut holes on a plate and dust with the confectioners' sugar. Serve warm.

23. Delicious Original Hash Browns

Preparation Time: 15 minutes
Cooking Time: 20 minutes
Servings: 4

Ingredients:

- 4 russet potatoes, peeled
- 1 teaspoon paprika
- Salt
- Freshly ground black pepper
- Cooking oil spray

Directions:

- Using a box grater or food processor, shred the potatoes. If your grater has different hole sizes, use the largest holes.

- Place the shredded potatoes in a large bowl of cold water. Let it sit for 5 minutes (Cold water helps remove excess starch from the potatoes.) Stir them to help dissolve the starch.

- Insert the crisper plate into the basket and the basket into the unit. Preheat the unit by selecting air fry, setting the temperature to 360°F, and setting the time to 3 minutes Select start/stop to begin.

- Dry out the potatoes and pat them with paper towels until the potatoes are completely dry. Season the potatoes with the paprika, salt, and pepper.

- Once the unit is preheated, spray the crisper plate with cooking oil. Spray the potatoes with the cooking oil and place them into the basket.

- Select air fry, set the temperature to 360°F, and set the time to 20 minutes Select start/stop to begin.

- After 5 minutes, remove the basket and shake the potatoes. Reinsert the basket to resume cooking. Continue shaking the basket every 5 minutes (a total of 4 times) until the potatoes are done.

- When the cooking is complete, remove the hash browns from the basket and serve warm.

24. Waffles and Chicken

Preparation Time: 15 minutes
Cooking Time: 30 minutes
Servings: 4

Ingredients:

- 8 whole chicken wings
- 1 teaspoon garlic powder
- Chicken seasoning, for preparing the chicken
- Freshly ground black pepper
- ½ cup all-purpose flour
- Cooking oil spray
- 8 frozen waffles
- Pure maple syrup, for serving (optional)

Directions:

- In a medium bowl, combine the chicken and garlic powder and season with chicken seasoning and pepper. Toss to coat.

- Transfer the chicken to a re-sealable plastic bag and add the flour. Seal the bag and shake it to coat the chicken thoroughly.

- Insert the crisper plate into the basket and the basket into the unit. Preheat the unit by selecting AIR FRY, setting the temperature to 400°F, and setting the time to 3 minutes Select START/STOP to begin.

- Once the unit is preheated, spray the crisper plate with cooking oil. Using tongs, transfer the chicken from the bag to the basket. It is okay to stack the chicken wings on top of each other. Spray them with cooking oil.

- Select air fry, set the temperature to 400°F, and set the time to 20 minutes Select start/stop to begin.

- After 5 minutes, remove the basket and shake the wings. Reinsert the basket to resume cooking. Remove and shake the basket every 5 minutes until the chicken is fully cooked.

- When the cooking is complete, remove the cooked chicken from the basket cover to keep warm.

- Rinse the basket and crisper plate with warm water. Insert them back into the unit.

- Select air fry, set the temperature to 360°F, and set the time to 3 minutes Select start/stop to begin.

- Once the unit is preheated, spray the crisper plate with cooking spray. Work in batches, place the frozen waffles into the basket. Do not stack them. Spray the waffles with cooking oil.

- Select air fry, set the temperature to 360°F, and set the time to 6 minutes Select start/stop to begin.

- Repeat steps 10 and 11 with the remaining waffles when the cooking is complete.

- Serve the waffles with the chicken and a touch of maple syrup, if desired.

Preparation Time: 10 minutes
Cooking Time: 20 minutes
Servings: 4

Ingredients:

- 1/3 Sheet frozen puff pastry, thawed
- Cooking oil spray
- ½ cup shredded Cheddar cheese
- 2 eggs
- ¼ teaspoon salt, divided
- 1 teaspoon minced fresh parsley (optional)

Directions:

- Insert the crisper plate into the basket and the basket into the unit. Preheat the unit by selecting bake, setting the temperature to 390°F, and setting the time to 3 minutes Select start/stop to begin.

- Lay the puff pastry sheet on a piece of parchment paper and cut it in half.

- Once the unit is preheated, spray the crisper plate with cooking oil. Transfer the 2 squares of pastry to the basket, keeping them on the parchment paper.

- Select bake, set the temperature to 390°F, and set the time to 20 minutes Select start/stop to begin.

- After 10 minutes, use a metal spoon to press down the center of each pastry square to make a well. Divide the cheese equally between the baked pastries. Carefully crack an egg on top of the cheese, and sprinkle each with the salt. Resume cooking for 7 to 10 minutes

- When the cooking is complete, the eggs will be cooked through. Sprinkle each with parsley (if using) and serve.

26. Early Morning Steak and Eggs

Preparation Time: 10 minutes
Cooking Time: 30 minutes
Servings: 4

Ingredients:

- Cooking oil spray

- 4 (4-ounce) New York strip steaks
- 1 teaspoon granulated garlic, divided
- 1 teaspoon salt, divided
- 1 teaspoon freshly ground black pepper, divided
- 4 eggs
- ½ teaspoon paprika

Directions:

- Insert the crisper plate into the basket and the basket into the unit. Preheat the unit by selecting air fry, setting the temperature to 360°F, and setting the time to 3 minutes Select start/stop to begin.

- Once the unit is preheated, spray the crisper plate with cooking oil. Place 2 steaks into the basket do not oil or season them at this time.

- Select air fry, set the temperature to 360°F, and set the time to 9 minutes Select start/stop to begin.

- After 5 minutes, open the unit and flip the steaks. Sprinkle each with ¼ teaspoon of granulated garlic, ¼ teaspoon of salt, and ¼ teaspoon of pepper. Resume cooking until the steaks register at least 145°F on a food thermometer.

- When the cooking is complete, transfer the steaks to a plate and tent with aluminum foil to keep warm. Repeat steps 2, 3, and 4 with the remaining steaks.

- Spray 4 ramekins with olive oil. Crack 1 egg into each ramekin. Sprinkle the eggs with the paprika and remaining ½ teaspoon each of salt and pepper. Work in batches, place 2 ramekins into the basket.

- Select BAKE, set the temperature to 330°F, and set the time to 5 minutes Select start/stop to begin. When the cooking is complete and the eggs are cooked to 160°F, remove the ramekins and repeat step 7 with the remaining 2 ramekins.

- Serve the eggs with the steaks.

27. Breakfast Potatoes

Preparation Time: 10 minutes

Cooking Time: 20 minutes
Serving: 6

Ingredients:

- 1½ teaspoons olive oil, divided, plus more for misting
- 4 large potatoes, skins on, cut into cubes
- 2 teaspoons seasoned salt, divided
- 1 teaspoon minced garlic, divided
- 2 large green or red bell peppers, cut into 1-inch chunks
- ½ onion, diced

Directions:

- Lightly mist the fryer basket with olive oil.

- In a medium bowl, toss the potatoes with ½ teaspoon of olive oil. Sprinkle with 1 teaspoon of seasoned salt and ½ teaspoon of minced garlic. Stir to coat.

- Place the seasoned potatoes in the fryer basket in a single layer.

- Cook for 5 minutes Shake the basket and cook for another 5 minutes

- Meanwhile, in a medium bowl, toss the bell peppers and onion with the remaining ½ teaspoon of olive oil.

- Sprinkle the peppers and onions with the remaining 1 teaspoon of seasoned salt and ½ teaspoon of minced garlic. Stir to coat.

- Add the seasoned peppers and onions to the fryer basket with the potatoes.

- Cook for 5 minutes Shake the basket and cook for an additional 5 minutes

28. Baked Potato Breakfast Boats

Preparation Time: 10 minutes
Cooking Time: 20 minutes
Serving: 4

Ingredients:

- 2 large russet potatoes, scrubbed
- Olive oil
- Salt
- Freshly ground black pepper
- 4 eggs

- ◆ 2 tablespoons chopped, cooked bacon
- ◆ 1 cup shredded cheddar cheese

Directions:

- Poke holes in the potatoes with a fork and microwave on full power for 5 minutes. Turn potatoes over and cook an additional 3 to 5 minutes, or until the potatoes are fork tender.

- Cut the potatoes in half lengthwise and use a spoon to scoop out the inside of the potato. Be careful to leave a layer of potato so that it makes a sturdy "boat. "Lightly spray the fryer basket with olive oil. Spray the skin side of the potatoes with oil and sprinkle with salt and pepper to taste.

- Place the potato skins in the fryer basket skin side down. Crack one egg into each potato skin.

- Sprinkle ½ tablespoon of bacon pieces and ¼ cup of shredded cheese on top of each egg. Sprinkle with salt and pepper to taste.

- Air fry until the yolk is slightly runny, 5 to 6 minutes, or until the yolk is fully cooked, 7 to 10 minutes

29. Greek Frittata

Preparation Time: 10 minutes
Cooking Time: 20 minutes
Serving: 4

Ingredients:

- ◆ Olive oil
- ◆ 5 eggs
- ◆ ¼ teaspoon salt
- ◆ 1/8Teaspoon freshly ground black pepper
- ◆ 1 cup baby spinach leaves, shredded
- ◆ ½ cup halved grape tomatoes
- ◆ ½ cup crumbled feta cheese

Directions:

- Spray a small round air fryer-friendly pan with olive oil.

- In a medium bowl, whisk together eggs, salt, and pepper and whisk to combine.

- Add the spinach and stir to combine.

- Pour ½ cup of the egg mixture into the pan.

- Sprinkle ¼ cup of the tomatoes and ¼ cup of the feta on top of the egg mixture.

- Cover the pan with aluminum foil and secure it around the edges.

- Place the pan carefully into the fryer basket.

- Air fry for 12 minutes

- Remove the foil from the pan and cook until the eggs are set, 5 to 7 minutes

- Remove the frittata from the pan and place on a serving platter. Repeat with the remaining ingredients.

30. Mini Shrimp Frittata

Preparation Time: 15 minutes
Cooking Time: 20 minutes
Serving: 4

Ingredients:

- ◆ 1 teaspoon olive oil, plus more for spraying
- ◆ ½ small red bell pepper, finely diced
- ◆ 1 teaspoon minced garlic
- ◆ 1 (4-ounce) can of tiny shrimp, Dry out
- ◆ Salt
- ◆ Freshly ground black pepper
- ◆ 4 eggs, beaten
- ◆ 4 teaspoons ricotta cheese

Directions:

- Spray four ramekins with olive oil. In a medium skillet over medium-low heat, heat 1 teaspoon of olive oil. Add the bell pepper and garlic and sauté until the pepper is soft, about 5 minutes

- Add the shrimp, season with salt and pepper, and cook until warm, 1 to 2 minutes Remove from the heat.

- Add the eggs and stir to combine. Pour one quarter of the mixture into each ramekin.

- Place 2 ramekins in the fryer basket and cook for 6 minutes. Remove the fryer basket from the air fryer and stir the mixture in each ramekin. Top each frittata with 1 teaspoon of ricotta cheese. Return the fryer basket to the air fryer and cook until eggs are set and the top is lightly browned, 4 to 5 minutes

- Repeat with the remaining two ramekins.

31. Spinach and Mushroom Mini Quiche

Preparation Time: 10 minutes
Cooking Time: 15 minutes
Serving: 4

Ingredients:

- 1 teaspoon olive oil, plus more for spraying
- 1 cup coarsely chopped mushrooms
- 1 cup fresh baby spinach, shredded
- 4 eggs, beaten
- ½ cup shredded Cheddar cheese
- ½ cup shredded mozzarella cheese
- ¼ teaspoon salt
- ¼ teaspoon black pepper

Directions:

- Spray 4 silicone baking cups with olive oil and set aside. In a medium sauté pan over medium heat, warm 1 teaspoon of olive oil. Add the mushrooms and sauté until soft, 3 to 4 minutes
- Add the spinach and cook until wilted, 1 to 2 minutes Set aside.
- In a medium bowl, whisk together the eggs, Cheddar cheese, mozzarella cheese, salt, and pepper. Gently fold the mushrooms and spinach into the egg mixture.
- Pour ¼ of the mixture into each silicone baking cup. Place the baking cups into the fryer basket and air fry for 5 minutes Stir the mixture in each ramekin slightly and air fry until the egg has set, an additional 3 to 5 minutes

32. Italian Egg Cups

Preparation Time: 5 minutes
Cooking Time: 10 minutes
Serving: 4

Ingredients:

- Olive Oil
- 1 cup marinara sauce
- 4 eggs
- 4 tablespoons shredded mozzarella cheese
- 4 teaspoons grated Parmesan cheese
- Salt
- Freshly ground black pepper
- Chopped fresh basil, for garnish

Directions:

- Lightly spray 4 individual ramekins with olive oil.
- Pour ¼ cup of marinara sauce into each ramekin.
- Crack one egg into each ramekin on top of the marinara sauce.
- Sprinkle 1 tablespoon of mozzarella and 1 tablespoon of Parmesan on top of each egg. Season it with salt and pepper.
- Cover each ramekin with aluminum foil. Place two of the ramekins in the fryer basket.
- Air fry for 5 minutes and remove the aluminum foil. Air fry until the top is lightly browned and the egg white is cooked, another 2 to 4 minutes If you prefer the yolk to be firmer, cook for 3 to 5 more minutes
- Repeat with the remaining two ramekins. Garnish with basil and serve.

33. Mexican Breakfast Pepper Rings

Preparation Time: 5 minutes
Cooking Time: 10 minutes
Serving: 4

Ingredients:

- Olive oil
- 1 large red, yellow, or orange bell pepper, cut into four ¾-inch rings
- 4 eggs
- Salt
- Freshly ground black pepper
- 2 teaspoons salsa

Directions:

- Lightly spray a small round air fryer–friendly pan with olive oil.
- Place 2 bell pepper rings on the pan. Crack one egg into each bell pepper ring. Season it with salt and black pepper.

- Spoon ½ teaspoon of salsa on top of each egg. Place the pan in the fryer basket. Air fry until the yolk is slightly runny, 5 to 6 minutes or until the yolk is fully cooked, 8 to 10 minutes

- Repeat with the remaining 2 pepper rings. Serve hot.

- Pair it With: Turkey sausage or turkey bacon make this a heartier morning meal.

- Air Fry like A Pro: Use a silicone spatula to easily move the rings from the pan to your plate.

34. Cajun Breakfast Muffins

Preparation Time: 10 minutes
Cooking Time: 10 minutes
Serving: 6

Ingredients:

- Olive oil
- 4 eggs, beaten
- 2¼ cups frozen hash browns, thawed
- 1 cup diced ham
- ½ cup shredded Cheddar cheese
- ½ teaspoon Cajun seasoning

Directions:

- Lightly spray 12 silicone muffin cups with olive oil.

- In a medium bowl, mix together the eggs, hash browns, ham, Cheddar cheese, and Cajun seasoning in a medium bowl.

- Spoon a heaping 1½ tablespoons of hash brown mixture into each muffin cup.

- Place the muffin cups in the fryer basket.

- Air fry until the muffins are golden brown on top and the center has set up, 8 to 10 minutes

- Make It Even Lower Calorie: Reduce or eliminate the cheese.

35. Hearty Blueberry Oatmeal

Preparation Time: 10 minutes
Cooking Time: 25 minutes
Serving: 6

Ingredients:

- 1½ cups quick oats
- 1¼ teaspoons ground cinnamon, divided
- ½ teaspoon baking powder
- Pinch salt
- 1 cup unsweetened vanilla almond milk
- ¼ cup honey
- 1 teaspoon vanilla extract
- 1 egg, beaten
- 2 cups blueberries
- Olive oil
- 1½ teaspoons sugar, divided
- 6 tablespoons low-fat whipped topping (optional)

Directions:

- In a large bowl, mix together the oats, 1 teaspoon of cinnamon, baking powder, and salt.

- In a medium bowl, whisk together the almond milk, honey, vanilla and egg.

- Pour the liquid ingredients into the oats mixture and stir to combine. Fold in the blueberries.

- Lightly spray a round air fryer–friendly pan with oil.

- Add half the blueberry mixture to the pan.

- Sprinkle 1/8 teaspoon of cinnamon and ½ teaspoon sugar over the top.

- Cover the pan with aluminum foil and place gently in the fryer basket. Air fry for 20 minutes remove the foil and air fry for an additional 5 minutes Transfer the mixture to a shallow bowl.

- Repeat with the remaining blueberry mixture, ½ teaspoon of sugar, and 1/8 teaspoon of cinnamon.

- To serve, spoon into bowls and top with whipped topping.

36. Spinach Egg Breakfast

Preparation Time: 10 Minutes
Cooking Time: 20 Minutes
Servings: 4

Ingredients:

- 3 eggs
- 1/4 cup coconut milk
- 1/4 cup parmesan cheese, grated
- 4 oz spinach, chopped
- 3 oz cottage cheese

Directions:

- Preheat the air fryer to 350 F.
- Add eggs, milk, half parmesan cheese, and cottage cheese in a bowl and whisk well. Add spinach and stir well.
- Pour mixture into the air fryer baking dish.
- Sprinkle remaining half parmesan cheese on top.
- Put it in the air fryer then cook for 20 minutes.
- Serve and enjoy.

37. Vegetable Quiche

Preparation Time: 10 Minutes
Cooking Time: 24 Minutes
Servings: 6

Ingredients:

- 8 eggs
- 1 cup of coconut milk
- 1 cup tomatoes, chopped
- 1 cup zucchini, chopped
- 1 tbsp butter
- 1 onion, chopped
- 1 cup Parmesan cheese, grated
- 1/2 tsp pepper
- 1 tsp salt

Directions:

- Preheat the air fryer to 370 F.
- Thaw butter in a pan then add onion and sauté until onion lightly brown.
- Add tomatoes and zucchini to the pan and sauté for 4-5 minutes.
- Transfer cooked vegetables into the air fryer baking dish.

- Beat eggs with cheese, milk, pepper, and salt in a bowl.
- Pour egg mixture over vegetables in a baking dish.
- Put it in the air fryer then cook for 24 minutes or until eggs are set.
- Slice and serve.

38. Breakfast Egg Tomato

Preparation Time: 10 Minutes
Cooking Time: 24 Minutes
Servings: 2

Ingredients:

- 2 eggs
- 2 large fresh tomatoes
- 1 tsp fresh parsley
- Pepper
- Salt

Directions:

- Preheat the air fryer to 325 F.
- Cut off the top of a tomato and spoon out the tomato innards.
- Break the egg in each tomato and place it in the air fryer basket and cook for 24 minutes.
- Season with parsley, pepper, and salt.
- Serve and enjoy.

39. Mushroom Leek Frittata

Preparation Time: 10 Minutes
Cooking Time: 32 Minutes
Servings: 4

Ingredients:

- 6 eggs
- 6 oz mushrooms, sliced
- 1 cup leeks, sliced
- Salt

Directions:

- Preheat the air fryer to 325 F.
- Heat another pan over medium heat. Spray pan with cooking spray.

- Add mushrooms, leeks, and salt in a pan sauté for 6 minutes.
- Break eggs in a bowl and whisk well.
- Transfer sautéed mushroom and leek mixture into the prepared baking dish.
- Pour egg over mushroom mixture.
- Put it in the air fryer then cook for 32 minutes.
- Serve and enjoy.

40. Perfect Breakfast Frittata

Preparation Time: 10 Minutes
Cooking Time: 32 Minutes
Servings: 2

Ingredients:

- 3 eggs
- 2 tbsp parmesan cheese, grated
- 2 tbsp sour cream
- 1/2 cup bell pepper, chopped
- 1/4 cup onion, chopped
- 1/2 tsp pepper
- 1/2 tsp salt

Directions:

- Add eggs in a mixing bowl and whisk with the remaining ingredients.
- Spray air fryer baking dish with cooking spray.
- Pour egg mixture into the prepared dish and place it in the air fryer and cook at 350 F for 5 minutes.
- Serve and enjoy.

41. Indian Cauliflower

Preparation Time: 10 Minutes
Cooking Time: 20 Minutes
Servings: 2

Ingredients:

- 3 cups cauliflower florets
- 2 tbsp water
- 2 tsp fresh lemon juice
- ½ tbsp ginger paste
- 1 tsp chili powder

- ¼ tsp turmeric
- ½ cup vegetable stock
- Salt and Pepper

Directions:

- Add all fixings into the air fryer baking dish and mix well.
- Put it in the air fryer then cook at 400 F for 10 minutes.
- Stir well and cook at 360 F for 10 minutes more.
- Stir well and serve.

42. Zucchini Salad

Preparation Time: 10 Minutes
Cooking Time: 25 Minutes
Servings: 4

Ingredients:

- 1 lb. zucchini, cut into slices
- 2 tbsp tomato paste
- ½ tbsp tarragon, chopped
- 1 yellow squash, diced
- ½ lb. carrots, peeled and diced
- 1 tbsp olive oil
- Pepper
- Salt

Directions:

- In air fryer baking dish mix together zucchini, tomato paste, tarragon, squash, carrots, pepper, and salt. Drizzle with olive oil.
- Put it in the air fryer then cook at 400 F for 25 minutes. Stir halfway through.
- Serve and enjoy.

43. Cinnamon Buns

Preparation Time: 10 Minutes
Cooking Time: 10 Minutes
Servings: 2

Ingredients:

- 8 oz. container crescent rolls, refrigerated
- 1 tbsp. ground cinnamon
- 2 oz. raisins

- 1/3 cup butter
- 2 tbsp. sugar, granulated
- 1/3 cup pecans, chopped
- Cooking spray (olive oil)
- Maple syrup – 2 tbsp.
- 1/3 cup brown sugar

Directions:

- In a saucepan, dissolve the butter completely. Transfer to a dish and blend the maple syrup and brown sugar.
- Layer one 8-inch pan with the olive oil spray.
- Distribute the sugar into the pan and empty the raisins and pecans inside, stirring to incorporate.
- In a glass dish, whisk the sugar and ground cinnamon.
- Open the can of crescent rolls and place on a cutting board.
- Slice the entire log of dough into eight individual pieces.
- Cover the top and bottom of the dough pieces in cinnamon and sugar, and transfer the pan to the air fryer.
- Adjust the settings to air crisp at 345° F for 5 minutes.
- Turn over the individual buns and steam for another 5 minutes.
- Take the pan out and move the buns to a serving plate.
- Drizzle the remaining sugar liquid on the buns and serve immediately.

44. Egg Cheddar Muffins

Preparation Time: 10 Minutes
Cooking Time: 15 Minutes
Servings: 4

Ingredients:

- 8 large eggs
- 2 medium carrots, peeled and shredded
- 1 small orange bell pepper, deseeded and diced
- ½ cup of frozen corn
- ½ cup frozen peas
- Salt and black pepper to taste
- ¼ cup grated cheddar cheese

Directions:

- Insert the drip pan at the bottom rack of the device and preheat the air fryer at Bake mode at 350 F for 3 to 4 minutes.
- Open the eggs into a bowl then whisk in the carrots, bell pepper, corn, peas, salt, black pepper, and half of the cheddar cheese.
- Lightly grease 6 muffin cups with some olive oil and fill in the egg mixture, two-thirds way up. Top with the remaining cheddar cheese.
- Open the oven and fit in the cooking tray on the middle rack. Place 3 muffin cups on the tray and close the oven. Set the timer for 15 minutes and cook until the timer reads to the end.
- Open the lid and check for doneness using a toothpick. If undone, cook further for 5 minutes.
- Remove the muffins cups and cook the second batch.
- Serve the egg muffins warm.

45. French toast Sticks with Sugar and Berries

Preparation Time: 10 Minutes
Cooking Time: 10 Minutes
Servings: 4

Ingredients:

- 4 (2-inch thick) bread slices
- 2 large eggs
- ¼ cup whole milk
- ¼ cup brown sugar
- 1 tbsp maple syrup
- 1 tsp cinnamon powder
- A pinch nutmeg powders
- 2 pinches icing sugar for topping
- Fresh blueberries and raspberries for topping

Directions:

- Insert the drip pan at the bottom rack of the device and preheat the air fryer at Air Fryer mode at 350 F for 3 to 4 minutes.

- Cut each bread slice into 4 long strips and set aside.

- Open the eggs into a bowl then whisk in the milk, maple syrup, cinnamon powder, and nutmeg powder.

- Place the cooking tray to your side. Working in batches, dip 7 to 8 bread strips into the egg mixture and arrange widthwise on the tray.

- Open the oven and fit in the cooking tray on the middle rack. Set the timer for 10 minutes, then cook until the timer reads to the end.

- Open the oven, remove the tray and check the toasts, which should not be wet but crispy and sweet.

- Transfer to serving plates and make the remaining toasts.

- To serve, sprinkle with the icing sugar and enjoy warm with the berries.

46. Tomato Mushroom Frittata

Preparation Time: 15 Minutes
Cooking Time: 15 Minutes
Servings: 4

Ingredients:

- 1 cup egg white
- 2 tbsp whole milk
- ¼ cup sliced tomato
- ¼ cup sliced mushrooms
- 2 tbsp chopped fresh chives
- Salt and black pepper to taste

Directions:

- Insert the drip pan at the bottom rack of the device and preheat the air fryer at Bake mode 320 F for 3 to 4 minutes.

- Lightly grease a 6-inch casserole dish with olive oil, add all the ingredients, and whisk until well distributed.

- Fit the cooking tray on the middle rack of the oven and place the dish on top.

- Close the oven, set the timer for 15 minutes, and bake until the frittata set.

- Remove from the oven, allow cooling for 2 to 3 minutes, and serve the frittata.

47. Potato and Carrot Hash Browns

Preparation Time: 30 Minutes
Cooking Time: 21 Minutes
Servings: 4

Ingredients:

- 4 large potatoes, peeled, finely grated, and steamed
- 1 large carrot, peeled and finely grated
- 2 tbsp corn flour
- Salt and black pepper to taste
- 1 tsp garlic powder
- 1 tsp onion powder
- 2 tsp red chili flakes
- 2 tsp olive oil, divided

Directions:

- In a bowl, mix all the fixings except the olive oil until well combined.

- Oil in the inner part of a 6-inch glass casserole dish with 1 teaspoon of olive oil and spread in the potato mixture. Use a spoon to level the top evenly.

- Refrigerate the mixture for 20 minutes or until firm.

- After 20 minutes, insert the drip pan at the bottom rack of the device and preheat the air fryer at Air Fryer mode at 350 F for 3 to 4 minutes.

- Remove from the dish from the refrigerator; divide the dough into 4 or 6 pieces and shape into rounds.

- Grease the cooking tray with the remaining olive oil and arrange the hash browns patties on top. Fit the cooking tray on the middle rack of the oven and close the oven.

- Set the timer for 15 minutes and air fry until the timer reads to the end. Open the oven and carefully flip the hash browns. Cook further with the timer set for 6 minutes or until uniformly air fried.

- Open the lid and remove the hash browns.

- Serve warm.

48. Breakfast Casserole

Preparation Time: 20 minutes
Cooking Time: 20 minutes
Servings: 4

Ingredients:

- 3 tbsp. brown sugar
- 1/2 cup of flour
- 1/2 tsp. cinnamon powder
- 4 tbsp. margarine
- 2 tbsp. white sugar
- 2 eggs
- 2-1/2 tbsp. white flour
- 1 tsp. baking powder
- 1 tsp. baking soda
- 2 tbsp. sugar
- 4 tbsp. margarine
- 1/2 cup of milk
- 1-1/3 cup of blueberries
- 1 tbsp. lemon zest

Directions:

- Preheat the Air Fryer Oven by selecting the pizza/bake mode.
- Adjust the temperature to 300°F
- In a bowl, mix the casserole ingredients, then pour it into the Air Fryer Oven baking pan.
- In a separate bowl, mix white sugar with flour, margarine, white sugar, and cinnamon.
- Mix until a crumbly mixture is achieved, spread over the blueberry's mixture.
- Transfer to the Air Fryer Oven and bake for 30 minutes

49. French Toast

Preparation Time: 5 minutes
Cooking Time: 5 minutes
Servings: 4

Ingredients:

- 2 slices of bread
- 1 tsp. Liquid vanilla
- 3 eggs
- 1 tbsp. Margarine

Directions:

- Preheat the Air Fryer Oven by setting it to toast/pizza mode.
- Adjust the temperature to 375°F; insert the pizza tray.
- In a bowl, whisk the eggs and vanilla
- Spread the margarine on the bread, transfer into the egg and allow to soak
- Place on the Air Fryer Oven pizza rack and set time to 6 minutes, flip after 3 minutes.

50. Raspberry Oatmeal

Preparation Time: 20 minutes
Cooking Time: 20 minutes
Servings: 4

Ingredients:

- 1 cups of shredded coconut
- 2 tsp. Stevia
- 1 tsp. Cinnamon powder
- 2 cups. Almond milk
- 1/2 cup of raspberries

Directions:

- Mix all the ingredients in a bowl
- Pour into the air fryer baking pan
- Transfer to the Air Fryer Oven
- Using the knob, select bake/pizza mode
- Adjust the temperature to 360°F.
- Bake for 15 minutes
- Serve and enjoy

51. Breakfast Egg and Tomatoes

Preparation Time: 5 minutes
Cooking Time: 25 minutes
Servings: 2

Ingredients:

- Salt and pepper to taste
- 2 eggs
- 2 large tomatoes

Directions:

- Preheat the air fryer by selecting the bake/pizza mode.

- Adjust the temperature to 375°F
- Cut off the top of the tomatoes, scoop out the seed and flesh.
- Break the egg into each tomato, transfer to the Air Fryer Oven baking tray.
- Bake for 24 minutes
- Serve and enjoy

52. Pancetta and Hotdog Omelet

Preparation Time: 5 minutes
Cooking Time: 15 minutes
Servings: 2

Ingredients:

- pancetta, chopped
- 1/4 tsp. dried rosemary
- 2 hot dogs, chopped
- 1/2 tsp. dried parsley
- 2 small onions, chopped

Directions:

- In a bowl, crack the egg.
- Add the remaining ingredients and mix, pour into the air fryer baking tray
- Preheat the Air Fryer Oven by selecting air fry
- Adjust temperature to 320°F
- Set time to 5 minutes
- Open the door and arrange your baking pan
- Air fry for 10 minutes
- Serve and enjoy

53. Sausage Omelet

Preparation Time: 5 minutes
Cooking Time: 18 minutes
Servings: 2

Ingredients:

- 2 sausage, chopped
- 1 yellow onion
- 1 bacon slice
- 4 eggs

Directions:

- Preheat the Air Fryer Oven by selecting air fry mode
- Adjust temperature to 320°F and time to 5 minutes
- In a bowl, mix all the ingredients.
- Pour into the air fryer baking tray
- Transfer into the Air Fryer Oven
- Air fry for 10 minutes
- Serve and enjoy!

54. Pepperoni Omelet

Preparation Time: 5 minutes
Cooking Time: 20 minutes
Servings: 2

Ingredients:

- 2 tbsp. milk
- 4 eggs
- 10 pepperoni slices
- Salt and ground black pepper to taste

Directions:

- Preheat the Air Fryer Oven by selecting air fry mode
- Adjust temperature to 350°F and time to 5 minutes
- In a bowl, mix all the ingredients.
- Pour into the Air fryer baking tray
- Transfer into the Air Fryer Oven
- Air fry for 12 minutes
- Serve and enjoy!

55. Zucchini Fritters

Preparation Time: 5 minutes
Cooking Time: 15 minutes
Servings: 4

Ingredients:

- 10 oz. zucchini
- 7 oz. halloumi cheese
- 2 eggs
- 1/4 cup all-purpose flour
- 1 tsp. dried dill
- Salt and black pepper to taste

Directions:

- Preheat the Air Fryer Oven by selecting bake/pizza mode
- Adjust temperature to 360°F and time to 5 minutes
- In a bowl, mix all the ingredients.
- Make small fritters from the mixture
- Place them on the Air fryer baking tray
- Transfer into the Air Fryer Oven
- Bake for 7 minutes
- Serve and enjoy!

56. Sausage Wraps

Preparation Time: 5 minutes
Cooking Time: 15 minutes
Servings: 2

Ingredients:

- 1 cup. Mozzarella cheese
- 8 sausage
- 8 crescent rolled dough

Directions:

- Preheat the Air Fryer Oven by selecting bake/ pizza mode
- Adjust temperature to 380°F and timer to 5 minutes
- Open the dough, arrange cheese at one end of the dough
- Add the sausage and roll, secure with a toothpick
- Arrange the sausage wrap in the Air fryer baking tray
- Transfer into the Air Fryer Oven
- Bake for 7 minutes
- Serve and enjoy

57. Beans and Eggs Recipes

Preparation Time: 5 minutes
Cooking Time: 22 minutes
Servings: 6

Ingredients:

- Cooking spray
- 12 eggs
- Salt and pepper

Directions:

- Spray a muffin pan with cooking spray.
- Crack an egg in each cup and make sure that you don't break the yolk.
- Place the muffin pan on the pizza rack on position 5 of the Air Fryer Oven and select the bake setting. Set the temperature to 350°F and the timer for 20 minutes. Press the start button to start.
- Check if the eggs are fully cooked by running the tip of a knife on one egg.
- Serve immediately after seasoning with salt and pepper.

58. Baked Eggs with Cheese

Preparation Time: 5 minutes
Cooking Time: 20 minutes
Servings: 6

Ingredients:

- Cooking spray
- 12 eggs
- 2/3 cup cheese, shredded
- Salt and pepper

Directions:

- Spray a muffin pan with cooking spray.
- Crack an egg in each cup and make sure that you don't break the yolk. Sprinkle some shredded cheese on each cup.
- Place the muffin pan on the pizza rack on shelf position 5 of the Air Fryer Oven and select the bake setting. Set the temperature to 350°F and the timer for 20 minutes. Press the start button to start.
- Check if the eggs are fully cooked by running the tip of a knife on one egg. Add more time if not cooked through.
- Serve immediately when seasoned with salt and pepper.

59. Scrambled Egg

Preparation Time: 8 minutes
Cooking Time: 12 minutes
Servings: 1

Ingredients:

♦ 2 eggs
♦ 2 tbsps. Butter
♦ 1/4 cup of cheese
♦ 1 tomato

Directions:

▪ Preheat the Air Fryer Oven by selecting air fry mode
▪ Adjust temperature to 290°F and time to 5 minutes
▪ Grease the baking tray with the butter.
▪ In a bowl, mix all the ingredients.
▪ Pour into the Air fryer baking tray
▪ Transfer into the Air Fryer Oven
▪ Air fry for 7 minutes

60. Sausage and Mushrooms Egg Casserole

Preparation Time: 15 minutes
Cooking Time: 40 minutes
Servings: 11

Ingredients:

♦ Cooking spray
♦ 12 oz. breakfast sausage
♦ 1 tbsp. butter
♦ 8 oz. cremini mushrooms, thinly sliced
♦ 12 eggs
♦ 1/2 cup whole milk
♦ 1 tbsp. salt
♦ 1/4 tbsp. black pepper
♦ 8 oz. Havarti cheese, shredded

Directions:

▪ Spray a baking dish with cooking spray and place two sheets of paper towels on a platter and set aside.
▪ Cook sausage on a skillet over medium-high heat for 7 minutes or until browned. Break the sausage into pieces using a rubber spatula.

▪ Transfer the cooked sausage to the platter with paper towels.
▪ Add butter to the skillet and cook mushrooms for 6 minutes or until the mushrooms have browned and shrunken.
▪ Whisk together with eggs, milk, salt, and pepper in a mixing bowl. Add the cooked sausage, mushrooms, and top with cheese. Mix until everything is well distributed.
▪ Pour the mixture on the prepared dish and place the dish on the pizza rack of the Air Fryer Oven and press bake.
▪ Set the temperature to 350°F and the timer for 40 minutes. Press the start button to start.
▪ When the casserole is done, check if it's fully cooked. Cut into squares and spoon on plates. Serve and enjoy.

61. Sausage and Cheese Egg Casserole

Preparation Time: 15 minutes
Cooking Time: 45 minutes
Servings: 10

Ingredients:

♦ Nonstick cooking spray
♦ 12 oz. breakfast sausage
♦ 12 eggs
♦ 1/2 cup whole milk
♦ 1 tbsp. salt
♦ 1/4 tbsp. black pepper
♦ 8 oz. cheddar cheese, shredded

Directions:

▪ Spray a baking dish with cooking spray and place two sheets of paper towels on a platter and set aside.
▪ Cook sausage on a skillet over medium-high heat for 7 minutes or until browned. Break the sausage into pieces using a rubber spatula.
▪ Transfer the cooked sausage to the platter with paper towels.
▪ Whisk together eggs, milk, salt, and pepper in a mixing bowl. Add the cooked sausage and top with shredded cheese. Mix until everything is well distributed.

- Pour the mixture on the prepared dish and place the dish on the pizza rack of Air Fryer Oven and press the bake setting.

- Set the temperature to 350°F and the timer for 45 minutes. Press the start button to start.

- When the casserole is done, cut into squares and spoon on plates. Serve and enjoy.

62. Spinach and Artichoke Egg Casserole

Preparation Time: 50 minutes
Cooking Time: 55 minutes
Servings: 11

Ingredients:

- Nonstick cooking spray
- 1 tbsp. olive oil
- 4 oz. baby spinach
- 1 can artichoke hertz
- 12 eggs
- Scallions, minced
- 1/2 cup sour cream
- 1/4 tbsp. garlic powder
- 1 tbsp. salt
- 1/4 tbsp. black pepper
- 4 oz. mozzarella cheese, shredded
- 4 oz. Italian blend

Directions:

- Spray a baking dish with cooking spray.

- Start heating the olive oil in a skillet over medium heat. Put the spinach and cook for 2 minutes or until the spinach softens.

- Add artichoke hertz and cook for 1 more minute. Remove from heat.

- In a mixing bowl, mix eggs, scallions, sour cream, garlic, salt, and pepper. Add cooked spinach, artichokes, and cheese.

- Fold until the vegetables are well distributed. Pour the mixture on the baking dish and place the dish on the pizza rack of your Air Fryer Oven. Select the bake setting.

- Set the temperature to 350°F and the timer for 45 minutes. Press the start button to start.

- When the casserole is done let rest for 10 minutes before serving. Cut into squares and spoon on plates. Serve and enjoy.

63. Green Bean Casserole Riceballs

Preparation Time: 30 minutes
Cooking Time: 30 minutes
Servings: 4

Ingredients:

- 1/2 cup whole milk ricotta
- 1/4 cup cream of mushroom soup
- 2 eggs, beaten
- 2 cup fried onions
- 1 cup sushi rice, cooked
- 1 pinch Salt and Pepper
- 2 cup all-purpose flour
- 1 cup Mozzarella cheese
- 2 (14.5-ounce) can green beans (cut)

Directions:

- In a large bowl, bring together the mozzarella, rice, ricotta, cream of mushroom soup and green beans.

- Toss to mix thoroughly. Season with salt and pepper to taste. Place the filling on the slightly salty side.

- Refrigerate for thirty minutes and install the dredging station.

- Place the fried onions in a zip-top plastic bag. Break the onions into morsels. Transfer to a shallow bowl.

- Roll the rice mixture into balls, roughly the mass of a billiard ball.

- Roll each ball in the flour, then the egg, and finally the onion morsels.

- Cook in the appliance at 380, until golden brown.

- Serve hot.

64. Beef & Bean Rolls

Preparation Time: 15 minutes
Cooking Time: 20 minutes
Servings: 4

Ingredients:

- 1 lb. ground beef, cooked
- 1/2 cup refried beans
- 2 teaspoons taco seasoning
- 4 corn tortillas
- 1/4 cup tomatoes, chopped
- 1/2 cup Mexican cheese, shredded

Directions:

- Mix beef and beans in a bowl.
- Season with taco seasoning.
- Top the tortillas with the beef mixture.
- Sprinkle tomatoes and cheese on top.
- Roll up the tortillas.
- Add the rolls to the air fryer tray.
- Select air fry setting.
- Cook at 340 degrees F for 4 minutes per side.

65. Pork & Green Beans

Preparation Time: 10 minutes
Cooking Time: 30 minutes
Servings: 4

Ingredients:

- 1/4 cup almond flour
- 1 teaspoon Creole seasoning
- 1/4 cup Parmesan cheese, grated
- 1 teaspoon paprika
- 1 teaspoon garlic powder
- 4 pork chops
- 4 cups green beans, trimmed and steamed
- Cooking spray

Directions:

- Preheat your air fryer to 375°F.
- Spray your air fryer tray with oil.
- In a bowl, mix all the ingredients except pork chops and green beans.
- Spray pork chops with oil.
- Coat with spice mixture.
- Air fry for 15 minutes, turning once.

66. Chicken Soup

Preparation Time: 20 minutes

Cooking Time: 1 hour & 16 minutes
Servings: 4

Ingredients:

- 4 chicken breasts, skinned and deboned
- 1 onion, sliced into rounds
- 2 tbsps. of extra virgin olive oil
- 16 ounces of chunky salsa
- 3 garlic cloves, grated
- 2 medium carrot, chopped
- 29 ounces of chicken stock
- 32 ounces of drained peas
- 29 ounces of canned diced tomatoes
- 1 Tbsp. of onion powder
- Fresh parsley for garnish
- 1 Tbsp. of chili powder
- 1 tsp. garlic powder
- 15 ounces of frozen corn
- Salt and black pepper, as desired

Directions:

- Set the Air Fryer to Sauté mode. Select one of the options, click the Timer Button, and dial to 6 minutes.
- Heat the oil, then add the sliced onions, stir and cook for 5 minutes. Stir in the garlic and cook for 1 minute.
- Add the chicken breast, canned tomatoes, salsa, chicken broth, salt, parsley, black pepper, chili powder, onion powder, and garlic. Stir.
- Close the cooker with the Pressure Lid and select the preset Pressure Poultry Mode. The short cooking program will have the chicken soup ready in 10 minutes.
- Release the pressure, then uncover the Air Fryer and transfer the chicken to a chopping board. Shred and set it aside.
- Add the frozen corn and pea to the Air Fryer, set in the Pressure Vegetable Mode (Short), and cook for 2-3 minutes.
- Combine the chicken soup and the beans mixture.
- Divide into bowls, garnish with parsley, and serve.

67. Parsnip Fries

Preparation Time: 10 minutes
Cooking Time: 30 minutes
Servings: 2

Ingredients:

- Big 3-4 Parsnips
- 1 tsp. Powdered garlic
- 1/2 tsp. Garlic, minced
- 1 tsp. Curcuma
- 2 tbsp. Grated Cheese with Parmesan

Directions:

- Heat the Air Fryer prior to cooking to a temperature of 400 degrees F
- Dice the same size of parsnip and toss with avocado oil, turmeric and garlic in a dish.
- Place the parsnip on a baking sheet and drizzle with the sea salt and parmesan cheese.
- Put it in an air fryer and cook for 15 minutes in the oven.
- Remove the baking sheet and flip the parsnip with a spatula after 15 minutes.
- Sprinkle with more parmesan cheese and return for another 15 minutes to the air fryer to bake.

68. Corn Soup

Preparation Time: 1 hour
Cooking Time: 1 hour & 15 minutes
Servings: 4

Ingredients:

- 2 Tbsps. of butter
- Extra virgin olive oil
- 2 leeks, chopped
- 1 Tbsp. of fresh chives, chopped
- 2 garlic cloves, grated
- 1-quart of chicken stock
- 6 ears of corn, kernels removed and cobs reserved
- 4 tarragon sprigs, chopped
- 2 bay leaves
- Boiled corn, for garnish
- Salt and black pepper, as desired

Directions:

- Set the Air Fryer to Sauté mode. Select one of the options, click the Timer Button, and dial to 6 minutes.
- Melt the butter, then add garlic and chopped leeks, stir and cook for 4 minutes.
- Add the corn, tarragon, bay leaves, 1/2 of the chicken broth, and cover with the Pressure Lid. Select the Pressure mode, choose vegetables, and cook for 3 minutes (Short).
- Relieve the pressure, uncover the Air Fryer, then throw away the bay leaves and corn on the cob.
- Transfer the other contents of the cooker to a food processor. Pulse to obtain a smooth soup, add the remaining stock, and stir again.
- Season with the salt and black pepper and stir.
- Divide the soup into equal portions and top with chives, boiled corn, and olive oil.
- Serve.

69. Butternut Squash Soup

Preparation Time: 20 minutes
Cooking Time: 1 hour & 56 minutes
Servings: 6

Ingredients:

- 1/2 cup green onions, thinly sliced
- 1-1/2 cup of half and half
- 3 tbsps. of butter
- 1/2 cup of carrots, diced
- 1-1/2 pounds of butternut squash, peeled, cut into cubes, and baked
- 1 garlic clove, grated
- 29 ounces of chicken stock
- 1/2 cup of chopped celery
- 1/2 tsp. of Italian seasoning
- 1/8 tsp. of red pepper flakes
- Green onions, chopped for garnish
- 15 ounces of canned diced tomatoes
- 1 cup of cooked, shredded chicken meat
- 1/8 tsp. of nutmeg, grated
- 1 cup of orzo, cooked
- Salt and black pepper, as desired

Directions:

- Set the Air Fryer to Sauté mode. Select one of the options, click the Timer Button, and dial to 6 minutes.
- Melt the butter in the Air Fryer. Add the chopped celery, onion, and carrot. Stir and fry for 5 minutes.
- Stir in the garlic and cook for 1 minute.
- Stir in the squash, tomato, chicken stock, pepper flakes, Italian seasoning, salt, black pepper, and nutmeg. Cover the cooker with the pressure lid.
- Select the Pressure mode, choose Vegetables, and cook for 12 minutes (Long).
- Release the pressure, uncover, and blend everything with a food processor.
- Set the Air Fryer to Pressure mode, add half and half, squash soup, barley, and chicken, stir and cook for 30 minutes (Medium).
- Divide the soup into bowls, garnish with green onions, and serve.

70. Potato and Cheese Soup

Preparation Time: 30 minutes
Cooking Time: 1 hour
Servings: 6

Ingredients:

- 2 tbsps. of butter
- 1 cup of corn
- 6 cups of diced potatoes
- 28 ounces of chicken stock
- 1/2 cup of chopped yellow onions
- 1/8 tsp. of red pepper flakes
- 2 tbsps. of dried parsley
- 2 tbsps. of cornstarch
- 6 bacon slices, cooked and chopped
- 2 tbsps. of water
- 3 ounces of cubed cream cheese
- 1 cup of shredded cheddar cheese
- 2 cups of half and half
- Salt and black pepper, as desired

Directions:

- Set the Air Fryer to Sauté mode. Select one of the options, click the Timer Button, and dial to 6 minutes.
- Melt the butter, add the yellow onions, stir and cook for 5 minutes.
- Stir in half of the chicken stock, salt, black pepper, parsley, and red pepper flakes. Place the potatoes in the mesh basket, cover with the Glass lid, and select 25 minutes (Medium) in the Steam Vegetable Mode.
- Uncover the Pressure Cooker & Air Fryer and transfer the potatoes to a bowl. In another bowl, mix the cornstarch with water and mix well. Add the mixture of cornstarch, cream cheese, and grated cheese to the cooker.
- Add the rest of the stock, corn, bacon, potatoes, half and half.
- Stir.
- Cover with the Glass Lid and select 25 minutes (Medium) in the Steam Vegetable Mode.
- Pour into bowls and serve hot.

71. Split Pea Soup

Preparation Time: 25 minutes
Cooking Time: 1 hour & 30 minutes
Servings: 6

Ingredients:

- 1 pound of ground chicken sausage
- 2 Tbsps. of butter
- 1/2 cup carrots, chopped
- 1 yellow onion, sliced into rounds
- 1/2 cup of chopped celery
- Salt and black pepper, as desired
- 2 garlic cloves, grated
- 29 ounces of chicken stock
- 16 ounces of split peas, rinsed
- 2 cups of water
- 1/4 tsp. red pepper flakes
- 1/2 cup half and half

Directions:

- Set the Air Fryer to Sauté mode. Select the Beef Mode (Medium). Add the sausage, brown on all sides and transfer to a plate.

- Set the cooker to Beef Mode again, add the butter to the Pressure Cooker & Air Fryer and melt.

- Add the celery and yellow onion, mix and cook for 4 minutes. Add the garlic, and cook for 1 minute. Add water, broth, a half and half, peas, and pepper flakes, cover with Glass Lid and cook for 20 minutes.

- Transfer the mixture to a food processor and blend.

- Divide the soup into equal portions, stir in the sausage and carrot

- Serve.

72. Beef and Rice Soup

Preparation Time: 15 minutes
Cooking Time: 50 minutes
Servings: 6

Ingredients:

- 3 garlic cloves, minced
- 1 Tbsp. of vegetable oil
- 1/2 cup of frozen peas
- 1-pound ground beef
- 1 celery stalk, chopped
- 28 ounces of beef stock
- 2 carrots, sliced thin
- 14 ounces of canned crushed tomatoes
- 1/2 cup white rice
- 12 ounces of spicy tomato juice
- 15 ounces of canned garbanzo beans, rinsed
- 1 yellow onion, sliced into rounds
- 1 potato, cubed
- Salt and black pepper, as desired

Directions:

- Set the Air Fryer to Sauté mode. Select Beef Mode (Medium).

- Add the meat and until brown, and transfer to a plate.

- Select 25 minutes (Medium) in the Steam Vegetable Mode. Add the oil, then celery, onion, and garlic. Stir and cook for 6 minutes.

- Add the tomato juice, peas, broth, tomato, rice, beans, carrots, potatoes, meat, salt, and black pepper. Cover with Glass lid and cook for the rest of the timer.

- Add extra salt and pepper, if required

- Transfer to bowls and serve hot.

73. Chicken Noodle Soup

Preparation Time: 20 minutes
Cooking Time: 32 minutes
Servings: 6

Ingredients:

- 1 celery stalk, chopped
- 1 yellow onion, sliced into rounds
- 6 cups of chicken stock
- 4 carrots, sliced
- 2 cups of cooked, shredded chicken
- 1 Tbsp. of butter
- Egg noodles, cooked
- Salt and black pepper, as desired

Directions:

- Set the Air Fryer to Sauté mode. Select one of the options, click the Timer Button, and dial to 6 minutes.

- Melt the butter, then add the onion, celery, and carrots—Cook for 5 minutes.

- Add the shredded chicken and stock. Cover with the Glass Lid and cook the soup for 25 minutes.

- Uncover the Air Fryer, add salt and pepper as desired.

- Divide the pasta into bowls, add the soup, and serve.

74. Chicken and Wild Rice Soup

Preparation Time: 20 minutes
Cooking Time: 50 minutes
Servings: 6

Ingredients:

- 1 cup of chopped celery

- 1 cup of half and half
- 1 cup of grated carrots
- 1 Tbsp. of dried parsley
- 1 cup of sliced yellow onion
- 1 cup of milk
- 2 Tbsps. of butter
- 2 chicken breasts, shredded
- 6 ounces of wild rice
- 28 ounces of chicken stock
- 2 Tbsps. of cornstarch
- Red pepper flakes
- 2 Tbsps. of water
- Salt and black pepper, as desired

Directions:

- Set the Air Fryer to Sauté mode. Select Chicken Mode (Medium).
- Melt the butter and add the carrot, onion, and celery—Cook for 5 minutes.
- Add the rice, chicken, broth, parsley, salt, and pepper, cover with Glass Lid and cook for 10 minutes.
- Uncover, add the cornstarch mixed with water, cheese, milk, and a half and a half. Keep cooking until the timer automatic timer runs out.
- Transfer to bowls and serve.

75. Creamy Tomato Soup

Preparation Time: 10 minutes
Cooking Time: 56 minutes
Servings: 8

Ingredients:

- 2 garlic cloves, grated
- 29 ounces of chicken stock
- 1 yellow onion, sliced into rounds
- 3 Tbsps. of butter
- 1 carrot, chopped
- 2 celery stalks, chopped
- 1/4 cup of fresh, chopped basil
- Salt and black pepper, as desired
- 3 pounds tomatoes, peeled and cut into quarters
- 1 Tbsp. of tomato paste

- 1/2 cup of shredded Parmesan cheese
- 1 cup of half and half

Directions:

- Set the Air Fryer to Sauté mode. Select Chicken Mode (Medium).
- Melt the butter, add onion, carrot, and celery, stir and cook for 3 minutes.
- Add the garlic, and cook for another 1 minute.
- Add the tomatoes, the tomato paste, broth, basil, salt, and pepper. Cover with Glass Lid, and cook for 15 minutes.
- Blend the soup with a food processor.
- Add the half and half and cheese
- Divide the soup into bowls and serve.

76. Bacon and Cheese Quiche

Preparation Time: 30 minutes
Cooking Time: 22 minutes
Servings: 6

Ingredients:

- 1 pie shell, frozen
- 6 strips of bacon
- 4 eggs
- 3/4 cup whole milk
- 1/4 cup heavy cream
- 1/2 tbsp. salt
- 1/4 tbsp. black pepper
- 2 oz. Gouda cheese, shredded

Directions:

- Poke the pie shell with a fork then place it on a baking sheet.
- Place the baking sheet on the pizza rack and select bake setting. Set the temperature to 400°F and the timer for 14 minutes. Press the start button to start.
- Take out from the oven and set aside.
- Line large dinner plates with paper towels and set aside.
- Cook bacon on a skillet over medium heat for 8 minutes or until browned and crispy.

- Transfer the bacon to the lined plates.

- In a mixing bowl, whisk eggs, milk, heavy cream. Salt and pepper. Add bacon and cheese to the egg mixture and fold until well mixed.

- Pour the mixture on a pie shell and cover the edges with strips of aluminum foil.

- Place the pie shell on the pizza rack of the Air Fryer Oven and select the bake setting.

- Set the temperature to 350°F and the timer for 55 minutes. Press the start button to start.

- When the quiche is well cooked it should be firm and golden brown. Remove from heat and let rest for 30 minutes before serving. Enjoy.

77. Goulash

Preparation Time: 45 minutes
Cooking Time: 17 minutes
Servings: 4-5

Ingredients:

- 2 bell peppers chopped
- Two diced tomatoes
- 1 lb. Chicken, ground
- 1/2 cup broth of chicken
- Pepper and salt

Directions:

- Pre-heat your fryer at 365°F and spray with cooking spray.

- For five minutes, cook the bell pepper.

- Using the diced tomatoes and ground chicken to throw in. Combine well then allow for another six minutes to cook.

- Pour the chicken broth inside, then season with salt and pepper to taste. Cook for six more minutes before serving.

78. Mac And Cheese

Preparation Time: 20-30 minutes
Cooking Time: 14 minutes
Servings: 4

Ingredients:

- Cauliflower with 1 head, chopped

- 3 tbsp. avocado oil
- 1/4 cup of almond milk unsweetened
- 1/4 Cup of heavy cream
- 1 cup shredded cheddar cheese

Directions:

- Pre-heat up to 400°F for your fryer.

- Drizzle over the cauliflower with some of the avocado oil and flip, thoroughly coating it. Season according to your taste.

- Place it in the fryer with the cauliflower.

- In a saucepan, add the remainder of the avocado oil, milk, cream, and cheddar. Cook on medium heat till the cheese has melted, stirring continuously.

- Pour over the cauliflower, cook for 14 minutes and serve until warmed.

79. Ham Hash

Preparation Time: 30 minutes
Cooking Time: 10 minutes
Servings: 4

Ingredients:

- 1 egg
- 1 Cup of ham, chopped
- 1/2 onion, chopped
- 1 tbsp. Butter
- 1/3 cup of grated parmesan

Directions:

- Pre-heat up to 350°F for your fryer.

- Before adding the ham, onion, and butter, whisk the egg well in a bowl. If needed, blend well and add seasoning.

- Scoop into three ramekins in equal parts, adding a sprinkle of parmesan on top.

- Set aside in a fryer and cook for 10 minutes. Take care of the ramekins and serve hot while removing them.

80. Mighty Egg Rolls

Preparation Time: 3 hours
Cooking Time: 10 minutes
Servings: 24

Ingredients:

- 1/4 cup of water
- 1/2 tsp almond flour
- 1 tsp. About salt
- 1/2 lb. Ground-based beef
- Two Eggs

Directions:

- Over medium heat, pour water into a saucepan and wait until it comes to a boil.

- Add the almond flour and salt into a bowl and dump the boiling water on top. Combine well then knead to form a soft dough with your fingertips. Set aside then.

- As required, season the ground beef, covering it evenly.

- Over medium heat, bring the beef into a skillet. Cook until browned and where possible, drain. Crack the egg and mix, then cook for four more minutes.

- Using a pin to roll the dough out and cut it into six equal-sized squares.

- Spoon into the middle of each square an equal amount of ground beef, and roll into cylinders.

- With cooking oil, spray your fryer and pre-heat to 350 F. For eight minutes, cook the rolls and enjoy

81. Mighty Meatballs

Preparation Time: 1 hour
Cooking Time: 10 minutes
Servings: 6-8

Ingredients:

- 1 cup of onion minced
- 1 lb. Ground-based beef
- Three egg yolks
- Mozzarella 1 cup, shredded
- 1 tbsp. Extra Virgin Olive Oil

Directions:

- Pre-heat the fryer at 375 degrees F. Grease yourself with olive oil.

- In a bowl, put the onion and ground beef and season as desired. Combine your hands with the egg yolks.

- Take a handful of beef and with your palm, press it flat out. Place a small amount of cheese on the meat to form a ball and wrap the meat around it. Make the majority of the cheese and beef.

- In the fryer, place all the meatballs and cook for ten minutes. Serve it wet.

82. Cilantro Drumsticks

Preparation Time: 20 minutes
Cooking Time: 20 minutes
Servings: 2

Ingredients:

- 8 drumsticks of chicken
- 1/2 cup of sauce with Chimichurri
- 1/4 Cup of Lemon Juice

Directions:

- Coat the chicken drumsticks with chimichurri sauce and cool for no less than an hour in an airtight container, preferably overnight.

- Pre-heat your fryer to 400°F when it's time to serve.

- Remove the chicken from the refrigerator and then allow it to return to room temperature for approximately 20 minutes.

- Cook in the fryer for eighteen minutes. Drizzle to taste and savor with lemon juice.

83. Pop Corn Chicken

Preparation Time: 20 minutes
Cooking Time: 15 minutes
Servings: 4

Ingredients:

- 1 lb. Skinless, boneless breast of chicken
- 1 tsp. Flakes of Chili
- 1 tsp. Powdered garlic
- ½ cup of flour with coconut
- 1 tbsp. Cooking Spray for Olive Oil

Directions:

- Pre-heat the fryer at 365 degrees F. Spray Olive oil.
- Chop the breasts of the chicken into cubes and put them in a bowl. Toss to taste with the chili flakes, garlic powder, and extra seasonings and make sure to coat them fully.
- Add the flour from the coconut and toss again.
- In the fryer, cook the chicken for ten minutes. Turnover and before eating, cook for another five minutes.

84. Crispy Chicken

Preparation Time: 10 minutes
Cooking Time: 6 minutes
Servings: 6

Ingredients:

- 1 lb. Skin of chicken
- 1 tsp. Butter
- 1/2 tsp. Chili Flakes
- 1 tsp. Dill

Directions:

- Pre-heat the 360 ° F fryer.
- Break the skin of the chicken into strips.
- Heat the butter and pour it over the skin of the chicken until it is melted. Toss to taste with chili flakes, dill, and any extra seasonings, making sure to coat well.
- In the fryer, cook the skins for three minutes. Turn them over and cook on the next side for another three minutes.
- They can be eaten hot or at room temperature, served immediately or saved for later.

85. Southern Cooked Chicken

Preparation Time: 1 hour 30 minutes
Cooking Time: 26 minutes
Servings: 4

Ingredients:

- About 2 x 6-oz. Boneless chicken breasts with skinless skin
- 2 tbsp. Hot Sauce Hot Sauce

- 1/2 tsp. Powdered onion
- 1 tbsp. Powdered chili
- 2 oz. Rinds of pork, finely ground

Directions:

- Lengthwise, break the chicken breasts in half and rub in the hot sauce. Combine the chili powder with the onion powder, then blend well with the meat. Enable it to marinate for at least an hour and a half.
- Using the ground pork rinds to coat and thoroughly cover the chicken breasts in the ground pork rinds. In your fryer, put the chicken.
- At 350 F, set the fryer and cook the chicken for 13 minutes. Turn over the chicken and then cook for another 13 minutes or until crispy on the other hand. With a meat thermometer, measure the chicken. It should exceed 165°F when fully cooked. Serve hot, with your choice of sides.

86. Lemon Pepper Chicken Legs

Preparation Time: 5 minutes
Cooking Time: 25 minutes
Servings: 5

Ingredients:

- 1/2 tsp. Powdered garlic
- 2 tsp. Powder for baking
- 8 legs of chicken
- 4 tbsp. Butter salted, melted
- 1 tbsp. lemon pepper seasoning

Directions:

- Blend the garlic powder and baking powder in a small bowl, then cover the chicken legs with this mixture. Place the chicken in your friend's basket.
- For twenty-five minutes, cook the chicken legs at 375°F. Turn them over halfway through and allow them on the other side to cook.
- Test a thermometer to ensure it has reached an optimal temperature of 165 ° F when the chicken has turned golden brown. Remove the fryer.

- Mix the seasoning of melted butter and lemon pepper together and toss with the legs of the chicken until the chicken is coated all over. Serve it wet.

87. Wrapped Bacon Shrimp

Preparation Time: 25 minutes
Cooking Time: 7 minutes
Servings: 5

Ingredients:

- Cleaned and deveined 14 shrimp (defrosted shrimp)
- Fourteen bacon slices

Directions:

- Preheat air fryer to the 380 degrees F
- Wrap the bacon with all the shrimp.
- Put the cooked bacon-wrapped shrimp in the refrigerator for about 20 minutes.
- Remove from the fridge and put for 5 minutes in the air fryer basket.
- Switch them over and continue baking for 2 minutes or more.
- Serve and enjoy

88. Goat Cheese Balls

Preparation Time: 10 minutes
Cooking Time: 8 minutes
Servings: 10

Ingredients:

- 2 Tbsp. Flour
- 1 beaten egg
- 8 oz. Soft Goat Cheese Log
- 1/2 of a c. Crumbs of panko bread
- 1/4 of a c. Harmony of Bee
- Sugar

Directions:

- Slice and roll the goat cheese into bits and balls
- Place them in a tray and freeze for thirty minutes.
- In a tub, break the shell.

- Take them out and then dip them inside the flour one by one after 30 minutes, then into the broken egg and eventually into the panko breadcrumbs.
- Then put them inside the air fryer basket and pray for the non-stick cooking spray balls.
- Set the air fryer to cook for approximately 8 minutes at 380f, until they are brown.
- Serve and enjoy

89. Ginger Carrots Sesame

Preparation Time: 10 minutes
Cooking Time: 20 minutes
Servings: 4

Ingredients:

- 2 cups of carrots sliced
- 2 tbsp. Oil with sesame seeds
- 1 tbsp. Ginger Minced
- 1 tbsp. Sauce of soy
- 1 tsp. Garlic, minced

Directions:

- In a cup, mix the sliced carrots, sesame oil, minced ginger, soy sauce and minced garlic.
- Through the air fry basket, pour the mixture in
- Set the air fryer to 375 for 8 minutes; after 4 minutes, shake the basket by cooking 4. Pour the carrots into a bowl after 8 minutes and garnish with the sesame and scallion seeds.

90. Chicken Finger Fiesta

Preparation Time: 10 minutes
Cooking Time: 16 minutes
Servings: 8

Ingredients:

- 3/4-pound boneless chicken breasts without skin
- 1/2 cup of buttermilk
- All-purpose flour, 1 cup
- 3 cups of maize chips, crushed
- 1 taco seasoning envelope

Directions:

- Preheat the fryer to 400 degrees F.
- Beat chicken breasts up to 1/2-inch thick with a meat mallet, then cut into 1-inch wide strips.
- Whisk in the buttermilk and pepper in a large cup.
- In another tub, place the flour.
- Combine the corn chips in a third bowl and the taco seasoning.
- Dip the chicken on either side in the flour to coat, shake off the excess, soak in the buttermilk mixture and then in the corn chip mixture.
- Arrange the chicken in batches and in a single layer in an air-fryer basket on a greased tray; brush with cooking spray.
- Cook on each side for 7-8 minutes. Repeat with the remaining chicken until the coating is golden brown, and the chicken is no longer pink. 9. Serve with dip or salsa from the ranch.

91. Blooming Onion

Preparation Time: 40 minutes
Cooking Time: 8 minutes
Servings: 1

Ingredients:

- 2 Beaten Eggs
- 1 Onion
- Flour, 2.5 cups
- 4 tsp. Old Bay Seasoning
- 1/2 Cup of Milk

Directions:

- Cut and rinse the onion under water, then peel the onion and cut the top off.
- Cut the onion into 8 sections of the same
- Preheat your air fryer to 400 degrees F
- Mix the flour and seasonings together inside a dish.
- In another separate cup, combine the egg and milk.
- Pour on the onion with the flour mixture. Using your hand to thoroughly mix

- Then shift the onion to the egg mixture and sprinkle it with more flour mixture and use a spoon to stir.
- Fry in the air for 8 minutes or until crispy.

92. Stuffed Mushrooms

Preparation Time: 15 minutes
Cooking Time: 10 minutes
Servings: 12

Ingredients:

- Breadcrumbs, 1/4 cup
- Pecorino-Romano, 1/4 cup grated
- 1 tsp. fresh parsley chopped
- 1 tsp. Chopped Stemmed New Mint
- 36 mushrooms with white buttons
- Pecorino-Romano, 2 tsp.

Directions:

- Blend together the breadcrumbs. A bowl of mozzarella, parsley, mint, 1 clove of garlic, 2 tablespoons of olive oil, 1/2 teaspoon of salt and 1/4 teaspoon of pepper
- Throw the mushrooms in another bowl with the remaining 2 tablespoons of olive oil and place them on a plate with the pouch facing up.
- Break the mixture of breadcrumb between the mushrooms, stuff the pouch and gently press it down to firm 4. Put the mushrooms in a single layer in the air fryer basket and set it to 360 F. Cook for 10 minutes until the filling is brown.
- For the rest of the mushrooms, repeat

SNACKS AND APPETIZERS

93. Pork Rind Tortillas

Preparation Time: 10 Minutes
Cooking Time: 5 Minutes
Servings: 4

Ingredients:

- 1-ounce pork rinds
- ¾ cup shredded mozzarella cheese
- Two tablespoons full-fat cream cheese
- One large egg

Directions:

- Place pork rinds into the food processor and pulse until finely ground.

- Place mozzarella into a large microwave-safe bowl. Breakdown cream cheese into small pieces and add them to the bowl. Microwave for 30 seconds, or wait until both kinds of cheese are melted. It can easily be stirred together into a ball. Add ground pork rinds and egg to the cheese mixture.

- Remain stirring until the mix forms a ball. If it cools too much and cheese hardens, microwave for ten more seconds.

- Separate the dough into four small balls. Put each ball of dough between two sheets of parchment and roll into a ¼" flat layer.

- Put the tortillas into the air fryer basket in a single layer, working in batches if necessary.

- Alter the temperature to 400°F and set the timer for 5 minutes.

- Tortillas will be crunchy and firm when fully cooked. Serve immediately.

94. Mozzarella Sticks

Preparation Time: 60 Minutes
Cooking Time: 10 Minutes
Servings: 4

Ingredients:

- 6 (1-ounce) mozzarella string cheese sticks
- ½ cup grated Parmesan cheese
- ½ ounce pork rinds, finely ground
- One teaspoon dried parsley
- Two large eggs

Directions:

- Put mozzarella sticks on a cutting board and cut in half. Freeze 45 minutes or until stable. If freezing overnight, remove frozen sticks after 1 hour, place it into an airtight zip-top storage bag, then put it again in the freezer for future use.

- In a large container, mix Parmesan, ground pork rinds, and parsley.

- In a medium bowl, whisk eggs.

- Dip a frozen mozzarella stick into beaten eggs and then into Parmesan mixture to coat. Repeat with remaining sticks. Position mozzarella sticks into the air fryer basket.

- Regulate the temperature to 400°F and set the timer for 10 minutes or until golden.

- Serve warm.

95. Mini Sweet Pepper Poppers

Preparation Time: 15 Minutes
Cooking Time: 8 Minutes
Servings: 4

Ingredients:

- Eight mini sweet peppers
- 4 ounces full-fat cream cheese, softened
- Four slices sugar-free bacon, cooked and crumbled
- ¼ cup shredded pepper jack cheese

Directions:

- Remove the tops from the peppers and portion each one in half lengthways. Practice a small knife to eliminate seeds and membranes.

- In a small bowl, blend cream cheese, bacon, and pepper jack.

- Place three teaspoons of the mix into each sweet pepper and press down smooth. Put it into the fryer basket.

- Regulate the temperature to 400°F and set the timer for 8 minutes.
- Serve warm.

96. Garlic Cheese Bread

Preparation Time: 10 Minutes
Cooking Time: 10 Minutes
Servings: 2

Ingredients:

- 1 cup shredded mozzarella cheese
- ¼ cup grated Parmesan cheese
- One large egg
- ½ teaspoon garlic powder

Directions:

- Mix all fixings in a large bowl. Torn a piece of parchment to fit your air fryer basket. Press the mixture into a circle on the parchment and place it into the air fryer basket.
- Regulate the temperature to 350°F and set the timer for 10 minutes.
- Serve warm.

97. Bacon-Wrapped Brie

Preparation Time: 5 Minutes
Cooking Time: 10 Minutes
Servings: 8

Ingredients:

- Four slices of sugar-free bacon
- 1 (8-ounce) round Brie

Directions:

- Put two slices of bacon to form an X. Then place the third slice of bacon parallel across the center of the X. Place the fourth slice of bacon straight up across the X. Then it should look like a plus sign (+) on top of an X. Position the Brie in the middle of the bacon.
- Wrap the bacon around the Brie, locking with a few toothpicks. Torn a piece of parchment to fit your air fryer basket and place the bacon-wrapped Brie on top. Put it inside the basket of the air fryer.
- Alter the temperature to 400°F, then change the timer for 10 minutes.
- When 3 minutes keep on the timer, cautiously flip Brie.
- When cooked, bacon will be crunchy, and cheese will be soft and melty. When serving it, cut into eight slices.

98. Smoky BBQ Roasted Almonds

Preparation Time: 5 Minutes
Cooking Time: 6 Minutes
Servings: 4

Ingredients:

- 1 cup of raw almonds
- Two teaspoons coconut oil
- One teaspoon chili powder
- ¼ teaspoon cumin
- ¼ teaspoon smoked paprika

Directions:

- In a large bowl, toss all fixings until almonds are evenly coated with oil and spices. Place almonds into the air fryer basket.
- Regulate the temperature to 320°F and set the timer for 6 minutes.
- Toss the fryer basket midway through the cooking time.
- Allow cooling completely.

99. Ranch Roasted Almonds

Preparation Time: 5 Minutes
Cooking Time: 6 Minutes
Servings: 8

Ingredients:

- 2 cups of raw almonds
- Two tablespoons unsalted butter, melted
- ½ (1-ounce) ranch dressing mix packet

Directions:

- In a large container, chuck almonds in butter to lightly coat. Sprinkle ranch mix over almonds and toss. Place almonds into the air fryer basket.

- Alter the temperature to 320°F and set the timer for 6 minutes.
- Shake the basket two- or three times during cooking.
- Let cool at least 20 minutes. Almonds will be soft but become crunchier during cooling—stock in an airtight vessel for up to 3 days.

100.   Pork Rind Nachos

Preparation Time: 5 Minutes
Cooking Time: 5 Minutes
Servings: 2

Ingredients:

- 1-ounce pork rinds
- 4 ounces shredded cooked chicken
- ½ cup shredded Monterey jack cheese
- ¼ cup sliced pickled jalapeños
- ¼ cup guacamole

Directions:

- Place pork rinds into 6" round baking pan. Cover with shredded chicken and Monterey jack cheese. Place pan into the air fryer basket.
- Adjust the temperature to 370°F and set the timer for 5 minutes or until cheese is melted.
- Top with jalapeños, guacamole, and sour cream. Serve immediately.

101.   Chicken Kebab

Preparation Time: 15 Minutes
Cooking Time: 15 Minutes
Servings: 6

Ingredients:

- Boneless Chicken Breast – 1.5 lb. cut into large, bite-sized pc
- Smoked Paprika – ½ tsp
- Turmeric – 1 tsp
- Ground Black Pepper – ½ tsp
- Plain Greek Yogurt – ¼ cup

Directions:

- Place chicken into a large bowl.
- Place Greek yogurt, smoked paprika, black pepper, and turmeric in a small blender container and process till you get a smooth mixture.
- Pour the blend over the chicken and coat it evenly.
- Allow chicken to marinate for 15 minutes.
- Put the chicken inside the basket of the air fryer.
- Set the air fryer to 370 degrees F and cook for 15 minutes.
- After 8 minutes, flip the chicken over and continue cooking.
- Once done, allow them to sit for several minutes and serve.

102.   Zucchini Parmesan Chips

Preparation Time: 10 Minutes
Cooking Time: 10 Minutes
Servings: 4

Ingredients:

- Zucchini - 2, medium-sized, thinly sliced
- Egg – 1, lightly beaten
- Italian-seasoned Breadcrumbs – ½ cup
- Parmesan Cheese – ½ cup grated
- Smoked Paprika – ½ tsp.

Directions:

- Slice the zucchinis as thinly as possible by means of a mandolin slicer or a knife. User a paper towel to dry the excess moisture.
- In a shallow container, beat the egg and add a pinch of salt and pepper. In another bowl, combine the breadcrumbs, smoked paprika, and grated cheese.
- Dip the zucchini slice in the egg mixture, followed by the breadcrumb's mixture. Coat evenly.
- Spray the coated zucchini slices with mist or cooking spray.
- Place the zucchini slices into the air fryer basket, do not overlap.
- Cook for 8 minutes at 350° F.

- Once done, enjoy and serve hot.

103. Cheese Stuffed Mushroom

Preparation Time: 6 Minutes
Cooking Time: 8 Minutes
Servings: 5

Ingredients:

- Fresh Mushroom – 8 oz. Large
- Parmesan Cheese – ¼ cup shredded
- Cream Cheese – 4 oz. Reduced-fat
- Worcestershire Sauce – 1 tsp
- White Cheddar Cheese – 1/8 cup

Directions:

- Cut the stem out of the mushroom, then melt the cream cheese.
- Combine cream cheese, parmesan cheese, white cheddar cheese, Worcestershire sauce, and salt & pepper in a bowl. Mix well.
- Stuff the mixture into the mushrooms.
- Place the mushrooms into the air fryer and cook for 8 minutes at 370 degrees F.
- Once done, serve and enjoy.

104. Spicy Bacon Wrapped Chicken

Preparation Time: 10 Minutes
Cooking Time: 13 Minutes
Servings: 4

Ingredients:

- Chicken Breast – 1 lb. cut into cubes.
- Bacon – 6 slices, cut into thirds
- Chili Powder – ½ tbsp.
- Cayenne Pepper – 1/8 tsp

Directions:

- Place a piece of chicken onto a piece of bacon. Roll it up and secure it with a toothpick.
- Blend the chili powder and cayenne pepper into a bowl. Coat the bacon-wrapped chicken into the mixture and set aside.

- Place the bacon-wrapped chicken into the air fryer basket and cook at 380 degrees F for 13 minutes.
- Once done, serve and enjoy.

105. Brussel Sprouts

Preparation Time: 2 Minutes
Cooking Time: 10 Minutes
Servings: 2

Ingredients:

- Brussel Sprouts – 2 cups, cut in half
- Balsamic Vinegar - 1 tbsp.
- Olive Oil – 1 tbsp.
- Sea salt - ¼ tbsp.

Directions:

- Toss the Brussel sprouts along with all the ingredients and place it in the air fryer for 10 minutes at 400 C.
- Keep checking on it every 2-3 minutes, making sure to get the right brownish color.
- Once done, enjoy and serve hot.

106. Buffalo Cauliflower

Preparation Time: 5 Minutes
Cooking Time: 10 Minutes
Servings: 4

Ingredients:

- Cauliflower Florets – 4 cups
- Panko Breadcrumbs – 1 cup
- Sea Salt – 1 tsp.
- Vegan Butter – ¼ cup, melted
- Vegan Buffalo Sauce – ¼ cup

Directions:

- Melt the vegan butter in a bowl.
- Add buffalo sauce into the butter and stir.
- Hold the stem and dip each floret into the buffalo mixture, making sure most floret is coated with sauce. Shake off the excess.
- Mix sea salt with breadcrumbs and coat the dipped floret evenly with it.

- Place the floret into the air fryer and cook for 10 minutes at 350°F. After 5 minutes, shake the florets, making sure they are evenly cooked.
- Once done, serve and enjoy.

107. Cauliflower Fritters

Preparation Time: 2 Minutes
Cooking Time: 13 Minutes
Servings: 4

Ingredients:

- Cauliflower Florets - 4 cups.
- Bread Crumbs - 1 cup
- Salt - 1 tsp.
- Butter - ¼ cup, melted.
- Buffalo sauce - ¼ cup

Directions:

- Twitch by melting the butter in the microwave for 10 seconds.
- Add the buffalo sauce into the butter and whisk well.
- Hold each cauliflower by its stem and dip it into the mixture.
- Next, coat the cauliflower into the bread crumbs.
- Place the coated cauliflowers into the air fryer.
- Cook 400 degrees F for 12 minutes.
- After 7 minutes, toss the cauliflowers and cook for another 6 minutes.
- Once done, serve hot and enjoy or with your favorite dip.

Nutritions:

Calories: 80
Fats: 6g
Protein: 6g
Carbs: 1g

108. Loaded Tater Tot Bites

Preparation Time: 5 Minutes
Cooking Time: 20 Minutes
Servings: 6

Ingredients:

- 24 tater tots, frozen
- 1 cup Swiss cheese, grated
- Six tablespoons Canadian bacon, cooked and chopped
- 1/4 cup Ranch dressing

Directions:

- Spritz the silicone muffin cups with non-stick cooking spray. Now, press the tater tots down into each cup.
- Divide the cheese, bacon, and Ranch dressing between tater tot cups.
- Cook in the preheated Air Fryer using 395 degrees for 10 minutes. Serve in paper cake cups. Bon appétit!

109. Italian-Style Tomato-Parmesan Crisps

Preparation Time: 5 Minutes
Cooking Time: 20 Minutes
Servings: 4

Ingredients:

- 4 Roma tomatoes, sliced
- Two tablespoons olive oil
- Sea salt and white pepper, to taste
- One teaspoon Italian seasoning mix
- Four tablespoons Parmesan cheese, grated

Directions:

- Begin by preheating your Air Fryer, then set it to 350 degrees F. Generously grease the Air Fryer basket with nonstick cooking oil.
- Toss the sliced tomatoes with the remaining *ingredient*. Transfer them to the cooking basket without overlapping.
- Cook in the warmed Air Fryer for 5 minutes. Shake the cooking basket and cook an additional 5 minutes. Work in batches.
- Serve with Mediterranean aioli for dipping, if desired. Bon appétit!

110. Roasted Parsnip Sticks with Salted Caramel

Preparation Time: 5 Minutes
Cooking Time: 25 Minutes
Servings: 4

Ingredients:

- 1-pound parsnip, trimmed, scrubbed, cut into sticks
- Two tablespoon avocado oil
- Two tablespoons granulated sugar
- Two tablespoons butter
- 1/4 teaspoon ground allspice

Directions:

- Toss the parsnip with the avocado oil; bake in the preheated Air Fryer at 380 degrees F for 15 minutes, and occasionally shake the cooking basket to ensure even cooking.
- Then, heat the sugar and one tablespoon of water in a small pan over medium heat. Cook until the sugar has dissolved; bring to a boil.
- Keep swirling the pan around until the sugar reaches a rich caramel color. Pour in 2 tablespoons of cold water. Now, add the butter, allspice, and salt. The mixture should be runny.
- Afterward, drizzle the salted caramel over the roasted parsnip sticks and enjoy!

111. Baked Cheese Crisps

Preparation Time: 5 Minutes
Cooking Time: 15 Minutes
Servings: 4

Ingredients:

- 1/2 cup Parmesan cheese, shredded
- 1 cup Cheddar cheese, shredded
- One teaspoon Italian seasoning
- 1/2 cup marinara sauce

Directions:

- Begin by preheating your Air Fryer and set it to 350 degrees F. Place a piece of parchment paper in the cooking basket.
- Mix the cheese with the Italian seasoning.
- Add around one tablespoon of the cheese mixture (per crisp to the basket, making sure

they are not touching—Bake for 6 minutes or until browned to your liking.

- Work in batches and place them on a large tray to cool slightly. Serve with the marinara sauce. Bon appétit!

112. Puerto Rican Tostones

Preparation Time: 5 Minutes
Cooking Time: 15 Minutes
Servings: 2

Ingredients:

- One ripe plantain, sliced
- One tablespoon sunflower oil
- A pinch of grated nutmeg
- A pinch of kosher salt

Directions:

- Toss the plantains with the oil, nutmeg, and salt in a bowl.
- Cook in the preheated Air Fryer at 400 degrees F for 10 minutes, shaking the cooking basket halfway through the cooking time.
- Regulate the seasonings to taste and serve immediately.

113. Cajun Cheese Sticks

Preparation Time: 5 Minutes
Cooking Time: 15 Minutes
Servings: 4

Ingredients:

- 1/2 cup all-purpose flour
- Two eggs
- 1/2 cup parmesan cheese, grated
- One tablespoon Cajun seasonings
- Eight cheese sticks, kid-friendly

Directions:

- To begin, set up your breading station. Place the all-purpose flour in a dish. In a separate dish, whisk the eggs.
- Finally, mix the parmesan cheese and Cajun seasoning in a third dish.

- Start by dredging the cheese sticks in the flour; then, dip them into the egg. Press the cheese sticks into the parmesan mixture, coating evenly.

- Place the breaded cheese sticks in the lightly greased Air Fryer basket. Cook with settings at 380 degrees F for 6 minutes.

- Serve with ketchup and enjoy!

114. Classic Deviled Eggs

Preparation Time: 5 Minutes
Cooking Time: 20 Minutes
Servings: 3

Ingredients:

- Five eggs
- Two tablespoons mayonnaise
- Two tablespoons sweet pickle relish
- Sea salt, to taste
- 1/2 teaspoon mixed peppercorns, crushed

Directions:

- Put the wire rack in the Air Fryer basket; lower the eggs onto the wire rack.

- Cook utilizing 270 degrees F for 15 minutes.

- Handover them to an ice-cold water bath to stop the cooking

- Peel the eggs underneath cold running water; slice them into halves.

- Puree the egg yolks with the mayo, sweet pickle relish, salt; spoon yolk mixture into egg whites. Assemble on a nice serving platter and garnish with the mixed peppercorns. Bon appétit!

115. Barbecue Little Smokies

Preparation Time: 5 Minutes
Cooking Time: 20 Minutes
Servings: 6

Ingredients:

- 1-pound beef cocktail wieners
- 10 ounces barbecue sauce

Directions:

- Twitch by preheating your Air Fryer to 380 degrees F.

- Prick holes into your sausages using a fork and transfer them to the baking pan.

- Cook for 13 minutes. Spoon the barbecue sauce into the pan and cook an additional 2 minutes.

- Serve with toothpicks. Bon appétit!

116. Paprika Potato Chips

Preparation Time: 5 Minutes
Cooking Time: 45 Minutes
Servings: 3

Ingredients:

- Three potatoes, thinly sliced
- One teaspoon sea salt
- One teaspoon garlic powder
- One teaspoon paprika
- 1/4 cup ketchup

Directions:

- Add the sliced potatoes to a bowl with salted water. Let them soak for 30 minutes. Drain and rinse your potatoes.

- Pat dry and toss with salt.

- Cook in the preheated Air Fryer set at 400 degrees F for 15 minutes, occasionally shaking the basket.

- Work in batches. Toss with the garlic powder and paprika. Serve with ketchup. Enjoy!

117. Cheddar Dip

Preparation Time: 5 Minutes
Cooking Time: 15 Minutes
Servings: 6

Ingredients:

- 8 oz. cheddar cheese; grated
- 12 oz. coconut cream
- 2 tsp. hot sauce

Directions:

- In a ramekin, mix the cream with hot sauce and cheese and whisk.

- Put the ramekin in the fryer and cook at 390°F for 12 minutes. Whisk, divide into bowls, and serve as a dip

118. Parmesan Sticks

Preparation Time: 5 minutes
Cooking Time: 15 minutes
Servings: 4

Ingredients:

- ¼ Teaspoon Black Pepper
- 4 Tablespoons Almond Flour
- 1 Egg
- ½ Cup Heavy Cream
- 8 Ounces Parmesan Cheese

Directions:

- Crack your egg into a bowl, beating it. Add in your almond flour and cream, mixing well.

- Sprinkle your cream mixture with black pepper, whisking well.

- Cut your cheese into short, thick sticks, and then dip it in the cream mixture. Place these sticks in a plastic bag and place them in the freezer. Let them freeze.

- Turn your air fryer to 400, and then place your frozen sticks on the air fryer rack, and then cook for eight minutes.

119. Garlic Mozzarella Sticks

Preparation Time: 1 hour and 5 minutes
Cooking Time: 10 minutes
Servings: 4

Ingredients:

- 1 Tablespoon Italian Seasoning
- 1 Cup Parmesan Cheese
- 8 String Cheeses, Diced
- 2 Eggs, Beaten
- 1 Clove Garlic, Minced

Directions:

- Start by combining your parmesan, garlic and Italian seasoning in a bowl. Dip your cheese into the egg, and mix well.

- Roll it into your cheese crumbles, and then press the crumbs into the cheese.

- Place them in the fridge for an hour, and then preheat your air fryer to 375.

- Spray your air fryer down with oil, and then arrange the cheese strings into the basket. Cook for eight to nine minutes at 365.

- Allow them to cool for at least five minutes before serving.

120. Zucchini Chips

Preparation Time: 5 minutes
Cooking Time: 20 minutes
Servings: 4

Ingredients:

- 2 Zucchini
- 1 Teaspoon Olive Oil
- 1 Teaspoon Paprika
- Sea Salt to Taste

Directions:

- Preheat your air fryer to 370, and then slice your zucchini.

- Sprinkle your salt and paprika over the zucchini. Sprinkle them down with oil, and then cook for thirteen minutes.

121. Pork Rinds

Preparation Time: 5 minutes
Cooking Time: 10 minutes
Servings: 8

Ingredients:

- ½ Teaspoon Black Pepper
- 1 Teaspoon Chili Flakes
- ½ Teaspoon Sea Salt, Fine
- 1 Teaspoon Olive Oil
- 1 lb. Pork Rinds

Directions:

- Start by heating your air fryer to 365, and then spray it down with olive oil.

- Place your pork rinds in your air fryer basket, and sprinkle with your seasoning. Mix well, and then cook for seven minutes.

- Shake gently, and then serve cooled.

122. Roasted Parsnips

Preparation Time: 5 minutes
Cooking Time: 40 minutes
Servings: 4

Ingredients:

- 2 lbs. Parsnips, Peeled & Cut into Chunks
- 2 Tablespoons Maple Syrup
- 1 Tablespoon Olive Oil
- 1 Tablespoon Parsley Flakes

Directions:

- Start by heating your air fryer to 360, and then add in your ingredients. Make sure that your parsnips are well coated.
- Cook for forty minutes, and then serve warm.

123. Honey Roasted Carrots

Preparation Time: 5 minutes
Cooking Time: 20 minutes
Servings: 4

Ingredients:

- 1 Tablespoon Honey, Raw
- 3 Cups Baby Carrots
- 1 Tablespoon Olive Oil
- Sea Salt & Black Pepper to Taste

Directions:

- Put all of the ingredients in a bowl, then heat your air fryer to 390.
- Cook for twelve minutes and serve warm.

124. Crisp Broccoli

Preparation Time: 5 minutes
Cooking Time: 20 minutes
Servings: 4

Ingredients:

- 1 Tablespoon Lemon Juice, Fresh
- 2 Teaspoon Olive Oil
- 1 Head Broccoli

Directions:

- Start by rinsing your broccoli and patting it dry. Cut it into florets, and then separate them. Make sure that if you use the stems it's cut into one-inch chunks and peeled.
- Toss your broccoli pieces with your lemon juice and olive oil until they're well coated. Roast your broccoli in the fryer in batches for ten for fourteen minutes. Each. They should be tender and crisp, and then serve warm.

125. Roasted Bell Pepper

Preparation Time: 5 minutes
Cooking Time: 20 minutes
Servings: 4

Ingredients:

- 1 Teaspoon Olive Oil
- ½ Teaspoon Thyme
- 4 Cloves Garlic, Minced
- 4 Bell Peppers, Cut into Fourths

Directions:

- Start by putting your peppers in your air fryer basket and drizzling with olive oil. Make sure they're coated well, and then roast for fifteen minutes.
- Sprinkle with thyme and garlic, roasting for an additional three to five minutes. They should be tender, and serve warm.

126. Curried Brussels Sprouts

- **Preparation Time:** 5 minutes
- **Cooking Time:** 25 minutes
- **Servings:** 4

Ingredients:

- 1 lb. Brussel Sprouts, end Trimmed & Halved
- 2 Teaspoons Olive Oil
- 1 Tablespoon Lemon Juice, Fresh
- 3 Teaspoons Curry Powder, Divided

Directions:

- Start by getting gout a large bowl and mix together your olive oil with a teaspoon of curry powder. Toss your Brussel sprouts in, mixing until well coated. Place them in your air fryer basket, roasting for twelve minutes. During this Cooking Time you'll need to shake your basket once.

- Sprinkle with the remaining curry powder and lemon juice, shaking your basket again. Roast for an additional three to five minutes. Your Brussel sprouts should be crisp and browned. Serve warm.

127. Garlic Asparagus

Preparation Time: 5 minutes
Cooking Time: 10 minutes
Servings: 4

Ingredients:

- 1 lb. Asparagus, Rinsed & Trimmed
- 2 Teaspoons Olive Oil
- 3 Cloves Garlic, Minced
- 2 Tablespoons Balsamic Vinegar
- ½ Teaspoon Thyme

Directions:

- Start by getting out a large bowl to toss your asparagus in olive oil before placing your vegetables in the air fryer basket.
- Sprinkle with garlic before roasting for eight to eleven minutes. Your asparagus should be tender but crisp.
- Drizzle with thyme and balsamic vinegar before serving warm.

128. Roasted Garlic

Preparation Time: 5 minutes
Cooking Time: 30 minutes
Servings: 10

Ingredients:

- 3 whole garlic bulbs, halved
- 3 tablespoons olive oil
- ¼ teaspoon kosher salt

Directions:

- Select the Bake function on the Air Fryer, adjust time to 30 minutes, then press Start/Cancel to heat up.

- Flavor garlic halves with olive oil and salt.
- Layer the food tray with parchment paper, then place garlic bulb halves face down onto the food tray.
- Insert the food tray at a low position in the warmed-up air fryer, then press Start/Cancel to start baking.
- Flip garlic halves face up after cooking for 20 minutes.
- Remove garlic halves when done and serve as a side, or make it into a paste to spread with butter over toast.

129. Dehydrated Candied Bacon

Preparation Time: 3 hours
Cooking Time: 4 hours and 10 minutes
Servings: 4

Ingredients:

- 6 slices bacon
- 3 tablespoons light brown sugar
- 2 tablespoons rice vinegar
- 2 tablespoons chili paste
- 1 tablespoon soy sauce

Directions:

- Mix brown sugar, rice vinegar, chili paste, and soy sauce together in a bowl.
- Add bacon slices and mix until all are evenly coated.
- Set aside for up to 3 hours or up until ready to dehydrate.
- Then put the bacon on the food tray.
- Set bacon on the air fryer 's wire rack, then insert the rack at mid-position in the air fryer toaster oven.
- Select the Dehydrate function on the Air Fryer, set time to 4 hours, then press Start.
- Remove the tray once done baking and let the bacon cool for 5 minutes, then serve.

130. Dehydrated Spiced Orange Slices

Preparation Time: 10 minutes
Cooking Time: 6 hours

Servings: 3

Ingredients:

- 2 large oranges, cut into 1/8-inch-thick slices
- ½ teaspoon ground star anise
- ½ teaspoon ground cinnamon
- 1 tbsp Choco-hazelnut spread

Directions:

- Dash seasonings on the orange slices.
- Place into the fry basket, then insert the basket at mid-position in the Air Fryer.
- Select the Dehydrate function, fix the time to 6 hours and temperature to 140°F, then press Start.
- Remove once done, and if desired serve with chocolate hazelnut spread.

131. Ranch Kale Chip

Preparation Time: 5 minutes
Cooking Time: 3 hours
Servings: 2

Ingredients:

- 3 whole kale leaves, cut into 2-inch squares
- 1 tbsp. olive oil
- 1 tbsp. ranch seasoning

Directions:

- In a small bowl, mix the olive oil and ranch seasoning.
- Mix ranch mixture with kale leaves until all are evenly coated.
- Put the kale leaves into the fry basket, then insert the fry basket at mid-position in the Air Fryer.
- Select the Dehydrate function, fix the time to 3 hours and temperature to 140°F, then press Start/Cancel.
- Remove when done and serve.

132. Taco Seasoned Kale Chips

Preparation Time: 5 minutes
Cooking Time: 3 hours
Servings: 2

Ingredients:

- 3 whole kale leaves, cut into 2-inch squares
- 1 tbsp.olive oil
- 1 tbsp. taco seasoning

Directions:

- Mix taco seasoning and olive oil in a small bowl.
- Combine taco seasoning mixture with kale leaves until all are evenly coated.
- Place kale leaves into the fry basket, then insert the fry basket at mid-position in the Air Fryer.
- Select the Dehydrate function, fix the time to 3 hours and temperature to 140°F, then press Start.
- Remove when done and serve.

133. Bacon-Wrapped Hot Dogs

Preparation Time: 5 minutes
Cooking Time: 20 minutes
Servings: 4

Ingredients:

- 4 strips thick-cut bacon
- 4 beef hot dogs
- 4 hot dog buns, slightly toasted

Directions:

- Wrap 1 piece of bacon around each hot dog, allowing the edges of the bacon to overlap slightly. Set aside.
- Select the Broil function on the Air Fryer, fix the time to 20 minutes, then press Start/Cancel to preheat.
- Line the food tray with foil, then set the wire rack on top of the food tray.
- Place the bacon-wrapped hot dogs on the wire rack, then insert the rack and food tray at top position in the preheated air fryer toaster oven. Press Start/Cancel.
- Flip the hot dogs halfway through cooking.
- Remove when done and place each hot dog in a hot dog bun.

- Serve with your choice of toppings.

134.   Avocado Baked Egg

Preparation Time: 5 minutes
Cooking Time: 20 minutes
Servings: 2

Ingredients:

- 1 large ripe avocado, halved and pitted
- 2 eggs
- ¼ tsp. salt
- ¼ tsp. black pepper
- 2 tbsp. grated Parmesan cheese

Directions:

- Put the avocado halves on the edges of the baking sheet. The rim of the baking sheet will stop them from rolling over.

- Scoop out some of the flesh from the avocado halves to make a hole large enough for 1 egg.

- Crack 1 egg into each of the halved avocados.

- Flavor with salt and pepper.

- Insert the wire rack at mid-position in the Air Fryer Toaster Oven. Select the Air Fry function, set timer to 22 minutes, then press Start to warm it up.

- In the preheated air fryer, place the baking sheet on top of the wire rack then press Start.

- After 12 minutes of cook time, sprinkle Parmesan cheese on the avocado halves.

- Remove the baked avocados when done and garnish with finely chopped chives, then serve.

135.   Air Fryer Buffalo Mushroom Poppers

Preparation Time: 5 minutes
Cooking Time: 10 minutes
Servings: 4

Ingredients:

- 1 pound Sparkling Total Button Mushroom
- ½ cup flour and panko mixture
- Grind Salt and Black Pepper

- 1/4 cup buffalo style hot sauce
- 2 eggs

Directions:

- Remove the stems from the mushroom peel. Finely chop and Put the cap on one side. Stir the chopped mushroom stem, salt, and pepper together in a small bowl. Fill each mushroom cap with about 1 tablespoon combination, rounding the filling to form a clean ball.

- Place Pancho in a shallow bowl. Place the dough in a 2d shallow bowl, and the eggs in a third shallow bowl. Coat mushrooms in flour, dip in egg mixture, and dredge in panko, pressing to adhere. Coat mushrooms properly with cooking spray.

- Place half of the mushrooms in an air fryer basket, and cook dinner at 350 ° F until golden brown and crispy. Transfer the cooked mushrooms to a huge bowl. Repeat with the last mushroom. Drizzle sauce over mushrooms toss to coat. Sprinkle with chives.

- Serve Mushroom Poppers.

136.   Air Fryer Potato Chips

Preparation Time: 5 minutes
Cooking Time: 10 minutes
Servings: 4

Ingredients:

- 1 medium russet potato, peeled,
- 1/8-inch-thick slices (about 3/4 lb.)
- 1 tbsp canola oil
- sea salt and freshly ground black pepper
- 1 tablespoon chopped Happened. Clean henna

Directions:

- Soak the potato slices in a large bowl of cold water, for 20 minutes. Pat dry the potatoes with paper towels.

- Dry-wipe the bowl then add oil, salt, and pepper. Add potatoes Toss gently to coat.

- Lightly grease air fryer basket with cooking spray. Place half a slice of potato in a basket, and prepare dinner in two batches at 375 ° F, until it becomes crispy within about 25 to 30 minutes.

- Cautiously remove the chips from the air fryer to the plate using a pair of tongs, Sprinkle over rosemary once or in an airtight plastic container.

137.   Air Fried Corn Dog Bites

Preparation Time: 5 minutes
Cooking Time: 10 minutes
Servings: 4

Ingredients:

- 2 uncured All Beef Hot Puppies
- ½ cup All-Purpose Flour
- Half Cup Bamboo Broach (About 2 1/8 oz.) or 12 craft sticks
- 1 1/2 cups minced corn flakes cereal
- 2 large eggs, lightly beaten

Directions:

- Slice each hot dog half lengthwise each length. Cut each half into 3 equal pieces. Put a craft stick or bamboo skewer at 1 end of each piece of a hot dog.

- Place the dough in a shallow dish. Place the overwhelmed eggs gently in another shallow dish. Place the cornflakes in a 0.33 shallow dish. Dip the hot dogs in the flour, adding extra. Dip in eggs, allowing any excess to drip off. Dredge into cornflake pieces, pressing to adhere.

- Lightly grease the air fryer basket with cooking spray. Place 6 corn dog bites in a basket Spray lightly with cooking spray. Cook at 375 ° F until the corn is golden brown and crispy, 10 minutes, cut the corn dog through cooking. Repeat with remaining corn dog bite.

- To serve, place three corn dog bites on each plate with 2 tablespoons of mustard, and serve immediately.

138.   Sauté in an Air Fryer

Preparation Time: 5 minutes
Cooking Time: 20 minutes

Servings: 4

Ingredients:

- Empanadas 1 tablespoon olive oil 3 ounces (85/15) lean floor red meat 1/4 cup finely chopped white onion three ounces.
- Finely cremini mushrooms 2 tablespoons chopped finely garlic 6 pitted green olives chopped, cinnamon half cup chopped tomatoes chopped
- 1/4 red bell pepper
- 1/4 teaspoon ground cumin
- 1/8 teaspoon ground 8 square gyoza wrappers 1 large egg, beaten gently

Directions:

- In a medium pan, heat the oil on medium-high. Add beef and onion Bake, crumble, until beginning to brown, three minutes.

- Add mushrooms Cook, stirring occasionally until the mushrooms are beginning to brown, 6 minutes. Add garlic, olives, paprika, cumin, and cinnamon Cook the dinner until the mushrooms become very soft and leave their liquid for 3 minutes. Stir in tomatoes, and cook dinner 1 minute, stirring occasionally. Transfer the filling to a bowl, and let cool for 5 minutes.

- Arrange the 4 goji covers on the work surface. Place about 1 tbsp of stuffing in the center of each cover. Brush the edges of the wrapper with eggs wrap the folds, wrapping the edges to seal. Repeat technique with closing cover and filling.

- Place 4 implants in one layer in an air fryer basket, and cook for 7 minutes, until well browned at 400 ° F. Repeat with the last empanadas.

139.   Air Fryer Churros with Chocolate Sauce

Preparation Time: 5 minutes
Cooking Time: 10 minutes
Servings: 4

Ingredients:

- 1/2 cup water 1/4 teaspoon kosher salt

- ◆ Unsalted butter, split half cup
- ◆ 2 tbsp. All-purpose flour
- ◆ 2 large eggs
- ◆ 1/3 cup granulated sugar cinnamon

Directions:

- Bring 1/4 cup of water, salt, and butter to a boil in a small saucepan over medium-high. Reduce heat from medium to low Add the flour, and stir vigorously with a wooden spoon until the dough is smooth about 30 seconds.

- Continue cooking, stirring continuously, until the dough starts to move away from the sides of the pan and leave a movie variety on the back of the pan for 2 to 3 minutes.

- Transfer the dough to a medium bowl. Stir continuously for about 1 minute, until slightly cooled. Add eggs, 1 at a time, stirring continuously until completely smooth after each addition. Transfer the mixture to a piping bag equipped with a medium celebrity tip. Chill 30 minutes.

- Pipe 6 (3 inches long) pieces into one layer in an air fryer basket. Cook at 380 ° F, about 10 minutes, until golden. Repeat with the last flour.

- In a medium bowl, collectively stir the sugar and cinnamon. Brush the cooked churros with the remaining 2 tablespoons of melted butter, and roll in a sugar mixture.

- Serve churros with chocolate sauce.

140.   Air Fryer Sweet Potato Tots

Preparation Time: 5 minutes
Cooking Time: 10 minutes
Servings: 4

Ingredients:

- ◆ 2 small (14 ounces total) candy potatoes, peeled
- ◆ 1 tbsp potato starch
- ◆ 1/8 teaspoon garlic powder
- ◆ 1 1/4 teaspoons kosher salt, split 3/4 cup no salt

Directions:

- Put a medium pan of water to a boil over high heat. Add the potatoes, and cook the dinner until the fork is tender about 15 minutes. Transfer potatoes to a plate to cool for about 15 minutes.

- Working on a medium bowl, grate a potato using a giant hole in a box grater. Gently toss with potato starch, garlic powder, and 1 teaspoon salt. Size combination in approximately 24 (1-inch) total-shaped cylinders.

- Lightly grease the air fryer with cooking spray. Put 1/2 of the children (about 12) in a layer in the basket, and spray with cooking spray. Cook to 400 ° F for 12 to 14 minutes, turning the children halfway through the Cooking Time. Remove from the fry basket and sprinkle with 1/8 teaspoon salt. Repeat with remaining children and salt. Serve directly with ketchup.

141.   Air-Fried Calzone

Preparation Time: 5 minutes
Cooking Time: 20 minutes
Servings: 4

Ingredients:

- ◆ 1 teaspoon olive oil
- ◆ 1/4 cup finely chopped pink onion (from 1 small onion) 3 oz.
- ◆ Baby spinach leaves (about three cups) 1/3 cup low-sodium marinara sauce 2 oz.
- ◆ Chopped rotisserie hen breast (about 1/3 cup)
- ◆ 1 1/2 ounces' flour 6 ounces freshly prepared wheat pizza pre-chopped (about 6 Karachi.) Part-time skim mozzarella cheese spray cooking

Directions:

- Heat the olive oil in a medium nonstick pan on medium-high. Add onion, stirring occasionally, until tender, and cook for 2 minutes. Add spinachCook for two and a half minutes, until dinner is covered. Remove pan from heat Stir in marinara sauce and chicken.

- Divide flour into 4 equal pieces. Gently roll each piece into a 6-inch circle on a flared surface. Place one-quarter of the spinach mixture more than half of each flour cycle. Top with one-quarter cheese. To bend the dough, fold the dough, shrink the seal. Coat calzone with cooking spray.

- Place the calzone in an air fryer basket, and prepare dinner at 325 ° F for 12 minutes, until the dough turns golden brown, flip the calzone after eight minutes.

142. Air-Fried Buffalo Cauliflower Bites

Preparation Time: 5 minutes
Cooking Time: 30 minutes
Servings: 4

Ingredients:

- ◆ 3 tablespoons ketchup without salt 2 tablespoons hot sauce (e.g. Frank's Red-hot)
- ◆ 1 giant egg white 3/4 cup Panko (Japanese-style cream) 1/2 (3-lb) Head.
- ◆ Cauliflower, trimmed and cooked in 1-inch florets (about 4 cups of florets).
- ◆ Cooking spray 1/4 cup low-fat buttercream 1/4-ounce crumbled blue cheese (about 1 tbsp) 1 small garlic clove, 1 teaspoon pink wine. Vinegar 1/4 teaspoon pepper.

Directions:

- In a small bowl, collectively ketchup, hot sauce, and egg whites until smooth. Place panko in a large bowl. Toss the cauliflower flower and ketchup combination collectively into another giant bowl until coated. Working in batches, tossing cauliflower to coat the panko. Coat cabbage well with cooking spray.

- Put the cabbage in an air fryer basket, and cook at 320 ° F for about 20 minutes, until golden brown and crisp. Repeat with the remaining cauliflower.

- When the cabbage cooks, stir together bitter cream, blue cheese, garlic, vinegar and pepper in a small bowl. Serve the cabbage with blue cheese sauce.

143. Artichoke Chicken

Preparation Time: 15 minutes
Cooking Time: 50 minutes
Servings: 8

Ingredients:

- ◆ 8 boneless skinless chicken breast halves
- ◆ 2 tbsp. of butter
- ◆ 2 jars (6 oz. each) marinated quartered artichoke hearts, drained
- ◆ 1 jar (4½ oz.) whole mushrooms, drained
- ◆ ½ cup of chopped onion
- ◆ 1/3 cup all-purpose flour
- ◆ 1½ tsp. of dried rosemary, crushed
- ◆ ¾ tsp. of salt
- ◆ ¼ tsp. of pepper
- ◆ 2 cups of chicken broth or (1 cup of broth and 1 cup of dry white wine)
- ◆ Hot cooked noodles
- ◆ Fresh parsley, minced

Directions:

- In a large skillet, brown the chicken in butter. After browning chicken, remove chicken to an ungreased 13x9-in. baking dish.

- Then arrange artichokes and mushrooms on top of chicken and set aside. Sauté the onion in pan juices (until crisp-tender).

- In a bowl, mix the rosemary, flour, salt and pepper. Stir into pan until blended.

- Add in the chicken broth and bring to a boil, cook and stir constantly until thickened and bubbly, for about 1 to 2 minutes.

- Remove from the heat, spoon over chicken and uncovered at 350° until a thermometer inserted in the chicken reads 170°, for about 35 to 40 minutes.

- Serve with pasta and sprinkle with parsley. Serve and enjoy!

144. Quentin's Peach-Bourbon Wings

Preparation Time: 35 minutes
Cooking Time: 15 minutes
Serving: 2

Ingredients:

- ◆ ½ cup of peach preserves

- 1 tbsp. of brown sugar
- 1 garlic clove, minced
- ¼ tsp. of salt
- 2 tbsp. of white vinegar
- 2 tbsp. of bourbon
- 1 tsp. of corn starch
- 1½ tsp. of water
- 2 lb. of chicken wings

Directions:

- Start by heating your Air fryer to 400°F. Place the preserves, brown sugar, garlic and salt in a food processor, process until blended.

- After blending the mixture, transfer to a small saucepan. Add vinegar and bourbon, bring to a boil.

- Reduce heat, simmer, uncovered, until slightly thickened, for about 4 to 6 minutes.

- Mix water and cornstarch in a bowl, until smooth. Stir into preserve mixture.

- Return to a boil. Cook and stir constantly for about 1 to 2 minutes (until thickened).

- Reserve ¼ cup of sauce for serving. Use a sharp knife, cut through the two joints on each chicken wing.

- Discard wing tips. Grease the basket of your Air fryer with cooking oil. (Work in batches as needed).

- Place chicken wing pieces in a single layer in the basket of your Air fryer. Set your Air fryer to cook for about 6 minutes.

- After the 6 minutes, turn and brush with preserve mixture. Return to your Air fryer, cook until browned and juices run clear, for about 6 to 8 minutes longer.

- Remove and keep warm. Repeat with remaining wing pieces.

- Serve wings immediately with reserved sauce.

- Serve and enjoy!

145. Chicken Breast

Preparation Time: 5 minutes
Cooking Time: 15 minutes
Servings: 4

Ingredients:

- 5 to 6 oz. chicken breasts split in half lengthwise
- Seasoning salt of choice
- Salt and pepper to taste

Directions:

- Set the Air fryer to 400°F. Cut the chicken breast in half and flavor with salt and pepper.

- Place the chicken in the basket of your Air fryer, set the temperature to 400°F.

- Close the basket and set the timer to cook for about 7 minutes. When the time is up.

- Take the chicken out and flip, cook for another 4 minutes longer.

- After the 4 minutes, remove and serve.

- Serve immediately and enjoy.

146. Rotisserie Style Whole Chicken

Preparation Time: 5 minutes
Cooking Time: 1 hour
Servings: 4

Ingredients:

- 1 whole chicken cleaned and blotted dry
- 2 tbsp. of Ghee (or coconut or olive oil)
- 1 tbsp. of TOG house seasoning

Directions:

- Remove giblet packet from chicken and pat dry. Rub Ghee/Oil all over the chicken. Season generously with TOG house seasoning.

- Place the chicken breast side down into your Air fryer. Set timer to cook at 350°F for about 30 minutes.

- After the 30 minutes, flip chicken over and cook at 350°F for an additional 30 minutes.

- Once the cooking is done, let rest for about 10 minutes.

- Serve immediately and enjoy!

147. Greek Stuffed Chicken Breast

Preparation Time: 10 minutes
Cooking Time: 15 minutes
Servings: 4

Ingredients:

- 26-oz. boneless skinless chicken breasts
- 1 cup of wild rice, prepared
- 4 oz. fat-free feta cheese
- 4 tbsp. of `Greek salad dressing

Directions:

- Slice the chicken breasts in half, making a total of 4 pieces of chicken.
- Between two pieces of parchment paper, pound the chicken breasts until thin.
- Mix prepared wild rice, 1 tbsp. of Greek dressing, and fat-free feta cheese together in a medium mixing bowl.
- Place ¼ rice mixture onto center of each chicken breast and roll covering mixture.
- Place each chicken breasts rolled side down into your Air fryer pan. Brush the remaining Greek dressing over the tops of your chicken breasts.
- Set timer to cook at 382°F for about 15 minutes. When the time is up.
- Serve immediately and enjoy!

148. Air Fried Buffalo Chicken Strips

Preparation Time: 5 minutes
Cooking Time: 15 minutes
Servings: 4

Ingredients:

- 12 ounces chicken breast strips
- ¼ cup of flour
- 1 egg (or liquid egg whites)
- Buffalo Sauce - (We used about 1/2 cup)
- Garlic salt and pepper to taste

Directions:

- In a separate bowl, place egg, and flour
- Spray a little cooking spray on the bottom of your Air fryer. Dip chicken in the flour, and then the egg, until well coated.
- Place the chicken in your Air fryer, spray the top of the chicken with a little more cooking spray.

- Set the timer to fry at 375°F for about 10 minutes. After the 10 minutes, flip and cook for an additional 3 to 5 minutes.
- When the time is up, remove chicken from your Air fryer. Place in a mixing bowl and toss in buffalo sauce until well coated.
- Serve with celery, carrots and ranch.
- Serve and enjoy!

149. Whole30 Lemon Pepper Chicken

Preparation Time: 5 minutes
Cooking Time: 15 minutes
Servings: 3

Ingredients:

- 1 chicken breast
- 2 lemons rind and juice
- 1 tablespoon of chicken seasoning
- 1 teaspoon of garlic puree
- Salt & pepper

Directions:

- Start by heating your Air fryer to 180°C. Set up your work station. Place a large sheet of silver foil on the work top.
- Add all the seasonings to it and the lemon rind. Lay out the chicken breasts onto a chopping board.
- Trim off any fatty bits and any little bones. Season each side with salt and pepper.
- Rub the chicken seasoning into both sides of the chicken breast so that it is slightly a different color.
- Place it in the silver foil sheet, rub it thoroughly so that it is fully seasoned. Seal it up very tight so that it can't breathe.
- Give it a slap with a rolling pin so that it will flatten it out and release more flavor.
- Place it in your Air fryer. Set your Air fryer to cook for about 15 minutes. After the 15 minutes, check to see if it is fully cooked in the middle before serving.
- Serve immediately and enjoy!

150. Roasted Chicken

Preparation Time: 5 minutes

Cooking Time: 1 hour and 10 minutes
Servings: 4

Ingredients:

- 1 whole chicken
- 1 tablespoon of avocado oil
- 2 tbsp. of primal palate super gyro seasoning
- 2 tablespoons of primal palate new bae seasoning
- 1 tablespoon of Himalayan pink salt

Directions:

- Start by heating your Air fryer to 375°F. Wash the chicken with clean water and Pat the chicken dry.

- Drizzle with avocado oil. Season with half the seasonings. Place the whole chicken in the basket of your Air fryer.

- Set timer to cook for about 30 minutes. Flip the chicken after 30 minutes and add the remaining seasoning.

- After flipping the chicken, set timer to cook the chicken for another 30 minutes.

- Once the chicken is done cooking, remove the chicken from the basket.

- Allow it to cool for about 5 minutes before slicing and serving.

- Serve and enjoy!

151. Pizza Stuffed Chicken

Preparation Time: 10 minutes
Cooking Time: 15 minutes
Servings: 4

Ingredients:

- 5 boneless skinless, chicken thighs
- ½ cup of pizza sauce
- 14 slices of turkey pepperoni
- ½ small red onion sliced
- 5 ounce of sliced mozzarella cheese

Directions:

- Open the chicken thighs and lay them flat on a piece of parchment paper.

- Place another piece of parchment paper on top of the chicken. Pound the chicken to create a thin piece.

- Spoon on a tbsp. of pizza sauce on each piece of the chicken and spread it equally. Put 3 pieces of turkey pepperoni on top of the sauce.

- Add a slice of Mozzarella cheese. Fold one side of the chicken over on to the other. Use a toothpick to hold the chicken together.

- Once cooked it stays together on its own. Preheat your Air fryer to 370°F for about 2 minutes.

- Smear the tray with oil, and lay the pieces out in a single layer. Add the chicken and set you Air fryer to cook for about 6 minutes.

- After the 6 minutes, Flip the chicken and cook for another 6 minutes. Add the cheese to melt on the top for the last 3 minutes,

- Always check chicken thighs to ensure they are heated to 165F.

- When the time is up, serve and enjoy!

152. Chicken Drumsticks

Preparation Time: 5 minutes
Cooking Time: 15 minutes
Servings: 4

Ingredients:

- 1 tsp. of salt
- 1 tsp. of black pepper
- 2 tbsp. of house Montreal chicken seasoning
- 600 grams of chicken drumsticks
- Oil

Directions:

- Start by warming up your Air fryer to 390°F.

- Generously rub the oil all over the chicken and season both sides of the chicken with the seasoning mix.

- Place the seasoned chicken into the Air fryer basket. Set your Air fryer to air-fry for about 10 minutes.

- Turn the chicken halfway through to brown evenly. Lessen the heat to 300°F and cook for additional 6 minutes.

- When the time is up, remove the chicken from your Air fryer, and allow the chicken to rest for about 2 minutes before serving.
- Serve and enjoy!

153. Air Fryer Crispy Chicken Wings

Preparation Time: 5 minutes
Cooking Time: 30 minutes
Servings: 12 chicken wings

Ingredients:

- 12 chicken wingettes
- ½ cup chicken broth
- ¼ cup melted butter
- Season all

Directions:

- Add the chicken wings in a pot and add the chicken broth.
- Close the lid and set the valve to sealing. set timer for 8 minutes.
- When the time has elapsed, quick-release pressure and transfer the chicken wings to an air fryer basket.
- Pour melted butter on the wings and mix the wings gently to coat them.
- Sprinkle season all then close the air fryer lid. Air crisp for 10 minutes, mix the wings and air fry for 10 more minutes.
- Serve and enjoy.

154. Air fryer Buffalo Chicken Pull-Apart Bread

Preparation Time: 15 minutes
Cooking Time: 5 minutes
Servings: 10

Ingredients:

- Round sourdough bread, slice diagonally into 1-inch cubes
- 1 cup mozzarella
- 1 lb buffalo chicken, shredded
- 8 slices Monterey Jack Cheese
- 2 tbsp butter, melted
- ½ cup crumbled blue cheese

- 1 green onion, chopped

Directions:

- Preheat your air fryer to 4000F for 5 minutes.
- Place mozzarella cheese on each bread cube then place buffalo chicken on mozzarella cheese.
- Place Monterey jack cheese on the chicken and coat the bread with butter.
- Place on the metal rack in the lowest position.
- Cook for the 5 minutes or until the cheese has melted.
- Top with blue cheese and green onions. Enjoy

155. Air fryer Blooming Onion

Preparation Time: 2 hours
Cooking Time: 20 minutes
Servings: 6

Ingredients:

- 1 onion, peeled and top cut off
- 2 eggs
- 2 tbsp milk
- 1 cup panko bread crumbs
- 1 tbsp paprika
- 1 tbsp garlic powder
- Olive oil

Directions:

- Place the cut side down of the onion and cut it into 8 slices.
- Place the onion in ice-cold water for 2 hours, face side down.
- In a mixing bowl, beat together egg and milk.
- Mix bread crumbs and seasoning in another mixing bowl.
- Coat the onion with the egg mixture then sprinkle panko bread crumbs all over the onion.
- Place in the air fryer basket and spray with olive oil.
- Cook in the air fryer at 3900F for 10 minutes.

- If not crispy enough cook for 5 more minutes. Serve and enjoy.

156. Air Fryer Bacon Wrapped Hot Dogs

Preparation Time: 10 minutes
Cooking Time: 12 minutes
Servings: 6

Ingredients:

- 6 hot dogs
- 6 slices of bacon

Directions:

- Wrap each hot dog with a bacon slice; roll from one end to another.
- Place the hot dogs in an air fryer basket then cook at 3900F for 12 minutes. Turn the hot dogs in the middle of the cooking period.
- Serve and enjoy.

157. Chocolate Oatmeal

Preparation Time: 5 minutes
Cooking Time: 5 minutes
Servings: 4

Ingredients:

- 2 cups quick oats
- 4 cups chocolate almond milk
- ½ cup chocolate chips
- Optional: strawberries

Directions:

- Spray the safe dish inside of the oven with non-stick spray.
- Add almond milk and quick oats then stir.
- Add 1½ cups water into the pot with trivet in then place oven safe dish on the trivet.
- Put the attached pressure cooker lid on and close the steam valve.
- Set for 5 minutes on high pressure. Quick release pressure and stir.
- Serve strawberries and chocolate chips.

158. Air fryer Apple Chips

Preparation Time: 5 minutes
Cooking Time: 8 minutes
Servings: 3

Ingredients:

- 3 crisp apples, large and sweet
- ¾ tbsp cinnamon, ground
- A pinch of salt

Directions:

- Wash the apple thoroughly in apple cider vinegar or warm water.
- Optional: core the apple or leave seeds in.
- Preheat your air fryer to 3900F.
- Meanwhile, cut apples using a sharp knife into 1/8 -inch rounds sideways.
- Mix salt and cinnamon in a small bowl.
- Rub the apple pieces with cinnamon mixture then arrange them in a single layer in your air fryer.
- Close and cook at 3900F for about 8 minutes. Flip half-way through.
- Repeat for the remaining batches.
- Once the crispiness is to your liking, place them in a cooling rack to cool.
- Serve and enjoy or store in a container, air-tight.

159. S'mores In An Air Fryer

Preparation Time: 2 minutes
Cooking Time: 8 minutes
Servings: 2

Ingredients:

- Graham crackers, half broken
- Marshmallows
- Hersey bars, same size to Graham Cracker pieces

Directions:

- Place the crackers halves into the basket of your air fryer.
- Top marshmallow on each cracker half.

- Cook for about 7-8 minutes at 3900F until marshmallows begin to crisp up.
- Carefully remove marshmallows then place Hersey bars on top.
- Place the crackers on top gently pushing down.
- Serve immediately and enjoy.

160. Air Fryer Sweet Potato Tots

Preparation Time: 20 minutes
Cooking Time: 1 hour
Servings: 4

Ingredients:

- 14 oz peeled sweet potatoes
- 1 tbsp potato starch
- 1/8 tbsp garlic powder
- 1¼ tbsp divided kosher salt
- ¾ cup ketchup, no-salt added
- Cooking spray

Directions:

- Boil water in a medium pot over high heat.
- Add potatoes and cook for about 15 minutes until fork tender.
- Transfer into a plate and cool for 15 minutes.
- Grate the potatoes over a bowl, medium, then toss with garlic powder, potato starch, and 1 tbsp salt.
- Shape the mixture into 24 cylinders, 1-inch tot-shaped.
- Coat your air fryer lightly with cooking spray then add 12 tots in one layer and spray using cooking spray.
- Cook for about 12-14 minutes at 4000F until browned lightly. Remove and splash with 1/8 tbsp salt. Repeat for the remaining tots. Serve with ketchup. Enjoy!

161. Air Fryer Doughnuts

Preparation Time: 35 minutes
Cooking Time: 1 hour 45 minutes
Servings: 8

Ingredients:

- ¼ cup warm water, 1000F
- 1 tbsp dry yeast, active
- ¼ cup + ½ tbsp divided granulated sugar
- 2 cups all-purpose flour, 8½ oz
- ¼ tbsp kosher salt
- ¼ cup whole milk, room temperature
- 2 tbsp melted butter, unsalted
- 1 beaten egg, large
- 1 cup, 4 oz, powdered sugar
- 4 tbsp tap water

Directions:

- Place water, ½ tbsp sugar, and yeast in a bowl, small, then stir together. Let sit for about 5 minutes until stir.
- Combine flour ¼ cup sugar, and salt in a bowl, medium, then add yeast mixture, butter, egg, and milk.
- Stir using a spoon, wooden, until dough comes together and is soft. Transfer onto a surface that is lightly floured.
- Knead for about 1-2 minutes until smooth then transfer into a greased bowl, lightly, and cover. Let rise for about 1 hour until volume doubled.
- Now place the raised dough on a surface lightly floured then cut 8 doughnuts form it. Use a round cutter, 3-inch, and 1-inch to remove the center.
- Transfer the cut doughnuts and holes on a surface lightly floured then wrap loosely with plastic wrap and let sit for about 30 minutes until doubled.
- Layer 2 doughnuts and 2 holes in an air fryer basket then cook for about 4-5 minutes at 4000F until golden brown.
- Repeat for the remaining doughnuts and doughnut holes.
- Meanwhile, whisk together water and sugar in a bowl, medium, until smooth.
- Dip doughnuts and holes to coat then place on a rack, wire, to drip off excess glaze.
- Let sit for 10 minutes for glaze to harden.
- Serve and enjoy.

162. Air Fryer Banana Bread

Preparation Time: 15 minutes
Cooking Time: 45 minutes
Servings: 8

Ingredients:

- 3 oz wheat flour, white-whole
- 1 tbsp cinnamon
- ½ tbsp kosher salt
- ¼ tbsp baking soda
- 12 oz mashed ripe bananas
- 2 lightly-beaten eggs, large
- ½ cup granulated sugar

Directions:

- Line a parchment paper on the bottom of a round cake pan, 6-inch, then coat with cooking spray. Whisk cinnamon, flour, baking soda, and salt together in a bowl, medium, and set aside.
- Whisk together eggs, bananas, yoghurt, sugar, vanilla, and oil in another medium bowl.
- Pour wet mixture into the flour mixture then stir until combined well.
- Now pour the batter into the pan and splash with walnuts.
- Heat your air fryer, 5.3-quart, at 3100F then insert the pan in.
- Cook for about 30 -35 minutes until browned. Make sure a toothpick comes out clean when inserted into the middle. Turn halfway through.
- Transfer and cool the bread on a wire rack for about 15 minutes. Slices and serve. Enjoy!

163. Air-fried Butter Cake

Preparation Time: 10 minutes
Cooking Time: 15 minutes
Servings: 4

Ingredients:

- Cooking spray
- 7 tbsp butter, room temperature
- ¼ cup white sugar
- 2 tbsp white sugar
- 1 egg
- 12/3 cups flour, all-purpose
- Salt to taste
- 6 tbsp milk

Directions:

- Preheat your air fryer to 3500F then spray tube pan, small-fluted, using cooking spray.
- Whisk together ¼ cup sugar and 2 tbsp butter in a medium bowl until creamy and light. Use a mixer, electric one, to whisk.
- Add egg then mix until fluffy and smooth.
- Stir in salt and flour then milk. Mix the batter thoroughly.
- Transfer the batter into prepared pan then level the surface with a spoon back.
- Place pan in the basket of your air fryer and cover.
- Cook for about 15 minutes until a toothpick comes out clean when inserted at the center.
- Remove the cake from the air fryer and cool for 5 minutes. Serve and enjoy.

164. Buttered Dinner Rolls

Preparation Time: 15 minutes
Cooking Time: 30 Minutes
Servings: 12

Ingredients:

- 1 cup milk
- 3 cups plain flour
- 7½ tablespoons unsalted butter
- 1 tablespoon coconut oil
- 1 tablespoon olive oil
- 1 teaspoon yeast
- Salt and black pepper, to taste

Directions:

- Preheat the Air fryer to 360-degree F and grease an Air fryer basket.
- Put olive oil, milk and coconut oil in a pan and cook for about 3 minutes.
- Remove from the heat and mix well.

- Mix together plain flour, yeast, butter, salt and black pepper in a large bowl.
- Knead well for about 5 minutes until a dough is formed.
- Cover the dough with a damp cloth and keep aside for about 5 minutes in a warm place.
- Knead the dough for about 5 minutes again with your hands.
- Cover the dough with a damp cloth and keep aside for about 30 minutes in a warm place.
- Divide the dough into 12 equal pieces and roll each into a ball.
- Arrange 6 balls into the Air fryer basket in a single layer and cook for about 15 minutes.
- Repeat with the remaining balls and serve warm.

165.   Shrimp And Artichoke Puffs

Preparation Time: 10 minutes
Cooking Time: 20 Minutes
Servings: 6

Ingredients:

- 1 (10-ounce) package frozen artichoke hearts, thawed
- 1 (3-ounce) package cream cheese, softened
- 1 cup shredded Coda cheese
- ½ cup mayonnaise
- 1 tablespoon lemon juice
- 1 teaspoon dried basil leaves
- 6 slices whole wheat bread
- 2 shallots, chopped
- 1 tablespoon olive oil
- ½ pound cooked shrimp

Directions:

- Preheat oven to 300°F. Using a 2-inch cookie cutter, cut rounds from bread slices. Place rounds on a baking sheet and bake at 300°F for 7 to 9 minutes, or until crisp, turning once. Remove from oven and cool on wire racks.
- In a heavy skillet, cook shallots in olive oil over medium heat until tender. Remove from heat. Chop shrimp and add to skillet along

with thawed, drained, and chopped artichoke hearts. Add both cheeses, mayonnaise, lemon juice, and basil; stir well to blend.

- Spoon 1 tablespoon shrimp mixture onto each bread round, covering the top and mounding the filling. Flash freeze on baking sheets. When frozen solid, pack in rigid containers, with waxed paper between layers. Label puffs and freeze.
- To reheat: Place frozen puffs on a baking sheet and bake at 400°F for 10 to 12 minutes or until topping is hot and bubbling.

166.   Homemade Doughnuts

Preparation Time: 30 minutes
Cooking Time: 25 Minutes
Servings: 4

Ingredients:

- 8 oz self-rising flour
- 1 tsp baking powder
- ½ cup milk
- 2 ½ tbsp butter
- 1 egg
- 2 oz brown sugar

Directions:

- Preheat Instant Vortex on Bake function to 350 F. Beat the butter with the sugar until smooth. Whisk in the egg and milk. In a bowl, combine flour with baking powder. Fold in the butter mixture.
- Form donut shapes and cut off the center with cookie cutters. Arrange on a lined baking sheet and cook in for 15 minutes. Serve with whipped cream or icing.

167.   Eggless Brownies

Preparation Time: 10 minutes
Cooking Time: 40 Minutes
Servings: 8

Ingredients:

- 1/4 cup walnuts, chopped
- 1/3 cup cocoa powder
- 2 tsp baking powder
- 1 cup of sugar

- 1 cup all-purpose flour
- 1/2 cup chocolate chips
- 2 tsp vanilla
- 1 tbsp milk
- 3/4 cup yogurt
- 1/2 cup butter, melted
- 1/4 tsp salt

Directions:

- Fit the Air fryer oven with the rack in position

- In a large mixing bowl, sift flour, cocoa powder, baking powder, and salt. Mix well and set aside.

- In another bowl, add butter, vanilla, milk, and yogurt and whisk until well combined.

- Add flour mixture into the butter mixture and mix until just combined.

- Fold in walnuts and chocolate chips.

- Pour batter into the prepared baking dish.

- Set to bake at 350 F for 45 minutes. After 5 minutes place the baking dish in the preheated oven.

- Slice and serve.

168. Apricot Crumble With Blackberries

Preparation Time: 20 minutes
Cooking Time: 30 Minutes
Servings: 4

Ingredients:

- 2 ½ cups fresh apricots, de-stoned and cubed
- 1 cup fresh blackberries
- ½ cup sugar
- 2 tbsp lemon Juice
- 1 cup flour
- 5 tbsp butter

Directions:

- Preheat Instant Vortex on Bake function to 360 F. Add the apricot cubes to a bowl and mix with lemon juice, 2 tbsp sugar, and blackberries. Scoop the mixture into a greased dish and spread it evenly.

- In another bowl, mix flour and remaining sugar. Add 1 tbsp of cold water and butter and keep mixing until you have a crumbly mixture. Pour over the fruit mixture and cook for 20 minutes.

169. Sweet Cream Cheese Wontons

Preparation Time: 20 minutes
Cooking Time: 5 Minutes
Servings: 16

Ingredients:

- 1 egg mixed with a bit of water
- Wonton wrappers
- ½ C. powdered erythritol
- 8 ounces softened cream cheese
- Olive oil

Directions:

- Preparing the Ingredients. Mix sweetener and cream cheese together.

- Lay out 4 wontons at a time and cover with a dish towel to prevent drying out.

- Place ½ of a teaspoon of cream cheese mixture into each wrapper.

- Dip finger into egg/water mixture and fold diagonally to form a triangle. Seal edges well.

- Repeat with remaining ingredients.

- Air Frying. Place filled wontons into the Instant Vortex air fryer oven and cook 5 minutes at 400 degrees, shaking halfway through cooking.

170. Cookie Custards

Preparation Time: 30 minutes
Cooking Time: 55 Minutes
Servings: 8

Ingredients:

- 2 tbsp. margarine
- A pinch of baking soda and baking powder
- 1 cup all-purpose flour
- ½ cup icing sugar
- ½ cup custard powder

Directions:

- Cream the margarine and sugar together. Add the remaining ingredients and fold them together.

- Prepare a baking tray by greasing it with butter. Make balls out of the dough, coat them with flour and place them in the tray.

- Preheat the fryer to 300 Fahrenheit for five minutes. You will need to place the baking tray in the basket and cover it. Cook till you find that the balls have turned golden brown. Remove the tray and leave it to cool outside for half an hour. Store in an airtight container.

171. Apple Wedges With Apricots

Preparation Time: 5 minutes
Cooking Time: 15 To 18 Minutes
Servings: 4

Ingredients:

- 4 large apples, peeled and sliced into 8 wedges
- 2 tablespoons olive oil
- ½ cup dried apricots, chopped
- 1 to 2 tablespoons sugar
- ½ teaspoon ground cinnamon

Directions:

- Toss the apple wedges with the olive oil in a mixing bowl until well coated.

- Place the apple wedges in the air fryer basket.

- Put the air fryer basket on the baking pan and slide into Rack Position 2, select Air Fry, set temperature to 350°F (180°C), and set time to 15 minutes.

- After about 12 minutes, remove from the oven. Sprinkle with the dried apricots and air fry for another 3 minutes.

- Meanwhile, thoroughly combine the sugar and cinnamon in a small bowl.

- Remove the apple wedges from the oven to a plate. Serve sprinkled with the sugar mixture.

172. Oatmeal Cake

Preparation Time: 3 hours
Cooking Time: 40 Minutes

Servings: 8

Ingredients:

- 2 eggs, beaten
- 1 tbsp cocoa powder
- 1/2 tsp salt
- 1 tsp baking soda
- 1/2 cup butter, softened
- 1 cup granulated sugar
- 1 cup brown sugar
- 1 3/4 cups flour
- 1 cup quick oats
- 3/4 cup mix nuts, chopped
- 2 cups chocolate chips
- 1 3/4 cup boiling water

Directions:

- Fit the Air fryer oven with the rack in position

- Combine together boiling water and oats in a large bowl.

- Add butter and sugar stir until butter melted.

- Add flour, baking soda, salt, cocoa powder, 1 cup chocolate chips, half chopped nuts, and egg. Mix until combine.

- Pour batter into the greased cake pan and sprinkle remaining nuts and chocolate chips over the top of cake batter.

- Set to bake at 350 F for 45 minutes. After 5 minutes place the baking dish in the preheated oven.

- Slice and serve.

173. Watermelon Jerky

Preparation Time: 5 minutes
Cooking Time: 12 hours
Servings: ½ cup

Ingredients:

- 1 cup seedless watermelon (1-inch) cubes

Directions:

- Arrange the watermelon cubes in a single layer in the Cook & Crisp Basket. Place the basket in the pot and close the Crisping Lid.

- Press Dehydrate, set the temperature to 135°F, and set the time to 12 hours. Select Start/Stop to begin.

- When dehydrating is complete, remove the basket from the pot and transfer the jerky to an airtight container.

TIP: Add a little zing to your watermelon jerky by sprinkling the watermelon with some sea salt and black pepper, paprika, cayenne pepper, or a squeeze of lime juice before placing it in the Air Fryer

174. Dried Mango

Preparation Time: 5 minutes
Cooking Time: 8 hours
Servings: 2

Ingredients:

- ½ mango, peeled, pitted, and cut into 3/8-inch slices

Directions:

- Arrange the mango slices flat in a single layer in the Cook & Crisp Basket. Place in the pot and close the Crisping Lid.

- Press Dehydrate, set the temperature to 135°F, and set the time to 8 hours. Select Start/Stop to begin.

- When dehydrating is complete, remove the basket from the pot and transfer the mango slices to an airtight container.

TIP: Use the Dehydrate feature to turn a variety of fruits into tasty snacks. Try apples, bananas, pineapple, and strawberries. Cook time and prep instructions for these foods are listed in the Dehydrate chart (here).

175. Beet Chips

Preparation Time: 5 minutes
Cooking Time: 8 hours
Servings: ½ cup

Ingredients:

- ½ beet, peeled and cut into 1/8-inch slices

Directions:

- Arrange the beet slices flat in a single layer in the Cook & Crisp Basket. Place in the pot and close the Crisping Lid.

- Press Dehydrate, set the temperature to 135°F, and set the time to 8 hours. Select Start/Stop to begin.

- When dehydrating is complete, remove the basket from the pot and transfer the beet chips to an airtight container.

TIP: Use a mandoline to ensure that the beet is sliced evenly into consistent 1/8-inch slices.

176. Maple Candied Bacon

Preparation Time: 5 minutes
Cooking Time: 40 minutes
Servings: 12

Ingredients:

- ½ cup maple syrup
- ¼ cup brown sugar
- Nonstick cooking spray
- 1 pound (12 slices) thick-cut bacon

Directions:

- Place the Reversible Rack in the pot. Close the Crisping Lid. Preheat the unit by selecting Air Crisp, setting the temperature to 400°F, and setting the time to 5 minutes.

- Meanwhile, in a small mixing bowl, mix together the maple syrup and brown sugar.

- Once the Air Fryer has preheated, carefully line the Reversible Rack with aluminum foil. Spray the foil with cooking spray.

- Arrange 4 to 6 slices of bacon on the rack in a single layer. Brush them with the maple syrup mixture.

- Close the Crisping Lid. Select Air Crisp and set the temperature to 400°F. Set the time to 10 minutes, then select Start/Stop to begin.

- After 10 minutes, flip the bacon and brush with more maple syrup mixture. Close the Crisping Lid, select Air Crisp, set the temperature to 400°F, and set the time to 10 minutes. Select Start/Stop to begin.

- Cooking is complete when your desired crispiness is reached. Remove the bacon from the Reversible Rack and transfer to a cooling rack for 10 minutes. Repeat steps 4 through 6 with the remaining bacon.

TIP: Do you like a little spice? Turn this recipe into a Spicy Maple Candied Bacon by adding ½ teaspoon of cayenne pepper to the maple-syrup-sugar mixture in step 2.

177. Chili-Ranch Chicken Wings

Preparation Time: 10 minutes
Cooking Time: 28 minutes
Servings: 4

Ingredients:

- ½ cup water
- ½ cup hot pepper sauce
- 2 tablespoons unsalted butter, melted
- 1½ tablespoons apple cider vinegar
- 2 pounds frozen chicken wings
- ½ (1-ounce) envelope ranch salad dressing mix
- ½ teaspoon paprika
- Nonstick cooking spray

Directions:

- Pour the water, hot pepper sauce, butter, and vinegar into the pot. Place the wings in the Cook & Crisp Basket and place the basket in the pot. Assemble the Pressure Lid, making sure the pressure release valve is in the Seal position.

- Select Pressure and set to High. Set the time to 5 minutes. Select Start/Stop to begin.

- When pressure cooking is complete, quick release the pressure by turning the pressure release valve to the Vent position. Carefully remove the lid when the unit has finished releasing pressure.

- Sprinkle the chicken wings with the dressing mix and paprika. Coat with cooking spray.

- Close the Crisping Lid. Select Air Crisp, set the temperature to 375°F, and set the time to 15 minutes. Select Start/Stop to begin.

- After 7 minutes, open the Crisping Lid, then lift the basket and shake the wings. Coat with cooking spray. Lower the basket back into

the pot and close the lid to resume cooking until the wings reach your desired crispiness.

TIP: Using fresh wings instead of frozen? Follow the instructions in the Air Crisp chart here.

178. Crispy Cheesy Arancini

Preparation Time: 15 minutes
Cooking Time: 44 minutes
Servings: 6

Ingredients:

- ½ cup extra-virgin olive oil, plus 1 tablespoon
- 1 small yellow onion, diced
- 2 garlic cloves, minced
- 5 cups chicken broth
- ½ cup white wine
- 2 cups arborio rice
- 1½ cups grated Parmesan cheese, plus more for garnish
- 1 cup frozen peas
- 1 teaspoon sea salt
- 1 teaspoon freshly ground black pepper
- 2 cups fresh bread crumbs
- 2 large eggs

Directions:

- Select Sear/Sauté and set to Medium High. Select Start/Stop to begin. Allow the pot to preheat for 5 minutes.

- Add 1 tablespoon of oil and the onion to the preheated pot. Cook until soft and translucent, stirring occasionally. Add the garlic and cook for 1 minute.

- Add the broth, wine, and rice to the pot; stir to incorporate. Assemble the Pressure Lid, making sure the pressure release valve is in the Seal position.

- Select Pressure and set to High. Set the time to 7 minutes. Press Start/Stop to begin.

- When pressure cooking is complete, allow pressure to naturally release for 10 minutes, then quick release any remaining pressure by turning the pressure release valve to the Vent position. Carefully remove the lid when the unit has finished releasing pressure.

- Add the Parmesan cheese, frozen peas, salt, and pepper. Stir vigorously until the rice begins to thicken. Transfer the risotto to a large mixing bowl and let cool.

- Meanwhile, clean the pot. In a medium mixing bowl, stir together the bread crumbs and the remaining ½ cup of olive oil. In a separate mixing bowl, lightly beat the eggs.

- Divide the risotto into 12 equal portions and form each one into a ball. Dip each risotto ball in the beaten eggs, then coat in the bread crumb mixture.

- Arrange half of the arancini in the Air Fryer Basket in a single layer.

- Close the Crisping Lid. Select Air Crisp, set the temperature to 400°F, and set the time to 10 minutes. Select Start/Stop to begin.

- Repeat steps 9 and 10 to cook the remaining arancini.

TIP: For best results, let the risotto cool before step 8 or use leftover risotto from Lemon Risotto and Roasted Carrots and skip steps 1 through 5.

179. Buffalo Chicken Meatballs

Preparation Time: 10 minutes
Cooking Time: 40 minutes
Servings: 6

Ingredients:

- 1-pound ground chicken
- 1 carrot, minced
- 2 celery stalks, minced
- ¼ cup crumbled blue cheese
- ¼ cup buffalo sauce
- ¼ cup bread crumbs
- 1 egg
- 2 tablespoons extra-virgin olive oil
- ½ cup water

Directions:

- Select Sear/Sauté and set to High. Select Start/Stop to begin. Allow the pot to preheat for 5 minutes.

- Meanwhile, in a large mixing bowl, mix together the chicken, carrot, celery, blue

cheese, buffalo sauce, bread crumbs, and egg. Shape the mixture into 1½-inch meatballs.

- Pour the olive oil into the preheated pot. Working in batches, place the meatballs in the pot and sear on all sides until browned. When each batch finishes cooking, transfer to a plate.

- Place the Cook & Crisp Basket in the pot. Add the water, then place all the meatballs in the basket.

- Assemble the Pressure Lid, making sure the pressure release valve is in the Seal position. Select Pressure and set to High. Set the time to 5 minutes. Select Start/Stop to begin.

- When pressure cooking is complete, quick release the pressure by turning the pressure release valve to the Vent position. Carefully remove the lid when the unit has finished releasing pressure.

- Close the Crisping Lid. Select Air Crisp, set the temperature to 360°F, and set the time to 10 minutes. Select Start/Stop to begin.

- After 5 minutes, open the lid, then lift the basket and shake the meatballs. Lower the basket back into the pot and close the lid to resume cooking until the meatballs achieve your desired crispiness.

180. Loaded Smashed Potatoes

Preparation Time: 10 minutes
Cooking Time: 30 minutes
Servings: 4

Ingredients:

- 12 ounces baby Yukon Gold potatoes
- 1 teaspoon extra-virgin olive oil
- ¼ cup sour cream
- ¼ cup shredded Cheddar cheese
- 2 slices bacon, cooked and crumbled
- 1 tablespoon chopped fresh chives
- Sea salt

Directions:

- Place the Cook & Crisp Basket in the pot. Close the Crisping Lid. Preheat the unit by selecting Air Crisp, setting the temperature to

350°F, and setting the time to 5 minutes. Press Start/Stop to begin.

- Meanwhile, toss the potatoes with the oil until evenly coated.

- Once the pot and basket are preheated, open the lid and add the potatoes to the basket. Close the lid, select Air Crisp, set the temperature to 350°F, and set the time to 30 minutes. Press Start/Stop to begin.

- After 15 minutes, open the lid, then lift the basket and shake the potatoes. Lower the basket back into the pot and close the lid to resume cooking.

- After 15 minutes, check the potatoes for your desired crispiness. They should be fork tender.

- Remove the potatoes from the basket. Use a large spoon to lightly crush the potatoes to split them. Top with the sour cream, cheese, bacon, and chives, and season with salt.

181.　Fried Dumplings

Preparation Time: 20 minutes
Cooking Time: 12 minutes
Servings: 8

Ingredients:

- 8 ounces ground pork
- 1 carrot, shredded
- ½ cup shredded Napa cabbage
- 1 large egg, beaten
- 1 garlic clove, minced
- 2 tablespoons reduced-sodium soy sauce
- ½ tablespoon sesame oil
- ½ tablespoon grated fresh ginger
- ½ teaspoon sea salt
- ½ teaspoon freshly ground black pepper
- 20 wonton wrappers
- 2 tablespoons vegetable oil

Directions:

- Place the Cook & Crisp Basket in the pot. Close the Crisping Lid. Preheat the unit by selecting Air Crisp, setting the temperature to 400°F, and setting the time to 5 minutes.

- Meanwhile, in a large mixing bowl, combine the pork, carrot, cabbage, egg, garlic, soy sauce, sesame oil, ginger, salt, and pepper.

- Place the wonton wrappers on a clean work surface and spoon 1 tablespoon of the pork mixture into the center of each wrapper. Gently rub the edges of the wrappers with water. Fold the dough over the filling to create a half-moon shape, pinching the edges to seal. Brush the dumplings with the vegetable oil.

- Place the dumplings in the Air Fryer Basket. Select Air Crisp, set the temperature to 400°F, and set the time to 12 minutes. Select Start/Stop to begin.

- After 6 minutes, open the lid, then lift the basket and shake the dumplings. Lower the basket back into the pot and close the lid to resume cooking until the dumplings achieve your desired crispiness.

TIP: Can't find wonton or dumpling wrappers at the grocery store? You can use egg roll wrappers instead. You can also swap out the ground pork in this recipe for ground chicken or beef.

182.　Spinach-Artichoke Bites

Preparation Time: 20 minutes
Cooking Time: 24 minutes
Servings: 8

Ingredients:

- ¼ cup frozen chopped spinach
- ¼ cup finely chopped artichoke hearts
- ¼ cup cottage cheese
- ¼ cup feta cheese
- 2 tablespoons grated Parmesan cheese
- 1 large egg white
- Zest of 1 lemon
- 1 teaspoon dried oregano
- ½ teaspoon sea salt
- ½ teaspoon freshly ground black pepper
- 4 (13-by-18-inch) sheets frozen phyllo dough, thawed
- 1 tablespoon extra-virgin olive oil

Directions:

- In a medium mixing bowl, combine the spinach, artichoke hearts, cottage cheese, feta cheese, Parmesan cheese, egg white, lemon zest, oregano, salt, and pepper.

- Place the Cook & Crisp Basket in the pot. Close the Crisping Lid. Preheat the unit by selecting Air Crisp, setting the temperature to 375°F, and setting the time to 5 minutes. Press Start/Stop to begin.

- Meanwhile, place 1 phyllo sheet on a clean work surface. Brush it all over with some of the olive oil. Place a second sheet of phyllo on top of the first and brush it with more oil. Continue layering to form a stack of 4 oiled sheets.

- Working from the short side, cut the stack of phyllo sheets into 8 (2¼-inch-wide) strips. Cut the strips in half to form 16 (2¼-inch-wide) strips.

- Spoon about 1 tablespoon of filling onto 1 short end of each strip. Fold one corner over the filling to create a triangle; continue folding back and forth to the end of the strip, creating a triangle-shaped phyllo packet. Repeat until you have formed 16 phyllo bites.

- Open the Crisping Lid and arrange half of the phyllo bites in the basket in a single layer. Close the lid, select Air Crisp, set the temperature to 350°F, and set the time to 12 minutes. Press Start/Stop to begin.

- After 6 minutes, open the lid and flip the bites over. Lower the basket back into the pot and close the lid to resume cooking.

- After 6 minutes, check the packets for your desired crispiness. If done, remove the bites from the basket.

- Repeat steps 6, 7, and 8 with the remaining bites.

TIP: If you have leftover filling, serve it with crackers or freeze it for later.

183. Loaded Cauliflower Soup

Preparation Time: 15 minutes
Cooking Time: 29 minutes
Servings: 8

Ingredients:

- 5 slices bacon, chopped
- 1 onion, chopped
- 3 garlic cloves, minced
- 1 head cauliflower, trimmed into florets
- 4 cups chicken broth
- 1 cup whole milk
- 1 teaspoon sea salt
- 1 teaspoon freshly ground black pepper
- 1½ cups shredded Cheddar cheese
- Sour cream, for serving (optional)
- Chopped fresh chives, for serving (optional)

Directions:

- Select Sear/Sauté and set to High. Select Start/Stop to begin. Allow the pot to preheat for 5 minutes.

- Put the bacon, onion, and garlic in the preheated pot. Cook, stirring occasionally, for 5 minutes. Reserve some of the bacon for garnish.

- Add the cauliflower and chicken broth to the pot. Assemble the Pressure Lid, making sure the pressure release valve is in the Seal position.

- Select Pressure and set to High. Set the time to 10 minutes, then select Start/Stop to begin.

- When pressure cooking is complete, quick release the pressure by moving the pressure release valve to the Vent position. Carefully remove the lid when the pressure has finished releasing.

- Add the milk and mash until the soup reaches your desired consistency. Season with the salt and black pepper. Sprinkle the cheese evenly over the top of the soup.

- Close the Crisping Lid. Select Broil and set the time to 5 minutes. Select Start/Stop to begin.

- When cooking is complete, top with the reserved crispy bacon and serve immediately, with sour cream and chives (if using).

FISH AND SEAFOOD

184.   Bacon Wrapped Shrimp

Preparation Time: 5 Minutes
Cooking Time: 5 Minutes
Servings: 4

Ingredients:

- 1¼ pound tiger shrimp, peeled and deveined
- 1-pound bacon

Directions:

- *Preparing the Ingredients.* With a slice of bacon, wrap each shrimp
- Refrigerate for about 20 minutes.
- Preheat the Air fryer oven to 390 degrees F.
- *Air Frying.* Arrange the shrimp in the Oven rack/basket. Place the Rack on the middle-shelf of the XL air fryer oven. Cook for about 5-7 minutes.

185.   Crispy Paprika Fish Fillets

Preparation Time: 5 Minutes
Cooking Time: 15 Minutes
Servings: 4

Ingredients:

- 1/2 cup seasoned breadcrumbs
- 1 tablespoon balsamic vinegar
- 1/2 teaspoon seasoned salt
- 1 teaspoon paprika
- 1/2 teaspoon ground black pepper
- 1 teaspoon celery seed
- 2 fish fillets, halved
- 1 egg, beaten

Directions:

- *Preparing the Ingredients.* Pour the vinegar, salt, breadcrumbs, paprika, celery seeds and ground black pepper to your food processor. Leave it for 30 seconds.

- Then cover the fish fillets using the beaten egg; then, put them into the breadcrumb's mixture.
- *Air Frying.* Cook it at 350 degrees F for around 15 minutes.

186.   Air Fryer Salmon

Preparation Time: 5 Minutes
Cooking Time: 10 Minutes
Servings: 2

Ingredients:

- 1/2 tsp. salt
- 1/2 tsp. garlic powder
- 1/2 tsp. smoked paprika
- Salmon

Directions:

- *Preparing the Ingredients.* Mix spices and sprinkle onto salmon.
- Place seasoned salmon into the XL air fryer oven.
- *Air Frying.* Set temperature to 400°F, and set time to 10 minutes.

187.   Sweet and Savory Breaded Shrimp

Preparation Time: 5 Minutes
Cooking Time: 20 Minutes
Servings: 2

Ingredients:

- 1/2 pound of fresh shrimp, peeled from their shells and rinsed
- 2 raw eggs
- 1/2 cup of breadcrumbs (we like Panko, but any brand or home recipe will do)
- 1/2 white onion, peeled and rinsed and finely chopped
- 1 teaspoon of ginger-garlic paste
- 1/2 teaspoon of turmeric powder
- 1/2 teaspoon of red chili powder
- 1/2 teaspoon of cumin powder
- 1/2 teaspoon of black pepper powder

- 1/2 teaspoon of dry mango powder
- Pinch of salt

Directions:

- *Preparing the Ingredients.* Cover the basket of the Air fryer oven with a lining of tin foil, leaving the edges uncovered to allow air to circulate through the basket.
- Preheat the Air fryer oven to 350 degrees.
- In a mixing bowl, whisk the eggs until fluffy and until the yolks and whites are fully combined.
- Dunk all the shrimp in the egg mixture, fully submerging.
- In a separate mixing bowl, combine the bread crumbs with all the dry ingredients until evenly blended.
- One by one, coat the egg-covered shrimp in the mixed dry ingredients so that fully covered, and place on the foil-lined air-fryer basket.
- *Air Frying.* Set the air-fryer timer to 20 minutes.
- Halfway through the cooking time, shake the handle of the air-fryer so that the breaded shrimp jostles inside and fry-coverage is even.
- After 20 minutes, when the fryer shuts off, the shrimp will be perfectly cooked and their breaded crust golden-brown and delicious! Using tongs, remove from the air fryer oven and set on a serving dish to cool.

188. Quick Paella

Preparation Time: 7 Minutes
Cooking Time: 15 Minutes
Servings: 4

Ingredients:

- 1 (10-ounce) package frozen cooked rice, thawed
- 1 (6-ounce) jar artichoke hearts, drained and chopped
- ¼ cup vegetable broth
- 1/2 teaspoon turmeric

- 1/2 teaspoon dried thyme
- 1 cup frozen cooked small shrimp
- 1/2 cup frozen baby peas
- 1 tomato, diced

Directions:

- *Preparing the Ingredients._* In a 6-by-6-by-2-inch pan, combine the rice, artichoke hearts, vegetable broth, turmeric, and thyme, and stir gently.
- *Air Frying.* Place in the Air fryer oven and bake for 8 to 9 minutes or until the rice is hot. Remove from the air fryer oven and gently stir in the shrimp, peas, and tomato. Cook for 5 to 8 minutes or until the shrimp and peas are hot and the paella is bubbling.

189. Coconut Shrimp

Preparation Time: 15 Minutes
Cooking Time: 5 Minutes
Servings: 4

Ingredients:

- 1 (8-ounce) can crushed pineapple
- 1/2 cup sour cream
- ¼ cup pineapple preserves
- 2 egg whites
- 2/3 cup cornstarch
- 2/3 cup sweetened coconut
- 1 cup panko bread crumbs
- 1-pound uncooked large shrimp, thawed if frozen, deveined and shelled
- Olive oil for misting

Directions:

- *Preparing the Ingredients.* Make sure to drain the pineapple well, getting the juice. With small bowl, combine the sour cream, pineapple, and preserves, then mix well. Put it aside.
- In another bowl, whisk the egg whites plus 2 tablespoons of pineapple liquid. The put the cornstarch on another plate. Blend the coconut plus the bread crumbs on extra plate.

- Dip the shrimp in the cornstarch, then dip into the egg white combination.

- Lastly into the coconut mixture. Put the shrimp in the air fryer rack and mist with oil.

- *Air Frying.* Cook it for 5 to 7 minutes or you may wait until the shrimp are golden brown.

190. Cilantro-Lime Fried Shrimp

Ingredients:

- 1-pound raw shrimp
- 1/2 cup chopped fresh cilantro
- Juice of 1 lime
- 1 egg
- 1/2 cup all-purpose flour
- ¾ cup bread crumbs
- Salt
- Pepper
- Cooking oil
- 1/2 cup cocktail sauce (optional)

Directions:

- *Preparing the Ingredients.* Place the shrimp in a plastic bag and add the cilantro and lime juice. Seal the bag. Shake to combine. Marinate in the refrigerator for 30 minutes.

- In a small bowl, beat the egg. In another small bowl, place the flour. Place the bread crumbs in a third small bowl, and season with salt and pepper to taste.

- Spray the air fryer rack/basket with cooking oil.

- Remove the shrimp from the plastic bag. Dip each in the flour, then the egg, and then the bread crumbs.

- *Air Frying.* Place the shrimp in the XL air fryer oven. It is okay to stack them. Spray the shrimp with cooking oil. Cook for 4 minutes.

- Open the air fryer oven and flip the shrimp. I recommend flipping individually instead of shaking to keep the breading intact. Cook for extra 4 minutes, or until crisp.

- Cool before serving. Serve with cocktail sauce if desired.

191. Lemony Tuna

Ingredients:

- 2 (6-ounce) cans water packed plain tuna
- 2 teaspoons Dijon mustard
- 1/2 cup breadcrumbs
- 1 tablespoon fresh lime juice
- 2 tablespoons fresh parsley, chopped
- 1 egg
- hot sauce
- 3 tablespoons canola oil
- Salt and freshly ground black pepper

Directions:

- *Preparing the ingredients.* Get majority of the liquid from the canned tuna.

- In a bowl, add the fish, mustard, crumbs, citrus juice, parsley, and hot sauce and mix till well combined. Add a little canola oil if it seems too dry. Add egg, salt and stir to combine. Make the patties from tuna mixture. Refrigerate the tuna patties for about 2 hours.

- *Air Frying.* Preheat the air fryer oven to 355 degrees F. Cook for about 10-12 minutes.

192. Grilled Soy Salmon Fillets

Preparation Time: 5 Minutes
Cooking Time: 8 Minutes
Servings: 4

Ingredients:

- 4 salmon fillets
- 1/4 teaspoon ground black pepper
- 1/2 teaspoon cayenne pepper
- 1/2 teaspoon salt
- 1 teaspoon onion powder
- 1 tablespoon fresh lemon juice
- 1/2 cup soy sauce
- 1/2 cup water
- 1 tablespoon honey
- 2 tablespoons extra-virgin olive oil

Directions:

- *Preparing the Ingredients.* Firstly, pat the salmon fillets dry using kitchen towels. Season the salmon with black pepper, cayenne pepper, salt, and onion powder.

- To make the marinade, combine together the lemon juice, soy sauce, water, honey, and olive oil. Marinate the salmon for at least 2 hours in your refrigerator.

- Arrange the fish fillets on a grill basket in your XL air fryer oven.

- *Air Frying.* Bake at 330 degrees for 8 to 9 minutes, or until salmon fillets are easily flaked with a fork.

- Work with batches and serve warm.

193.   Old Bay Crab Cakes

Preparation Time: 10 Minutes
Cooking Time: 20 Minutes
Servings: 4

Ingredients:

- 2 slices dried bread, crusts removed
- Small amount of milk
- 1 tablespoon mayonnaise
- 1 tablespoon Worcestershire sauce
- 1 tablespoon baking powder
- 1 tablespoon parsley flakes
- 1 teaspoon Old Bay® Seasoning
- 1/4 teaspoon salt
- 1 egg
- 1-pound lump crabmeat

Directions:

- *Preparing the Ingredients.* Crush your bread over a large bowl until it is broken down into small pieces.

- Add milk and stir until bread crumbs are moistened. Mix in mayo and Worcestershire sauce. Add remaining ingredients and mix well. Shape into 4 patties.

- *Air Frying.* Cook at 360 degrees for 20 minutes, flip half way through.

194.   Scallops and Spring Veggies

Preparation Time: 10 Minutes

Cooking Time: 8 Minutes
Servings: 4

Ingredients:

- 1/2 pound asparagus ends trimmed, cut into 2-inch pieces
- 1 cup sugar snap peas
- 1-pound sea scallops
- 1 tablespoon lemon juice
- 2 teaspoons olive oil
- 1/2 teaspoon dried thyme
- Pinch salt
- Freshly ground black pepper

Directions:

- *Preparing the Ingredients.* Place the sugar snap peas plus the asparagus in the Oven rack/basket. Place the Rack on the middle-shelf of the XL air fryer oven.

- *Air Frying.* Cook for 2 to 3 minutes or until the vegetables are just starting to get tender.

- Meanwhile, check the scallops for a small muscle attached to the side, and pull it off and discard.

- In a medium bowl, blend the scallops with the lemon juice, olive oil, thyme, salt, and pepper. Place into the Oven rack/basket on top of the vegetables. Place the Rack on the middle-shelf of the XL air fryer oven.

- *Air Frying.* Steam for 5 to 7 minutes. Until the scallops are just firm, and the vegetables are tender. Serve immediately.

195.   Fried Calamari

Preparation Time: 8 Minutes
Cooking Time: 7 Minutes
Servings: 8

Ingredients:

- 1/2 tsp. salt
- 1/2 tsp. Old Bay seasoning
- 1/3 C. plain cornmeal
- 1/2 C. semolina flour
- 1/2 C. almond flour

- 5-6 C. olive oil
- 1 1/2 pounds baby squid

Directions:

- *Preparing the Ingredients.* Rinse squid in cold water and slice tentacles, keeping just ¼-inch of the hood in one piece.
- Combine 1-2 pinches of pepper, salt, Old Bay seasoning, cornmeal, and both flours together. Dredge squid pieces into flour mixture and place into the XL air fryer oven.
- *Air Frying.* Spray liberally with olive oil. Cook 15 minutes at 345 degrees till coating turns a golden brown.

196. Soy and Ginger Shrimp

Preparation Time: 8 Minutes
Cooking Time: 10 Minutes
Servings: 4

Ingredients:

- 2 tablespoons olive oil
- 2 tablespoons scallions, finely chopped
- 2 cloves garlic, chopped
- 1 teaspoon fresh ginger, grated
- 1 tablespoon dry white wine
- 1 tablespoon balsamic vinegar
- 1/4 cup soy sauce
- 1 tablespoon sugar
- 1-pound shrimp
- Salt and ground black pepper, to taste

Directions:

- *Preparing the Ingredients.* To make the marinade, warm the oil in a saucepan; cook all ingredients, except the shrimp, salt, and black pepper. Now, let it cool.
- Marinate the shrimp, covered, at least an hour, in the refrigerator.
- *Air Frying.* After that, bake the shrimp at 350 degrees F for 8 to 10 minutes (depending on the size), turning once or twice. Season prepared shrimp with salt and black pepper and serve right away.

197. Crispy Cheesy Fish Fingers

Preparation Time: 10 Minutes
Cooking Time: 20 Minutes
Servings: 4

Ingredients:

- Large codfish filet, approximately 6-8 ounces, fresh or frozen and thawed, cut into 1 1/2-inch strips
- 2 raw eggs
- 1/2 cup of breadcrumbs (we like Panko, but any brand or home recipe will do)
- 2 tablespoons of shredded or powdered parmesan cheese
- 1 tablespoons of shredded cheddar cheese
- Pinch of salt and pepper

Directions:

- *Preparing the Ingredients.* Cover the basket of the Air fryer oven with a lining of tin foil, leaving the edges uncovered to allow air to circulate through the basket.
- Preheat the air fryer oven to 350 degrees.
- In a large mixing bowl, beat the eggs until fluffy and until the yolks and whites are fully combined.
- Dunk all the fish strips in the beaten eggs, fully submerging.
- In a separate mixing bowl, combine the bread crumbs with the parmesan, cheddar, and salt and pepper, until evenly mixed.
- One by one, coat the egg-covered fish strips in the mixed dry ingredients so that they're fully covered, and place on the foil-lined Oven rack/basket. Place the Rack on the middle-shelf of the XL air fryer oven.
- *Air Frying.* Set the air-fryer timer to 20 minutes.
- Halfway through the cooking time, shake the handle of the air-fryer so that the breaded fish jostles inside and fry-coverage is even.
- After 20 minutes, when the fryer shuts off, the fish strips will be perfectly cooked and their breaded crust golden-brown and

delicious! Using tongs, remove from the air fryer oven and set on a serving dish to cool.

198. Panko-Crusted Tilapia

Preparation Time: 5 Minutes
Cooking Time: 10 Minutes
Servings: 3

Ingredients:

- 2 tsp. Italian seasoning
- 2 tsp. lemon pepper
- 1/3 C. panko breadcrumbs
- 1/3 C. egg whites
- 1/3 C. almond flour
- 3 tilapia fillets
- Olive oil

Directions:

- *Preparing the Ingredients.* Place panko, egg whites, and flour into separate bowls. Mix lemon pepper and Italian seasoning in with breadcrumbs.
- Pat tilapia fillets dry. Dredge in flour, then egg, then breadcrumb mixture.
- *Air Frying.* Add to the Oven rack/basket and spray lightly with olive oil. Place the Rack on the middle-shelf of the XL air fryer oven.
- Cook 10-11 minutes at 400 degrees, making sure to flip halfway through cooking.

199. Fish Cake with Mango Relish

Preparation Time: 5 Minutes
Cooking Time: 10 Minutes
Servings: 4

Ingredients:

- 1 lb. White Fish Fillets
- 3 Tbsps. Ground Coconut
- 1 Ripened Mango
- 1/2 Tsps. Chili Paste
- Tbsps. Fresh Parsley
- 1 Green Onion
- 1 Lime
- 1 Tsp. Salt

- 1 Egg

Directions:

- *Preparing the Ingredients.* To make the relish, peel and dice the mango into cubes. Combine with a half teaspoon of chili paste, a tablespoon of parsley, and the zest and juice of half a lime.
- In a food processor, pulse the fish until it forms a smooth texture. Place into a bowl and add the salt, egg, chopped green onion, parsley, two tablespoons of the coconut, and the remainder of the chili paste and lime zest and juice. Combine well
- Portion the mixture into 10 equal balls and flatten them into small patties. Pour the reserved tablespoon of coconut onto a dish and roll the patties over to coat.
- Preheat the Air fryer oven to 390 degrees
- *Air Frying.* Place the fish cakes into the Air fryer oven and cook for 8 minutes.
- Serve hot with mango relish

200. Firecracker Shrimp

Preparation Time: 10 Minutes
Cooking Time: 8 Minutes
Servings: 4

Ingredients:

- 1-pound raw shrimp, peeled and deveined
- Salt
- Pepper
- 1 egg
- 1/2 cup all-purpose flour
- ¾ cup panko bread crumbs
- Cooking oil
- For the firecracker sauce
- 1/3 cup sour cream
- 2 tablespoons Sriracha
- ¼ cup sweet chili sauce

Directions:

- *Preparing the Ingredients.* With salt and pepper, season the shrimp to taste. In a small bowl, beat the egg. In another small bowl, place the flour. In a third small bowl, add the panko bread crumbs.

- Spray the Oven rack/basket with cooking oil. Dip the shrimp in the flour, then the egg, and then the bread crumbs. Place the shrimp in the Oven rack/basket. It is okay to stack them. Spray the shrimp with cooking oil. Place the Rack on the middle-shelf of the XL air fryer oven.

- *Air Frying.* Cook for 4 minutes. Open the Air fryer oven and flip the shrimp. I recommend flipping individually instead of shaking to keep the breading intact. Cook for extra 4 minutes or until crisp.

- While the shrimp is cooking, make the firecracker sauce: In a small bowl, combine the sour cream, Sriracha, and sweet chili sauce. Mix well. Serve with the shrimp.

201.   Sesame Seeds Coated Fish

Preparation Time: 10 Minutes
Cooking Time: 8 Minutes
Servings: 5

Ingredients:

- 3 tablespoons plain flour
- 2 eggs
- 1/2 cup sesame seeds, toasted
- 1/2 cup breadcrumbs
- 1/8 teaspoon dried rosemary, crushed
- Pinch of salt
- Pinch of black pepper
- 3 tablespoons olive oil
- 5 frozen fish fillets (white fish of your choice)

Directions:

- *Preparing the Ingredients.* In a shallow dish, place flour. In another shallow dish, whisk the eggs. In a third shallow dish, add remaining ingredients except fish fillets and mix till a crumbly mixture form.

- Coat the fillets with flour and shake off the excess flour.

- Next, dip the fillets in the egg.

- Then coat the fillets with sesame seeds mixture generously.

- Preheat the Air fryer oven to 390 degrees F.

- *Air Frying.* Line an Air fryer rack/basket with a piece of foil. Arrange the fillets into prepared basket.

- Cook for about 14 minutes, flipping once after 10 minutes.

202.   Creamy Breaded Shrimp

Preparation Time: 15 Minutes
Cooking Time: 20 Minutes
Servings: 3

Ingredients:

- ¼ cup all-purpose flour
- 1 cup panko breadcrumbs
- 1-pound shrimp, peeled and deveined
- ½ cup mayonnaise
- ¼ cup sweet chili sauce
- 1 tablespoon Sriracha sauce

Directions:

- Preheat the Air fryer to 400 o F and grease an Air fryer basket.

- Place flour in a shallow bowl and mix the mayonnaise, chili sauce, and Sriracha sauce in another bowl.

- Place the breadcrumbs in a third bowl.

- Coat each shrimp with the flour, dip into mayonnaise mixture and finally, dredge in the breadcrumbs.

- Arrange half of the coated shrimps into the Air fryer basket and cook for about 10 minutes.

- Dish out the coated shrimps onto serving plates and repeat with the remaining mixture.

203.   Coconut Crusted Shrimp

Preparation Time: 15 Minutes
Cooking Time: 40 Minutes
Servings: 3

Ingredients:

- 8 ounces coconut milk
- ½ cup sweetened coconut, shredded
- ½ cup panko breadcrumbs
- 1-pound large shrimp, peeled and deveined
- Salt and black pepper, to taste

Directions:

- Preheat the Air fryer to 350 o F and grease an Air fryer basket.
- Place the coconut milk in a shallow bowl.
- Mix coconut, breadcrumbs, salt, and black pepper in another bowl.
- Dip each shrimp into coconut milk and finally, dredge in the coconut mixture.
- Arrange half of the shrimps into the Air fryer basket and cook for about 20 minutes.
- Dish out the shrimps onto serving plates and repeat with the remaining mixture to serve.

204. Shrimp Scampi

Preparation Time: 15 Minutes
Cooking Time: 7 Minutes
Servings: 6

Ingredients:

- 4 tablespoons salted butter
- 1-pound shrimp, peeled and deveined
- 2 tablespoons fresh basil, chopped
- 1 tablespoon fresh chives, chopped
- 1 tablespoon fresh lemon juice
- 1 tablespoon garlic, minced
- 2 teaspoons red pepper flakes, crushed
- 2 tablespoons dry white wine

Directions:

- Preheat the Air fryer to 325 o F and grease an Air fryer pan.
- Heat butter, lemon juice, garlic, and red pepper flakes in a pan and return the pan to Air fryer basket.
- Cook for about 2 minutes and stir in shrimp, basil, chives and wine.

- Cook for about 5 minutes and dish out the mixture onto serving plates.
- Serve hot.

205. Rice Flour Coated Shrimp

Preparation Time: 20 Minutes
Cooking Time: 20 Minutes
Servings: 3

Ingredients:

- 3 tablespoons rice flour
- 1-pound shrimp, peeled and deveined
- 2 tablespoons olive oil
- 1 teaspoon powdered sugar
- Salt and black pepper, as required

Directions:

- Preheat the Air fryer to 325 o F and grease an Air fryer basket.
- Mix rice flour, olive oil, sugar, salt, and black pepper in a bowl.
- Stir in the shrimp and transfer half of the shrimp to the Air fryer basket.
- Cook for about 10 minutes, flipping once in between.
- Dish out the mixture onto serving plates and repeat with the remaining mixture.

206. Shrimp Kebabs

Preparation Time: 15 Minutes
Cooking Time: 10 Minutes
Servings: 2

Ingredients:

- ¾ pound shrimp, peeled and deveined
- 1 tablespoon fresh cilantro, chopped
- Wooden skewers, presoaked
- 2 tablespoons fresh lemon juice
- 1 teaspoon garlic, minced
- ½ teaspoon paprika
- ½ teaspoon ground cumin
- Salt and ground black pepper, as required

Directions:

- Preheat the Air fryer to 350 o F and grease an Air fryer basket.
- Mix lemon juice, garlic, and spices in a bowl.
- Stir in the shrimp and mix to coat well.
- Thread the shrimp onto presoaked wooden skewers and transfer to the Air fryer basket.
- Cook for about 10 minutes, flipping once in between.
- Dish out the mixture onto serving plates and serve garnished with fresh cilantro.

207. Garlic Parmesan Shrimp

Preparation Time: 20 Minutes
Cooking Time: 10 Minutes
Servings: 2

Ingredients:

- 1-pound shrimp, deveined and peeled
- ½ cup parmesan cheese, grated
- ¼ cup cilantro, diced
- 1 tablespoon olive oil
- 1 teaspoon salt
- 1 teaspoon fresh cracked pepper
- 1 tablespoon lemon juice
- 6 garlic cloves, diced

Directions:

- Preheat the Air fryer to 350 o F and grease an Air fryer basket.
- Drizzle shrimp with olive oil and lemon juice and season with garlic, salt and cracked pepper.
- Cover the bowl with plastic wrap and refrigerate for about 3 hours.
- Stir in the parmesan cheese and cilantro to the bowl and transfer to the Air fryer basket.
- Cook for about 10 minutes and serve immediately.

208. Breaded Shrimp with Lemon

Preparation Time: 15 Minutes
Cooking Time: 14 Minutes
Servings: 3

Ingredients:

- ½ cup plain flour
- 2 egg whites
- 1 cup breadcrumbs
- 1-pound large shrimp, peeled and deveined
- Salt and ground black pepper, as required
- ¼ teaspoon lemon zest
- ¼ teaspoon cayenne pepper
- ¼ teaspoon red pepper flakes, crushed
- 2 tablespoons vegetable oil

Directions:

- Preheat the Air fryer to 400 o F and grease an Air fryer basket.
- Mix flour, salt, and black pepper in a shallow bowl.
- Whisk the egg whites in a second bowl and mix the breadcrumbs, lime zest and spices in a third bowl.
- Coat each shrimp with the flour, dip into egg whites and finally, dredge in the breadcrumbs.
- Drizzle the shrimp evenly with olive oil and arrange half of the coated shrimps into the Air fryer basket.
- Cook for about 7 minutes and dish out the coated shrimps onto serving plates.
- Repeat with the remaining mixture and serve hot.

209. Buttered Salmon

Preparation Time: 10 Minutes
Cooking Time: 10 Minutes
Servings: 2

Ingredients:

- 2 (6-ounce) salmon fillets
- Salt and freshly ground black pepper, to taste
- 1 tablespoon butter, melted

Directions:

- Season each salmon fillet with salt and black pepper and then, coat with the butter.

- Press "Power Button" of Digital Air Fry Oven and turn the dial to select "Air Fry" mode.
- Press "Time Button" and again turn the dial to set the cooking time to 10 minutes.
- Now push "Temp Button" and rotate the dial to set the temperature at 360 degrees F.
- Press "Start/Pause" button to start.
- When the unit beeps to show that it is preheated, open the lid and grease the air fry basket.
- Arrange the salmon fillets into the prepared air fry basket and insert in the oven.
- When cooking time is complete, open the lid and transfer the salmon fillets onto serving plates.
- Serve hot.

210. Herbed Salmon

Preparation Time: 10 Minutes
Cooking Time: 10 Minutes
Servings: 2

Ingredients:

- 1 tablespoon fresh lime juice
- ½ tablespoons olive oil
- Salt and freshly ground black pepper, to taste
- 1 garlic clove, minced
- ½ teaspoon fresh thyme leaves, chopped
- ½ teaspoon fresh rosemary, chopped
- 2 (7-ounce) salmon fillets

Directions:

- In a bowl, add all the ingredients except the salmon and mix well.
- Add the salmon fillets and coat with the mixture generously.
- Press "Power Button" of Digital Air Fry Oven and turn the dial to select "Air Bake" mode.
- Press "Time Button" and again turn the dial to set the cooking time to 10 minutes.
- Now push "Temp Button" and rotate the dial to set the temperature at 400 degrees F.

- Press "Start/Pause" button to start.
- When the unit beeps to show that it is preheated, open the lid.
- Arrange the salmon fillets over the greased wire rack and insert in the oven.
- Flip the fillets once halfway through.
- When cooking time is complete, open the lid and transfer the salmon fillets onto serving plates.
- Serve hot.

211. Ranch Tilapia

Preparation Time: 15 Minutes
Cooking Time: 13 Minutes
Servings: 4

Ingredients:

- ¾ cup cornflakes, crushed
- 1 (1-ounce) packet dry ranch-style dressing mix
- 2½ tablespoons vegetable oil
- 2 eggs
- 4 (6-ounce) tilapia fillets

Directions:

- In a shallow bowl, crack the eggs and beat slightly.
- In another bowl, add the cornflakes, ranch dressing, and oil and mix until a crumbly mixture form.
- Dip the fish fillets into egg and then, coat with the breadcrumb's mixture.
- Press "Power Button" of Digital Air Fry Oven and turn the dial to select "Air Fry" mode.
- Press "Time Button" and again turn the dial to set the cooking time to 13 minutes.
- Now push "Temp Button" and rotate the dial to set the temperature at 356 degrees F.
- Press "Start/Pause" button to start.
- When the unit beeps to show that it is preheated, open the lid and grease the air fry basket.

- Arrange the tilapia fillets into the prepared air fry basket and insert in the oven. When cooking time is complete, open the lid and transfer the fillets onto serving plates.

- Serve hot.

212. Grilled Sardines

Preparation Time: 5 Minutes
Cooking Time: 21 Minutes
Servings: 2

Ingredients:

- Five sardines
- Herbs of Provence

Directions:

- Preheat the air fryer to 1600C.

- Spray the basket and place your sardines in the basket of your fryer.

- Set the timer for 14 minutes. After 7 minutes, remember to turn the sardines so that they are roasted on both sides.

213. Zucchini with Tuna

Preparation Time: 10-20 Minutes
Cooking Time: 15-30 Minutes
Servings: 2

Ingredients:

- Four medium zucchinis
- 120g of tuna in oil (canned) drained
- 30g grated cheese
- Tsp pine nuts
- Salt, pepper to taste

Directions:

- Cut the zucchini in half lengthways and empty it with a small spoon (set aside the pulp that will be used for the filling); place them in the basket.

- In a food processor, put the zucchini pulp, drained tuna, pine nuts, and grated cheese. Blend everything until you get a homogeneous and dense mixture.

- Fill the zucchini. Set the air fryer to 1800C.

- Simmer for 20 min. Depending on the size of the zucchini. Let cool before serving

214. Caramelized Salmon Fillet

Preparation Time: 10 Minutes
Cooking Time: 30 Minutes
Servings: 4

Ingredients:

- Two salmon fillets
- 60g cane sugar
- 4 tbsp soy sauce
- 50g sesame seeds
- Unlimited Ginger

Directions:

- Preheat the air fryer at 1800C for 5 minutes.

- Put the sugar and soy sauce in the basket.

- Cook everything for 5 minutes.

- In the meantime, wash the fish well, pass it through sesame to cover it completely, and place it inside the tank and add the fresh ginger.

- Cook for 12 minutes.

- Turn the fish over and finish cooking for another 8 minutes.

215. Breaded Swordfish

Preparation Time: 20 Minutes
Cooking Time: 30 Minutes
Servings: 8

Ingredients:

- 500g swordfish ranches
- Breadcrumbs to taste
- 1 tsp peanut oil
- 1 tsp olive oil
- ½ lemon juice

Directions:

- Clean and rinse the fish; grease each slice and pass it in lightly salted breadcrumbs to cover it completely.

- Preheat the air fryer at 1600C for 5 minutes.

- Place the breaded fish in the basket—Cook the fish for 10 minutes.
- Turn the fish over and cook for additional 8 minutes.
- Meanwhile, prepare the marinade with olive oil, lemon juice, salt, pepper, and chopped parsley; mix with a fork.
- Once ready, place the fish slices on the plate and pour 1 to 2 tablespoons of marinade.

216. Deep Fried Prawns

Preparation Time: 20 Minutes
Cooking Time: 15 Minutes
Servings: 6

Ingredients:

- 12 prawns
- Two eggs
- Flour to taste
- Breadcrumbs
- 1 tsp oil

Directions:

- Remove the head of the prawns and shell carefully.
- Pass the prawns first in the flour, then in the beaten egg, and then in the breadcrumbs.
- Preheat the air fryer for 1 minute at 1500C.
- Add the prawns and cook for 4 minutes. If the prawns are large, it will be necessary to cook six at a time.
- Turn the prawns and cook for another 4 minutes.
- They should be served with a yogurt or mayonnaise sauce.

217. Mussels with Pepper

Preparation Time: 20 Minutes
Cooking Time: 15 Minutes
Servings: 6

Ingredients:

- 700g mussels
- One clove garlic
- 1 tsp oil
- Pepper to taste
- Parsley Taste

Directions:

- Clean and scrape the mold cover and remove the byssus (the "beard" that comes out of the mold).
- Pour the oil, clean the mussels, and the crushed garlic in the basket.
- Set the temperature to 2000C and simmer for 12 minutes.
- Towards the end of cooking, add black pepper and chopped parsley.
- Finally, distribute the mussel juice well at the bottom of the basket, stirring the basket.

218. Scallops in Butter with Leaves

Preparation Time: 20 Minutes
Cooking Time: 30 Minutes
Servings: 4

Ingredients:

- 400g scallops
- 20g butter
- One clove garlic
- Leaves to taste
- ½ lemon juice

Directions:

- Wash the scallops and dry them on a paper towel.
- Place the butter and chopped garlic inside the basket. Set the temperature to 1500C.
- Melt the butter for 2 to 3 minutes.
- Add the scallops, salt, pepper, and cook for 8 minutes.
- Then add the lemon juice, parsley, and finish cooking for another 3 to 4 minutes.
- Very good as an appetizer to serve inside the shells.

219. Monkfish with Olives and Capers

Preparation Time: 20 Minutes
Cooking Time: 45 Minutes
Servings: 4

Ingredients:

- One monkfish
- Ten cherry tomatoes
- 50 g cailletier olives
- Five capers

Directions:

- Spread aluminum foil inside the basket and place the monkfish clean and skinless.
- Add chopped tomatoes, olives, capers, oil, and salt.
- Set the temperature to 1600C.
- Cook the monkfish for around 40 minutes.

220. Shrimp, Zucchini and Cherry Tomato Sauce

Preparation Time: 10 Minutes
Cooking Time: 30 Minutes
Servings: 4

Ingredients:

- Two zucchinis
- 300 shrimp
- Seven cherry tomatoes
- Salt to taste
- One clove garlic

Directions:

- Pour the oil, add the garlic clove, and diced zucchini.
- Cook for 15 minutes at 1500C.
- Add the shrimp and the pieces of tomato, salt, and spices.
- Cook for another 5 to 10 minutes or until the shrimp water evaporates.

221. Salmon with Pistachio Bark

Preparation Time: 20 Minutes
Cooking Time: 30 Minutes
Servings: 4

Ingredients:

- 600 g salmon fillet

- 50g pistachios
- Salt to taste

Directions:

- Place the parchment paper on the bottom of the basket and place the salmon fillet in it (it can be cooked whole or already divided into four portions).
- Cut the pistachios into thick pieces; grease the top of the fish, salt (little because the pistachios are already salted), and cover everything with the pistachios.
- Set the air fryer to 1800C and simmer for 25 minutes.

222. Salmon in Papillote with Orange

Preparation Time: 20 Minutes
Cooking Time: 30 Minutes
Servings: 4

Ingredients:

- 600g salmon fillet
- Four oranges
- Two cloves of garlic
- Chives to taste
- One lemon

Directions:

- Pour the freshly squeezed orange juice, the lemon juice, the zest of the two oranges into a bowl. Add two tablespoons of oil, salt, and garlic. Dip the previously washed salmon fillet and leave it in the marinade for one hour, preferably in the refrigerator
- Place the steak and part of your marinade on a sheet of foil. Salt and sprinkle with chives and a few slices of orange.
- Set to 1600C. Simmer for 30 minutes. Open the sheet, let it evaporate, and serve with a nice garnish of fresh orange.

223. Salted Marinated Salmon

Preparation Time: 10 Minutes
Cooking Time: 30 Minutes
Servings: 2

Ingredients:

- 500g salmon fillet
- 1 kg of coarse salt

Directions:

- Place the baking paper on the basket and the salmon on top (skin side up) covered with coarse salt.
- Set the air fryer to 1500C.
- Cook everything for 25 to 30 minutes. At the end of cooking, remove the salt from the fish and serve with a drizzle of oil.

224. Sautéed Trout with Almonds

Preparation Time: 30 Minutes
Cooking Time: 30 Minutes
Servings: 4

Ingredients:

- 700 g salmon trout
- 15 black peppercorns
- Dill leaves to taste
- 30g almonds
- Salt to taste

Directions:

- Cut the trout into cubes and marinate it for half an hour with the ingredients (except salt).
- Cook for 17 minutes at 1600C. Pour a drizzle of oil and serve.

225. Stuffed Cuttlefish

Preparation Time: 20 Minutes
Cooking Time: 30 Minutes
Servings: 4

Ingredients:

- Eight small cuttlefish
- 50 g of breadcrumbs
- Garlic to taste
- Parsley to taste
- One egg

Directions:

- Clean the cuttlefish, cut, and separate the tentacles. In a blender, pour the breadcrumbs, the parsley (without the branches), the egg, the salt, a drizzle of olive oil, and the sepia tentacles.
- Blend until you get a dense mixture. Fill the sepia with the mixture obtained.
- Place the cuttlefish in the bowl.
- Set the air fryer to 1500C and cook for 20 minutes. At the end of cooking, add a drizzle of olive oil and serve.

226. Rabas

Preparation Time: 5 Minutes
Cooking Time: 12 Minutes
Servings: 4

Ingredients:

- 16 rabas
- One egg
- Breadcrumbs
- Salt, pepper, sweet paprika

Directions:

- Put the rabas boil for 2 minutes.
- Remove and dry well.
- Beat the egg and season to taste. You can put salt, pepper, and sweet paprika—place in the egg.
- Bread with breadcrumbs. Place in sticks.
- Place in the fryer for 5 minutes at 1600C. Remove
- Spray with a cooking spray and place five more minutes at 2000C.

227. Roasted Salmon with Vegetables

Preparation Time: 15 Minutes
Cooking Time: 14 Minutes
Servings: 2

Ingredients:

- One large carrot, peeled and sliced
- One fennel bulb, thinly sliced
- One small onion, thinly sliced
- ¼ cup low-fat sour cream

- 2 (5-ounce / 142-g) salmon fillets

Directions:

- Preheat the air fryer to 400°F (205°C).

- In a bowl, mix the carrot, fennel bulb, and onion. Toss well.

- Transfer the vegetable mixture to a 6-inch metal pan, then put the pan in the air fryer basket.

- Roast in the preheated air fryer for 4 minutes, or until the vegetables are fork-tender.

- Remove the pan from the air fryer. Add the sour cream to the pan and season with ground pepper, then spread the salmon fillets on top.

- Return the pan to the air fryer and roast for an additional 10 minutes, or until the fish flakes easily when tested with a fork.

- Let the salmon and vegetables cool for 5 minutes before serving.

228. Quick Coconut Shrimp

Preparation Time: 10 Minutes
Cooking Time: 8 Minutes
Servings: 4

Ingredients:

- ¼ cup all-purpose flour

- One egg

- 1/3 cup shredded unsweetened coconut

- 1/4 cup panko bread crumbs

- 1 pound (454 g) raw shrimp, peeled, deveined, and patted dry

Directions:

- Heat the air fryer to 400°F (205°C).

- On a plate, place the flour.

- In a small bowl, whisk the egg until frothy.

- In a separate bowl, mix the coconut, bread crumbs, salt, and pepper.

- Dredge the shrimp in the flour, shake off any excess, dip them in the egg, and finally coat them in the coconut-bread mixture.

- Spray the air fryer basket with cooking spray. Put the breaded shrimp in the basket and spray with cooking spray.

- Cook in the warmed air fryer for 8 minutes, flipping the shrimp once during cooking, or until the shrimp are opaque and crisp.

- Remove from the basket and serve on a plate.

229. Lemon-Pepper Tilapia Fillets

Preparation Time: 5 Minutes
Cooking Time: 15 Minutes
Servings: 4

Ingredients:

- Four tilapia fillets

- One teaspoon garlic powder

- One teaspoon paprika

- One teaspoon dried basil

- Lemon-pepper seasoning, to taste

Directions:

- Heat the air fryer to 400°F (205°C).

- Add the olive oil, garlic powder, paprika, basil, lemon-pepper seasoning, fillets to a large bowl, and toss well to coat the fillets thoroughly.

- Transfer the coated fillets to the air fryer basket.

- Cook in the warmed air fryer for 8 minutes. Flip the fillets and cook for 7 minutes more until the fish flakes easily with a fork.

- Divide the fillets among four serving plates and serve hot.

230. Blackened Shrimp with Lemon Juice

Preparation Time: 5 Minutes
Cooking Time: 10 Minutes
Servings: 4

Ingredients:

- 1 pound (454 g) raw shrimp, peeled, deveined, and patted dry

- One teaspoon paprika

- ½ teaspoon cayenne pepper

- ½ teaspoon dried oregano
- Juice of ½ lemon

Directions:

- Heat the air fryer to 400°F (205°C).
- Put the shrimp in a sealable plastic bag. Add the paprika, cayenne pepper, oregano, lemon juice, salt, and pepper to the shrimp. Lid the bag and shake to coat the shrimp with the spices evenly.
- Spray the air fryer basket with cooking spray. Arrange the shrimp in the basket.
- Cook in the warmed air fryer for 7 minutes, shaking the basket once during cooking, or until the shrimp is blackened.
- Let the shrimp cool for 5 minutes and serve warm.

231. Fried Catfish with Fish Fry

Preparation Time: 5 Minutes
Cooking Time: 13 Minutes
Servings: 4

Ingredients:

- Four catfish fillets rinsed and patted dry
- ¼ cup seasoned fish fry
- One tablespoon chopped parsley
- One tablespoon olive oil

Directions:

- Warm the air fryer to 400°F (205°C).
- Put the fillets and seasoned fish fry in a Ziploc bag. Cover the bag and shake well until the fish is nicely coated.
- Brush both sides of each piece of fish with olive oil. Put the fillets in the air fryer basket.
- Cook in the preheated air fryer for 13 minutes. Flip the fillets once during cooking or until the fish is cooked through.
- Remove from the basket and garnish with chopped parsley.

232. Pecan-Crusted Catfish Fillets

Preparation Time: 5 Minutes
Cooking Time: 12 Minutes

Servings: 4

Ingredients:

- ½ cup pecan meal
- 4 (4-ounce / 113-g) catfish fillets, rinsed and patted dry
- Fresh oregano, for garnish (optional)
- Pecan halves, for garnish (optional)

Directions:

- Warm the air fryer to 375°F (190°C). Grease the air fryer basket with half of the avocado oil and set aside.
- Stir together the pecan meal, salt, and pepper in a large bowl. Roll the fillets with the mixture, pressing, so the fish is well coated.
- Brush the fillets with the remaining avocado oil and transfer to the air fryer basket.
- Cook in the preheated air fryer for 12 minutes, flipping the fillets halfway through, or until the fish flakes easily with a fork.
- Remove from the basket to a large plate. Sprinkle the oregano and pecan halves on top for garnish, if desired.

233. Fish Fillets with Parmesan Cheese

Preparation Time: 5 Minutes
Cooking Time: 10 to 12 Minutes
Servings: 4

Ingredients:

- 1 cup Parmesan cheese, grated
- One egg whisked
- One teaspoon garlic powder
- ½ teaspoon shallot powder
- Four white fish fillets

Directions:

- Preheat the air fryer to 370°F (188°C).
- In a shallow dish, put the Parmesan cheese. Mix the whisked egg, garlic powder, and shallot powder in a bowl, and stir to combine.
- On a clean surface, season the fillets generously with salt and pepper. Dredge the

fillets into the egg mixture, then roll over the cheese until thickly coated.

- Assemble the fillets in the air fryer basket and air fry until golden brown, about 10 to 12 minutes.

- Let the fish fillets cool for 5 minutes before serving.

234. Air-Fried Sardines

Preparation Time: 10 Minutes
Cooking Time: 12 Minutes
Servings: 4

Ingredients:

- 1½ pounds (680 g) sardines, rinsed and patted dry

- One tablespoon lemon juice

- One tablespoon Italian seasoning mix

Directions:

- Warm the air fryer to 350°F (180°C).

- In a large bowl, toss the sardines with olive oil, lemon juice, Italian seasoning mix, soy sauce, salt, and pepper. Let the sardines marinate for 30 minutes.

- Put the marinated sardines in the air fryer basket and air fry for about 12 minutes until flaky, flipping the fish halfway through.

- Transfer to a plate and serve hot.

235. Garlicky Shrimp

Preparation Time: 5 Minutes
Cooking Time: 3 to 4 Minutes
Servings: 4

Ingredients:

- 1½ pounds (680 g) shrimp, shelled and deveined

- Three cloves garlic, minced

- One teaspoon smoked cayenne pepper

- ½ teaspoon ginger, freshly grated

- ½ tablespoon fresh basil leaves, chopped

Directions:

- Warm the air fryer to 390°F (199°C).

- Mix all the ingredients in a large bowl and toss until well incorporated. Let the shrimp sit for 30 minutes.

- Put it in the basket and air fry for 3 to 4 minutes, or until the shrimp are opaque. Serve hot.

236. Tuna Steaks with Red Onions

Preparation Time: 10 Minutes
Cooking Time: 10 Minutes
Servings: 4

Ingredients:

- Four tuna steaks

- ½ pound (227 g) red onions

- One teaspoon dried rosemary

- One tablespoon cayenne pepper

- One lemon, sliced

Directions:

- Warm the air fryer to 400°F (205°C) and spray the basket with cooking spray.

- Place the tuna steaks in the basket and scatter the onions all over. Sprinkle with the olive oil and sprinkle with rosemary, cayenne pepper, salt, and black pepper.

- Bake in batches in the preheated air fryer for 10 minutes until cooked through.

- Garnish with the lemon slices and serve warm.

237. Parmesan Haddock Fillets

Preparation Time: 5 Minutes
Cooking Time: 11 to 13 Minutes
Servings: 2

Ingredients:

- ½ cup Parmesan cheese, freshly grated

- One teaspoon dried parsley flake

- One egg

- ¼ teaspoon cayenne pepper

- Two haddock fillets patted dry

Directions:

- Warm the air fryer to 360°F (182°C).

- Stir together the Parmesan cheese and parsley flakes in a shallow dish. Beat the egg with the cayenne pepper, sea salt, and pepper in a bowl.

- Dunk the haddock fillets into the egg, and then roll over the Parmesan mixture until fully coated on both sides.

- Handover the fillets to the air fryer basket and drizzle with the olive oil

- Cook in the preheated air fryer for 11 to 13 minutes, or until the flesh is opaque.

- Remove from the basket to a plate and serve.

238.　Shrimp Skewers with Vermouth

Preparation Time: 10 Minutes
Cooking Time: 5 Minutes
Servings: 4

Ingredients:

- 1½ pounds (680 g) shrimp
- ¼ cup vermouth
- Two cloves garlic, crushed
- One lemon, cut into wedges

Directions:

- Warm the air fryer to 400°F (205°C).

- Toss the shrimp with the vermouth, olive oil, garlic, salt, and pepper in a bowl and then put it in the fridge to marinate for 1 hour.

- Remove the shrimp from the refrigerator and discard the marinade. Skewer the shrimp by piercing through the center and transfer to the basket.

- Cook in the warmed air fryer for 5 minutes, flipping the shrimp halfway through.

- Relish with the lemon wedges and serve hot.

239.　Lobster Tails with Green Olives

Preparation Time: 10 Minutes
Cooking Time: 7 Minutes
Servings: 5

Ingredients:

- 2 pounds (907 g) fresh lobster tails, cleaned and halved, in shells

- One teaspoon onion powder
- One teaspoon cayenne pepper
- Two garlic cloves, minced
- 1 cup of green olives

Directions:

- Warm the air fryer to 390°F (199°C) and spray the basket with cooking spray.

- Put all the ingredients except for the green olives in a sealable plastic bag. Seal the bag and shake until the lobster tails are coated completely.

- Arrange the coated lobster tails in the greased basket. Cook in batches in the preheated air fryer for 6 to 7 minutes, shaking the basket halfway through.

- Remove from the basket and serve with green olives.

240.　Salmon

Preparation Time: 10 minutes
Cooking Time: 12 minutes
Servings: 4

Ingredients:

- 4 (6-oz.) salmon fillets
- Salt and ground black pepper, as required

Directions:

- Season the salmon fillets with salt and black pepper evenly.

- Press "Power Button" of Air Fry Oven and turn the dial to select the "Air Broil" mode.

- Press the Time button and again turn the dial to set the cooking time to 12 minutes.

- Press "Start/Pause" button to start.

- When the unit beeps to show that it is preheated, open the lid.

- Arrange the fish fillets over the greased "Wire Rack" and insert in the oven.

- Serve hot.

241.　Buttered Salmon

Preparation Time: 10 minutes
Cooking Time: 10 minutes

Servings: 2

Ingredients:

- 2 (6-oz.) salmon fillets
- Salt and ground black pepper, as required
- 1 tablespoon butter, melted

Direction:

- Season each salmon fillet with salt and black pepper and then, coat with the butter.
- Press "Power Button" of Air Fry Oven and turn the dial to select the "Air Fry" mode.
- Press the Time button and again turn the dial to set the cooking time to 10 minutes.
- Now push the Temp button and rotate the dial to set the temperature at 360 degrees F.
- Press "Start/Pause" button to start.
- When the unit beeps to show that it is preheated, open the lid.
- Arrange the salmon fillets in greased "Air Fry Basket" and insert in the oven.
- Serve hot.

242.   Cajun Salmon

Preparation Time: 10 minutes
Cooking Time: 7 minutes
Servings: 2

Ingredients:

- 2 (7-oz.) (¾-inch thick) salmon fillets
- 1 tablespoon Cajun seasoning
- ½ teaspoon sugar
- 1 tablespoon fresh lemon juice

Directions:

- Sprinkle the salmon fillets with Cajun seasoning and sugar evenly.
- Press "Power Button" of Air Fry Oven and turn the dial to select the "Air Fry" mode.
- Press the Time button and again turn the dial to set the cooking time to 7 minutes.
- Now push the Temp button and rotate the dial to set the temperature at 356 degrees F.
- Press "Start/Pause" button to start.

- When the unit beeps to show that it is preheated, open the lid.
- Arrange the salmon fillets, skin-side up in greased "Air Fry Basket" and insert in the oven.
- Drizzle with the lemon juice and serve hot.

243.   Spicy Salmon

Preparation Time: 10 minutes
Cooking Time: 11 minutes
Servings: 2

Ingredients:

- 1 teaspoon smoked paprika
- 1 teaspoon cayenne pepper
- 1 teaspoon onion powder
- 1 teaspoon garlic powder
- Salt and ground black pepper, as required
- 2 (6-oz.) (1½-inch thick) salmon fillets
- 2 teaspoons olive oil

Directions:

- Add the spices in a bowl and mix well.
- Drizzle the salmon fillets with oil and then, rub with the spice mixture.
- Press "Power Button" of Air Fry Oven and turn the dial to select the "Air Fry" mode.
- Press the Time button and again turn the dial to set the cooking time to 11 minutes.
- Now push the Temp button and rotate the dial to set the temperature at 390 degrees F.
- Press "Start/Pause" button to start.
- When the unit beeps to show that it is preheated, open the lid.
- Arrange the salmon fillets in greased "Air Fry Basket" and insert in the oven.
- Serve hot.

244.   Lemony Salmon

Preparation Time: 10 minutes
Cooking Time: 8 minutes
Servings: 3

Ingredients:

- 1½ lbs. salmon
- ½ teaspoon red chili powder
- Salt and ground black pepper, as required
- 1 lemon, cut into slices
- 1 tablespoon fresh dill, chopped

Directions:

- Season the salmon with chili powder, salt, and black pepper.
- Press "Power Button" of Air Fry Oven and turn the dial to select the "Air Fry" mode.
- Press the Time button and again turn the dial to set the cooking time to 8 minutes.
- Now push the Temp button and rotate the dial to set the temperature at 375 degrees F.
- Press "Start/Pause" button to start.
- When the unit beeps to show that it is preheated, open the lid.
- Arrange the salmon fillets in greased "Air Fry Basket" and insert in the oven.
- Garnish with fresh dill and serve hot.

245.   Honey Glazed Salmon

Preparation Time: 10 minutes
Cooking Time: 8 minutes
Servings: 2

Ingredients:

- 2 (6-oz.) salmon fillets
- Salt, as required
- 2 tablespoons honey

Directions:

- Sprinkle the salmon fillets with salt and then, coat with honey.
- Press "Power Button" of Air Fry Oven and turn the dial to select the "Air Fry" mode.
- Press the Time button and again turn the dial to set the cooking time to 8 minutes.
- Now push the Temp button and rotate the dial to set the temperature at 355 degrees F.
- Press "Start/Pause" button to start.
- When the unit beeps to show that it is preheated, open the lid.

- Arrange the salmon fillets in greased "Air Fry Basket" and insert in the oven.
- Serve hot.

246.   Sweet & Sour Glazed Salmon

Preparation Time: 12 minutes
Cooking Time: 20 minutes
Servings: 2

Ingredients:

- 1/3 cup soy sauce
- 1/3 cup honey
- 3 teaspoons rice wine vinegar
- 1 teaspoon water
- 4 (3½-oz.) salmon fillets

Directions:

- In a small bowl, mix together the soy sauce, honey, vinegar, and water.
- In another small bowl, reserve about half of the mixture.
- Add salmon fillets in the remaining mixture and coat well.
- Cover the bowl and refrigerate to marinate for about 2 hours.
- Press "Power Button" of Air Fry Oven and turn the dial to select the "Air Fry" mode.
- Press the Time button and again turn the dial to set the cooking time to 12 minutes.
- Now push the Temp button and rotate the dial to set the temperature at 355 degrees F.
- Press "Start/Pause" button to start.
- When the unit beeps to show that it is preheated, open the lid.
- Arrange the salmon fillets in greased "Air Fry Basket" and insert in the oven.
- Flip the salmon fillets once halfway through and coat with the reserved marinade after every 3 minutes.
- Serve hot.

247.   Salmon Parcel

Preparation Time: 15 minutes
Cooking Time: 23 minutes

Servings: 2

Ingredients:

- 2 (4-oz.) salmon fillets
- 6 asparagus stalks
- ¼ cup white sauce
- 1 teaspoon oil
- ¼ cup champagne
- Salt and ground black pepper, as required

Directions:

- In a bowl, mix together all the ingredients.
- Divide the salmon mixture over 2 pieces of foil evenly.
- Seal the foil around the salmon mixture to form the packet.
- Press "Power Button" of Air Fry Oven and turn the dial to select the "Air Fry" mode.
- Press the Time button and again turn the dial to set the cooking time to 13 minutes.
- Now push the Temp button and rotate the dial to set the temperature at 355 degrees F.
- Press "Start/Pause" button to start.
- When the unit beeps to show that it is preheated, open the lid.
- Arrange the salmon parcels in "Air Fry Basket" and insert in the oven.
- Serve hot.

248. Salmon with Broccoli

Preparation Time: 15 minutes
Cooking Time: 12 minutes
Servings: 2

Ingredients:

- 1½ cups small broccoli florets
- 2 tablespoons vegetable oil, divided
- Salt and ground black pepper, as required
- 1 (½-inch) piece fresh ginger, grated
- 1 tablespoon soy sauce
- 1 teaspoon rice vinegar
- 1 teaspoon light brown sugar
- ¼ teaspoon cornstarch

- 2 (6-oz.) skin-on salmon fillets
- 1 scallion, thinly sliced

Directions:

- In a bowl, mix together the broccoli, 1 tablespoon of oil, salt, and black pepper.
- In another bowl, mix well the ginger, soy sauce, vinegar, sugar, and cornstarch.
- Coat the salmon fillets with remaining oil and then with the ginger mixture.
- Press "Power Button" of Air Fry Oven and turn the dial to select the "Air Fry" mode.
- Press the Time button and again turn the dial to set the cooking time to 12 minutes.
- Now push the Temp button and rotate the dial to set the temperature at 375 degrees F.
- Press "Start/Pause" button to start.
- When the unit beeps to show that it is preheated, open the lid.
- Arrange the broccoli florets in greased "Air Fry Basket" and top with the salmon fillets.
- Insert the basket in the oven.
- Serve hot.

249. Salmon with Prawns & Pasta

Preparation Time: 20 minutes
Cooking Time: 18 minutes
Servings: 4

Ingredients:

- 14 oz. pasta (of your choice)
- 4 tablespoons pesto, divided
- 4 (4-oz.) salmon steaks
- 2 tablespoons olive oil
- ½ lb. cherry tomatoes, chopped
- 8 large prawns, peeled and deveined
- 2 tablespoons fresh lemon juice
- 2 tablespoons fresh thyme, chopped

Directions:

- In a large pan of salted boiling water, add the pasta and cook for about 8-10 minutes or until desired doneness.

- Meanwhile, in the bottom of a baking pan, spread 1 tablespoon of pesto.
- Place salmon steaks and tomatoes over pesto in a single layer and drizzle with the oil.
- Arrange the prawns on top in a single layer.
- Drizzle with lemon juice and sprinkle with thyme.
- Press "Power Button" of Air Fry Oven and turn the dial to select the "Air Fry" mode.
- Press the Time button and again turn the dial to set the cooking time to 8 minutes.
- Now push the Temp button and rotate the dial to set the temperature at 390 degrees F.
- Press "Start/Pause" button to start.
- When the unit beeps to show that it is preheated, open the lid.
- Arrange the baking pan in "Air Fry Basket" and insert in the oven.
- Drain the pasta and transfer into a large bowl.
- Add the remaining pesto and toss to coat well.
- Divide the pasta onto serving plate and top with salmon mixture.
- Serve immediately.

250. Salmon Burgers

Preparation Time: 20 minutes
Cooking Time: 22 minutes
Servings: 6

Ingredients:

- 3 large russet potatoes, peeled and cubed
- 1 (6-oz.) cooked salmon fillet
- 1 egg
- ¾ cup frozen vegetables (of your choice), parboiled and drained
- 2 tablespoons fresh parsley, chopped
- 1 teaspoon fresh dill, chopped
- Salt and ground black pepper, as required
- 1 cup breadcrumbs
- ¼ cup olive oil

Directions:

- In a pan of the boiling water, cook the potatoes for about 10 minutes.
- Drain the potatoes well.
- Transfer the potatoes into a bowl and mash with a potato masher.
- Set aside to cool completely.
- In another bowl, add the salmon and flake with a fork.
- Add the cooked potatoes, egg, parboiled vegetables, parsley, dill, salt and black pepper and mix until well combined.
- Make 6 equal-sized patties from the mixture.
- Coat patties with breadcrumb evenly and then drizzle with the oil evenly.
- Press "Power Button" of Air Fry Oven and turn the dial to select the "Air Fry" mode.
- Press the Time button and again turn the dial to set the cooking time to 12 minutes.
- Now push the Temp button and rotate the dial to set the temperature at 355 degrees F.
- Press "Start/Pause" button to start.
- When the unit beeps to show that it is preheated, open the lid.
- Arrange the patties in greased "Air Fry Basket" and insert in the oven.
- Flip the patties once halfway through.
- Serve hot.

251. Ranch Tilapia

Preparation Time: 15 minutes
Cooking Time: 13 minutes
Servings: 4

Ingredients:

- ¾ cup cornflakes, crushed
- 1 (1-oz.) packet dry ranch-style dressing mix
- 2½ tablespoons vegetable oil
- 2 eggs
- 4 (6-oz.) tilapia fillets

Directions:

- In a shallow bowl, beat the eggs.

- In another bowl, add the cornflakes, ranch dressing, and oil and mix until a crumbly mixture form.

- Dip the fish fillets into egg and then, coat with the breadcrumb's mixture.

- Press "Power Button" of Air Fry Oven and turn the dial to select the "Air Fry" mode.

- Press the Time button and again turn the dial to set the cooking time to 13 minutes.

- Now push the Temp button and rotate the dial to set the temperature at 356 degrees F.

- Press "Start/Pause" button to start.

- When the unit beeps to show that it is preheated, open the lid.

- Arrange the tilapia fillets in greased "Air Fry Basket" and insert in the oven.

- Serve hot.

252. Chinese Cod

Preparation Time: 15 minutes
Cooking Time: 15 minutes
Servings: 2

Ingredients:

- 2 (7-oz.) cod fillets
- Salt and ground black pepper, as required
- ¼ teaspoon sesame oil
- 1 cup water
- 5 little squares rock sugar
- 5 tablespoons light soy sauce
- 1 teaspoon dark soy sauce
- 2 scallions (green part), sliced
- ¼ cup fresh cilantro, chopped
- 3 tablespoons olive oil
- 5 ginger slices

Directions:

- Season each cod fillet evenly with salt, and black pepper and drizzle with sesame oil.

- Set aside at room temperature for about 15-20 minutes.

- Dip the fish fillets into egg and then, coat with the breadcrumb's mixture.

- Press "Power Button" of Air Fry Oven and turn the dial to select the "Air Fry" mode.

- Press the Time button and again turn the dial to set the cooking time to 12 minutes.

- Now push the Temp button and rotate the dial to set the temperature at 355 degrees F.

- Press "Start/Pause" button to start.

- When the unit beeps to show that it is preheated, open the lid.

- Arrange the cod fillets in greased "Air Fry Basket" and insert in the oven.

- Meanwhile, in a small pan, add the water and bring it to a boil.

- Add the rock sugar and both soy sauces and cook until sugar is dissolved, stirring continuously.

- Remove from the heat and set aside.

- Remove the cod fillets from oven and transfer onto serving plates.

- Top each fillet with scallion and cilantro.

- In a small frying pan, heat the olive oil over medium heat and sauté the ginger slices for about 2-3 minutes.

- Remove the frying pan from heat and discard the ginger slices.

- Carefully, pour the hot oil evenly over cod fillets.

- Top with the sauce mixture and serve.

253. Cod Parcel

Preparation Time: 20 minutes
Cooking Time: 15 minutes
Servings: 2

Ingredients:

- 2 tablespoons butter, melted
- 1 tablespoon fresh lemon juice
- ½ teaspoon dried tarragon
- Salt and ground black pepper, as required
- ½ cup red bell peppers, seeded and thinly sliced
- ½ cup carrots, peeled and julienned
- ½ cup fennel bulbs, julienned

- 2 (5-oz.) frozen cod fillets, thawed
- 1 tablespoon olive oil

Directions:

- In a large bowl, mix together the butter, lemon juice, tarragon, salt, and black pepper.
- Add the bell pepper, carrot, and fennel bulb and generously coat with the mixture.
- Arrange 2 large parchment squares onto a smooth surface.
- Coat the cod fillets with oil and then, sprinkle evenly with salt and black pepper.
- Arrange 1 cod fillet onto each parchment square and top each evenly with the vegetables.
- Top with any remaining sauce from the bowl.
- Fold the parchment paper and crimp the sides to secure fish and vegetables.
- Press "Power Button" of Air Fry Oven and turn the dial to select the "Air Fry" mode.
- Press the Time button and again turn the dial to set the cooking time to 15 minutes.
- Now push the Temp button and rotate the dial to set the temperature at 350 degrees F.
- Press "Start/Pause" button to start.
- When the unit beeps to show that it is preheated, open the lid.
- Arrange the cod parcels in "Air Fry Basket" and insert in the oven.
- Serve hot.

254. Cod Burgers

Preparation Time: 15 minutes
Cooking Time: 7 minutes
Servings: 6

Ingredients:

- ½ lb. cod fillets
- ½ teaspoon fresh lime zest, grated finely
- ½ egg
- ½ teaspoon red chili paste
- Salt, to taste
- ½ tablespoon fresh lime juice

- 3 tablespoons coconut, grated and divided
- 1 small scallion, chopped finely
- 1 tablespoon fresh parsley, chopped

Directions:

- In a food processor, add cod filets, lime zest, egg, chili paste, salt and lime juice and pulse until smooth.
- Transfer the cod mixture into a bowl.
- Add 1½ tablespoons coconut, scallion and parsley and mix until well combined.
- Make 6 equal-sized patties from the mixture.
- In a shallow dish, place the remaining coconut.
- Coat the patties in coconut evenly.
- Press "Power Button" of Air Fry Oven and turn the dial to select the "Air Fry" mode.
- Press the Time button and again turn the dial to set the cooking time to 7 minutes.
- Now push the Temp button and rotate the dial to set the temperature at 375 degrees F.
- Press "Start/Pause" button to start.
- When the unit beeps to show that it is preheated, open the lid.
- Arrange the patties in greased "Air Fry Basket" and insert in the oven.
- Serve hot.

255. Spicy Catfish

Preparation Time: 15 minutes
Cooking Time: 13 minutes
Servings: 2

Ingredients:

- 2 tablespoons almond flour
- 1 teaspoon red chili powder
- ½ teaspoon paprika
- ½ teaspoon garlic powder
- Salt, as required
- 2 (6-oz.) catfish fillets
- 1 tablespoon olive oil

Directions:

- In a bowl, mix together the flour, paprika, garlic powder and salt.
- Add the catfish fillets and coat with the mixture evenly.
- Now, coat each fillet with oil.
- Press "Power Button" of Air Fry Oven and turn the dial to select the "Air Fry" mode.
- Press the Time button and again turn the dial to set the cooking time to 13 minutes.
- Now push the Temp button and rotate the dial to set the temperature at 400 degrees F.
- Press "Start/Pause" button to start.
- When the unit beeps to show that it is preheated, open the lid.
- Arrange the fish fillets in greased "Air Fry Basket" and insert in the oven.
- Flip the fish fillets once halfway through.
- Serve hot.

256. Seasoned Catfish

Preparation Time: 15 minutes
Cooking Time: 23 minutes
Servings: 4

Ingredients:

- 4 (4-oz.) catfish fillets
- 2 tablespoons Italian seasoning
- Salt and ground black pepper, as required
- 1 tablespoon olive oil
- 1 tablespoon fresh parsley, chopped

Directions:

- Rub the fish fillets with seasoning, salt and black pepper generously and then, coat with oil.
- Press "Power Button" of Air Fry Oven and turn the dial to select the "Air Fry" mode.
- Press the Time button and again turn the dial to set the cooking time to 20 minutes.
- Now push the Temp button and rotate the dial to set the temperature at 400 degrees F.
- Press "Start/Pause" button to start.
- When the unit beeps to show that it is preheated, open the lid.

- Arrange the fish fillets in greased "Air Fry Basket" and insert in the oven.
- Flip the fish fillets once halfway through.
- Serve hot with the garnishing of parsley.

257. Crispy Catfish

Preparation Time: 15 minutes
Cooking Time: 15 minutes
Servings: 5

Ingredients:

- 5 (6-oz.) catfish fillets
- 1 cup milk
- 2 teaspoons fresh lemon juice
- ½ cup yellow mustard
- ½ cup cornmeal
- ¼ cup all-purpose flour
- 2 tablespoons dried parsley flakes
- ¼ teaspoon red chili powder
- ¼ teaspoon cayenne pepper
- ¼ teaspoon onion powder
- ¼ teaspoon garlic powder
- Salt and ground black pepper, as required
- Olive oil cooking spray

Directions:

- In a large bowl, place the catfish, milk, and lemon juice and refrigerate for about 15 minutes.
- In a shallow bowl, add the mustard.
- In another bowl, mix together the cornmeal, flour, parsley flakes, and spices.
- Remove the catfish fillets from milk mixture and with paper towels, pat them dry.
- Coat each fish fillet with mustard and then, roll into cornmeal mixture.
- Then, spray each fillet with the cooking spray.
- Press "Power Button" of Air Fry Oven and turn the dial to select the "Air Fry" mode.
- Press the Time button and again turn the dial to set the cooking time to 15 minutes.

- Now push the Temp button and rotate the dial to set the temperature at 400 degrees F.
- Press "Start/Pause" button to start.
- When the unit beeps to show that it is preheated, open the lid.
- Arrange the catfish fillets in greased "Air Fry Basket" and insert in the oven.
- After 10 minutes of cooking, flip the fillets and spray with the cooking spray.
- Serve hot.

258.   Cornmeal Coated Catfish

Preparation Time: 15 minutes
Cooking Time: 14 minutes
Servings: 4

Ingredients:

- 2 tablespoons cornmeal
- 2 teaspoons Cajun seasoning
- ½ teaspoon paprika
- ½ teaspoon garlic powder
- Salt, as required
- 2 (6-oz.) catfish fillets
- 1 tablespoon olive oil

Directions:

- In a bowl, mix together the cornmeal, Cajun seasoning, paprika, garlic powder, and salt.
- Add the catfish fillets and coat with the mixture.
- Now, coat each fillet with oil.
- Press "Power Button" of Air Fry Oven and turn the dial to select the "Air Fry" mode.
- Press the Time button and again turn the dial to set the cooking time to 14 minutes.
- Now push the Temp button and rotate the dial to set the temperature at 400 degrees F.
- Press "Start/Pause" button to start.
- When the unit beeps to show that it is preheated, open the lid.
- Arrange the catfish fillets in greased "Air Fry Basket" and insert in the oven.

- After 10 minutes of cooking, flip the fillets and spray with the cooking spray.
- Serve hot

259.   Breaded Flounder

Preparation Time: 15 minutes
Cooking Time: 12 minutes
Servings: 3

Ingredients:

- 1 egg
- 1 cup dry breadcrumbs
- ¼ cup vegetable oil
- 3 (6-oz.) flounder fillets
- 1 lemon, sliced

Directions:

- In a shallow bowl, beat the egg
- In another bowl, add the breadcrumbs and oil and mix until crumbly mixture is formed.
- Dip flounder fillets into the beaten egg and then, coat with the breadcrumb mixture.
- Press "Power Button" of Air Fry Oven and turn the dial to select the "Air Fry" mode.
- Press the Time button and again turn the dial to set the cooking time to 12 minutes.
- Now push the Temp button and rotate the dial to set the temperature at 356 degrees F.
- Press "Start/Pause" button to start.
- When the unit beeps to show that it is preheated, open the lid.
- Arrange the flounder fillets in greased "Air Fry Basket" and insert in the oven.
- Garnish with the lemon slices and serve hot.

260.   Coconut-Shrimp Po' Boys

Preparation Time: 10 minutes
Cooking Time: 12 minutes
Servings: 4

Ingredients:

- ½ cup cornstarch
- 2 eggs
- 2 tablespoons milk

- ¾ cup shredded coconut
- ½ cup panko breadcrumbs
- pound (454 g) shrimp, peeled and deveined
- Old Bay seasoning, to taste
- Oil for misting or cooking spray
- large hoagie rolls
- Honey mustard or light mayonnaise
- 1½ cups shredded lettuce
- 1 large tomato, thinly sliced

Directions:

- Place cornstarch in a shallow dish or plate.
- In another shallow dish, beat together eggs and milk.
- In a third dish mix the coconut and panko crumbs.
- Sprinkle shrimp with Old Bay seasoning.
- Dip shrimp in cornstarch to coat lightly, dip in egg mixture, shake off excess, and roll in coconut mixture to coat well.
- Spray both sides of coated shrimp with oil or cooking spray.
- Select Air Fry. Set temperature to 390°F (199°C), and set time to 5 minutes.
- Repeat to cook remaining shrimp.
- Split each hoagie lengthwise, leaving one long edge intact.
- Place in air fryer cooking tray and cook at 390°F (199°C), and set time to 1 to 2 minutes or until heated through.
- Remove buns, break apart, and place on 4 plates, cut side up.
- Spread with honey mustard and/or mayonnaise.
- Top with shredded lettuce, tomato slices, and coconut shrimp.

261.   Crumb Coated Fish Fillet

Preparation Time: 10 minutes
Cooking Time: 6 minutes
Servings: 4

Ingredients:

- 1-pound (454 g) fish fillets
- ½ teaspoon hot sauce
- 1 tablespoon coarse brown mustard
- 1 teaspoon Worcestershire sauce
- Salt, to taste
- For the Crumb Coating:
- ¾ cup panko breadcrumbs
- ¼ cup stone-ground cornmeal
- ¼ teaspoon salt
- Oil for misting or cooking spray

Directions:

- Cut fish fillets crosswise into slices 1-inch wide.
- Mix the hot sauce, mustard, and Worcestershire sauce together to make a paste and rub on all sides of the fish. Season to taste with salt.
- Mix crumb coating ingredients together and spread on a sheet of wax paper.
- Roll the fish fillets in the crumb mixture.
- Spray all sides with olive oil or cooking spray and place in air fryer cooking tray in a single layer.
- Select Broil. Set temperature to 390°F (199°C), and set time to 6 to 9 minutes, until fish flakes easily.

262.   Sea Scallops

Preparation Time: 5 minutes
Cooking Time: 16 minutes
Servings: 4

Ingredients:

- 1½ pounds (680 g) sea scallops
- Salt and pepper, to taste
- 2 eggs
- ½ cup flour
- ½ cup plain breadcrumbs
- Oil for misting or cooking spray

Directions:

- Rinse scallops and remove the tough side muscle. Sprinkle to taste with salt and pepper.

- Beat eggs together in a shallow dish. Place flour in a second shallow dish and breadcrumbs in a third.

- Preheat air fryer to 390°F (199°C).

- Dip scallops in flour, then eggs, and then roll in breadcrumbs. Mist with oil or cooking spray.

- Place scallops in air fryer cooking tray in a single layer, leaving some space between. You should be able to cook about a dozen at a time.

- Select Air Fry. Set temperature to 390°F (199°C), and set time to 6 to 8 minutes, watching carefully so as not to overcook. Scallops are done when they turn opaque all the way through. They will feel slightly firm when pressed with tines of a fork.

- Repeat step 6 to cook remaining scallops.

263. Marinaded Crispy Shrimp

Preparation Time: 10 minutes
Cooking Time: 16 minutes
Servings: 4

Ingredients:

- 1-pound (454 g) shrimp, peeled, deveined, and butterflied (last tail section of shell intact)
For the Marinade:

- (5-ounce / 142-g) can evaporated milk
- eggs, beaten
- tablespoons white vinegar
- 1 tablespoon baking powder
- For the Coating:
- 1 cup crushed panko breadcrumbs
- ½ teaspoon paprika
- ½ teaspoon Old Bay seasoning
- ¼ teaspoon garlic powder
- Oil for misting or cooking spray

Directions:

- Stir together all marinade ingredients until well mixed. Add shrimp and stir to coat. Refrigerate for 1 hour.

- When ready to cook, preheat air fryer to 390°F (199°C).

- Combine coating ingredients in shallow dish.

- Remove shrimp from marinade, roll in crumb mixture, and spray with olive oil or cooking spray.

- Cooking in two batches, place shrimp in air fryer cooking tray in single layer, close but not overlapping. Select Air Fry. Set temperature to 390°F (199°C), and set time to 6 to 8 minutes, until light golden brown and crispy.

- Repeat step 5 to cook remaining shrimp.

264. Shrimp and Grits

Preparation Time: 15 minutes
Cooking Time: 20 minutes
Servings: 4

Ingredients:

- pound (454 g) raw shelled shrimp, deveined
For the Marinade:

- 2 tablespoons lemon juice
- 2 tablespoons Worcestershire sauce
- 1 tablespoon olive oil
- 1 teaspoon Old Bay seasoning
- ½ teaspoon hot sauce
For the Grits:

- ¾ cup quick cooking grits (not instant)
- 3 cups water
- ½ teaspoon salt
- 1 tablespoon butter
- ½ cup chopped green bell pepper
- ½ cup chopped celery
- ½ cup chopped onion
- ½ teaspoon oregano
- ¼ teaspoon Old Bay seasoning
- 2 ounces (57 g) sharp Cheddar cheese, grated

Directions:

- Stir together all marinade ingredients. Pour marinade over shrimp and set aside.

- For grits, heat water and salt to boil in saucepan on stovetop. Stir in grits, lower heat to medium-low, and cook about 5 minutes or until thick and done.

- Place butter, bell pepper, celery, and onion in air fryer cooking tray. Select Roast. Set temperature to 390°F (199°C), and set time to 2 minutes and stir. Roast 6 or 7 minutes longer, until crisp tender.

- Add oregano and 1 teaspoon Old Bay to cooked vegetables. Stir in grits and cheese and select Broil. Set temperature to 390°F (199°C), and set time to 1 minute. Stir and broil 1 to 2 minutes longer to melt cheese.

- Remove baking pan from air fryer. Cover with plate to keep warm while shrimp cooks.

- Drain marinade from shrimp. Place shrimp in air fryer cooking tray and select Air Fry. Set temperature to 360°F (182°C), and set time to 3 minutes. Stir or shake cooking tray. Air-fry 2 to 4 more minutes, until done.

- To serve, spoon grits onto plates and top with shrimp.

265. Lush Stuffed Shrimp

Preparation Time: 15 minutes
Cooking Time: 24 minutes
Servings: 4

Ingredients:

- 16 tail-on shrimp, peeled and deveined (last tail section intact)
- ¾ cup crushed panko breadcrumbs
- Oil for misting or cooking spray

For the Stuffing:

- 2 (6-ounce / 170-g) cans lump crabmeat
- 2 tablespoons chopped shallots
- 2 tablespoons chopped green onions
- 2 tablespoons chopped celery
- 2 tablespoons chopped green bell pepper
- ½ cup crushed saltine crackers
- 1 teaspoon Old Bay seasoning

- 1 teaspoon garlic powder
- ¼ teaspoon ground thyme
- 2 teaspoons dried parsley flakes
- 2 teaspoons fresh lemon juice
- 2 teaspoons Worcestershire sauce
- 1 egg, beaten

Directions:

- Rinse shrimp. Remove tail section (shell) from 4 shrimp, discard, and chop the meat finely.

- To prepare the remaining 12 shrimp, cut a deep slit down the back side so that the meat lies open flat. Do not cut all the way through.

- Preheat air fryer to 360°F (182°C).

- Place chopped shrimp in a large bowl with all of the stuffing ingredients and stir to combine.

- Divide stuffing into 12 portions, about 2 tablespoons each.

- Place one stuffing portion onto the back of each shrimp and form into a ball or oblong shape. Press firmly so that stuffing sticks together and adheres to shrimp.

- Gently roll each stuffed shrimp in panko crumbs and mist with oil or cooking spray.

- Place 6 shrimp in air fryer cooking tray and select Air Fry. Set temperature to 360°F (182°C), and set time to 10 minutes. Mist with oil or spray and cook 2 minutes longer or until stuffing cooks through inside and is crispy outside.

- Repeat step 8 to cook remaining shrimp.

266. Calamari with Garlic and Sherry Wine

Preparation Time: 10 minutes
Cooking Time: 5 minutes
Servings: 4

Ingredients:

- 1-pound (454 g) calamari, sliced into rings
- 2 tablespoons butter, melted
- 4 garlic cloves, smashed

- 2 tablespoons sherry wine
- 2 tablespoons fresh lemon juice
- Coarse sea salt and ground black pepper, to taste
- 1 teaspoon paprika
- 1 teaspoon dried oregano

Directions:

- Toss all ingredients in a lightly greased Air Fryer cooking tray.
- Select Air Fry. Set temperature to 400°F (204°C), and set time to 5 minutes, tossing the cooking tray halfway through the cooking time.
- Bon appétit!

267. Lemon Shrimp with Broccoli

Preparation Time: 10 minutes
Cooking Time: 6 minutes
Servings: 4

Ingredients:

- 1 pound (454 g) raw shrimp, peeled and deveined
- ½ pound (227 g) broccoli florets
- 1 tablespoon olive oil
- 1 garlic clove, minced
- 3 tablespoons freshly squeezed lemon juice
- Coarse sea salt and ground black pepper, to taste
- 1 teaspoon paprika

Directions:

- Toss all ingredients in a lightly greased Air Fryer cooking tray.
- Select Air Fry. Set temperature to 400°F (204°C), and set time to 6 minutes, tossing the cooking tray halfway through the cooking time.
- Bon appétit!

268. King Prawn Salad

Preparation Time: 10 minutes
Cooking Time: 6 minutes
Servings: 4

Ingredients:

- 1½ pounds (680 g) king prawns, peeled and deveined
- Coarse sea salt and ground black pepper, to taste
- 1 tablespoon fresh lemon juice
- 1 cup mayonnaise
- 1 teaspoon Dijon mustard
- 1 tablespoon fresh parsley, roughly chopped
- 1 teaspoon fresh dill, minced
- 1 shallot, chopped

Directions:

- Toss the prawns with the salt and black pepper in a lightly greased Air Fryer cooking tray.
- Select Air Fry. Set temperature to 400°F (204°C), and set time to 6 minutes, tossing the cooking tray halfway through the cooking time.
- Add the prawns to a salad bowl; add in the remaining ingredients and stir to combine well.
- Bon appétit!

269. Cod Fish Fingers

Preparation Time: 15 minutes
Cooking Time: 12 minutes
Servings: 4

Ingredients:

- 2 eggs
- ½ cup all-purpose flour
- Sea salt and ground black pepper, to taste
- ½ teaspoon onion powder
- ¼ teaspoon garlic powder
- ¼ cup plain breadcrumbs
- 1½ tablespoons olive oil
- pound (454 g) cod fish fillets, slice into pieces

Directions:

- In a mixing bowl, thoroughly combine the eggs, flour, and spices. In a separate bowl, thoroughly combine the breadcrumbs and olive oil.

- Mix to combine well.

- Now, dip the fish pieces into the flour mixture to coat; roll the fish pieces over the breadcrumb mixture until they are well coated on all sides.

- Select Broil. Set temperature to 400°F (204°C), and set time to 10 minutes, turning them over halfway through the cooking time.

- Bon appétit!

270.   English Muffin Tuna Melts

Preparation Time: 10 minutes
Cooking Time: 14 minutes
Servings: 4

Ingredients:

- 1-pound (454 g) tuna, boneless and chopped
- ½ cup all-purpose flour
- ½ cup breadcrumbs
- 2 tablespoons buttermilk
- 2 eggs, whisked
- Kosher salt and ground black pepper, to taste
- ½ teaspoon cayenne pepper
- 1 tablespoon olive oil
- 4 Mozzarella cheese slices
- 4 English muffins

Directions:

- Mix all ingredients, except for the cheese and English muffins, in a bowl. Shape the mixture into four patties and place them in a lightly oiled Air Fryer cooking tray.

- Select Broil. Set temperature to 400°F (204°C), and set time to about 14 minutes, turning them over halfway through the cooking time.

- Place the cheese slices on the warm patties and serve on hamburger buns and enjoy!

271.   Mahi-Mahi Fillets

Preparation Time: 10 minutes
Cooking Time: 12 minutes
Servings: 4

Ingredients:

- 1-pound (454 g) mahi-mahi fillets
- 2 tablespoons butter, at room temperature
- 2 tablespoons fresh lemon juice
- Kosher salt and freshly ground black pepper, to taste
- 1 teaspoon smoked paprika
- 1 teaspoon garlic, minced
- 1 teaspoon dried basil
- 1 teaspoon dried oregano

Directions:

- Toss the fish fillets with the remaining ingredients and place them in a lightly oiled Air Fryer cooking tray.

- Select Broil. Set temperature to 400°F (204°C), and set time to about 14 minutes, turning them over halfway through the cooking time.

- Bon appétit!

272.   Codfish Fillet Tacos

Preparation Time: 10 minutes
Cooking Time: 14 minutes
Servings: 4

Ingredients:

- 1-pound (454 g) codfish fillets
- 1 tablespoon olive oil
- 1 avocado, pitted, peeled and mashed
- 4 tablespoons mayonnaise
- 1 teaspoon mustard
- 1 shallot, chopped
- 1 habanero pepper, chopped
- 8 small corn tortillas

Directions:

- Toss the fish fillets with the olive oil; place them in a lightly oiled Air Fryer cooking tray.

- Select Broil. Set temperature to 400°F (204°C), and set time to about 14 minutes, turning them over halfway through the cooking time.

- Assemble your tacos with the chopped fish and remaining ingredients and serve warm. Bon appétit!

273. Chili and Paprika Squid with Capers

Preparation Time: 10 minutes
Cooking Time: 6 minutes
Servings: 5

Ingredients:

- 1½ pounds (680 g) squid, cut into pieces
- 1 chili pepper, chopped
- 1 small lemon, squeezed
- 2 tablespoons olive oil
- 1 tablespoon capers, drained
- 3 garlic cloves, minced
- 1 tablespoon coriander, chopped
- 2 tablespoons parsley, chopped
- 1 teaspoon sweet paprika
- Sea salt and ground black pepper, to taste

Directions:

- Toss all ingredients in a lightly greased Air Fryer cooking tray.
- Select Air Fry. Set temperature to 400°F (204°C), and set time to 5 minutes, tossing the cooking tray halfway through the cooking time.
- Bon appétit!

274. Cilantro Garlic Swordfish Steak

Preparation Time: 10 minutes
Cooking Time: 10 minutes
Servings: 4

Ingredients:

- 1-pound (454 g) swordfish steaks
- 4 garlic cloves, peeled
- 4 tablespoons olive oil
- 2 tablespoons fresh lemon juice, more for later
- 1 tablespoon fresh cilantro, roughly chopped
- 1 teaspoon Spanish paprika

- Sea salt and ground black pepper, to taste

Directions:

- Toss the swordfish steaks with the remaining ingredients and place them in a lightly oiled Air Fryer cooking tray.
- Select Broil. Set temperature to 400°F (204°C), and set time to about 10 minutes, turning them over halfway through the cooking time.
- Bon appétit!

275. Peppercorn Halibut Steaks

Preparation Time: 5 minutes
Cooking Time: 12 minutes
Servings: 4

Ingredients:

- 1-pound (454 g) halibut steaks
- ¼ cup butter
- Sea salt, to taste
- 2 tablespoons fresh chives, chopped
- 1 teaspoon garlic, minced
- 1 teaspoon mixed peppercorns, ground

Directions:

- Toss the halibut steaks with the rest of the ingredients and place them in a lightly oiled Air Fryer cooking tray.
- Select Broil. Set temperature to 400°F (204°C), and set time to about 12 minutes, turning them over halfway through the cooking time.
- Bon appétit!

276. Orange Roughy Fillets

Preparation Time: 5 minutes
Cooking Time: 10 minutes
Servings: 4

Ingredients:

- 1-pound (454 g) orange Roughy fillets
- 2 tablespoons butter
- 2 cloves garlic, minced
- Sea salt and red pepper flakes, to taste

Directions:

- Toss the fish fillets with the remaining ingredients and place them in a lightly oiled Air Fryer cooking tray.
- Select Broil. Set temperature to 400°F (204°C), and set time to about 10 minutes, turning them over halfway through the cooking time.
- Bon appétit!

277. Restaurant-Style Fried Calamari Rings

Preparation Time: 10 minutes
Cooking Time: 5 minutes
Servings: 4

Ingredients:

- 1 cup all-purpose flour
- ½ cup tortilla chips, crushed
- 1 teaspoon mustard powder
- 1 tablespoon dried parsley
- Sea salt and freshly ground black pepper, to taste
- 1 teaspoon cayenne pepper
- 2 tablespoons olive oil
- 1-pound (454 g) calamari, sliced into rings

Directions:

- In a mixing bowl, thoroughly combine the flour, tortilla chips, spices, and olive oil. Mix to combine well.
- Now, dip your calamari into the flour mixture to coat.
- Select Air Fry. Set temperature to 400°F (204°C), and set time to 5 minutes, turning them over halfway through the cooking time.
- Bon appétit!

278. Air-Fried Shrimp

Preparation Time: 15 minutes
Cooking Time: 6 minutes
Servings: 4

Ingredients:

- 1½ pounds (680 g) raw shrimp, peeled and deveined
- tablespoon olive oil
- 1 teaspoon garlic, minced
- 1 teaspoon cayenne pepper
- ½ teaspoon lemon pepper
- Sea salt, to taste

Directions:

- Toss all ingredients in a lightly greased Air Fryer cooking tray.
- Select Air Fry. Set temperature to 400°F (204°C), and set time to 6 minutes, tossing the cooking tray halfway through the cooking time.
- Bon appétit!

279. Exotic Fried Prawns

Preparation Time: 10 minutes
Cooking Time: 9 minutes
Servings: 4

Ingredients:

- 1½ pounds (680 g) prawns, peeled and deveined
- 2 garlic cloves, minced
- 2 tablespoons fresh chives, chopped
- ½ cup whole-wheat flour
- ½ teaspoon sweet paprika
- 1 teaspoon hot paprika
- 2 tablespoons coconut oil
- 2 tablespoons lemon juice

Directions:

- Toss all ingredients in a lightly greased Air Fryer cooking tray.
- Select Air Fry. Set temperature to 400°F (204°C), and set time to 9 minutes, tossing the cooking tray halfway through the cooking time. Bon appétit!

280. Parmesan-crusted Hake with Garlic Sauce

Preparation Time: 5 minutes

Cooking Time: 10 minutes
Servings: 3

Ingredients:

- 6 tablespoons mayonnaise
- tablespoon fresh lime juice
- 1 teaspoon Dijon mustard
- 1 cup grated Parmesan cheese
- Salt, to taste
- ¼ teaspoon ground black pepper, or more to taste
- 3 hake fillets, patted dry
- Nonstick cooking spray
- Garlic Sauce:
- ¼ cup plain Greek yogurt
- tablespoons olive oil
- 2 cloves garlic, minced
- ½ teaspoon minced tarragon leaves

Directions:

- Mix the mayo, lime juice, and mustard in a shallow bowl and whisk to combine. In another shallow bowl, stir together the grated Parmesan cheese, salt, and pepper.
- Dredge each fillet in the mayo mixture, then roll them in the cheese mixture until they are evenly coated on both sides.
- Spray the air fryer basket with nonstick cooking spray. Place the fillets in the pan.
- Put the air fryer basket on the baking pan and slide into Rack Position 2, select Air Fry, set temperature to 395°F (202°C), and set time to 10 minutes.
- Flip the fillets halfway through the cooking time.
- Meanwhile, in a small bowl, whisk all the ingredients for the sauce until well incorporated.
- When cooking is complete, the fish should flake apart with a fork. Remove the fillets from the oven and serve warm alongside the sauce.

281. Glazed Tuna and Fruit Kebabs

Preparation Time: 7 minutes
Cooking Time: 10 minutes
Servings: 3

Ingredients:

Kebabs:

- 1-pound (454 g) tuna steaks, cut into 1-inch cubes
- ½ cup canned pineapple chunks, drained, juice reserved
- ½ cup large red grapes
Marinade:

- 1 tablespoon honey
- 1 teaspoon olive oil
- 2 teaspoons grated fresh ginger
- Pinch cayenne pepper

Directions:

- Make the kebabs: Thread, alternating tuna cubes, pineapple chunks, and red grapes, onto the metal skewers.
- Make the marinade: Whisk together the honey, olive oil, ginger, and cayenne pepper in a small bowl. Brush generously the marinade over the kebabs and allow to sit for 10 minutes.
- When ready, transfer the kebabs to the air fryer basket.
- Put the air fryer basket on the baking pan and slide into Rack Position 2, select Air Fry, set temperature to 370°F (188°C), and set time to 10 minutes.
- After 5 minutes, remove from the oven and flip the kebabs and brush with the remaining marinade. Return the pan to the oven and continue cooking for an additional 5 minutes.
- When cooking is complete, the kebabs should reach an internal temperature of 145°F (63°C) on a meat thermometer. Remove from the oven and discard any remaining marinade. Serve hot.

282. Crispy Cheesy Fish Fingers

Preparation Time: 5 minutes
Cooking Time: 21 minutes

Servings: 4

Ingredients:

- Large codfish filet, approximately 6-8 ounces, fresh or frozen and thawed, cut into 1 ½-inch strips
- 2 raw eggs
- ½ cup of breadcrumbs (we like Panko, but any brand or home recipe will do)
- 2 tablespoons of shredded or powdered parmesan cheese
- 2 tablespoons of shredded cheddar cheese
- Pinch of salt and pepper

Directions:

- Preparing the Ingredients. Cover the basket of the Instant Vortex air fryer oven with a lining of tin foil, leaving the edges uncovered to allow air to circulate through the basket.
- Preheat the air fryer oven to 350 degrees.
- In a large mixing bowl, beat the eggs until fluffy and until the yolks and whites are fully combined.
- Dunk all the fish strips in the beaten eggs, fully submerging.
- In a separate mixing bowl, combine the bread crumbs with the parmesan, cheddar, and salt and pepper, until evenly mixed.
- One by one, coat the egg-covered fish strips in the mixed dry ingredients so that they're fully covered, and place on the foil-lined Oven rack/basket. Place the Rack on the middle-shelf of the Instant Vortex air fryer oven.
- Air Frying. Set the air-fryer timer to 20 minutes.
- Halfway through the cooking time, shake the handle of the air-fryer so that the breaded fish jostles inside and fry-coverage is even.
- After 20 minutes, when the fryer shuts off, the fish strips will be perfectly cooked and their breaded crust golden-brown and delicious! Using tongs, remove from the air fryer oven and set on a serving dish to cool.

283. Flavorful Baked Halibut

Preparation Time: 8 minutes
Cooking Time: 12 minutes
Servings: 4

Ingredients:

- 1 lb. halibut fillets
- 1/4 tsp garlic powder
- 1/4 tsp paprika
- 1/4 tsp smoked paprika
- 1/4 tsp pepper
- 1/4 cup olive oil
- 1 lemon juice
- 1/2 tsp salt

Directions:

- Fit the Air fryer oven with the rack in position
- Place fish fillets into the baking dish.
- In a small bowl, mix lemon juice, oil, paprika, smoked paprika, garlic powder, and salt.
- Brush lemon juice mixture over fish fillets.
- Set to bake at 425 F for 17 minutes. After 5 minutes place the baking dish in the preheated oven.
- Serve and enjoy.

284. Tender & Juicy Cajun Cod

Preparation Time: 15 minutes
Cooking Time: 16 minutes
Servings: 6

Ingredients:

- 3 cod fillets, cut in half
- 1 tbsp Cajun seasoning
- 1 tbsp garlic, minced
- 1 tbsp olive oil
- 1/4 cup butter, melted
- Pepper
- Salt

Directions:

- Fit the Air fryer oven with the rack in position

- Season fish fillets with pepper and salt and place in a 9*13-inch baking dish.
- Mix together the remaining ingredients and pour over fish fillets.
- Set to bake at 400 F for 20 minutes. After 5 minutes place the baking dish in the preheated oven.
- Serve and enjoy.

285. Easy Scallops

Preparation Time: 9 minutes
Cooking Time: 4 minutes
Servings: 2

Ingredients:

- 12 medium sea scallops, rinsed and patted dry
- 1 teaspoon fine sea salt
- ¾ teaspoon ground black pepper, plus more for garnish
- Fresh thyme leaves, for garnish (optional)
- Avocado oil spray

Directions:

- Coat the air fryer basket with avocado oil spray.
- Place the scallops in a medium bowl and spritz with avocado oil spray. Sprinkle the salt and pepper to season.
- Transfer the seasoned scallops to the basket, spacing them apart.
- Put the air fryer basket on the baking pan and slide into Rack Position 2, select Air Fry, set temperature to 390°F (199°C), and set time to 4 minutes.
- Flip the scallops halfway through the cooking time.
- When cooking is complete, the scallops should reach an internal temperature of just 145°F (63°C) on a meat thermometer. Sprinkle the pepper and thyme leaves on top for garnish, if desired. Serve immediately.

286. Garlic-Butter Catfish

Preparation Time: 9 minutes
Cooking Time: 21 minutes
Servings: 2

Ingredients:

- 2 catfish fillets
- 2 tsp blackening seasoning
- Juice of 1 lime
- 2 tbsp butter, melted
- 1 garlic clove, mashed
- 1 tbsp cilantro

Directions:

- In a bowl, blend in garlic, lime juice, cilantro, and butter. Pour half of the mixture over the fillets and sprinkle with blackening seasoning.
- Place the fillets in the basket and fit in the baking tray; cook for 15 minutes at 360 F on Air Fry function. Serve the fish with remaining sauce.

287. Tropical Shrimp Skewers

Preparation Time: 15 minutes
Cooking Time: 5 minutes
Servings: 4

Ingredients:

- 1 tbsp. lime juice
- 1 tbsp. honey
- ¼ tsp red pepper flakes
- ¼ tsp pepper
- ¼ tsp ginger
- Nonstick cooking spray
- 1 lb. medium shrimp, peel, devein & leave tails on
- 3 cups peaches, drain & chop
- ½ green bell pepper, chopped fine
- ¼ cup scallions, chopped

Directions:

- Soak 8 small wooden skewers in water for 15 minutes.
- In a small bowl, whisk together lime juice, honey and spices. Transfer 2 tablespoons of the mixture to a medium bowl.

- Place the baking pan in position 2 of the oven. Lightly spray fryer basket with cooking spray. Set oven to broil on 400°F for 10 minutes.

- Thread 5 shrimp on each skewer and brush both sides with marinade. Place in basket and after 5 minutes, place on the baking pan. Cook 4-5 minutes or until shrimp turn pink.

- Add peaches, bell pepper, and scallions to reserved honey mixture, mix well. Divide salsa evenly between serving plates and top with 2 skewers each. Serve immediately.

288. Spicy Orange Shrimp

Preparation Time: 9 minutes
Cooking Time: 12 minutes
Servings: 4

Ingredients:

- 1/3 cup orange juice
- 3 teaspoons minced garlic
- 1 teaspoon Old Bay seasoning
- ¼ to ½ teaspoon cayenne pepper
- 1 pound (454 g) medium shrimp, thawed, deveined, peeled, with tails off, and patted dry
- Cooking spray

Directions:

- Stir together the orange juice, garlic, Old Bay seasoning, and cayenne pepper in a medium bowl. Add the shrimp to the bowl and toss to coat well.

- Cover the bowl with plastic wrap and marinate in the refrigerator for 30 minutes.

- Spritz the air fryer basket with cooking spray. Place the shrimp in the pan and spray with cooking spray.

- Put the air fryer basket on the baking pan and slide into Rack Position 2, select Air Fry, set temperature to 400°F (205°C), and set time to 12 minutes.

- Flip the shrimp halfway through the cooking time.

- When cooked, the shrimp should be opaque and crisp. Remove from the oven and serve hot.

289. Lemon Pepper Tilapia Fillets

Preparation Time: 5 minutes
Cooking Time: 15 minutes
Servings: 4

Ingredients:

- 2 lb. tilapia fillets
- 1 tbsp Italian seasoning
- 1 tbsp canola oil
- 1 tbsp lemon pepper
- Salt to taste
- 2-3 butter buds

Directions:

- Preheat your Air fryer oven to 400 F on Bake function. Drizzle tilapia fillets with canola oil. In a bowl, mix salt, lemon pepper, butter buds, and Italian seasoning; spread on the fish. Place the fillet on a baking tray and press Start. Cook for 10 minutes until tender and crispy. Serve warm.

290. Tasty Parmesan Shrimp

Preparation Time: 15 minutes
Cooking Time: 12 minutes
Servings: 4

Ingredients:

- 1 lb. shrimp, peeled and deveined
- 1/4 cup parmesan cheese, grated
- 4 garlic cloves, minced
- 1 tbsp olive oil
- 1/4 tsp oregano
- 1/2 tsp pepper
- 1/2 tsp onion powder
- 1/2 tsp basil

Directions:

- Fit the Air fryer oven with the rack in position 2.

- Add all ingredients into the large bowl and toss well.
- Add shrimp to the air fryer basket then place an air fryer basket in the baking pan.
- Place a baking pan on the oven rack. Set to air fry at 350 F for 10 minutes.
- Serve and enjoy.

291. Rosemary Garlic Shrimp

Preparation Time: 9 minutes
Cooking Time: 10 minutes
Servings: 4

Ingredients:

- 1 lb. shrimp, peeled and deveined
- 2 garlic cloves, minced
- 1/2 tbsp fresh rosemary, chopped
- 1 tbsp olive oil
- Pepper
- Salt

Directions:

- Fit the Air fryer oven with the rack in position
- Add shrimp and remaining ingredients in a large bowl and toss well.
- Pour shrimp mixture into the baking dish.
- Set to bake at 400 F for 15 minutes. After 5 minutes place the baking dish in the preheated oven.
- Serve and enjoy.

292. Spicy Halibut

Preparation Time: 15 minutes
Cooking Time: 12 minutes
Servings: 4

Ingredients:

- 1 lb. halibut fillets
- 1/2 tsp chili powder
- 1/2 tsp smoked paprika
- 1/4 cup olive oil
- 1/4 tsp garlic powder
- Pepper

- Salt

Directions:

- Fit the Air fryer oven with the rack in position
- Place halibut fillets in a baking dish.
- In a small bowl, mix oil, garlic powder, paprika, pepper, chili powder, and salt.
- Brush fish fillets with oil mixture.
- Set to bake at 425 F for 17 minutes. After 5 minutes place the baking dish in the preheated oven.
- Serve and enjoy.

293. Seafood Spring Rolls

Preparation Time: 5 minutes
Cooking Time: 20 minutes
Servings: 4

Ingredients:

- 1 tablespoon olive oil
- 2 teaspoons minced garlic
- 1 cup matchstick cut carrots
- 2 cups finely sliced cabbage
- 2 (4-ounce / 113-g) cans tiny shrimp, drained
- 2 teaspoons soy sauce
- Salt and freshly ground black pepper, to taste
- 16 square spring roll wrappers
- Cooking spray

Directions:

- Spray the air fryer basket with cooking spray. Set aside.
- Heat the olive oil in a medium skillet over medium heat until it shimmers.
- Add the garlic to the skillet and cook for 30 seconds. Stir in the cabbage and carrots and sauté for about 5 minutes, stirring occasionally, or until the vegetables are lightly tender.
- Fold in the shrimp and soy sauce and sprinkle with salt and pepper, then stir to combine. Sauté for another 2 minutes, or until the

moisture is evaporated. Remove from the heat and set aside to cool.

- Put a spring roll wrapper on a work surface and spoon 1 tablespoon of the shrimp mixture onto the lower end of the wrapper.

- Roll the wrapper away from you halfway, and then fold in the right and left sides, like an envelope. Continue to roll to the very end, using a little water to seal the edge. Repeat with the remaining wrappers and filling.

- Place the spring rolls in the air fryer basket in a single layer, leaving space between each spring roll. Mist them lightly with cooking spray.

- Put the air fryer basket on the baking pan and slide into Rack Position 2, select Air Fry, set temperature to 375°F (190°C), and set time to 10 minutes.

- Flip the rolls halfway through the cooking time.

- When cooking is complete, the spring rolls will be heated through and start to brown. If necessary, continue cooking for 5 minutes more. Remove from the oven and cool for a few minutes before serving.

294. Roasted Halibut Steaks with Parsley

Preparation Time: 15 minutes
Cooking Time: 10 minutes
Servings: 4

Ingredients:

- 1-pound (454 g) halibut steaks
- ¼ cup vegetable oil
- 2½ tablespoons Worcester sauce
- 2 tablespoons honey
- 2 tablespoons vermouth
- 1 tablespoon freshly squeezed lemon juice
- 1 tablespoon fresh parsley leaves, coarsely chopped
- Salt and pepper, to taste
- 1 teaspoon dried basil

Directions:

- Put all the ingredients in a large mixing dish and gently stir until the fish is coated evenly. Transfer the fish to the air fryer basket.

- Put the air fryer basket on the baking pan and slide into Rack Position 2, select Roast, set temperature to 390°F (199°C), and set time to 10 minutes.

- Flip the fish halfway through cooking time.

- When cooking is complete, the fish should reach an internal temperature of at least 145°F (63°C) on a meat thermometer. Remove from the oven and let the fish cool for 5 minutes before serving.

295. Greek Cod with Asparagus

Preparation Time: 6 minutes
Cooking Time: 20 minutes
Servings: 2

Ingredients:

- 1 lb. cod, cut into 4 pieces
- 8 asparagus spears
- 1 leek, sliced
- 1 onion, quartered
- 2 tomatoes, halved
- 1/2 tsp oregano
- 1/2 tsp red chili flakes
- 1/2 cup olives, chopped
- 1 tbsp olive oil
- 1/4 tsp pepper
- 1/4 tsp salt

Directions:

- Fit the Air fryer oven with the rack in position

- Arrange fish pieces, olives, asparagus, leek, onion, and tomatoes in a baking dish.

- Season with oregano, chili flakes, pepper, and salt and drizzle with olive oil.

- Set to bake at 400 F for 25 minutes. After 5 minutes place the baking dish in the preheated oven.

- Serve and enjoy.

296. Roasted Scallops with Snow Peas

Preparation Time: 15 minutes
Cooking Time: 8 minutes
Servings: 4

Ingredients:

- 1-pound (454 g) sea scallops
- 3 tablespoons hoisin sauce
- ½ cup toasted sesame seeds
- 6 ounces (170 g) snow peas, trimmed
- 3 teaspoons vegetable oil, divided
- 1 teaspoon soy sauce
- 1 teaspoon sesame oil
- 1 cup roasted mushrooms

Directions:

- Brush the scallops with the hoisin sauce. Put the sesame seeds in a shallow dish. Roll the scallops in the sesame seeds until evenly coated.
- Combine the snow peas with 1 teaspoon of vegetable oil, the sesame oil, and soy sauce in a medium bowl and toss to coat.
- Grease the baking pan with the remaining 2 teaspoons of vegetable oil. Put the scallops in the middle of the pan and arrange the snow peas around the scallops in a single layer.
- Slide the baking pan into Rack Position 2, select Roast, set temperature to 375°F (190°C), and set time to 8 minutes.
- After 5 minutes, remove the pan and flip the scallops. Fold in the mushrooms and stir well. Return the pan to the oven and continue cooking.
- When done, remove from the oven and cool for 5 minutes. Serve warm.

297. Fired Shrimp with Mayonnaise Sauce

Preparation Time: 15 minutes
Cooking Time: 7 minutes
Servings: 4

Ingredients:

Shrimp

- 12 jumbo shrimp
- ½ teaspoon garlic salt
- ¼ teaspoon freshly cracked mixed peppercorns

Sauce:

- 4 tablespoons mayonnaise
- 1 teaspoon grated lemon rind
- 1 teaspoon Dijon mustard
- 1 teaspoon chipotle powder
- ½ teaspoon cumin powder

Directions:

- In a medium bowl, season the shrimp with garlic salt and cracked mixed peppercorns.
- Place the shrimp in the air fryer basket.
- Put the air fryer basket on the baking pan and slide into Rack Position 2, select Air Fry, set temperature to 395°F (202°C), and set time to 7 minutes.
- After 5 minutes, remove from the oven and flip the shrimp. Return to the oven and continue cooking for 2 minutes more, or until they are pink and no longer opaque.
- Meanwhile, stir together all the ingredients for the sauce in a small bowl until well mixed.
- When cooking is complete, remove the shrimp from the oven and serve alongside the sauce.

298. Baked Halibut Steaks with Parsley

Preparation Time: 15 minutes
Cooking Time: 12 minutes
Servings: 4

Ingredients:

- 1-pound (454 g) halibut steaks
- ¼ cup vegetable oil
- 2½ tablespoons Worcester sauce
- 2 tablespoons honey
- 2 tablespoons vermouth
- 1 tablespoon freshly squeezed lemon juice
- 1 tablespoon fresh parsley leaves, coarsely chopped

- Salt and pepper, to taste
- 1 teaspoon dried basil

Directions:

- Put all the ingredients in a large mixing dish and gently stir until the fish is coated evenly. Transfer the fish to the baking pan.

- Slide the baking pan into Rack Position 1, select Convection Bake, set temperature to 375°F (190°C), and set time to 10 minutes.

- Flip the fish halfway through cooking time.

- When cooking is complete, the fish should reach an internal temperature of at least 145°F (63°C) on a meat thermometer. Remove from the oven and let the fish cool for 5 minutes before serving.

299. Air Fryer Salmon

Preparation Time: 15 minutes
Cooking Time: 10 minutes
Servings: 2

Ingredients:

- ½ tsp. salt
- ½ tsp. garlic powder
- ½ tsp. smoked paprika
- Salmon

Directions:

- Preparing the Ingredients. Mix spices and sprinkle onto salmon.

- Place seasoned salmon into the Instant Vortex air fryer oven.

- Air Frying. Set temperature to 400°F, and set time to 10 minutes.

MEAT

300. Pork Satay

Preparation Time: 15 minutes
Cooking Time: 9-14 minutes
Servings: 4

Ingredients:

- 1 (1-pound) pork tenderloin, cut into 11/2-inch cubes
- ¼ cup minced onion
- 2 garlic cloves, minced
- 1 jalapeño pepper, minced
- 2 tablespoons freshly squeezed lime juice
- 2 tablespoons coconut milk
- 2 tablespoons unsalted peanut butter
- 2 teaspoons curry powder

Directions:

- In a medium bowl, mix the pork, onion, garlic, jalapeño, lime juice, coconut milk, peanut butter, and curry powder until well combined. Let stand for 10 minutes at room temperature.

- With a slotted spoon, remove the pork from the marinade. Reserve the marinade.

- Thread the pork onto about 8 bamboo (see Tip, here) or metal skewers. Grill for 9 to 14 minutes, brushing once with the reserved marinade, until the pork reaches at least 145°F on a meat thermometer. Discard any remaining marinade. Serve immediately.

301. Pork Burgers with Red Cabbage Salad

Preparation Time: 20 minutes
Cooking Time: 7-9 minutes
Servings: 4

Ingredients:

- 1/2 cup Greek yogurt
- 2 tablespoons low-sodium mustard, divided
- 1 tablespoon lemon juice
- ¼ cup sliced red cabbage
- ¼ cup grated carrots
- 1-pound lean ground pork
- 1/2 teaspoon paprika
- 1 cup mixed baby lettuce greens
- 2 small tomatoes, sliced
- 8 small low-sodium whole-wheat sandwich buns, cut in half

Directions:

- In a small bowl, combine the yogurt, 1 tablespoon mustard, lemon juice, cabbage, and carrots mix and refrigerate.

- In a medium bowl, combine the pork, remaining 1 tablespoon mustard, and paprika. Form into 8 small patties.

- Put the sliders into the air fryer basket. Grill for 7 to 9 minutes, or until the sliders register 165°F as tested with a meat thermometer.

- Assemble the burgers by placing some of the lettuce greens on a bun bottom. Top with a tomato slice, the -burgers, and the cabbage mixture. Add the bun top and serve immediately.

302. Crispy Mustard Pork Tenderloin

Preparation Time: 10 minutes
Cooking Time: 12-16 minutes
Servings: 4

Ingredients:

- 3 tablespoons low-sodium grainy mustard
- 2 teaspoons olive oil
- ¼ teaspoon dry mustard powder
- 1 (1-pound) pork tenderloin, silver skin and excess fat trimmed and discarded (see Tip, here)
- 2 slices low-sodium whole-wheat bread, crumbled
- ¼ cup ground walnuts (see Tip)
- 2 tablespoons cornstarch

Directions:

- In a small bowl, stir together the mustard, olive oil, and mustard powder. Spread this mixture over the pork.

- On a plate, mix the bread crumbs, walnuts, and cornstarch. Dip the mustard-coated pork into the crumb -mixture to coat.

- Air-fry the pork for 12 to 16 minutes, or until it registers at least 145°F on a meat thermometer. Slice to serve.

303. Apple Pork Tenderloin

Preparation Time: 10 minutes
Cooking Time: 14-19 minutes
Servings: 4

Ingredients:

- 1 (1-pound) pork tenderloin, cut into 4 pieces (see Tip)
- 1 tablespoon apple butter
- 2 teaspoons olive oil
- 2 Granny Smith apples or Jonagold apples, sliced
- 3 celery stalks, sliced
- 1 onion, sliced
- 1/2 teaspoon dried marjoram
- 1/3 cup apple juice

Directions:

- Rub each piece of pork with the apple butter and olive oil.

- In a medium metal bowl, mix the pork, apples, celery, onion, marjoram, and apple juice.

- Place the bowl into the air fryer and roast for 14 to 19 minutes, or until the pork reaches at least 145°F on a meat thermometer and the apples and vegetables are tender. Stir once during cooking. Serve immediately.

304. Espresso-Grilled Pork Tenderloin

Preparation Time: 15 minutes
Cooking Time: 9-11 minutes
Servings: 4

Ingredients:

- 1 tablespoon packed brown sugar
- 2 teaspoons espresso powder
- 1 teaspoon ground paprika

- 1/2 teaspoon dried marjoram
- 1 tablespoon honey
- 1 tablespoon freshly squeezed lemon juice
- 2 teaspoons olive oil
- 1 (1-pound) pork tenderloin

Directions:

- In a small bowl, mix the brown sugar, espresso powder, paprika, and marjoram.

- Stir in the honey, lemon juice, and olive oil until well mixed.

- Spread the honey mixture over the pork and let stand for 10 minutes at room temperature.

- Roast the tenderloin in the air fryer basket for 9 to 11 minutes, or until the pork registers at least 145°F on a meat thermometer. Slice the meat to serve.

305. Pork and Potatoes

Preparation Time: 5 minutes
Cooking Time: 25 minutes
Servings: 4

Ingredients:

- 2 cups creamer potatoes, rinsed and dried
- 2 teaspoons olive oil (see Tip)
- 1 (1-pound) pork tenderloin, cut into 1-inch cubes
- 1 onion, chopped
- 1 red bell pepper, chopped
- 2 garlic cloves, minced
- 1/2 teaspoon dried oregano
- 2 tablespoons low-sodium chicken broth

Directions:

- In a medium bowl, toss the potatoes and olive oil to coat.

- Transfer the potatoes to the air fryer basket. Roast for 15 minutes.

- In a medium metal bowl, mix the potatoes, pork, onion, red bell pepper, garlic, and oregano.

- Drizzle with the chicken broth. Put the bowl in the air fryer basket. Roast for about 10 minutes more, shaking the basket once during cooking, until the pork reaches at least 145°F on a meat thermometer and the potatoes are tender. Serve immediately.

306. Pork and Fruit Kebabs

Preparation Time: 15 minutes
Cooking Time: 9-12 minutes
Servings: 4

Ingredients:

- 1/3 cup apricot jam
- 2 tablespoons freshly squeezed lemon juice
- 2 teaspoons olive oil
- 1/2 teaspoon dried tarragon
- 1 (1-pound) pork tenderloin, cut into 1-inch cubes
- 4 plums, pitted and quartered (see Tip)
- 4 small apricots, pitted and halved (see Tip)

Directions:

- In a large bowl, mix the jam, lemon juice, olive oil, and tarragon.

- Add the pork and stir to coat. Let stand for 10 minutes at room temperature.

- Alternating the items, thread the pork, plums, and -apricots onto 4 metal skewers that fit into the air fryer. Brush with any remaining jam mixture. Discard any remaining marinade.

- Grill the kebabs in the air fryer for 9 to 12 minutes, or until the pork reaches 145°F on a meat thermometer and the fruit is tender. Serve immediately.

307. Steak and Vegetable Kebabs

Preparation Time: 15 minutes
Cooking Time: 5 to 7 minutes
Servings: 4

Ingredients:

- 2 tablespoons balsamic vinegar
- 2 teaspoons olive oil
- 1/2 teaspoon dried marjoram
- 1/8 teaspoon freshly ground black pepper
- ¾ pound round steak, cut into 1-inch pieces
- 1 red bell pepper, sliced

- 16 button mushrooms
- 1 cup cherry tomatoes

Directions:

- In a medium bowl, stir together the balsamic vinegar, olive oil, marjoram, and black pepper.

- Add the steak and stir to coat. Let stand for 10 minutes at room temperature.

- Alternating items, thread the beef, red bell pepper, mushrooms, and tomatoes onto 8 bamboo (see Tip, here) or metal skewers that fit in the air fryer.

- Grill in the air fryer for 5 to 7 minutes, or until the beef is browned and reaches at least 145°F on a meat thermo-meter. Serve immediately.

308. Spicy Grilled Steak

Preparation Time: 7 minutes
Cooking Time: 6 to 9 minutes
Servings: 4

Ingredients:

- 2 tablespoons low-sodium salsa
- 1 tablespoon minced chipotle pepper
- 1 tablespoon apple cider vinegar
- 1 teaspoon ground cumin
- 1/8 teaspoon freshly ground black pepper
- 1/8 teaspoon red pepper flakes
- ¾ pound sirloin tip steak, cut into 4 pieces and gently pounded to about 1/3 inch thick

Directions:

- In a small bowl, thoroughly mix the salsa, chipotle pepper, cider vinegar, cumin, black pepper, and red pepper flakes. Rub this mixture into both sides of each steak piece. Let stand for 15 minutes at room temperature.

- Grill the steaks in the air fryer, two at a time, for 6 to 9 minutes, or until they reach at least 145°F on a meat thermometer.

- Remove the steaks to a clean plate and cover with aluminum foil to keep warm. Repeat with the remaining steaks.

- Slice the steaks thinly against the grain and serve.

309. Greek Vegetable Skillet

Preparation Time: 10 minutes
Cooking Time: 9 to 19 minutes
Servings: 4

Ingredients:

- 1/2 pound 96 percent lean ground beef
- 2 medium tomatoes, chopped
- 1 onion, chopped
- 2 garlic cloves, minced
- 2 cups fresh baby spinach (see Tip)
- 2 tablespoons freshly squeezed lemon juice
- 1/3 cup low-sodium beef broth
- 2 tablespoons crumbled low-sodium feta cheese

Directions:

- In a 6-by-2-inch metal pan, crumble the beef. Cook in the air fryer for 3 to 7 minutes, stirring once during cooking, until browned. Drain off any fat or liquid.

- Add the tomatoes, onion, and garlic to the pan. Air-fry for 4 to 8 minutes more, or until the onion is tender.

- Add the spinach, lemon juice, and beef broth. Air-fry for 2 to 4 minutes more, or until the spinach is wilted.

- Sprinkle with the feta cheese and serve immediately

310. Light Herbed Meatballs

Preparation Time: 10 minutes
Cooking Time: 12 to 17 minutes
Servings: 24

Ingredients:

- 1 medium onion, minced
- 2 garlic cloves, minced
- 1 teaspoon olive oil
- 1 slice low-sodium whole-wheat bread, crumbled
- 3 tablespoons 1 percent milk
- 1 teaspoon dried marjoram
- 1 teaspoon dried basil
- 1-pound 96 percent lean ground beef

Directions:

- In a 6-by-2-inch pan, combine the onion, garlic, and olive oil. Air-fry for 2 to 4 minutes, or until the vegetables are crisp-tender.

- Transfer the vegetables to a medium bowl, and add the bread crumbs, milk, marjoram, and basil. Mix well.

- Add the ground beef. With your hands, work the mixture gently but thoroughly until combined. Form the meat mixture into about 24 (1-inch) meatballs.

- Bake the meatballs, in batches, in the air fryer basket for 12 to 17 minutes, or until they reach 160°F on a meat thermometer. Serve immediately.

311. Brown Rice and Beef-Stuffed Bell Peppers

Preparation Time: 10 minutes
Cooking Time: 11 to 16 minutes
Servings: 4

Ingredients:

- 4 medium bell peppers, any colors, rinsed, tops removed
- 1 medium onion, chopped
- 1/2 cup grated carrot
- 2 teaspoons olive oil
- 2 medium beefsteak tomatoes, chopped
- 1 cup cooked brown rice
- 1 cup chopped cooked low-sodium roast beef (see Tip)
- 1 teaspoon dried marjoram

Directions:

- Remove the stems from the bell pepper tops and chop the tops.

- In a 6-by-2-inch pan, combine the chopped bell pepper tops, onion, carrot, and olive oil. Cook for 2 to 4 minutes, or until the vegetables are crisp-tender.

- Transfer the vegetables to a medium bowl. Add the -tomatoes, brown rice, roast beef, and marjoram. Stir to mix.

- Stuff the vegetable mixture into the bell peppers. Place the bell peppers in the air fryer basket. Bake for 11 to 16 minutes, or until the peppers are tender and the filling is hot. Serve immediately.

312. Beef and Broccoli

Preparation Time: 10 minutes
Cooking Time: 14 to 18 minutes
Servings: 4

Ingredients:

- 2 tablespoons cornstarch
- 1/2 cup low-sodium beef broth
- 1 teaspoon low-sodium soy sauce
- 12 ounces sirloin strip steak, cut into 1-inch cubes
- 21/2 cups broccoli florets
- 1 onion, chopped
- 1 cup sliced cremini mushrooms (see Tip)
- 1 tablespoon grated fresh ginger
- Brown rice, cooked (optional)

Directions:

- In a medium bowl, stir together the cornstarch, beef broth, and soy sauce.

- Add the beef and toss to coat. Let stand for 5 minutes at room temperature.

- With a slotted spoon, transfer the beef from the broth mixture into a medium metal bowl. Reserve the broth.

- Add the broccoli, onion, mushrooms, and ginger to the beef. Place the bowl into the air fryer and cook for 12 to 15 minutes, or until the beef reaches at least 145°F on a meat thermometer and the vegetables are tender.

- Add the reserved broth and cook for 2 to 3 minutes more, or until the sauce boils.

- Serve immediately over hot cooked brown rice, if desired.

313. Beef and Fruit Stir-Fry

Preparation Time: 15 minutes

Cooking Time: 6 to 11 minutes
Servings: 4

Ingredients:

- 12 ounces sirloin tip steak, thinly sliced
- 1 tablespoon freshly squeezed lime juice
- 1 cup canned mandarin orange segments, drained, juice reserved (see Tip)
- 1 cup canned pineapple chunks, drained, juice reserved (see Tip)
- 1 teaspoon low-sodium soy sauce
- 1 tablespoon cornstarch
- 1 teaspoon olive oil
- 2 scallions, white and green parts, sliced
- Brown rice, cooked (optional)

Directions:

- In a medium bowl, mix the steak with the lime juice. Set aside.

- In a small bowl, thoroughly mix 3 tablespoons of reserved mandarin orange juice, 3 tablespoons of reserved pineapple juice, the soy sauce, and cornstarch.

- Drain the beef and transfer it to a medium metal bowl, reserving the juice. Stir the reserved juice into the mandarin-pineapple juice mixture. Set aside.

- Add the olive oil and scallions to the steak. Place the metal bowl in the air fryer and cook for 3 to 4 minutes, or until the steak is almost cooked, shaking the basket once during cooking.

- Stir in the mandarin oranges, pineapple, and juice -mixture. Cook for 3 to 7 minutes more, or until the sauce is bubbling and the beef is tender and reaches at least 145°F on a meat thermometer.

- Stir and serve over hot cooked brown rice, if desired.

314. Beef Strip with Snow Pea and Mushrooms

Preparation Time: 8 Minutes
Cooking Time: 22 Minutes
Servings: 2

Ingredients:

- 2 beef steaks (cut into strips)
- 2 tbsp. soy sauce
- 7 oz. snow pea
- 1 medium yellow onion (cut into rings)
- 1 tbsp. olive oil
- 8 oz. white mushroom (cut into halves)
- Salt and black pepper to taste

Directions:

- Preheat the air fryer to 3500F.
- Pour the olive oil and soy sauce, into a bowl then whisk. Toss in the beef strip to coat.
- In a separate bowl, mix the mushroom, snow pea, onions, salt, and pepper. Transfer the contents in the bowl to a pan and fit it into the air fryer. Set the timer for 16 minutes and start cooking.
- Turn up the air fryer's temperature to 4000F, add the beef strip, and cook for another 6 minutes.
- Serve.

315. Beef Fillet with Garlic Mayo

Preparation Time: 10 Minutes
Cooking Time: 40 Minutes
Servings: 8

Ingredients:

- 3 lb. beef fillet
- 1 cup mayonnaise
- 4 tbsp. Dijon mustard
- 1/3 cup sour cream
- 1/4 cup chopped tarragon
- 2 tbsp. chopped chives
- 2 cloves garlic (minced)
- Salt and black pepper, to taste

Directions:

- Preheat the air fryer to 3700F.
- Season beef using salt and pepper, transfer to the air fryer, and cook for 20 minutes. Remove and set aside.

- In a bowl, whisk the mustard and tarragon. Add the beef and toss, return to the air fryer and cook for 20 minutes.
- In a separate bowl, mix the garlic, sour cream, mayonnaise, chives, salt, and pepper. Whisk and set aside.
- Serve the beef with the garlic-mayo spread.

316. Mustard Marina Ted Beef

Preparation Time: 10 Minutes
Cooking Time: 45 Minutes
Servings: 6

Ingredients:

- 3 lb. beef roast
- 6 bacon strips
- 1-3/4 beef stock
- 2 tbsp. butter
- 3/4 cup red wine
- 1 tbsp. horseradish
- 3 cloves garlic (minced)
- 1 tbsp. mustard
- Salt and pepper, to taste

Directions:

- Preheat the air fryer to 4000F.
- In a bowl, add the butter, horseradish, mustard, garlic, salt, garlic, and mix. Rub the beef with the mixture.
- Arrange the bacon on a cutting board, add the meat on top and wrap the beef with the bacon strips. Put it into the air fryer then cook for 15 minutes. Remove the beef roast and transfer to a pan.
- Add the stock and wine to the pan, lower the temperature to 3600F and cook for 30minutes.
- Carve the beef and serve.

317. Chinese Steak and Broccoli

Preparation Time: 30 Minutes
Cooking Time: 12 Minutes
Servings: 8

Ingredients:

- 3/4 lb. steak cut into strips
- 1/3 cup oyster sauce
- 1/3 cup sherry
- 1 lb. broccoli florets
- 1 tsp. soy sauce
- 2 tsp. sesame oil
- 1 tsp. sugar
- 1 garlic clove (minced)
- 1 tbsp. olive oil

Directions:

- Preheat the air fryer to 3800F.
- In a bowl, mix the oyster sauce, sesame oil, sherry, soy sauce, and sugar. Add the beef and mix; leave to marinate for 30 minutes.
- Transfer the meat to a pan that fits into the air fryer, add the broccoli, garlic, oil, and toss together. Cook for 12 minutes.
- Uncover the air fryer, serve, and enjoy.

318. Beef Brisket and Onion Sauce

Preparation Time: 10 Minutes
Cooking Time: 2 Hours
Servings: 6

Ingredients:

- 4 lb. beef brisket
- 1 lb. yellow onion (chopped)
- 1/2 lb. chopped celery
- 1 lb. chopped carrot
- 4 cups of water
- 8 earl gray tea bags
- Salt and black pepper to taste
- 4 lb. beef brisket
- 1 lb. yellow onion (chopped)
- 1/2 lb. chopped celery
- 1 lb. chopped carrot
- 4 cups of water
- 8 earl gray tea bags
- Salt and black pepper to taste

Directions:

- Preheat the air fryer to 3000F.
- Put water in a pan that fits into the air fryer. Add the onions, celery, carrots, salt, and pepper. Stir and allow to simmer over medium-high heat.
- Add the beef brisket, 8 earl grey tea bags, and stir. Put it into the air fryer then cook for 1 hour 30 minutes.
- Meanwhile, place a pan over medium-high heat, add vegetable oil, and heat until shimmering. Add the sweet onion and sauté for 10 minutes. Add the remaining sauce ingredients and cook for 10 minutes. Remove and discard the teabags.
- Cut and serve the beef brisket with the onion sauce.

319. Simple Beef Sirloin Roast

Preparation Time: 10 minutes
Cooking Time: 50 minutes
Servings: 8

Ingredients:

- 2½ pounds sirloin roast
- Salt and ground black pepper, as required

Directions:

- Rub the roast with salt and black pepper generously.
- Insert the rotisserie rod through the roast.
- Insert the rotisserie forks, one on each side of the rod to secure the rod to the chicken.
- Arrange the drip pan in the bottom of Air fryer cooking chamber.
- Select "Roast" and then adjust the temperature to 350 degrees F.
- Set the timer for 50 minutes and press the "Start".
- When the display shows "Add Food" press the red lever down and load the left side of the rod into the Vortex.
- Now, slide the rod's left side into the groove along the metal bar so it doesn't move.
- Then, close the door and touch "Rotate".

- When cooking time is complete, press the red lever to release the rod.

- Remove from the Vortex and place the roast onto a platter for about 10 minutes before slicing.

- With a sharp knife, cut the roast into desired sized slices and serve.

320. Seasoned Beef Roast

Preparation Time: 10 minutes
Cooking Time: 45 minutes
Servings: 10

Ingredients:

- 3 pounds beef top roast
- 1 tablespoon olive oil
- 2 tablespoons Montreal steak seasoning

Directions:

- Coat the roast with oil and then rub with the seasoning generously.

- With kitchen twines, tie the roast to keep it compact.

- Arrange the roast onto the cooking tray.

- Arrange the drip pan in the bottom of Air fryer cooking chamber.

- Select "Air Fry" and then adjust the temperature to 360 degrees F.

- Set the timer for 45 minutes and press the "Start".

- When the display shows "Add Food" insert the cooking tray in the center position.

- When the display shows "Turn Food" do nothing.

- When cooking time is complete, remove the tray from Vortex and place the roast onto a platter for about 10 minutes before slicing.

- With a sharp knife, cut the roast into desired sized slices and serve.

321. Bacon Wrapped Filet Mignon

Preparation Time: 10 minutes
Cooking Time: 15 minutes
Servings: 2

Ingredients:

- 2 bacon slices
- 2 (4-ounce) filet mignon
- Salt and ground black pepper, as required
- Olive oil cooking spray

Directions:

- Wrap 1 bacon slice around each filet mignon and secure with toothpicks.

- Season the filets with the salt and black pepper lightly.

- Arrange the filet mignon onto a coking rack and spray with cooking spray.

- Arrange the drip pan in the bottom of Air fryer cooking chamber.

- Select "Air Fry" and then adjust the temperature to 375 degrees F.

- Set the timer for 15 minutes and press the "Start".

- When the display shows "Add Food" insert the cooking rack in the center position.

- When the display shows "Turn Food" turn the filets.

- When cooking time is complete, remove the rack from Vortex and serve hot.

322. Beef Burgers

Preparation Time: 15 minutes
Cooking Time: 18 minutes
Servings: 4

Ingredients:

- For Burgers:
- 1-pound ground beef
- ½ cup panko breadcrumbs
- ¼ cup onion, chopped finely
- 3 tablespoons Dijon mustard
- 3 teaspoons low-sodium soy sauce
- 2 teaspoons fresh rosemary, chopped finely
- Salt, to taste
- For Topping:
- 2 tablespoons Dijon mustard
- 1 tablespoon brown sugar
- 1 teaspoon soy sauce
- 4 Gruyere cheese slices

Directions:

- In a large bowl, add all the ingredients and mix until well combined.
- Make 4 equal-sized patties from the mixture.
- Arrange the patties onto a cooking tray.
- Arrange the drip pan in the bottom of Air fryer cooking chamber.
- Select "Air Fry" and then adjust the temperature to 370 degrees F.
- Set the timer for 15 minutes and press the "Start".
- When the display shows "Add Food" insert the cooking rack in the center position.
- When the display shows "Turn Food" turn the burgers.
- Meanwhile, for sauce: in a small bowl, add the mustard, brown sugar and soy sauce and mix well.
- When cooking time is complete, remove the tray from Vortex and coat the burgers with the sauce.
- Top each burger with 1 cheese slice.
- Return the tray to the cooking chamber and select "Broil".
- Set the timer for 3 minutes and press the "Start".
- When cooking time is complete, remove the tray from Vortex and serve hot.

Protein 44.4 g

323. Beef Jerky

Preparation Time: 15 minutes
Cooking Time: 3 hours
Servings: 4

Ingredients:

- 1½ pounds beef round, trimmed
- ½ cup Worcestershire sauce
- ½ cup low-sodium soy sauce
- 2 teaspoons honey
- 1 teaspoon liquid smoke
- 2 teaspoons onion powder
- ½ teaspoon red pepper flakes

- Ground black pepper, as required

Directions:

- In a zip-top bag, place the beef and freeze for 1-2 hours to firm up.
- Place the meat onto a cutting board and cut against the grain into 1/8-¼-inch strips.
- In a large bowl, add the remaining ingredients and mix until well combined.
- Add the steak slices and coat with the mixture generously.
- Refrigerate to marinate for about 4-6 hours.
- Remove the beef slices from bowl and with paper towels, pat dry them.
- Divide the steak strips onto the cooking trays and arrange in an even layer.
- Select "Dehydrate" and then adjust the temperature to 160 degrees F.
- Set the timer for 3 hours and press the "Start".
- When the display shows "Add Food" insert 1 tray in the top position and another in the center position.
- After 1½ hours, switch the position of cooking trays.
- Meanwhile, in a small pan, add the remaining ingredients over medium heat and cook for about 10 minutes, stirring occasionally.
- When cooking time is complete, remove the trays from Vortex.

324. Sweet & Spicy Meatballs

Preparation Time: 20 minutes
Cooking Time: 30 minutes
Servings: 8

Ingredients:

- For Meatballs:
- 2 pounds lean ground beef
- 2/3 cup quick-cooking oats
- ½ cup Ritz crackers, crushed
- 1 (5-ounce) can evaporated milk
- 2 large eggs, beaten lightly
- 1 teaspoon honey
- 1 tablespoon dried onion, minced

- 1 teaspoon garlic powder
- 1 teaspoon ground cumin
- Salt and ground black pepper, as required
- For Sauce:
- 1/3 cup orange marmalade
- 1/3 cup honey
- 1/3 cup brown sugar
- 2 tablespoons cornstarch
- 2 tablespoons soy sauce
- 1-2 tablespoons hot sauce
- 1 tablespoon Worcestershire sauce

Directions:

- For meatballs: in a large bowl, add all the ingredients and mix until well combined.
- Make 1½-inch balls from the mixture.
- Arrange half of the meatballs onto a cooking tray in a single layer.
- Arrange the drip pan in the bottom of Air fryer cooking chamber.
- Select "Air Fry" and then adjust the temperature to 380 degrees F.
- Set the timer for 15 minutes and press the "Start".
- When the display shows "Add Food" insert the cooking tray in the center position.
- When the display shows "Turn Food" turn the meatballs.
- When cooking time is complete, remove the tray from Vortex.
- Repeat with the remaining meatballs.
- Meanwhile, for sauce: in a small pan, add all the ingredients over medium heat and cook until thickened, stirring continuously.
- Serve the meatballs with the topping of sauce.

325. Spiced Pork Shoulder

Preparation Time: 15 minutes
Cooking Time: 55 minutes
Servings: 6

Ingredients:

- 1 teaspoon ground cumin

- 1 teaspoon cayenne pepper
- 1 teaspoon garlic powder
- Salt and ground black pepper, as required
- 2 pounds skin-on pork shoulder

Directions:

- In a small bowl, mix together the spices, salt and black pepper.
- Arrange the pork shoulder onto a cutting board, skin-side down.
- Season the inner side of pork shoulder with salt and black pepper.
- With kitchen twines, tie the pork shoulder into a long round cylinder shape.
- Season the outer side of pork shoulder with spice mixture.
- Insert the rotisserie rod through the pork shoulder.
- Insert the rotisserie forks, one on each side of the rod to secure the pork shoulder.
- Arrange the drip pan in the bottom of Air fryer cooking chamber.
- Select "Roast" and then adjust the temperature to 350 degrees F.
- Set the timer for 55 minutes and press the "Start".
- When the display shows "Add Food" press the red lever down and load the left side of the rod into the Vortex.
- Now, slide the rod's left side into the groove along the metal bar so it doesn't move.
- Then, close the door and touch "Rotate".
- When cooking time is complete, press the red lever to release the rod.
- Remove the pork from Vortex and place onto a platter for about 10 minutes before slicing.
- With a sharp knife, cut the pork shoulder into desired sized slices and serve.

326. Seasoned Pork Tenderloin

Preparation Time: 10 minutes
Cooking Time: 45 minutes
Servings: 5

Ingredients:

- 1½ pounds pork tenderloin
- 2-3 tablespoons BBQ pork seasoning

Directions:

- Rub the pork with seasoning generously.
- Insert the rotisserie rod through the pork tenderloin.
- Insert the rotisserie forks, one on each side of the rod to secure the pork tenderloin.
- Arrange the drip pan in the bottom of Air fryer cooking chamber.
- Select "Roast" and then adjust the temperature to 360 degrees F.
- Set the timer for 45 minutes and press the "Start".
- When the display shows "Add Food" press the red lever down and load the left side of the rod into the Vortex.
- Now, slide the rod's left side into the groove along the metal bar so it doesn't move.
- Then, close the door and touch "Rotate".
- When cooking time is complete, press the red lever to release the rod.
- Remove the pork from Vortex and place onto a platter for about 10 minutes before slicing.
- With a sharp knife, cut the roast into desired sized slices and serve.

327. Garlicky Pork Tenderloin

Preparation Time: 15 minutes
Cooking Time: 20 minutes
Servings: 5

Ingredients:

- 1½ pounds pork tenderloin
- Nonstick cooking spray
- 2 small heads roasted garlic
- Salt and ground black pepper, as required

Directions:

- Lightly, spray all the sides of pork with cooking spray and then, season with salt and black pepper.
- Now, rub the pork with roasted garlic.
- Arrange the roast onto the lightly greased cooking tray.
- Arrange the drip pan in the bottom of Air fryer cooking chamber.
- Select "Air Fry" and then adjust the temperature to 400 degrees F.
- Set the timer for 20 minutes and press the "Start".
- When the display shows "Add Food" insert the cooking tray in the center position.
- When the display shows "Turn Food" turn the pork.
- When cooking time is complete, remove the tray from Vortex and place the roast onto a platter for about 10 minutes before slicing.
- With a sharp knife, cut the roast into desired sized slices and serve.

328. Glazed Pork Tenderloin

Preparation Time: 15 minutes
Cooking Time: 20 minutes
Servings: 3

Ingredients:

- 1-pound pork tenderloin
- 2 tablespoons Sriracha
- 2 tablespoons honey
- Salt, as required

Directions:

- Insert the rotisserie rod through the pork tenderloin.
- Insert the rotisserie forks, one on each side of the rod to secure the pork tenderloin.
- In a small bowl, add the Sriracha, honey and salt and mix well.
- Brush the pork tenderloin with honey mixture evenly.
- Arrange the drip pan in the bottom of Air fryer cooking chamber.

- Select "Air Fry" and then adjust the temperature to 350 degrees F.
- Set the timer for 20 minutes and press the "Start".
- When the display shows "Add Food" press the red lever down and load the left side of the rod into the Vortex.
- Now, slide the rod's left side into the groove along the metal bar so it doesn't move.
- Then, close the door and touch "Rotate".
- When cooking time is complete, press the red lever to release the rod.
- Remove the pork from Vortex and place onto a platter for about 10 minutes before slicing.
- With a sharp knife, cut the roast into desired sized slices and serve.

329.   Honey Mustard Pork Tenderloin

Preparation Time: 15 minutes
Cooking Time: 25 minutes
Servings: 3

Ingredients:

- 1-pound pork tenderloin
- 1 tablespoon garlic, minced
- 2 tablespoons soy sauce
- 2 tablespoons honey
- 1 tablespoon Dijon mustard
- 1 tablespoon grain mustard
- 1 teaspoon Sriracha sauce

Directions:

- In a large bowl, add all the ingredients except pork and mix well.
- Add the pork tenderloin and coat with the mixture generously.
- Refrigerate to marinate for 2-3 hours.
- Remove the pork tenderloin from bowl, reserving the marinade.
- Place the pork tenderloin onto the lightly greased cooking tray.
- Arrange the drip pan in the bottom of Air fryer cooking chamber.

- Select "Air Fry" and then adjust the temperature to 380 degrees F.
- Set the timer for 25 minutes and press the "Start".
- When the display shows "Add Food" insert the cooking tray in the center position.
- When the display shows "Turn Food" turn the pork and oat with the reserved marinade.
- When cooking time is complete, remove the tray from Vortex and place the pork tenderloin onto a platter for about 10 minutes before slicing.
- With a sharp knife, cut the pork tenderloin into desired sized slices and serve.

330.   Seasoned Pork Chops

Preparation Time: 10 minutes
Cooking Time: 12 minutes
Servings: 4

Ingredients:

- 4 (6-ounce) boneless pork chops
- 2 tablespoons pork rub
- 1 tablespoon olive oil

Directions:

- Coat both sides of the pork chops with the oil and then, rub with the pork rub.
- Place the pork chops onto the lightly greased cooking tray.
- Arrange the drip pan in the bottom of Air fryer cooking chamber.
- Select "Air Fry" and then adjust the temperature to 400 degrees F.
- Set the timer for 12 minutes and press the "Start".
- When the display shows "Add Food" insert the cooking tray in the center position.
- When the display shows "Turn Food" turn the pork chops.
- When cooking time is complete, remove the tray from Vortex and serve hot.

331.   Breaded Pork Chops

Preparation Time: 15 minutes
Cooking Time: 28 minutes
Servings: 2

Ingredients:

- 2 (5-ounce) boneless pork chops
- 1 cup buttermilk
- ½ cup flour
- 1 teaspoon garlic powder
- Salt and ground black pepper, as required
- Olive oil cooking spray

Directions:

- In a bowl, place the chops and buttermilk and refrigerate, covered for about 12 hours.
- Remove the chops from the bowl of buttermilk, discarding the buttermilk.
- In a shallow dish, mix together the flour, garlic powder, salt, and black pepper.
- Coat the chops with flour mixture generously.
- Place the pork chops onto the cooking tray and spray with the cooking spray.
- Arrange the drip pan in the bottom of Air fryer cooking chamber.
- Select "Air Fry" and then adjust the temperature to 380 degrees F.
- Set the timer for 28 minutes and press the "Start".
- When the display shows "Add Food" insert the cooking tray in the center position.
- When the display shows "Turn Food" turn the pork chops.
- When cooking time is complete, remove the tray from Vortex and serve hot.

332. Crusted Rack Of Lamb

Preparation Time: 15 minutes
Cooking Time: 19 minutes
Servings: 4

Ingredients:

- 1 rack of lamb, trimmed all fat and frenched
- Salt and ground black pepper, as required
- 1/3 cup pistachios, chopped finely
- 2 tablespoons panko breadcrumbs
- 2 teaspoons fresh thyme, chopped finely
- 1 teaspoon fresh rosemary, chopped finely
- 1 tablespoon butter, melted
- 1 tablespoon Dijon mustard

Directions:

- Insert the rotisserie rod through the rack on the meaty side of the ribs, right next to the bone.
- Insert the rotisserie forks, one on each side of the rod to secure the rack.
- Season the rack with salt and black pepper evenly.
- Arrange the drip pan in the bottom of Air fryer cooking chamber.
- Select "Air Fry" and then adjust the temperature to 380 degrees F.
- Set the timer for 12 minutes and press the "Start".
- When the display shows "Add Food" press the red lever down and load the left side of the rod into the Vortex.
- Now, slide the rod's left side into the groove along the metal bar so it doesn't move.
- Then, close the door and touch "Rotate".
- Meanwhile, in a small bowl, mix together the remaining ingredients except the mustard.
- When cooking time is complete, press the red lever to release the rod.
- Remove the rack from Vortex and brush the meaty side with the mustard.
- Then, coat the pistachio mixture on all sides of the rack and press firmly.
- Now, place the rack of lamb onto the cooking tray, meat side up.
- Select "Air Fry" and adjust the temperature to 380 degrees F.
- Set the timer for 7 minutes and press the "Start".
- When the display shows "Add Food" insert the cooking tray in the center position.
- When the display shows "Turn Food" do nothing.

- When cooking time is complete, remove the tray from Vortex and place the rack onto a cutting board for at least 10 minutes.

- Cut the rack into individual chops and serve.

333. Lamb Burgers

Preparation Time: 15 minutes
Cooking Time: 8 minutes
Servings: 6

Ingredients:

- 2 pounds ground lamb
- 1 tablespoon onion powder
- Salt and ground black pepper, as required

Directions:

- In a bowl, add all the ingredients and mix well.

- Make 6 equal-sized patties from the mixture.

- Arrange the patties onto a cooking tray.

- Arrange the drip pan in the bottom of Air fryer cooking chamber.

- Select "Air Fry" and then adjust the temperature to 360 degrees F.

- Set the timer for 8 minutes and press the "Start".

- When the display shows "Add Food" insert the cooking rack in the center position.

- When the display shows "Turn Food" turn the burgers.

- When cooking time is complete, remove the tray from Vortex and serve hot.

334. Pork Taquitos

Preparation Time: 10 minutes
Cooking Time: 16 minutes
Servings: 8

Ingredients:

- 1 juiced lime
- 10 whole wheat tortillas
- 2 ½ C. shredded mozzarella cheese
- 30 ounces of cooked and shredded pork tenderloin

Directions:

- Preparing the Ingredients. Ensure your air fryer is preheated to 380 degrees.

- Drizzle pork with lime juice and gently mix.

- Heat up tortillas in the microwave with a dampened paper towel to soften.

- Add about 3 ounces of pork and ¼ cup of shredded cheese to each tortilla. Tightly roll them up.

- Spray the Pro Breeze air fryer basket with a bit of olive oil.

- Air Frying. Set temperature to 380°F, and set time to 10 minutes. Air fry taquitos 7-10 minutes till tortillas turn a slight golden color, making sure to flip halfway through cooking process.

335. Air Fried Baby Back Ribs

Preparation Time: 10 minutes
Cooking Time: 1 hour and 20 minutes
Servings: 4

Ingredients:

- 1 rack baby back ribs
- 1 tbsp olive oil
- 1 tbsp liquid smoke flavoring
- 1 tbsp brown sugar
- ½ tsp salt
- ½ tsp ground black pepper
- ½ tsp garlic powder
- ½ tsp onion powder
- ½ tsp chili powder
- 1 cup BBQ sauce

Directions:

- Clean the baby back ribs by removing the membrane the covers it. Trim the ribs such that it will fit inside the air fryer.

- In a bowl, mix the olive oil and liquid smoke. Brush the mixture all over the ribs.

- Preheat the air fryer to 3000F for 5 minutes.

- Place the ribs inside the air fryer.

- Select the Bake function and adjust the cooking time to 1 hour and 20 minutes.

- Meanwhile, mix the remaining ingredients in a saucepan and simmer over medium flame until slightly thick.

- Five minutes before the cooking time ends, brush the ribs with the sauce.

336.   Prime Rib Roast

Preparation Time: 10 minutes
Cooking Time: 2 hours
Servings: 6

Ingredients:

- 1 3-lb beef rib roast
- 12 cloves of garlic, minced
- 6 sprigs fresh thyme
- Salt and pepper to taste
- 2 ½ tbsp paprika
- 2 tbsp garlic powder
- 1 tbsp black pepper
- 1 tbsp onion powder
- 1 tbsp cayenne pepper
- 1 tbsp dried thyme

Directions:

- Preheat the air fryer to 3700F for 5 minutes.
- Pat dry the beef rib roast and place on a plate.
- In a bowl, mix together the remaining ingredients.
- Rub the seasoning mix on to the roast and make sure that all surfaces are coated with the seasoning.
- Place in the bake pan.
- Select the Bake setting and adjust the cooking time to 2 hours.

337.   Strip Steak with Potatoes

Preparation Time: 5 minutes
Cooking Time: 60 minutes
Servings: 6

Ingredients:

- 2 lbs. New York Strop steak, cut into 1-inch pieces
- 2 russet potatoes, halved
- Salt and pepper to taste

- 2 tbsp Worcestershire sauce
- Canola oil for brushing
- Fresh chives for garnish

Directions:

- Preheat the air fryer to 4000F for 5 minutes.
- Place all ingredients in a bake tray and toss using your hands to coat potatoes and steaks with the seasonings.
- Place in the air fryer and select the AirFry setting.
- Adjust the cooking time to 60 minutes.
- Halfway through the cooking time, stir the potatoes and beef.

338.   Air Fryer Steak Bites and Mushrooms

Preparation Time: 10 minutes
Cooking Time: 25 minutes
Servings: 3

Ingredients:

- 1 lb. steak cut into chunks
- 8 oz mushrooms, halved
- 2 tbsp butter, melted
- 1 tsp Worcestershire sauce
- ½ tsp garlic powder
- Salt and pepper to taste
- A dash of pepper flakes

Directions:

- Preheat the air fryer to 4000F for 5 minutes.
- Toss everything in a bowl. Make sure that the mushrooms and beef are coated with the seasonings.
- Place the steaks and mushrooms on the crisper tray.
- Select the AirFry setting and adjust the cooking time to 25 minutes.

339.   Air Fried Beef Kabobs

Preparation Time: 5 minutes
Cooking Time: 25 minutes
Servings: 4

Ingredients:

- 1 ½ lbs. sirloin steak, cut into 1-inch thick
- 4 tbsp olive oil
- 1 tbsp lemon juice
- ½ tbsp chili powder
- ½ tsp cumin
- Salt and pepper to taste
- 1 large bell pepper, seeded and sliced into squares
- 1 large onion, quartered

Directions:

- Preheat the air fryer to 4000F for 5 minutes.
- Place the beef, olive oil, lemon juice, chili powder, cumin, salt and pepper in a bowl and toss to coat.
- Skewer the seasoned beef, bell pepper, and onion on bamboo or metal skewers.
- Place inside the air fryer and onto the crisper tray.
- Select the AirFry setting and adjust the cooking time to 25 minutes.

340. Air fryer Beef Steak

Preparation Time: 10 minutes
Cooking Time: 20 minutes
Servings: 4

Ingredients:

- 2 lb. Ribeye steak
- Salt and pepper to taste
- 1 tbsp. Olive oil

Directions:

- Preheat the Air fryer by selecting air fry mode
- Adjust temperature to 356°F and timer to 5 minutes
- Season the steak with olive oil, salt, and pepper.
- Place on the Air fryer pizza tray
- Transfer into the Air fryer
- Air fry for 7 minutes, flip and cook for additional 6 minutes
- Serve and enjoy

341. Mushroom Meatloaf

Preparation Time: 15 minutes
Cooking Time: 30 minutes
Servings: 4

Ingredients:

- 14 oz. Lean ground beef
- 1 chorizo sausage, chopped
- 1 egg
- 1 small onion, chopped
- Salt and freshly ground black pepper, to taste
- 3 Tbsp. Olive oil
- 2 tbsp. fresh mushrooms, sliced thinly
- 1 garlic clove, minced
- 2 tbsp. fresh cilantro, chopped
- 3 tbsp breadcrumbs

Directions:

- Preheat the Air fryer by selecting pizza/bake mode
- Adjust temperature to 390°F and time to 10 minutes
- Combine all the ingredients in a bowl except the mushroom.
- Pour into the Air fryer baking tray, smoothen with a spatula
- Arrange the mushroom on top
- Transfer into the Air fryer
- Bake for 25 minutes
- Serve and enjoy!

342. Carrot and Beef Cocktail Balls

Preparation Time: 15 minutes
Cooking Time: 60 minutes
Servings: 4

Ingredients:

- 1 lb. ground beef
- 2 carrots,
- 1 red onion, peeled and chopped
- 3/4 cup breadcrumbs
- Salt and black pepper to taste
- 1/2 tsp dried rosemary, crushed
- 2 cloves garlic, minced
- 1/2 tsp dried basil

- ♦ 1 Egg
- ♦ 1 tsp dried oregano

Directions:

- Pulse carrot, onion, and garlic in a food processor
- Pour into a bowl, add the remaining ingredients except for flour
- Form into a ball, refrigerate for 20 minutes
- Roll in flour and arrange on the Air fryer baking tray
- Transfer to the Air fryer and select the air fryer mode.
- Adjust temperature to 390°F
- Set time to 20 minutes
- Serve with toothpicks

343.   Marinated Cajun Beef

Preparation Time: 10 minutes
Cooking Time: 1hour 25 minutes
Servings: 2

Ingredients:

- ♦ 1lb. Beef tenderloins
- ♦ 1/3 cup beef broth
- ♦ 1/2 tsp. garlic powder
- ♦ 2 tbsp Cajun seasoning, crushed
- ♦ 1-1/2 tbsp. Olive oil
- ♦ 1/2 tbsp pear cider vinegar
- ♦ 1/3 tsp cayenne pepper
- ♦ 1 tsp. Salt
- ♦ 1 tsp. Freshly ground black pepper

Directions:

- Add all the ingredients to a bowl.
- Add the beef and leave to marinate for 40 minutes
- Place on the Air fryer pizza tray
- Transfer to the Air fryer
- Select the air fryer/grill mode
- Adjust temperature to 390°F
- Grill for 22 minutes, flipping halfway through

- Serve and enjoy

344.   Beef and Potatoes

Preparation Time: 5 minutes
Cooking Time: 15 minutes
Servings: 2

Ingredients:

- ♦ 1 lb. Ground beef
- ♦ 3 cups of mashed potatoes
- ♦ 1 cup sour cream
- ♦ 2 eggs
- ♦ 2 tbsp. Garlic powder

Directions:

- Preheat the Air fryer by selecting bake/pizza mode
- Adjust temperature to 350°F and time to 5 minutes
- Combine all the ingredients in a bowl.
- Pour into the Air fryer baking tray
- Transfer into the Air fryer
- Bake for 6 minutes
- Serve and enjoy!

345.   Breaded Beef Schnitzel

Preparation Time: 10 minutes
Cooking Time: 20 minutes
Servings: 2

Ingredients:

- ♦ 4 beef schnitzel
- ♦ 2 tbsp. Olive oil
- ♦ 1 egg
- ♦ 5 cups of breadcrumbs

Directions:

- Preheat the Air fryer by selecting grill mode
- Adjust temperature to 350°F and time to 5 minutes
- Whisk egg and olive oil in a bowl
- Add breadcrumbs to another bowl
- Dip the beef schnitzel in the egg mixture.
- then coat with the breadcrumb mixture

- Arrange on the grilling plate
- Transfer into the Air fryer
- Grill for 12 minutes, flipping halfway
- Serve and enjoy!

346.   Steak with Olive Tapenade

Preparation Time: 15 minutes
Cooking Time: 15 minutes
Servings: 4

Ingredients:

Steak

- 1-1/4 lb. sirloin steak
- 1 tablespoon olive oil
- Salt and pepper to taste

Tapenade

- 1/2 cup red onion, chopped
- 1 clove garlic, minced
- 1 green bell pepper, chopped
- 1 tablespoon fresh parsley, chopped
- 2 tablespoons capers
- 1 cup kalamata olives, pitted and sliced
- 2 tablespoons olive oil
- 3 tablespoons lemon juice
- Salt and pepper to taste

Directions:

- Preheat your air fryer to 400 degrees F for 5 minutes.
- Brush steaks with oil.
- Season with salt and pepper.
- Add to the air fryer oven.
- Choose air fry option.
- Cook the steaks for 5 to 6 minutes per side.
- Mix the tapenade ingredients.
- Serve steak with tapenade.

347.   Steak Salad

Preparation Time: 1 hour and 20 minutes
Cooking Time: 10 minutes
Servings: 4

Ingredients:

Steak

- 2 rib eye steaks, sliced into strips
- 2 teaspoons garlic, minced
- 1/4 cup soy sauce
- 1/4 cup honey
- 1/4 cup bourbon
- 1/4 cup Worcestershire sauce
- 1/4 cup brown sugar
- 1/2 teaspoon red pepper flakes

Salad

- 4 cups Romaine lettuce
- 1/4 cup red onions, sliced
- 1/2 cucumber, diced
- 1 cup cherry tomatoes, sliced in half
- 1/2 mozzarella cheese, shredded

Directions:

- Add the steaks to a bowl.
- In another bowl, mix the steak ingredients.
- Pour mixture into the steak strips.
- Cover and marinate in the refrigerator for 1 hour.
- Preheat your air fryer at 400 degrees F for 5 minutes.
- Select air fry option.
- Cook the steak strips for 5 minutes per side.
- Toss the salad ingredients in a large bowl.
- Top with the steak strips.

348.   Meatballs

Preparation Time 7 minutes
Cooking Time: 8 minutes
Servings: 4

Ingredients:

- 1/2 lb. ground beef
- 1/2 cup ground pork
- 1 onion, chopped
- 2 cloves garlic, minced
- 2 teaspoons dried basil
- 2 teaspoons dried oregano
- 2 teaspoons dried parsley
- 1 cup breadcrumbs

- ♦ 1 egg, beaten
- ♦ 1/2 cup Parmesan cheese
- ♦ Salt and pepper to taste
- ♦ Cooking spray

Directions:

- Combine all the ingredients in a large bowl.
- Mix well.
- Form balls from the mixture.
- Spray with oil.
- Add the meatballs to the air fryer oven.
- Choose air fry option.
- Cook at 350 degrees F for 4 minutes per side.

349. Beef Enchilada

Preparation Time: 10 minutes
Cooking Time: 10 minutes
Servings: 2

Ingredients:

- ♦ 1 cup lean ground beef, cooked
- ♦ 2 teaspoons taco seasoning
- ♦ 1/4 cup tomatoes, chopped
- ♦ 1/4 cup black beans
- ♦ 1/4 cup enchilada sauce
- ♦ 2 tortillas

Directions:

- Season the ground beef with taco seasoning.
- Mix with the tomatoes and black beans.
- Top the tortillas with the beef mixture.
- Sprinkle cheese on top.
- Roll up the tortillas.
- Place in the air fryer.
- Brush with the enchilada sauce.
- Select air fry setting.
- Cook at 350 degrees F for 5 minutes per side.

350. Rib Eye Steak

Preparation Time: 10 minutes
Cooking Time: 10 minutes
Servings: 2

Ingredients:

- ♦ 2 rib eye steaks
- ♦ 2 tablespoons butter, melted
- ♦ Salt and pepper to taste

Directions:

- Brush steaks with melted butter.
- Season with salt and pepper.
- Preheat your air fryer oven to 400 degrees F.
- Add the steaks to the air fryer oven.
- Set it to air fry.
- Cook at 5 minutes per side.

351. Beef Teriyaki

Preparation Time: 11 minutes
Cooking Time: 9 minutes
Servings: 2

Ingredients:

- ♦ 1 tablespoon soy sauce
- ♦ 2 tablespoons olive oil
- ♦ Pepper to taste
- ♦ 1 lb. sirloin steak, sliced into strips
- ♦ 1 onion, sliced
- ♦ 1 red bell pepper, sliced into strips
- ♦ 1 green bell pepper, sliced into strips
- ♦ 1 yellow bell pepper, sliced into strips
- ♦ 1 cup teriyaki sauce

Directions:

- Mix the soy sauce, olive oil and pepper in a bowl.
- Pour half of the mixture into another bowl.
- Stir in the steak strips into the first bowl.
- Add the onion and peppers to the other bowl.
- Preheat your air fryer to 400 degrees F.
- Add the steak and vegetables to the air fryer tray.
- Select roasting setting.
- Cook for 5 to 7 minutes.
- Stir in the teriyaki sauce.
- Cook for another 2 minutes.

352.   New York Strip Steak

Preparation Time: 1 hour
Cooking Time: 20 minutes
Servings: 2

Ingredients:

- 2 New York strip steaks
- Salt and pepper
- 2 tablespoons olive oil
- Herbed butter
- 1/2 cup butter
- 1 teaspoon garlic, minced
- 1 teaspoon lemon juice
- 1 tablespoon rosemary, chopped
- 1 tablespoon parsley, chopped
- 1 teaspoon thyme, chopped
- Salt and pepper to taste

Directions:

- Combine the herbed butter ingredients in a bowl.
- Form a log from the mixture. Wrap with plastic.
- Refrigerate for 1 hour.
- Sprinkle both sides of steaks with salt and pepper.
- Preheat your air fryer to 400 degrees F for 5 minutes.
- Choose air fry setting.
- Cook the steaks for 5 minutes per side.
- Top with the butter log and let butter melt before serving.

353.   Steak Bites

Preparation Time: 7 minutes
Cooking Time: 8 minutes
Servings: 4

Ingredients:

- 1 lb. steak, sliced into cubes
- Steak rub
- 1 tablespoon olive oil
- 1 teaspoon onion powder
- 1 teaspoon garlic powder

- 1 teaspoon Montreal steak seasoning
- 1/2 teaspoon cayenne pepper
- Salt and pepper to taste

Directions:

- Select roast setting in your air fryer oven.
- Preheat your air fryer oven to 400 degrees F.
- Mix the olive oil, onion powder, garlic powder, steak seasoning, cayenne pepper, salt and pepper.
- Rub the steak with the mixture.
- Add the steaks to the air fryer oven.
- Cook for 5 minutes.
- Turn and cook for another 3 minutes.

354.   Steak with Basil & Garlic Butter

Preparation Time: 20 minutes
Cooking Time: 10 minutes
Servings: 2

Ingredients:

- 2 rib eye steaks
- 2 tablespoons olive oil
- Salt and pepper to taste
- 3 rosemary sprigs
- Garlic Basil Butter:
- 1/2 teaspoon garlic powder
- 4 teaspoons fresh basil, chopped
- 1/2 cup butter
- 1 teaspoon fresh parsley, chopped

Directions:

- Brush both sides of steaks with oil.
- Season with salt and pepper.
- Add the steak to the air fryer oven.
- Top with the rosemary sprigs.
- Add to the air fryer oven.
- Choose air fry setting.
- Cook at 400 degrees F for 5 minutes per side.
- Mix the garlic basil butter ingredients.
- Spread mixture on top of the steaks before serving.

355. Steak with Chimichurri

Preparation Time: 8 minutes
Cooking Time: 12 minutes
Servings: 4

Ingredients:

- 2 lb. flank steak
- 2 tablespoons butter
- Salt and pepper to taste
- Chimichurri Sauce
- 1/4 cup olive oil
- 2 tablespoons red wine vinegar
- 1/2 cup cilantro, chopped
- 1/2 cup parsley, chopped
- 1/2 onion, sliced
- 1 clove garlic
- 1/2 teaspoon red pepper flakes
- Salt and pepper to taste

Directions:

- Preheat your air fryer oven to 400 degrees F.
- Select air fry option.
- Coat your flank steak with butter.
- Season with salt and pepper.
- Place inside the air fryer oven.
- Cook for 6 minutes per side.
- Add the chimichurri ingredients to the food processor.
- Pulse until smooth.
- Spread steak with the chimichurri and serve.

356. Beef Kebab

Preparation Time: 2 hours
Cooking Time: 30 minutes
Servings: 8

Ingredients:

- 2 cups teriyaki sauce, divided
- 1-1/2 lb. sirloin steak, sliced into cubes
- 1 onion, diced
- 1 green bell pepper, sliced

Directions:

- Add half of the teriyaki sauce to a sealable plastic bag.
- Add steak cubes to the bag.
- Turn to coat evenly.
- Refrigerate for 2 hours.
- Thread steak cubes and vegetables onto skewers.
- Brush with the remaining sauce.
- Place in the air fryer oven.
- Choose grill or roast option.
- Cook at 400 degrees F for 5 minutes per side.

357. Barbecue Meatballs

Preparation Time: 5 minutes
Cooking Time: 10 minutes
Servings: 6

Ingredients:

- 1 pack frozen meatballs
- 1 cup barbecue sauce

Directions:

- Spread meatballs onto the air fryer tray.
- Turn to air fry setting.
- Cook at 350 degrees F for 5 minutes.
- Pour the barbecue sauce into a pan over medium heat.
- Heat the sauce for 5 minutes.
- Toss meatballs in the sauce and serve.

358. Beef Burger with Bacon

Preparation Time
Cooking Time: 20 minutes
Servings: 4

Ingredients:

Patty

- 1/2 cup onion, chopped
- 1-1/2 lb. lean ground beef
- 1 teaspoon Worcestershire sauce
- 1 teaspoon soy sauce
- 1 teaspoon dried parsley
- 1 teaspoon garlic powder

Burger

- 4 slices bacon, cooked
- 4 burger rolls

Directions:

- In a bowl, combine the patty ingredients.
- Form patties from the mixture.
- Place the patties inside the air fryer oven.
- Select grill setting.
- Cook at 400 degrees F for 8 minutes.
- Flip and cook for another 3 minutes.
- Serve in burger buns with bacon.

359. Steak with Rosemary Butter

Preparation Time: 1 hour
Cooking Time: 20 minutes
Servings: 2

Ingredients:

- 2 rib eye or t-bone steaks
- Salt and pepper to taste
- 1/4 cup butter
- 1 tablespoon rosemary, chopped

Directions:

- Preheat your air fryer oven to 400 degrees F for 5 minutes.
- Choose air fry setting.
- Season steaks with salt and pepper.
- In a bowl, mix butter and rosemary.
- Form round shapes from the mixture.
- Wrap with plastic.
- Refrigerate for 1 hour.
- Cook the steaks in the air fryer oven for 6 minutes per side.
- Top with the herbed butter before serving.

360. Sirloin Steak with Mustard Butter

Preparation Time: 1 hour
Cooking Time: 20 minutes
Servings: 2

Ingredients:

- 2 sirloin steaks
- 2 tablespoons olive oil
- Salt and pepper to taste
- Mustard butter
- 2 tablespoons butter
- 1 tablespoon scallion, chopped
- 1 teaspoon mustard
- Salt and pepper to taste

Directions:

- Preheat your air fryer to 400 degrees F for 5 minutes.
- Brush steaks with oil.
- Season with salt and pepper.
- Choose air fry setting in your air fryer oven.
- Cook the steaks for 6 minutes per side.
- Mix the mustard butter ingredients in a bowl.
- Press onto a small circular dish.
- Cover and refrigerate for 1 hour.
- Top the steaks with the mustard butter and serve.

361. Bourbon Steaks

Preparation Time: 1 hour
Cooking Time: 20 minutes
Servings: 4

Ingredients:

- 1 lb. steak, sliced into cubes

Marinade

- 1/2 cup vegetable oil
- 1/2 cup bourbon
- 1/2 cup Worcestershire sauce
- 1/2 cup mustard
- 1/2 cup brown sugar

Directions:

- Mix the marinade ingredients in a bowl.
- Add the steak cubes to the marinade.
- Cover and marinate for 1 hour in the refrigerator.
- Transfer steak cubes to the air fryer tray.
- Select grill setting.

- Set it to 400 degrees F.
- Cook for 5 minutes.
- Turn and cook for another 5 minutes.

362. Rib Eye Steak with Buttered Garlic & Chives

Preparation Time: 1 hour
Cooking Time: 20 minutes
Servings: 2

Ingredients:

- 2 rib eye steaks
- Olive oil
- Salt and pepper to taste
- Garlic & chive butter
- 1/2 cup butter
- 1 clove garlic, minced
- 1 tablespoon chives, chopped

Directions:

- Combine the butter ingredients in a bowl.
- Refrigerate for 1 hour.
- Preheat your air fryer to 400 degrees F for 5 minutes.
- Rub steaks with oil and season with salt and pepper.
- Place inside the air fryer oven.
- Choose air fry option.
- Air fry the steaks for 6 minutes.
- Turn and cook for another 6 minutes.
- Top the steaks with the butter compound and serve.

363. Sesame Beef Stir Fry

Preparation Time: 10 minutes
Cooking Time: 15 minutes
Servings: 2

Ingredients:

Stir Fry

- 1 lb. flank steak, sliced into strips
- 1/2 cup red onions, sliced
- 1/2 cup carrots, shredded
- 1/2 cup snow peas
- 1/2 cup broccoli florets

Sauce

- 2 cloves garlic, minced
- 1/4 cup hoisin sauce
- 1 tablespoon soy sauce
- 1 teaspoon ground ginger
- 1 teaspoon sesame oil
- 1/4 cup water

Directions:

- Preheat your air fryer to 400 degrees F for 5 minutes.
- Choose grill setting.
- Mix the sauce ingredients in a bowl. Set aside.
- Add the steaks to the air fryer tray.
- Cook for 5 minutes per side.
- Stir in the rest of the stir fry ingredients.
- Cook for 3 minutes.
- Add the sauce and stir.
- Cook for 7 minutes, stirring once or twice.

364. Steak with Pastrami Butter

Preparation Time: 9 minutes
Cooking Time: 11 minutes
Servings: 2

Ingredients:

- 2 sirloin steaks
- 2 tablespoons butter
- Salt and pepper to taste
- 1/4 cup butter
- 2 teaspoons pastrami spice blend

Directions:

- Preheat your air fryer oven to 400 degrees F for 5 minutes.
- Spread 2 tablespoons butter on both sides of steaks.
- Sprinkle with salt and pepper.
- Place the steaks inside the air fryer oven.
- Turn to air fry setting.
- Cook steaks for 6 minutes per side.

- Mix the butter and pastrami spice blend.
- Serve on top of the steaks.

365. Spicy Thai Beef Stir-Fry

Preparation Time: 15 minutes
Cooking Time: 9 minutes
Servings: 4

Ingredients

- 1-pound sirloin steaks, thinly sliced
- 2 tablespoons lime juice, divided
- 1/3 cup crunchy peanut butter
- ½ cup beef broth
- 1 tablespoon olive oil
- 1½ cups broccoli florets
- 2 cloves garlic, sliced
- 1 to 2 red chile peppers, sliced

Directions:

- Preparing the Ingredients. In a medium bowl, combine the steak with 1 tablespoon of the lime juice. Set aside.

- Combine the peanut butter and beef broth in a small bowl and mix well. Drain the beef and add the juice from the bowl into the peanut butter mixture.

- In a 6-inch metal bowl, combine the olive oil, steak, and broccoli.

- Air Frying. Cook for 3 to 4 minutes or until the steak is almost cooked and the broccoli is crisp and tender, shaking the basket once during cooking time.

- Add the garlic, chile peppers, and the peanut butter mixture and stir.

- Cook for 3 to 5 minutes or until the sauce is bubbling and the broccoli is tender.

- Serve over hot rice.

366. Copycat Taco Bell Crunch Wraps

Preparation Time: 10 minutes
Cooking Time: 2 minutes
Servings: 6

Ingredients:

- 6 wheat tostadas

- 2 C. sour cream
- 2 C. Mexican blend cheese
- 2 C. shredded lettuce
- 12 ounces low-sodium nacho cheese
- 3 Roma tomatoes
- 6 12-inch wheat tortillas
- 1 1/3 C. water
- 2 packets low-sodium taco seasoning
- 2 pounds of lean ground beef

Directions:

- Preparing the Ingredients. Ensure your air fryer is preheated to 400 degrees.

- Make beef according to taco seasoning packets.

- Place 2/3 C. prepared beef, 4 tbsp. cheese, 1 tostada, 1/3 C. sour cream, 1/3 C. lettuce, 1/6th of tomatoes and 1/3 C. cheese on each tortilla.

- Fold up tortillas edges and repeat with remaining ingredients.

- Lay the folded sides of tortillas down into the air fryer and spray with olive oil.

- Air Frying. Set temperature to 400°F, and set time to 2 minutes. Cook 2 minutes till browned.

367. Meat Lovers' Pizza

Preparation Time: 10 minutes
Cooking Time: 12 minutes
Servings: 2

Ingredients:

- 1 pre-prepared 7-inch pizza pie crust, defrosted if necessary.
- 1/3 cup of marinara sauce.
- 2 ounces of grilled steak, sliced into bite-sized pieces
- 2 ounces of salami, sliced fine
- 2 ounces of pepperoni, sliced fine
- ¼ cup of American cheese
- ¼ cup of shredded mozzarella cheese

Directions:

- Preparing the ingredients. Preheat the Air fryer oven to 350 degrees.

- Lay the pizza dough flat on a sheet of parchment paper or tin foil, cut large enough to hold the entire pie crust, but small enough that it will leave the edges of the air frying rack/basket uncovered to allow for air circulation.

- Using a fork, stab the pizza dough several times across the surface – piercing the pie crust will allow air to circulate throughout the crust and ensure even cooking.

- With a deep soup spoon, ladle the marinara sauce onto the pizza dough, and spread evenly in expanding circles over the surface of the pie-crust. Be sure to leave at least ½ inch of bare dough around the edges, to ensure that extra-crispy crunchy first bite of the crust!

- Distribute the pieces of steak and the slices of salami and pepperoni evenly over the sauce-covered dough, then sprinkle the cheese in an even layer on top.

- Set the Air fryer oven timer to 12 minutes, and place the pizza with foil or paper on the fryer's basket surface. Again, be sure to leave the edges of the basket uncovered to allow for proper air circulation, and don't let your bare fingers touch the hot surface.

- After 12 minutes, when the Air fryer oven shuts off, the cheese should be perfectly melted and lightly crisped, and the pie crust should be golden brown.

- Using a spatula – or two, if necessary, remove the pizza from the Oven rack/basket and set on a serving plate.

- Wait a few minutes until the pie is cool enough to handle, then cut into slices and serve.

368. Country Fried Steak

Preparation Time: 5 minutes
Cooking Time: 12 minutes
Servings: 2

Ingredients:

- 1 tsp. pepper

- 2 C. almond milk
- 2 tbsp. almond flour
- 6 ounces ground sausage meat
- 1 tsp. pepper
- 1 tsp. salt
- 1 tsp. garlic powder
- 1 tsp. onion powder
- 1 C. panko breadcrumbs
- 1 C. almond flour
- 3 beaten eggs
- 6 ounces sirloin steak, pounded till thin

Directions:

- Preparing the Ingredients. Season panko breadcrumbs with spices.

- Dredge steak in flour, then egg, and then seasoned panko mixture.

- Place into air fryer rack/basket.

- Air Frying. Set temperature to 370°F, and set time to 12 minutes.

- To make sausage gravy, cook sausage and drain off fat, but reserve 2 tablespoons.

- Add flour to sausage and mix until incorporated. Gradually mix in milk over medium to high heat till it becomes thick.

- Season mixture with pepper and cook 3 minutes longer.

- Serve steak topped with gravy and enjoy!

369. Beef & veggie Spring Rolls

Preparation Time: 5 minutes
Cooking Time: 12 minutes
Servings: 10

Ingredients:

- 2-ounce Asian rice noodles
- 1 tablespoon sesame oil
- 7-ounce ground beef
- 1 small onion, chopped
- 3 garlic cloves, crushed
- 1 cup fresh mixed vegetables
- 1 teaspoon soy sauce
- 1 packet spring roll skins
- 2 tablespoons water

- ◆ Olive oil, as required

Directions:

- ■ Preparing the Ingredients. Soak the noodles in warm water till soft.
- ■ Drain and cut into small lengths. In a pan heat the oil and add the onion and garlic and sauté for about 4-5 minutes.
- ■ Add beef and cook for about 4-5 minutes.
- ■ Add vegetables and cook for about 5-7 minutes or till cooked through.
- ■ Stir in soy sauce and remove from the heat.
- ■ Immediately, stir in the noodles and keep aside till all the juices have been absorbed.
- ■ Preheat the Air fryer oven to 350 degrees F. and preheat the oven to 350 degrees F also.
- ■ Place the spring rolls skin onto a smooth surface.
- ■ Add a line of the filling diagonally across.
- ■ Fold the top point over the filling and then fold in both sides.
- ■ On the final point, brush it with water before rolling to seal.
- ■ Brush the spring rolls with oil.
- ■ Air Frying. Arrange the rolls in batches in the Air fryer oven and Cook for about 8 minutes.
- ■ Repeat with remaining rolls.
- ■ Now, place spring rolls onto a baking sheet.
- ■ Bake for about 6 minutes per side

370. Air Fryer Roast Beef

Preparation Time: 5 minutes
Cooking Time: 45 minutes
Servings: 6

Ingredients:

- ◆ Roast beef
- ◆ 1 tbsp. olive oil
- ◆ Seasonings of choice

Directions:

- ■ Preparing the Ingredients. Ensure your air fryer is preheated to 160 degrees.

- ■ Place roast in bowl and toss with olive oil and desired seasonings.
- ■ Put seasoned roast into the Air fryer oven.
- ■ Air Frying. Set temperature to 160°F, and set time to 30 minutes and cook 30 minutes.
- ■ Turn roast when the timer sounds and cook another 15 minutes.

371. Crispy Mongolian Beef

Preparation Time: 5 minutes
Cooking Time: 10 minutes
Servings: 6

Ingredients:

- ◆ Olive oil
- ◆ ½ C. almond flour
- ◆ 2 pounds beef tenderloin or beef chuck, sliced into strips

Sauce:

- ◆ ½ C. chopped green onion
- ◆ 1 tsp. red chili flakes
- ◆ 1 tsp. almond flour
- ◆ ½ C. brown sugar
- ◆ 1 tsp. hoisin sauce
- ◆ ½ C. water
- ◆ ½ C. rice vinegar
- ◆ ½ C. low-sodium soy sauce
- ◆ 1 tbsp. chopped garlic
- ◆ 1 tbsp. finely chopped ginger
- ◆ 2 tbsp. olive oil

Directions:

- ■ Preparing the Ingredients. Toss strips of beef in almond flour, ensuring they are coated well. Add to the Air fryer oven.
- ■ Air Frying. Set temperature to 300°F, and set time to 10 minutes, and cook 10 minutes at 300 degrees.
- ■ Meanwhile, add all sauce ingredients to the pan and bring to a boil. Mix well.
- ■ Add beef strips to the sauce and cook 2 minutes.
- ■ Serve over cauliflower rice!

372. Swedish Meatballs

Preparation Time: 10 minutes
Cooking Time: 14 minutes
Servings: 4

Ingredients:

For the meatballs

- 1 pound 93% lean ground beef
- 1 (1-ounce) packet Lipton Onion Recipe Soup & Dip Mix
- 1/3 cup bread crumbs
- 1 egg, beaten
- Salt
- Pepper

For the gravy

- 1 cup beef broth
- 1/3 cup heavy cream
- 1 tablespoon all-purpose flour

Directions:

- Preparing the Ingredients. In a large bowl, combine the ground beef, onion soup mix, bread crumbs, egg, and salt and pepper to taste. Mix thoroughly.

- Using 2 tablespoons of the meat mixture, create each meatball by rolling the beef mixture around in your hands. This should yield about 10 meatballs.

- Air Frying. Place the meatballs in the Air fryer oven. It is okay to stack them. Set temperature to 360°F. Cook for 14 minutes.

- While the meatballs cook, prepare the gravy. Heat a saucepan over medium-high heat.

- Add the beef broth and heavy cream. Stir for 1 to 2 minutes.

- Add the flour and stir. Cover and allow the sauce to simmer for 3 to 4 minutes, or until thick.

- Drizzle the gravy over the meatballs and serve.

373. Tender Beef with Sour Cream Sauce

Preparation Time: 5 minutes
Cooking Time: 12 minutes
Servings: 2

Ingredients:

- 9 ounces tender beef, chopped
- 1 cup scallions, chopped
- 2 cloves garlic, smashed
- 3/4 cup sour cream
- 3/4 teaspoon salt
- 1/4 teaspoon black pepper, or to taste
- 1/2 teaspoon dried dill weed

Directions:

- Preparing the Ingredients. Add the beef, scallions, and garlic to the baking dish.

- Air Frying. Cook for about 5 minutes at 390 degrees F.

- Once the meat is starting to tender, pour in the sour cream. Stir in the salt, black pepper, and dill.

- Now, cook 7 minutes longer.

374. Air Fryer Burgers

Preparation Time: 5 minutes
Cooking Time: 10 minutes
Servings: 4

Ingredients:

- 1-pound lean ground beef
- 1 tsp. dried parsley
- ½ tsp. dried oregano
- ½ tsp. pepper
- ½ tsp. salt
- ½ tsp. onion powder
- ½ tsp. garlic powder
- Few drops of liquid smoke
- 1 tsp. Worcestershire sauce

Directions:

- Preparing the Ingredients. Ensure your air fryer is preheated to 350 degrees.

- Mix all seasonings together till combined.

- Place beef in a bowl and add seasonings. Mix well, but do not overmix.

- Make 4 patties from the mixture and using your thumb, making an indent in the center of each patty.

- Add patties to air fryer rack/basket.
- Air Frying. Set temperature to 350°F, and set time to 10 minutes, and cook 10 minutes. No need to turn.

375. Beef Steaks with Beans

Preparation Time: 5 minutes
Cooking Time: 10 minutes
Servings: 4

Ingredients:

- 4 beef steaks, trim the fat and cut into strips
- 1 cup green onions, chopped
- 2 cloves garlic, minced
- 1 red bell pepper, seeded and thinly sliced
- 1 can tomatoes, crushed
- 1 can cannellini beans
- 3/4 cup beef broth
- 1/4 teaspoon dried basil
- 1/2 teaspoon cayenne pepper
- 1/2 teaspoon sea salt
- 1/4 teaspoon ground black pepper, or to taste

Directions:

- Preparing the Ingredients. Add the steaks, green onions and garlic to the Oven rack/basket. Place the Rack on the middle-shelf of the Air fryer oven.
- Air Frying. Cook at 390 degrees F for 10 minutes, working in batches.
- Stir in the remaining ingredients and cook for an additional 5 minutes.

376. Parmesan-crusted Pork Loin

Preparation Time: 8 minutes
Cooking Time: 20 minutes
Servings: 4

Ingredients:

- 1-pound pork loin
- 1 teaspoon salt
- 1/2 tablespoon garlic powder
- 1/2 tablespoon onion powder
- 2 tablespoons parmesan cheese
- 1 tablespoon olive oil

Directions:

- Start by preheating toaster oven to 475°F
- Place pan in the oven and let it heat while the oven preheats
- Mix all ingredients in a shallow dish and roll the pork loin until it is fully coated.
- Remove pan and sear the pork in the pan on each side, once seared, bake pork in the pan for 20 minutes.
- Serve Warm.

377. Crispy Breaded Pork Chop

Preparation Time: 10 minutes
Cooking Time: 12 minutes
Servings: 6

Ingredients:

- olive oil spray
- 6 3/4-inch-thick center-cut boneless pork chops, fat trimmed (5 oz each)
- kosher salt
- 1 large egg, beaten
- 1/2 cup panko crumbs, check labels for GF
- 1/3 cup crushed cornflakes crumbs
- 2 tbsp grated parmesan cheese
- 1 1/4 tsp sweet paprika
- 1/2 tsp garlic powder
- 1/2 tsp onion powder
- 1/4 tsp chili powder
- 1/8 tsp black pepper

Directions:

- Preheat the Instant Pot Duo Crisp Air Fryer for 12 minutes at 400°F
- On both sides, season pork chops with half teaspoon kosher salt
- Combine cornflake crumbs, panko, parmesan cheese, 3/4 tsp kosher salt, garlic powder, paprika, onion powder, chili powder, and black pepper in a large bowl
- Place the egg beat in another bowl
- Dip the pork in the egg & then crumb mixture

- When the air fryer is ready, place 3 of the chops into the Instant Pot Duo Crisp Air Fryer Basket and spritz the top with oil
- Close the Air Fryer lid and cook for 12 minutes turning halfway, spritzing both sides with oil
- Set aside and repeat with the remaining

378. BBQ Pork Ribs

Preparation Time: 10 minutes
Cooking Time: 12 minutes
Servings: 6

Ingredients:

- 1 slab baby back pork ribs, cut into pieces ½ cup BBQ sauce
- ½ tsp paprika
- Salt

Directions:

- Add pork ribs in a mixing bowl
- Add BBQ sauce, paprika, and salt over pork ribs and coat well and set aside for 30 minutes
- Preheat the instant vortex air fryer oven to 350 F
- Arrange marinated pork ribs on instant vortex air fryer oven pan and cook for 10-12 minutes
- Turn halfway through.
- Serve and enjoy.

379. Honey Mustard Pork Tenderloin

Preparation Time: 10 minutes
Cooking Time: 26 minutes
Servings: 4

Ingredients:

- 1 lb. pork tenderloin
- 1 tsp sriracha sauce
- 1 tbsp garlic, minced
- 2 tbsp soy sauce
- 1 ½ tbsp honey
- ¾ tbsp Dijon mustard
- 1 tbsp mustard

Directions:

- Add sriracha sauce, garlic, soy sauce, honey, Dijon mustard, and mustard into the large zip-lock bag and mix well
- Add pork tenderloin into the bag
- Seal bag and place in the refrigerator for overnight
- Preheat the instant vortex air fryer oven to 380 F. Spray instant vortex air fryer tray with cooking spray then place marinated pork tenderloin on a tray and air fry for 26 minutes
- Turn pork tenderloin after every 5 minutes
- Slice and serve.

380. Pork Chops

Preparation Time: 10 minutes
Cooking Time: 16 minutes
Servings: 4

Ingredients:

- 4 pork chops, boneless
- 2 tsp olive oil
- ½ tsp celery seed
- ½ tsp parsley
- ½ tsp granulated onion
- ½ tsp granulated garlic
- ¼ tsp sugar
- ½ tsp salt

Directions:

- In a small bowl, mix together oil, celery seed, parsley, granulated onion, granulated garlic, sugar, and salt, rub seasoning mixture all over the pork chops
- Place pork chops on the air fryer oven pan and cook at 350 F for 8 minutes
- turn pork chops to other side and cook for 8 minutes more
- Serve and enjoy.

381. Sweet & Sour Pork

Preparation Time: 10 minutes
Cooking Time: 27 minutes
Servings: 4

Ingredients:

- 2 pounds Pork cut into chunks
- 2 large Eggs
- 1 teaspoon Pure Sesame Oil (optional)
- 1 cup Potato Starch (or cornstarch) 1/2 teaspoon Sea Salt
- 1/4 teaspoon Freshly Ground Black Pepper 1/16 teaspoon Chinese Five Spice
- 3 Tablespoons Canola Oil
- Oil Mister

Directions:

- In a mixing bowl, combine salt, potato starch, Chinese Five Spice, and peppers
- In another bowl, beat the eggs & add sesame oil, then dredge the pieces of Pork into the Potato Starch and remove the excess
- Then dip each piece into the egg mixture, shake off excess, and then back into the Potato Starch mixture
- Place pork pieces into the Instant Pot Duo Crisp Air Fryer Basket after spray the pork with oil, close the Air Fryer oven door and cook at 340°F for approximately 8 to 12 minutes (or until pork is cooked), shaking the basket a couple of times for evenly distribution

382. Pork Tenderloin

Preparation Time: 10 minutes
Cooking Time: 45 minutes
Servings: 5

Ingredients:

- 1½ pounds pork tenderloin
- 2-3 tablespoons BBQ pork seasoning

Directions:

- Rub the pork with seasoning generously
- Insert the rotisserie rod through the pork tenderloin, insert the rotisserie forks, one on each side of the rod to secure the pork tenderloin
- Arrange the drip pan in the bottom of Air fryer cooking chamber
- Select "Roast" and then adjust the temperature to 360 degrees F

- Set the timer for 45 minutes and press the "Start"
- When the display shows "Add Food" press the red lever down and load the left side of the rod into the Vortex. Now, slide the rod's left side into the groove along the metal bar so it doesn't move, then, close the door and touch "Rotate"
- Press the red lever to release the rod when cooking time is complete
- Remove the pork from Vortex and place onto a platter for about 10 minutes before slicing, with a sharp knife, cut the roast into desired sized slices and serve.

383. Glazed Pork Tenderloin

Preparation Time: 15 minutes
Cooking Time: 20 minutes
Servings: 3

Ingredients:

- 1-pound pork tenderloin
- 2 tablespoons Sriracha
- 2 tablespoons honey
- Salt, as required

Directions:

- Insert the rotisserie rod through the pork tenderloin, insert the rotisserie forks, one on each side of the rod to secure the pork tenderloin
- In a small bowl, add the Sriracha, honey and salt and mix well, brush the pork tenderloin with honey mixture evenly
- Arrange the drip pan in the bottom of Air fryer cooking chamber, select "Air Fry" and then adjust the temperature to 350 degrees F
- Set the timer for 20 minutes and press the "Start", when the display shows "Add Food" press the red lever down and load the left side of the rod into the Vortex
- Now, slide the rod's left side into the groove along the metal bar so it doesn't move, then, close the door and touch "Rotate"
- Press the red lever to release the rod when cooking time is complete, remove the pork

from Vortex and place onto a platter for about 10 minutes before slicing

- With a sharp knife, cut the roast into desired sized slices and serve.

384. Breaded Pork Chops

Preparation Time: 15 minutes
Cooking Time: 28 minutes
Servings: 2

Ingredients:

- 2 (5-ounce) boneless pork chops
- 1 cup buttermilk
- ½ cup flour
- 1 teaspoon garlic powder
- Salt and ground black pepper, as required Olive oil cooking spray

Directions:

- In a bowl, place the chops and buttermilk and refrigerate, covered for about 12 hours, remove the chops from the bowl of buttermilk, discarding the buttermilk
- In a shallow dish, mix together the flour, garlic powder, salt, and black pepper
- Coat the chops with flour mixture generously
- Place the pork chops onto the cooking tray and spray with the cooking spray, arrange the drip pan in the bottom of Air fryer cooking chamber
- Select "Air Fry" and then adjust the temperature to 380 degrees F., set the timer for 28 minutes and press the "Start"
- When the display shows "Add Food" insert the cooking tray in the center position, when the display shows "Turn Food" turn the pork chops
- When cooking time is complete, remove the tray from Vortex and serve hot.

385. Seasoned Pork Chops

Preparation Time: 10 minutes
Cooking Time: 12 minutes
Servings: 4

Ingredients:

- 4 (6-ounce) boneless pork chops
- 2 tablespoons pork rub
- 1 tablespoon olive oil

Directions:

- Coat both sides of the pork chops with the oil and then, rub with the pork rub, place the pork chops onto the lightly greased cooking tray
- Arrange the drip pan in the bottom of Air fryer cooking chamber
- Select "Air Fry" and then adjust the temperature to 400 degrees F
- Set the timer for 12 minutes and press the "Start", when the display shows "Add Food" insert the cooking tray in the center position
- When the display shows "Turn Food" turn the pork chops, when cooking time is complete, remove the tray from Vortex and serve hot.

386. Spiced Pork Shoulder

Preparation Time: 15 minutes
Cooking Time: 55 minutes
Servings: 6

Ingredients:

- 1 teaspoon ground cumin
- 1 teaspoon cayenne pepper
- 1 teaspoon garlic powder
- Salt and ground black pepper, as required
- 2 pounds skin-on pork shoulder

Directions:

- In a small bowl, mix together the spices, salt and black pepper, arrange the pork shoulder onto a cutting board, skin-side down
- Season the inner side of pork shoulder with salt and black pepper, with kitchen twines, tie the pork shoulder into a long round cylinder shape
- Season the outer side of pork shoulder with spice mixture, insert the rotisserie rod through the pork shoulder
- Insert the rotisserie forks, one on each side of the rod to secure the pork shoulder

- Arrange the drip pan in the bottom of Air fryer cooking chamber, select "Roast" and then adjust the temperature to 350 degrees F. set the timer for 55 minutes and press the "Start"

- When the display shows "Add Food" press the red lever down and load the left side of the rod into the Vortex

- Now, slide the rod's left side into the groove along the metal bar so it doesn't move, then, close the door and touch "Rotate"

- Press the red lever to release the rod when cooking time is complete, remove the pork from Vortex and place onto a platter for about 10 minutes before slicing

- With a sharp knife, cut the pork shoulder into desired sized slices and serve.

387.   Sweet and Sour Pork

Preparation Time: 20 minutes
Cooking Time: 20 minutes
Servings: 4

Ingredients:

- 2 pounds pork cut into chunks
- 2 large Eggs
- 1 tsp olive oil
- 1 cup cornstarch
- Salt and freshly ground black pepper to taste
- 1/4 tsp. Chinese spice
- Oil Mister

Directions:

- Preheat the Air fryer by selecting grill mode

- Adjust temperature to 350°F and time to 5 minutes

- Whisk egg and olive oil in a bowl

- Add breadcrumbs to another bowl

- Dip the beef schnitzel in the egg mixture then coat with the breadcrumb mixture

- Arrange on the Air fryer ing plate

- Transfer into the Air fryer

- Grill for 12 minutes, flipping halfway

- Serve and enjoy!

388.   Pork Ratatouille

Preparation Time: 5 minutes
Cooking Time: 35 minutes
Servings: 4

Ingredients:

- 4 pork sausages

For Ratatouille

- 1 pepper, chopped
- 15 oz tomatoes, chopped
- 2 zucchinis, chopped
- 1 red chili, chopped
- 1 eggplant, chopped
- 2 sprigs fresh thyme
- 1 medium red onion, chopped
- 1 tbsp. balsamic vinegar
- 2 garlic cloves, minced

Directions:

- Preheat the Air fryer by selecting pizza/bake mode

- Adjust temperature to 392°F and time to 10 minutes

- Combine zucchini, eggplant, onions, and oil in the cooking tray.

- Transfer to the Air fryer , bake for 20 minutes

- Remove and add the remaining Ratatouille ingredients.

- Transfer to the Air fryer and cook for an additional 20 minutes

- Remove and season with salt and pepper.

- Add the sausage to the Pizza tray

- Cook for 15 minutes, flipping halfway

- Serve and enjoy

389.   Cheddar Pork Meatballs

Preparation Time: 20 minutes
Cooking Time: 15 minutes
Servings: 6

Ingredients:

- 1 lb. ground pork
- 1/2 tsp. maple syrup

- 1 large onion, chopped
- 2 tsp mustard
- Salt and black pepper to taste
- 1/2 cup chopped basil leaves
- 2 tbsp. grated cheddar cheese

Directions:

- Preheat the Air fryer by selecting air fry mode
- Adjust temperature to 390°F and time to 5 minutes
- Combine all the ingredients in a bowl.
- Form into small balls
- Arrange on the Air fryer baking tray
- Transfer into the Air fryer
- Air fry for 10 minutes, flip and cook for additional 5 minutes
- Serve and enjoy!

390. Almond Pork Bite

Preparation Time: 25 minutes
Cooking Time: 20 minutes
Servings: 10

Ingredients:

- 16 oz. sausage meat
- 1 whole egg, beaten
- 1/3 cup chopped onion
- 2 tbsp. almonds, chopped
- 1/2 tsp pepper
- 2 tbsp. dried sage
- 1/3 cup sliced apples, sliced
- 1/2 tsp salt

Directions:

- Preheat the Air fryer by selecting grill mode
- Adjust temperature to 350°F and time to 5 minutes
- Combine all the ingredients in a bowl.
- Pour into a Ziploc bag and marinate for 15 minutes
- Form into cutlets
- Arrange on the Air fryer grilling plate
- Transfer into the Air fryer

- Grill for 20 minutes
- Serve and enjoy!

391. Stuffed Pork Chops

Preparation Time: 10 minutes
Cooking Time: 50 minutes
Servings: 4

Ingredients:

- 8 pork chops
- 2 tbsp. olive
- 1/4 tsp. pepper
- 4 cups stuffing mix
- 1/2 tsp salt
- 4 garlic cloves, minced
- 2 tbsp sage leaves

Directions:

- Preheat the Air fryer by selecting Air Fryer mode
- Adjust temperature to 350°F and time to 5 minutes
- Cut a hole in the pork chops, fill the hole with stuffing mix
- In a bowl, combine the remaining ingredients.
- Add the pork chops and leave to marinate for 10 minutes
- Arrange on the Air fryer grilling plate
- Transfer into the Air fryer
- Air fry for 20 minutes
- Serve and enjoy!

392. Crispy Breaded Pork

Preparation Time: 15 minutes
Cooking Time: 15 minutes
Servings: 6

Ingredients:

- 6 (3/4- inch thick) center-cut boneless pork chops
- olive oil spray
- 1-1/4 tsp. sweet paprika
- kosher salt
- 1/2 tsp onion powder

- 1 large egg, beaten
- 1/2 cup panko crumbs
- 1/3 cup crushed cornflakes crumbs
- 1/4 tsp. chili powder
- 2 tbsp. grated parmesan cheese
- 1/2 tsp garlic powder
- 1/8 tsp. black pepper

Directions:

- Preheat the Air fryer by selecting Air Fryer mode
- Adjust temperature to 390°F and time to 5 minutes
- Season the pork chops on both sides with salt
- In a bowl, combine the remaining ingredients except for the egg.
- Beat the egg in another bowl
- Dip pork chops in eggs then in breadcrumb mixture
- Arrange on the Air fryer baking tray, sprinkle with oil
- Transfer into the Air fryer
- Air fry for 6 minutes per sides

393. Lemongrass Pork Chops

Preparation Time: 20 minutes
Cooking Time: 2 hours 30 minutes
Servings: 4

Ingredients:

- 3 pork chops
- 4 stalks lemongrass, trimmed and chopped
- 1-1/4 tsp. soy sauce
- 2 garlic cloves, minced
- 1-1/2 tbsp sugar
- 2 shallots, chopped
- 2 tbsp olive oil
- 1-1/4 tsp. fish sauce
- 1-1/2 tsp black pepper

Directions:

- Combine all the ingredients in a bowl
- add the pork chops and leave to marinate for 2 hours

- Preheat the Air fryer by selecting Grill/air fry mode
- Adjust temperature to 390°F and time to 5 minutes
- Remove the pork chops and arrange on the grilling plate
- Transfer into the Air fryer
- Air fry for 6 minutes, flip and air fry for additional 7 minutes
- Serve and enjoy!

394. Pork Taquitos

Preparation Time: 10 minutes
Cooking Time: 16 minutes
Servings: 8

Ingredients:

- 1 juiced lime
- 10 whole wheat tortillas
- 2 ½ C. shredded mozzarella cheese
- 30 ounces of cooked and shredded pork tenderloin

Directions:

- Ensure your air fryer oven is preheated to 380 degrees.
- Drizzle pork with lime juice and gently mix.
- Heat up tortillas in the microwave with a dampened paper towel to soften.
- Add about 3 ounces of pork and ¼ cup of shredded cheese to each tortilla. Tightly roll them up.
- Spray the air fryer basket with a bit of olive oil.
- Set temperature to 380°F, and set time to 10 minutes. Air fry taquitos 7-10 minutes till tortillas turn a slight golden color, making sure to flip halfway through cooking process.

395. Apricot Glazed Pork Tenderloins

Preparation Time: 5 minutes
Cooking Time: 30 minutes
Servings: 3

Ingredients:

- 1 teaspoon salt
- 1/2 teaspoon pepper
- 1-lb pork tenderloin
- 2 tablespoons minced fresh rosemary or 1 tablespoon dried rosemary, crushed
- 2 tablespoons olive oil, divided
- garlic cloves, minced
- Apricot Glaze Ingredients
- 1 cup apricot preserves
- 4 tablespoons lemon juice

Directions:

- Mix well pepper, salt, garlic, oil, and rosemary. Brush all over pork. If needed cut pork crosswise in half to fit in air fryer.
- Lightly grease baking pan of air fryer with cooking spray. Add pork.
- For 3 minutes per side, brown pork in a preheated 390°F air fryer.
- Meanwhile, mix well all glaze Ingredients in a small bowl. Baste pork every 5 minutes.
- Cook for 20 minutes at 330°F.
- Serve and enjoy.

396. Pork Tenders With Bell Peppers

Preparation Time: 5 minutes
Cooking Time: 15 minutes
Servings: 4

Ingredients:

- 11 Ozs Pork Tenderloin
- 1 Bell Pepper, in thin strips
- 1 Red Onion, sliced
- 2 Tsps Provencal Herbs
- Black Pepper to taste
- 1 Tbsp Olive Oil
- 1/2 Tbsp Mustard
- * Round Oven Dish

Directions:

- Preheat the air fryer oven to 390 degrees.
- In the oven dish, mix the bell pepper strips with the onion, herbs, and some salt and pepper to taste.

- Add half a tablespoon of olive oil to the mixture
- Cut the pork tenderloin into four pieces and rub with salt, pepper and mustard.
- Thinly coat the pieces with remaining olive oil and place them upright in the oven dish on top of the pepper mixture
- Place the bowl into the air fryer oven. Set the timer to 15 minutes and roast the meat and the vegetables
- Turn the meat and mix the peppers halfway through
- Serve with a fresh salad

397. Barbecue Flavored Pork Ribs

Preparation Time: 5 minutes
Cooking Time: 15 minutes
Servings: 6

Ingredients:

- ¼ cup honey, divided
- ¾ cup BBQ sauce
- 2 tablespoons tomato ketchup
- 1 tablespoon Worcestershire sauce
- 1 tablespoon soy sauce
- ½ teaspoon garlic powder
- Freshly ground white pepper, to taste
- 1¾ pound pork ribs

Directions:

- In a large bowl, mix together 3 tablespoons of honey and remaining ingredients except pork ribs.
- Refrigerate to marinate for about 20 minutes.
- Preheat the air fryer oven to 355 degrees F.
- Place the ribs in an Air fryer basket.
- Cook for about 13 minutes.
- Remove the ribs from the air fryer oven and coat with remaining honey.
- Serve hot.

398. Balsamic Glazed Pork Chops

Preparation Time: 5 minutes
Cooking Time: 50 minutes
Servings: 4

Ingredients:

- ¾ cup balsamic vinegar
- 1 ½ tablespoons sugar
- 1 tablespoon butter
- 3 tablespoons olive oil
- tablespoons salt
- 3 pork rib chops

Directions:

- Place all ingredients in bowl and allow the meat to marinate in the fridge for at least 2 hours.
- Preheat the air fryer oven to 390°F.
- Place the grill pan accessory in the air fryer.
- Grill the pork chops for 20 minutes making sure to flip the meat every 10 minutes for even grilling.
- Meanwhile, pour the balsamic vinegar on a saucepan and allow to simmer for at least 10 minutes until the sauce thickens.
- Brush the meat with the glaze before serving.

399.   Rustic Pork Ribs

Preparation Time: 5 minutes
Cooking Time: 15 minutes
Servings: 4

Ingredients:

- 1 rack of pork ribs
- 3 tablespoons dry red wine
- 1 tablespoon soy sauce
- 1/2 teaspoon dried thyme
- 1/2 teaspoon onion powder
- 1/2 teaspoon garlic powder
- 1/2 teaspoon ground black pepper
- 1 teaspoon smoke salt
- 1 tablespoon cornstarch
- 1/2 teaspoon olive oil

Directions:

- Begin by preheating your air fryer oven to 390 degrees F. Place all ingredients in a mixing bowl and let them marinate at least 1 hour.

- Pour into the Oven rack/basket. Place the Rack on the middle-shelf of the Air fryer oven. Set temperature to 390°F, and set time to 25 minutes. Cook the marinated ribs approximately 25 minutes.
- Serve hot.

400.   Keto Parmesan Crusted Pork Chops

Preparation Time: 10 minutes
Cooking Time: 15 minutes
Servings: 8

Ingredients:

- 3 tbsp. grated parmesan cheese
- 1 C. pork rind crumbs
- 2 beaten eggs
- ¼ tsp. chili powder
- ½ tsp. onion powder
- 1 tsp. smoked paprika
- ¼ tsp. pepper
- ½ tsp. salt
- 4-6 thick boneless pork chops

Directions:

- Ensure your air fryer oven is preheated to 400 degrees.
- With pepper and salt, season both sides of pork chops.
- In a food processor, pulse pork rinds into crumbs. Mix crumbs with other seasonings.
- Beat eggs and add to another bowl.
- Dip pork chops into eggs then into pork rind crumb mixture.
- Spray down air fryer with olive oil and add pork chops to the basket. Set temperature to 400°F, and set time to 15 minutes.

401.   Crispy Fried Pork Chops the Southern Way

Preparation Time: 10 minutes
Cooking Time: 25 minutes
Servings: 4

Ingredients:

- ½ cup all-purpose flour
- ½ cup low fat buttermilk
- ½ teaspoon black pepper
- ½ teaspoon Tabasco sauce
- teaspoon paprika
- 3 bone-in pork chops

Directions:

- Place the buttermilk and hot sauce in a Ziploc bag and add the pork chops. Allow to marinate for at least an hour in the fridge.
- In a bowl, combine the flour, paprika, and black pepper.
- Remove pork from the Ziploc bag and dredge in the flour mixture.
- Preheat the air fryer oven to 390°F.
- Spray the pork chops with cooking oil.
- Pour into the Oven rack/basket. Place the Rack on the middle-shelf of the Air fryer oven. Set temperature to 390°F, and set time to 25 minutes.

402. Fried Pork Quesadilla

Preparation Time: 10 minutes
Cooking Time: 12 minutes
Servings: 2

Ingredients:

- Two 6-inch corn or flour tortilla shells
- 1 medium-sized pork shoulder, approximately 4 ounces, sliced
- ½ medium-sized white onion, sliced
- ½ medium-sized red pepper, sliced
- ½ medium sized green pepper, sliced
- ½ medium sized yellow pepper, sliced
- ¼ cup of shredded pepper-jack cheese
- ¼ cup of shredded mozzarella cheese

Directions:

- Preheat the air fryer oven to 350 degrees.
- In the oven on high heat for 20 minutes, grill the pork, onion, and peppers in foil in the same pan, allowing the moisture from the vegetables and the juice from the pork mingle together. Remove pork and vegetables in foil

from the oven. While they're cooling, sprinkle half the shredded cheese over one of the tortillas, then cover with the pieces of pork, onions, and peppers, and then layer on the rest of the shredded cheese. Top with the second tortilla. Place directly on hot surface of the air fryer basket.

- Set the air fryer timer for 6 minutes. After 6 minutes, when the air fryer shuts off, flip the tortillas onto the other side with a spatula; the cheese should be melted enough that it won't fall apart, but be careful anyway not to spill any toppings!
- Reset the air fryer to 350 degrees for another 6 minutes.
- After 6 minutes, when the air fryer shuts off, the tortillas should be browned and crisp, and the pork, onion, peppers and cheese will be crispy and hot and delicious. Remove with tongs and let sit on a serving plate to cool for a few minutes before slicing.

403. Pork Wonton Wonderful

Preparation Time: 10 minutes
Cooking Time: 25 minutes
Servings: 3

Ingredients:

- 8 wanton wrappers (Leasa brand works great, though any will do)
- 4 ounces of raw minced pork
- 1 medium-sized green apple
- 1 cup of water, for wetting the wanton wrappers
- 1 tablespoon of vegetable oil
- ½ tablespoon of oyster sauce
- 1 tablespoon of soy sauce
- Large pinch of ground white pepper

Directions:

- Cover the basket of the air fryer oven with a lining of tin foil, leaving the edges uncovered to allow air to circulate through the basket. Preheat the air fryer to 350 degrees.
- In a small mixing bowl, combine the oyster sauce, soy sauce, and white pepper, then add in the minced pork and stir thoroughly.

Cover and set in the fridge to marinate for at least 15 minutes. Core the apple, and slice into small cubes – smaller than bite-sized chunks.

- Add the apples to the marinating meat mixture, and combine thoroughly. Spread the wonton wrappers, and fill each with a large spoonful of the filling. Wrap the wontons into triangles, so that the wrappers fully cover the filling, and seal with a drop of the water.

- Coat each filled and wrapped wonton thoroughly with the vegetable oil, to help ensure a nice crispy fry. Place the wontons on the foil-lined air-fryer basket.

- Set the air fryer oven timer to 25 minutes. Halfway through cooking time, shake the handle of the air fryer basket vigorously to jostle the wontons and ensure even frying. After 25 minutes, when the air fryer oven shuts off, the wontons will be crispy golden-brown on the outside and juicy and delicious on the inside. Serve directly from the air fryer basket and enjoy while hot.

404. Cilantro-Mint Pork BBQ Thai Style

Preparation Time: 5 minutes
Cooking Time: 15 minutes
Servings: 3

Ingredients:

- 1 minced hot chile
- 1 minced shallot
- 1-pound ground pork
- 2 tablespoons fish sauce
- 2 tablespoons lime juice
- 3 tablespoons basil
- tablespoons chopped mint
- 3 tablespoons cilantro

Directions:

- In a shallow dish, mix well all Ingredients with hands. Form into 1-inch ovals.

- Thread ovals in skewers. Place on skewer rack in air fryer.

- For 15 minutes, cook on 360°F. Halfway through cooking time, turnover skewers. If needed, cook in batches.

- Serve and enjoy.

405. Tuscan Pork Chops

Preparation Time: 10 minutes
Cooking Time: 10 minutes
Servings: 4

Ingredients:

- 1/4 cup all-purpose flour
- 1 teaspoon salt
- 3/4 teaspoons seasoned pepper
- 4 (1-inch-thick) boneless pork chops
- 1 tablespoon olive oil
- 3 to 4 garlic cloves
- 1/3 cup balsamic vinegar
- 1/3 cup chicken broth
- 3 plum tomatoes, seeded and diced
- tablespoons capers

Directions:

- Combine flour, salt, and pepper

- Press pork chops into flour mixture on both sides until evenly covered.

- Cook in your air fryer oven at 360 degrees for 14 minutes, flipping half way through.

- While the pork chops cook, warm olive oil in a medium skillet.

- Add garlic and sauté for 1 minute; then mix in vinegar and chicken broth.

- Add capers and tomatoes and turn to high heat.

- Bring the sauce to a boil, stirring regularly, then add pork chops, cooking for one minute.

- Remove from heat and cover for about 5 minutes to allow the pork to absorb some of the sauce; serve hot.

406. Italian Parmesan Breaded Pork Chops

Preparation Time: 5 minutes
Cooking Time: 25 minutes

Servings: 5

Ingredients:

- 5 (3½- to 5-ounce) pork chops (bone-in or boneless)
- 1 teaspoon Italian seasoning
- Seasoning salt
- Pepper
- ¼ cup all-purpose flour
- 2 tablespoons Italian bread crumbs
- 3 tablespoons finely grated Parmesan cheese
- Cooking oil

Directions:

- Season the pork chops with the Italian seasoning and seasoning salt and pepper to taste.
- Sprinkle the flour on both sides of the pork chops, then coat both sides with the bread crumbs and Parmesan cheese.
- Place the pork chops in the air fryer basket. Stacking them is okay. Spray the pork chops with cooking oil. Cook for 6 minutes.
- Open the air fryer and flip the pork chops. Cook for an additional 6 minutes.
- Cool before serving. Instead of seasoning salt, you can use either chicken or pork rub for additional flavor. You can find these rubs in the spice aisle of the grocery store.

407.   Crispy Roast Garlic-Salt Pork

Preparation Time: 5 minutes
Cooking Time: 45 minutes
Servings: 4

Ingredients:

- 1 teaspoon Chinese five spice powder
- 1 teaspoon white pepper
- 2 pounds pork belly
- 2 teaspoons garlic salt

Directions:

- Preheat the air fryer oven to 390°F.
- Mix all the spices in a bowl to create the dry rub.

- Score the skin of the pork belly with a knife and season the entire pork with the spice rub.
- Place in the air fryer basket and cook for 40 to 45 minutes until the skin is crispy.
- Chop before serving.

408.   Peanut Satay Pork

Preparation Time: 5 minutes
Cooking Time: 12 minutes
Servings: 5

Ingredients:

- 11 Ozs Pork Fillet, sliced into bite sized strips
- 4 Cloves Garlic, crushed
- 1 Tsp Ginger Powder
- 2 Tsps Chili Paste
- 2 Tbsps Sweet Soy Sauce (Kecap Manis)
- 2 Tbsps Vegetable Oil
- 1 Shallot, finely chopped
- 1 Tsp Ground Coriander
- 3/4 Cup Coconut Milk
- 1/3 Cup Peanuts, ground

Directions:

- Mix half of the garlic in a dish with the ginger, a tablespoon of sweet soy sauce, and a tablespoon of the oil. Combine the meat into the mixture and leave to marinate for 15 minutes
- Preheat the air fryer oven to 390 degrees
- Place the marinated meat into the air fryer oven basket. Set the timer to 12 minutes and roast the meat until brown and done. Turn once while roasting
- In the meantime, make the peanut sauce by heating the remaining tablespoon of oil in a saucepan and gently sauté the shallot with the garlic. Add the coriander and fry until fragrant
- Mix the coconut milk and the peanuts with the chili paste and remaining soy sauce with the shallot mixture and gently boil for 5 minutes, while stirring
- Drizzle over the cooked meat and serve with rice

409. Crispy Breaded Pork Chops

Preparation Time: 10 minutes
Cooking Time: 15 minutes
Servings: 8

Ingredients:

- 1/8 tsp. pepper
- ¼ tsp. chili powder
- ½ tsp. onion powder
- ½ tsp. garlic powder
- 1 ¼ tsp. sweet paprika
- 2 tbsp. grated parmesan cheese
- 1/3 C. crushed cornflake crumbs
- ½ C. panko breadcrumbs
- 1 beaten egg
- 6 center-cut boneless pork chops

Directions:

- Ensure that your air fryer is preheated to 400 degrees. Spray the basket with olive oil.
- With ½ teaspoon salt and pepper, season both sides of pork chops.
- Combine ¾ teaspoon salt with pepper, chili powder, onion powder, garlic powder, paprika, cornflake crumbs, panko breadcrumbs and parmesan cheese.
- Beat egg in another bowl.
- Dip pork chops into the egg and then crumb mixture.
- Add pork chops to air fryer and spritz with olive oil.
- Pour into the Oven rack/basket. Place the Rack on the middle-shelf of the Air fryer oven. Set temperature to 400°F, and set time to 12 minutes. Cook 12 minutes, making sure to flip over halfway through cooking process.
- Only add 3 chops in at a time and repeat the process with remaining pork chops.

410. Ginger, Garlic And Pork Dumplings

Preparation Time: 10 minutes
Cooking Time: 15 minutes
Servings: 8

Ingredients:

- ¼ teaspoon crushed red pepper
- ½ teaspoon sugar
- 1 tablespoon chopped fresh ginger
- 1 tablespoon chopped garlic
- 1 teaspoon canola oil
- 1 teaspoon toasted sesame oil
- 18 dumpling wrappers
- 2 tablespoons rice vinegar
- 2 teaspoons soy sauce
- 4 cups bok choy, chopped
- 4 ounces ground pork

Directions:

- Heat oil in a skillet and sauté the ginger and garlic until fragrant. Stir in the ground pork and cook for 5 minutes.
- Stir in the bok choy and crushed red pepper. Season with salt and pepper to taste. Allow to cool.
- Place the meat mixture in the middle of the dumpling wrappers. Fold the wrappers to seal the meat mixture in.
- Place the bok choy in the grill pan.
- Cook the dumplings in the air fryer at 330°F for 15 minutes.
- Meanwhile, prepare the dipping sauce by combining the remaining Ingredients in a bowl.

411. Caramelized Pork Shoulder

Preparation Time: 10 minutes
Cooking Time: 20 minutes
Servings: 8

Ingredients:

- 1/3 cup soy sauce
- 2 tablespoons sugar
- 1 tablespoon honey
- 2-pound pork shoulder, cut into 1½-inch thick slices

Directions:

- In a bowl, mix together all ingredients except pork.
- Add pork and coat with marinade generously.

- Cover and refrigerate o marinate for about 2-8 hours.
- Preheat the air fryer oven to 335 degrees F.
- Place the pork in an Air fryer basket.
- Cook for about 10 minutes.
- Now, set the air fryer oven to 390 degrees F. Cook for about 10 minutes

412. Curry Pork Roast in Coconut Sauce

Preparation Time: 10 minutes
Cooking Time: 60 minutes
Servings: 6

Ingredients:

- ½ teaspoon curry powder
- ½ teaspoon ground turmeric powder
- 1 can unsweetened coconut milk
- 1 tablespoons sugar
- 2 tablespoons fish sauce
- 2 tablespoons soy sauce
- 3 pounds pork shoulder
- Salt and pepper to taste

Directions:

- Place all Ingredients in bowl and allow the meat to marinate in the fridge for at least 2 hours.
- Preheat the air fryer to 390°F.
- Place the grill pan accessory in the air fryer.
- Grill the meat for 20 minutes making sure to flip the pork every 10 minutes for even grilling and cook in batches.
- Meanwhile, pour the marinade in a saucepan and allow to simmer for 10 minutes until the sauce thickens.
- Baste the pork with the sauce before serving.

413. Chinese Salt and Pepper Pork Chop Stir-fry

Preparation Time: 10 minutes
Cooking Time: 15 minutes
Servings: 4

Ingredients:

Pork Chops:

- Olive oil
- ¾ C. almond flour
- ¼ tsp. pepper
- ½ tsp. salt
- 1 egg white
- Pork Chops

Stir-fry:

- ¼ tsp. pepper
- 1 tsp. sea salt
- 2 tbsp. olive oil
- 2 sliced scallions
- 2 sliced jalapeno peppers

Directions:

- Coat the air fryer oven basket with olive oil.
- Whisk pepper, salt, and egg white together till foamy.
- Cut pork chops into pieces, leaving just a bit on bones. Pat dry.
- Add pieces of pork to egg white mixture, coating well. Let sit for marinade 20 minutes.
- Put marinated chops into a large bowl and add almond flour. Dredge and shake off excess and place into air fryer.
- Set temperature to 360°F, and set time to 12 minutes. Cook 12 minutes at 360 degrees.
- Turn up the heat to 400 degrees and cook another 6 minutes till pork chops are nice and crisp.
- To make stir-fry, remove jalapeno seeds and chop up. Chop scallions and mix with jalapeno pieces.
- Heat a skillet with olive oil. Stir-fry pepper, salt, scallions, and jalapenos 60 seconds. Then add fried pork pieces to skills and toss with scallion mixture. Stir-fry 1-2 minutes till well coated and hot.

414. Baked Sweet & Tangy Pork Chops

Preparation Time: 25 minutes
Cooking Time: 35 Minutes
Servings: 2

Ingredients:

- 2 pork chops
- 2 tbsp brown sugar
- 2 tbsp ketchup
- 2 onion sliced
- Pepper
- Salt

Directions:

- Fit the Air fryer oven with the rack in position
- Season pork chops with pepper and salt.
- Place pork chops in a baking dish.
- Mix ketchup and brown sugar and pour over pork chops.
- Top with onion slices.
- Set to bake at 375 F for 40 minutes. After 5 minutes place the baking dish in the preheated oven.
- Serve and enjoy.

415.   Cajun Burger Patties

Preparation Time: 18 minutes
Cooking Time: 10 Minutes
Servings: 2

Ingredients:

- 1 egg, lightly beaten
- 1/2 lb ground pork
- 1/2 cup breadcrumbs
- 1 tbsp Cajun seasoning
- Pepper
- Salt

Directions:

- Fit the Air fryer oven with the rack in position 2.
- Line the air fryer basket with parchment paper.
- Add all ingredients into the large bowl and mix until well combined.
- Make two equal shapes of patties from meat mixture and place in the air fryer basket then place an air fryer basket in the baking pan.

- Place a baking pan on the oven rack. Set to air fry at 360 F for 10 minutes.
- Serve and enjoy.

416.   Minty Chicken-fried Pork Chops

Preparation Time: 15 minutes
Cooking Time: 30 Minutes
Servings: 6

Ingredients:

- 4 medium-sized pork chops, approximately 3.5 ounces each
- 1 cup of breadcrumbs (Panko brand works well)
- 2 medium-sized eggs
- Pinch of salt and pepper
- ½ tablespoon of mint, either dried and ground; or fresh, rinsed and finely chopped

Directions:

- Preparing the Ingredients. Cover the basket of the Instant Vortex air fryer oven with a lining of tin foil, leaving the edges uncovered to allow air to circulate through the basket. Preheat the Instant Vortex air fryer oven to 350 degrees.
- In a mixing bowl, beat the eggs until fluffy and until the yolks and whites are fully combined, and set aside.
- In a separate mixing bowl, combine the breadcrumbs, mint, salt, and pepper, and set aside. One by one, dip each raw pork chop into the bowl with dry ingredients, coating all sides; then submerge into the bowl with wet ingredients, then dip again into the dry ingredients. This double coating will ensure an extra crisp air-fry. Lay the coated pork chops on the foil covering the Oven rack/basket, in a single flat layer. Place the Rack on the middle-shelf of the Instant Vortex air fryer oven.
- Air Frying. Set the Instant Vortex air fryer oven timer for 15 minutes. After 15 minutes, the Instant Vortex air fryer oven will turn off, and the pork should be mid-way cooked and the breaded coating starting to brown. Using tongs, turn each piece of steak over to ensure

a full all-over fry. Reset the air fryer oven to 320 degrees for 15 minutes.

- After 15 minutes, when the air fryer shuts off, remove the fried pork chops using tongs and set on a serving plate. Eat as soon as cool enough to handle – and enjoy!

417.   Teriyaki Pork Ribs With Tomato Sauce

Preparation Time: 15 minutes
Cooking Time: 20 Minutes + Marinating Time
Servings: 3

Ingredients:

- 1-pound pork ribs
- Salt and black pepper to taste
- 1 tbsp sugar
- 1 tsp ginger juice
- 1 tsp five-spice powder
- 1 tbsp teriyaki sauce
- 1 tbsp soy sauce
- 1 garlic clove, minced
- 2 tbsp honey
- 1 tbsp tomato sauce
- 1 tbsp olive oil

Directions:

- In a bowl, mix pepper, sugar, five-spice powder, salt, ginger juice, and teriyaki sauce. Add pork ribs to the marinade and let sit for 2 hours.

- Add ribs to the greased basket and fit in the baking tray; cook for 8 minutes on Air Fry function at 350 F. In a separate bowl, mix soy sauce, garlic, honey, 1 tbsp of water, and tomato sauce.

- In a pan over medium heat, heat olive oil and fry garlic for 30 seconds. Add fried pork ribs and pour in the sauce. Stir-fry for a few minutes and serve.

418.   Meat and Rice Stuffed Bell Peppers

Preparation Time: 20 minutes
Cooking Time: 18 minutes
Servings: 4

Ingredients:

- ¾ pound (340 g) lean ground beef
- 4 ounces (113 g) lean ground pork
- ¼ cup onion, minced
- 1 (15-ounce / 425-g) can crushed tomatoes
- 1 teaspoon Worcestershire sauce
- 1 teaspoon barbecue seasoning
- 1 teaspoon honey
- ½ teaspoon dried basil
- ½ cup cooked brown rice
- ½ teaspoon garlic powder
- ½ teaspoon oregano
- ½ teaspoon salt
- 2 small bell peppers, cut in half, stems removed, deseeded
- Cooking spray

Directions:

- Spritz a baking pan with cooking spray.

- Arrange the beef, pork, and onion in the baking pan.

- Select Bake of the oven. Set temperature to 360°F (182°C) and set time to 8 minutes. Press Start to begin preheating.

- Once preheated, place the pan into the oven. Break the ground meat into chunks halfway through the cooking.

- When cooking is complete, the ground meat should be lightly browned.

- Meanwhile, combine the tomatoes, Worcestershire sauce, barbecue seasoning, honey, and basil in a saucepan. Stir to mix well.

- Transfer the cooked meat mixture to a large bowl and add the cooked rice, garlic powder, oregano, salt, and ¼ cup of the tomato mixture. Stir to mix well.

- Stuff the pepper halves with the mixture, then arrange the pepper halves in the perforated pan.

- Select Air Fry of the oven. Set time to 10 minutes. Place the pan into the oven.

- When cooking is complete, the peppers should be lightly charred.

- Serve the stuffed peppers with the remaining tomato sauce on top.

419. Sumptuous Beef and Pork Sausage Meatloaf

Preparation Time: 10 minutes
Cooking Time: 25 minutes
Servings: 4

Ingredients:

- ¾ pound (340 g) ground chuck
- 4 ounces (113 g) ground pork sausage
- 2 eggs, beaten
- 1 cup Parmesan cheese, grated
- 1 cup chopped shallot
- 3 tablespoons plain milk
- 1 tablespoon oyster sauce
- 1 tablespoon fresh parsley
- 1 teaspoon garlic paste
- 1 teaspoon chopped porcini mushrooms
- ½ teaspoon cumin powder
- Seasoned salt and crushed red pepper flakes, to taste

Directions:

- In a large bowl, combine all the ingredients until well blended.
- Place the meat mixture in the baking pan. Use a spatula to press the mixture to fill the pan.
- Select Bake of the oven. Set temperature to 360°F (182°C) and set time to 25 minutes. Press Start to begin preheating.
- Once preheated, place the pan into the oven.
- When cooking is complete, the meatloaf should be well browned.
- Let the meatloaf rest for 5 minutes. Transfer to a serving dish and slice. Serve warm.

420. Apple-Glazed Pork

Preparation Time: 15 minutes
Cooking Time: 19 minutes
Servings: 4

Ingredients:

- 1 sliced apple

- 1 small onion, sliced
- 2 tablespoons apple cider vinegar, divided
- ½ teaspoon thyme
- ½ teaspoon rosemary
- ¼ teaspoon brown sugar
- 3 tablespoons olive oil, divided
- ¼ teaspoon smoked paprika
- 4 pork chops
- Salt and ground black pepper, to taste

Directions:

- Combine the apple slices, onion, 1 tablespoon of vinegar, thyme, rosemary, brown sugar, and 2 tablespoons of olive oil in a baking pan. Stir to mix well.
- Select Bake of the oven. Set temperature to 350°F (180°C) and set time to 4 minutes. Press Start to begin preheating.
- Once preheated, place the pan into the oven. Stir the mixture halfway through.
- Meanwhile, combine the remaining vinegar and olive oil, and paprika in a large bowl. Sprinkle with salt and ground black pepper. Stir to mix well. Dredge the pork in the mixture and toss to coat well.
- Place the pork in the perforated pan.
- When cooking is complete, remove the baking pan from the oven and place in the perforated pan.
- Select Air Fry of the oven and set time to 10 minutes. Flip the pork chops halfway through.
- When cooking is complete, the pork should be lightly browned.
- Remove the pork from the oven and baste with baked apple mixture on both sides. Put the pork back to the oven and air fry for an additional 5 minutes. Flip halfway through.
- Serve immediately.

421. Citrus Carnitas

Preparation Time: 1 hour 10 minutes
Cooking Time: 25 minutes
Servings: 6

Ingredients:

- 2½ pounds (1.1 kg) boneless country-style pork ribs, cut into 2-inch pieces
- 3 tablespoons olive brine
- 1 tablespoon minced fresh oregano leaves
- 1/3 cup orange juice
- 1 teaspoon ground cumin
- 1 tablespoon minced garlic
- 1 teaspoon salt
- 1 teaspoon ground black pepper
- Cooking spray

Directions:

- Combine all the ingredients in a large bowl. Toss to coat the pork ribs well. Wrap the bowl in plastic and refrigerate for at least an hour to marinate.
- Spritz a perforated pan with cooking spray.
- Arrange the marinated pork ribs in the pan and spritz with cooking spray.
- Select Air Fry of the oven. Set temperature to 400°F (205°C) and set time to 25 minutes. Press Start to begin preheating.
- Once preheated, place the pan into the oven. Flip the ribs halfway through.
- When cooking is complete, the ribs should be well browned.
- Serve immediately.

422.   Easy Ranch Pork Chops

Preparation Time: 10 minutes
Cooking Time: 32 minutes
Servings: 6

Ingredients:

- 6 pork chops, boneless
- 2 tbsp olive oil
- 1 oz ranch seasoning

Directions:

- Fit the Air fryer oven with the rack in position
- Brush pork chops with oil and rub with ranch seasoning.
- Place pork chops in a baking pan.

- Set to bake at 400 F for 40 minutes. After 5 minutes place the baking pan in the preheated oven.
- Serve and enjoy.

423.   Easy Lamb Chops with Asparagus

Preparation Time: 5 minutes
Cooking Time: 17 minutes
Servings: 4

Ingredients:

- 4 asparagus spears, trimmed
- 2 tablespoons olive oil, divided
- 1-pound (454 g) lamb chops
- 1 garlic clove, minced
- 2 teaspoons chopped fresh thyme, for serving
- Salt and ground black pepper, to taste

Directions:

- Spritz the air fryer basket with cooking spray.
- On a large plate, brush the asparagus with 1 tablespoon olive oil, then sprinkle with salt. Set aside.
- On a separate plate, brush the lamb chops with remaining olive oil and sprinkle with salt and ground black pepper.
- Arrange the lamb chops in the pan.
- Put the air fryer basket on the baking pan and slide into Rack Position 2, select Air Fry, set temperature to 400°F (205°C) and set time to 15 minutes.
- Flip the lamb chops and add the asparagus and garlic halfway through.
- When cooking is complete, the lamb should be well browned and the asparagus should be tender.
- Serve them on a plate with thyme on top.

424.   Beef Steak Momo's Recipe

Preparation Time: 15 minutes
Cooking Time: 12 minutes
Servings: 3

Ingredients:

- 2 tsp. ginger-garlic paste
- 2 tsp. soya sauce
- 1 ½ cup all-purpose flour
- ½ tsp. salt
- 5 tbsp. water
- For filling:
- 2 cups minced beef steak
- 2 tbsp. oil
- 2 tsp. vinegar

Directions:

- Squeeze the dough and cover it with plastic wrap and set aside. Next, cook the ingredients for the filling and try to ensure that the beef is covered well with the sauce. Roll the dough and cut it into a square. Place the filling in the center.

- Now, wrap the dough to cover the filling and pinch the edges together. Pre heat the Air fryer oven at 200° F for 5 minutes. Place the wontons in the fry basket and close it. Let them cook at the same temperature for another 20 minutes. Recommended sides are chili sauce or ketchup.

425. Bacon-Wrapped Sausage with Tomato Relish

Preparation Time: 15 minutes
Cooking Time: 32 minutes
Servings: 4

Ingredients:

- 8 pork sausages
- 8 bacon strips
- Relish:
- 8 large tomatoes, chopped
- 1 small onion, peeled
- 1 clove garlic, peeled
- 1 tablespoon white wine vinegar
- 3 tablespoons chopped parsley
- 1 teaspoon smoked paprika
- 2 tablespoons sugar

- Salt and ground black pepper, to taste

Directions:

- Purée the tomatoes, onion, and garlic in a food processor until well mixed and smooth.

- Pour the purée in a saucepan and drizzle with white wine vinegar. Sprinkle with salt and ground black pepper. Simmer over medium heat for 10 minutes.

- Add the parsley, paprika, and sugar to the saucepan and cook for 10 more minutes or until it has a thick consistency. Keep stirring during the cooking. Refrigerate for an hour to chill.

- Wrap the sausage with bacon strips and secure with toothpicks, then place them in the basket.

- Put the air fryer basket on the baking pan and slide into Rack Position 2, select Air Fry, set temperature to 350°F (180°C) and set time to 12 minutes.

- Flip the bacon-wrapped sausage halfway through.

- When cooking is complete, the bacon should be crispy and browned.

- Transfer the bacon-wrapped sausage on a plate and baste with the relish or just serve with the relish alongside.

426. Juicy Pork Ribs Ole

Preparation Time: 9 minutes
Cooking Time: 26 minutes
Servings: 4

Ingredients:

- 1 rack of pork ribs
- 1/2 cup low-fat milk
- 1 tablespoon envelope taco seasoning mix
- 1 can tomato sauce
- 1/2 teaspoon ground black pepper
- 1 teaspoon seasoned salt
- 1 tablespoon cornstarch
- 1 teaspoon canola oil

Directions:

- Preparing the ingredients. Place all ingredients in a mixing dish; let them marinate for 1 hour.
- Air Frying. Cook the marinated ribs approximately 25 minutes at 390 degrees F
- Work with batches. Enjoy.

427. Spicy Meatballs

Preparation Time: 8 minutes
Cooking Time: 31 minutes
Servings: 4

Ingredients:

- 1 lb. ground beef
- 4 oz cream cheese
- 1 tsp dried basil
- 2 tbsp Worcestershire sauce
- 1/3 cup milk
- 1/2 cup cheddar cheese, shredded
- 3/4 cup breadcrumbs
- 2 jalapenos, minced
- 1/2 onion, minced
- 1 tsp salt

Directions:

- Fit the Air fryer oven with the rack in position
- Add all ingredients into the mixing bowl and mix until well combined.
- Make small balls from the meat mixture and place it into the parchment-lined baking pan.
- Set to bake at 400 F for 35 minutes. After 5 minutes place the baking pan in the preheated oven.
- Serve and enjoy.

428. Barbecue Pork Club Sandwich with Mustard

Preparation Time: 15 minutes
Cooking Time: 12 minutes
Servings: 3

Ingredients:

- 2 slices of white bread

- 1 tbsp. softened butter
- ½ lb. cut pork (Get the meat cut into cubes)
- 1 small capsicum
- ¼ tbsp. red chili sauce
- 1 tbsp. tomato ketchup
- ½ cup water.
- ¼ tbsp. Worcestershire sauce
- ½ tsp. olive oil
- ½ flake garlic crushed
- ¼ cup chopped onion
- ¼ tsp. mustard powder
- ½ tbsp. sugar
- A pinch of salt and black pepper to taste

Directions:

- Take the slices of bread and remove the edges. Now cut the slices horizontally. Cook the ingredients for the sauce and wait till it thickens. Now, add the pork to the sauce and stir till it obtains the flavors. Roast the capsicum and peel the skin off. Cut the capsicum into slices.
- Mix the ingredients together and apply it to the bread slices.
- Pre-heat the Air fryer oven for 5 minutes at 300 Fahrenheit. Open the basket of the Fryer and place the prepared Classic Sandwiches in it such that no two Classic Sandwiches are touching each other. Now keep the fryer at 250 degrees for around 15 minutes.
- Turn the Classic Sandwiches in between the cooking process to cook both slices. Serve the Classic Sandwiches with tomato ketchup or mint sauce.

429. Festive Stuffed Pork Chops

Preparation Time: 15 minutes
Cooking Time: 41 minutes
Servings: 4

Ingredients:

- 4 pork chops
- Salt and black pepper to taste
- 4 cups stuffing mix

- 2 tbsp olive oil
- 4 garlic cloves, minced
- 2 tbsp fresh sage leaves, chopped

Directions:

- Cut a hole in pork chops and fill chops with stuffing mix. In a bowl, mix sage, garlic, oil, salt, and pepper. Rub the chops with the marinade and let sit for 10 minutes.

- Preheat Instant Vortex on Bake function to 380 F. Put the chops in a baking tray and place in the oven. Press Start and cook for 25 minutes. Serve and enjoy!

430. Meat Lovers' Pizza

Preparation Time: 10 minutes
Cooking Time: 12 minutes
Servings: 2

Ingredients:

- 1 pre-prepared 7-inch pizza pie crust, defrosted if necessary.

- 1/3 cup of marinara sauce.

- 2 ounces of grilled steak, sliced into bite-sized pieces

- 2 ounces of salami, sliced fine

- 2 ounces of pepperoni, sliced fine

- ¼ cup of American cheese

- ¼ cup of shredded mozzarella cheese

Directions:

- Preparing the ingredients. Preheat the Instant Vortex air fryer oven to 350 degrees. Lay the pizza dough flat on a sheet of parchment paper or tin foil, cut large enough to hold the entire pie crust, but small enough that it will leave the edges of the air frying rack/basket uncovered to allow for air circulation.

- Using a fork, stab the pizza dough several times across the surface – piercing the pie crust will allow air to circulate throughout the crust and ensure even cooking. With a deep soup spoon, ladle the marinara sauce onto the pizza dough, and spread evenly in expanding circles over the surface of the pie-crust. Be sure to leave at least ½ inch of bare

dough around the edges, to ensure that extra-crispy crunchy first bite of the crust!

- Distribute the pieces of steak and the slices of salami and pepperoni evenly over the sauce-covered dough, then sprinkle the cheese in an even layer on top.

- Air Frying. Set the Instant Vortex air fryer oven timer to 12 minutes, and place the pizza with foil or paper on the fryer's basket surface. Again, be sure to leave the edges of the basket uncovered to allow for proper air circulation, and don't let your bare fingers touch the hot surface.

- After 12 minutes, when the Instant Vortex air fryer oven shuts off, the cheese should be perfectly melted and lightly crisped, and the pie crust should be golden brown.

- Using a spatula – or two, if necessary, remove the pizza from the Oven rack/basket and set on a serving plate. Wait a few minutes until the pie is cool enough to handle, then cut into slices and serve.

431. Smoked Ham with Sweet Glaze

Preparation Time: 15 minutes
Cooking Time: 31 minutes
Servings: 4

Ingredients:

- 2 pears, chopped
- 1 lb. smoked ham
- 1 ½ cups brown sugar
- ¾ tbsp allspice
- 1 tbsp balsamic vinegar
- 1 tsp black pepper

Directions:

- Preheat Air fryer oven to 330 F on Air Fry function. Place pears, brown sugar, balsamic vinegar, allspices, and pepper in a small pot over medium heat. Stir and bring to a boil then reduce the heat to low. Simmer for 8-10 minutes until the glaze is thickened.

- Place the ham in a greased baking dish. With a knife, score only the fatty surface of the ham in a diamond pattern. Pour the pear mixture over the ham and cook for 20-25 minutes until golden and glazed. Let sit for a few minutes before slicing and serving.

432. Pork Neck with Salad

Preparation Time: 11 minutes
Cooking Time: 12 minutes
Servings: 2

Ingredients:

For Pork:

- 1 tablespoon soy sauce
- 1 tablespoon fish sauce
- ½ tablespoon oyster sauce
- ½ pound pork neck

For Salad:

- 1 ripe tomato, sliced tickly
- 8-10 Thai shallots, sliced
- 1 scallion, chopped
- 1 bunch fresh basil leaves
- 1 bunch fresh cilantro leaves

For Dressing:

- 3 tablespoons fish sauce
- 2 tablespoons olive oil
- 1 teaspoon apple cider vinegar
- 1 tablespoon palm sugar
- 2 bird eye chilies
- 1 tablespoon garlic, minced

Directions:

- Preparing the ingredients. For pork in a bowl, mix together all ingredients except pork.
- Add pork neck and coat with marinade evenly. Refrigerate for about 2-3 hours.
- Preheat the Instant Vortex air fryer oven to 340 degrees F.
- Air Frying. Place the pork neck onto a grill pan. Cook for about 12 minutes.
- Meanwhile, in a large salad bowl, mix together all salad ingredients.
- In a bowl, add all dressing ingredients and beat till well combined.

- Remove pork neck from Air fryer oven and cut into desired slices.
- Place pork slices over salad.

433. Beef Steak Oregano Fingers

Preparation Time: 15 minutes
Cooking Time: 12 minutes
Servings: 3

Ingredients:

- 1 lb. boneless beef steak cut into Oregano Fingers
- 2 cup dry breadcrumbs
- 4 tbsp. lemon juice
- 2 tsp. salt
- 1 tsp. pepper powder
- 1 tsp. red chili powder
- 6 tbsp. corn flour
- 4 eggs
- 2 tsp. oregano
- 2 tsp. red chili flakes
- 1 ½ tbsp. ginger-garlic paste

Directions:

- Mix all the ingredients for the marinade and put the beef Oregano Fingers inside and let it rest overnight. Mix the breadcrumbs, oregano and red chili flakes well and place the marinated Oregano Fingers on this mixture.
- Cover it with plastic wrap and leave it till right before you serve to cook. Pre heat the Air fryer oven at 160 degrees Fahrenheit for 5 minutes. Place the Oregano Fingers in the fry basket and close it. Let them cook at the same temperature for another 15 minutes or so. Toss the Oregano Fingers well so that they are cooked uniformly.

434. Lamb Marinade Cutlet with Capsicum

Preparation Time: 15 minutes
Cooking Time: 12 minutes
Servings: 3

Ingredients:

- 2 cups sliced lamb
- 1 big capsicum (Cut this capsicum into big cubes)
- 2 cup fresh green coriander
- ½ cup mint leaves
- 4 tsp. fennel
- 2 tbsp. ginger-garlic paste
- 1 small onion
- 6-7 flakes garlic (optional)
- Salt to taste
- 1 onion (Cut it into quarters. Now separate the layers carefully.)
- 5 tbsp. gram flour
- A pinch of salt to taste
- 3 tbsp. lemon juice

Directions:

- You will first need to make the sauce. Add the ingredients to a blender and make a thick paste. Slit the pieces of lamb and stuff half the paste into the cavity obtained. Take the remaining paste and add it to the gram flour and salt. Toss the pieces of lamb in this mixture and set aside. Apply a little bit of the mixture on the capsicum and onion.

- Place these on a stick along with the lamb pieces. Pre heat the Air fryer oven at 290 Fahrenheit for around 5 minutes. Open the basket. Arrange the satay sticks properly. Close the basket.

- Keep the sticks with the lamb at 180 degrees for around half an hour while the sticks with the vegetables are to be kept at the same temperature for only 7 minutes.

- Turn the sticks in between so that one side does not get burnt and also to provide a uniform cook.

435. Amazing Bacon & Potato Platter

Preparation Time: 12 minutes
Cooking Time: 41 minutes
Servings: 4

Ingredients:

- 4 potatoes, halved
- 6 garlic cloves, squashed
- 4 streaky cut rashers bacon
- 1 tbsp olive oil

Directions:

- In a mixing bowl, mix garlic, bacon, potatoes, and olive oil; toss to coat. Place the mixture in the basket and fit in the baking tray; roast for 25-30 minutes at 400 F on Air Fry, shaking once.

436. Chipotle Pork Chops

Preparation Time: 15 minutes
Cooking Time: 20 minutes
Servings: 4

Ingredients:

- 4 pork chops
- 1 lime, juiced
- Salt and black pepper to taste
- 1 tsp garlic powder
- 2 cups white rice, cooked
- 1 can (14.5 oz) tomato sauce
- 1 onion, chopped
- 3 garlic cloves, minced
- ½ tsp dried oregano
- 1 tsp chipotle chili powder

Directions:

- Season pork chops with salt, pepper, and garlic powder. In a bowl, mix onion, garlic, chipotle powder, oregano, and tomato sauce. Toss in the pork to coat. Let marinate for 1 hour.

- Remove the chops from the mixture and place them in a greased baking dish. Select Bake function, adjust the temperature to 380 F, and press Start. Cook for 25 minutes. Serve with rice.

437. Morning Ham & Cheese Sandwich

Preparation Time: 5 minutes
Cooking Time: 7 minutes
Servings: 4

Ingredients:

- 8 slices whole wheat bread
- 4 slices lean pork ham
- 4 slices cheese
- 8 slices tomato

Directions:

- Lay four slices of bread on a flat surface. Spread the slices with cheese, tomato, turkey, and ham. Cover with the remaining slices to form sandwiches. Add the sandwiches to the cooking basket and cook for 10 minutes at 360 F on Air Fry function. Serve.

438. Air-Fried Ravioli

Preparation Time: 15 minutes
Cooking Time: 15 minutes
Servings: 6

Ingredients:

- seasoned breadcrumbs (1 cup)
- shredded parmesan cheese (.25 cup)
- dried basil (2 tsp.)
- AP flour (.5 cup)
- eggs - lightly beaten (2 large)
- frozen beef ravioli - thawed (9 oz. pkg.)
- cooking spray (as needed)
- warmed marinara sauce (1 cup)

Directions:

- Preheat the air fryer unit to 350° F/177° C.
- In a shallow bowl, mix the breadcrumbs with the parmesan cheese, and basil.
- Measure and add flour and whisked eggs into individual shallow bowls.
- Pat the ravioli in flour to cover both sides, shaking off the excess.
- Dip them into the eggs, then in the crumb mixture, pushing it in slightly to help the coating stick during the cooking cycle.
- Prepare them in batches. Arrange the ravioli on a greased tray (not bunched) in the basket of the air fryer. Lightly spray them using a

baking oil spray. Air fry the ravioli until golden brown (3-4 min.).

- Flip them around and spritz with a little cooking spray.
- Cook until they're nicely browned (3-4 min.). Immediately sprinkle with basil and more parmesan cheese.
- Serve warm with marinara sauce.

439. Delicious Air-Fried Roast Beef

Preparation Time: 10 minutes
Cooking Time: 12 minutes
Servings: 6

Ingredients:

- beef roast (2 lb.)
- olive oil (1 tbsp.)
- option: onion (1 medium)
- salt and pepper (1 tsp. of each)
- rosemary & thyme - fresh or dried (2 tsp. of each/as desired)

Directions:

- Set the vortex air fryer temperature at 390° F/199° C.
- Dab the beef roast dry using a few paper towels. Spritz it using a bit of oil and seasonings. Rub in the mixture.
- Place the roast on a tray and place it on the bottom rung.
- Cook for 15 minutes. Check the temperature for doneness as desired. Rare 125° F - medium 135° F - medium 145° F - medium-well 150° F or well 160° F.
- Remove the beef from the fryer and cover with a layer of foil. Wait for at least ten minutes before serving.
- Thinly carve the roast - against the grain and serve with veggies.

440. Ground Beef Wellington

Preparation Time: 15 minutes
Cooking Time: 35 minutes
Servings: 2

Ingredients:

- butter (1 tbsp.)
- fresh mushrooms (.5 cup)
- all-purpose flour (2 tsp.)
- pepper - divided (.25 tsp.)
- half-and-half cream (.5 cup)
- egg yolk (1 large)
- finely chopped onion (2 tbsp.)
- salt (.25 tsp.)
- ground beef (.5 lb.)
- refrigerated crescent rolls (4 oz. tube)
- optional for egg wash: egg - lightly beaten (1 large)
- dried parsley flakes (1 tsp.)

Directions:

- Set the air fryer unit at 300° F/149° C.
- Melt the butter in a saucepan using the med-high temperature setting.
- Chop and add the mushrooms. Air fry them stirring until tender (5-6 min.).
- Dust it with the pepper (1/8 tsp.) And flour until incorporated.
- Slowly mix in the cream. Once boiling, simmer and stir for two minutes or until thickened. Transfer the pan from the burner and place it to the side for now.
- Whisk the egg yolk and mix with the onion, two tablespoons mushroom sauce, salt, and the rest of the pepper.
- Crumble the beef over the mixture and combine. Shape into two loaves.
- Unroll the package of dough and break it into two rectangles. Press its perforations to seal.
- Arrange the meatloaf on each rectangle. Close the edges with a pinch to seal. Brush with a beaten egg.
- Arrange the wellingtons (not touching) on a greased tray in the basket of the air fryer. Cook until golden brown, and a thermometer inserted into the loaf reads 160° F/71° C (18-22 min.).
- In the meantime, warm the rest of the sauce using the low-temperature setting, and mix in

the parsley. Serve the delicious sauce with wellingtons.

441. Mini Chimichangas

Preparation Time: 10 minutes
Cooking Time: 60 minutes
Servings: 14

Ingredients:

- ground beef (1 lb.)
- onion (1 medium)
- taco seasoning (1 envelope)
- water (.75 cup)
- Monterey jack cheese - shredded (3 cups)
- sour cream (1 cup)
- green chiles (4 oz. can)
- egg roll wrappers (14)
- large egg white (1)
- cooking spray (as needed)
- salsa - to serve

Directions:

- Warm the air fryer unit at 375° F/191° C.
- Chop the onion. Drain and chop the chiles.
- Cook the beef and onions using the medium-temperature setting until the meat is done (pink is gone) and drain.
- Mix in the water and taco seasoning. Wait for the mixture to boil. Lower the setting and simmer with the lid off the pan for five minutes, occasionally stirring. Transfer the pan from the burner and cool it slightly.
- Toss the cheese with the chiles and sour cream. Fold in the beef mixture.
- Put an egg roll wrapper on a cutting board with one point facing you. Place some of the filling (1/3 cup) in the center. Fold the bottom one-third of the wrapper over the filling and tuck in the sides.
- Brush the top point with egg white and roll it up to close.
- Continue the process with the rest of the wrappers and filling.

- Using batches, arrange the chimichangas on a greased tray in the fryer basket (single-layered) with a spritz of baking oil spray.

- Air fry the chimichangas until golden brown (3-4 min. Per side). Serve warm with salsa and additional sour cream.

442. Steak Fajita

Preparation Time: 15 minutes
Cooking Time: 20 minutes
Servings: 6

Ingredients:

- tomatoes (2 large)
- red onion (.5 cup)
- lime juice (.25 cup)
- jalapeno pepper, seeded and minced
- fresh cilantro (3 tbsp.)
- ground cumin - divided (2 tsp.)
- salt - divided (.75 tsp.)
- beef flank steak (1 @ about 1.5 lb.)
- onion (1 large)
- whole-wheat tortillas (6 @ 8-inches each) warmed

Directions:

- Set the air fryer unit to reach 400° F/204° C.

- Dice the red onion. Remove the seeds and chop the tomatoes. Slice the whole onion in half to slice. Remove the seeds and mince the jalapeno and cilantro.

- For the salsa, place the first five fixings in a mixing container and stir in one teaspoon cumin and ¼ of a teaspoon of salt. Let stand until serving time.

- Sprinkle the steak with the rest of the salt and cumin. Place it on a greased tray in the fryer basket. Air fry until the beef reaches the desired doneness. Check it at the thickest part using a thermometer; (for medium-rare, should read 135° F; medium, 140° F; medium-well, 145° F). It should take about six to eight minutes per side. Transfer it from the basket and let them stand for five minutes.

- In the meantime, place onion on the tray in the fryer basket. Cook until tender and crispy (2-3 min.), stirring once. Thinly slice the steak across the grain and serve in tortillas with onion and salsa.

- Serve with avocado and lime wedges.

443. Taquitos

Preparation Time: 15 minutes
Cooking Time: 21 minutes
Servings: 10

Ingredients:

- eggs (2 large)
- dry breadcrumbs (.5 cup)
- taco seasoning (3 tbsp.)
- ground beef - 90% lean (1 lb.)
- corn tortillas (10 @ 6 inches - warmed)
- cooking spray (as needed)
- optional: salsa & guacamole

Directions:

- Warm the air fryer unit to reach 350° F/177° C.

- Combine the eggs with the breadcrumbs and taco seasoning. Fold in the beef and mix it lightly - but thoroughly.

- Spoon 1/4 cup of the beef mixture down the middle of each tortilla.

- Tightly roll and secure with toothpicks.

- Air fry them in batches. Arrange the taquitos on a greased tray in the fryer basket (single-layered) with a spritz of cooking oil spray.

- Fry them for six minutes. Flip them over and continue to cook until they're golden brown and crispy (6-7 min.). Discard toothpicks before serving. If desired, serve with salsa and guacamole.

444. Vortex Cheeseburger Sliders

Preparation Time: 15 minutes
Cooking Time: 11 minutes
Servings: 4

Ingredients:

- ground beef/pork/turkey or a mixture (1 lb.)
- Hawaiian rolls (1 pkg.)
- onion (half of 1)
- garlic powder (1 tsp.)
- ranch dressing powder (1 pouch/as desired)
- Worcestershire sauce (1 tbsp.)
- pepper & salt (as desired)

Directions:

- Preheat the vortex air fryer to reach 400° F/204° C.
- Finely chop the onion. Combine all of the fixings in a mixing container.
- Grab a chunk of meat (golf ball-sized) and roll it into a ball. Once done, flatten them.
- Arrange them in the air fryer. Flip them after four minutes (total of 8 - 15 minutes depending on you want them cooked**).
- Cover with cheese and toast for another minute.
- Cover the buns with butter and toast (2-3 min.) Assemble the burgers and serve.

445. Pork Chops

Preparation Time: 15 minutes
Cooking Time: 10 minutes
Servings: 4

Ingredients:

- boneless pork loin chops (4 @ 6 oz. each)
- parmesan cheese - grated (.25 cup)
- almond flour (.33 cup)
- paprika (1 tsp.)
- garlic powder (1 tsp.)
- creole seasoning (1 tsp.)

Directions:

- Preheat the air fryer unit to reach 375° F/191° C.
- Spritz the fryer basket using a cooking spray.
- Use a shallow container and add the almond flour with the cheese, garlic powder, creole seasoning, and paprika.

- Coat chops with the flour mixture, and shake off the excess.
- Prepare them in batches as needed. Place the chops (not stacked) in the air fryer basket with a spritz of cooking oil spray.
- Air fry until it's browned as desired (12-15 min.) Or until a thermometer reads 145° F/63° C. Turn about halfway through the cooking cycle and spritz with additional cooking spray.
- Remove and keep warm. Repeat with the remaining chops and serve.

446. Sweet Bacon Wrapped Pork Tenderloin - Keto-Friendly

Preparation Time: 15 minutes
Cooking Time: 10 minutes
Servings: 4

Ingredients:

- bacon (5 slices/10 oz.)
- pork tenderloin (1 lb.)
- Dijon/honey mustard (3 tbsp.)
- brown sugar (.25 cup)
- salt (.5 tsp.)
- black pepper (.25 tsp.)

Direction:

- Warm the air fryer to 400° F/204° C using the air fry function.
- Cook the bacon in long strips for a few minutes until they are halfway cooked.
- Leave the air fryer preheating (300° F/149° C) using the bake function.
- Dry the meat using several paper towels.
- Whisk the sugar with the pepper, salt, and mustard. Continue stirring until the sugar liquefies into the mustard.
- Prepare the pork loin with a drizzle of sauce over the pork. Don't touch the spoon on the pork. Wrap the bacon around the tenderloin.
- Bake for ten minutes on the lowest rack setting. Check the internal temp - add a few more minutes if it has not reached 145° F/63° C.

- If the bacon isn't as crispy as you would like it - move to the top rack to finish cooking (1-2 min.).
- Serve with your favorite sides.

447. Sweet & Sour Pork

Preparation Time: 15 minutes
Cooking Time: 25 minutes
Servings: 2

Ingredients:

- unsweetened crushed pineapple, undrained (.5 cup)
- Dijon mustard (1.5 tsp.)
- cider vinegar (.5 cup)
- sugar (.25 cup)
- dark brown sugar - tightly packed (.25 cup)
- ketchup (.25 cup)
- soy sauce - low-sodium (1 tbsp.)
- garlic powder (.5 tsp.)
- pork tenderloin (.75 lb.)
- salt & pepper (.125 tsp.)

Directions:

- Combine the first eight ingredients up to the line (**).
- Once it's all boiling, lower the temperature setting and simmer with the lid off until thickened (6-8 min.), stirring occasionally.
- Warm the air fryer to reach 350° F/177° C.
- Sprinkle the pork using salt and pepper. Slice it in half.
- Arrange the pork on a greased tray in the fryer basket with a spritz of baking oil spray.
- Air fry until the pork begins to brown around edges (7-8 min.).
- Turn it over and pour two tablespoons of the sauce over the pork.
- Continue to fry until a thermometer inserted into the pork's thickest part reaches at least 145° F/63° C (10-12 min.).
- Let pork stand for five minutes before slicing.

- Serve with the rest of the sauce and top with sliced green onions.

LAMB RECIPES

448.   Herb Encrusted Lamb Chops

Preparation Time: 5 minutes
Cooking Time: 15 minutes
Servings: 2

Ingredients:

- 1 teaspoon oregano
- 1 teaspoon coriander
- 1 teaspoon thyme
- 1 teaspoon rosemary
- ½ teaspoon salt
- ¼ teaspoon pepper
- 2 tablespoons lemon juice
- 2 tablespoons olive oil
- 1-pound lamb chops

Directions:

- In a closeable bag, combine the oregano, coriander, thyme, rosemary, salt, pepper, lemon juice, and olive oil and shake well so it mixes.
- Place the chops in the bag and squish around so the mixture is on them. Refrigerate 1 hour.
- Preheat the air fryer to 390 degrees F for 5 minutes.
- Place the chops in the basket that has been sprayed with cooking spray.
- Cook for 3 minutes and pause. Flip the chops to the other side and cook for another 4 minutes for medium rare. If you want them more well done, cook 4 minutes, pause, turn and cook 5 more minutes.

449.   Herbed Rack of Lamb

Preparation Time: 15 minutes
Cooking Time: 35 minutes
Servings: 2

Ingredients:

- 1 tablespoon olive oil
- 1 clove garlic, peeled and minced

- 1 ½ teaspoons fresh ground pepper
- 1 tablespoon fresh rosemary, chopped
- 1 tablespoon fresh thyme, chopped
- ¾ cup breadcrumbs
- 1 egg
- 1 to 2 pounds rack of lamb

Directions:

- Place the olive oil in a small dish and add the garlic. Mix well.
- Brush the garlic on the rack of lamb and season with pepper.
- In one bowl combine the rosemary, thyme, and breadcrumbs and break the egg and whisk in another bowl.
- Preheat air fryer 350 degrees F for 5 minutes. Spray with cooking spray.
- Dip the rack in the egg and then place in the breadcrumb mixture and coat the rack.
- Place rack in the air fryer basket and cook 20 minutes.
- Raise the temperature to 400 degrees F and set for 5 more minutes.
- Tear a piece of aluminum foil that will fit to wrap the rack. Take it out of the basket with tongs and put it in the middle of the foil. Carefully wrap and let sit about 10 minutes. Unwrap and serve.

450.   Lemon and Cumin Coated Rack of Lamb

Preparation Time: 15 minutes
Cooking Time: 200 minutes
Servings: 4

Ingredients:

- 1 ½ to 1 ¾ pound Frenched rack of lamb
- Salt and pepper to taste
- ½ cup breadcrumbs
- 1 teaspoon cumin seed
- 1 teaspoon ground cumin
- ½ teaspoon salt
- 1 teaspoon garlic, peeled and grated
- Lemon zest (1/4 of a lemon)
- 1 teaspoon vegetable or olive oil

- 1 egg, beaten

Directions:

- Season the lamb rack with pepper and salt to taste and set it aside.

- In a large bowl, combine the breadcrumbs, cumin seed, ground cumin, salt, garlic, lemon zest, and oil and set aside.

- In another bowl, beat the egg.

- Preheat to air fryer to 250 degrees F for 5 minutes

- Dip the rack in the egg to coat and then into the breadcrumb mixture. Make sure it is well coated.

- Spray the basket of the air fryer using cooking spray and put the rack in. You may have to bend it a little to get it to fit.

- Set for 250 degrees and cook 25 minutes.

- Increase temperature to 400 degrees F and cook another 5 minutes. Check internal temperature to make sure it is 145 degrees for medium-rare or more.

- Remove rack when done and cover with foil for 10 minutes before separating ribs into individual servings.

451.   Macadamia Rack of Lamb

Preparation Time: 20 minutes
Cooking Time: 32 minutes
Servings: 4

Ingredients:

- 1 tablespoon olive oil
- 1 clove garlic, peeled and minced
- 1 ½ to 1 ¾ pound rack of lamb
- Salt and pepper to taste
- ¾ cup unsalted macadamia nuts
- 1 tablespoon fresh rosemary, chopped
- 1 tablespoon breadcrumbs
- 1 egg, beaten

Directions:

- Mix together the olive oil and garlic and brush it all over the rack of lamb. Season with salt and pepper.

- Preheat the air fryer 250 degrees F for 8 minutes.

- Chop the macadamia nuts as fine as possible and put them in a bowl.

- Mix in the rosemary and breadcrumbs and set it aside.

- Beat the egg in another bowl.

- Dip the rack in the egg mixture to coat completely.

- Place the rack in the breadcrumb mixture and coat well.

- Spray the basket of the air fryer using cooking spray and place the rack inside.

- Cook at 250 degrees for 25 minutes and then increase to 400 and cook another 5 to 10 minutes or until done.

- Cover with foil paper for 10 minutes, uncover and separate into chops and serve.

452.   Tandoori Lamb

Preparation Time: 10 minutes
Cooking Time: 20 minutes
Servings: 4

Ingredients:

- ½ onion, peeled and quartered
- 5 cloves garlic, peeled
- 4 slices fresh ginger, peeled
- 1 teaspoon ground fennel
- 1 teaspoon Garam Masala
- 1 teaspoon ground cinnamon
- ½ teaspoon ground cardamom
- ½ teaspoon cayenne
- 1 teaspoon salt
- 1-pound boneless lamb sirloin steaks

Directions:

- Place the onion, garlic, ginger, fennel, Garam Masala, cinnamon, cardamom, cayenne, and salt in a blender and pulse 4 to 6 times until ground.

- Place the lamb steaks in a large bowl and slash the meat so the spices will permeate into it.

- Pour the spice mix over top and rub it on both sides. Let sit room temperature 30 minutes or cover and refrigerate overnight.

- Preheat the air fryer to 350 degrees F for 10 minutes.

- Spray the basket using cooking spray and place lamb steaks in without letting them overlap much. You may have to do this in batches.

- Cook 7 minutes, turn and cook another 8 minutes.

- Test with the meat thermometer to make sure they are done. The medium-well will be 150 degrees F.

453. Asian Inspired Sichuan Lamb

Preparation Time: 5 minutes
Cooking Time: 10 minutes
Servings: 4

Ingredients:

- 1 ½ tablespoons cumin seed (do not use ground cumin)
- 1 teaspoon Sichuan peppers or ½ teaspoon cayenne
- 2 tablespoons vegetable oil
- 1 tablespoon garlic, peeled and minced
- 1 tablespoon light soy sauce
- 2 red chili peppers, seeded and chopped (use gloves)
- ¼ teaspoon granulated sugar
- ½ teaspoon salt
- 1-pound lamb shoulder, cut in ½ to 1-inch pieces
- 2 green onions, chopped
- 1 handful fresh cilantro, chopped

Directions:

- Turn on the burner to medium high on the stove and heat up a dry skillet. Pour in the cumin seed and Sichuan peppers or cayenne and toast until fragrant. Turn off the burner and set aside until they are cool. Grind them in a grinder or mortar and pestle.

- In a large bowl that will contain the marinade and the lamb, combine the vegetable oil,

garlic, soy sauce, chili peppers, granulated sugar and salt. Pour in the cumin/pepper combination and mix well.

- Using a fork, poke holes in the lamb all over the top and bottom. Place the lamb in the marinade, cover and refrigerate. You can also use a closeable plastic bag.

- Preheat the air fryer to 360 degrees for 5 minutes.

- Spray the basket with cooking spray.

- Remove the lamb pieces from the marinade with tongs or slotted spoon and place in basket of the air fryer in a single layer. You may need to do more than 1 batch.

- Cook for 10 minutes, flipping over 1 half way through. Make sure the lamb's internal temperature is 145 degrees F with a meat thermometer. Put on a serving platter and repeat with rest of the lamb.

- Sprinkle the chopped green onions and cilantro over top, stir and serve.

454. Garlic Sauced Lamb Chops

Preparation Time: 15 minutes
Cooking Time: 25 minutes
Servings: 4

Ingredients:

- 1 garlic bulb
- 1 teaspoon + 3 tablespoons olive oil
- 1 tablespoon fresh oregano, chopped fine
- ¼ teaspoon ground pepper
- ½ teaspoon sea salt
- 8 lamb chops

Directions:

- Preheat the air fryer to 400 degrees F 5 minutes and while it is preheating take excess paper from the garlic bulb.

- Coat the garlic bulb with the 1 teaspoon of olive oil and drop it in the basket that has treated with cooking spray. Roast for 12 minutes.

- Combine the 3 tablespoons of olive oil, oregano, salt and pepper and lightly coat the lamb chops on both with the resulting oil. Let them sit at room temperature for 5 minutes.

- Remove the garlic bulb from the basket and if it is cool, preheat again to 400 degrees for 3 minutes.

- Spray the air fryer basket with cooking oil and place 4 chops in cooking at 400 degrees F for 5 minutes. Place them on a platter and cover to keep them warm while you do the other chops.

- Squeeze each garlic clove between the thumb and index finger into a small bowl.

- Taste and add salt and pepper and mix. Serve along the chops like serving ketchup.

455. BBQ Lamb

Preparation Time: 2 hours
Cooking Time: 1hour 40 minutes
Servings: 8

Ingredients:

- 4 lbs. boneless leg of lamb, cut into 2-inch chunks
- 2-1/2 tbsps. herb salt
- 2 tbsps. olive oil

Directions:

- Preheat the Air fryer by selecting air fryer mode
- Adjust the temperature to 390°F, set time to 5 minutes
- Season the meat with salt and olive oil
- Arrange on the Air fryer baking tray
- Transfer to the Air fryer
- Air fry for 15 minutes, flipping halfway through
- Serve and enjoy

456. Lamb Meatballs

Preparation Time: 10 minutes
Cooking Time: 30 minutes
Servings: 12

Ingredients:

- 1 lb. ground lamb

- 1/2 cup breadcrumbs
- 1 lemon, juiced and zested
- 1/4 cup milk
- 2 egg yolks
- 1 tsp ground cumin
- 1 tsp dried oregano
- 1/2 tsp salt
- 1 tsp ground coriander
- 1/2 tsp black pepper
- 3 garlic cloves, minced
- 1/4 cup fresh parsley, chopped
- 1/2 cup crumbled feta cheese

Directions:

- Preheat the Air fryer by selecting Broil mode
- Adjust the temperature to 390°F, set time to 5 minutes
- Combine all the ingredients in a bowl
- Form into 12 balls
- Arrange on the Air fryer baking tray
- Transfer to the Air fryer
- Cook for 12 minutes
- Serve and enjoy

457. Glazed Lamb Chops

Preparation Time: 20 minutes
Cooking Time: 35 minutes
Servings: 4

Ingredients:

- 4 (4-ounce) lamb loin chops
- 1 tbsp Dijon mustard
- 1 tsp honey
- 1/2 tbsp fresh lime juice
- 1/2 tsp olive oil
- Salt and ground black pepper, as required

Directions:

- Preheat the Air fryer by selecting air fryer mode
- Adjust the temperature to 3900 F, set time to 5 minutes
- Combine all the ingredients in a bowl
- Add the pork chops and toss to coat

- Arrange on the Air fryer baking tray
- Transfer to the Air fryer
- Air fry for 15 minutes, flipping halfway through
- Serve and enjoy

458. Garlic Lamb Shank

Preparation Time: 10 minutes
Cooking Time: 40 minutes
Servings: 4

Ingredients:

- 17 oz. lamb shanks
- 2 tbsp garlic, peeled and coarsely chopped
- 1 tsp kosher salt
- 1/2 cup chicken stock
- 1 tbsp dried parsley
- 1 tsp dried rosemary
- 4 oz. chive stems, chopped
- 1 tsp butter
- 1 tsp nutmeg
- 1/2 tsp ground black pepper

Directions:

- Make the cuts in the lamb shank and fill the cuts with the chopped garlic.
- Sprinkle the lamb shank with the kosher salt, dried parsley, dried rosemary, nutmeg, and ground black pepper.
- Stir the spices on the lamb shank gently.
- Preheat the Air fryer by selecting air fry mode.
- Adjust the temperature to 380°F, set time to 5 minutes
- put the butter, chives, and chicken stock in the air fryer baking tray.
- Add the lamb shank and air fry the meat for 24 minutes.
- Serve and enjoy

459. Indian Meatball with Lamb

Preparation Time: 20 minutes
Cooking Time: 24 minutes
Servings: 8

Ingredients:

- 1 lb. ground lamb
- 1 garlic clove, minced
- 1 egg
- 1 tbsp butter
- 4 oz. chive stems, grated
- 1/4 tbsp turmeric
- 1/3 tsp cayenne pepper
- 1/4 tsp bay leaf
- 1 tsp ground coriander
- 1 tsp salt
- 1 tsp ground black pepper

Directions:

- Combine all the ingredients together in a bowl
- Preheat the Air fryer by selecting the air fry mode
- Adjust the temperature to 390°F and set time to 5 minutes
- Put the butter in the Air fryer baking tray and melt it.
- Form the meatballs
- Place them in the air fryer baking tray.
- Transfer to the Air fryer
- Cook the dish for 14 minutes.
- Stir the meatballs twice during the cooking

460. Roasted Lamb

Preparation Time: 30 minutes
Cooking Time: 1hour 13 minutes
Servings: 4

Ingredients:

- 2-1/2 pounds lamb leg roast, slits carved
- 1 tbsp olive oil
- 2 garlic cloves, sliced into smaller slithers
- 1 tbsp dried rosemary
- Cracked Himalayan rock salt and cracked peppercorns, to taste

Directions:

- Make the cuts in the lamb roast and insert them with garlic.
- Sprinkle the lamb roast with kosher salt, rosemary, and ground black pepper.
- Brush with oil.
- Preheat the Air fryer by selecting air fry mode.
- Adjust the temperature to 380°F, set time to 5 minutes
- Place the lamb roast on the Baking Pan
- Transfer to the Air fryer .
- Air fry for 1 hour 15 minutes
- Serve and enjoy

461. Lamb Gyro

Preparation Time: 30 minutes
Cooking Time: 35 minutes
Servings: 4

Ingredients:

- 1-pound ground lamb
- 1/2 onion sliced
- 1/4 cup mint, minced
- 1/4 red onion, minced
- 1/8 tsp rosemary
- 1/2 tsp salt
- 1/2 tsp black pepper
- 3/4 cup hummus
- 4 slices pita bread
- 1/2 cucumber, peeled and sliced into thin rounds
- 1 cup romaine lettuce, shredded
- 1 Roma tomato, diced
- 1/4 cup parsley, minced
- 2 cloves garlic, minced
- 12 mint leaves, minced

Directions:

- Preheat the Air fryer by selecting broil mode
- Adjust the temperature to 3700F, set time to 5 minutes
- Mix lamb with onions, mint, parsley, garlic, salt, rosemary, and pepper
- Form into patties

- Arrange in a lined Air fryer baking tray
- Transfer to the Air fryer
- Air fry for 20 minutes, flipping halfway through
- Assemble the gyro with the remaining ingredients
- Serve and enjoy

462. Lemon Lamb Rack

Preparation Time: 10 minutes
Cooking Time: 40 minutes
Servings: 4

Ingredients:

- 1/4 cup olive oil
- 3 tbsp garlic, minced
- 1/3 cup dry white wine
- 1 tbsp lemon zest, grated
- 2 tbsps. lemon juice
- 1-1/2 tsp dried oregano, crushed
- 1 tsp thyme leaves, minced
- Salt and black pepper
- 4 lamb rack
- 1 lemon, sliced

Directions:

- Whisk everything in a baking pan to coat the chicken breasts well.
- Place the lemon slices on top of the chicken breasts.
- Spread the mustard mixture over the toasted bread slices.
- Press "Power Button" of Air Fry Oven and turn the dial to select the "Bake" mode.
- Press the Time button and again turn the dial to set the cooking time to 30 minutes.
- Now push the Temp button and rotate the dial to set the temperature at 370 degrees F.
- Once preheated, place the baking pan inside and close its lid.
- Serve warm.
- Preheat the Air fryer by selecting air fryer mode

- Adjust the temperature to 3700F, set time to 5 minutes
- Whisk all the ingredients together in a bowl
- Pour into air fryer baking tray
- Add the lamb rack
- Top with lemon
- Transfer to the Air fryer
- Air fry for 30 minutes, flipping halfway through
- Serve and enjoy

463. Béchamel Baked Lamb

Preparation Time: 10 minutes
Cooking Time: 60 minutes
Servings: 8

Ingredients:

- 2 tablespoons olive oil
- 1 large onion, diced
- 2 lbs. ground lamb
- 2 teaspoons salt
- 6 cloves garlic, chopped
- 1/2 cup red wine
- 6 cloves garlic, chopped
- 3 teaspoons ground cinnamon
- 2 teaspoons ground cumin
- 2 teaspoons dried oregano
- 1 teaspoon black pepper
- 1 can 28 oz. crushed tomatoes
- 1 tablespoon tomato paste

Béchamel:

- 3 tablespoons olive oil
- 1/4 cup flour
- 2 ½ cups milk
- 1/2 teaspoon ground nutmeg
- ¾ teaspoon salt
- ¼ teaspoon white pepper
- 1/2 cup grated Parmesan cheese
- ½ cup plain Greek yogurt
- 2 extra-large eggs, beaten
- 3/4-lb. penne pasta, boiled

Directions:

- Put a suitable wok over moderate heat and add oil to heat.
- Toss in onion, salt, and lamb meat then stir cook for 12 minutes.
- Stir in red wine and cook for 2 minutes.
- Add cinnamon, garlic, oregano, cumin, and pepper, then stir cook for 2 minutes.
- Add tomato paste and tomatoes and cook for 20 minutes on a simmer.
- Toss in penne pasta then spread this mixture in a casserole dish.
- Prepare the lamb béchamel sauce in a suitable pot.
- Add oil to heat, then stir in flour and cook for 1 minute.
- Pour in milk and stir cook until it thickens.
- Stir in parmesan, white pepper, nutmeg, egg, yogurt, and salt.
- Spread this sauce over the lamb Bolognese.
- Press "Power Button" of Air Fry Oven and turn the dial to select the "Bake" mode.
- Press the Time button and again turn the dial to set the cooking time to 30 minutes.
- Now push the Temp button and rotate the dial to set the temperature at 350 degrees F.
- Once preheated, place casserole dish in the oven and close its lid.
- Serve warm.

464. Lamb Moussaka Bake

Preparation Time: 10 minutes
Cooking Time: 50 minutes
Servings: 6

Ingredients:

- ¼ cup olive oil
- 1 eggplant, diced
- 1 onion, diced
- 2 garlic cloves, crushed
- 1 lb. lamb mince
- ½ teaspoon cinnamon
- ¼ teaspoon ground cumin
- 1 teaspoon fresh rosemary
- 2 cups tomato pasta sauce

- 2 oz. butter
- ¼ cup flour
- 2 cups milk, hot
- ½ cup tasty cheese, grated
- 1 egg
- 1 pinch nutmeg
- Salt and black pepper to taste
- 7 oz. pasta, boiled

Directions:

- Put a wok on moderate heat and add oil to heat.
- Stir in eggplant, then sauté for 5 minutes.
- Add lamb, spices, rosemary, garlic, and onion, then stir cook for 8 minutes.
- Stir in pasta, and tomato paste and cook on a simmer for 5 minutes.
- Spread this lamb mixture in a casserole dish.
- Prepare the white sauce in a suitable pot.
- Add oil to heat, then stir in flour and cook for 1 minute.
- Pour in milk and stir cook until it thickens.
- Stir in cheese, egg, nutmeg, salt, and black pepper.
- Spread this white sauce over the lamb pasta mixture.
- Press "Power Button" of Air Fry Oven and turn the dial to select the "Bake" mode.
- Press the Time button and again turn the dial to set the cooking time to 30 minutes.
- Now push the Temp button and rotate the dial to set the temperature at 350 degrees F.
- Once preheated, place casserole dish in the oven and close its lid.
- Serve warm.

Fiber 0.2 g
Sugar 0.1 g
Protein 42.5 g

465.　Spring Lamb Skewers

Preparation Time: 10 minutes
Cooking Time: 15 minutes
Servings: 4

Ingredients:

- 3 garlic cloves, minced
- 4 tablespoon rapeseed oil
- 2 tablespoon cider vinegar
- large bunch thyme
- 1 ¼ lb. boneless lamb leg, diced

For the salad

- 1 cucumber, chopped
- 6 radishes, halved and sliced
- 1 fennel bulb, sliced
- 1/2 teaspoon caster sugar
- 4 tablespoon cider vinegar
- 1 handful dill sprigs

Directions:

- Toss lamb with all its thyme, oil, vinegar, and garlic.
- Marinate the thyme lamb for 2 hours in a closed container in the refrigerator.
- Thread the marinated lamb on the skewers.
- Place these skewers in an Air fryer basket.
- Press "Power Button" of Air Fry Oven and turn the dial to select the "Air fry" mode.
- Press the Time button and again turn the dial to set the cooking time to 15 minutes.
- Now push the Temp button and rotate the dial to set the temperature at 350 degrees F.
- Once preheated, place the Air fryer basket in the oven and close its lid.
- Flip the skewers when cooked halfway through then resume cooking.
- Meanwhile, toss the salad ingredients in a salad bowl.
- Serve the skewers with salad.

466.　Mint Lamb Kebobs

Preparation Time: 10 minutes
Cooking Time: 15 minutes
Servings: 4

Ingredients:

- ½ cup yogurt
- 1½ tablespoon mint

- 1 teaspoon ground cumin
- 10.5 oz. diced lean lamb
- ½ small onion, cubed
- 2 large pitta bread, cubed
- 2 handfuls lettuce, chopped

Directions:

- Whisk yogurt with mint and cumin in a suitable bowl.
- Toss in lamb cubes and mix well to coat. Marinate for 30 minutes.
- Alternatively, thread the lamb, onion and bread on the skewers.
- Place these lamb skewers in the Air fry basket.
- Press "Power Button" of Air Fry Oven and turn the dial to select the "Air fryer" mode.
- Press the Time button and again turn the dial to set the cooking time to 15 minutes.
- Now push the Temp button and rotate the dial to set the temperature at 370 degrees F.
- Once preheated, place Air fryer basket in the oven and close its lid.
- Flip the skewers when cooked halfway through then resume cooking.
- Serve warm.

467. Jerk Lamb Kebobs

Preparation Time: 10 minutes
Cooking Time: 18 minutes
Servings: 6

Ingredients:

- 2 lbs. lamb steaks
- 2 tablespoon jerk paste or marinade
- zest and juice of 1 lime
- 1 tablespoon honey
- handful thyme leaves, chopped

Directions:

- Mix lamb with jerk paste, lime juice, zest, honey and thyme.
- Toss well to coat then marinate for 30 minutes.

- Alternatively, thread the lamb on the skewers.
- Place these lamb skewers in the Air fry basket.
- Press "Power Button" of Air Fry Oven and turn the dial to select the "Air fryer" mode.
- Press the Time button and again turn the dial to set the cooking time to 18 minutes.
- Now push the Temp button and rotate the dial to set the temperature at 360 degrees F.
- Once preheated, place Air fryer basket in the oven and close its lid.
- Flip the skewers when cooked halfway through then resume cooking.
- Serve warm.

468. Lamb Chops with Rosemary Sauce

Preparation Time: 10 minutes
Cooking Time: 52 minutes
Servings: 8

Ingredients:

- 8 lamb loin chops
- 1 small onion, peeled and chopped
- Salt and black pepper, to taste

For the sauce:

- 1 onion, peeled and chopped
- 1 tablespoon rosemary leaves
- 1 oz butter
- 1 oz plain flour
- 6 Fl oz milk
- 6 fl oz vegetable stock
- 2 tablespoons cream, whipping
- Salt and black pepper, to taste

Directions:

- Place the lamb loin chops, and onion in a baking tray, then drizzle salt and black pepper on top.
- Press "Power Button" of Air Fry Oven and turn the dial to select the "Bake" mode.
- Press the Time button and again turn the dial to set the cooking time to 45 minutes.

- Now push the Temp button and rotate the dial to set the temperature at 350 degrees F.
- Once preheated, place the lamb baking tray in the oven and close its lid.
- Prepare the white sauce by melting butter in a saucepan then stir in onions.
- Sauté for 5 minutes, then stir flour and stir cook for 2 minutes.
- Stir in the rest of the ingredients and mix well.
- Pour the sauce over baked chops and serve.

469.   Roast Lamb Shoulder

Preparation Time: 10 minutes
Cooking Time: 60 minutes
Servings: 2

Ingredients:

- 1 lb. boneless lamb shoulder roast
- 4 cloves garlic, minced
- 1 tablespoon rosemary, chopped
- 2 teaspoon thyme leaves
- 3 tablespoon olive oil, divided
- Salt
- Black pepper
- 2 lb. baby potatoes halved

Directions:

- Toss potatoes with all the herbs, seasonings, and oil in a baking tray.
- Press "Power Button" of Air Fry Oven and turn the dial to select the "Air Roast" mode.
- Press the Time button and again turn the dial to set the cooking time to 60 minutes.
- Now push the Temp button and rotate the dial to set the temperature at 370 degrees F.
- Once preheated, place the lamb baking tray in the oven and close its lid.
- Slice and serve warm.

470.   Garlicky Lamb Chops

Preparation Time: 10 minutes
Cooking Time: 45 minutes
Servings: 8

Ingredients:

- 8 medium lamb chops
- 1/4 cup olive oil
- 3 thin lemon slices
- 2 garlic cloves, crushed
- 1 teaspoon dried oregano
- 1 teaspoon salt
- 1/2 teaspoon black pepper

Directions:

- Place the medium lamb chops in a baking tray and rub them with olive oil.
- Add lemon slices, garlic, oregano, salt, and black pepper on top of the lamb chops.
- Press "Power Button" of Air Fry Oven and turn the dial to select the "Air Roast" mode.
- Press the Time button and again turn the dial to set the cooking time to 45 minutes.
- Now push the Temp button and rotate the dial to set the temperature at 400 degrees F.
- Once preheated, place the lamb baking tray in the oven and close its lid.
- Slice and serve warm.

471.   New England Lamb

Preparation Time: 10 minutes
Cooking Time: 60 minutes
Servings: 6

Ingredients:

- 2 tablespoon canola oil
- 2 lbs. boneless leg of lamb, diced
- 1 onion, chopped
- 2 leeks white portion only, sliced
- 2 carrots, sliced
- 2 tablespoons minced fresh parsley, divided
- 1/2 teaspoon dried rosemary, crushed
- 1/2 teaspoon salt
- 1/4 teaspoon black pepper
- 1/4 teaspoon dried thyme, crushed
- 3 potatoes, peeled and sliced
- 3 tablespoons butter, melted

Directions:

- Toss the lamb cubes with all the veggies, oil, and seasonings in a baking tray.
- Press "Power Button" of Air Fry Oven and turn the dial to select the "Air Roast" mode.
- Press the Time button and again turn the dial to set the cooking time to 60 minutes.
- Now push the Temp button and rotate the dial to set the temperature at 350 degrees F.
- Once preheated, place the lamb baking tray in the oven and close its lid.
- Slice and serve warm.

472. Onion Lamb Kebabs

Preparation Time: 10 minutes
Cooking Time: 20 minutes
Servings: 4

Ingredients:

- 18 oz lamb kebab
- 1 teaspoon chili powder
- 1 teaspoon cumin powder
- 1 egg
- 2 oz onion, chopped
- 2 teaspoon sesame oil

Directions:

- Whisk onion with egg, chili powder, oil, cumin powder, and salt in a bowl.
- Add lamb to coat well then thread it on the skewers.
- Place these lamb skewers in the Air fryer basket.
- Press "Power Button" of Air Fry Oven and turn the dial to select the "Air Fry" mode.
- Press the Time button and again turn the dial to set the cooking time to 20 minutes.
- Now push the Temp button and rotate the dial to set the temperature at 395 degrees F.
- Once preheated, place the Air fryer basket in the oven and close its lid.
- Slice and serve warm.

473. Zucchini Lamb Meatballs

Preparation Time: 10 minutes
Cooking Time: 15 minutes

Servings: 4

Ingredients:

- 1 lb. ground lamb
- avocado oil spray
- 1/2 tablespoon garlic ghee
- 1 red bell pepper diced
- 1/3 cup red onion diced
- 1/3 cup cilantro diced
- 1/3 cup zucchini diced
- 1 tablespoon gyro seasoning
- 1/2 teaspoon turmeric
- 1/2 teaspoon cumin
- 1/2 teaspoon coriander
- 2 garlic cloves minced
- Salt and black pepper to taste

Directions:

- Mix the lamb minced with all the meatball ingredients in a bowl.
- Make small meatballs out of this mixture and place them in the Air fryer basket.
- Press "Power Button" of Air Fry Oven and turn the dial to select the "Air Fry" mode.
- Press the Time button and again turn the dial to set the cooking time to 15 minutes.
- Now push the Temp button and rotate the dial to set the temperature at 370 degrees F.
- Once preheated, place the Air fryer basket in the oven and close its lid.
- Slice and serve warm.

474. Mint Lamb with Roasted Hazelnuts

Preparation Time: 10 minutes
Cooking Time: 25 minutes
Servings: 2

Ingredients:

- ¼ cup hazelnuts, toasted
- 2/3 lb. shoulder of lamb cut into strips
- 1 tablespoon hazelnut oil
- 2 tablespoon fresh mint leaves chopped
- ½ cup frozen peas
- ¼ cup of water

- ½ cup white wine
- Salt and black pepper to taste

Directions:

- Toss lamb with hazelnuts, spices, and all the ingredients in a baking pan.
- Press "Power Button" of Air Fry Oven and turn the dial to select the "Bake" mode.
- Press the Time button and again turn the dial to set the cooking time to 25 minutes.
- Now push the Temp button and rotate the dial to set the temperature at 370 degrees F.
- Once preheated, place the baking pan in the oven and close its lid.
- Slice and serve warm.

475. Lamb Rack with Lemon Crust

Preparation Time: 10 minutes
Cooking Time: 25 minutes
Servings: 5

Ingredients:

- 1.7 lbs. frenched rack of lamb
- Salt and black pepper, to taste
- 0.13-lb. dry breadcrumbs
- 1 teaspoon grated garlic
- 1/2 teaspoon salt
- 1 teaspoon cumin seeds
- 1 teaspoon ground cumin
- 1 teaspoon oil
- ½ teaspoon Grated lemon rind
- 1 egg, beaten

Directions:

- Place the lamb rack in a baking tray and pour the whisked egg on top.
- Whisk rest of the crusting ingredients in a bowl and spread over the lamb.
- Press "Power Button" of Air Fry Oven and turn the dial to select the "Air Fry" mode.
- Press the Time button and again turn the dial to set the cooking time to 25 minutes.
- Now push the Temp button and rotate the dial to set the temperature at 350 degrees F.

- Once preheated, place the lamb baking tray in the oven and close its lid.
- Slice and serve warm.

476. Braised Lamb Shanks

Preparation Time: 10 minutes
Cooking Time: 20 minutes
Servings: 4

Ingredients:

- 4 lamb shanks
- 1½ teaspoons salt
- ½ teaspoon black pepper
- 4 garlic cloves, crushed
- 2 tablespoons olive oil
- 4 to 6 sprigs fresh rosemary
- 3 cups beef broth, divided
- 2 tablespoons balsamic vinegar

Directions:

- Place the sham shanks in a baking pan.
- Whisk rest of the ingredients in a bowl and pour over the shanks.
- Place these shanks in the Air fryer basket.
- Press "Power Button" of Air Fry Oven and turn the dial to select the "Air Fry" mode.
- Press the Time button and again turn the dial to set the cooking time to 20 minutes.
- Now push the Temp button and rotate the dial to set the temperature at 360 degrees F.
- Once preheated, place the Air fryer basket in the oven and close its lid.
- Slice and serve warm.

477. Za'atar Lamb Chops

Preparation Time: 10 minutes
Cooking Time: 10 minutes
Servings: 8

Ingredients:

- 8 lamb loin chops, bone-in
- 3 garlic cloves, crushed
- 1 teaspoon olive oil
- 1/2 fresh lemon
- 1 1/4 teaspoon salt

- ◆ 1 tablespoon Za'atar
- ◆ Black pepper, to taste

Directions:

- Rub the lamb chops with oil, zaatar, salt, lemon juice, garlic, and black pepper.
- Place these chops in the Air fryer basket.
- Press "Power Button" of Air Fry Oven and turn the dial to select the "Air Fry" mode.
- Press the Time button and again turn the dial to set the cooking time to 10 minutes.
- Now push the Temp button and rotate the dial to set the temperature at 400 degrees F.
- Once preheated, place the air fryer basket in the oven and close its lid.
- Flip the chops when cooked halfway through then resume cooking.
- Serve warm.

478.   Lamb Sirloin Steak

Preparation Time: 10 minutes
Cooking Time: 15 minutes
Servings: 2

Ingredients:

- ◆ 1/2 onion
- ◆ 4 slices ginger
- ◆ 5 cloves garlic
- ◆ 1 teaspoon garam masala
- ◆ 1 teaspoon fennel, ground
- ◆ 1 teaspoon cinnamon ground
- ◆ 1/2 teaspoon cardamom ground
- ◆ 1 teaspoon cayenne
- ◆ 1 teaspoon salt
- ◆ 1-lb. boneless lamb sirloin steaks

Directions:

- In a blender, jug add all the ingredients except the chops.
- Rub the chops with this blended mixture and marinate for 30 minutes.
- Transfer the chops to the Air fryer basket.
- Press "Power Button" of Air Fry Oven and turn the dial to select the "Air Fry" mode.

- Press the Time button and again turn the dial to set the cooking time to 15 minutes.
- Now push the Temp button and rotate the dial to set the temperature at 330 degrees F.
- Once preheated, place the Air fryer basket in the oven and close its lid.
- Flip the chops when cooked halfway through then resume cooking.
- Serve warm.

479.   Lemony Lamb Chops

Preparation Time: 10 minutes
Cooking Time: 25 minutes
Servings: 2

Ingredients:

- ◆ 2 medium lamb chops
- ◆ ¼ cup lemon juice

Directions:

- Liberally rub the lamb chops with lemon juice.
- Place the lemony chops in the Air fryer basket.
- Press "Power Button" of Air Fry Oven and turn the dial to select the "Air Fry" mode.
- Press the Time button and again turn the dial to set the cooking time to 25 minutes.
- Now push the Temp button and rotate the dial to set the temperature at 350 degrees F.
- Once preheated, place the Air fryer basket in the oven and close its lid.
- Flip the chops when cooked halfway through then resume cooking.
- Serve warm.

480.   Garlicky Rosemary Lamb Chops

Preparation Time: 10 minutes
Cooking Time: 12 minutes
Servings: 4

Ingredients:

- ◆ 4 lamb chops
- ◆ 2 teaspoon olive oil
- ◆ 1 teaspoon fresh rosemary

- ♦ 2 garlic cloves, minced
- ♦ 2 teaspoon garlic puree
- ♦ Salt & black pepper

Directions:

- Place lamb chops in the Air fryer basket.
- Rub them with olive oil, rosemary, garlic, garlic puree, salt, and black pepper
- Press "Power Button" of Air Fry Oven and turn the dial to select the "Air Fry" mode.
- Press the Time button and again turn the dial to set the cooking time to 12 minutes.
- Now push the Temp button and rotate the dial to set the temperature at 350 degrees F.
- Once preheated, place the Air fryer basket in the oven and close its lid.
- Flip the chops when cooked halfway through then resume cooking.
- Serve warm.

481. Lamb Tomato Bake

Preparation Time: 10 minutes
Cooking Time: 35 minutes
Servings: 6

Ingredients:

- ♦ 25 oz. potatoes, boiled
- ♦ 14 oz. lean lamb mince
- ♦ 1 teaspoon cinnamon
- ♦ 23 oz. jar tomato pasta

Sauce

- ♦ 12 oz. white sauce
- ♦ 1 tablespoon olive oil

Directions:

- Mash the potatoes in a bowl and stir in white sauce and cinnamon.
- Sauté lamb mince with olive oil in a frying pan until brown.
- Layer a casserole dish with tomato pasta sauce.
- Top the sauce with lamb mince.
- Spread the potato mash over the lamb in an even layer.

- Press "Power Button" of Air Fry Oven and turn the dial to select the "Bake" mode.
- Press the Time button and again turn the dial to set the cooking time to 35 minutes.
- Now push the Temp button and rotate the dial to set the temperature at 350 degrees F.
- Once preheated, place casserole dish in the oven and close its lid.
- Serve warm.

482. Lamb Baked with Tomato Topping

Preparation Time: 10 minutes
Cooking Time: 1hr 40 minutes
Servings: 8

Ingredients:

- ♦ 8 lamb shoulder chops, trimmed
- ♦ 1/4 cup plain flour
- ♦ 1 tablespoon olive oil
- ♦ 1 large brown onion, chopped
- ♦ 2 garlic cloves, crushed
- ♦ 3 medium carrots, peeled and diced
- ♦ 2 tablespoons tomato paste
- ♦ 2 1/2 cups beef stock
- ♦ 2 dried bay leaves
- ♦ 1 cup frozen peas
- ♦ 3 cups potato gems

Directions:

- Dust the lamb chops with flour and sear it in a pan layered with olive oil.
- Sear the lamb chops for 4 minutes per side.
- Transfer the chops to a baking tray.
- Add onion, garlic, and carrot to the same pan.
- Sauté for 5 minutes, then stir in tomato paste, stock and all other ingredients.
- Stir cook for 4 minutes then pour this sauce over the chops.
- Press "Power Button" of Air Fry Oven and turn the dial to select the "Bake" mode.
- Press the Time button and again turn the dial to set the cooking time to 1 hr. 30 minutes.

- Now push the Temp button and rotate the dial to set the temperature at 350 degrees F.
- Once preheated, place the baking pan in the oven and close its lid.
- Serve warm.

483. Lamb Potato Chips Baked

Preparation Time: 10 minutes
Cooking Time: 25 minutes
Servings: 4

Ingredients:

- ½ lb. minced lamb
- 1 tbs parsley chopped
- 2 teaspoon curry powder
- 1 pinch salt and black pepper
- 1 lb. potato cooked, mashed
- 1 oz. cheese grated
- 1 ½ oz. potato chips crushed

Directions:

- Mix lamb, curry powder, seasoning and parsley.
- Spread this lamb mixture in a casserole dish.
- Top the lamb mixture with potato mash, cheese, and potato chips.
- Press "Power Button" of Air Fry Oven and turn the dial to select the "Bake" mode.
- Press the Time button and again turn the dial to set the cooking time to 20 minutes.
- Now push the Temp button and rotate the dial to set the temperature at 350 degrees F.
- Once preheated, place casserole dish in the oven and close its lid.
- Serve warm.

484. Greek Macaroni Bake

Preparation Time: 10 minutes
Cooking Time: 46 minutes
Servings: 6

Ingredients:

- 1 tablespoon olive oil
- 1 large onion, chopped finely
- 2 garlic cloves, minced

- 1 lb. lean lamb mince
- 1 teaspoon ground cinnamon
- 1 beef or lamb stock cube
- 2 cups tomatoes chopped
- 1 tablespoon dried oregano
- 14 oz. macaroni, boiled
- 9 0z. tub ricotta
- 2 tablespoons parmesan, grated
- 2 tablespoons milk
- bread, to serve optional

Directions:

- Sauté onion with oil in a frying pan for 10 minutes.
- Stir in garlic and cook for 1 minute, then remove it from the heat.
- Toss lamb mince then sauté until brown.
- Stir in cinnamon, tomatoes, oregano, and stock cubes.
- Cook this mixture on a simmer for 15 minutes.
- Meanwhile, blend ricotta with parmesan, milk and garlic in a blender.
- Spread the lamb tomatoes mixture in a casserole dish and top it with ricotta mixture.
- Press "Power Button" of Air Fry Oven and turn the dial to select the "Bake" mode.
- Press the Time button and again turn the dial to set the cooking time to 30 minutes.
- Now push the Temp button and rotate the dial to set the temperature at 350 degrees F.
- Once preheated, place casserole dish in the oven and close its lid.
- Serve warm.

485. Greek lamb Farfalle

Preparation Time: 10 minutes
Cooking Time: 20 minutes
Servings: 4

Ingredients:

- 1 tablespoon olive oil
- 1 onion, finely chopped
- 2 garlic cloves, finely chopped

- 2 teaspoon dried oregano
- 1 lb. pack lamb mince
- ¾ lb. tin chopped tomatoes
- ¼ cup pitted black olives
- ½ cup frozen spinach, defrosted
- 2 tablespoons dill, stems removed and chopped
- 9 0z. farfalle, boiled
- 1 ball half-fat mozzarella, torn

Directions:

- Sauté onion and garlic with oil in a pan over moderate heat for 5 minutes.
- Stir in tomatoes, spinach, dill, lamb, and olives, then stir cook for 5 minutes.
- Spread the lamb in a casserole dish and toss in the pasta.
- Top the pasta lamb mix with mozzarella cheese.
- Press "Power Button" of Air Fry Oven and turn the dial to select the "Bake" mode.
- Press the Time button and again turn the dial to set the cooking time to 10 minutes.
- Now push the Temp button and rotate the dial to set the temperature at 350 degrees F.
- Once preheated, place casserole dish in the oven and close its lid.
- Serve warm.

486. Lamb Orzo Bake

Preparation Time: 10 minutes
Cooking Time: 2hr. 15 minutes
Servings: 6

Ingredients:

Lamb

- 1 tablespoon olive oil
- 1 2/3 lbs. lamb shoulder, diced
- 2 onions, chopped
- 2 teaspoon dried oregano and thyme
- 1 teaspoon dried mint
- 3 bay leaves
- ½ teaspoon ground cumin
- 1 teaspoon smoked paprika

Pasta

- 14 oz. tin cherry tomatoes
- 2.6 cups vegetable stock, hot
- 10.5 oz. orzo pasta
- 2 ½ oz. peppadew peppers halved
- 2 ½ 0z. pitted kalamata olives halved
- 2 oz. sun-blushed tomatoes, chopped
- ¼ cup feta, crumbled
- Finely grated zest 1 lemon

Directions:

- Rub the lamb shoulder with all its seasonings and oil.
- Place the lamb should in a baking tray.
- Press "Power Button" of Air Fry Oven and turn the dial to select the "Bake" mode.
- Press the Time button and again turn the dial to set the cooking time to 1 hr. 45 minutes.
- Now push the Temp button and rotate the dial to set the temperature at 350 degrees F.
- Once preheated, place the lamb baking tray in the oven and close its lid.
- Meanwhile, cook orzo, with hot stock, peppers, tomatoes, olives, salt and black pepper in a cooking pot for 30 minutes.
- Serve the lamb with orzo.

487. Minced Lamb Casserole

Preparation Time: 10 minutes
Cooking Time: 30 minutes
Servings: 4

Ingredients:

- 2 tablespoons olive oil
- 1 medium onion, chopped
- ½ lb. ground lamb
- 4 fresh mushrooms, sliced
- 1 cup small pasta shells, cooked
- 2 cups bottled marinara sauce
- 1 teaspoon butter
- 4 teaspoons flour
- 1 cup milk
- 1 egg, beaten
- 1 cup cheddar cheese, grated

Directions:

- Put a wok on moderate heat and add oil to heat.

- Toss in onion and sauté until soft.

- Stir in mushrooms and lamb, then cook until meat is brown.

- Add marinara sauce and cook it to a simmer.

- Stir in pasta then spread this mixture in a casserole dish.

- Prepare the sauce by melting butter in a saucepan over moderate heat.

- Stir in flour and whisk well, pour in the milk.

- Mix well and whisk ¼ cup sauce with egg then return it to the saucepan.

- Stir cook for 1 minute then pour this sauce over the lamb.

- Drizzle cheese over the lamb casserole.

- Press "Power Button" of Air Fry Oven and turn the dial to select the "Bake" mode.

- Press the Time button and again turn the dial to set the cooking time to 30 minutes.

- Now push the Temp button and rotate the dial to set the temperature at 350 degrees F.

- Once preheated, place casserole dish in the oven and close its lid.

- Serve warm.

POULTRY

488. Cheesy Chicken in Leek-Tomato Sauce

Preparation Time: 10 Minutes
Cooking Time: 20 Minutes
Servings: 4

Ingredients:

- 2 large-sized chicken breasts, cut in half lengthwise
- Salt and ground black pepper, to taste
- 4 ounces Cheddar cheese, cut into sticks
- 1 tablespoon sesame oil
- 1 cup leeks, chopped
- 2 cloves garlic, minced
- 2/3 cup roasted vegetable stock
- 2/3 cup tomato puree
- 1 teaspoon dried rosemary
- 1 teaspoon dried thyme

Directions:

- Preparing the Ingredients. Firstly, season chicken breasts with the salt and black pepper; place a piece of Cheddar cheese in the middle. Then, tie it using a kitchen string; drizzle with sesame oil and reserve.
- Add the leeks and garlic to the oven safe bowl.
- Air Frying. Cook in the Air fryer at 390 degrees F for 5 minutes or until tender.
- Add the reserved chicken. Throw in the other ingredients and cook for 12 to 13 minutes more or until the chicken is done. Enjoy!

489. Mexican Chicken Burgers

Preparation Time: 10 Minutes
Cooking Time: 10 Minutes
Servings: 6

Ingredients:

- 1 jalapeno pepper
- 1 tsp. cayenne pepper
- 1 tbsp. mustard powder
- 1 tbsp. oregano
- 1 tbsp. thyme
- 3 tbsp. smoked paprika
- 1 beaten egg
- 1 small head of cauliflower
- 4 chicken breasts

Directions:

- Preparing the Ingredients. Ensure your Air fryer is preheated to 350 degrees.
- Add seasonings to a blender. Slice cauliflower into florets and add to blender.
- Pulse till mixture resembles that of breadcrumbs.
- Take out ¾ of cauliflower mixture and add to a bowl. Set to the side. In another bowl, beat your egg and set to the side.
- Remove skin and bones from chicken breasts and add to blender with remaining cauliflower mixture. Season with pepper and salt.
- Take out mixture and form into burger shapes. Roll each patty in cauliflower crumbs, then the egg, and back into crumbs again.
- Air Frying. Place coated patties into the Air fryer. Set temperature to 350°F, and set time to 10 minutes.
- Flip over at 10-minute mark. They are done when crispy!

490. Fried Chicken Livers

Preparation Time: 5 Minutes
Cooking Time: 10 Minutes
Servings: 4

Ingredients:

- 1-pound chicken livers
- 1 cup flour
- 1/2 cup cornmeal
- 2 teaspoons your favorite seasoning blend
- 3 eggs
- 2 tablespoons milk

Directions:

- *Preparing the Ingredients.* Clean and rinse the livers, pat dry.
- Beat eggs in a shallow bowl and mix in milk.
- In another bowl combine flour, cornmeal, and seasoning, mixing until even.
- Dip the livers in the egg mix, then toss them in the flour mix.
- *Air Frying.* Air-fry at 375 degrees for 10 minutes using your Air fryer. Toss at least once halfway through.

491.　Crispy Southern Fried Chicken

Preparation Time: 10 Minutes
Cooking Time: 25 Minutes
Servings: 4

Ingredients:

- 1 tsp. cayenne pepper
- 2 tbsp. mustard powder
- 2 tbsp. oregano
- 2 tbsp. thyme
- 3 tbsp. coconut milk
- 1 beaten egg
- ¼ C. cauliflower
- ¼ C. gluten-free oats
- 8 chicken drumsticks

Directions:

- *Preparing the Ingredients.* Ensure the Air fryer is preheated to 350 degrees.
- Lay out chicken and season with pepper and salt on all sides.
- Add all other ingredients to a blender, blending till a smooth-like breadcrumb mixture is created. Place in a bowl and add a beaten egg to another bowl.
- Dip chicken into breadcrumbs, then into the egg, and breadcrumbs once more.
- *Air Frying.* Place coated drumsticks into the Air fryer. Set temperature to 350°F, and set time to 20 minutes and cook 20 minutes. Bump up the temperature to 390 degrees and cook another 5 minutes till crispy.

492.　Tex-Mex Turkey Burgers

Preparation Time: 10 Minutes

Cooking Time: 15 Minutes
Servings: 4

Ingredients:

- 1/3 cup finely crushed corn tortilla chips
- 1 egg, beaten
- ¼ cup salsa
- 1/3 cup shredded pepper Jack cheese
- Pinch salt
- Freshly ground black pepper
- 1-pound ground turkey
- 1 tablespoon olive oil
- 1 teaspoon paprika

Directions:

- Preparing the Ingredients. In a medium bowl, combine the tortilla chips, egg, salsa, cheese, salt, and pepper, and mix well.
- Add the turkey and mix gently but thoroughly with clean hands.
- Form the meat mixture into patties about ½ inch thick. Make an indentation in the center of each patty with your thumb, so the burgers don't puff up while cooking.
- Brush the patties on both sides with the olive oil and sprinkle with paprika.
- Air Frying. Put in the Air fryer basket. Grill for 14 to 16 minutes or until the meat registers at least 165°F.

493.　Air Fryer Turkey Breast

Preparation Time: 5 Minutes
Cooking Time: 60 Minutes
Servings: 6

Ingredients:

- Pepper and salt
- 1 oven-ready turkey breast
- Turkey seasonings of choice

Directions:

- *Preparing the Ingredients.* Preheat the Air fryer to 350 degrees.
- Season turkey with pepper, salt, and other desired seasonings.

- Place turkey in the Air fryer basket.
- *Air Frying.* Set temperature to 350°F, and set time to 60 minutes. Cook 60 minutes. The meat should be at 165 degrees when done.
- Allow to rest 10-15 minutes before slicing. Enjoy!

494.   Mustard Chicken Tenders

Preparation Time: 5 Minutes
Cooking Time: 20 Minutes
Servings: 4

Ingredients:

- ½ C. coconut flour
- 1 tbsp. spicy brown mustard
- 2 beaten eggs
- 1 pound of chicken tenders

Directions:

- Preparing the Ingredients. Season tenders with pepper and salt.
- Place a thin layer of mustard onto tenders and then dredge in flour and dip in egg.
- Air Frying. Add to the Air fryer, set temperature to 390°F, and set time to 20 minutes.

495.   Chicken Nuggets

Preparation Time: 10 Minutes
Cooking Time: 20 Minutes
Servings: 4

Ingredients:

- 1-pound boneless, skinless chicken breasts
- Chicken seasoning or rub
- Salt
- Pepper
- 2 eggs
- 6 tablespoons bread crumbs
- 2 tablespoons panko bread crumbs
- Cooking oil

Directions:

- *Preparing the Ingredients.* Cut the chicken breasts into 1-inch pieces.

- In a large bowl, combine the chicken pieces with chicken seasoning, salt, and pepper to taste.
- In a small bowl, beat the eggs. In another bowl, combine the bread crumbs and panko.
- Dip the chicken pieces in the eggs and then the bread crumbs.
- Place the nuggets in the Air fryer. Do not overcrowd the basket. Cook in batches. Spray the nuggets with cooking oil.
- *Air Frying.* Cook for 4 minutes. Open the Air fryer and shake the basket. Cook for an additional 4 minutes. Remove the cooked nuggets from the Air fryer, then repeat steps 5 and 6 for the remaining chicken nuggets. Cool before serving.

496.   Cheesy Chicken Fritters

Preparation Time: 5 Minutes
Cooking Time: 20 Minutes
Servings: 8

Ingredients:

Chicken Fritters:

- ½ tsp. salt
- 1/8 tsp. pepper
- 1 ½ tbsp. fresh dill
- 1 1/3 C. shredded mozzarella cheese
- 1/3 C. coconut flour
- 1/3 C. vegan mayo
- 2 eggs
- 1 ½ pounds chicken breasts

Garlic Dip:

- 1/8 tsp. pepper
- ¼ tsp. salt
- ½ tbsp. lemon juice
- 1 pressed garlic clove
- 1/3 C. vegan mayo

Directions:

- Preparing the Ingredients. Slice chicken breasts into 1/3" pieces and place in a bowl. Add all remaining fritter ingredients to the bowl and stir well. Cover and chill 2 hours or overnight.

- Ensure your air fryer is preheated to 350 degrees. Spray basket with a bit of olive oil.

- Air Frying. Add marinated chicken to the Air fryer. Set temperature to 350°F, and set time to 20 minutes and cook 20 minutes, making sure to turn halfway through cooking process.

- To make the dipping sauce, combine all the dip ingredients until smooth.

497. Thai Basil Chicken

Preparation Time: 5 Minutes
Cooking Time: 20 Minutes
Servings: 4

Ingredients:

- 4 Chicken Breasts
- 1 Onion
- 2 Bell Peppers
- 2 Hot Peppers
- 1 Tbsp Olive Oil
- 3 Tbsps. Fish Sauce
- 2 Tbsps. Oyster Sauce
- 3 Tbsps. Sweet Chili Sauce
- 1 Tbsp Soy Sauce
- 1 Quart Chicken Broth
- 1 Tbsp Garlic Powder
- 1 Tbsp Chili Powder
- 1 Cup Thai Basil

Directions:

- *Preparing the Ingredients.* Wash the breasts and boil them in the chicken broth for 10 minutes, then lower to simmer for another 10 minutes until tender. Take them out of the broth and allow to cool

- Using two forks, tear the chicken into shreds. Toss the shreds with the garlic powder, chili powder, and salt and pepper to taste

- *Air Frying.* Preheat the Air fryer to 390 degrees and cook the chicken shreds for 20 minutes, at which point they will get dark brown and crispy. They will soften up as they absorb the juices from cooking with the veggies

- While the chicken is cooking, cut the onions and peppers into thin slices. Add the olive oil to a wok and heat for a minute on medium high heat. Toss in all the veggies and sauté for 5 minutes

- Add in the fish sauce, oyster sauce, soy sauce, sweet chili sauce, and stir well for 1 minute. Add the chicken and basil leaves and stir until the leaves have wilted

- Serve over jasmine rice.

498. Air Fryer Chicken Parmesan

Preparation Time: 5 Minutes
Cooking Time: 9 Minutes
Servings: 4

Ingredients:

- ½ C. keto marinara
- 6 tbsp. mozzarella cheese
- 1 tbsp. melted ghee
- 2 tbsp. grated parmesan cheese
- 6 tbsp. gluten-free seasoned breadcrumbs
- 1 8-ounce chicken breasts

Directions:

- *Preparing the Ingredients.* Ensure air fryer is preheated to 360 degrees. Spray the basket with olive oil.

- Mix parmesan cheese and breadcrumbs together. Melt ghee.

- Brush melted ghee onto the chicken and dip into breadcrumb mixture.

- Place coated chicken in the air fryer and top with olive oil.

- *Air Frying.* Set temperature to 360°F, and set time to 6 minutes. Cook 2 breasts for 6 minutes and top each breast with a tablespoon of sauce and 1½ tablespoons of mozzarella cheese. Cook another 3 minutes to melt cheese.

- Keep cooked pieces warm as you repeat the process with remaining breasts.

499. Ricotta and Parsley Stuffed Turkey Breasts

Preparation Time: 5 Minutes

Cooking Time: 25 Minutes
Servings: 4

Ingredients:

- 1 turkey breast, quartered
- 1 cup Ricotta cheese
- 1/4 cup fresh Italian parsley, chopped
- 1 teaspoon garlic powder
- 1/2 teaspoon cumin powder
- 1 egg, beaten
- 1 teaspoon paprika
- Salt and ground black pepper, to taste
- Crushed tortilla chips
- 1 ½ tablespoons extra-virgin olive oil

Directions:

- *Preparing the Ingredients.* Firstly, flatten out each piece of turkey breast with a rolling pin. Prepare three mixing bowls.
- In a shallow bowl, combine Ricotta cheese with the parsley, garlic powder, and cumin powder.
- Place the Ricotta/parsley mixture in the middle of each piece. Repeat with the remaining pieces of the turkey breast and roll them up.
- In another shallow bowl, whisk the egg together with paprika. In the third shallow bowl, combine the salt, pepper, and crushed tortilla chips.
- Dip each roll in the whisked egg, then, roll them over the tortilla chips mixture.
- Transfer prepared rolls to the Air fryer basket. Drizzle olive oil over all.
- *Air Frying.* Cook at 350 degrees F for 25 minutes, working in batches. Serve warm, garnished with some extra parsley, if desired.

500.   Chicken Popcorn

Preparation Time: 10 Minutes
Cooking Time: 10 Minutes
Servings: 6

Ingredients:

- 4 eggs

- 1 1/2 lbs. chicken breasts, cut into small chunks
- 1 tsp paprika
- 1/2 tsp garlic powder
- 1 tsp onion powder
- 2 1/2 cups pork rind, crushed
- 1/4 cup coconut flour
- Pepper
- Salt

Directions:

- In a small bowl, mix together coconut flour, pepper, and salt.
- In another bowl, whisk eggs until combined.
- Take one more bowl and mix together pork panko, paprika, garlic powder, and onion powder.
- Add chicken pieces in a large mixing bowl. Sprinkle coconut flour mixture over chicken and toss well.
- Dip chicken pieces in the egg mixture and coat with pork panko mixture and place on a plate.
- Spray air fryer basket with cooking spray.
- Preheat the air fryer to 400 F.
- Add half prepared chicken in air fryer basket and cook for 10-12 minutes. Shake basket halfway through.
- Cook remaining half using the same method.
- Serve and enjoy.

501.   Zaatar Chicken

Preparation Time: 10 Minutes
Cooking Time: 35 Minutes
Servings: 4

Ingredients:

- 4 chicken thighs
- 2 sprigs thyme
- 1 onion, cut into chunks
- 2 1/2 tbsp zaatar
- 1/2 tsp cinnamon
- 2 garlic cloves, smashed
- 1 lemon juice

- ♦ 1 lemon zest
- ♦ 1/4 cup olive oil
- ♦ 1/4 tsp pepper
- ♦ 1 tsp salt

Directions:

- Add oil, lemon juice, lemon zest, cinnamon, garlic, pepper, 2 tbsp zaatar, and salt in a large zip-lock bag and shake well.
- Add chicken, thyme, and onion to bag and shake well to coat. Place in refrigerator for overnight.
- Preheat the air fryer to 380 F.
- Add marinated chicken in air fryer basket and cook at 380 F for 15 minutes.
- Turn chicken to another side and sprinkle with remaining za'atar spice and cook at 380 F for 15-18 minutes more.
- Serve and enjoy.

502. Teriyaki Chicken

Preparation Time: 10 Minutes
Cooking Time: 20 Minutes
Servings: 6

Ingredients:

- ♦ 6 chicken drumsticks
- ♦ 1 cup keto teriyaki sauce
- ♦ 1 tbsp sesame seeds, toasted
- ♦ 2 tbsp green onion, sliced

Directions:

- Add chicken and teriyaki sauce into the large zip-lock bag. Shake well and place in the refrigerator for 1 hour.
- Preheat the air fryer to 360 F.
- Add marinated chicken drumsticks into the air fryer basket and cook for 20 minutes. Shake basket twice.
- Garnish with green onion and sesame seeds.
- Serve and enjoy.

503. Warm Chicken and Spinach Salad

Preparation Time: 10 Minutes

Cooking Time: 20 Minutes
Servings: 4

Ingredients:

- ♦ 3 (5-ounce) boneless, skinless chicken breasts, cut into 1-inch cubes
- ♦ 5 teaspoons extra-virgin olive oil
- ♦ ½ teaspoon dried thyme
- ♦ 1 medium red onion, sliced
- ♦ 1 red bell pepper, sliced
- ♦ 1 small zucchini, cut into strips
- ♦ 3 tablespoons freshly squeezed lemon juice
- ♦ 6 cups fresh baby spinach leaves

Directions:

- Insert the crisper plate into the basket and the basket into the unit. Preheat the unit by selecting AIR ROAST, setting the temperature to 375°F, and setting the time to 3 minutes. Select START/STOP to begin.
- In a large bowl, combine the chicken, olive oil, and thyme. Toss to coat. Transfer to a medium metal bowl that fits into the basket.
- Once the unit is preheated, place the bowl into the basket.
- Select AIR ROAST, set the temperature to 375°F, and set the time to 20 minutes. Select START/STOP to begin.
- After 8 minutes, add the red onion, red bell pepper, and zucchini to the bowl. Resume cooking. After about 6 minutes more, stir the chicken and vegetables. Resume cooking.
- When the cooking is complete, a food thermometer inserted into the chicken should register at least 165°F. Remove the bowl from the unit and stir in the lemon juice.
- Put the spinach in a serving bowl and top with the chicken mixture. Toss to combine and serve immediately.

504. Chicken Fajitas

Preparation Time: 10 Minutes
Cooking Time: 10 to 14 Minutes
Servings: 4

Ingredients:

- Cooking oil spray
- 4 boneless, skinless chicken breasts, sliced crosswise
- 1 small red onion, sliced
- 2 red bell peppers, seeded and sliced
- ½ cup spicy ranch salad dressing, divided
- ½ teaspoon dried oregano
- 8 corn tortillas
- 2 cups torn butter lettuce leaves
- 2 avocados, peeled, pitted, and chopped

Directions:

- Insert the crisper plate into the basket and the basket into the unit. Preheat the unit by selecting BAKE, setting the temperature to 375°F, and setting the time to 3 minutes. Select START/STOP to begin.

- Once the unit is preheated, spray the crisper plate with cooking oil. Place the chicken, red onion, and red bell pepper into the basket. Drizzle with 1 tablespoon of the salad dressing and season with the oregano. Toss to combine.

- Select BAKE, set the temperature to 375°F, and set the time to 14 minutes. Select START/STOP to begin.

- After 10 minutes, check the chicken. If a food thermometer inserted into the chicken registers at least 165°F, it is done. If not, resume cooking.

- When the cooking is complete, transfer the chicken and vegetables to a bowl and toss with the remaining salad dressing.

- Serve the chicken mixture family-style with the tortillas, lettuce, and avocados, and let everyone make their own plates.

505. Spicy Chicken Meatballs

Preparation Time: 10 Minutes
Cooking Time: 25 Minutes
Servings: 4

Ingredients:

- 1 medium red onion, minced
- 2 garlic cloves, minced
- 1 jalapeño pepper, minced

- 2 teaspoons extra-virgin olive oil
- 3 tablespoons ground almonds
- 1 egg
- 1 teaspoon dried thyme
- 1-pound ground chicken breast
- Cooking oil spray

Directions:

- Insert the crisper plate into the basket and the basket into the unit. Preheat the unit by selecting BAKE, setting the temperature to 400°F, and setting the time to 3 minutes. Select START/STOP to begin.

- In a 6-by-2-inch round pan, combine the red onion, garlic, jalapeño, and olive oil.

- Once the unit is preheated, place the pan into the basket.

- Select BAKE, set the temperature to 400°F, and set the time to 4 minutes. Select START/STOP to begin.

- When the cooking is complete, the vegetables should be crisp-tender. Transfer to a medium bowl.

- Mix the almonds, egg, and thyme into the vegetable mixture. Add the chicken and mix until just combined. Form the chicken mixture into about 24 (1-inch) balls.

- Insert the crisper plate into the basket and the basket into the unit. Preheat the unit by selecting BAKE, setting the temperature to 400°F, and setting the time to 3 minutes. Select START/STOP to begin.

- Once the unit is preheated, spray the crisper plate with cooking oil. Working in batches, place half the meatballs in a single layer, not touching, into the basket.

- Select BAKE, set the temperature to 400°F, and set the time to 10 minutes. Select START/STOP to begin.

- When the cooking is complete, a food thermometer inserted into the meatballs should register at least 165°F.

- Repeat steps 8 and 9 with the remaining meatballs. Serve warm.

506. Italian Chicken Parmesan

Preparation Time: 10 Minutes
Cooking Time: 20 Minutes
Servings: 4

Ingredients:

- 2 (4-ounce) boneless, skinless chicken breasts
- 2 egg whites, beaten
- 1 cup Italian bread crumbs
- ½ cup grated Parmesan cheese
- 2 teaspoons Italian seasoning
- Salt
- Freshly ground black pepper
- Cooking oil spray
- ¾ cup marinara sauce
- ½ cup shredded mozzarella cheese

Directions:

- With your knife blade parallel to the cutting board, cut the chicken breasts in half horizontally to create 4 thin cutlets. On a solid surface, pound the cutlets to flatten them. You can use your hands, a rolling pin, a kitchen mallet, or a meat hammer.

- Pour the egg whites into a bowl large enough to dip the chicken.

- In another bowl large enough to dip a chicken cutlet in, stir together the bread crumbs, Parmesan cheese, and Italian seasoning, and season with salt and pepper.

- Dip each cutlet into the egg whites and into the breadcrumb mixture to coat.

- Insert the crisper plate into the basket and the basket into the unit. Preheat the unit by selecting AIR FRY, setting the temperature to 375°F, and setting the time to 3 minutes. Select START/STOP to begin.

- Once the unit is preheated, spray the crisper plate with cooking oil. Working in batches, place 2 chicken cutlets into the basket. Spray the top of the chicken with cooking oil.

- Select AIR FRY, set the temperature to 375°F, and set the time to 7 minutes. Select START/STOP to begin.

- When the cooking is complete, repeat steps 6 and 7 with the remaining cutlets.

- Top the chicken cutlets with the marinara sauce and shredded mozzarella cheese. If the chicken will fit into the basket without stacking, you can prepare all 4 at once. Otherwise, do these 2 cutlets at a time.

- Select AIR FRY, set the temperature to 375°F, and set the time to 3 minutes. Select START/STOP to begin.

- The cooking is complete when the cheese is melted and the chicken reaches an internal temperature of 165°F. Cool for 5 minutes before serving.

507.   Easy General Tso's Chicken

Preparation Time: 10 Minutes
Cooking Time: 14 Minutes
Servings: 4

Ingredients:

- 1 tablespoon sesame oil
- 1 teaspoon minced garlic
- ½ teaspoon ground ginger
- 1 cup chicken broth
- 4 tablespoons soy sauce, divided
- ½ teaspoon sriracha, plus more for serving
- 2 tablespoons hoisin sauce
- 4 tablespoons cornstarch, divided
- 4 boneless, skinless chicken breasts, cut into 1-inch pieces
- Olive oil spray
- 2 medium scallions, sliced, green parts only
- Sesame seeds, for garnish

Directions:

- In a small saucepan over low heat, combine the sesame oil, garlic, and ginger and cook for 1 minute.

- Add the chicken broth, 2 tablespoons of soy sauce, the sriracha, and hoisin. Whisk to combine.

- Whisk in 2 tablespoons of cornstarch and continue cooking over low heat until the sauce starts to thicken, about 5 minutes. Remove the pan from the heat, cover it, and set aside.

- Insert the crisper plate into the basket and the basket into the unit. Preheat the unit by selecting BAKE, setting the temperature to 400°F, and setting the time to 3 minutes. Select START/STOP to begin.

- In a medium bowl, toss together the chicken, remaining 2 tablespoons of soy sauce, and remaining 2 tablespoons of cornstarch.

- Once the unit is preheated, spray the crisper plate with olive oil. Place the chicken into the basket and spray it with olive oil.

- Select BAKE, set the temperature to 400°F, and set the time to 9 minutes. Select START/STOP to begin.

- After 5 minutes, remove the basket, shake, and spray the chicken with more olive oil. Reinsert the basket to resume cooking.

- When the cooking is complete, a food thermometer inserted into the chicken should register at least 165°F. Transfer the chicken to a large bowl and toss it with the sauce. Garnish with the scallions and sesame seeds and serve.

508. Spicy Coconut Chicken Wings

Preparation Time: 45 Minutes
Cooking Time: 20 Minutes
Servings: 4

Ingredients:

- 16 chicken drumettes (party wings)
- ¼ cup full-fat coconut milk
- 1 tablespoon sriracha
- 1 teaspoon onion powder
- 1 teaspoon garlic powder
- Salt
- Freshly ground black pepper
- 1/3 cup shredded unsweetened coconut
- ½ cup all-purpose flour
- Cooking oil spray
- 1 cup mango, cut into ½-inch chunks
- ¼ cup fresh cilantro, chopped
- ½ cup red onion, chopped
- 2 garlic cloves, minced
- Juice of ½ lime

Directions:

- Place the drumettes in a resealable plastic bag.

- In a small bowl, whisk the coconut milk and sriracha.

- Drizzle the drumettes with the sriracha–coconut milk mixture. Season the drumettes with the onion powder, garlic powder, salt, and pepper. Seal the bag. Shake it thoroughly to combine the seasonings and coat the chicken. Marinate for at least 30 minutes, preferably overnight, in the refrigerator.

- When the drumettes are almost done marinating, in a large bowl, stir together the shredded coconut and flour.

- Dip the drumettes into the coconut-flour mixture. Press the flour mixture onto the chicken with your hands.

- Insert the crisper plate into the basket and the basket into the unit. Preheat the unit by selecting AIR FRY, setting the temperature to 400°F, and setting the time to 3 minutes. Select START/STOP to begin.

- Once the unit is preheated, spray the crisper plate and the basket with cooking oil. Place the drumettes in the air fryer. It is okay to stack them. Spray the drumettes with cooking oil, being sure to cover the bottom layer.

- Select AIR FRY, set the temperature to 400°F, and set the time to 20 minutes. Select START/STOP to begin.

- After 5 minutes, remove the basket and shake it to ensure all pieces cook through. Reinsert the basket to resume cooking. Remove and shake the basket every 5 minutes, twice more, until a food thermometer inserted into the drumettes registers 165°F.

- When the cooking is complete, let the chicken cool for 5 minutes.

- While the chicken cooks and cools, make the salsa. In a small bowl, combine the mango, cilantro, red onion, garlic, and lime juice. Mix well until fully combined. Serve with the wings.

509. Chili Ranch Chicken Wings

Preparation Time: 40 Minutes
Cooking Time: 40 Minutes
Servings: 4

Ingredients:

- 2 tablespoons water
- 2 tablespoons hot pepper sauce
- 2 tablespoons unsalted butter, melted
- 2 tablespoons apple cider vinegar
- 1 (1-ounce) envelope ranch salad dressing mix
- 1 teaspoon paprika
- 4 pounds chicken wings, tips removed
- Cooking oil spray

Directions:

- In a large bowl, whisk the water, hot pepper sauce, melted butter, vinegar, salad dressing mix, and paprika until combined.

- Add the wings and toss to coat. At this point, you can cover the bowl and marinate the wings in the refrigerator for 4 to 24 hours for best results. However, you can just let the wings stand for 30 minutes in the refrigerator.

- Insert the crisper plate into the basket and the basket into the unit. Preheat the unit by selecting AIR FRY, setting the temperature to 400°F, and setting the time to 3 minutes. Select START/STOP to begin.

- Once the unit is preheated, spray the crisper plate with cooking oil. Working in batches, put half the wings into the basket; it is okay to stack them. Refrigerate the remaining wings.

- Select AIR FRY, set the temperature to 400°F, and set the time to 20 minutes. Select START/STOP to begin.

- After 5 minutes, remove the basket and shake it. Reinsert the basket to resume cooking. Remove and shake the basket every 5 minutes, three more times, until the chicken is browned and glazed and a food thermometer inserted into the wings registers 165°F.

- Repeat steps 4, 5, and 6 with the remaining wings.

- When the cooking is complete, serve warm.

510. Crispy Chicken Thighs with Roasted Carrots

Preparation Time: 10 Minutes
Cooking Time: 22 Minutes
Servings: 4

Ingredients:

- 4 bone-in, skin-on chicken thighs
- 2 carrots, cut into 2-inch pieces
- 2 tablespoons extra-virgin olive oil
- 2 teaspoons poultry spice
- 1 teaspoon sea salt, divided
- 2 teaspoons chopped fresh rosemary leaves
- Cooking oil spray
- 2 cups cooked white rice

Directions:

- Brush the chicken thighs and carrots with olive oil. Sprinkle both with the poultry spice, salt, and rosemary.

- Insert the crisper plate into the basket and the basket into the unit. Preheat the unit by selecting AIR FRY, setting the temperature to 400°F, and setting the time to 3 minutes. Select START/STOP to begin.

- Once the unit is preheated, spray the crisper plate with cooking oil. Place the carrots into the basket. Add the wire rack and arrange the chicken thighs on the rack.

- Select AIR FRY, set the temperature to 400°F, and set the time to 20 minutes. Select START/STOP to begin.

- When the cooking is complete, check the chicken temperature. If a food thermometer inserted into the chicken registers 165°F, remove the chicken from the air fryer, place it on a clean plate, and cover with aluminum foil to keep warm. Otherwise, resume cooking for 1 to 2 minutes longer.

- The carrots can cook for 18 to 22 minutes and will be tender and caramelized; cooking time isn't as crucial for root vegetables.

- Serve the chicken and carrots with the hot cooked rice.

511. Buffalo Chicken Strips

Preparation Time: 15 Minutes
Cooking Time: 13 To 17 Minutes
Servings: 4

Ingredients:

- ¾ cup all-purpose flour
- 2 eggs
- 2 tablespoons water
- 1 cup seasoned panko bread crumbs
- 2 teaspoons granulated garlic
- 1 teaspoon salt
- 1 teaspoon freshly ground black pepper
- 16 chicken breast strips, or 3 large boneless, skinless chicken breasts, cut into 1-inch strips
- Olive oil spray
- ¼ cup Buffalo sauce, plus more as needed

Directions:

- Put the flour in a small bowl.
- In another small bowl, whisk the eggs and the water.
- In a third bowl, stir together the panko, granulated garlic, salt, and pepper.
- Dip each chicken strip in the flour, in the egg, and in the panko mixture to coat. Press the crumbs onto the chicken with your fingers.
- Insert the crisper plate into the basket and the basket into the unit. Preheat the unit by selecting AIR FRY, setting the temperature to 375°F, and setting the time to 3 minutes. Select START/STOP to begin.
- Once the unit is preheated, place a parchment paper liner into the basket. Working in batches if needed, place the chicken strips into the basket. Do not stack unless using a wire rack for the second layer. Spray the top of the chicken with olive oil.
- Select AIR FRY, set the temperature to 375°F, and set the time to 17 minutes. Select START/STOP to begin.
- After 10 or 12 minutes, remove the basket, flip the chicken, and spray again with olive oil. Reinsert the basket to resume cooking.
- When the cooking is complete, the chicken should be golden brown and crispy and a food thermometer inserted into the chicken should register 165°F.
- Repeat steps 6, 7, and 8 with any remaining chicken.
- Transfer the chicken to a large bowl. Drizzle the Buffalo sauce over the top of the cooked chicken, toss to coat, and serve.

512. Chicken Satay

Preparation Time: 12 Minutes
Cooking Time: 12 to 18 Minutes
Servings: 4

Ingredients:

- ½ cup crunchy peanut butter
- 1/3 cup chicken broth
- 3 tablespoons low-sodium soy sauce
- 2 tablespoons freshly squeezed lemon juice
- 2 garlic cloves, minced
- 2 tablespoons extra-virgin olive oil
- 1 teaspoon curry powder
- 1-pound chicken tenders
- Cooking oil spray

Directions:

- In a medium bowl, whisk the peanut butter, broth, soy sauce, lemon juice, garlic, olive oil, and curry powder until smooth.
- Place 2 tablespoons of this mixture into a small bowl. Transfer the remaining sauce to a serving bowl and set aside.
- Add the chicken tenders to the bowl with the 2 tablespoons of sauce and stir to coat. Let stand for a few minutes to marinate.
- Insert the crisper plate into the basket and the basket into the unit. Preheat the unit by selecting AIR FRY, setting the temperature to 390°F, and setting the time to 3 minutes. Select START/STOP to begin.
- Run a 6-inch bamboo skewer lengthwise through each chicken tender.

- Once the unit is preheated, spray the crisper plate with cooking oil. Working in batches, place half the chicken skewers into the basket in a single layer without overlapping.

- Select AIR FRY, set the temperature to 390°F, and set the time to 9 minutes. Select START/STOP to begin.

- After 6 minutes, check the chicken. If a food thermometer inserted into the chicken registers 165°F, it is done. If not, resume cooking.

- Repeat steps 6, 7, and 8 with the remaining chicken.

- When the cooking is complete, serve the chicken with the reserved sauce.

513. Crispy Chicken Tenders

Preparation Time: 10 Minutes
Cooking Time: 15 Minutes
Servings: 4

Ingredients:

- 1 cup panko bread crumbs
- 1 tablespoon paprika
- ½ teaspoon salt
- ¼ teaspoon freshly ground black pepper
- 16 chicken tenders
- ½ cup mayonnaise
- Olive oil spray

Directions:

- In a medium bowl, stir together the panko, paprika, salt, and pepper.

- In a large bowl, toss together the chicken tenders and mayonnaise to coat. Transfer the coated chicken pieces to the bowl of seasoned panko and dredge to coat thoroughly. Press the coating onto the chicken with your fingers.

- Insert the crisper plate into the basket and the basket into the unit. Preheat the unit by selecting AIR FRY, setting the temperature to 350°F, and setting the time to 3 minutes. Select START/STOP to begin.

- Once the unit is preheated, place a parchment paper liner into the basket. Place

the chicken into the basket and spray it with olive oil.

- Select AIR FRY, set the temperature to 350°F, and set the time to 15 minutes. Select START/STOP to begin.

- When the cooking is complete, the tenders will be golden brown and a food thermometer inserted into the chicken should register 165°F. For more even browning, remove the basket halfway through cooking and flip the tenders. Give them an extra spray of olive oil and reinsert the basket to resume cooking. This ensures they are crispy and brown all over.

- When the cooking is complete, serve.

514. Chicken Cordon Bleu

Preparation Time: 15 Minutes
Cooking Time: 15 Minutes
Servings: 4

Ingredients:

- 4 chicken breast filets
- ¼ cup chopped ham
- 1/3 cup grated Swiss cheese, or Gruyere cheese
- ¼ cup all-purpose flour
- Pinch salt
- Freshly ground black pepper
- ½ teaspoon dried marjoram
- 1 egg
- 1 cup panko bread crumbs
- Olive oil spray

Directions:

- Put the chicken breast filets on a work surface and gently press them with the palm of your hand to make them a bit thinner. Don't tear the meat.

- In a small bowl, combine the ham and cheese. Divide this mixture among the chicken filets. Wrap the chicken around the filling to enclose it, using toothpicks to hold the chicken together.

- In a shallow bowl, stir together the flour, salt, pepper, and marjoram.

- In another bowl, beat the egg.

- Spread the panko on a plate.

- Dip the chicken in the flour mixture, in the egg, and in the panko to coat thoroughly. Press the crumbs into the chicken so they stick well.

- Insert the crisper plate into the basket and the basket into the unit. Preheat the unit by selecting BAKE, setting the temperature to 375°F, and setting the time to 3 minutes. Select START/STOP to begin.

- Once the unit is preheated, spray the crisper plate with olive oil. Place the chicken into the basket and spray it with olive oil.

- Select BAKE, set the temperature to 375°F, and set the time to 15 minutes. Select START/STOP to begin.

- When the cooking is complete, the chicken should be cooked through and a food thermometer inserted into the chicken should register 165°F. Carefully remove the toothpicks and serve.

515. Spicy Air-Crisped Chicken and Potatoes

Preparation Time: 5 Minutes
Cooking Time: 25 Minutes
Servings: 4

Ingredients:

- 4 bone-in, skin-on chicken thighs
- ½ teaspoon kosher salt or ¼ teaspoon fine salt
- 2 tablespoons melted unsalted butter
- 2 teaspoons Worcestershire sauce
- 2 teaspoons curry powder
- 1 teaspoon dried oregano leaves
- ½ teaspoon dry mustard
- ½ teaspoon granulated garlic
- ¼ teaspoon paprika
- ¼ teaspoon hot pepper sauce, such as Tabasco
- Cooking oil spray
- 4 medium Yukon gold potatoes, chopped
- 1 tablespoon extra-virgin olive oil

Directions:

- Sprinkle the chicken thighs on both sides with salt.

- In a medium bowl, stir together the melted butter, Worcestershire sauce, curry powder, oregano, dry mustard, granulated garlic, paprika, and hot pepper sauce. Add the thighs to the sauce and stir to coat.

- Insert the crisper plate into the basket and the basket into the unit. Preheat the unit by selecting AIR FRY, setting the temperature to 400°F, and setting the time to 3 minutes. Select START/STOP to begin.

- Once the unit is preheated, spray the crisper plate with cooking oil. In the basket, combine the potatoes and olive oil and toss to coat.

- Add the wire rack to the air fryer and place the chicken thighs on top.

- Select AIR FRY, set the temperature to 400°F, and set the time to 25 minutes. Select START/STOP to begin.

- After 19 minutes check the chicken thighs. If a food thermometer inserted into the chicken registers 165°F, transfer them to a clean plate, and cover with aluminum foil to keep warm. If they aren't cooked to 165°F, resume cooking for another 1 to 2 minutes until they are done. Remove them from the unit along with the rack.

- Remove the basket and shake it to distribute the potatoes. Reinsert the basket to resume cooking for 3 to 6 minutes, or until the potatoes are crisp and golden brown.

- When the cooking is complete, serve the chicken with the potatoes.

516. Korean Chicken Wings

Preparation Time: 10 Minutes
Cooking Time: 25 Minutes
Servings: 4

Ingredients:

- ¼ cup gochujang, or red pepper paste
- ¼ cup mayonnaise
- 2 tablespoons honey
- 1 tablespoon sesame oil
- 2 teaspoons minced garlic
- 1 tablespoon sugar
- 2 teaspoons ground ginger
- 3 pounds whole chicken wings

- Olive oil spray
- 1 teaspoon salt
- ½ teaspoon freshly ground black pepper

Directions:

- In a large bowl, whisk the gochujang, mayonnaise, honey, sesame oil, garlic, sugar, and ginger. Set aside.

- Insert the crisper plate into the basket and the basket into the unit. Preheat the unit by selecting AIR FRY, setting the temperature to 400°F, and setting the time to 3 minutes. Select START/STOP to begin.

- To prepare the chicken wings, cut the wings in half. The meatier part is the drumette. Cut off and discard the wing tip from the flat part (or save the wing tips in the freezer to make chicken stock).

- Once the unit is preheated, spray the crisper plate with olive oil. Working in batches, place half the chicken wings into the basket, spray them with olive oil, and sprinkle with the salt and pepper.

- Select AIR FRY, set the temperature to 400°F, and set the time to 20 minutes. Select START/STOP to begin.

- After 10 minutes, remove the basket, flip the wings, and spray them with more olive oil. Reinsert the basket to resume cooking.

- Cook the wings to an internal temperature of 165°F, then transfer them to the bowl with the prepared sauce and toss to coat.

- Repeat steps 4, 5, 6, and 7 for the remaining chicken wings.

- Return the coated wings to the basket and air fry for 4 to 6 minutes more until the sauce has glazed the wings and the chicken is crisp. After 3 minutes, check the wings to make sure they aren't burning. Serve hot.

517. Paprika Chicken Wings

Preparation Time: 15 Minutes
Cooking Time: 24 Minutes
Servings: 6

Ingredients:

- 1 ½ lb. chicken wings
- 1/4 teaspoon sea salt
- 1/2 teaspoon black pepper
- 1/2 teaspoon smoked paprika
- 1/2 teaspoon garlic powder

Directions:

- Mix smoked paprika, black pepper, salt, garlic powder, baking powder, and onion powder in a small bowl.

- Add all the chicken wings to a large bowl and drizzle the spice mixture over the wings.

- Toss well and transfer the wings to an Air Fryer basket.

- Return the Air Fryer basket to the Air Fryer.

- Select the Air Fry mode at 400 degrees F for 24 minutes.

- Toss the wings once cooked halfway through.

- Serve warm.

518. Breaded Chicken Legs

Preparation Time: 20 Minutes
Cooking Time: 24 Minutes
Servings: 6

Ingredients:

- 12 chicken legs
- Two tablespoons seasoned salt
- Four tablespoons olive oil
- One bag chicken breading

Directions:

- Toss drumsticks with olive oil and drizzle seasoning on top

- Mix well to coat and coat the drumsticks with breadcrumbs.

- Place the coated drumsticks in the Air Fryer basket and spray them with cooking oil.

- Return the Air Fryer basket to the Air Fryer.

- Select the Air Fry mode at 400 degrees F for 24 minutes.

- Flip the drumsticks once cooked halfway through, then resume cooking.

- Serve warm.

519. Herbed Chicken Breast

Preparation Time: 15 Minutes
Cooking Time: 22 Minutes
Servings: 4

Ingredients:

- Four boneless skinless chicken breasts
- 1/2 teaspoon garlic powder
- 1/2 teaspoon salt
- 1/8 teaspoon black pepper
- 1/2 teaspoon dried oregano

Directions:

- Mix garlic powder, oregano, black pepper, and salt in a small bowl.
- Spray the chicken breast with cooking spray.
- Rub the chicken with the seasoning mix liberally.
- Place the seasoned chicken breast in the Air Fryer basket.
- Return the Air Fryer basket to the Air Fryer.
- Select the Air Fry mode at 360 degrees F for 22 minutes.
- Flip the chicken once cooked halfway through, drizzle the remaining seasoning.
- Resume cooking and cook until the chicken is golden.
- Serve warm.

520. Tangy Chicken Drumsticks

Preparation Time: 15 Minutes
Cooking Time: 20 Minutes
Servings: 4

Ingredients:

- One teaspoon paprika
- Eight chicken drumsticks
- Two tablespoons olive oil
- One teaspoon of sea salt
- One teaspoon fresh cracked pepper

Directions:

- Mix and whisk all the spices and herbs in a small bowl.
- Toss the drumsticks with olive oil and the spice mixture to coat well in a bowl.
- At 400 degrees F, preheat your Ninja Air Fryer on Air Fry mode.
- Spread the drumsticks in the Air Fryer basket.
- Return the Air Fryer basket to the Air Fryer.
- Select the Air Fry mode at 400 degrees F for 20 minutes.
- Flip the drumsticks once cooked halfway through.
- Serve warm.

521. Seasoned Turkey Leg

Preparation Time: 10 Minutes
Cooking Time: 27 Minutes
Servings: 2

Ingredients:

- 1 lb. turkey leg
- One teaspoon poultry seasoning
- One teaspoon garlic salt

Directions:

- Rub the turkey leg with poultry seasoning and garlic salt.
- Place the turkey leg in the Air Fryer basket.
- Return the Air Fryer basket to the Air Fryer.
- Select the Air Fry mode at 350 degrees F for 27 minutes.
- Flip the turkey leg once cooked halfway through.
- Serve warm.

522. Balsamic Chicken Thighs

Preparation Time: 15 Minutes
Cooking Time: 14 Minutes
Servings: 4

Ingredients:

- Four boneless skinless chicken thighs
- 1/4 cup lemon juice

- 1/4 cup coarse ground mustard
- 1/4 cup balsamic vinaigrette
- One teaspoon kosher salt

Directions:

- Mix lemon juice, mustard, vinaigrette, salt, rosemary, and black pepper in a bowl.
- Add chicken thighs and mix well to coat.
- Cover and refrigerate for 2 hours for marination.
- Set the seasoned chicken in the Air Fryer basket and spray with cooking oil.
- Return the Air Fryer basket to the Air Fryer.
- Select the Air Fry mode at 400 degrees F for 14 minutes.
- Flip the chicken once cooked halfway through. And resume cooking.
- Serve warm.

523. Turkey Breasts

Preparation Time: 5 minutes
Cooking Time: 1 hour
Servings: 4

Ingredients:

- Boneless turkey breast – 3 lbs.
- Mayonnaise – ¼ cup
- Poultry seasoning – 2 tsps.
- Salt and pepper to taste
- Garlic powder – ½ tsp.

Directions:

- Preheat the air fryer to 360F. Season the turkey with mayonnaise, seasoning, salt, garlic powder, and black pepper. Cook the turkey in the air fryer for 1 hour at 360F.
- Turning after every 15 minutes. The turkey is done when it reaches 165F.

524. BBQ Chicken Breasts

Preparation Time: 5 minutes
Cooking Time: 15 minutes
Servings: 4

Ingredients:

- Boneless, skinless chicken breast – 4, about 6 oz. each
- BBQ seasoning – 2 tbsps.
- Cooking spray

Directions:

- Rub the chicken with BBQ seasoning and marinate in the refrigerator for 45 minutes. Preheat the air fryer at 400F. Grease the basket with oil and place the chicken.
- Then spray oil on top. Cook for 13 to 14 minutes. Flipping at the halfway mark. Serve.

525. Rotisserie Chicken

Preparation Time: *5 minutes*
Cooking Time: *1 hour*
Servings: 4

Ingredients:

- Whole chicken – 1, cleaned and patted dry
- Olive oil – 2 tbsps.
- Seasoned salt – 1 tbsp.

Directions:

- Remove the giblet packet from the cavity. Rub the chicken with oil and salt. Place in the air fryer basket, breast-side down. Cook at 350F for 30 minutes.
- Then flip and cook another 30 minutes. Chicken is done when it reaches 165F.

526. Honey-Mustard Chicken Breasts

Preparation Time: *5 minutes*
Cooking Time: 25 minutes
Servings: 6

Ingredients:

- Boneless, skinless chicken breasts – 6 (6-oz, each)
- Fresh rosemary – 2 tbsps. minced
- Honey – 3 tbsps.
- Dijon mustard – 1 tbsp.
- Salt and pepper to taste

Directions:

- Combine the mustard, honey, pepper, rosemary and salt in a bowl. Rub the chicken with this mixture.
- Grease the air fryer basket with oil. Air fry the chicken at 350F for 20 to 24 minutes or until the chicken reaches 165F. Serve.

527. Chicken Parmesan Wings

Preparation Time: *5 minutes*
Cooking Time: 15 minutes
Servings: 4

Ingredients:

- Chicken wings – 2 lbs. cut into drumettes, pat dried
- Parmesan – ½ cup, plus 6 tbsps. grated
- Herbs de Provence – 1 tsp.
- Paprika – 1 tsp.
- Salt to taste

Directions:

- Combine the parmesan, herbs, paprika, and salt in a bowl and rub the chicken with this mixture. Preheat the air fryer at 350F.
- Grease the basket with cooking spray. Cook for 15 minutes. Flip once at the halfway mark. Garnish with parmesan and serve.

528. Air Fryer Chicken

Preparation Time: 5 minutes
Cooking Time: 30 minutes
Servings: 4

Ingredients:

- Chicken wings – 2 lbs.
- Salt and pepper to taste
- Cooking spray

Directions:

- Flavor the chicken wings with salt and pepper. Grease the air fryer basket with cooking spray. Add chicken wings and cook at 400F for 35 minutes.
- Flip 3 times during cooking for even cooking. Serve.

529. Whole Chicken

Preparation Time: 5 minutes
Cooking Time: 40 minutes
Servings: 6

Ingredients:

- Whole chicken – 1 (2 ½ pounds) washed and pat dried
- Dry rub – 2 tbsps.
- Salt – 1 tsp.
- Cooking spray

Directions:

- Preheat the air fryer at 350F. Rub the dry rub on the chicken. Then rub with salt. Cook it at 350°F for 45 minutes. After 30 minutes, flip the chicken and finish cooking.
- Chicken is done when it reaches 165F.

530. Honey Duck Breasts

Preparation Time: *5 minutes*
Cooking Time: 25 minutes
Servings: 2

Ingredients:

- Smoked duck breast – 1, halved
- Honey – 1 tsp.
- Tomato paste – 1 tsp.
- Mustard – 1 tbsp.
- Apple vinegar – ½ tsp.

Directions:

- Mix tomato paste, honey, mustard, and vinegar in a bowl. Whisk well. Add duck breast pieces and coat well. Cook in the air fryer at 370F for 15 minutes.
- Remove the duck breast from the air fryer and add to the honey mixture. Coat again. Cook again at 370F for 6 minutes. Serve.

531. Creamy Coconut Chicken

Preparation Time: *5 minutes*
Cooking Time: 20 minutes
Servings: 4

Ingredients:

- Big chicken legs – 4
- Turmeric powder – 5 tsps.
- Ginger – 2 tbsps. grated
- Salt and black pepper to taste
- Coconut cream – 4 tbsps.

Directions:

- In a bowl, mix salt, pepper, ginger, turmeric, and cream. Whisk. Add chicken pieces, coat and marinate for 2 hours.
- Transfer chicken to the preheated air fryer and cook at 370F for 25 minutes. Serve.

532.   Buffalo Chicken Tenders

Preparation Time: *5 minutes*
Cooking Time: 20 minutes
Servings: 4

Ingredients:

- Boneless, skinless chicken tenders – 1 pound
- Hot sauce – ¼ cup
- Pork rinds – 1 ½ ounces, finely ground
- Chili powder – 1 tsp.
- Garlic powder – 1 tsp.

Directions:

1. Put the chicken breasts in a bowl and pour hot sauce over them. Toss to coat. Mix ground pork rinds, chili powder and garlic powder in another bowl.
2. Place each tender in the ground pork rinds, and coat well. With wet hands, press down the pork rinds into the chicken. Place the tender in a single layer into the air fryer basket. Cook at 375F for 20 minutes. Flip once. Serve.

533.   Teriyaki Wings

Preparation Time: *5 minutes*
Cooking Time: 20 minutes
Servings: 4

Ingredients:

- Chicken wings – 2 pounds

- Teriyaki sauce – ½ cup
- Minced garlic – 2 tsp.
- Ground ginger - ¼ tsp.
- Baking powder – 2 tsp.

Directions:

- Except for the baking powder, place all ingredients in a bowl and marinate for 1 hour in the refrigerator. Place wings into the air fryer basket and sprinkle with baking powder.
- Gently rub into wings. Cook at 400F for 25 minutes. Shake the basket two- or three-times during cooking. Serve.

534.   Lemony Drumsticks

Preparation Time: 5 minutes
Cooking Time: 20 minutes
Servings: 2

Ingredients:

- Baking powder – 2 tsps.
- Garlic powder – ½ tsp.
- Chicken drumsticks – 8
- Salted butter – 4 tbsps. melted
- Lemon pepper seasoning – 1 tbsp.

Directions:

- Sprinkle garlic powder and baking powder over drumsticks and rub into chicken skin. Place drumsticks into the air fryer basket. Cook at 375F for 25 minutes. Flip the drumsticks once halfway through the Cooking Time.
- Remove when cooked. Mix seasoning and butter in a bowl. Add drumsticks to the bowl and toss to coat. Serve.

535.   Parmesan Chicken Tenders

Preparation Time: *5 minutes*
Cooking Time: 10 minutes
Servings: 4

Ingredients:

- 1 pound chicken tenderloins
- 3 large egg whites

- ½ cup Italian-style bread crumbs
- ¼ cup grated Parmesan cheese

Directions:

- Preparing the Ingredients. Spray the Cuisinart air fryer basket with olive oil. Trim off any white fat from the chicken tenders. In a bowl, whisk the egg whites until frothy. In a separate small mixing bowl, combine the bread crumbs and Parmesan cheese. Mix well.

- Dip the chicken tenders into the egg mixture, then into the Parmesan and bread crumbs. Shake off any excess breading. Place the chicken tenders in the greased Cuisinart air fryer basket in a single layer. Generously spray the chicken with olive oil to avoid powdery, uncooked breading.

- Air Frying. Set the temperature of your Air fryer to 370°F. Set the timer and bake for 4 minutes. Using tongs, flip the chicken tenders and bake for 4 minutes more. Check that the chicken has reached an internal temperature of 165°F. Add Cooking Time if needed. Once the chicken is fully cooked, plate, serve, and enjoy.

536. Easy Lemon Chicken Thighs

Preparation Time: *5 minutes*
Cooking Time: 10 minutes
Servings: 4

Ingredients:

- Salt and black pepper to taste
- 2 tablespoons olive oil
- 2 tablespoons Italian seasoning
- 2 tablespoons freshly squeezed lemon juice
- 1 lemon, sliced

Directions:

- Place the chicken thighs in a medium mixing bowl and season them with the salt and pepper. Add the olive oil, Italian seasoning, and lemon juice and toss until the chicken thighs are thoroughly coated with oil. Add the sliced lemons. Place the chicken thighs into the air fryer basket in a single layer.

- Set the temperature of your AF to 350°F. Set the timer and cook for 10 minutes. Using tongs, flip the chicken. Reset the timer and cook for 10 minutes more. Check that the chicken has reached an internal temperature of 165°F. Add Cooking Time if needed. Once the chicken is fully cooked, plate, serve, and enjoy.

537. Air Fryer Grilled Chicken Breasts

Preparation Time: *5 minutes*
Cooking Time: 14 minutes
Servings: 4

Ingredients:

- ½ teaspoon garlic powder
- salt and black pepper to taste
- 1 teaspoon dried parsley
- 2 tablespoons olive oil, divided
- 3 boneless, skinless chicken breasts

Directions:

- Preparing the Ingredients. In a small bowl, combine together the garlic powder, salt, pepper, and parsley. Using 1 tablespoon of olive oil and half of the seasoning mix, rub each chicken breast with oil and seasonings. Place the chicken breast in the air fryer basket.

- Air Frying. Set the temperature of your Air fryer to 370°F. Set the timer and grill for 7 minutes.

- Using tongs, flip the chicken and brush the remaining olive oil and spices onto the chicken. Reset the timer and grill for 7 minutes more. Check that the chicken has reached an internal temperature of 165°F. Add Cooking Time if needed.

- When the chicken is cooked, transfer it to a platter and serve.

538. Air Fried Smothered Turkey Wings

Preparation Time: 10 minutes
Cooking Time: 1 hour and 15 minutes
Servings: 2

Ingredients:

- ♦ 4 turkey wings
- ♦ ½ tbsp salt
- ♦ ½ tbsp ground pepper
- ♦ ½ tbsp onion powder
- ♦ ½ tbsp garlic powder
- ♦ ¼ cup butter
- ♦ 1/3 cup olive oil
- ♦ 1 onion, chopped
- ♦ ½ cup all-purpose flour
- ♦ 1 chicken bouillon cube
- ♦ ½ tsp liquid smoke
- ♦ 4 ½ cups water

Directions:

- Preheat your air fryer to 5 minutes.
- In a bowl, mix together the turkey wings, salt, pepper, onion, powder, and garlic powder. Rub all mixture into the turkey wings.
- Place the wings in the crisper or air fryer basket and select the AirFry cooking mode. Make sure to adjust the cooking time to 4300F and the time to 1 hour and 15 minutes. Make sure to flip the wings halfway through the cooking time.
- Meanwhile, heat a saucepan over medium flame and add the butter and olive oil. Stir in the onions and sauté for 30 sec to 1 min.
- Stir in the oil purpose flour and mix until a roux is formed. Cook for 3 minutes over low to medium flame.
- Slowly stir in the bouillon cube, liquid smoke, and water. Whisk to remove the clumps. Cook for 5 minutes until the gravy thickens. Set aside.
- Once the turkey wings are cooked, pour over the gravy on the turkey wings.
- Serve.

539.   Air Fried Turkey Breast

Preparation Time: 10 minutes
Cooking Time: 20 minutes
Servings: 10

Ingredients:

- ♦ 4 pounds turkey breast
- ♦ 1 tbsp olive oil
- ♦ 2 teaspoons butter
- ♦ ½ tbsp turkey seasoning

Directions:

- Preheat the air fryer to 3500F for 5 minutes.
- Rub all seasonings on the turkey breasts.
- Place the seasoned turkey in the air fryer and select the AirFry function. Adjust the cooking time to 20 minutes.
- Make sure to flip the turkey breasts halfway through the cooking time.
- Cook until the internal temperature reads at 1600F.

540.   Air Fried Whole Rotisserie Chicken

Preparation Time: 20 minutes
Cooking Time: 50 minutes
Servings: 6

Ingredients:

- ♦ 2 tbsp olive oil
- ♦ 1 tbsp salt
- ♦ 1 tbsp black pepper
- ♦ 1 tsp garlic powder
- ♦ 1 tsp paprika
- ♦ ½ tsp dried basil
- ♦ ½ tsp dried oregano
- ♦ ½ tsp dried thyme
- ♦ 1 5-lb whole chicken

Directions:

- Preheat the air fryer to 3500F for 5 minutes.
- Combine all seasonings in a bowl. Mix until well combined.
- Brush the chicken with the seasoning.
- Skewer the rotisserie chicken through the rotisserie spit.
- Place inside the Power Air Fryer 360 and select the Rotisserie setting.
- Cook for 50 minutes until the internal temperature reads at 1650F.

541. Air Fried Roast Rosemary Chicken

Preparation Time: 10 minutes
Cooking Time: 1 hour and 15 minutes
Servings: 6

Ingredients:

- ¼ cup salt
- 10 cups water
- 1 5-lb whole chicken
- 1 tbsp dried rosemary

Directions:

- Dissolve salt in water in a large bowl.
- Add in the chicken and rosemary and allow the chicken to soak in the brine overnight.
- Preheat the air fryer for 5 minutes.
- Place the chicken in the crisper tray. Make sure that the drip tray is placed underneath.
- Select the AirFry setting and adjust the temperature to 1 hour and 15 minutes.
- Cook the chicken for 1 hour and 15 minutes.

542. Crispy Panko Chicken Breasts

Preparation Time: 30 minutes
Cooking Time: 20 minutes
Serving: 2

Ingredients:

- 1-pound boneless chicken breasts, skin removed
- 1 tsp salt
- ½ tsp black pepper
- 1 tsp garlic powder
- 1 tsp onion powder
- 1 egg beaten
- 1 cup panko bread crumbs

Directions:

- Preheat the air fryer for 5 minutes.
- Season the chicken breasts with salt, black pepper, garlic powder, and onion powder.
- Place the beaten egg in one bowl and the panko crumbs in another.
- Dip the seasoned chicken in the egg and dredge in panko bread crumbs. Spray with cooking oil.
- Place the chicken in the crisper tray.
- Select the AirFry setting and cook for 20 minutes.
- Make sure to flip the chicken halfway through the cooking time for even cooking.

543. Baked Chicken Wings

Preparation Time: 12 minutes
Cooking Time: 30 minutes
Servings: 4

Ingredients:

- 2 lbs. chicken wings
- 1 tsp baking powder
- 1 tsp salt
- 1tbsp butter
- 1/3 cup hot wing sauce

Directions:

- Preheat the air fryer to 4000F for 5 minutes.
- Dry the chicken wings with paper towel and sprinkle with baking powder and salt.
- Place the chicken wings on the crisper tray. Make sure to leave enough space for the air to circulate.
- Select the AirFry setting and adjust the cooking time to 30 minutes.
- Meanwhile, heat the butter in a saucepan over medium flame. Add the hot wing sauce. Stir for 5 minutes.
- Serve the air fried wings with the hot sauce.

544. Crunchy Chicken Drumsticks

Preparation Time: 5 minutes
Cooking Time: 25 minutes
Servings: 6

Ingredients:

- 6 chicken drumsticks
- ½ tsp salt
- ½ tsp pepper
- ½ tsp garlic powder

- ♦ ½ tbsp onion powder
- ♦ ½ tbsp oregano
- ♦ 1 tbsp parsley
- ♦ 1 cup panko bread crumbs

Directions:

- Preheat the air fryer to 4000F for 5 minutes.
- Season the chicken with salt, pepper, garlic powder, onion powder, oregano, and parsley.
- Spray seasoned chicken with cooking oil and dredge in panko bread crumbs.
- Place on the crisper tray.
- Select the AirFry setting and cook for 25 minutes.

545.   Southern Fried Chicken

Preparation Time: 20 minutes
Servings: 6
Cooking Time: 30 minutes

Ingredients:

- ♦ 2 lbs. chicken legs
- ♦ 2 tsp salt
- ♦ 1 ½ tsp black pepper
- ♦ 1 ½ tsp paprika
- ♦ 1 tsp onion powder
- ♦ 1 tsp Italian seasoning
- ♦ ¼ cup cornstarch
- ♦ 1 cup self-rising flour
- ♦ 1 tbsp hot sauce
- ♦ 2 eggs, beaten
- ♦ 2 tbsp milk
- ♦ ¼ cup water

Directions:

- Preheat the air fryer to 4000F for 5 minutes.
- Season the chicken legs with salt, pepper, paprika, onion powder, and Italian seasoning.
- Place the cornstarch in a separate container. Do the same thing with the flour.
- To the eggs, place them in bowl and add in the hot sauce, milk, and water. Beat until well combined.

- Dredge the seasoned chicken legs in cornstarch then dip in egg mixture before dredging in flour. Do this twice.
- Oil the surface of the chicken with cooking spray.
- Place on the crisper basket or tray.
- Select the AirFry setting and adjust the cooking time to 30 minutes.
- Flip the chicken legs halfway through the cooking time.

546.   Buttermilk Fried Chicken

Preparation Time: 3 hours
Cooking Time: 25 minutes
Servings: 4

Ingredients:

- ♦ 1 4-lb chicken, cut into bite-sized pieces
- ♦ 2 cups buttermilk
- ♦ 1 ½ cups all-purpose flour
- ♦ 2 tsp paprika
- ♦ 1 tsp salt
- ♦ A dash of ground black pepper
- ♦ 2 eggs, beaten

Directions:

- Preheat the air fryer to 4000F for 5 minutes.
- Place the chicken in a Ziploc bag and add the buttermilk. Place in the fridge for at least 2 hours.
- Prepare the dredging station by putting the flour, paprika, salt, and black pepper in a bowl.
- Place the beaten eggs in another bowl.
- Dip the chicken in the beaten eggs and dredge in seasoned flour.
- Place on the crisper tray.
- Select the Air Fry setting and adjust the cooking time to 25 minutes.

547.   General Tso's Chicken

Preparation Time: 30 minutes
Cooking Time: 30 minutes
Servings: 6

Ingredients:

- 1 large egg, beaten
- 1 lb. boneless chicken thighs, dried and cut into chunks
- 1/3 cup cornstarch
- ¼ tsp salt
- ¼ tsp ground white pepper
- 7 tbsp chicken broth
- 2 tbsp soy sauce
- 2 tbsp ketchup
- 2 tsp sugar
- 2 tsp rice vinegar
- 1 ½ tbsp canola oil
- 3 chiles de arbol, chopped
- 1 tbsp ginger, chopped
- 1 tbsp garlic, chopped
- 2 tbsp green onions, chopped
- 1 tsp toasted sesame oil

Directions:

- Preheat the air fryer to 4000F for 5 minutes.
- Beat the egg in a bowl and add in the chicken. Dip the chicken for 10 minutes.
- In another bowl, combine the cornstarch, salt, and white pepper. Dredge the chicken in the cornstarch mixture and place on a crisper tray.
- Press the AirFry setting and adjust the cooking time to 30 minutes.
- Give the cooked chicken a shake for even cooking.
- Meanwhile, place the broth, soy sauce, ketchup, sugar, vinegar, canola oil, chiles, ginger, and garlic in a saucepan. Heat for 10 minutes until the sauce thickens.
- Once the chicken pieces are cooked, place in a bowl and add in the sauce. Toss to coat. Add in the green onions and sesame oil.

548. Korean-Style Chicken Wings

Preparation Time: 20 minutes
Cooking Time: 30 minutes
Servings: 4

Ingredients:

- 2 pounds chicken wings

- ¾ cup cornstarch
- 1 tsp garlic powder
- 1 tsp onion powder
- ¼ tsp salt
- 3 tbsp honey
- 2 tbsp gochujang
- 2 tbsp brown sugar
- 1 tbsp soy sauce
- 1 tsp grated fresh ginger
- 1 tsp grated garlic
- ½ tsp salt
- Green onions, chopped

Directions:

- Preheat the air fryer to 4000F for 5 minutes.
- Dry the wings with paper towel and place in a large bowl.
- In another bowl, mix together the cornstarch, garlic powder, onion powder, and salt.
- Dredge the wings with the cornstarch mixture and make sure that all parts of the wings are coated with cornstarch.
- Remove the excess starch by shaking the chicken.
- Place on the crisper basket and select the AirFry setting and adjust the cooking time to 30
- Make the sauce by mixing the honey, gochujang, brown sugar, soy sauce, ginger, garlic, and salt. Place in a saucepan and cook for 5 minutes.
- Once the chicken is done, transfer in a bowl and pour over the sauce.
- Toss to coat and garnish with green onions.

549. Orange Chicken

Preparation Time: 5 minutes
Cooking Time: 30 minutes
Servings: 4

Ingredients:

- 2 lbs. boneless chicken breasts, skin removed
- Salt and pepper to taste
- 2 cups orange juice

- ♦ ¼ cup chicken broth
- ♦ ¼ cup soy sauce
- ♦ 3 tbsp honey
- ♦ 1 tsp garlic powder
- ♦ 2 tsp grated ginger
- ♦ ½ tbsp orange zest

Directions:

- Preheat the air fryer to 4000F for 5 minutes.
- Season the chicken with salt and pepper to taste.
- Place in the crisper tray.
- Select the AirFry setting and adjust the cooking time to 30 minutes.
- Meanwhile, mix the remaining ingredients in a saucepan and bring to a boil until it thickens.
- Once the chicken is cooked, place in a bowl and pour over the sauce. Toss to coat the chicken with the sauce.

550.   Firecracker Chicken

Preparation Time: 20 minutes
Cooking Time: 25 minutes
Servings: 4

Ingredients:

- ♦ 1 ¼ lb. boneless chicken breast, cut into 1-inch pieces
- ♦ Salt and pepper to taste
- ♦ 1/3 cup cornstarch
- ♦ 2 eggs, beaten
- ♦ 1/3 cup buffalo hot sauce
- ♦ ½ cup brown sugar
- ♦ 1 tbsp rice vinegar
- ♦ ¼ tsp red pepper flakes
- ♦ ¼ cup green onions, chopped

Directions:

- Preheat the air fryer to 4000F for 5 minutes.
- Place the chicken pieces on a plate and season with salt and pepper to taste.
- Sprinkle cornstarch all over the chicken and toss to coat evenly.

- Dip the chicken with beaten eggs.
- Place on the crisper tray.
- Select the AirFry setting and adjust the cooking time to 25 minutes.
- Meanwhile, mix the buffalo hot sauce, sugar, vinegar, and pepper flakes. Heat for 10 minutes until the sauce thickens.
- Once the chicken is cooked, place in a bowl and pour over the sauce. Toss to coat and garnish with green onions.

551.   One-Pot Chicken and Tomato Spiced Curry

Preparation Time: 20 minutes
Cooking Time: 6 hours
Servings: 6

Ingredients:

- ♦ ½ lb. chicken breast, cut into chunks
- ♦ 1 onion, chopped
- ♦ 2 garlic cloves, chopped
- ♦ 1-inch ginger, peeled and grated
- ♦ 2 tbsp curry paste
- ♦ ½ cup chopped tomatoes
- ♦ ½ cup basmati rice
- ♦ A handful of coriander, chopped

Directions:

- Preheat the air fryer to 4000F for 5 minutes.
- Place all ingredients in a deep casserole dish. Mix until well combined.
- Place inside the air fryer.
- Select the Slow Cook setting and adjust the cooking time to 6 hours.

552.   Italian Baked Chicken

Preparation Time: 15 minutes
Cooking Time: 60 minutes
Servings: 6

Ingredients:

- ♦ 2 lbs. boneless chicken breast
- ♦ Salt and pepper to taste
- ♦ 2 tsp dry oregano
- ♦ 1 tsp fresh thyme

- 1 tsp sweet paprika
- 4 garlic cloves, minced
- 3 tbsp olive oil
- Juice from ½ lemon
- 1 medium red onion, chopped
- 6 tomatoes, chopped
- Handful chopped parsley
- Handful basil leaves

Directions:

- Preheat the air fryer to 4000F for 5 minutes.
- Season the chicken with salt, pepper, oregano, thyme, paprika, and garlic cloves. Add in the olive oil and lemon juice.
- Place the onions in the bottom of a casserole dish. Pour in the tomatoes. Add the seasoned chicken slices on top.
- Place inside the air fryer.
- Select the Bake setting and adjust the cooking time to 60 minutes.
- Garnish with parsley and basil leaves.

553. Garlic Butter Chicken

Preparation Time: 20 minutes
Cooking Time: 60 minutes
Servings: 6

Ingredients:

- 1 ½ lb. chicken breasts
- ¼ cup soy sauce
- 1 tbsp hot sauce
- 1 tbsp olive oil
- 3 tbsp butter, melted
- 5 cloves garlic, minced
- 1 tsp fresh thyme, chopped
- 1 tsp fresh rosemary, chopped
- 1 tsp fresh oregano, chopped
- Salt and pepper to taste
- Crushed red pepper flakes
- ½ lb. potatoes, quartered

Directions:

- Marinate the chicken in soy sauce and hot sauce. Place inside the fridge and allow to marinate for 2 hours.

- Preheat the air fryer to 4000F for 5 minutes.
- In a casserole dish, place the chicken, olive oil, butter, garlic, thyme, rosemary, oregano, salt, pepper, and red pepper flakes.
- Place inside the air fryer and select the Bake button. Adjust the cooking time to 60 minutes.
- After 10 minutes, take the casserole dish out and baste the chicken with the oil. Add in the potatoes and baste with oil.
- Put back in the oven and cook for the remaining time.

554. Spinach Chicken Casserole

Preparation Time: 30 minutes
Cooking Time: 60 minutes
Servings: 5

Ingredients:

- 2 large boneless chicken breasts, cut into bite-sized pieces
- Salt and pepper to taste
- 1 tsp garlic powder
- ½ tsp red pepper flakes
- ½ tsp Italian seasoning
- 2 cups spinach, rinsed and torn
- 8 ounces cream cheese, softened
- 4 ounces Mozzarella cheese, shredded

Directions:

- Preheat the air fryer to 3500F for 5 minutes.
- Pat dry the chicken breasts and season with salt, pepper, and garlic powder.
- Place the spinach in a casserole dish that will fit inside the air fryer. Place seasoned chicken on top of the spinach.
- Top with cream cheese and mozzarella cheese.
- Place inside the air fryer and select the Bake function.
- Adjust the cooking time to 60 minutes.

555. Air Fried Southern Style Chicken

Preparation Time: 30 minutes
Cooking Time: 15 minutes

Servings: 4

Ingredients:

- 2 cups crushed Ritz crackers
- 1 tbsp minced parsley
- 1 tsp garlic salt
- 1 tsp paprika
- ½ tsp pepper
- ¼ tsp ground cumin
- 1 large egg, beaten
- 1 fryer chicken, cut up into bite-sized pieces
- Cooking spray

Directions:

- Preheat the air fryer to 3750F for 5 minutes.
- In a bowl, mix the first 7 ingredients.
- Place the egg in another owl.
- Dip the chicken in egg and dredge in the Ritz cracker mixture.
- Spray with cooking oil then place inside the air fryer.
- Select the AirFry setting and adjust the cooking time to 15 minutes.

556. Parmesan Baked Chicken Breast

Preparation Time: 5 minutes
Cooking Time: 20 minutes
Servings: 2

Ingredients:

- 1 lb. skinless and boneless chicken breast
- 1 ½ tbsp garlic powder
- 2 tbsp lemon juice
- Salt and ground black pepper to taste
- 3 dashed cayenne pepper
- ½ cup grated parmesan cheese
- Cooking spray
- Lemon wedges for garnish

Directions:

- Preheat the air fryer to 3500F for 5 minutes.
- Season the chicken with garlic powder, lemon juice, salt, pepper, and cayenne pepper.

- Dredge in parmesan cheese then spray with cooking oil.
- Place the chicken on the crisper tray.
- Select the AirFry setting and adjust the cooking time to 20 minutes.

557. Garlic Chicken

Preparation Time: 10 minutes
Cooking Time: 15 minutes
Servings: 4

Ingredients:

- 3 tbsp butter
- 2 cloves garlic, minced
- 4 skinless and boneless chicken breasts, halved
- ¼ cup Italian-seasoned bread crumbs
- ¼ cup parmesan cheese, grated

Directions:

- Preheat the air fryer to 3500F for 5 minutes.
- Heat the butter in a saucepan and add the garlic.
- Stir in the chicken breasts and allow to sear for 2 minutes on each side.
- Place in a casserole dish and sprinkle with bread crumbs and parmesan cheese on top.
- Place in the air fryer and select the AirFry setting. Adjust the cooking time to 15 minutes.

558. Rosemary Turkey Breast

Preparation Time: 2 hours 20 minutes
Cooking Time: 30 minutes
Servings: 6

Ingredients:

- ½ teaspoon dried rosemary
- 2 minced garlic cloves
- 2 teaspoons salt
- 1 teaspoon ground black pepper
- 1/4 cup olive oil
- 2 1/2 pounds (1.1 kg) turkey breast
- ¼ cup pure maple syrup
- 1 tablespoon stone-ground brown mustard
- 1 tablespoon melted vegan butter

Directions:

- Combine the rosemary, garlic, salt, ground black pepper, and olive oil in a large bowl. Stir to mix well.
- Dunk the turkey breast in the mixture and wrap the bowl in plastic. Refrigerate for 2 hours to marinate.
- Remove the bowl from the refrigerator and let sit for half an hour before cooking.
- Spritz the air fry basket with cooking spray.
- Remove the turkey from the marinade and place in the air fry basket.
- Select Air Fry, Super Convection. Set temperature to 400°F (205°C) and set time to 20 minutes. Press Start/Stop to begin preheating.
- Once preheated, place the basket on the air fry position. Flip the breast halfway through.
- When cooking is complete, the breast should be well browned.
- Meanwhile, combine the remaining ingredients in a small bowl. Stir to mix well.
- Pour half of the butter mixture over the turkey breast in the oven and air fry for 10 more minutes. Flip the breast and pour the remaining half of butter mixture over halfway through.
- Transfer the turkey on a plate and slice to serve.

559. Glazed Duck with Cherry Sauce

Preparation Time: 20 minutes
Cooking Time: 32 minutes
Servings: 12

Ingredients:

- 1 whole duck (about 5 pounds / 2.3 kg in total), split in half, back and rib bones removed, fat trimmed
- 1 teaspoon olive oil
- Salt and freshly ground black pepper, to taste

Cherry Sauce:

- 1 tablespoon butter
- 1 shallot, minced
- ½ cup sherry
- 1 cup chicken stock
- 1 teaspoon white wine vinegar
- ¾ cup cherry preserves
- 1 teaspoon fresh thyme leaves
- Salt and freshly ground black pepper, to taste

Directions:

- On a clean work surface, rub the duck with olive oil, then sprinkle with salt and ground black pepper to season.
- Place the duck in the air fry basket, breast side up.
- Select Air Fry, Super Convection. Set temperature to 400°F (205°C) and set time to 25 minutes. Press Start/Stop to begin preheating.
- Once preheated, place the basket on the air fry position. Flip the ducks halfway through the cooking time.
- Meanwhile, make the cherry sauce: Heat the butter in a skillet over medium-high heat or until melted.
- Add the shallot and sauté for 5 minutes or until lightly browned.
- Add the sherry and simmer for 6 minutes or until it reduces in half.
- Add the chicken stick, white wine vinegar, and cherry preserves. Stir to combine well. Simmer for 6 more minutes or until thickened.
- Fold in the thyme leaves and sprinkle with salt and ground black pepper. Stir to mix well.
- When the cooking of the duck is complete, glaze the duck with a quarter of the cherry sauce, then air fry for another 4 minutes.
- Flip the duck and glaze with another quarter of the cherry sauce. Air fry for an additional 3 minutes.
- Transfer the duck on a large plate and serve with remaining cherry sauce.

560. Braised Chicken with Hot Peppers

Preparation Time: 10 minutes
Cooking Time: 27 minutes
Servings: 4

Ingredients:

- 4 bone-in, skin-on chicken thighs (about 1½ pounds / 680 g)
- 1½ teaspoon kosher salt, divided
- 1 link sweet Italian sausage (about 4 ounces / 113 g), whole
- 8 ounces (227 g) miniature bell peppers, halved and deseeded
- 1 small onion, thinly sliced
- 2 garlic cloves, minced
- 1 tablespoon olive oil
- 4 hot pickled cherry peppers, deseeded and quartered, along with 2 tablespoons pickling liquid from the jar
- ¼ cup chicken stock
- Cooking spray

Directions:

- Salt the chicken thighs on both sides with 1 teaspoon of kosher salt. Spritz a baking pan with cooking spray and place the thighs skin-side down on the pan. Add the sausage.
- Select Roast, Super Convection, set temperature to 375°F (190°C), and set time to 27 minutes. Press Start/Stop to begin preheating.
- Once preheated, place the pan on the roast position.
- While the chicken and sausage cook, place the bell peppers, onion, and garlic in a large bowl. Sprinkle with the remaining kosher salt and add the olive oil. Toss to coat.
- After 10 minutes, remove the pan from the oven and flip the chicken thighs and sausage. Add the pepper mixture to the pan. Return the pan to the oven and continue cooking.
- After another 10 minutes, remove the pan from the oven and add the pickled peppers, pickling liquid, and stock. Stir the pickled peppers into the peppers and onion. Return the pan to the oven and continue cooking.

- When cooking is complete, the peppers and onion should be soft and the chicken should read 165°F (74°C) on a meat thermometer. Remove the pan from the oven. Slice the sausage into thin pieces and stir it into the pepper mixture. Spoon the peppers over four plates. Top with a chicken thigh.

561. Strawberry-Glazed Turkey

Preparation Time: 15 minutes
Cooking Time: 37 minutes
Serving 2

Ingredients:

- 2 pounds (907 g) turkey breast
- 1 tablespoon olive oil
- Salt and ground black pepper, to taste
- 1 cup fresh strawberries

Directions:

- Rub the turkey bread with olive oil on a clean work surface, then sprinkle with salt and ground black pepper.
- Transfer the turkey in the air fry basket and spritz with cooking spray.
- Select Air Fry, Super Convection. Set temperature to 375°F (190°C) and set time to 30 minutes. Press Start/Stop to begin preheating.
- Once preheated, place the basket on the air fry position. Flip the turkey breast halfway through.
- Meanwhile, put the strawberries in a food processor and pulse until smooth.
- When cooking is complete, spread the puréed strawberries over the turkey and fry for 7 more minutes.
- Serve immediately.

562. Turkey and Cauliflower Meatloaf

Preparation Time: 15 minutes
Cooking Time: 50 minutes
Servings: 6

Ingredients:

- 2 pounds (907 g) lean ground turkey

- 11/3 cups riced cauliflower
- 2 large eggs, lightly beaten
- 1/4 cup almond flour
- 2/3 cup chopped yellow or white onion
- 1 teaspoon ground dried turmeric
- 1 teaspoon ground cumin
- 1 teaspoon ground coriander
- 1 tablespoon minced garlic
- 1 teaspoon salt
- 1 teaspoon ground black pepper
- Cooking spray

Directions:

- Spritz a loaf pan with cooking spray.

- Combine all the ingredients in a large bowl. Stir to mix well. Pour half of the mixture in the prepared loaf pan and press with a spatula to coat the bottom evenly. Spritz the mixture with cooking spray.

- Select Bake, Super Convection, set temperature to 350°F (180°C) and set time to 25 minutes. Press Start/Stop to begin preheating.

- Once preheated, place the pan on the bake position.

- When cooking is complete, the meat should be well browned and the internal temperature should reach at least 165°F (74°C).

- Remove the loaf pan from the oven and serve immediately.

563.   Deep Fried Duck Leg Quarters

Preparation Time: 5 minutes
Cooking Time: 45 minutes
Servings: 4

Ingredients:

- 4 (½-pound / 227-g) skin-on duck leg quarters
- 2 medium garlic cloves, minced
- ½ teaspoon salt
- ½ teaspoon ground black pepper

Directions:

- Spritz the air fry basket with cooking spray.

- On a clean work surface, rub the duck leg quarters with garlic, salt, and black pepper.

- Arrange the leg quarters in the air fry basket and spritz with cooking spray.

- Select Air Fry, Super Convection. Set temperature to 300°F (150°C) and set time to 30 minutes. Press Start/Stop to begin preheating.

- Once preheated, place the basket on the air fry position.

- After 30 minutes, remove the basket from the oven. Flip the leg quarters. Increase temperature to 375°F (190°C) and set time to 15 minutes. Return the basket to the oven and continue cooking.

- When cooking is complete, the leg quarters should be well browned and crispy.

- Remove the duck leg quarters from the oven and allow to cool for 10 minutes before serving.

564.   Duck Breasts with Marmalade Balsamic Glaze

Preparation Time: 5 minutes
Cooking Time: 13 minutes
Servings: 4

Ingredients:

- 4 (6-ounce / 170-g) skin-on duck breasts
- 1 teaspoon salt
- ¼ cup orange marmalade
- 1 tablespoon white balsamic vinegar
- ¾ teaspoon ground black pepper

Directions:

- Cut 10 slits into the skin of the duck breasts, then sprinkle with salt on both sides.

- Place the breasts in the air fry basket, skin side up.

- Select Air Fry, Super Convection. Set temperature to 400°F (205°C) and set time to 10 minutes. Press Start/Stop to begin preheating.

- Once preheated, place the basket on the air fry position.

- Meanwhile, combine the remaining ingredients in a small bowl. Stir to mix well.
- When cooking is complete, brush the duck skin with the marmalade mixture. Flip the breast and air fry for 3 more minutes or until the skin is crispy and the breast is well browned.
- Serve immediately.

565. Thai Game Hens with Cucumber and Chile Salad

Preparation Time: 25 minutes
Cooking Time: 25 minutes
Servings: 6

Ingredients:

- 2 (1¼-pound / 567-g) Cornish game hens, giblets discarded
- 1 tablespoon fish sauce
- 6 tablespoons chopped fresh cilantro
- 2 teaspoons lime zest
- 1 teaspoon ground coriander
- 2 garlic cloves, minced
- 2 tablespoons packed light brown sugar
- 2 teaspoons vegetable oil
- Salt and ground black pepper, to taste
- 1 English cucumber, halved lengthwise and sliced thin
- 1 Thai chile, stemmed, deseeded, and minced
- 2 tablespoons chopped dry-roasted peanuts
- 1 small shallot, sliced thinly
- 1 tablespoon lime juice
- Lime wedges, for serving
- Cooking spray

Directions:

- Arrange a game hen on a clean work surface, remove the backbone with kitchen shears, then pound the hen breast to flat. Cut the breast in half. Repeat with the remaining game hen.
- Loose the breast and thigh skin with your fingers, then pat the game hens dry and pierce about 10 holes into the fat deposits of the hens. Tuck the wings under the hens.

- Combine 2 teaspoons of fish sauce, ¼ cup of cilantro, lime zest, coriander, garlic, 4 teaspoons of sugar, 1 teaspoon of vegetable oil, ½ teaspoon of salt, and 1/8 teaspoon of ground black pepper in a small bowl. Stir to mix well.
- Rub the fish sauce mixture under the breast and thigh skin of the game hens, then let sit for 10 minutes to marinate.
- Spritz the air fry basket with cooking spray.
- Arrange the marinated game hens in the basket, skin side down.
- Select Air Fry, Super Convection. Set temperature to 400°F (205°C) and set time to 25 minutes. Press Start/Stop to begin preheating.
- Once preheated, place the basket on the air fry position. Flip the game hens halfway through the cooking time.
- When cooking is complete, the hen skin should be golden brown and the internal temperature of the hens should read at least 165°F (74°C).
- Meanwhile, combine all the remaining ingredients, except for the lime wedges, in a large bowl and sprinkle with salt and black pepper. Toss to mix well.
- Transfer the fried hens on a large plate, then sit the salad aside and squeeze the lime wedges over before serving.

566. Rosemary Turkey Scotch Eggs

Preparation Time: 15 minutes
Cooking Time: 12 minutes
Servings: 4

Ingredients:

- 1 egg
- 1 cup panko bread crumbs
- ½ teaspoon rosemary
- 1-pound (454 g) ground turkey
- 4 hard-boiled eggs, peeled
- Salt and ground black pepper, to taste
- Cooking spray

Directions:

- Spritz the air fry basket with cooking spray.
- Whisk the egg with salt in a bowl. Combine the bread crumbs with rosemary in a shallow dish.
- Stir the ground turkey with salt and ground black pepper in a separate large bowl, then divide the ground turkey into four portions.
- Wrap each hard-boiled egg with a portion of ground turkey. Dredge in the whisked egg, then roll over the bread crumb mixture.
- Place the wrapped eggs in the air fry basket and spritz with cooking spray.
- Select Air Fry, Super Convection. Set temperature to 400°F (205°C) and set time to 12 minutes. Press Start/Stop to begin preheating.
- Once preheated, place the basket on the air fry position. Flip the eggs halfway through.
- When cooking is complete, the scotch eggs should be golden brown and crunchy.
- Serve immediately.

567. Bacon-Wrapped Turkey with Carrots

Preparation Time: 10 minutes
Cooking Time: 25 minutes
Serving 4

Ingredients:

- 2 (12-ounce / 340-g) turkey tenderloins
- 1 teaspoon kosher salt, divided
- 6 slices bacon
- 3 tablespoons balsamic vinegar
- 2 tablespoons honey
- 1 tablespoon Dijon mustard
- ½ teaspoon dried thyme
- 6 large carrots, peeled and cut into ¼-inch rounds
- 1 tablespoon olive oil

Directions:

- Sprinkle the turkey with ¾ teaspoon of the salt. Wrap each tenderloin with 3 strips of bacon, securing the bacon with toothpicks. Place the turkey in a baking pan.

- In a small bowl, mix the balsamic vinegar, honey, mustard, and thyme.
- Place the carrots in a medium bowl and drizzle with the oil. Add 1 tablespoon of the balsamic mixture and ¼ teaspoon of kosher salt and toss to coat. Place these on the pan around the turkey tenderloins. Baste the tenderloins with about one-half of the remaining balsamic mixture.
- Select Roast, Super Convection, set temperature to 375°F (190°C), and set time to 25 minutes. Press Start/Stop to begin preheating.
- Once preheated, place the pan on the roast position.
- After 13 minutes, remove the pan from the oven. Gently stir the carrots. Flip the tenderloins and baste with the remaining balsamic mixture. Return the pan to the oven and continue cooking.
- When cooking is complete, the carrots should tender and the center of the tenderloins should register 165°F (74°C) on a meat thermometer. Remove the pan from the oven. Slice the turkey and serve with the carrots.

568. Chicken Ciabatta Sandwiches

Preparation Time: 12 minutes
Cooking Time: 13 minutes
Servings: 4

Ingredients:

- 2 (8-ounce / 227-g) boneless, skinless chicken breasts
- 1 teaspoon kosher salt, divided
- 1 cup all-purpose flour
- 1 teaspoon Italian seasoning
- 2 large eggs
- 2 tablespoons plain yogurt
- 2 cups panko bread crumbs
- 1 1/3 cups grated Parmesan cheese, divided
- 2 tablespoons olive oil
- 4 ciabatta rolls, split in half
- ½ cup marinara sauce
- ½ cup shredded Mozzarella cheese

Directions:

- Lay the chicken breasts on a cutting board and cut each one in half parallel to the board so you have 4 fairly even, flat fillets. Place a piece of plastic wrap over the chicken pieces and use a rolling pin to gently pound them to an even thickness, about ½-inch thick. Season the chicken on both sides with ½ teaspoon of kosher salt.

- Place the flour on a plate and add the remaining kosher salt and the Italian seasoning. Mix with a fork to distribute evenly. In a wide bowl, whisk together the eggs with the yogurt. In a small bowl combine the panko, 1 cup of Parmesan cheese, and olive oil. Place this in a shallow bowl.

- Lightly dredge both sides of the chicken pieces in the seasoned flour, and then dip them in the egg wash to coat completely, letting the excess drip off. Finally, dredge the chicken in the bread crumbs. Carefully place the breaded chicken pieces in the air fry basket.

- Select Air Fry, Super Convection, set temperature to 375°F (190°C), and set time to 10 minutes. Press Start/Stop to begin preheating.

- Once preheated, place the air fry basket into the oven.

- After 5 minutes, remove the air fry basket from the oven. Carefully turn the chicken over. Return the air fry basket to the oven and continue cooking. When cooking is complete, remove the air fry basket from the oven.

- Unfold the rolls on the air fry basket and spread each half with 1 tablespoon of marinara sauce. Place a chicken breast piece on the bottoms of the buns and sprinkle the remaining Parmesan cheese over the chicken pieces. Divide the Mozzarella among the top halves of the buns.

- Select Broil, Super Convection, set temperature to High, and set time to 3 minutes. Press Start/Stop to begin preheating.

- Once preheated, place the basket on the broil position. Check the sandwiches halfway through. When cooking is complete, the Mozzarella cheese should be melted and bubbly.

- Remove the air fry basket from the oven. Close the sandwiches and serve.

569. Balsamic Chicken Breast Roast

Preparation Time: 35 minutes
Cooking Time: 40 minutes
Servings: 2

Ingredients:

- ¼ cup balsamic vinegar
- 2 teaspoons dried oregano
- 2 garlic cloves, minced
- 1 tablespoon olive oil
- 1/8 teaspoon salt
- ½ teaspoon freshly ground black pepper
- 2 (4-ounce / 113-g) boneless, skinless, chicken-breast halves
- Cooking spray

Directions:

- In a small bowl, add the vinegar, oregano, garlic, olive oil, salt, and pepper. Mix to combine.

- Put the chicken in a resealable plastic bag. Pour the vinegar mixture in the bag with the chicken, seal the bag, and shake to coat the chicken. Refrigerate for 30 minutes to marinate.

- Spritz a baking pan with cooking spray. Put the chicken in the prepared baking pan and pour the marinade over the chicken.

- Select Bake, Super Convection, set temperature to 400°F (205°C) and set time to 40 minutes. Press Start/Stop to begin preheating.

- Once preheated, place the pan on the bake position.

- After 20 minutes, remove the pan from the oven. Flip the chicken. Return the pan to the oven and continue cooking.

- When cooking is complete, the internal temperature of the chicken should registers at least 165°F (74°C).
- Let sit for 5 minutes, then serve.

570. Chicken Skewers with Corn Salad

Preparation Time: 17 minutes
Cooking Time: 10 minutes
Servings: 4

Ingredients:

- 1 pound (454 g) boneless, skinless chicken breast, cut into 1½-inch chunks
- 1 green bell pepper, deseeded and cut into 1-inch pieces
- 1 red bell pepper, deseeded and cut into 1-inch pieces
- 1 large onion, cut into large chunks
- 2 tablespoons fajita seasoning
- 3 tablespoons vegetable oil, divided
- 2 teaspoons kosher salt, divided
- 2 cups corn, drained
- ¼ teaspoon granulated garlic
- 1 teaspoon freshly squeezed lime juice
- 1 tablespoon mayonnaise
- 3 tablespoons grated Parmesan cheese

Special Equipment:

- 12 wooden skewers, soaked in water for at least 30 minutes

Directions:

- Place the chicken, bell peppers, and onion in a large bowl. Add the fajita seasoning, 2 tablespoons of vegetable oil, and 1½ teaspoons of kosher salt. Toss to coat evenly.
- Alternate the chicken and vegetables on the skewers, making about 12 skewers.
- Place the corn in a medium bowl and add the remaining vegetable oil. Add the remaining kosher salt and the garlic, and toss to coat. Place the corn in an even layer on a baking pan and place the skewers on top.
- Select Roast, Super Convection, set temperature to 375°F (190°C), and set time

to 10 minutes. Press Start/Stop to begin preheating.
- Once preheated, place the pan on the roast position.
- After about 5 minutes, remove the pan from the oven and turn the skewers. Return the pan to the oven and continue cooking.
- When cooking is complete, remove the pan from the oven. Place the skewers on a platter. Put the corn back to the bowl and combine with the lime juice, mayonnaise, and Parmesan cheese. Stir to mix well. Serve the skewers with the corn.

571. Cheesy Turkey Burgers

Preparation Time: 10 minutes
Cooking Time: 25 minutes
Servings: 4

Ingredients:

- 2 medium yellow onions
- 1 tablespoon olive oil
- 1½ teaspoons kosher salt, divided
- 11/4 pound (567 g) ground turkey
- 1/3 cup mayonnaise
- 1 tablespoon Dijon mustard
- 2 teaspoons Worcestershire sauce
- 4 slices sharp Cheddar cheese (about 4 ounces / 113 g in total)
- 4 hamburger buns, sliced

Directions:

- Trim the onions and cut them in half through the root. Cut one of the halves in half. Grate one quarter. Place the grated onion in a large bowl. Thinly slice the remaining onions and place in a medium bowl with the oil and ½ teaspoon of kosher salt. Toss to coat. Place the onions in a single layer on a baking pan.
- Select Roast, Super Convection, set temperature to 350°F (180°C), and set time to 10 minutes. Press Start/Stop to begin preheating.
- Once preheated, place the pan on the roast position.

- While the onions are cooking, add the turkey to the grated onion. Add the remaining kosher salt, mayonnaise, mustard, and Worcestershire sauce. Mix just until combined, being careful not to overwork the turkey. Divide the mixture into 4 patties, each about ¾-inch thick.

- When cooking is complete, remove the pan from the oven. Move the onions to one side of the pan and place the burgers on the pan. Poke your finger into the center of each burger to make a deep indentation.

- Select Broil, Super Convection, set temperature to High, and set time to 12 minutes. Press Start/Stop to begin preheating.

- Once preheated, place the pan on the broil position. After 6 minutes, remove the pan. Turn the burgers and stir the onions. Return the pan to the oven and continue cooking. After about 4 minutes, remove the pan and place the cheese slices on the burgers. Return the pan to the oven and continue cooking for about 1 minute, or until the cheese is melted and the center of the burgers has reached at least 165°F (74°C) on a meat thermometer.

- When cooking is complete, remove the pan from the oven. Loosely cover the burgers with foil.

- Lay out the buns, cut-side up, on the oven rack. Select Broil, Super Convection, set temperature to High, and set time to 3 minutes. Place the pan on the broil position. Check the buns after 2 minutes; they should be lightly browned.

- Remove the buns from the oven. Assemble the burgers and serve.

572.   Chicken and Sweet Potato Curry

Preparation Time: 10 minutes
Cooking Time: 20 minutes
Servings: 4

Ingredients:

- 1 pound (454 g) boneless, skinless chicken thighs
- 1 teaspoon kosher salt, divided

- ¼ cup unsalted butter, melted
- 1 tablespoon curry powder
- 2 medium sweet potatoes, peeled and cut in 1-inch cubes
- 12 ounces (340 g) Brussels sprouts, halved

Directions:

- Sprinkle the chicken thighs with ½ teaspoon of kosher salt. Place them in the single layer on a baking pan.

- In a small bowl, stir together the butter and curry powder.

- Place the sweet potatoes and Brussels sprouts in a large bowl. Drizzle half the curry butter over the vegetables and add the remaining kosher salt. Toss to coat. Transfer the vegetables to the baking pan and place in a single layer around the chicken. Brush half of the remaining curry butter over the chicken.

- Select Roast, Super Convection, set temperature to 400°F (205°C), and set time to 20 minutes. Press Start/Stop to begin preheating.

- Once preheated, place the pan on the roast position.

- After 10 minutes, remove the pan from the oven and turn over the chicken thighs. Baste them with the remaining curry butter. Return the pan to the oven and continue cooking.

- Cooking is complete when the sweet potatoes are tender and the chicken is cooked through and reads 165°F (74°C) on a meat thermometer.

573.   Chicken Shawarma

Preparation Time: 10 minutes
Cooking Time: 18 minutes
Servings: 4

Ingredients:

- 1½ pounds (680 g) boneless, skinless chicken thighs
- 1¼ teaspoon kosher salt, divided
- 2 tablespoons plus 1 teaspoon olive oil, divided
- 2/3 cup plus 2 tablespoons plain Greek yogurt, divided

- 2 tablespoons freshly squeezed lemon juice (about 1 medium lemon)
- 4 garlic cloves, minced, divided
- 1 tablespoon Shawarma Seasoning
- 4 pita breads, cut in half
- 2 cups cherry tomatoes
- ½ small cucumber, peeled, deseeded, and chopped
- 1 tablespoon chopped fresh parsley

Directions:

- Sprinkle the chicken thighs on both sides with 1 teaspoon of kosher salt. Place in a resealable plastic bag and set aside while you make the marinade.

- In a small bowl, mix 2 tablespoons of olive oil, 2 tablespoons of yogurt, the lemon juice, 3 garlic cloves, and Shawarma Seasoning until thoroughly combined. Pour the marinade over the chicken. Seal the bag, squeezing out as much air as possible. And massage the chicken to coat it with the sauce. Set aside.

- Wrap 2 pita breads each in two pieces of aluminum foil and place on a baking pan.

- Select Bake, Super Convection, set temperature to 300°F (150°C), and set time to 6 minutes. Press Start/Stop to begin preheating.

- Once the oven has preheated, place the pan on the bake position. After 3 minutes, remove the pan from the oven and turn over the foil packets. Return the pan to the oven and continue cooking. When cooking is complete, remove the pan from the oven and place the foil-wrapped pitas on the top of the oven to keep warm.

- Remove the chicken from the marinade, letting the excess drip off into the bag. Place them on the baking pan. Arrange the tomatoes around the sides of the chicken. Discard the marinade.

- Select Broil, Super Convection, set temperature to High, and set time to 12 minutes. Press Start/Stop to begin preheating.

- Once preheated, place the pan on the broil position.

- After 6 minutes, remove the pan from the oven and turn over the chicken. Return the pan to the oven and continue cooking.

- Wrap the cucumber in a paper towel to remove as much moisture as possible. Place them in a small bowl. Add the remaining yogurt, kosher salt, olive oil, garlic clove, and parsley. Whisk until combined.

- When cooking is complete, the chicken should be browned, crisp along its edges, and sizzling. Remove the pan from the oven and place the chicken on a cutting board. Cut each thigh into several pieces. Unwrap the pitas. Spread a tablespoon of sauce into a pita half. Add some chicken and add 2 roasted tomatoes. Serve.

574. Cheesy Marinara Chicken Breasts

Preparation Time: 30 minutes
Cooking Time: 1 hour
Servings: 2

Ingredients:

- 1 large egg
- ¼ cup almond meal
- 2 (6-ounce / 170-g) boneless, skinless chicken breast halves
- 1 (8-ounce / 227-g) jar marinara sauce, divided
- 4 tablespoons shredded Mozzarella cheese, divided
- 4 tablespoons grated Parmesan cheese, divided
- 4 tablespoons chopped fresh basil, divided
- Salt and freshly ground black pepper, to taste
- Cooking spray

Directions:

- Spritz the air fry basket with cooking spray.
- In a shallow bowl, beat the egg.
- In a separate shallow bowl, place the almond meal.
- Dip 1 chicken breast half into the egg, then into the almond meal to coat. Place the

coated chicken in the air fry basket. Repeat with the remaining 1 chicken breast half.

- Select Bake, Super Convection, set temperature to 350°F (180°C) and set time to 40 minutes. Press Start/Stop to begin preheating.

- Once preheated, place the basket on the bake position.

- After 20 minutes, remove the basket from the oven and flip the chicken. Return the basket to oven and continue cooking.

- When cooking is complete, the chicken should no longer pink and the juices run clear.

- In a baking pan, pour half of marinara sauce.

- Place the cooked chicken in the sauce. Cover with the remaining marinara.

- Sprinkle 2 tablespoons of Mozzarella cheese and 2 tablespoons of soy Parmesan cheese on each chicken breast. Top each with 2 tablespoons of basil.

- Place the baking pan back in the oven and set the baking time to 20 minutes. Flip the chicken halfway through the cooking time.

- When cooking is complete, an instant-read thermometer inserted into the center of the chicken should read at least 165°F (74°C).

- Remove the pan from oven and divide between 2 plates. Season with salt and pepper and serve.

575. Chicken Thighs with Radish Slaw

Preparation Time: 10 minutes
Cooking Time: 27 minutes
Servings: 4

Ingredients:

- 4 bone-in, skin-on chicken thighs
- 1½ teaspoon kosher salt, divided
- 1 tablespoon smoked paprika
- ½ teaspoon granulated garlic
- ½ teaspoon dried oregano
- ¼ teaspoon freshly ground black pepper
- 3 cups shredded cabbage
- ½ small red onion, thinly sliced
- 4 large radishes, julienned
- 3 tablespoons red wine vinegar
- 2 tablespoons olive oil
- Cooking spray

Directions:

- Salt the chicken thighs on both sides with 1 teaspoon of kosher salt. In a small bowl, combine the paprika, garlic, oregano, and black pepper. Sprinkle half this mixture over the skin sides of the thighs. Spritz a baking pan with cooking spray and place the thighs skin-side down on the pan. Sprinkle the remaining spice mixture over the other sides of the chicken pieces.

- Select Roast, Super Convection, set temperature to 375°F (190°C), and set time to 27 minutes. Press Start/Stop to begin preheating.

- Once preheated, place the pan on the roast position.

- After 10 minutes, remove the pan from the oven and turn over the chicken thighs. Return the pan to the oven and continue cooking.

- While the chicken cooks, place the cabbage, onion, and radishes in a large bowl. Sprinkle with the remaining kosher salt, vinegar, and olive oil. Toss to coat.

- After another 9 to 10 minutes, remove the pan from the oven and place the chicken thighs on a cutting board. Place the cabbage mixture in the pan and toss with the chicken fat and spices.

- Spread the cabbage in an even layer on the pan and place the chicken on it, skin-side up. Place the pan on the roast position and continue cooking. Roast, Super Convection for another 7 to 8 minutes.

- When cooking is complete, the cabbage is just becoming tender. Remove the pan from the oven. Taste and adjust the seasoning if necessary. Serve.

576. Chicken with Potatoes and Corn

Preparation Time: 10 minutes

Cooking Time: 25 minutes
Servings: 4

Ingredients:

- 4 bone-in, skin-on chicken thighs
- 2 teaspoons kosher salt, divided
- 1 cup Bisquick baking mix
- ½ cup butter, melted, divided
- 1 pound (454 g) small red potatoes, quartered
- 3 ears corn, shucked and cut into rounds 1- to 1½-inches thick
- 1/3 cup heavy whipping cream
- ½ teaspoon freshly ground black pepper

Directions:

- Sprinkle the chicken on all sides with 1 teaspoon of kosher salt. Place the baking mix in a shallow dish. Brush the thighs on all sides with ¼ cup of butter, then dredge them in the baking mix, coating them all on sides. Place the chicken in the center of a baking pan.
- Place the potatoes in a large bowl with 2 tablespoons of butter and toss to coat. Place them on one side of the chicken on the pan.
- Place the corn in a medium bowl and drizzle with the remaining butter. Sprinkle with ¼ teaspoon of kosher salt and toss to coat. Place on the pan on the other side of the chicken.
- Select Roast, Super Convection, set temperature to 375°F (190°C), and set time to 25 minutes. Press Start/Stop to begin preheating.
- Once preheated, place the pan on the roast position.
- After 20 minutes, remove the pan from the oven and transfer the potatoes back to the bowl. Return the pan to oven and continue cooking.
- As the chicken continues cooking, add the cream, black pepper, and remaining kosher salt to the potatoes. Lightly mash the potatoes with a potato masher.
- When cooking is complete, the corn should be tender and the chicken cooked through,

reading 165°F (74°C) on a meat thermometer. Remove the pan from the oven and serve the chicken with the smashed potatoes and corn on the side.

577. Pineapple Chicken

Preparation Time: 10 minutes
Cooking Time: 10 minutes
Servings: 6

Ingredients:

- 1½ pounds (680 g) boneless, skinless chicken breasts, cut into 1-inch chunks
- ¾ cup soy sauce
- 2 tablespoons ketchup
- 2 tablespoons brown sugar
- 2 tablespoons rice vinegar
- 1 red bell pepper, cut into 1-inch chunks
- 1 green bell pepper, cut into 1-inch chunks
- 6 scallions, cut into 1-inch pieces
- 1 cup (¾-inch chunks) fresh pineapple, rinsed and drained
- Cooking spray

Directions:

- Place the chicken in a large bowl. Add the soy sauce, ketchup, brown sugar, vinegar, red and green peppers, and scallions. Toss to coat.
- Spritz a baking pan with cooking spray and place the chicken and vegetables on the pan.
- Select Roast, Super Convection, set temperature to 375°F (190°C), and set time to 10 minutes. Press Start/Stop to begin preheating.
- Once preheated, place the pan on the roast position.
- After 6 minutes, remove the pan from the oven. Add the pineapple chunks to the pan and stir. Return the pan to the oven and continue cooking.
- When cooking is complete, remove the pan from the oven. Serve with steamed rice, if desired.

578. Buttermilk Marinated Chicken

Preparation Time: 10 minutes

Cooking Time: 25 minutes
Servings: 6

Ingredients:

- 3-lb. whole chicken
- 1 tablespoon salt
- 1-pint buttermilk

Directions:

- Place the whole chicken in a large bowl and drizzle salt on top.
- Pour the buttermilk over it and leave the chicken soaked overnight.
- Cover the chicken bowl and refrigerate overnight.
- Remove the chicken from the marinade and fix it on the rotisserie rod in the Air fryer oven.
- Turn the dial to select the "Air Roast" mode.
- Hit the Time button and again use the dial to set the cooking time to 25 minutes.
- Now push the Temp button and rotate the dial to set the temperature at 370 degrees F.
- Close its lid and allow the chicken to roast.
- Serve warm.

579. Thyme Turkey Breast

Preparation Time: 10 minutes
Cooking Time: 40 minutes
Servings: 4

Ingredients:

- 2 lb. turkey breast
- Salt, to taste
- Black pepper, to taste
- 4 tablespoon butter, melted
- 3 cloves garlic, minced
- 1 teaspoon thyme, chopped
- 1 teaspoon rosemary, chopped

Directions:

- Mix butter with salt, black pepper, garlic, thyme, and rosemary in a bowl.
- Rub this seasoning over the turkey breast liberally and place in the Air Fryer basket.

- Turn the dial to select the "Air Fry" mode.
- Hit the Time button and again use the dial to set the cooking time to 40 minutes.
- Now push the Temp button and rotate the dial to set the temperature at 375 degrees F.
- Once preheated, place the Air fryer basket inside the oven.
- Slice and serve fresh.

580. Roasted Duck

Preparation Time: 10 minutes
Cooking Time: 3 hours
Servings: 12

Ingredients:

- 6 lb. whole Pekin duck
- salt
- 5 garlic cloves chopped
- 1 lemon, chopped

Glaze

- 1/2 cup balsamic vinegar
- 1 lemon, juiced
- 1/4 cup honey

Directions:

- Place the Pekin duck in a baking tray and add garlic, lemon, and salt on top.
- Whisk honey, vinegar, and honey in a bowl.
- Brush this glaze over the duck liberally. Marinate overnight in the refrigerator.
- Remove the duck from the marinade and fix it on the rotisserie rod in the Air fryer oven.
- Turn the dial to select the "Air Roast" mode.
- Hit the Time button and again use the dial to set the cooking time to 3 hours.
- Now push the Temp button and rotate the dial to set the temperature at 350 degrees F.
- Close its lid and allow the duck to roast.
- Serve warm.

581. Chicken Drumsticks

Preparation Time: 10 minutes
Cooking Time: 20 minutes
Servings: 8

Ingredients:

- 8 chicken drumsticks
- 2 tablespoon olive oil
- 1 teaspoon salt
- 1 teaspoon pepper
- 1 teaspoon garlic powder
- 1 teaspoon paprika
- 1/2 teaspoon cumin

Directions:

- Mix olive oil with salt, black pepper, garlic powder, paprika, and cumin in a bowl.
- Rub this mixture liberally over all the drumsticks.
- Place these drumsticks in the Air fryer basket.
- Turn the dial to select the "Air Fry" mode.
- Hit the Time button and again use the dial to set the cooking time to 20 minutes.
- Now push the Temp button and rotate the dial to set the temperature at 375 degrees F.
- Once preheated, place the Air fryer basket inside the oven.
- Flip the drumsticks when cooked halfway through.
- Resume air frying for another rest of the 10 minutes.
- Serve warm.

582. Blackened Chicken Bake

Preparation Time: 10 minutes
Cooking Time: 18 minutes
Servings: 4

Ingredients:

- 4 chicken breasts
- 2 teaspoon olive oil

Seasoning:

- 1 1/2 tablespoon brown sugar
- 1 teaspoon paprika
- 1 teaspoon dried oregano
- 1/4 teaspoon garlic powder
- 1/2 teaspoon salt and pepper

Garnish:

- Chopped parsley

Directions:

- Mix olive oil with brown sugar, paprika, oregano, garlic powder, salt, and black pepper in a bowl.
- Place the chicken breasts in the baking tray of the Ninja Oven.
- Pour and rub this mixture liberally over all the chicken breasts.
- Turn the dial to select the "Bake" mode.
- Hit the Time button and again use the dial to set the cooking time to 18 minutes.
- Now push the Temp button and rotate the dial to set the temperature at 425 degrees F.
- Once preheated, place the baking tray inside the oven.
- Serve warm.

583. Crusted Chicken Drumsticks

Preparation Time: 10 minutes
Cooking Time: 10 minutes
Servings: 4

Ingredients:

- 1 lb. chicken drumsticks
- 1/2 cup buttermilk
- 1/2 cup panko breadcrumbs
- 1/2 cup flour
- 1/4 teaspoon baking powder
- Spice Mixture
- 1/2 teaspoon salt
- 1/2 teaspoon celery salt
- 1/4 teaspoon oregano
- 1/4 teaspoon cayenne
- 1 teaspoon paprika
- 1/4 teaspoon garlic powder
- 1/4 teaspoon dried thyme
- 1/2 teaspoon ground ginger
- 1/2 teaspoon white pepper
- 1/2 teaspoon black pepper
- 3 tablespoon butter melted

Directions:

- Soak chicken in the buttermilk and cover to marinate overnight in the refrigerator.
- Mix spices with flour, breadcrumbs, and baking powder in a shallow tray.
- Remove the chicken from the milk and coat them well with the flour spice mixture
- Place the chicken drumsticks in the Air fryer basket of the Ninja Oven.
- Pour the melted butter over the drumsticks
- Turn the dial to select the "Air fry" mode.
- Hit the Time button and again use the dial to set the cooking time to 10 minutes.
- Now push the Temp button and rotate the dial to set the temperature at 425 degrees F.
- Once preheated, place the baking tray inside the oven.
- Flip the drumsticks and resume cooking for another 10 minutes.
- Serve warm.

584.   Roasted Turkey Breast

Preparation Time: 10 minutes
Cooking Time: 50 minutes
Servings: 6

Ingredients:

- 3 lb. boneless turkey breast
- ¼ cup mayonnaise
- 2 teaspoon poultry seasoning
- 1 teaspoon salt
- ½ teaspoon garlic powder
- ¼ teaspoon black pepper

Directions:

- Whisk all the ingredients, including turkey in a bowl, and coat it well.
- Place the boneless turkey breast in the Air fryer basket.
- Rotate the dial to select the "Air fry" mode.
- Press the Time button and again use the dial to set the cooking time to 50 minutes.
- Now press the Temp button and rotate the dial to set the temperature at 350 degrees F.

- Once preheated, place the air fryer basket in the Ninja oven and Close its lid to bake.
- Slice and serve.

585.   Brine Soaked Turkey

Preparation Time: 10 minutes
Cooking Time: 45 minutes
Servings: 8

Ingredients:

- 7 lb. bone-in, skin-on turkey breast

Brine:

- 1/2 cup salt
- 1 lemon
- 1/2 onion
- 3 cloves garlic, smashed
- 5 sprigs fresh thyme
- 3 bay leaves
- black pepper

Turkey Breast:

- 4 tablespoon butter, softened
- 1/2 teaspoon black pepper
- 1/2 teaspoon garlic powder
- 1/4 teaspoon dried thyme
- 1/4 teaspoon dried oregano

Directions:

- Mix the turkey brine ingredients in a pot and soak the turkey in the brine overnight.
- Next day, remove the soaked turkey from the brine.
- Whisk the butter, black pepper, garlic powder, oregano, and thyme.
- Brush the butter mixture over the turkey then place it in a baking tray.
- Press "Power Button" of Air Fry Oven and turn the dial to select the "Air Roast" mode.
- Press the Time button and again turn the dial to set the cooking time to 45 minutes.
- Now push the Temp button and rotate the dial to set the temperature at 370 degrees F.
- Once preheated, place the turkey baking tray in the oven and close its lid.

- Slice and serve warm.

586. Turkey Meatballs

Preparation Time: 10 minutes
Cooking Time: 20 minutes
Servings: 6

Ingredients:

- 1.5 lb. turkey mince
- 1 red bell pepper, deseeded and chopped
- 1 large egg, beaten
- 4 tablespoons parsley, minced
- 1 tablespoon cilantro, minced
- Salt, to taste
- Black pepper, to taste

Directions:

- Toss all the meatball ingredients in a bowl and mix well.
- Make small meatballs out this mixture and place them in the air fryer basket.
- Press "Power Button" of Air Fry Oven and turn the dial to select the "Air Fry" mode.
- Press the Time button and again turn the dial to set the cooking time to 20 minutes.
- Now push the Temp button and rotate the dial to set the temperature at 375 degrees F.
- Once preheated, place the air fryer basket inside and close its lid.
- Serve warm.

587. Lemon Pepper Turkey

Preparation Time: 10 minutes
Cooking Time: 45 minutes
Servings: 6

Ingredients:

- 3 lbs. turkey breast
- 2 tablespoons oil
- 1 tablespoon Worcestershire sauce
- 1 teaspoon lemon pepper
- 1/2 teaspoon salt

Directions:

- Whisk everything in a bowl and coat the turkey liberally.
- Place the turkey in the Air fryer basket.
- Press "Power Button" of Air Fry Oven and turn the dial to select the "Air Fry" mode.
- Press the Time button and again turn the dial to set the cooking time to 45 minutes.
- Now push the Temp button and rotate the dial to set the temperature at 375 degrees F.
- Once preheated, place the air fryer basket inside and close its lid.
- Serve warm.

588. Ground Chicken Meatballs

Preparation Time: 10 minutes
Cooking Time: 10 minutes
Servings: 4

Ingredients:

- 1-lb. ground chicken
- 1/3 cup panko
- 1 teaspoon salt
- 2 teaspoons chives
- 1/2 teaspoon garlic powder
- 1 teaspoon thyme
- 1 egg

Directions:

- Toss all the meatball ingredients in a bowl and mix well.
- Make small meatballs out this mixture and place them in the air fryer basket.
- Press "Power Button" of Air Fry Oven and turn the dial to select the "Air Fry" mode.
- Press the Time button and again turn the dial to set the cooking time to 10 minutes.
- Now push the Temp button and rotate the dial to set the temperature at 350 degrees F.
- Once preheated, place the air fryer basket inside and close its lid.
- Serve warm.

589. Parmesan Chicken Meatballs

Preparation Time: 10 minutes
Cooking Time: 12 minutes

Servings: 4

Ingredients:

- 1-lb. ground chicken
- 1 large egg, beaten
- ½ cup Parmesan cheese, grated
- ½ cup pork rinds, ground
- 1 teaspoon garlic powder
- 1 teaspoon paprika
- 1 teaspoon kosher salt
- ½ teaspoon pepper

Crust:

- ½ cup pork rinds, ground

Directions:

- Toss all the meatball ingredients in a bowl and mix well.
- Make small meatballs out this mixture and roll them in the pork rinds.
- Place the coated meatballs in the air fryer basket.
- Press "Power Button" of Air Fry Oven and turn the dial to select the "Bake" mode.
- Press the Time button and again turn the dial to set the cooking time to 12 minutes.
- Now push the Temp button and rotate the dial to set the temperature at 400 degrees F.
- Once preheated, place the air fryer basket inside and close its lid.
- Serve warm.

590. Easy Italian Meatballs

Preparation Time: 10 minutes
Cooking Time: 13 minutes
Servings: 4

Ingredients:

- 2-lb. lean ground turkey
- ¼ cup onion, minced
- 2 cloves garlic, minced
- 2 tablespoons parsley, chopped
- 2 eggs
- 1½ cup parmesan cheese, grated
- ½ teaspoon red pepper flakes

- ½ teaspoon Italian seasoning
- Salt and black pepper to taste

Directions:

- Toss all the meatball ingredients in a bowl and mix well.
- Make small meatballs out this mixture and place them in the air fryer basket.
- Press "Power Button" of Air Fry Oven and turn the dial to select the "Air Fry" mode.
- Press the Time button and again turn the dial to set the cooking time to 13 minutes.
- Now push the Temp button and rotate the dial to set the temperature at 350 degrees F.
- Once preheated, place the air fryer basket inside and close its lid.
- Flip the meatballs when cooked halfway through.
- Serve warm.

Nutrition per serving:

Calories 472
Total Fat 25.8 g
Saturated Fat .4 g
Cholesterol 268 mg
Sodium 503 mg
Total Carbs 1.7 g
Fiber 0.3 g
Sugar 0.6 g
Protein 59.6 g

591. Oregano Chicken Breast

Preparation Time: 10 minutes
Cooking Time: 25 minutes
Servings: 6

Ingredients:

- 2 lbs. chicken breasts, minced
- 1 tablespoon avocado oil
- 1 teaspoon smoked paprika
- 1 teaspoon garlic powder
- 1 teaspoon oregano
- 1/2 teaspoon salt
- Black pepper, to taste

Directions:

- Toss all the meatball ingredients in a bowl and mix well.
- Make small meatballs out this mixture and place them in the air fryer basket.
- Press "Power Button" of Air Fry Oven and turn the dial to select the "Air Fry" mode.
- Press the Time button and again turn the dial to set the cooking time to 25 minutes.
- Now push the Temp button and rotate the dial to set the temperature at 375 degrees F.
- Once preheated, place the air fryer basket inside and close its lid.
- Serve warm.

592. Lemon Chicken Breasts

Preparation Time: 10 minutes
Cooking Time: 30 minutes
Servings: 4

Ingredients:

- 1/4 cup olive oil
- 3 tablespoons garlic, minced
- 1/3 cup dry white wine
- 1 tablespoon lemon zest, grated
- 2 tablespoons lemon juice
- 1 1/2 teaspoons dried oregano, crushed
- 1 teaspoon thyme leaves, minced
- Salt and black pepper
- 4 skin-on boneless chicken breasts
- 1 lemon, sliced

Directions:

- Whisk everything in a baking pan to coat the chicken breasts well.
- Place the lemon slices on top of the chicken breasts.
- Spread the mustard mixture over the toasted bread slices.
- Press "Power Button" of Air Fry Oven and turn the dial to select the "Bake" mode.
- Press the Time button and again turn the dial to set the cooking time to 30 minutes.

- Now push the Temp button and rotate the dial to set the temperature at 370 degrees F.
- Once preheated, place the baking pan inside and close its lid.
- Serve warm.

593. Healthy Chicken Tenders

Preparation Time: 10 minutes
Cooking Time: 10 minutes
Serving: 3

Ingredients:

- 1 egg
- 1 lb. chicken breast, boneless & cut into strips
- 1 tsp garlic powder
- 2 tsp Italian seasoning
- 1/3 cup pecans, chopped
- 2/3 cup almond flour
- 1 tbsp water
- 1/2 tsp sea salt

Directions:

- In a small bowl, whisk together egg and 1 tablespoon of water.
- In a shallow bowl, mix together almond flour, pecans, Italian seasoning, garlic powder, and salt.
- Dip each chicken strip in egg then coat with almond flour mixture.
- Place the cooking tray in the air fryer basket.
- Select Air Fry mode.
- Set time to 10 minutes and temperature 350 F then press START.
- The air fryer display will prompt you to ADD FOOD once the temperature is reached then place coated chicken strips in the air fryer basket.
- Turn chicken strips halfway through.
- Serve and enjoy.

594. Sweet & Tangy Chicken

Preparation Time: 10 minutes
Cooking Time: 15 minutes
Serving: 3

Ingredients:

- 1 lb. chicken breast, boneless and cut into bite-size pieces
- 1 tbsp sesame seeds, toasted
- 2 garlic cloves, minced
- 1 tsp fresh ginger, chopped
- 1 tsp orange zest, grated
- 2 tbsp orange juice
- 1 tbsp sesame oil
- 2 tbsp vinegar
- 1/4 cup coconut amino
- 1 tsp garlic powder
- 3 1/2 tbsp arrowroot

Directions:

- Toss chicken with 3 tablespoons of arrowroot and garlic powder.
- Place the cooking tray in the air fryer basket.
- Select Air Fry mode.
- Set time to 12 minutes and temperature 370 F then press START.
- The air fryer display will prompt you to ADD FOOD once the temperature is reached then add chicken pieces in the air fryer basket. Spray chicken pieces with cooking spray.
- Toss chicken halfway through.
- Meanwhile, for sauce, in a small saucepan, whisk together vinegar, garlic, ginger, orange zest, sesame oil, orange juice, and coconut aminos. Whisk in remaining arrowroot and cook over medium heat until sauce thicken. Remove from heat.
- Once the chicken is done, toss in a mixing bowl with sauce.
- Sprinkle with sesame seeds and serve.

595. Parmesan Chicken Breast

Preparation Time: 10 minutes
Cooking Time: 14 minutes
Serving: 4

Ingredients:

- 2 eggs, lightly beaten
- 1 lb. chicken breast, skinless & boneless
- 1 cup parmesan cheese, grated
- 1/2 cup almond flour
- 1/2 tsp garlic powder
- 1 tsp Italian seasoning
- Pepper
- Salt

Directions:

- In a shallow bowl, add eggs and whisk well.
- In a separate shallow dish, mix together parmesan cheese, Italian seasoning, garlic powder, almond flour, pepper, and salt.
- Dip chicken breast into the egg mixture and coat with parmesan cheese mixture.
- Place the cooking tray in the air fryer basket.
- Select Air Fry mode.
- Set time to 14 minutes and temperature 360 F then press START.
- The air fryer display will prompt you to ADD FOOD once the temperature is reached then place coated chicken breasts in the air fryer basket.
- Serve and enjoy.

596. Garlic Herb Turkey Breast

Preparation Time: 10 minutes
Cooking Time: 40 minutes
Serving: 6

Ingredients:

- 3 lbs. turkey breast, boneless & thawed
- 2 garlic cloves, minced
- 1 tbsp fresh parsley, chopped
- 1 tbsp fresh rosemary, chopped
- 1 tsp pepper
- 1 tsp salt

Directions:

- In a small bowl, mix together garlic, parsley, rosemary, pepper, and salt and rub all over turkey breast.
- Place the cooking tray in the air fryer basket.
- Select Air Fry mode.

- Set time to 40 minutes and temperature 350 F then press START.
- The air fryer display will prompt you to ADD FOOD once the temperature is reached then place turkey breast in the air fryer basket.
- Remove turkey breast from the air fryer and let it cool for 10 minutes.
- Slice and serve.

597. Simple & Juicy Chicken Breasts

Preparation Time: 10 minutes
Cooking Time: 30 minutes
Serving: 2

Ingredients:

- 2 chicken breasts, skinless & boneless
- 1/2 tsp garlic powder
- 1 tbsp olive oil
- 1/4 tsp pepper
- 1/2 tsp salt

Directions:

- Brush chicken breasts with oil and season with garlic powder, pepper, and salt.
- Place the cooking tray in the air fryer basket.
- Select Air Fry mode.
- Set time to 30 minutes and temperature 360 F then press START.
- The air fryer display will prompt you to ADD FOOD once the temperature is reached then place chicken breasts in the air fryer basket. Turn chicken after 20 minutes.
- Serve and enjoy.

598. Cauliflower Chicken Casserole

Preparation Time: 10 minutes
Cooking Time: 30 minutes
Serving: 4

Ingredients:

- 1 lb. cooked chicken, shredded
- 4 oz cream cheese, softened
- 4 cups cauliflower florets
- 1/8 tsp black pepper
- 1/4 cup Greek yogurt

- 1 cup cheddar cheese, shredded
- 1/2 cup salsa
- 1/2 tsp kosher salt

Directions:

- Add cauliflower florets into the baking dish and microwave for 10 minutes.
- Add cream cheese and microwave for 30 seconds more. Mix well.
- Add chicken, yogurt, cheddar cheese, salsa, pepper, and salt and stir everything well.
- Select Bake mode.
- Set time to 20 minutes and temperature 375 F then press START.
- The air fryer display will prompt you to ADD FOOD once the temperature is reached then place the baking dish in the air fryer basket.
- Serve and enjoy.

599. Flavorful Greek Chicken

Preparation Time: 10 minutes
Cooking Time: 30 minutes
Serving: 4

Ingredients:

- 1 lb. chicken breasts, skinless & boneless

For marinade:

- 1 tsp onion powder
- 1/4 tsp basil
- 1/4 tsp oregano
- 3 garlic cloves, minced
- 1 tbsp lemon juice
- 3 tbsp olive oil
- 1/2 tsp dill
- 1/4 tsp pepper
- 1/2 tsp salt

Directions:

- Add all marinade ingredients into the bowl and mix well.
- Add chicken into the marinade and coat well. Cover and place in the refrigerator overnight.
- Arrange marinated chicken into the baking dish. Cover dish with foil.

- Select Bake mode.
- Set time to 30 minutes and temperature 400 F then press START.
- The air fryer display will prompt you to ADD FOOD once the temperature is reached then place baking dish in the air fryer basket.
- Serve and enjoy.

600. Simple Baked Chicken Breast

Preparation Time: 10 minutes
Cooking Time: 25 minutes
Serving: 6

Ingredients:

- 6 chicken breasts, skinless & boneless
- 1/4 tsp pepper
- 1/4 tsp paprika
- 1 tsp Italian seasoning
- 2 tbsp olive oil
- 1/2 tsp garlic salt

Directions:

- Brush chicken with oil.
- Mix together Italian seasoning, garlic salt, paprika, and pepper and rub all over the chicken.
- Arrange chicken breasts into the baking dish. Cover dish with foil.
- Select Bake mode.
- Set time to 25 minutes and temperature 400 F then press START.
- The air fryer display will prompt you to ADD FOOD once the temperature is reached then place the baking dish in the air fryer basket.
- Serve and enjoy.

601. Baked Chicken Thighs

Preparation Time: 10 minutes
Cooking Time: 35 minutes
Serving: 6

Ingredients:

- 6 chicken thighs
- 2 tsp poultry seasoning
- 2 tbsp olive oil

- Pepper
- Salt

Directions:

- Brush chicken with oil and rub with poultry seasoning, pepper, and salt.
- Arrange chicken into the baking dish. Cover dish with foil.
- Select Bake mode.
- Set time to 35 minutes and temperature 400 F then press START.
- The air fryer display will prompt you to ADD FOOD once the temperature is reached then place the baking dish in the air fryer basket.
- Serve and enjoy.

602. Tasty Chicken Wings

Preparation Time: 10 minutes
Cooking Time: 45 minutes
Serving: 6

Ingredients:

- 3 lbs. chicken wings
- 2 tbsp olive oil
- 1/2 cup dry BBQ spice rub

Directions:

- Brush chicken wings with olive oil and place in a large bowl.
- Add BBQ spice over chicken wings and toss well.
- Select Bake mode.
- Set time to 45 minutes and temperature 400 F then press START.
- The air fryer display will prompt you to ADD FOOD once the temperature is reached then add chicken wings in the air fryer basket.
- Serve and enjoy.

603. Italian Turkey Tenderloin

Preparation Time: 10 minutes
Cooking Time: 45 minutes
Serving: 4

Ingredients:

- 1 1/2 lbs. turkey breast tenderloin
- 1/2 tbsp olive oil
- 1 tsp Italian seasoning
- 1/4 tsp pepper
- 1/2 tsp salt

Directions:

- Brush turkey tenderloin with olive oil and rub with Italian seasoning, pepper, and salt.
- Select Bake mode.
- Set time to 45 minutes and temperature 390 F then press START.
- The air fryer display will prompt you to ADD FOOD once the temperature is reached then place turkey tenderloin in the air fryer basket.
- Serve and enjoy.

604. Pesto Parmesan Chicken

Preparation Time: 10 minutes
Cooking Time: 25 minutes
Serving: 4

Ingredients:

- 4 chicken breasts, skinless & boneless
- 1/2 cup parmesan cheese, shredded
- 1/2 cup basil pesto
- Pepper
- Salt

Directions:

- Season chicken with pepper and salt and place into the baking dish.
- Spread pesto on top of the chicken and sprinkle with shredded cheese.
- Select Bake mode.
- Set time to 25 minutes and temperature 400 F then press START.
- The air fryer display will prompt you to ADD FOOD once the temperature is reached then place the baking dish in the air fryer basket.
- Serve and enjoy.

605. Lemon Chicken Breasts

Preparation Time: 10 minutes
Cooking Time: 30 minutes

Serving: 4

Ingredients:

- 4 chicken breasts, skinless and boneless
- 4 tsp butter, sliced
- 1/2 tsp paprika
- 1 tsp garlic powder
- 1 tsp lemon pepper seasoning
- 4 tsp lemon juice
- Pepper
- Salt

Directions:

- Season chicken with pepper and salt and place into the baking dish. Pour lemon juice over chicken.
- Mix together paprika, garlic powder, and lemon pepper seasoning and sprinkle over chicken.
- Add butter slices on top of the chicken.
- Select Bake mode.
- Set time to 30 minutes and temperature 350 F then press START.
- The air fryer display will prompt you to ADD FOOD once the temperature is reached then place the baking dish in the air fryer basket.
- Serve and enjoy.

606. Spicy Chicken Wings

Preparation Time: 10 minutes
Cooking Time: 20 minutes
Serving: 4

Ingredients:

- 12 chicken wings
- 1 tbsp chili powder
- 1/2 tbsp baking powder
- 1 tsp granulated garlic
- 1/2 tsp sea salt

Directions:

- Add chicken wings into the large bowl and toss with remaining ingredients.
- Select Air Fry mode.

- Set time to 20 minutes and temperature 400 F then press START.
- The air fryer display will prompt you to ADD FOOD once the temperature is reached then place chicken wings in the air fryer basket.
- Serve and enjoy.

607. Meatballs

Preparation Time: 10 minutes
Cooking Time: 20 minutes
Serving: 6

Ingredients:

- 1 lb. ground turkey
- 1 tbsp basil, chopped
- 1/3 cup coconut flour
- 2 cups zucchini, grated
- 1 tbsp dried onion flakes
- 2 eggs, lightly beaten
- 1 tbsp nutritional yeast
- 1 tsp dried oregano
- 1 tbsp garlic, minced
- 1 tsp cumin
- Pepper
- Salt

Directions:

- Add all ingredients into the bowl and mix until just combined.
- Make small balls from the meat mixture.
- Select Bake mode.
- Set time to 20 minutes and temperature 400 F then press START.
- The air fryer display will prompt you to ADD FOOD once the temperature is reached then place meatballs in the air fryer basket.
- Serve and enjoy.

608. Hot Chicken Wings

Preparation Time: 10 minutes
Cooking Time: 25 minutes
Serving: 4

Ingredients:

- 2 lbs. chicken wings

- 1/2 tsp Worcestershire sauce
- 1/2 tsp Tabasco
- 6 tbsp butter, melted
- 12 oz hot sauce

Directions:

- Select Air Fry mode.
- Set time to 25 minutes and temperature 375 F then press START.
- The air fryer display will prompt you to ADD FOOD once the temperature is reached then place chicken wings in the air fryer basket.
- Meanwhile, in a bowl, mix together hot sauce, Worcestershire sauce, and butter. Set aside.
- Add chicken wings into the sauce bowl and toss well.
- Serve and enjoy.

609. Fajita Chicken

Preparation Time: 10 minutes
Cooking Time: 15 minutes
Serving: 4

Ingredients:

- 4 chicken breasts, make horizontal cuts on each piece
- 2 tbsp fajita seasoning
- 2 tbsp olive oil
- 1 onion, sliced
- 1 bell pepper, sliced

Directions:

- Brush chicken with oil and season with fajita seasoning.
- Select Bake mode.
- Set time to 15 minutes and temperature 375 F then press START.
- The air fryer display will prompt you to ADD FOOD once the temperature is reached then add chicken, onion, and bell pepper in the air fryer basket.
- Serve and enjoy.

610. Turkey Balls

Preparation Time: 10 minutes
Cooking Time: 12 minutes
Serving: 4

Ingredients:

- 1 egg
- 1 lb. ground turkey
- 1/4 cup celery, chopped
- 1/4 cup carrots, grated
- 1 garlic clove, minced
- 2 green onion, chopped
- 2 tbsp coconut flour
- Pepper
- Salt

Directions:

- Add all ingredients into the large bowl and mix until just combined.
- Make small balls from the meat mixture.
- Select Air Fry mode.
- Set time to 12 minutes and temperature 400 F then press START.
- The air fryer display will prompt you to ADD FOOD once the temperature is reached then place meatballs in the air fryer basket.
- Serve and enjoy.

611.   Herb Wings

Preparation Time: 10 minutes
Cooking Time: 15 minutes
Serving: 4

Ingredients:

- 2 lbs. chicken wings
- 1 tsp paprika
- 1/2 cup parmesan cheese, grated
- 1 tsp herb de Provence
- Salt

Directions:

- In a small bowl, mix together cheese, herb de Provence, paprika, and salt.
- Coat chicken wings with cheese mixture.
- Select Air Fry mode.

- Set time to 15 minutes and temperature 350 F then press START.
- The air fryer display will prompt you to ADD FOOD once the temperature is reached then place chicken wings in the air fryer basket.
- Serve and enjoy.

612.   Rosemary Garlic Chicken

Preparation Time: 10 minutes
Cooking Time: 25 minutes
Serving: 4

Ingredients:

- 1 lb. chicken breasts, skinless, boneless, and cubed
- 2 tbsp chives, chopped
- 1 tbsp fresh lemon juice
- 1 tsp garlic powder
- 1 tbsp rosemary, chopped
- 1 tbsp garlic, minced
- 2 tbsp olive oil

Directions:

- Add all ingredients into the bowl and toss well.
- Select Air Fry mode.
- Set time to 25 minutes and temperature 370 F then press START.
- The air fryer display will prompt you to ADD FOOD once the temperature is reached then add the chicken mixture in the air fryer basket.
- Serve and enjoy.

613.   Air Fried Chicken Potatoes with Sun-Dried Tomato

Preparation Time: 15 minutes
Cooking Time: 10 minutes
Servings: 2

Ingredients:

- 2 teaspoons minced fresh oregano, divided
- 2 teaspoons minced fresh thyme, divided
- 2 teaspoons extra-virgin olive oil, plus extra as needed

- 1-pound (454 g) fingerling potatoes, unpeeled
- 1 (12-ounce / 340-g) bone-in split chicken breasts, trimmed
- 1 garlic clove, minced
- ¼ cup oil-packed sun-dried tomatoes, patted dry and chopped
- 1½ tablespoons red wine vinegar
- 1 tablespoon capers, rinsed and minced
- 1 small shallot, minced
- Salt and ground black pepper, to taste

Directions:

- Combine 1 teaspoon of oregano, 1 teaspoon of thyme, ¼ teaspoon of salt, ¼ teaspoon of ground black pepper, 1 teaspoons of olive oil in a large bowl. Add the potatoes and toss to coat well.
- Combine the chicken with remaining thyme, oregano, and olive oil. Sprinkle with garlic, salt, and pepper. Toss to coat well.
- Place the potatoes in the perforated pan, then arrange the chicken on top of the potatoes.
- Select Air Fry of the oven. Set temperature to 350°F (180°C) and set time to 25 minutes. Press Start to begin preheating.
- Once preheated, place the pan into the oven. Flip the chicken and potatoes halfway through.
- When cooking is complete, the internal temperature of the chicken should reach at least 165 °F (74 °C) and the potatoes should be wilted.
- Meanwhile, combine the sun-dried tomatoes, vinegar, capers, and shallot in a separate large bowl. Sprinkle with salt and ground black pepper. Toss to mix well.
- Remove the chicken and potatoes from the oven and allow to cool for 10 minutes. Serve with the sun-dried tomato mix.

614. Air Fried Chicken Wings with Buffalo Sauce

Preparation Time: 10 minutes
Cooking Time: 20 minutes

Servings: 6

Ingredients:

- 16 chicken drumettes (party wings)
- Chicken seasoning or rub, to taste
- 1 teaspoon garlic powder
- Ground black pepper, to taste
- ¼ cup buffalo wings sauce
- Cooking spray

Directions:

- Spritz a perforated pan with cooking spray.
- Rub the chicken wings with chicken seasoning, garlic powder, and ground black pepper on a clean work surface.
- Arrange the chicken wings in the perforated pan. Spritz with cooking spray.
- Select Air Fry of the oven. Set temperature to 400°F (205°C) and set time to 10 minutes. Press Start to begin preheating.
- Once preheated, place the pan into the oven. Flip the chicken wings halfway through.
- When cooking is complete, the chicken wings should be lightly browned.
- Transfer the chicken wings in a large bowl, then pour in the buffalo wings sauce and toss to coat well.
- Put the wings back to the oven and set time to 7 minutes. Flip the wings halfway through.
- When cooking is complete, the wings should be heated through. Serve immediately.

615. Apricot-Glazed Chicken Drumsticks

Preparation Time: 15 minutes
Cooking Time: 30 minutes
Servings: 3

Ingredients:

For the Glaze:

- ½ cup apricot preserves
- ½ teaspoon tamari
- ¼ teaspoon chili powder
- 2 teaspoons Dijon mustard

For the Chicken:

- 6 chicken drumsticks
- ½ teaspoon seasoning salt
- 1 teaspoon salt
- ½ teaspoon ground black pepper
- Cooking spray

Directions:

Make the glaze:

- Combine the ingredients for the glaze in a saucepan, then heat over low heat for 10 minutes or until thickened.
- Turn off the heat and sit until ready to use.

Make the Chicken:

- Spritz a perforated pan with cooking spray.
- Combine the seasoning salt, salt, and pepper in a small bowl. Stir to mix well.
- Place the chicken drumsticks in the perforated pan. Spritz with cooking spray and sprinkle with the salt mixture on both sides.
- Select Air Fry of the oven. Set temperature to 370°F (188°C) and set time to 20 minutes. Press Start to begin preheating.
- Once preheated, place the pan into the oven. Flip the chicken halfway through.
- When cooking is complete, the chicken should be well browned.
- Baste the chicken with the glaze and air fry for 2 more minutes or until the chicken tenderloin is glossy.
- Serve immediately.

616. Bell Pepper Stuffed Chicken Roll-Ups

Preparation Time: 10 minutes
Cooking Time: 12 minutes
Servings: 4

Ingredients:

- 2 (4-ounce / 113-g) boneless, skinless chicken breasts, slice in half horizontally
- 1 tablespoon olive oil
- Juice of ½ lime

- 2 tablespoons taco seasoning
- ½ green bell pepper, cut into strips
- ½ red bell pepper, cut into strips
- ¼ onion, sliced

Directions:

- Unfold the chicken breast slices on a clean work surface. Rub with olive oil, then drizzle with lime juice and sprinkle with taco seasoning.
- Top the chicken slices with equal amount of bell peppers and onion. Roll them up and secure with toothpicks.
- Arrange the chicken roll-ups in the perforated pan.
- Select Air Fry of the oven. Set temperature to 400°F (205°C) and set time to 12 minutes. Press Start to begin preheating.
- Once preheated, place the pan into the oven. Flip the chicken roll-ups halfway through.
- When cooking is complete, the internal temperature of the chicken should reach at least 165°F (74°C).
- Remove the chicken from the oven. Discard the toothpicks and serve immediately.

617. Bacon-Wrapped and Cheese-Stuffed Chicken

Preparation Time: 10 minutes
Cooking Time: 20 minutes
Servings: 4

Ingredients:

- 4 (5-ounce / 142-g) boneless, skinless chicken breasts, pounded to ¼ inch thick
- 1 cup cream cheese
- 4 tablespoons chopped fresh chives
- 8 slices thin-cut bacon
- Sprig of fresh cilantro, for garnish
- Cooking spray

Directions:

- Spritz a perforated pan with cooking spray.
- On a clean work surface, slice the chicken horizontally to make a 1-inch incision on top

of each chicken breast with a knife, then cut into the chicken to make a pocket. Leave a ½-inch border along the sides and bottom.

- Combine the cream cheese and chives in a bowl. Stir to mix well, then gently pour the mixture into the chicken pockets.

- Wrap each stuffed chicken breast with 2 bacon slices, then secure the ends with toothpicks.

- Arrange them in the perforated pan.

- Select Air Fry of the oven. Set temperature to 400°F (205°C) and set time to 20 minutes. Press Start to begin preheating.

- Once preheated, place the pan into the oven. Flip the bacon-wrapped chicken halfway through the cooking time.

- When cooking is complete, the bacon should be browned and crispy.

- Transfer them on a large plate and serve with cilantro on top.

618. Bacon-Wrapped Chicken Breasts Rolls

Preparation Time: 10 minutes
Cooking Time: 15 minutes
Servings: 4

Ingredients:

- ¼ cup chopped fresh chives
- 2 tablespoons lemon juice
- 1 teaspoon dried sage
- 1 teaspoon fresh rosemary leaves
- ½ cup fresh parsley leaves
- 4 cloves garlic, peeled
- 1 teaspoon ground fennel
- 1 teaspoons sea salt
- ½ teaspoon red pepper flakes
- 1 (4-ounce / 113-g) boneless, skinless chicken breasts, pounded to ¼ inch thick
- 8 slices bacon
- Sprigs of fresh rosemary, for garnish
- Cooking spray

Directions:

- Spritz a perforated pan with cooking spray.

- Put the chives, lemon juice, sage, rosemary, parsley, garlic, fennel, salt, and red pepper flakes in a food processor, then pulse to purée until smooth.

- Unfold the chicken breasts on a clean work surface, then brush the top side of the chicken breasts with the sauce.

- Roll the chicken breasts up from the shorter side, then wrap each chicken rolls with 2 bacon slices to cover. Secure with toothpicks.

- Arrange the rolls in the perforated pan.

- Select Air Fry of the oven. Set temperature to 340°F (171°C) and set time to 10 minutes. Press Start to begin preheating.

- Once preheated, place the pan into the oven. Flip the rolls halfway through.

- After 10 minutes, increase temperature to 390°F (199°C) and set time to 5 minutes.

- When cooking is complete, the bacon should be browned and crispy.

- Transfer the rolls to a large plate. Discard the toothpicks and spread with rosemary sprigs before serving.

619. Barbecue   Chicken and Coleslaw Tostadas

Preparation Time: 15 minutes
Cooking Time: 10 minutes
Servings: 2

Ingredients:

Coleslaw:

- ¼ cup sour cream
- ¼ small green cabbage, finely chopped
- ½ tablespoon white vinegar
- ½ teaspoon garlic powder
- ½ teaspoon salt
- ¼ teaspoon ground black pepper

Tostadas:

- 2 cups pulled rotisserie chicken
- ½ cup barbecue sauce
- 4 corn tortillas
- ½ cup shredded Mozzarella cheese
- Cooking spray

Directions:

Make the Coleslaw:

- Combine the ingredients for the coleslaw in a large bowl. Toss to mix well.
- Refrigerate until ready to serve.

Make the Tostadas:

- Spritz a perforated pan with cooking spray.
- Toss the chicken with barbecue sauce in a separate large bowl to combine well. Set aside.
- Place one tortilla in the perforated pan and spritz with cooking spray.
- Select Air Fry of the oven. Set temperature to 370°F (188°C) and set time to 10 minutes. Press Start to begin preheating.
- Once preheated, place the pan into the oven. Flip the tortilla and spread the barbecue chicken and cheese over halfway through.
- When cooking is complete, the tortilla should be browned and the cheese should be melted.
- Serve the tostadas with coleslaw on top.

620. Bruschetta Chicken

Preparation Time: 10 minutes
Cooking Time: 10 minutes
Servings: 4

Ingredients:

Bruschetta Stuffing:

- 1 tomato, diced
- 2 tablespoons balsamic vinegar
- 1 teaspoon Italian seasoning
- 3 tablespoons chopped fresh basil
- 2 garlic cloves, minced
- 2 tablespoons extra-virgin olive oil

Chicken:

- 4 (4-ounce / 113-g) boneless, skinless chicken breasts, cut 4 slits each
- 1 teaspoon Italian seasoning
- Chicken seasoning or rub, to taste
- Cooking spray

Directions:

- Spritz a perforated pan with cooking spray.
- Combine the ingredients for the bruschetta stuffing in a bowl. Stir to mix well. Set aside.
- Rub the chicken breasts with Italian seasoning and chicken seasoning on a clean work surface.
- Arrange the chicken breasts, slits side up, in the perforated pan and spritz with cooking spray.
- Select Air Fry of the oven. Set temperature to 370°F (188°C) and set time to 10 minutes. Press Start to begin preheating.
- Once preheated, place the pan into the oven. Flip the breast and fill the slits with the bruschetta stuffing halfway through.
- When cooking is complete, the chicken should be well browned.
- Serve immediately.

621. Cheese-Encrusted Chicken Tenderloins with Peanuts

Preparation Time: 10 minutes
Cooking Time: 12 minutes
Servings: 4

Ingredients:

- ½ cup grated Parmesan cheese
- ½ teaspoon garlic powder
- 1 teaspoon red pepper flakes
- Sea salt and ground black pepper, to taste
- 2 tablespoons peanut oil
- 1½ pounds (680 g) chicken tenderloins
- 2 tablespoons peanuts, roasted and roughly chopped
- Cooking spray

Directions:

- Spritz a perforated pan with cooking spray.
- Combine the Parmesan cheese, garlic powder, red pepper flakes, salt, black pepper, and peanut oil in a large bowl. Stir to mix well.
- Dip the chicken tenderloins in the cheese mixture, then press to coat well. Shake the excess off.

- Transfer the chicken tenderloins in the perforated pan.
- Select Air Fry of the oven. Set temperature to 360°F (182°C) and set time to 12 minutes. Press Start to begin preheating.
- Once preheated, place the pan into the oven. Flip the tenderloin halfway through.
- When cooking is complete, the tenderloin should be well browned.
- Transfer the chicken tenderloins on a large plate and top with roasted peanuts before serving.

622. Lechon Kawali

Preparation Time: 10 minutes
Cooking Time: 32 minutes
Servings: 4

Ingredients:

- 1-pound (454 g) pork belly, cut into three thick chunks
- 6 garlic cloves
- 2 bay leaves
- 2 tablespoons soy sauce
- 1 teaspoon kosher salt
- 1 teaspoon ground black pepper
- 3 cups water
- Cooking spray

Directions:

- Put all the ingredients in a pressure cooker, then put the lid on and cook on high for 15 minutes.
- Natural release the pressure and release any remaining pressure, transfer the tender pork belly on a clean work surface. Allow to cool under room temperature until you can handle.
- Generously spritz a perforated pan with cooking spray.
- Cut each chunk into two slices, then put the pork slices in the pan.
- Select Air Fry of the oven. Set temperature to 400°F (205°C) and set time to 15 minutes. Press Start to begin preheating.

- Once preheated, place the pan into the oven.
- After 7 minutes, remove the pan from the oven. Flip the pork. Return the pan to the oven and continue cooking.
- When cooking is complete, the pork fat should be crispy.
- Serve immediately.

623. Cheesy Pepperoni and Chicken Pizza

Preparation Time: 15 minutes
Cooking Time: 15 minutes
Servings: 6

Ingredients:

- 2 cups cooked chicken, cubed
- 1 cup pizza sauce
- 20 slices pepperoni
- ¼ cup grated Parmesan cheese
- 1 cup shredded Mozzarella cheese
- Cooking spray

Directions:

- Spritz a baking pan with cooking spray.
- Arrange the chicken cubes in the prepared baking pan, then top the cubes with pizza sauce and pepperoni. Stir to coat the cubes and pepperoni with sauce. Scatter the cheeses on top.
- Select Air Fry of the oven. Set temperature to 375°F (190°C) and set time to 15 minutes. Press Start to begin preheating.
- Once preheated, place the pan into the oven.
- When cooking is complete, the pizza should be frothy and the cheeses should be melted.
- Serve immediately.

624. Chicken and Ham Meatballs with Dijon Sauce

Preparation Time: 15 minutes
Cooking Time: 12 minutes
Servings: 3

Ingredients:

Meatballs:

- ½ pound (227 g) ham, diced
- ½ pound (227 g) ground chicken
- ½ cup grated Swiss cheese
- 1 large egg, beaten
- 3 cloves garlic, minced
- ¼ cup chopped onions
- 1½ teaspoons sea salt
- 1 teaspoon ground black pepper
- Cooking spray

Dijon Sauce:

- 3 tablespoons Dijon mustard
- 2 tablespoons lemon juice
- ¼ cup chicken broth, warmed
- ¾ teaspoon sea salt
- ¼ teaspoon ground black pepper
- Chopped fresh thyme leaves, for garnish

Directions:

- Spritz a perforated pan with cooking spray.
- Combine the ingredients for the meatballs in a large bowl. Stir to mix well, then shape the mixture in twelve 1½-inch meatballs.
- Arrange the meatballs in the perforated pan.
- Select Air Fry of the oven. Set temperature to 390°F (199°C) and set time to 15 minutes. Press Start to begin preheating.
- Once preheated, place the pan into the oven. Flip the balls halfway through.
- When cooking is complete, the balls should be lightly browned.
- Meanwhile, combine the ingredients, except for the thyme leaves, for the sauce in a small bowl. Stir to mix well.
- Transfer the cooked meatballs on a large plate, then baste the sauce over. Garnish with thyme leaves and serve.

625. Chicken Rochambeau with Mushroom Sauce

Preparation Time: 25 minutes
Cooking Time: 32 minutes
Servings: 4

Ingredients:

- 1 tablespoon melted butter
- ¼ cup all-purpose flour
- 4 chicken tenders, cut in half crosswise
- 4 slices ham, ¼-inch thick, large enough to cover an English muffin
- 4 English muffins, split in halves
- Salt and ground black pepper, to taste
- Cooking spray

Mushroom Sauce:

- 2 tablespoons butter
- ½ cup chopped mushrooms
- ½ cup chopped green onions
- 2 tablespoons flour
- 1 cup chicken broth
- 1½ teaspoons Worcestershire sauce
- ¼ teaspoon garlic powder

Directions:

- Put the butter in a baking pan. Combine the flour, salt, and ground black pepper in a shallow dish. Roll the chicken tenders over to coat well.
- Arrange the chicken in the baking pan and flip to coat with the melted butter.
- Select Broil of the oven. Set temperature to 390°F (199°C) and set time to 10 minutes. Press Start to begin preheating.
- Once preheated, place the pan into the oven. Flip the tenders halfway through.
- When cooking is complete, the juices of chicken tenders should run clear.
- Meanwhile, make the mushroom sauce: melt 2 tablespoons of butter in a saucepan over medium-high heat.
- Add the mushrooms and onions to the saucepan and sauté for 3 minutes or until the onions are translucent.
- Gently mix in the flour, broth, Worcestershire sauce, and garlic powder until smooth.
- Reduce the heat to low and simmer for 5 minutes or until it has a thick consistency. Set the sauce aside until ready to serve.

- When broiling is complete, remove the baking pan from the oven and set the ham slices into the perforated pan.

- Select Air Fry of the oven. Set time to 5 minutes. Press Start. Flip the ham slices halfway through.

- When cooking is complete, the ham slices should be heated through.

- Remove the ham slices from the oven and set in the English muffin halves and warm for 1 minute.

- Arrange each ham slice on top of each muffin half, then place each chicken tender over the ham slice.

- Transfer to the oven and set time to 2 minutes on Air Fry.

- Serve with the sauce on top.

626. Chicken Thighs in Waffles

Preparation Time: 80 minutes
Cooking Time: 21 minutes
Servings: 4

Ingredients:

For the chicken:

- 4 chicken thighs, skin on
- 1 cup low-fat buttermilk
- ½ cup all-purpose flour
- ½ teaspoon garlic powder
- ½ teaspoon mustard powder
- 1 teaspoon kosher salt
- ½ teaspoon freshly ground black pepper
- ¼ cup honey, for serving
- Cooking spray

For the waffles:

- ½ cup all-purpose flour
- ½ cup whole wheat pastry flour
- 1 large egg, beaten
- 1 cup low-fat buttermilk
- 1 teaspoon baking powder
- 2 tablespoons canola oil
- ½ teaspoon kosher salt
- 1 tablespoon granulated sugar

Directions:

- Combine the chicken thighs with buttermilk in a large bowl. Wrap the bowl in plastic and refrigerate to marinate for at least an hour.

- Spritz a perforated pan with cooking spray.

- Combine the flour, mustard powder, garlic powder, salt, and black pepper in a shallow dish. Stir to mix well.

- Remove the thighs from the buttermilk and pat dry with paper towels. Sit the bowl of buttermilk aside.

- Dip the thighs in the flour mixture first, then into the buttermilk, and then into the flour mixture. Shake the excess off.

- Arrange the thighs in the perforated pan and spritz with cooking spray.

- Select Air Fry of the oven. Set temperature to 360°F (182°C) and set time to 20 minutes. Press Start to begin preheating.

- Once preheated, place the pan into the oven. Flip the thighs halfway through.

- When cooking is complete, an instant-read thermometer inserted in the thickest part of the chicken thighs should register at least 165 °F (74 °C).

- Meanwhile, make the waffles: combine the ingredients for the waffles in a large bowl. Stir to mix well, then arrange the mixture in a waffle iron and cook until a golden and fragrant waffle forms.

- Remove the waffles from the waffle iron and slice into 4 pieces. Remove the chicken thighs from the oven and allow to cool for 5 minutes.

- Arrange each chicken thigh on each waffle piece and drizzle with 1 tablespoon of honey. Serve warm.

627. Crispy Chicken Skin

Preparation Time: 5 minutes
Cooking Time: 6 minutes
Servings: 4

Ingredients:

- 1-pound (454 g) chicken skin, cut into slices
- 1 teaspoon melted butter
- ½ teaspoon crushed chili flakes

- ◆ 1 teaspoon dried dill
- ◆ Salt and ground black pepper, to taste

Directions:

- Combine all the ingredients in a large bowl. Toss to coat the chicken skin well.
- Transfer the skin in the perforated pan.
- Select Air Fry of the oven. Set temperature to 360°F (182°C) and set time to 6 minutes. Press Start to begin preheating.
- Once preheated, place the pan into the oven. Stir the skin halfway through.
- When cooking is complete, the skin should be crispy.
- Serve immediately.

628. Sausage Ratatouille

Preparation Time: 10 minutes
Cooking Time: 26 minutes
Servings: 4

Ingredients:

- ◆ 4 pork sausages

Ratatouille:

- ◆ 2 zucchinis, sliced
- ◆ 1 eggplant, sliced
- ◆ 15 ounces (425 g) tomatoes, sliced
- ◆ 1 red bell pepper, sliced
- ◆ 1 medium red onion, sliced
- ◆ 1 cup canned butter beans, drained
- ◆ 1 tablespoon balsamic vinegar
- ◆ 2 garlic cloves, minced
- ◆ 1 red chili, chopped
- ◆ 2 tablespoons fresh thyme, chopped
- ◆ 2 2 tablespoons olive oil

Directions:

- Place the sausages in the perforated pan.
- Select Air Fry of the oven. Set temperature to 390°F (199°C) and set time to 10 minutes. Press Start to begin preheating.
- Once preheated, place the pan into the oven.

- After 7 minutes, remove the pan from the oven. Flip the sausages. Return the pan to the oven and continue cooking.
- When cooking is complete, the sausages should be lightly browned.
- Meanwhile, make the ratatouille: arrange the vegetable slices on the prepared baking pan alternatively, then add the remaining ingredients on top.
- Transfer the air fried sausage to a plate, then arrange the baking pan in the oven.
- Select Bake. Set time to 15 minutes and bake until the vegetables are tender. Give the vegetables a stir halfway through the baking.
- Serve the ratatouille with the sausage on top.

629. Korean Flavor Glazed Chicken Wings

Preparation Time: 10 minutes
Cooking Time: 26 minutes
Servings: 4

Ingredients:

Wings:

- ◆ 2 pounds (907 g) chicken wings
- ◆ 1 teaspoon salt
- ◆ 1 teaspoon ground black pepper

Sauce:

- ◆ 2 tablespoons gochujang
- ◆ 1 tablespoon mayonnaise
- ◆ 1 tablespoon minced ginger
- ◆ 1 tablespoon minced garlic
- ◆ 1 teaspoon agave nectar
- ◆ 2 packets Splenda
- ◆ 1 tablespoon sesame oil

For Garnish:

- ◆ 2 teaspoons sesame seeds
- ◆ ¼ cup chopped green onions

Directions:

- Line a baking pan with aluminum foil, then arrange the rack on the pan.

- On a clean work surface, rub the chicken wings with salt and ground black pepper, then arrange the seasoned wings on the rack.

- Select Air Fry of the oven. Set temperature to 400°F (205°C) and set time to 20 minutes. Press Start to begin preheating.

- Once preheated, place the pan into the oven. Flip the wings halfway through.

- When cooking is complete, the wings should be well browned.

- Meanwhile, combine the ingredients for the sauce in a small bowl. Stir to mix well. Reserve half of the sauce in a separate bowl until ready to serve.

- Remove the air fried chicken wings from the oven and toss with remaining half of the sauce to coat well.

- Place the wings back to the oven. Select Air Fry. Set time to 5 minutes.

- When cooking is complete, the internal temperature of the wings should reach at least 165°F (74°C).

- Remove the wings from the oven and place on a large plate. Sprinkle with sesame seeds and green onions. Serve with reserved sauce.

630. Lettuce Chicken Tacos with Peanut Sauce

Preparation Time: 10 minutes
Cooking Time: 6 minutes
Servings: 4

Ingredients:

- 1-pound (454 g) ground chicken
- 2 cloves garlic, minced
- ¼ cup diced onions
- ¼ teaspoon sea salt
- Cooking spray

Peanut Sauce:

- ¼ cup creamy peanut butter, at room temperature
- 2 tablespoons tamari
- 1½ teaspoons hot sauce
- 2 tablespoons lime juice
- 2 tablespoons grated fresh ginger
- 2 tablespoons chicken broth
- 2 teaspoons sugar

For Serving:

- 2 small heads butter lettuce, leaves separated
- Lime slices (optional)

Directions:

- Spritz a baking pan with cooking spray.

- Combine the ground chicken, garlic, and onions in the baking pan, then sprinkle with salt. Use a fork to break the ground chicken and combine them well.

- Select Bake of the oven. Set temperature to 350°F (180°C) and set time to 5 minutes. Press Start to begin preheating.

- Once preheated, place the pan into the oven. Stir them halfway through the cooking time.

- When cooking is complete, the chicken should be lightly browned.

- Meanwhile, combine the ingredients for the sauce in a small bowl. Stir to mix well.

- Pour the sauce in the pan of chicken, then bake for 1 more minute or until heated through.

- Unfold the lettuce leaves on a large serving plate, then divide the chicken mixture on the lettuce leaves. Drizzle with lime juice and serve immediately.

631. Lime Chicken with Cilantro

Preparation Time: 35 minutes
Cooking Time: 10 minutes
Servings: 4

Ingredients:

- 4 (4-ounce / 113-g) boneless, skinless chicken breasts
- ½ cup chopped fresh cilantro
- Juice of 1 lime
- Chicken seasoning or rub, to taste
- Salt and ground black pepper, to taste
- Cooking spray

Directions:

- Put the chicken breasts in the large bowl, then add the cilantro, lime juice, chicken seasoning, salt, and black pepper. Toss to coat well.

- Wrap the bowl in plastic and refrigerate to marinate for at least 30 minutes.

- Spritz a perforated pan with cooking spray.

- Remove the marinated chicken breasts from the bowl and place in the perforated pan. Spritz with cooking spray.

- Select Air Fry of the oven. Set temperature to 400°F (205°C) and set time to 10 minutes. Press Start to begin preheating.

- Once preheated, place the pan into the oven. Flip the breasts halfway through.

- When cooking is complete, the internal temperature of the chicken should reach at least 165 °F (74 °C).

- Serve immediately.

632. Nice Goulash

Preparation Time: 5 minutes
Cooking Time: 17 minutes
Servings: 2

Ingredients:

- 2 red bell peppers, chopped
- 1-pound (454 g) ground chicken
- 2 medium tomatoes, diced
- ½ cup chicken broth
- Salt and ground black pepper, to taste
- Cooking spray

Directions:

- Spritz a baking pan with cooking spray.
- Set the bell pepper in the baking pan.
- Select Broil of the oven. Set temperature to 365°F (185°C) and set time to 5 minutes. Press Start to begin preheating.
- Once preheated, place the pan into the oven. Stir the bell pepper halfway through.
- When broiling is complete, the bell pepper should be tender.
- Add the ground chicken and diced tomatoes in the baking pan and stir to mix well.

- Set the time of oven to 12 minutes. Press Start. Stir the mixture and mix in the chicken broth, salt and ground black pepper halfway through.

- When cooking is complete, the chicken should be well browned.

- Serve immediately.

633. Oven-fried Herbed Chicken

Preparation Time: 5 minutes
Cooking Time: 15 minutes
Servings: 2

Ingredients:

- 1/2 cup buttermilk
- 2 cloves garlic, minced
- 1-1/2 teaspoons salt
- 1 tablespoon oil
- 1/2-pound boneless, skinless chicken breasts
- 1 cup rolled oats
- 1/2 teaspoon red pepper flakes
- 1/2 cup grated parmesan cheese
- 1/4 cup fresh basil leaves or rosemary needles
- Olive oil spray

Directions:

- Mix together buttermilk, oil, 1/2 teaspoon salt, and garlic in a shallow bowl.

- Roll chicken in buttermilk and refrigerate in bowl overnight.

- Preheat your toaster oven to 425°F.

- Mix together the oats, red pepper, salt, parmesan, and basil, and mix roughly to break up oats.

- Place the mixture on a plate.

- Remove the chicken from the buttermilk mixture and let any excess drip off.

- Roll the chicken in the oat mixture and transfer to a baking sheet lightly coated with olive oil spray.

- Spray the chicken with oil spray and bake for 15 minutes.

634. Award Winning Breaded Chicken

Preparation Time: 8 minutes
Cooking Time: 21 minutes
Servings: 4

Ingredients:

- 1 1/2 tsp. olive oil
- 1 tsp. red pepper flakes, crushed
- 1/3 tsp. chicken bouillon granules
- 1/3 tsp. shallot powder
- 1 1/2 tablespoons tamari soy sauce
- 1/3 tsp. cumin powder
- 1½ tablespoons mayo 1 tsp. kosher salt
- For the chicken:
- 2 beaten eggs Breadcrumbs
- 1½ chicken breasts, boneless and skinless
- 1 ½ tablespoons plain flour

Directions:

- Margarine fly the chicken breasts, and then, marinate them for at least 55 minutes. Coat the chicken with plain flour; then, coat with the beaten eggs; finally, roll them in the breadcrumbs.
- Lightly grease the cooking basket. Air-fry the breaded chicken at 345 °F for 12 minutes, flipping them halfway.

635. Cheese and Garlic Stuffed Chicken Breasts

Preparation Time: 15 minutes
Cooking Time: 22 minutes
Servings: 2

Ingredients:

- 1/2 cup Cottage cheese
- 2 eggs, beaten
- 2 medium-sized chicken breasts, halved
- 2 tablespoons fresh coriander, chopped
- 1tsp. fine sea salt
- Seasoned breadcrumbs
- 1/3 tsp. freshly ground black pepper, to savor
- 3 cloves garlic, finely minced

Directions:

- Firstly, flatten out the chicken breast using a meat tenderizer.

- In a medium-sized mixing dish, combine the Cottage cheese with the garlic, coriander, salt, and black pepper.
- Spread 1/3 of the mixture over the first chicken breast. Repeat with the remaining ingredients. Roll the chicken around the filling; make sure to secure with toothpicks.
- Now, whisk the egg in a shallow bowl. In another shallow bowl, combine the salt, ground black pepper, and seasoned breadcrumbs.
- Coat the chicken breasts with the whisked egg; now, roll them in the breadcrumbs.
- Cook in the air fryer cooking basket at 365 °F for 22 minutes. Serve immediately.

636. Lemon Duck Legs

Preparation Time: 15 minutes
Cooking Time: 26 minutes
Servings: 6

Ingredients:

- 1 lemon
- 2-pound duck legs
- 1 teaspoon ground coriander
- 1 teaspoon ground nutmeg
- 1 teaspoon kosher salt
- ½ teaspoon dried rosemary
- 1 tablespoon olive oil
- 1 teaspoon stevia extract
- ¼ teaspoon sage

Directions:

- Squeeze the juice from the lemon and grate the zest.
- Combine the lemon juice and lemon zest together in the big mixing bowl.
- Add the ground coriander, ground nutmeg, kosher salt, dried rosemary, and sage.
- Sprinkle the liquid with the olive oil and stevia extract.
- Whisk it carefully and put the duck legs there.
- Stir the duck legs and leave them for 15 minutes to marinate.
- Meanwhile, preheat the air fryer to 380 F.

- Put the marinated duck legs in the air fryer and cook them for 25 minutes.
- Turn the duck legs into another side after 15 minutes of cooking.
- When the duck legs are cooked – let them cool little.
- Serve and enjoy!

637. Chicken Lasagna with Eggplants

Preparation Time: 5 minutes
Cooking Time: 17 minutes
Servings: 10

Ingredients:

- 6 oz Cheddar cheese, shredded
- 7 oz Parmesan cheese, shredded
- 2 eggplants
- 1-pound ground chicken
- 1 teaspoon paprika
- 1 teaspoon salt
- ½ teaspoon cayenne pepper
- ½ cup heavy cream
- 2 teaspoon butter
- 4 oz chive stems, diced

Directions:

- Take the air fryer basket tray and spread it with the butter.
- Then peel the eggplants and slice them.
- Separate the sliced eggplants into 3 parts.
- Combine the ground chicken with the paprika, salt, cayenne pepper, and diced chives.
- Mix the mixture up.
- Separate the ground chicken mixture into 2 parts.
- Make the layer of the first part of the sliced eggplant in the air fryer basket tray.
- Then make the layer of the ground chicken mixture.
- After this, sprinkle the ground chicken layer with the half of the shredded Cheddar cheese,

- Then cover the cheese with the second part of the sliced eggplant.
- The next step is to make the layer of the ground chicken and all shredded Cheddar cheese,
- Cover the cheese layer with the last part of the sliced eggplants.
- Then sprinkle the eggplants with shredded Parmesan cheese.
- Pour the heavy cream and add butter.
- Preheat the air fryer to 365 F.
- Cook the lasagna for 17 minutes.
- When the time is over – let the lasagna chill gently.
- Serve it!

638. Chicken & Rice Casserole

Preparation Time: 5 minutes
Cooking Time: 41 minutes
Servings: 6

Ingredients:

- 2 lbs. bone-in chicken thighs
- Salt and black pepper
- 1 teaspoon olive oil
- 5 cloves garlic, chopped
- 2 large onions, chopped
- 2 large red bell peppers, chopped
- 1 tablespoon sweet Hungarian paprika
- 1 teaspoon hot Hungarian paprika
- 2 tablespoons tomato paste
- 2 cups chicken broth
- 3 cups brown rice, thawed
- 2 tablespoons parsley, chopped
- 6 tablespoons sour cream

Directions:

- Mix broth, tomato paste, and all the spices in a bowl.
- Add chicken and mix well to coat.
- Spread the rice in a casserole dish and add chicken along with its marinade.
- Top the casserole with the rest of the ingredients.

- Press "Power Button" of Air Fry Oven and turn the dial to select the "Bake" mode.
- Press the Time button and again turn the dial to set the cooking time to 40 minutes.
- Now push the Temp button and rotate the dial to set the temperature at 350 degrees F.
- Once preheated, place the baking pan inside and close its lid.
- Serve warm.

639. Maple Chicken Thighs

Preparation Time: 16 minutes
Cooking Time: 14 minutes
Servings: 4

Ingredients:

- 4 large chicken thighs, bone-in
- 2 tablespoons French mustard
- 2 tablespoons Dijon mustard
- 1 clove minced garlic
- 1/2 teaspoon dried marjoram
- 2 tablespoons maple syrup

Directions:

- Mix chicken with everything in a bowl and coat it well.
- Place the chicken along with its marinade in the baking pan.
- Press "Power Button" of Air Fry Oven and turn the dial to select the "Bake" mode.
- Press the Time button and again turn the dial to set the cooking time to 30 minutes.
- Now push the Temp button and rotate the dial to set the temperature at 370 degrees F.
- Once preheated, place the baking pan inside and close its lid.
- Serve warm.

640. Parmesan Chicken Meatballs

Preparation Time: 15 minutes
Cooking Time: 12 minutes
Servings: 4

Ingredients:

- 1-lb. ground chicken

- 1 large egg, beaten
- ½ cup Parmesan cheese, grated
- ½ cup pork rinds, ground
- 1 teaspoon garlic powder
- 1 teaspoon paprika
- 1 teaspoon kosher salt
- ½ teaspoon pepper

Crust:

- ½ cup pork rinds, ground

Directions:

- Toss all the meatball ingredients in a bowl and mix well.
- Make small meatballs out this mixture and roll them in the pork rinds.
- Place the coated meatballs in the air fryer basket.
- Press "Power Button" of Air Fry Oven and turn the dial to select the "Bake" mode.
- Press the Time button and again turn the dial to set the cooking time to 12 minutes.
- Now push the Temp button and rotate the dial to set the temperature at 400 degrees F.
- Once preheated, place the air fryer basket inside and close its lid.
- Serve warm.

641. BBQ Chicken Breasts

Preparation Time: 15 minutes
Cooking Time: 16 minutes
Servings: 4

Ingredients:

- 4 boneless skinless chicken breasts about 6 oz each
- 1-2 Tbsp BBQ seasoning

Directions:

- Cover both sides of chicken breast with the BBQ seasoning. Cover and marinate the in the refrigerator for 45 minutes.
- Choose the Air Fry option and set the temperature to 400°F. Push start and let it preheat for 5 minutes.

- Upon preheating, place the chicken breast in the Instant Vortex Air Fryer basket, making sure they do not overlap. Spray with oil.
- Cook for 13-14 minutes
- flipping halfway.
- Remove chicken when the chicken reaches an internal temperature of 160°F. Place on a plate and allow to rest for 5 minutes before slicing.

642. Chicken Parmesan

Preparation Time: 5 minutes
Cooking Time: 10 minutes
Servings: 4

Ingredients:

- 2 (6-oz. boneless, skinless chicken breasts
- 1 oz. pork rinds, crushed
- ½ cup grated Parmesan cheese, divided.
- 1 cup low-carb, no-sugar-added pasta sauce.
- 1 cup shredded mozzarella cheese, divided.
- 4 tbsp. full-fat mayonnaise, divided.
- ½ tsp. garlic powder.
- ¼ tsp. dried oregano.
- ½ tsp. dried parsley.

Directions:

- Slice each chicken breast in half lengthwise and lb. out to 3/4-inch thickness. Sprinkle with garlic powder, oregano and parsley
- Spread 1 tbsp. mayonnaise on top of each piece of chicken, then sprinkle ¼ cup mozzarella on each piece.
- Mix the crushed pork rinds and Parmesan. Sprinkle the mixture on top of mozzarella
- Pour sauce into 6-inch round baking pan and place chicken on top. Place pan into the air fryer basket. Adjust the temperature to 320 Degrees F and set the timer for 25 minutes
- Cheese will be browned and internal temperature of the chicken will be at least 165 Degrees F when fully cooked. Serve warm.

643. Delicious Chicken Burgers

Preparation Time: 15 minutes
Cooking Time: 31 minutes

Servings: 4

Ingredients:

- 4 boneless, skinless chicken breasts
- 1¾ ounces plain flour
- 2 eggs
- 4 hamburger buns, split and toasted
- 4 mozzarella cheese slices
- 1 teaspoon mustard powder
- ½ teaspoon paprika
- 1 teaspoon Worcestershire sauce
- ¼ teaspoon dried parsley
- ¼ teaspoon dried tarragon
- ¼ teaspoon dried oregano
- 1 teaspoon dried garlic
- 1 teaspoon chicken seasoning
- ½ teaspoon cayenne pepper
- Salt and black pepper, as required

Directions:

- Preheat the Air fryer to 355-degree F and grease an Air fryer basket.
- Put the chicken breasts, mustard, paprika, Worcestershire sauce, salt, and black pepper in a food processor and pulse until minced.
- Make 4 equal-sized patties from the mixture.
- Place the flour in a shallow bowl and whisk the egg in a second bowl.
- Combine dried herbs and spices in a third bowl.
- Coat each chicken patty with flour, dip into whisked egg and then coat with breadcrumb mixture.
- Arrange the chicken patties into the Air fryer basket in a single layer and cook for about 30 minutes, flipping once in between.
- Place half bun in a plate, layer with lettuce leaf, patty and cheese slice.
- Cover with bun top and dish out to serve warm.

644. Turkey-Stuffed Peppers

Preparation Time: 15 minutes
Cooking Time: 11 minutes
Servings: 6

Ingredients:

- 1-pound lean ground turkey
- 1 tablespoon olive oil
- 2 cloves garlic, minced
- 1/3 onion, minced
- 1 tablespoon cilantro (optional)
- 1 teaspoon garlic powder
- 1 teaspoon cumin powder
- 1/2 teaspoon salt
- Pepper to taste
- 3 large red bell peppers
- 1 cup chicken broth
- 1/4 cup tomato sauce
- 1-1/2 cups cooked brown rice
- 1/4 cup shredded cheddar
- 6 green onions

Directions:

- Start by preheating toaster oven to 400°F.
- Heat a skillet on medium heat.
- Add olive oil to the skillet, then mix in onion and garlic.
- Sauté for about 5 minutes, or until the onion starts to look opaque.
- Add the turkey to the skillet and season with cumin, garlic powder, salt, and pepper.
- Brown the meat until thoroughly cooked, then mix in chicken broth and tomato sauce.
- Reduce heat and simmer for about 5 minutes, stirring occasionally.
- Add the brown rice and continue stirring until it is evenly spread through the mix.
- Cut the bell peppers lengthwise down the middle and remove all of the seeds.
- Grease a pan or line it with parchment paper and lay all peppers in the pan with the outside facing down.
- Spoon the meat mixture evenly into each pepper and use the back of the spoon to level.
- Bake for 30 minutes.
- Remove pan from oven and sprinkle cheddar over each pepper, then put it back in for another 3 minutes, or until the cheese is melted.
- While the cheese melts, dice the green onions. Remove pan from oven and sprinkle onions over each pepper and serve.

645. Herb-Roasted Chicken Tenders

Preparation Time: 11 minutes
Cooking Time: 9 minutes
Servings: 2

Ingredients:

- 7 ounces chicken tenders
- 1 tablespoon olive oil
- 1/2 teaspoon Herbes de Provence
- 2 tablespoons Dijon mustard
- 1 tablespoon honey
- Salt and pepper

Directions:

- Start by preheating toaster oven to 450°F.
- Brush bottom of pan with 1/2 tablespoon olive oil.
- Season the chicken with herbs, salt, and pepper.
- Place the chicken in a single flat layer in the pan and drizzle the remaining olive oil over it.
- Bake for about 10 minutes.
- While the chicken is baking, mix together the mustard and honey for a tasty condiment.

646. Ranch Chicken Wings

Preparation Time: 15 minutes
Cooking Time: 9 minutes
Servings: 3

Ingredients:

- 1/4 cup almond meal
- 1/4 cup flaxseed meal
- 2 tablespoons butter, melted
- 6 tablespoons parmesan cheese, preferably freshly grated
- 1 tablespoon Ranch seasoning mix
- 2 tablespoons oyster sauce

- 6 chicken wings, bone-in

Directions:

- Start by preheating your Air Fryer to 370 degrees F.

- In a resealable bag, place the almond meal, flaxseed meal, butter, parmesan, Ranch seasoning mix, and oyster sauce. Add the chicken wings and shake to coat on all sides.

- Arrange the chicken wings in the Air Fryer basket. Spritz the chicken wings with a nonstick cooking spray.

- Cook for 11 minutes. Turn them over and cook an additional 11 minutes. Serve warm with your favorite dipping sauce, if desired. Enjoy!

647. Chicken Legs with Dilled Brussels Sprouts

Preparation Time: 15 minutes
Cooking Time: 11 minutes
Servings: 2

Ingredients:

- 2 chicken legs
- 1/2 teaspoon paprika
- 1/2 teaspoon kosher salt
- 1/2 teaspoon black pepper
- 1/2-pound Brussels sprouts
- 1 teaspoon dill, fresh or dried

Directions:

- Start by preheating your Air Fryer to 370 degrees F.

- Now, season your chicken with paprika, salt, and pepper. Transfer the chicken legs to the cooking basket. Cook for 10 minutes.

- Flip the chicken legs and cook an additional 10 minutes. Reserve.

- Add the Brussels sprouts to the cooking basket; sprinkle with dill. Cook at 380 degrees F for 15 minutes, shaking the basket halfway through.

- Serve with the reserved chicken legs.

648. Lime and Mustard Marinated Chicken

Preparation Time: 15 minutes
Cooking Time: 9 minutes
Servings: 4

Ingredients:

- 1/2 teaspoon stone-ground mustard
- 1/2 teaspoon minced fresh oregano
- 1/3 cup freshly squeezed lime juice
- 2 small-sized chicken breasts, skin-on
- 1 teaspoon kosher salt
- 1teaspoon freshly cracked mixed peppercorns

Directions:

- Preheat your Air Fryer to 345 degrees F.

- Toss all of the above ingredients in a medium-sized mixing dish; allow it to marinate overnight.

- Cook in the preheated Air Fryer for 26 minutes.

649. Chicken with Veggies and Rice

Preparation Time: 15 minutes
Cooking Time: 20 minutes
Servings: 3

Ingredients:

- 3 cups cold boiled white rice
- 1 cup cooked chicken, diced
- ½ cup frozen carrots
- ½ cup frozen peas
- ½ cup onion, chopped
- 6 tablespoons soy sauce
- 1 tablespoon vegetable oil

Directions:

- Preheat the Air fryer to 360-degree F and grease a 7" nonstick pan.

- Mix the rice, soy sauce, and vegetable oil in a bowl.

- Stir in the remaining ingredients and mix until well combined.

- Transfer the rice mixture into the pan and place in the Air fryer.

- Cook for about 20 minutes and dish out to serve immediately.

650. Spicy Egg and Ground Turkey Bake

Preparation Time: 15 minutes
Cooking Time: 9 minutes
Servings: 6

Ingredients:

- 1½ pounds ground turkey
- 6 whole eggs, well beaten
- 1/3 teaspoon smoked paprika
- 2 egg whites, beaten
- Tabasco sauce, for drizzling
- 2 tablespoons sesame oil
- 2 leeks, chopped
- 3 cloves garlic, finely minced
- 1 teaspoon ground black pepper
- 1/2 teaspoon sea salt

Directions:

- Warm the oil in a pan over moderate heat; then, sweat the leeks and garlic until tender; stir periodically.
- Next, grease 6 oven safe ramekins with pan spray. Divide the sautéed mixture among six ramekins.
- In a bowl, beat the eggs and egg whites using a wire whisk. Stir in the smoked paprika, salt and black pepper; whisk until everything is thoroughly combined. Divide the egg mixture among the ramekins.
- Air-fry approximately 22 minutes at 345 degrees F. Drizzle Tabasco sauce over each portion and serve.

651. Orange Chicken Rice

Preparation Time: 15 minutes
Cooking Time: 41 minutes
Servings: 4

Ingredients:

- 3 tablespoons olive oil
- 1 medium onion, chopped
- 1 3/4 cups chicken broth
- 1 cup brown basmati rice
- Zest and juice of 2 oranges
- Salt to taste
- 4 (6-oz.) boneless, skinless chicken thighs
- Black pepper, to taste
- 2 tablespoons fresh mint, chopped
- 2 tablespoons pine nuts, toasted

Directions:

- Spread the rice in a casserole dish and place the chicken on top.
- Toss the rest of the ingredients in a bowl and liberally pour over the chicken.
- Press "Power Button" of Air Fry Oven and turn the dial to select the "Bake" mode.
- Press the Time button and again turn the dial to set the cooking time to 55 minutes.
- Now push the Temp button and rotate the dial to set the temperature at 350 degrees F.
- Once preheated, place the casserole dish inside and close its lid.
- Serve warm.

652. Garlic Chicken Potatoes

Preparation Time: 15 minutes
Cooking Time: 16 minutes
Servings: 4

Ingredients:

- 2 lbs. red potatoes, quartered
- 3 tablespoons olive oil
- 1/2 teaspoon cumin seeds
- Salt and black pepper, to taste
- 4 garlic cloves, chopped
- 2 tablespoons brown sugar
- 1 lemon (1/2 juiced and 1/2 cut into wedges)
- Pinch of red pepper flakes
- 4 skinless, boneless chicken breasts
- 2 tablespoons cilantro, chopped

Directions:

- Place the chicken, lemon, garlic, and potatoes in a baking pan.
- Toss the spices, herbs, oil, and sugar in a bowl.

- Add this mixture to the chicken and veggies then toss well to coat.
- Press "Power Button" of Air Fry Oven and turn the dial to select the "Bake" mode.
- Press the Time button and again turn the dial to set the cooking time to 30 minutes.
- Now push the Temp button and rotate the dial to set the temperature at 400 degrees F.
- Once preheated, place the baking pan inside and close its lid.
- Serve warm.

VEGAN AND VEGETARIAN RECIPES

653. Grilled Cauliflower

Preparation Time: 15 minutes
Cooking Time: 40 minutes
Servings: 4

Ingredients:

- 1 large head of cauliflower, leaves removed and stem trimmed
- Salt, as required
- 4 tablespoons unsalted butter
- ¼ cup hot sauce
- 1 tablespoon ketchup
- 1 tablespoon soy sauce
- 1/2 cup mayonnaise
- 2 tablespoons white miso
- 1 tablespoon fresh lemon juice
- 1/2 teaspoon ground black pepper
- 2 scallions, thinly sliced

Directions:

- Sprinkle the cauliflower with salt evenly.
- Arrange the cauliflower head in a large microwave-safe bowl.
- With a plastic wrap, cover the bowl.
- With a knife, pierce the plastic a few times to vent.
- Microwave on high for about 5 minutes.
- Remove from the microwave and set aside to cool slightly.
- In a small saucepan, add butter, hot sauce, ketchup and soy sauce over medium heat and cook for about 2-3 minutes, stirring occasionally.
- Brush the cauliflower head with warm sauce evenly.
- Place the water tray in the bottom of Smokeless Electric Grill.
- Place about 2 cups of lukewarm water into the water tray.
- Place the drip pan over water tray and then arrange the heating element.
- Now, place the grilling pan over heating element.
- Plugin the Smokeless Electric Grill and press the 'Power' button to turn it on.
- Then press 'Fan" button.
- Set the temperature settings according to manufacturer's directions.
- Cover the grill with lid and let it preheat.
- After preheating, remove the lid and grease the grilling pan.
- Place the cauliflower head over the grilling pan.
- Cover with the lid and cook for about 10 minutes.
- Turn the cauliflower over and brush with warm sauce.
- Cover with the lid and cook for about 25 minutes, flipping and brushing with warm sauce after every 10
- Transfer cauliflower to a plate and let cool slightly.
- In a bowl, place the mayonnaise, miso, lemon juice, and pepper and beat until smooth.
- Spread the mayonnaise mixture onto a plate and arrange the cauliflower on top.
- Garnish with scallions and serve.

654. Stuffed Zucchini

Preparation Time: 20 minutes
Cooking Time: 24 minutes
Servings: 6

Ingredients:

- 3 medium zucchinis, sliced in half lengthwise
- 1 teaspoon vegetable oil
- Salt and ground black pepper, as required
- 3 cup corn, cut off the cob
- 1 cup Parmesan cheese, shredded
- 2/3 cup sour cream
- ¼ teaspoon hot sauce

♦ Olive oil cooking spray

Directions:

- Cut the ends off the zucchini and slice in half lengthwise.

- Scoop out the pulp from each half of zucchini, leaving the shell.

- For filling: in a large pan of boiling water, add the corn over medium heat and cook for about 5-7 minutes.

- Drain the corn and set aside to cool.

- In a large bowl, add corn, half of the parmesan cheese, sour cream and hot sauce and mix well.

- Spray the zucchini shells with cooking spray evenly.

- Place the water tray in the bottom of Smokeless Electric Grill.

- Place about 2 cups of lukewarm water into the water tray.

- Place the drip pan over water tray and then arrange the heating element.

- Now, place the grilling pan over heating element.

- Plugin the smokeless electric grill and press the 'power' button to turn it on.

- Then press 'fan" button.

- Set the temperature settings according to manufacturer's directions.

- Cover the grill with lid and let it preheat.

- After preheating, remove the lid and grease the grilling pan.

- Place the zucchini halves over the grilling pan, flesh side down.

- Cover with the lid and cook for about 8-10 minutes.

- Remove the zucchini halves from grill.

- Spoon filling into each zucchini half evenly and sprinkle with remaining parmesan cheese.

- Place the zucchini halves over the grilling pan.

- Cover with the lid and cook for about 8 minutes.

- Serve hot.

655.　Vinegar Veggies

Preparation Time: 15 minutes
Cooking Time: 10 minutes
Servings: 4

Ingredients:

♦ 3 golden beets, trimmed, peeled and sliced thinly
♦ 3 carrots, peeled and sliced lengthwise
♦ 1 cup zucchini, sliced
♦ 1 onion, sliced
♦ 1/2 cup yam, sliced thinly
♦ 2 tablespoon fresh rosemary
♦ 1 garlic clove, minced
♦ Salt and ground black pepper, as required
♦ 3 tablespoons vegetable oil
♦ 2 teaspoons balsamic vinegar

Directions:

- Place all ingredients in a bowl and toss to coat well.

- Refrigerate to marinate for at least 30 minutes.

- Place the water tray in the bottom of Smokeless Electric Grill.

- Place about 2 cups of lukewarm water into the water tray.

- Place the drip pan over water tray and then arrange the heating element.

- Now, place the grilling pan over heating element.

- Plugin the Smokeless Electric Grill and press the 'Power' button to turn it on.

- Then press 'Fan" button.

- Set the temperature settings according to manufacturer's directions.

- Cover the grill with lid and let it preheat.

- After preheating, remove the lid and grease the grilling pan.

- Place the vegetables over the grilling pan.

- Cover with the lid and cook for about 5 minutes per side.

- Serve hot.

656. Garlicky Mixed Veggies

Preparation Time: 15 minutes
Cooking Time: 8 minutes
Servings: 4

Ingredients:

- 1 bunch fresh asparagus, trimmed
- 6 ounces fresh mushrooms, halved
- 6 Campari tomatoes, halved
- 1 red onion, cut into 1-inch chunks
- 3 garlic cloves, minced
- 2 tablespoons olive oil
- Salt and ground black pepper, as required

Directions:

- In a large bowl, add all ingredients and toss to coat well.
- Place the water tray in the bottom of Smokeless Electric Grill.
- Place about 2 cups of lukewarm water into the water tray.
- Place the drip pan over water tray and then arrange the heating element.
- Now, place the grilling pan over heating element.
- Plugin the Smokeless Electric Grill and press the 'Power' button to turn it on.
- Then press 'Fan" button.
- Set the temperature settings according to manufacturer's directions.
- Cover the grill with lid and let it preheat.
- After preheating, remove the lid and grease the grilling pan.
- Place the vegetables over the grilling pan.
- Cover with the lid and cook for about 8 minutes, flipping occasionally.

657. Mediterranean Veggies

Preparation Time: 5 minutes
Cooking Time: 10 minutes
Servings: 4

Ingredients:

- 1 cup mixed bell peppers, chopped
- 1 cup eggplant, chopped
- 1 cup zucchini, chopped
- 1 cup mushrooms, chopped
- 1/2 cup onion, chopped
- 1/2 cup sun-dried tomato vinaigrette dressing

Directions:

- In a large bowl, add all ingredients and toss to coat well.
- Refrigerate to marinate for about 1 hour.
- Place the water tray in the bottom of Smokeless Electric Grill.
- Place about 2 cups of lukewarm water into the water tray.
- Place the drip pan over water tray and then arrange the heating element.
- Now, place the grilling pan over heating element.
- Plugin the Smokeless Electric Grill and press the 'Power' button to turn it on.
- Then press 'Fan" button.
- Set the temperature settings according to manufacturer's directions.
- Cover the grill with lid and let it preheat.
- After preheating, remove the lid and grease the grilling pan.
- Place the vegetables over the grilling pan.
- Cover with the lid and cook for about 8-10 minutes, flipping occasionally.
- Serve hot.

658. Marinated Veggie Skewers

Preparation Time: 20 minutes
Cooking Time: 10 minutes
Servings: 4

Ingredients:

- For Marinade:
- 2 garlic cloves, minced
- 2 teaspoons fresh basil, minced
- 2 teaspoons fresh oregano, minced
- 1/2 teaspoon cayenne pepper
- Sea Salt and ground black pepper, as required

- 2 tablespoons fresh lemon juice
- 2 tablespoons olive oil
- For Veggies:
- 2 large zucchinis, cut into thick slices
- 8 large button mushrooms, quartered
- 1 yellow bell pepper, seeded and cubed
- 1 red bell pepper, seeded and cubed

Directions:

- For marinade: in a large bowl, add all the ingredients and mix until well combined.
- Add the vegetables and toss to coat well.
- Cover and refrigerate to marinate for at least 6-8 hours.
- Remove the vegetables from the bowl and thread onto pre-soaked wooden skewers.
- Place the water tray in the bottom of Smokeless Electric Grill.
- Place about 2 cups of lukewarm water into the water tray.
- Place the drip pan over water tray and then arrange the heating element.
- Now, place the grilling pan over heating element.
- Plugin the Smokeless Electric Grill and press the 'Power' button to turn it on.
- Then press 'Fan" button.
- Set the temperature settings according to manufacturer's directions.
- Cover the grill with lid and let it preheat.
- After preheating, remove the lid and grease the grilling pan.
- Place the skewers over the grilling pan.
- Cover with the lid and cook for about 8-10 minutes, flipping occasionally.
- **Serve hot.**

659. Pineapple & Veggie Skewers

Preparation Time: 20 minutes
Cooking Time: 15 minutes
Servings: 6

Ingredients:

- 1/3 cup olive oil

- 1 1/2 teaspoons dried basil
- ¾ teaspoon dried oregano
- Salt and ground black pepper, as required
- 2 zucchinis, cut into 1-inch slices
- 2 yellow squash, cut into 1-inch slices
- 1/2 pound whole fresh mushrooms
- 1 red bell pepper, cut into chunks
- 1 red onion, cut into chunks
- 12 cherry tomatoes
- 1 fresh pineapple, cut into chunks

Directions:

- In a bowl, add oil, herbs, salt and black pepper and mix well.
- Thread the veggies and pineapple onto pre-soaked wooden skewers.
- Brush the veggies and pineapple with oil mixture evenly.
- Place the water tray in the bottom of Smokeless Electric Grill.
- Place about 2 cups of lukewarm water into the water tray.
- Place the drip pan over water tray and then arrange the heating element.
- Now, place the grilling pan over heating element.
- Plugin the Smokeless Electric Grill and press the 'Power' button to turn it on.
- Then press 'Fan" button.
- Set the temperature settings according to manufacturer's directions.
- Cover the grill with lid and let it preheat.
- After preheating, remove the lid and grease the grilling pan.
- Place the skewers over the grilling pan.
- Cover with the lid and cook for about 10-15 minutes, flipping occasionally.
- Serve hot.

660. Buttered Corn

Preparation Time: 10 minutes
Cooking Time: 20 minutes
Servings: 6

Ingredients:

- 6 fresh whole corn on the cob
- 1/2 cup butter, melted
- Salt, as required

Directions:

- Husk the corn and remove all the silk.
- Brush each corn with melted butter and sprinkle with salt.
- Place the water tray in the bottom of Smokeless Electric Grill.
- Place about 2 cups of lukewarm water into the water tray.
- Place the drip pan over water tray and then arrange the heating element.
- Now, place the grilling pan over heating element.
- Plugin the Smokeless Electric Grill and press the 'Power' button to turn it on.
- Then press 'Fan" button.
- Set the temperature settings according to manufacturer's directions.
- Cover the grill with lid and let it preheat.
- After preheating, remove the lid and grease the grilling pan.
- Place the corn over the grilling pan.
- Cover with the lid and cook for about 20 minutes, rotating after every 5 minutes and brushing with butter once halfway through.
- Serve warm.

661.   Guacamole

Preparation Time: 15 minutes
Cooking Time: 4 minutes
Servings: 4

Ingredients:

- 2 ripe avocados, halved and pitted
- 2 teaspoons vegetable oil
- 3 tablespoons fresh lime juice
- 1 garlic clove, crushed
- ¼ teaspoon ground chipotle chile
- Salt, as required

- ¼ cup red onion, chopped finely
- ¼ cup fresh cilantro, chopped finely

Directions:

- Brush the cut sides of each avocado half with oil.
- Place the water tray in the bottom of Smokeless Electric Grill.
- Place about 2 cups of lukewarm water into the water tray.
- Place the drip pan over water tray and then arrange the heating element.
- Now, place the grilling pan over heating element.
- Plugin the Smokeless Electric Grill and press the 'Power' button to turn it on.
- Then press 'Fan" button.
- Set the temperature settings according to manufacturer's directions.
- Cover the grill with lid and let it preheat.
- After preheating, remove the lid and grease the grilling pan.
- Place the avocado halves over the grilling pan, cut side down.
- Cook, uncovered for about 2-4 minutes.
- Transfer the avocados onto cutting board and let them cool slightly.
- Remove the peel and transfer the flesh into a bowl.
- Add the lime juice, garlic, chipotle and salt and with a fork, mash until almost smooth.
- Stir in onion and cilantro and refrigerate, covered for about 1 hour before serving.

662.   Tofu Nuggets

Preparation Time: 15 minutes
Cooking Time: 25 minutes
Servings: 4

Ingredients:

TOFU

- 14 oz. tofu, sliced into cubes
- Cooking spray
- ¼ cup flour

- 1 teaspoon garlic powder
- 1/2 teaspoon paprika
- 1/2 teaspoon ground cumin
- Salt to taste

Sauce

- 1 tablespoon avocado oil
- 2 tablespoons sugar
- 3 tablespoons soy sauce
- 2 tablespoons honey
- 1 teaspoon garlic powder
- 1 tablespoon ginger, grated
- Pepper to taste

Directions:

- Spray tofu cubes with oil.
- Mix remaining ingredients in a bowl.
- Coat tofu evenly with this mixture.
- Add the tofu cubes to the air fryer.
- Set it to air fry.
- Cook at 350 degrees F for 10 minutes.
- Toss and cook for 15 minutes.
- In a bowl, mix the sauce ingredients.
- Toss the tofu in the sauce and serve.

Serving Suggestions: Garnish with sesame seeds and chopped chives.

Preparation & Cooking Tips: Use maple syrup if honey is not available.

663. Zucchini Lasagna

Preparation Time: 15 minutes
Cooking Time: 15 minutes
Servings: 4

Ingredients:

- 1 zucchini, sliced thinly lengthwise and divided
- 1/2 cup marinara sauce, divided
- ¼ cup ricotta, divided
- 1 cup fresh basil leaves, chopped and divided
- ¼ cup spinach leaves, chopped and divided

Directions:

- Layer half of the zucchini slices in a small loaf pan.

- Spread with half of marinara sauce and ricotta.
- Top with half of spinach and basil.
- Repeat layers with the remaining ingredients.
- Cover the pan with foil.
- Place inside the air fryer.
- Set it to bake.
- Cook at 400 degrees F for 10 minutes.
- Remove foil and cook for another 5 minutes.

Serving Suggestions: Garnish with fresh basil.

Preparation & Cooking Tips: Make this ahead of time by freezing and baking when ready to serve.

664. Veggie Rolls

Preparation Time: 20 minutes
Cooking Time: 20 minutes
Servings: 5

Ingredients:

- 1 tablespoon olive oil
- 1 clove garlic, minced
- 1 teaspoon ginger, minced
- 3 scallions, chopped
- 1/2 lb. mushrooms, chopped
- 2 cups cabbage, chopped
- 8 oz. water chestnuts, diced
- Salt and pepper to taste
- 6 spring roll wrappers
- 1 tablespoon water

Directions:

- Add oil to a pan over medium heat.
- Cook the garlic, ginger, scallions and mushrooms for 2 minutes.
- Stir in the remaining vegetables.
- Season with salt and pepper.
- Cook for 3 minutes, stirring.
- Transfer to a strainer.
- Add vegetables on top of the wrappers.
- Roll up the wrappers.
- Seal the edges with water.
- Place the rolls inside the air fryer.

- Choose air fry setting.
- Cook at 360 degrees F for 15 minutes.

Serving Suggestions: Serve with vinegar dipping sauce.

Preparation & Cooking Tips: Cook in batches.

665. Onion Rings

Preparation Time: 10 minutes
Cooking Time: 10 minutes
Servings: 3

Ingredients:

- 2 white onions, sliced into rings
- 1 cup flour
- 2 eggs, beaten
- 1 cup breadcrumbs

Directions:

- Cover the onion rings with flour.
- Dip in the egg.
- Dredge with breadcrumbs.
- Add to the air fryer.
- Set it to air fry.
- Cook at 400 degrees F for 10 minutes.

Serving Suggestions: Serve with tartar sauce.

Preparation & Cooking Tips: Make ahead of time and freeze. Air fry when ready to serve.

666. Cheesy Egg Rolls

Preparation Time: 15 minutes
Cooking Time: 12 minutes
Servings: 12

Ingredients:

- 12 spring roll wrappers
- 12 slices provolone cheese
- 3 eggs, cooked and sliced
- 1 carrot, sliced into thin strips
- 1 tablespoon water

Directions:

- Top the wrappers with cheese, eggs and carrot strips.
- Roll up the wrappers and seal with water.
- Place inside the air fryer.
- Set it to air fry.
- Cook at 390 degrees F for 12 minutes, turning once or twice.

Serving Suggestions: Serve with ketchup or sweet chili sauce.

Preparation & Cooking Tips: You can also use cheddar cheese for this recipe.

667. Cauliflower Bites

Preparation Time: 15 minutes
Cooking Time: 10 minutes
Servings: 6

Ingredients:

Cauliflower bites

- 4 cups cauliflower rice
- 1 egg, beaten
- 1 cup Parmesan cheese, grated
- 1 cup cheddar, shredded
- 2 tablespoons chives, chopped
- ¼ cup breadcrumbs
- Salt and pepper to taste

SAUCE

- 1/2 cup ketchup
- 2 tablespoons hot sauce

Directions:

- Combine cauliflower bites ingredients in a bowl.
- Mix well.
- Form balls from the mixture.
- Choose air fry setting.
- Add cauliflower bites to the air fryer.
- Cook at 375 degrees F for 10 minutes.
- Mix ketchup and hot sauce.
- Serve cauliflower bites with dip.

Serving Suggestions: Garnish with chopped parsley.

Preparation & Cooking Tips: You can make your own cauliflower rice by pulsing cauliflower florets in a food processor.

668. Baked Potatoes

Preparation Time: 20 minutes
Cooking Time: 45 minutes
Servings: 6

Ingredients:

- 6 potatoes
- 1 tablespoon olive oil
- Salt to taste
- 1 cup butter
- 1/2 cup milk
- 1/2 cup sour cream
- 1 1/2 cup cheddar, shredded and divided

Directions:

- Poke the potatoes using a fork.
- Add to the air fryer.
- Set it to bake.
- Cook at 400 degrees F for 40 minutes.
- Take out of the oven.
- Slice the potato in half
- Scoop out the potato flesh.
- Mix potato flesh with the remaining ingredients.
- Put the mixture back to the potato shells.
- Bake in the air fryer for 5 minutes.

Serving Suggestions: Garnish with chopped green onions.

Preparation & Cooking Tips: Use large Russet potatoes.

669. Vegetarian Pizza

Preparation Time: 15 minutes
Cooking Time: 10 minutes
Servings: 1

Ingredients:

- 1 pizza crust
- 1 tablespoon olive oil
- ¼ cup tomato sauce
- 1 cup mushrooms
- 1/2 cup black olives, sliced
- 1 clove garlic, minced
- 1/2 teaspoon oregano
- Salt and pepper to taste
- 1 cup mozzarella, shredded

Directions:

- Brush pizza crust with oil.
- Spread tomato sauce on top.
- Arrange mushrooms and olives on top.
- Sprinkle with garlic and oregano.
- Season with salt and pepper.
- Top with mozzarella cheese.
- Place inside the air fryer.
- Set it to bake.
- Cook at 400 degrees F for 10 minutes.

Serving Suggestions: Garnish with fresh basil leaves.

Preparation & Cooking Tips: Use 8-inch diameter pizza crust.

670. Brussels Sprout Chips

Preparation Time: 10 minutes

Cooking Time: 15 minutes

Servings: 2

Ingredients:

- 2 cups Brussels sprouts, sliced thinly
- 1 tablespoon olive oil
- 1 teaspoon garlic powder
- Salt and pepper to taste
- 2 tablespoons Parmesan cheese, grated

Directions:

- Toss the Brussels sprouts in oil.
- Sprinkle with garlic powder, salt, pepper and Parmesan cheese.
- Choose bake function.
- Add the Brussels sprouts in the air fryer.
- Cook at 350 degrees F for 8 minutes.
- Flip and cook for 7 more minutes.

Serving Suggestions: Serve with Caesar dressing for dipping.

Preparation & Cooking Tips: You can also use this recipe for other vegetables like cauliflower or broccoli.

671. Tangy Sweet Potatoes

Preparation Time: 5 minutes
Cooking Time: 22 minutes
Servings: 4

Ingredients:

- 5 garnet sweet potatoes, peeled and diced
- 11/2 tablespoons fresh lime juice
- 1 tablespoon butter, melted
- 2 teaspoons tamarind paste
- 11/2 teaspoon ground allspice
- 1/3 teaspoon white pepper
- 1/2 teaspoon turmeric powder
- A few drops liquid stevia

Directions:

- In a large mixing bowl, combine all the ingredients and toss until the sweet potatoes are evenly coated. Place the sweet potatoes in the air fry basket.
- Place the basket on the air fry position.
- Select Air Fry, set temperature to 400°F (205°C), and set time to 22 minutes. Stir the potatoes twice during cooking.
- When cooking is complete, the potatoes should be crispy on the outside and soft on the inside. Let the potatoes cool for 5 minutes before serving.

672. Green Beans with Sesame Seeds

Preparation Time: 5 minutes
Cooking Time: 8 minutes
Servings: 4

Ingredients:

- 1 tablespoon reduced-sodium soy sauce or tamari
- 1/2 tablespoon Sriracha sauce
- 4 teaspoons toasted sesame oil, divided
- 12 ounces (340 g) trimmed green beans
- 1/2 tablespoon toasted sesame seeds

Directions:

- Whisk together the Sriracha sauce, soy sauce, and 1 teaspoon of sesame oil in a small bowl until smooth. Set aside.
- Toss the green beans with the remaining sesame oil in a large bowl until evenly coated.
- Place the green beans in the air fry basket in a single layer.
- Place the basket on the air fry position.
- Select Air Fry, set temperature to 375°F (190°C), and set time to 8 minutes. Stir the green beans halfway through the cooking time.
- When cooking is complete, the green beans should be lightly charred and tender. Remove from the air fryer grill to a platter. Pour the prepared sauce over the top of green beans and toss well. Serve sprinkled with the toasted sesame seeds.

673. Easy Cinnamon Squash

Preparation Time: 5 minutes
Cooking Time: 15 minutes
Servings: 4

Ingredients:

- 1 medium acorn squash, halved crosswise and deseeded
- 1 teaspoon coconut oil
- 1 teaspoon light brown sugar
- Few dashes of ground cinnamon
- Few dashes of ground nutmeg

Directions:

- On a clean work surface, rub the cut sides of the acorn squash with coconut oil. Scatter with the cinnamon, nutmeg, and brown sugar.
- Put the squash halves in the air fry basket, cut-side up.
- Place the basket on the air fry position.
- Select Air Fry, set temperature to 325°F (163°C), and set time to 15 minutes.
- When cooking is complete, the squash halves should be just tender when pierced in the

center with a paring knife. Remove the basket from the air fryer grill. Rest for 5 to 10 minutes and serve warm.

674. Golden Garlicky Potatoes

Preparation Time: 5 minutes
Cooking Time: 18 minutes
Servings: 4

Ingredients:

- 2 cup sliced frozen potatoes, thawed
- 3 cloves garlic, minced
- Pinch salt
- Freshly ground black pepper, to taste
- ¾ cup heavy cream

Directions:

- Toss the potatoes with the salt, garlic, and black pepper in a baking pan until evenly coated. Pour the heavy cream over the top.
- Place the pan on the bake position.
- Select Bake, set temperature to 380°F (193°C), and set time to 15 minutes.
- When cooking is complete, the potatoes should be tender and the top golden brown. Check for doneness and bake for another 5 minutes if needed. Remove from the air fryer grill and serve hot.

675. Crispy Cheesy Asparagus

Preparation Time: 15 minutes
Cooking Time: 6 minutes
Servings: 4

Ingredients:

- 2 egg whites
- ¼ cup water
- ¼ cup plus 2 tablespoons grated Parmesan cheese, divided
- ¾ cup panko bread crumbs
- ¼ teaspoon salt
- 12 ounces (340 g) fresh asparagus spears , woody ends trimmed
- Cooking spray

Directions:

- In a shallow dish, whisk together the egg whites and water until slightly foamy. In a separate shallow dish, thoroughly combine ¼ cup of Parmesan cheese, bread crumbs, and salt.
- Dip the asparagus in the egg white, then roll in the cheese mixture to coat well.
- Place the asparagus in the air fry basket in a single layer, leaving space between each spear. Spritz the asparagus with cooking spray.
- Place the basket on the air fry position.
- Select Air Fry, set temperature to 390°F (199°C), and set time to 6 minutes.
- When cooking is complete, the asparagus should be golden brown and crisp. Remove the basket from the air fryer grill. Sprinkle with the remaining 2 tablespoons of cheese and serve hot.

676. Simple Balsamic-Glazed Carrots

Preparation Time: 5 minutes
Cooking Time: 18 minutes
Servings: 4

Ingredients:

- 3 medium-size carrots, cut into 2-inch × 1/2-inch sticks
- 1 tablespoon orange juice
- 2 teaspoons balsamic vinegar
- 1 teaspoon maple syrup
- 1 teaspoon avocado oil
- 1/2 teaspoon dried rosemary
- ¼ teaspoon sea salt
- ¼ teaspoon lemon zest

Directions:

- Put the carrots in a baking pan and sprinkle with the balsamic vinegar, orange juice, maple syrup, and avocado oil, and sea salt, rosemary, finished by the lemon zest. Toss well.

- Place the pan on the toast position.

- Select Toast, set temperature to 392°F (200°C), and set time to 18 minutes. Stir the carrots several times during the cooking process.

- When cooking is complete, the carrots should be nicely glazed and tender. Remove from the air fryer grill and serve hot.

677. Easy Crispy Zucchini

Preparation Time: 5 minutes
Cooking Time: 14 minutes
Servings: 4

Ingredients:

- 2 small zucchini, cut into 2-inch × 1/2-inch sticks
- 3 tablespoons chickpea flour
- 2 teaspoons arrowroot (or cornstarch)
- 1/2 teaspoon garlic granules
- ¼ teaspoon sea salt
- 1/8 teaspoon freshly ground black pepper
- 1 tablespoon water
- Cooking spray

Directions:

- Combine the zucchini sticks with the chickpea flour, garlic granules, salt, arrowroot, and pepper in a medium bowl and toss to coat. Add the water and stir to mix well.

- Spritz the air fry basket with cooking spray and spread out the zucchini sticks in the basket. Mist the zucchini sticks with cooking spray.

- Place the basket on the air fry position.

- Select Air Fry, set temperature to 392°F (200°C), and set time to 14 minutes. Stir the sticks halfway through the cooking time.

- When cooking is complete, the zucchini sticks should be crispy and nicely browned. Remove from the air fryer grill and serve warm.

678. *Crispy* Sweet Brussels sprouts

Preparation Time: 10 minutes
Cooking Time: 11 minutes
Servings: 4

Ingredients:

- 21/2 cups trimmed Brussels sprouts
Sauce:

- 11/2 teaspoons mellow white miso
- 11/2 tablespoons maple syrup
- 1 teaspoon toasted sesame oil
- 1 teaspoons tamari or shoyu
- 1 teaspoon grated fresh ginger
- 2 large garlic cloves, finely minced
- ¼ to 1/2 teaspoon red chili flakes
- Cooking spray

Directions:

- Spritz the air fry basket with cooking spray.

- Arrange the Brussels sprouts in the air fry basket and spray them with cooking spray.

- Place the basket on the air fry position.

- Select Air Fry, set temperature to 392°F (200°C), and set time to 11 minutes.

- After 6 minutes, remove the basket from the air fryer grill. Flip the Brussels sprouts and spritz with cooking spray again. Return to the air fryer grill and continue cooking for 5 minutes more.

- Meanwhile, make the sauce: Stir together the maple syrup and miso in a medium bowl. Add the sesame oil, ginger, garlic, tamari, and red chili flakes and whisk to combine.

- When cooking is complete, the Brussels sprouts should be crisp-tender. Transfer the Brussels sprouts to the bowl of sauce, tossing to coat well. If you prefer a saltier taste, you can add additional 1/2 teaspoon tamari to the sauce. Serve immediately.

679. Russet Potatoes with Yogurt and Chives

Preparation Time: 5 minutes
Cooking Time: 35 minutes
Servings: 4

Ingredients:

- 4 (7-ounce / 198-g) russet potatoes, rinsed
- Olive oil spray
- 1/2 teaspoon kosher salt, divided
- 1/2 cup 2% plain Greek yogurt
- ¼ cup minced fresh chives
- Freshly ground black pepper, to taste

Directions:

- Pat the potatoes dry and pierce them all over with a fork. Spritz the potatoes with olive oil spray. Sprinkle with ¼ teaspoon of the salt.
- Transfer the potatoes to the air fry basket.
- Place the basket on the bake position.
- Select Bake, set temperature to 400°F (205°C), and set time to 35 minutes.
- When cooking is complete, the potatoes should be fork-tender. Remove from the air fryer grill and split open the potatoes. Top with the chives, yogurt, the remaining ¼ teaspoon of salt, and finish with the black pepper. Serve immediately.

680. Golden Squash Croquettes

Preparation Time: 5 minutes
Cooking Time: 17 minutes
Servings: 4

Ingredients:

- 1/3 butternut squash, peeled and grated
- 1/3 cup all-purpose flour
- 2 eggs, whisked
- 4 cloves garlic, minced
- 11/2 tablespoons olive oil
- 1 teaspoon fine sea salt
- 1/3 teaspoon freshly ground black pepper, or more to taste
- 1/3 teaspoon dried sage
- A pinch of ground allspice

Directions:

- Line the air fry basket with parchment paper. Set aside.

- In a mixing bowl, stir together all the ingredients until well combined.
- Make the squash croquettes: Use a small cookie scoop to drop tablespoonfuls of the squash mixture onto a lightly floured surface and shape into balls with your hands. Transfer them to the air fry basket.
- Place the basket on the air fry position.
- Select Air Fry, set temperature to 345°F (174°C), and set time to 17 minutes.
- When cooking is complete, the squash croquettes should be golden brown. Remove from the air fryer grill to a plate and serve warm.

681. Golden Cheesy Corn Casserole

Preparation Time: 5 minutes
Cooking Time: 15 minutes
Servings: 4

Ingredients:

- 2 cups frozen yellow corn
- 1 egg, beaten
- 3 tablespoons flour
- 1/2 cup grated Swiss or Havarti cheese
- 1/2 cup light cream
- ¼ cup milk
- Pinch salt
- Freshly ground black pepper, to taste
- 2 tablespoons butter, cut into cubes
- Nonstick cooking spray

Directions:

- Spritz a baking pan with nonstick cooking spray.
- Stir together the remaining ingredients except the butter in a medium bowl until well incorporated. Transfer the mixture to the prepared baking pan and scatter with the butter cubes.
- Place the pan on the bake position.
- Select Bake, set temperature to 320°F (160°C), and set time to 15 minutes.

- When cooking is complete, the top should be golden brown and a toothpick inserted in the center should come out clean. Remove the pan from the air fryer grill. Let the casserole cool for 5 minutes before slicing into wedges and serving.

682. Breaded Cheesy Broccoli Gratin

Preparation Time: 5 minutes
Cooking Time: 14 minutes
Servings: 2

Ingredients

- 1/3 cup fat-free milk
- 1 tablespoon all-purpose or gluten-free flour
- 1/2 tablespoon olive oil
- 1/2 teaspoon ground sage
- ¼ teaspoon kosher salt
- 1/8 teaspoon freshly ground black pepper
- 2 cups roughly chopped broccoli florets
- 6 tablespoons shredded Cheddar cheese
- 2 tablespoons panko bread crumbs
- 1 tablespoon grated Parmesan cheese
- Olive oil spray

Directions:

- Spritz a baking dish with olive oil spray.
- Mix the milk, olive oil, flour, salt, sage, and pepper in a medium bowl and whisk to combine. Stir in the broccoli florets, bread crumbs, Parmesan cheese, and Cheddar cheese and toss to coat.
- Pour the broccoli mixture into the prepared baking dish.
- Place the baking dish on the bake position.
- Select Bake, set temperature to 330°F (166°C), and set time to 14 minutes.
- When cooking is complete, the top should be golden brown and the broccoli should be tender. Remove from the air fryer grill and serve immediately.

683. Broccoli with Hot Sauce

Preparation Time: 5 minutes
Cooking Time: 14 minutes

Servings: 6

Ingredients:

Broccoli:

- 1 medium-sized head broccoli, cut into florets
- 11/2 tablespoons olive oil
- 1 teaspoon shallot powder
- 1 teaspoon porcini powder
- 1/2 teaspoon freshly grated lemon zest
- 1/2 teaspoon hot paprika
- 1/2 teaspoon granulated garlic
- 1/3 teaspoon fine sea salt
- 1/3 teaspoon celery seeds

Hot Sauce:

- 1/2 cup tomato sauce
- 1 tablespoon balsamic vinegar
- 1/2 teaspoon ground allspice

Directions:

- In a mixing bowl, combine all the ingredients for the broccoli and toss to coat. Transfer the broccoli to the air fry basket.
- Place the basket on the air fry position.
- Select Air Fry, set temperature to 360°F (182°C), and set time to 14 minutes.
- Meanwhile, make the hot sauce by whisking together the balsamic vinegar, tomato sauce, and allspice in a small bowl.
- When cooking is complete, remove the broccoli from the air fryer grill and serve with the hot sauce.

684. Crispy Brussels sprouts with Sage

Preparation Time: 5 minutes
Cooking Time: 15 minutes
Servings: 4

Ingredients:

- 1 pound (454 g) Brussels sprouts, halved
- 1 cup bread crumbs
- 2 tablespoons grated Grana Padano cheese

- 1 tablespoon paprika
- 2 tablespoons canola oil
- 1 tablespoon chopped sage

Directions:

- Line the air fry basket with parchment paper. Set aside.
- In a small bowl, thoroughly mix the cheese, bread crumbs, and paprika. In a large bowl, place the Brussels sprouts and drizzle the canola oil over the top. Sprinkle with the bread crumb mixture and toss to coat.
- Transfer the Brussels sprouts to the prepared basket.
- Place the basket on the toast position.
- Select Toast, set temperature to 400°F (205°C), and set time to 15 minutes. Stir the Brussels a few times during cooking.
- When cooking is complete, the Brussels sprouts should be lightly browned and crisp. Transfer the Brussels sprouts to a plate and sprinkle the sage on top before serving.

685. Cheesy Buttered Broccoli

Preparation Time: 5 minutes
Cooking Time: 4 minutes
Servings: 4

Ingredients:

- 1 pound (454 g) broccoli florets
- 1 medium shallot, minced
- 2 tablespoons olive oil
- 2 tablespoons unsalted butter, melted
- 2 teaspoons minced garlic
- ¼ cup grated Parmesan cheese

Directions:

- Combine the broccoli florets with the butter, garlic, shallot, olive oil, and Parmesan cheese in a medium bowl and toss until the broccoli florets are thoroughly coated.
- Place the broccoli florets in the air fry basket in a single layer.
- Place the basket on the toast position.

- Select Toast, set temperature to 360°F (182°C), and set time to 4 minutes.
- When cooking is complete, the broccoli florets should be crisp-tender. Remove from the air fryer grill and serve warm.

686.   Crisp Green Bean Chips

Preparation Time: 9 minutes
Cooking Time: 8 hours
Servings: 4

Ingredients:

- 2 1/2 lbs. green beans, frozen & thawed
- 2 1/2 tbsp coconut oil, melted
- 1/2 tsp garlic powder
- 1/2 tsp onion powder
- 2 tsp salt

Directions:

- Add green beans into the large bowl. Pour melted oil over green beans and sprinkle with garlic powder, onion powder, and salt and mix well.
- Arrange green beans onto the cooking tray and place the cooking tray in vortex plus air fryer oven.
- Select DEHYDRATE mode, then set the temperature to 135 F and the time to 8 hours, then press start.
- Store green beans in an airtight container.

687. Zucchini Chips

Preparation Time: 10 minutes
Cooking Time: 10 hours
Servings: 4

Ingredients:

- 4 cups zucchini slices
- 1/2 tsp crushed red pepper flakes
- 1/2 tbsp onion powder
- 1/2 tbsp garlic powder
- 1 tbsp dried parsley
- 1 tbsp dried basil
- 1 tbsp dried oregano

- 2 tbsp olive oil
- 2 tbsp balsamic vinegar
- 1/2 tsp black pepper
- 1/2 tsp salt

Directions:

- Add sliced zucchini and remaining ingredients into the mixing bowl and toss until well coated.
- Arrange zucchini slices onto the cooking tray and place the cooking tray in vortex plus air fryer oven.
- Select DEHYDRATE mode, then set the temperature to 120 F and the time to 10 hours, then press start.
- Store zucchini chips in an airtight container.

688. Healthy Cashew Almond Crackers

Preparation Time: 10 minutes
Cooking Time: 9 hours
Servings: 12

Ingredients:

- 1 cup ground almonds
- 1 cup ground cashews
- 1/2 cup water
- 1/3 cup ground flax
- 3/4 tsp dried garlic
- 2 tsp rosemary
- Salt

Directions:

- Add all ingredients except into the large bowl and mix well.
- Spread mixture onto the parchment-lined cooking tray, about 1/3-inch thick.
- Place the cooking tray in vortex plus air fryer oven.
- Select DEHYDRATE mode, then set the temperature to 140 F and the time to 1 hour, then press start.
- After a one-hour change temperature to 115 F and the timer to 8 hours.

- Cut into pieces and serve.

689. Walnut Crackers

Preparation Time: 10 minutes
Cooking Time: 9 hours
Servings: 12

Ingredients:

- 2 cup walnuts, soak in water for overnight
- 1 tsp oregano
- 1/4 cup olives, sliced
- 1/3 cup sun-dried tomatoes, chopped
- 1/4 cup water
- 1/2 cup ground flax
- Salt

Directions:

- Add walnuts in the food processor and process until ground finely.
- Separately blend together olives and sun-dried tomatoes.
- Mix together ground walnuts, blended olives & sun-dried tomatoes, ground flax, water, and salt until dough is formed.
- Spread dough onto the parchment-lined cooking tray, about 1/4-inch thick.
- Place the cooking tray in vortex plus air fryer oven.
- Select DEHYDRATE mode, then set the temperature to 140 F and the time to 1 hour, then press start.
- After a one-hour change temperature to 115 F and the timer to 8 hours.
- Cut into pieces and serve.

690. Herbed Eggplant

Preparation Time: 15 minutes
Cooking Time: 15 minutes
Servings: 2

Ingredients:

- ½ teaspoon dried marjoram, crushed
- ½ teaspoon dried oregano, crushed
- ½ teaspoon dried thyme, crushed

- ½ teaspoon garlic powder
- Salt and ground black pepper, as required
- 1 large eggplant, cubed
- Olive oil cooking spray

Directions:

- Set the temperature of air fryer to 390F. Grease an air fryer basket.
- In a small bowl, mix well herbs, garlic powder, salt, and black pepper.
- Spray the eggplant cubes evenly with cooking spray and then, rub with the herbs mixture.
- Arrange eggplant cubes into the prepared air fryer basket in a single layer.
- Air fry for about 6 minutes
- Flip and spray the eggplant cubes with cooking spray.
- Air fry for another 6 minutes
- Flip and again, spray the eggplant cubes with cooking spray.
- Air fry for 2-3 more minutes
- Remove from air fryer and transfer the eggplant cubes onto serving plates.

691.   Roasted Vegetables with Basil

Preparation Time: 15 minutes
Cooking Time: 21 minutes
Servings: 2

Ingredients:

- 1 small eggplant, halved and sliced
- 1 yellow bell pepper, sliced into 1-inch strips
- 1 red bell pepper, sliced into 1-inch strips
- 2 garlic cloves, quartered
- 1 red onion, sliced
- 1 tablespoon extra-virgin olive oil
- Salt and freshly ground black pepper, to taste
- ½ cup chopped fresh basil, for garnish

Directions:

- Grease a nonstick baking dish with cooking spray.

- Place the eggplant, bell peppers, garlic, and red onion in the greased baking dish. Drizzle with the olive oil and toss to coat well. Spritz any uncoated surfaces with cooking spray.
- Select Bake, set temperature to 350F, and set time to 20 minutes. Select Start to begin preheating.
- Once preheated, place the baking dish into the oven. Flip the vegetables halfway through the cooking time.
- When done, remove from the oven and sprinkle with salt and pepper.
- Sprinkle the basil on top for garnish and serve.

692.   Cinnamon Celery Roots

Preparation Time: 10 minutes
Cooking Time: 21 minutes
Servings: 4

Ingredients:

- 2 celery roots, peeled and diced
- 1 teaspoon extra-virgin olive oil
- 1 teaspoon butter, melted
- ½ teaspoon ground cinnamon
- Sea salt and freshly ground black pepper, to taste

Directions:

- Line a baking sheet with aluminum foil.
- Toss the celery roots with the olive oil in a large bowl until well coated. Transfer them to the prepared baking sheet.
- Select Roast, set temperature to 350°F (180°C), and set time to 20 minutes. Select Start to begin preheating.
- Once preheated, place the baking sheet into the oven.
- When done, the celery roots should be very tender. Remove from the oven to a serving bowl. Stir in the butter and cinnamon and mash them with a potato masher until fluffy.
- Season with salt and pepper to taste. Serve immediately.

693.   Cheesy Broccoli Tots

Preparation Time: 19 minutes
Cooking Time: 16 minutes
Servings: 4

Ingredients:

- 12 ounces frozen broccoli, thawed, drained, and patted dry
- 1 large egg, lightly beaten
- ½ cup seasoned whole-wheat bread crumbs
- ¼ cup shredded reduced-fat sharp Cheddar cheese
- ¼ cup grated Parmesan cheese
- 1½ teaspoons minced garlic
- Salt and freshly ground black pepper, to taste
- Cooking spray

Directions:

- Spritz a perforated pan lightly with cooking spray.
- Place the remaining ingredients into a food processor and process until the mixture resembles a coarse meal. Transfer the mixture to a bowl.
- Using a tablespoon, scoop out the broccoli mixture and form into 24 oval "tater tot" shapes with your hands.
- Put the tots in the prepared perforated pan in a single layer, spacing them 1 inch apart. Mist the tots lightly with cooking spray.
- Select Air Fry, set temperature to 375°F, and set time to 15 minutes. Select Start to begin preheating.
- Once preheated, place the pan into the oven. Flip the tots halfway through the cooking time.
- When done, the tots will be lightly browned and crispy. Remove from the oven and serve on a plate.

694. Crispy Roasted Broccoli

Preparation Time: 10 minutes
Cooking Time: 8 minutes
Servings: 2

Ingredients:

- ¼ teaspoon Masala
- ½ teaspoon Red chili powder
- ½ teaspoon Salt
- ¼ teaspoon Turmeric powder
- 1 tablespoon Chickpea flour
- 2 tablespoon Yogurt
- 1-pound broccoli

Directions:

- Cut broccoli up into florets. Soak in a bowl of water with 2 teaspoons of salt for at least half an hour to remove impurities.
- Take out broccoli florets from water and let drain. Wipe down thoroughly.
- Mix all other ingredients together to create a marinade.
- Toss broccoli florets in the marinade. Cover and chill 15-30 minutes.
- Preheat the air fryer oven to 390 degrees.
- Place marinated broccoli florets into the fryer basket, set temperature to 350°F, and set time to 10 minutes.
- Florets will be crispy when done.

695. Air Fried Yellow Squash, Zucchini & Carrots

Preparation Time: 5 minutes
Cooking Time: 36 minutes
Servings: 4

Ingredients:

- 1 tablespoon Chopped tarragon leaves
- ½ teaspoon White pepper
- 1 teaspoon Salt
- 1-pound yellow squash
- 1-pound zucchini
- 6 teaspoon Olive oil
- ½ pound carrots

Directions:

- Stem and root the end of squash and zucchini and cut in ¾-inch half-moons. Peel and cut carrots into 1-inch cubes. Combine carrot cubes with 2 teaspoons of olive oil, tossing to combine.

- Pour into the air fryer oven basket, set temperature to 400°f, and set time to 5 minutes. As carrots cook, drizzle remaining olive oil over squash and zucchini pieces, then season with pepper and salt. Toss well to coat.

- Add squash and zucchini when the timer for carrots goes off. Cook 30 minutes, making sure to toss 2-3 times during the cooking process. Once done, take out veggies and toss with tarragon. Serve up warm.

696.　Pesto Roasted Tomatoes

Preparation Time: 15 minutes
Cooking Time: 14 minutes
Servings: 4

Ingredients:

- Large heirloom tomatoes – 3, cut into ½ inch thick slices.

- Pesto – 1 cup

- Feta cheese – 8 oz. cut into ½ inch thick slices

- Red onion – ½ cup, sliced thinly

- Olive oil – 1 tbsp.

Directions:

- Spread some pesto on each slice of tomato. Top each tomato slice with a feta slice and onion and drizzle with oil. Arrange the tomatoes onto the greased rack and spray with cooking spray.

- Arrange the drip pan in the bottom of the Instant Vortex Air Fryer Oven cooking chamber. Select "Air Fry" and then adjust the temperature to 390 °F. Set the time for 14 minutes and press "Start".

- When the display shows "Add Food" insert the rack in the center position. When the display shows "Turn Food" do not turn food. When cooking time is complete, remove the rack from the Vortex Oven. Serve warm.

697.　Herbed Potatoes

Preparation Time: 15 minutes
Cooking Time: 21 minutes
Servings: 4

Ingredients:

- Small red potatoes – 1 lb. cut into 1-inch pieces

- Olive oil – 1 tbsp.

- Fresh thyme – 1 tsp. chopped

- Fresh rosemary – 1 tsp. chopped

- Fresh oregano – 1 tsp. chopped

- Salt and ground black pepper, as required

- Lemon zest – 1 tbsp. grated

Directions:

- In a bowl, add all ingredients except lemon zest and toss to coat well. Place the potatoes in the rotisserie basket and attach the lid. Arrange the drip pan in the bottom of the Instant Vortex Air Fryer Oven cooking chamber.

- Select "Air Fry" and then adjust the temperature to 400 °F. Set the time for 20 minutes and press "Start". Then, close the door and touch "Rotate". When the display shows "Add Food" arrange the rotisserie basket, on the rotisserie spit. Then, close the door and touch "Rotate".

- When cooking time is complete, press the red lever to release the rod. Remove from the Vortex and transfer the potatoes into a bowl. Add the lemon zest and toss to coat well. Serve immediately.

698.　Seasoned Potatoes

Preparation Time: 5 minutes
Cooking Time: 41 minutes
Servings: 1

Ingredients:

- Russet potatoes – 2, scrubbed

- Butter – ½ tbsp. melted

- Garlic & herb blend seasoning – ½ tsp.

- Garlic powder – ½ tsp.

- Salt, as required

Directions:

- In a small bowl, mix together spices and salt. With a fork, prick the potatoes. Coat the potatoes with butter and sprinkle with spice mixture. Arrange the potatoes onto the cooking rack.

- Arrange the drip pan in the bottom of the Instant Vortex Air Fryer Oven cooking chamber. Select "Air Fry" and then adjust the temperature to 400 °F. Set the time for 40 minutes and press "Start".

- When the display shows "Add Food" insert the cooking rack in the center position. When the display shows "Turn Food" do nothing. When cooking time is complete, remove the tray from the Vortex Oven. Serve hot.

699. Cheesy Spinach

Preparation Time: 15 minutes
Cooking Time: 17 minutes
Servings: 3

Ingredients:

- Frozen spinach – 1 (10-oz.) package, thawed
- Onion – ½ cup, chopped
- Garlic – 2 tsps. Minced
- Cream cheese – 4 oz. chopped
- Ground nutmeg – ½ tsp.
- Salt and ground black pepper, as required
- Parmesan cheese – ¼ cup, shredded

Directions:

- In a bowl, mix together spinach, onion, garlic, cream cheese, nutmeg, salt, and black pepper. Place the spinach mixture into a baking dish that will fit in the Vortex Air Fryer Oven.

- Arrange the drip pan in the bottom of the Instant Vortex Air Fryer Oven cooking chamber. Select "Air Fry" and then adjust the temperature to 355 °F. Set the time for 15 minutes and press "Start".

- When the display shows "Add Food" insert the baking dish in the center position. When the display shows "Turn Food" do not turn

food. When cooking time is complete, remove the baking dish from the Vortex Oven. Serve hot.

700. Spicy Zucchini

Preparation Time: 15 minutes
Cooking Time: 12 minutes
Servings: 3

Ingredients:

- Zucchini – 1 lb. cut into ½-inch thick slices lengthwise
- Olive oil – 1 tbsp.
- Garlic powder – ½ tsp.
- Cayenne pepper – ½ tsp.
- Salt and ground black pepper, as required

Directions:

- Add all the ingredients into a bowl and toss to coat well. Arrange the zucchini slices onto a cooking tray. Arrange the drip pan in the bottom of the Instant Vortex Air Fryer Oven cooking chamber.

- Select "Air Fry" and then adjust the temperature to 400 °F. Set the time for 12 minutes and press "Start". When the display shows "Add Food" insert the cooking tray in the center position.

- When the display shows "Turn Food" do nothing. When cooking time is complete, remove the tray from the Vortex Oven. Serve hot.

701. Seasoned Yellow Squash

Preparation Time: 15 minutes
Cooking Time: 6 minutes
Servings: 2

Ingredients:

- Large yellow squash – 4, cut into slices
- Olive oil – ¼ cup
- Onion – ½, sliced
- Italian seasoning – ¾ tsp.
- Garlic salt – ½ tsp.
- Seasoned salt – ¼ tsp.

Directions:

- In a large bowl, mix together all the ingredients. Place the veggie mixture in the greased cooking tray. Arrange the drip pan in the bottom of Instant Vortex Air Fryer Oven cooking chamber.

- Select "Air Fry" and then adjust the temperature to 400 °F. Set the time for 10 minutes and press "Start". When the display shows "Add Food" insert the cooking tray in the center position. When the display shows "Turn Food" turn the vegetables. When cooking time is complete, remove the tray from the Vortex Oven. Serve hot.

702. Buttered Asparagus

Preparation Time: 15 minutes
Cooking Time: 11 minutes
Servings: 3

Ingredients:

- Fresh thick asparagus spears – 1 lb. trimmed

- Butter – 1 tbsp. melted

- Salt and ground black pepper, as required

Directions:

- Add all the ingredients into a bowl and toss to coat well. Arrange the asparagus onto a cooking tray. Arrange the drip pan in the bottom of Instant Vortex Air Fryer Oven cooking chamber.

- Select "Air Fry" and then adjust the temperature to 350 °F. Set the time for 10 minutes and press "Start". When the display shows "Add Food" insert the cooking tray in the center position.

- When the display shows "Turn Food" turn the asparagus. When cooking time is complete, remove the tray from Vortex Oven. Serve hot.

703. Balsamic Brussels Sprouts

Preparation Time: 15 minutes
Cooking Time: 21 minutes
Servings: 4

Ingredients:

- Brussels Sprouts – 1 lb. ends trimmed and cut into bite-sized pieces

- Balsamic vinegar – 1 tbsp.

- Olive oil – 1 tbsp.

- Salt and ground black pepper, as required

Directions:

- Add all the ingredients into a bowl and toss to coat well. Place the Brussels Sprouts in the rotisserie basket and attach the lid. Arrange the drip pan in the bottom of Instant Vortex Air Fryer Oven cooking chamber.

- Select "Air Fry" and then adjust the temperature to 350 °F. Set the time for 20 minutes and press "Start". Then, close the door and touch "Rotate". When the display shows "Add Food" arrange the rotisserie basket, on the rotisserie spit. Then, close the door and touch "Rotate".

- When cooking time is complete, press the red lever to release the rod. Remove from the Vortex Oven. Serve hot.

704. Parmesan Broccoli

Preparation Time: 5 minutes
Cooking Time: 6 minutes
Servings: 4

Ingredients:

- Small broccoli florets – 1 lb.

- Garlic – 1 tbsp. minced

- Olive oil – 2 tbsps.

- Parmesan cheese – ¼ cup, grated

Directions:

- Add all the ingredients into a bowl and toss to coat well. Arrange the broccoli florets onto a cooking tray. Arrange the drip pan in the bottom of the Instant Vortex Air Fryer Oven cooking chamber.

- Select "Air Fry" and then adjust the temperature to 350 °F. Set the time for 6 minutes and press "Start". When the display shows "Add Food" insert the cooking tray in the center position. When the display shows "Turn Food" turn the broccoli florets. When cooking time is complete, remove the tray from Vortex Oven. Serve hot.

705. Buttered Broccoli

Preparation Time: 15 minutes
Cooking Time: 9 minutes
Servings: 4

Ingredients:

- Broccoli florets – 1 lb.
- Butter – 1 tbsp. melted
- Red pepper flakes – ½ tsp. crushed
- Salt and ground black pepper, as required

Directions:

- Add all the ingredients into a bowl and toss to coat well. Place the broccoli florets in the rotisserie basket and attach the lid. Arrange the drip pan in the bottom of the Instant Vortex Air Fryer Oven cooking chamber.
- Select "Air Fry" and then adjust the temperature to 400 °F. Set the time for 15 minutes and press "Start". Then, close the door and touch "Rotate". When the display shows "Add Food" arrange the rotisserie basket, on the rotisserie spit. Then, close the door and touch "Rotate". When cooking time is complete, press the red lever to release the rod. Remove from the Vortex Oven. Serve immediately.

706. Roasted Veggie and Tofu

Preparation Time: 10 minutes
Cooking Time: 11 minutes
Servings: 4

Ingredients:

- 1/3 cup Asian-Style sauce
- 1 teaspoon cornstarch
- ½ teaspoon red pepper flakes, or more to taste
- 1 pound (454 g) firm or extra-firm tofu, cut into 1-inch cubes
- 1 small carrot, peeled and cut into ¼-inch-thick coins
- 1 small green bell pepper, cut into bite-size pieces
- 2 scallions, sliced, whites and green parts separated
- 2 tablespoons roasted unsalted peanuts

Direction

- In a large bowl, whisk together the sauce, cornstarch, and red pepper flakes. Fold in the tofu, carrot, pepper, and the white parts of the scallions and toss to coat. Spread the mixture evenly on the sheet pan.
- Select Roast. Set temperature to 375°F (190°C) and set time to 10 minutes. Press Start to begin preheating.
- Once preheated, place the pan into the oven. Stir the ingredients once halfway through the cooking time.
- When done, remove the pan from the oven. Serve sprinkled with the peanuts and scallion greens.

707. Black Bean and Salsa Tacos

Preparation Time: 12 minutes
Cooking Time: 7 minutes
Servings: 4

Ingredients:

- 1 (15-ounce / 425-g) can black beans, drained and rinsed
- ½ cup prepared salsa
- 1½ teaspoons chili powder
- 4 ounces (113 g) grated Monterey Jack cheese
- 2 tablespoons minced onion
- 8 (6-inch) flour tortillas
- 2 tablespoons vegetable or extra-virgin olive oil
- Shredded lettuce, for serving

Directions:

- In a medium bowl, add the beans, salsa and chili powder. Coarsely mash them with a potato masher. Fold in the cheese and onion and stir until combined.

- Arrange the flour tortillas on a cutting board and spoon 2 to 3 tablespoons of the filling into each tortilla. Fold the tortillas over, pressing lightly to even out the filling. Brush the tacos on one side with half the olive oil and put them, oiled side down, on the sheet pan. Brush the top side with the remaining olive oil.

- Select Air Fry. Set temperature to 400°F (205°C) and set time to 7 minutes. Press Start to begin preheating.

- Once preheated, place the pan into the oven. Flip the tacos halfway through the cooking time.

- Remove the pan from the oven and allow to cool for 5 minutes. Serve with the shredded lettuce on the side.

708. Thai Curried Veggies

Preparation Time: 10 minutes
Cooking Time: 8 minutes
Servings: 4

Ingredients:

- 1 small head Napa cabbage, shredded, divided
- 1 medium carrot, cut into thin coins
- 8 ounces (227 g) snow peas
- 1 red or green bell pepper, sliced into thin strips
- 1 tablespoon vegetable oil
- 2 tablespoons soy sauce
- 1 tablespoon sesame oil
- 2 tablespoons brown sugar
- 2 tablespoons freshly squeezed lime juice
- 2 teaspoons red or green Thai curry paste
- 1 serrano chile, deseeded and minced
- 1 cup frozen mango slices, thawed
- ½ cup chopped roasted peanuts or cashews

Directions:

- Put half the Napa cabbage in a large bowl, along with the carrot, snow peas, and bell pepper. Drizzle with the vegetable oil and

toss to coat. Spread them evenly on the sheet pan.

- Select Roast. Set temperature to 375°F (190°C) and set time to 8 minutes. Press Start to begin preheating.

- Once preheated, place the pan into the oven.

- Meanwhile, whisk together the soy sauce, sesame oil, brown sugar, lime juice, and curry paste in a small bowl.

- When done, the vegetables should be tender and crisp. Remove the pan and put the vegetables back into the bowl. Add the chile, mango slices, and the remaining cabbage. Pour over the dressing and toss to coat. Top with the roasted nuts and serve.

709. Eggplant and Bell Peppers with Basil

Preparation Time: 15 minutes
Cooking Time: 21 minutes
Servings: 2

Ingredients:

- 1 small eggplant, halved and sliced
- 1 yellow bell pepper, cut into thick strips
- 1 red bell pepper, cut into thick strips
- 2 garlic cloves, quartered
- 1 red onion, sliced
- 1 tablespoon extra-virgin olive oil
- Salt and freshly ground black pepper, to taste
- ½ cup chopped fresh basil, for garnish
- Cooking spray

Directions:

- Grease a nonstick baking dish with cooking spray.

- Place the eggplant, bell peppers, garlic, and red onion in the greased baking dish. Drizzle with the olive oil and toss to coat well. Spritz any uncoated surfaces with cooking spray.

- Select Bake. Set temperature to 350°F (180°C) and set time to 20 minutes. Press Start to begin preheating.

- Once preheated, place the baking dish into the oven. Flip the vegetables halfway through the cooking time.
- When done, remove from the oven and sprinkle with salt and pepper.
- Sprinkle the basil on top for garnish and serve.

710.   Vinegary Asparagus

Preparation Time: 15 minutes
Cooking Time: 10 minutes
Servings: 4

Ingredients:

- 4 tablespoons olive oil, plus more for greasing
- 4 tablespoons balsamic vinegar
- 1½ pounds (680 g) asparagus spears, trimmed
- Salt and freshly ground black pepper, to taste

Directions:

- Grease the perforated pan with olive oil.
- In a shallow bowl, stir together the 4 tablespoons of olive oil and balsamic vinegar to make a marinade.
- Put the asparagus spears in the bowl so they are thoroughly covered by the marinade and allow to marinate for 5 minutes.
- Put the asparagus in the greased pan in a single layer and season with salt and pepper.
- Select Air Fry. Set temperature to 350°F (180°C) and set time to 10 minutes. Press Start to begin preheating.
- Once preheated, place the pan into the oven. Flip the asparagus halfway through the cooking time.
- When done, the asparagus should be tender and lightly browned. Cool for 5 minutes before serving.

711.   Baked Eggs with Spinach and Basil

Preparation Time: 10 minutes
Cooking Time: 12 minutes
Servings: 2

Ingredients:

- 2 tablespoons olive oil
- 4 eggs, whisked
- 5 ounces (142 g) fresh spinach, chopped
- 1 medium-sized tomato, chopped
- 1 teaspoon fresh lemon juice
- ½ teaspoon ground black pepper
- ½ teaspoon coarse salt
- ½ cup roughly chopped fresh basil leaves, for garnish

Directions:

- Generously grease a baking pan with olive oil.
- Stir together the remaining ingredients except the basil leaves in the greased baking pan until well incorporated.
- Select Bake. Set temperature to 280°F (137°C) and set time to 10 minutes. Press Start to begin preheating.
- Once preheated, place the pan into the oven.
- When cooking is complete, the eggs should be completely set and the vegetables should be tender. Remove from the oven and serve garnished with the fresh basil leaves.

712.   Cheesy Broccoli with Rosemary

Preparation Time: 5 minutes
Cooking Time: 18 minutes
Servings: 4

Ingredients:

- 1 large-sized head broccoli, stemmed and cut into small florets
- 2 ½ tablespoons canola oil
- 2 teaspoons dried basil
- 2 teaspoons dried rosemary
- Salt and ground black pepper, to taste
- 1/3 Cup grated yellow cheese

Directions:

- Bring a pot of lightly salted water to a boil. Add the broccoli florets to the boiling water and let boil for about 3 minutes.

- Drain the broccoli florets well and transfer to a large bowl. Add the canola oil, basil, rosemary, salt, and black pepper to the bowl and toss until the broccoli is fully coated. Place the broccoli in the perforated pan.

- Select Air Fry. Set temperature to 390°F (199°C) and set time to 15 minutes. Press Start to begin preheating.

- Once preheated, place the pan into the oven. Stir the broccoli halfway through the cooking time.

- When cooking is complete, the broccoli should be crisp. Remove the pan from the oven. Serve the broccoli warm with grated cheese sprinkled on top.

713. Kale with Tahini-Lemon Dressing

Preparation Time: 5 minutes
Cooking Time: 15 minutes
Servings: 4

Ingredients:

Dressing:

- ¼ cup tahini
- ¼ cup fresh lemon juice
- 2 tablespoons olive oil
- 1 teaspoon sesame seeds
- ½ teaspoon garlic powder
- ¼ teaspoon cayenne pepper

Kale:

- 4 cups packed torn kale leaves (stems and ribs removed and leaves torn into palm-size pieces)
- Kosher salt and freshly ground black pepper, to taste

Directions:

- Make the dressing: Whisk together the tahini, lemon juice, olive oil, sesame seeds, garlic powder, and cayenne pepper in a large bowl until well mixed.

- Add the kale and massage the dressing thoroughly all over the leaves. Sprinkle the salt and pepper to season.

- Place the kale in the perforated pan in a single layer.

- Select Air Fry. Set temperature to 350°F (180°C) and set time to 15 minutes. Press Start to begin preheating.

- Once preheated, place the pan into the oven.

- When cooking is complete, the leaves should be slightly wilted and crispy. Remove from the oven and serve on a plate.

714. Vegetable Mélange with Garlic

Preparation Time: 10 minutes
Cooking Time: 16 minutes
Servings: 4

Ingredients:

- 1 (8-ounce / 227-g) package sliced mushrooms
- 1 yellow summer squash, sliced
- 1 red bell pepper, sliced
- 2 cloves garlic, sliced
- 1 tablespoon olive oil
- ½ teaspoon dried basil
- ½ teaspoon dried thyme
- ½ teaspoon dried tarragon

Directions:

- Toss the mushrooms, squash, and bell pepper with the garlic and olive oil in a large bowl until well coated. Mix in the basil, thyme, and tarragon and toss again.

- Spread the vegetables evenly in the perforated pan.

- Select Roast. Set temperature to 350°F (180°C) and set time to 16 minutes. Press Start to begin preheating.

- Once preheated, place the pan into the oven.

- When cooking is complete, the vegetables should be fork-tender. Remove the pan from the oven. Cool for 5 minutes before serving.

715. Garlic Carrots with Sesame Seeds

Preparation Time: 5 minutes
Cooking Time: 16 minutes
Servings: 6

Ingredients:

- 1-pound (454 g) baby carrots
- 1 tablespoon sesame oil
- ½ teaspoon dried dill
- Pinch salt
- Freshly ground black pepper, to taste
- 6 cloves garlic, peeled
- 3 tablespoons sesame seeds

Directions:

- In a medium bowl, drizzle the baby carrots with the sesame oil. Sprinkle with the dill, salt, and pepper and toss to coat well.
- Place the baby carrots in the perforated pan.
- Select Roast. Set temperature to 380°F (193°C) and set time to 16 minutes. Press Start to begin preheating.
- Once preheated, place the pan into the oven.
- After 8 minutes, remove the pan from the oven and stir in the garlic. Return the pan to the oven and continue roasting for 8 minutes more.
- When cooking is complete, the carrots should be lightly browned. Remove the pan from the oven and serve sprinkled with the sesame seeds.

716. Thai-Flavored Brussels Sprouts

Preparation Time: 5 minutes
Cooking Time: 21 minutes
Servings: 2

Ingredients:

- ¼ cup Thai sweet chili sauce
- 2 tablespoons black vinegar or balsamic vinegar
- ½ teaspoon hot sauce
- 2 small shallots, cut into ¼-inch-thick slices
- 8 ounces (227 g) Brussels sprouts, trimmed (large sprouts halved)

- Kosher salt and freshly ground black pepper, to taste
- 2 teaspoons lightly packed fresh cilantro leaves, for garnish

Directions:

- Place the chili sauce, vinegar, and hot sauce in a large bowl and whisk to combine.
- Add the shallots and Brussels sprouts and toss to coat. Sprinkle with the salt and pepper. Transfer the Brussels sprouts and sauce to a baking pan.
- Select Roast. Set temperature to 390°F (199°C) and set time to 20 minutes. Press Start to begin preheating.
- Once preheated, place the pan into the oven. Stir the Brussels sprouts twice during cooking.
- When cooking is complete, the Brussels sprouts should be crisp-tender. Remove from the oven. Sprinkle the cilantro on top for garnish and serve warm.

717. Honey Eggplant with Yogurt Sauce

Preparation Time: 5 minutes
Cooking Time: 15 minutes
Servings: 2

Ingredients:

- 1 medium eggplant, quartered and cut crosswise into ½-inch-thick slices
- 2 tablespoons vegetable oil
- Kosher salt and freshly ground black pepper, to taste
- ½ cup plain yogurt (not Greek)
- 2 tablespoons harissa paste
- 1 garlic clove, grated
- 2 teaspoons honey

Directions:

- Toss the eggplant slices with the vegetable oil, salt, and pepper in a large bowl until well coated.
- Lay the eggplant slices in the perforated pan.

- Select Air Fry. Set temperature to 400°F (205°C) and set time to 15 minutes. Press Start to begin preheating.

- Once preheated, place the pan into the oven. Stir the slices two to three times during cooking.

- Meanwhile, make the yogurt sauce by whisking together the yogurt, harissa paste, and garlic in a small bowl.

- When cooking is complete, the eggplant slices should be golden brown. Spread the yogurt sauce on a platter, and pile the eggplant slices over the top. Serve drizzled with the honey.

718. Parmesan Cabbage Wedges

Preparation Time: 5 minutes
Cooking Time: 21 minutes
Servings: 4

Ingredients:

- 4 tablespoons melted butter
- 1 head cabbage, cut into wedges
- 1 cup shredded Parmesan cheese
- Salt and black pepper, to taste
- ½ cup shredded Mozzarella cheese

Directions:

- Brush the melted butter over the cut sides of cabbage wedges and sprinkle both sides with the Parmesan cheese. Season with salt and pepper to taste.

- Place the cabbage wedges in the perforated pan.

- Select Air Fry. Set temperature to 380°F (193°C) and set time to 20 minutes. Press Start to begin preheating.

- Once preheated, place the pan into the oven. Flip the cabbage halfway through the cooking time.

- When cooking is complete, the cabbage wedges should be lightly browned. Transfer the cabbage wedges to a plate and serve with the Mozzarella cheese sprinkled on top.

719. Sesame Mushrooms with Thyme

Preparation Time: 5 minutes
Cooking Time: 15 minutes
Servings: 2

Ingredients:

- 1 tablespoon soy sauce
- 2 teaspoons toasted sesame oil
- 2 teaspoons vegetable oil, divided
- 1 garlic clove, minced
- 7 ounces (198 g) maitake (hen of the woods) mushrooms
- ½ teaspoon flaky sea salt
- ½ teaspoon sesame seeds
- ½ teaspoon finely chopped fresh thyme leaves

Directions:

- Whisk together the soy sauce, sesame oil, 1 teaspoon of vegetable oil, and garlic in a small bowl.

- Arrange the mushrooms in the perforated pan in a single layer. Drizzle the soy sauce mixture over the mushrooms.

- Select Roast. Set temperature to 300°F (150°C) and set time to 15 minutes. Press Start to begin preheating.

- Once preheated, place the pan into the oven.

- After 10 minutes, remove the pan from the oven. Flip the mushrooms and sprinkle the sea salt, sesame seeds, and thyme leaves on top. Drizzle the remaining 2 teaspoons of vegetable oil all over. Return to the oven and continue roasting for an additional 5 minutes.

- When cooking is complete, remove the mushrooms from the oven to a plate and serve hot.

720. Ratatouille with Bread Crumb Topping

Preparation Time: 10 minutes
Cooking Time: 12 minutes
Servings: 6

Ingredients:

- 1 medium zucchini, sliced ½-inch thick

- 1 small eggplant, peeled and sliced ½-inch thick
- 2 teaspoons kosher salt, divided
- 2 tablespoons extra-virgin olive oil, divided
- 2 garlic cloves, minced
- 1 small onion, chopped
- 1 small red bell pepper, cut into ½-inch chunks
- 1 small green bell pepper, cut into ½-inch chunks
- ½ teaspoon dried oregano
- ¼ teaspoon freshly ground black pepper
- 1-pint cherry tomatoes
- 2 tablespoons minced fresh basil
- 1 cup panko bread crumbs
- ½ cup grated Parmesan cheese (optional)

Directions:

- Season one side of the zucchini and eggplant slices with ¾ teaspoon of salt. Put the slices, salted side down, on a rack set over a baking sheet. Sprinkle the other sides with ¾ teaspoon of salt. Allow to sit for 10 minutes, or until the slices begin to exude water. When ready, rinse and dry them. Cut the zucchini slices into quarters and the eggplant slices into eighths.
- Pour the zucchini and eggplant into a large bowl, along with 2 tablespoons of olive oil, garlic, onion, bell peppers, oregano, and black pepper. Toss to coat well. Arrange the vegetables on the sheet pan.
- Select Roast. Set temperature to 375°F (190°C) and set time to 12 minutes. Press Start to begin preheating.
- Once preheated, place the pan into the oven.
- Meanwhile, add the tomatoes and basil to the large bowl. Sprinkle with the remaining ½ teaspoon of salt and 1 tablespoon of olive oil. Toss well and set aside.
- Stir together the remaining 1 tablespoon of olive oil, panko, and Parmesan cheese (if desired) in a small bowl.

- After 6 minutes, remove the pan and add the tomato mixture to the sheet pan and stir to mix well. Scatter the panko mixture on top. Return the pan to the oven and continue cooking for 6 minutes, or until the vegetables are softened and the topping is golden brown.
- Cool for 5 minutes before serving.

721. Butternut Squash and Parsnip with Thyme

Preparation Time: 5 minutes
Cooking Time: 16 minutes
Servings: 2

Ingredients:

- 1 parsnip, sliced
- 1 cup sliced butternut squash
- 1 small red onion, cut into wedges
- ½ chopped celery stalk
- 1 tablespoon chopped fresh thyme
- 2 teaspoons olive oil
- Salt and black pepper, to taste

Directions:

- Toss all the ingredients in a large bowl until the vegetables are well coated.
- Transfer the vegetables to the perforated pan.
- Select Air Fry. Set temperature to 380°F (193°C) and set time to 16 minutes. Press Start to begin preheating.
- Once preheated, place the pan into the oven. Stir the vegetables halfway through the cooking time.
- When cooking is complete, the vegetables should be golden brown and tender. Remove from the oven and serve warm.

722. Butternut Squash with Goat Cheese

Preparation Time: 5 minutes
Cooking Time: 21 minutes
Servings: 2

Ingredients:

- 1-pound (454 g) butternut squash, cut into wedges
- 2 tablespoons olive oil
- 1 tablespoon dried rosemary
- Salt, to salt
- 1 cup crumbled goat cheese
- 1 tablespoon maple syrup

Directions:

- Toss the squash wedges with the olive oil, rosemary, and salt in a large bowl until well coated.
- Transfer the squash wedges to the perforated pan, spreading them out in as even a layer as possible.
- Select Air Fry. Set temperature to 350°F (180°C) and set time to 20 minutes. Press Start to begin preheating.
- Once preheated, place the pan into the oven.
- After 10 minutes, remove from the oven and flip the squash. Return the pan to the oven and continue cooking for 10 minutes.
- When cooking is complete, the squash should be golden brown. Remove the pan from the oven. Sprinkle the goat cheese on top and serve drizzled with the maple syrup.

723. Ginger-Pepper Broccoli

Preparation Time: 5 minutes
Cooking Time: 10 minutes
Servings: 2

Ingredients:

- 12 ounces (340 g) broccoli florets
- 2 tablespoons Asian hot chili oil
- 1 teaspoon ground Sichuan peppercorns (or black pepper)
- 2 garlic cloves, finely chopped
- 1 (2-inch) piece fresh ginger, peeled and finely chopped
- Kosher salt and freshly ground black pepper

Directions:

- Toss the broccoli florets with the chili oil, Sichuan peppercorns, garlic, ginger, salt, and

pepper in a mixing bowl until thoroughly coated.
- Transfer the broccoli florets to the perforated pan.
- Select Air Fry. Set temperature to 375°F (190°C) and set time to 10 minutes. Press Start to begin preheating.
- Once preheated, place the pan into the oven. Stir the broccoli florets halfway through the cooking time.
- When cooking is complete, the broccoli florets should be lightly browned and tender. Remove the broccoli from the oven and serve on a plate.

724. Parmesan Brussels Sprouts

Preparation Time: 10 minutes
Cooking Time: 21 minutes
Servings: 4

Ingredients:

- 1 pound (454 g) fresh Brussels sprouts, trimmed
- 1 tablespoon olive oil
- ½ teaspoon salt
- 1/8 teaspoon pepper
- ¼ cup grated Parmesan cheese

Directions:

- In a large bowl, combine the Brussels sprouts with olive oil, salt, and pepper and toss until evenly coated.
- Spread the Brussels sprouts evenly in the perforated pan.
- Select Air Fry. Set temperature to 330°F (166°C) and set time to 20 minutes. Press Start to begin preheating.
- Once preheated, place the pan into the oven. Stir the Brussels sprouts twice during cooking.
- When cooking is complete, the Brussels sprouts should be golden brown and crisp. Remove the pan from the oven. Sprinkle the grated Parmesan cheese on top and serve warm.

725. Roasted Veggie Rice with Eggs

Preparation Time: 5 minutes
Cooking Time: 12 minutes
Servings: 4

Ingredients:

- 2 teaspoons melted butter
- 1 cup chopped mushrooms
- 1 cup cooked rice
- 1 cup peas
- 1 carrot, chopped
- 1 red onion, chopped
- 1 garlic clove, minced
- Salt and black pepper, to taste
- 2 hard-boiled eggs, grated
- 1 tablespoon soy sauce

Directions:

- Coat a baking dish with melted butter.
- Stir together the mushrooms, cooked rice, peas, carrot, onion, garlic, salt, and pepper in a large bowl until well mixed. Pour the mixture into the prepared baking dish.
- Select Roast. Set temperature to 380°F (193°C) and set time to 12 minutes. Press Start to begin preheating.
- Once preheated, place the baking dish into the oven.
- When cooking is complete, remove from the oven. Divide the mixture among four plates. Serve warm with a sprinkle of grated eggs and a drizzle of soy sauce.

726. Air Fried Carrots, Yellow Squash & Zucchini

Preparation Time: 15 minutes
Cooking Time: 21 minutes
Servings: 4

Ingredients:

- 1 tbsp. chopped tarragon leaves
- ½ tsp. white pepper
- 1 tsp. salt
- 1-pound yellow squash
- 1-pound zucchini
- 6 tsp. olive oil
- ½ pound carrots

Directions:

- Preparing the ingredients. Stem and root the end of squash and zucchini and cut in ¾-inch half-moons. Peel and cut carrots into 1-inch cubes
- Combine carrot cubes with 2 teaspoons of olive oil, tossing to combine.
- Air Frying. Pour into the Oven rack/basket. Place the Rack on the middle-shelf of the Instant Vortex air fryer oven. Set temperature to 400°F, and set time to 5 minutes.
- As carrots cook, drizzle remaining olive oil over squash and zucchini pieces, then season with pepper and salt. Toss well to coat.
- Add squash and zucchini when the timer for carrots goes off. Cook 30 minutes, making sure to toss 2-3 times during the cooking process.
- Once done, take out veggies and toss with tarragon. Serve up warm!

727. Potato Flat Cakes

Preparation Time: 15 minutes
Cooking Time: 12 minutes
Servings: 3

Ingredients:

- 2 or 3 green chilies finely chopped
- 1 ½ tbsp. lemon juice
- Salt and pepper to taste
- 2 tbsp. garam masala
- 2 cups sliced potato
- 3 tsp. ginger finely chopped
- 1-2 tbsp. fresh coriander leaves

Directions:

- Mix the ingredients in a clean bowl and add water to it. Make sure that the paste is not too watery but is enough to apply on the potato slices.

- Pre heat the oven at 160 degrees Fahrenheit for 5 minutes. Place the French Cuisine Galettes in the fry basket and let them cook for another 25 minutes at the same temperature. Keep rolling them over to get a uniform cook. Serve either with mint sauce or ketchup.

728. Cayenne Spicy Green Beans

Preparation Time: 5 minutes
Cooking Time: 12 minutes
Servings: 4

Ingredients:

- 1 cup panko breadcrumbs
- 2 whole eggs, beaten
- ½ cup Parmesan cheese, grated
- ½ cup flour
- 1 tsp cayenne pepper
- 1 ½ pounds green beans
- Salt to taste

Directions:

- In a bowl, mix panko breadcrumbs, Parmesan cheese, cayenne pepper, salt, and pepper. Roll the green beans in flour and dip in eggs. Dredge beans in the parmesan-panko mix. Place the prepared beans in the greased cooking basket and fit in the baking tray; cook for 15 minutes on Air Fry function at 350 F, shaking once. Serve and enjoy!

729. Cabbage Fritters

Preparation Time: 15 minutes
Cooking Time: 19 minutes
Servings: 3

Ingredients:

- 1-2 tbsp. fresh coriander leaves
- 2 or 3 green chilies finely chopped
- 1 ½ tbsp. lemon juice
- Salt and pepper to taste
- 2 tbsp. garam masala
- 2 cups cabbage
- 1 ½ cup coarsely crushed peanuts

- 3 tsp. ginger finely chopped

Directions:

- Mix the ingredients in a clean bowl.
- Mold this mixture into round and flat fritters.
- Wet the fritters slightly with water. Coat each fritter with the crushed peanuts.
- Pre heat the Instant Vortex smart oven at 160 degrees Fahrenheit for 5 minutes. Place the fritters in the fry basket and let them cook for another 25 minutes at the same temperature. Keep rolling them over to get a uniform cook. Serve either with mint sauce or ketchup.

730. Okra Spicy Lemon Kebab

Preparation Time: 15 minutes
Cooking Time: 19 minutes
Servings: 4

Ingredients:

- 3 tsp. lemon juice
- 2 tsp. garam masala
- 4 tbsp. chopped coriander
- 3 tbsp. cream
- 3 tbsp. chopped capsicum
- 3 eggs
- 2 cups sliced okra
- 3 onions chopped
- 5 green chilies-roughly chopped
- 1 ½ tbsp. ginger paste
- 1 ½ tsp. garlic paste
- 1 ½ tsp. salt
- 2 ½ tbsp. white sesame seeds

Directions:

- Grind the ingredients except for the egg and form a smooth paste. Coat the okra in the paste. Now, beat the eggs and add a little salt to it.
- Dip the coated vegetables in the egg mixture and then transfer to the sesame seeds and coat the okra well. Place the vegetables on a stick.

- Pre heat the Instant Vortex smart oven at 160 degrees Fahrenheit for around 5 minutes. Place the sticks in the basket and let them cook for another 25 minutes at the same temperature. Turn the sticks over in between the cooking process to get a uniform cook.

731. Spaghetti Squash Lasagna

Preparation Time: 15 minutes
Cooking Time: 16 minutes
Servings: 4

Ingredients:

- 3 lb. spaghetti squash, halved lengthwise & seeded
- 4 tbsp. water, divided
- 1 tbsp. extra-virgin olive oil
- 1 bunch broccolini, chopped
- 4 cloves garlic, chopped fine
- ¼ tsp crushed red pepper flakes
- 1 cup mozzarella cheese, grated &divided
- ¼ cup parmesan cheese, grated & divided
- ¾ tsp Italian seasoning
- ½ tsp salt
- ¼ tsp ground pepper

Directions:

- Place squash, cut side down, in a microwave safe dish. Add 2 tablespoons water and microwave on high until tender, about 10 minutes.
- Heat oil in a large skillet over medium heat. Add broccoli, garlic, and red pepper. Cook, stirring frequently, 2 minutes.
- Add remaining water and cook until broccolini is tender, about 3-5 minutes. Transfer to a large bowl.
- With a fork, scrape the squash from the shells into the bowl with the broccolini. Place the shells in an 8x11-inch baking pan.
- Add ¾ cup mozzarella, 2 tablespoons parmesan, and seasonings to the squash mixture and stir to combine. Spoon evenly into the shells and top with remaining cheese.

- Place rack in position 1 and set oven to bake on 450°F for 15 minutes. After 5 minutes, place the squash in the oven and cook 10 minutes.
- Set the oven to broil on high and move the pan to position 2. Broil until cheese starts to brown, about 2 minutes. Serve immediately.

732. Sandwiches with Tomato, Nuts & Cheese

Preparation Time: 15 minutes
Cooking Time: 45 minutes
Servings: 2

Ingredients:

- 1 heirloom tomato
- 1 (4-oz) block feta cheese
- 1 small red onion, thinly sliced
- 1 clove garlic
- Salt to taste
- 2 tsp + ¼ cup olive oil
- 1 ½ tbsp toasted pine nuts
- ¼ cup chopped parsley
- ¼ cup grated Parmesan cheese
- ¼ cup chopped basil

Directions:

- Add basil, pine nuts, garlic, and salt to a food processor. Process while slowly adding ¼ cup of olive oil. Once finished, pour basil pesto into a bowl and refrigerate for 30 minutes.
- Preheat Instant Vortex on Air Fry function to 390 F. Slice the feta cheese and tomato into ½-inch slices. Remove the pesto from the fridge and spread half of it on the tomato slices. Top with feta cheese slices and onion. Drizzle the remaining olive oil on top.
- Place the tomatoes in the fryer basket and fit in the baking tray; cook for 12 minutes. Remove to a serving platter and top with the remaining pesto. Serve.

733. Simple Ratatouille

Preparation Time: 15 minutes

Cooking Time: 16 minutes
Servings: 2

Ingredients:

- 2 Roma tomatoes, thinly sliced
- 1 zucchini, thinly sliced
- 2 yellow bell peppers, sliced
- 2 garlic cloves, minced
- 2 tablespoons olive oil
- 2 tablespoons Herbes de Provence
- 1 tablespoon vinegar
- Salt and black pepper, to taste

Directions:

- Place the tomatoes, zucchini, bell peppers, garlic, olive oil, Herbes de Provence, and vinegar in a large bowl and toss until the vegetables are evenly coated. Sprinkle with salt and pepper and toss again. Pour the vegetable mixture into the baking pan.
- Slide the baking pan into Rack Position 2, select Roast, set temperature to 390°F (199°C) and set time to 16 minutes.
- Stir the vegetables halfway through.
- When cooking is complete, the vegetables should be tender.
- Let the vegetable mixture stand for 5 minutes in the oven before removing and serving.

734. Cottage Cheese and Mushroom Mexican Burritos

Preparation Time: 15 minutes
Cooking Time: 12 minutes
Servings: 3

Ingredients:

- ½ cup mushrooms thinly sliced
- 1 cup cottage cheese cut in too long and slightly thick Oregano Fingers
- A pinch of salt to taste
- ½ tsp. red chili flakes
- 1 tsp. freshly ground peppercorns
- ½ cup pickled jalapenos
- 1-2 lettuce leaves shredded.

- ½ cup red kidney beans (soaked overnight)
- ½ small onion chopped
- 1 tbsp. olive oil
- 2 tbsp. tomato puree
- ¼ tsp. red chili powder
- 1 tsp. of salt to taste
- 4-5 flour tortillas
- 1 or 2 spring onions chopped finely. Also cut the greens.
- Take one tomato. Remove the seeds and chop it into small pieces.
- 1 green chili chopped.
- 1 cup of cheddar cheese grated.
- 1 cup boiled rice (not necessary).
- A few flour tortillas to put the filing in.

Directions:

- Cook the beans along with the onion and garlic and mash them finely.
- Now, make the sauce you will need for the burrito. Ensure that you create a slightly thick sauce.
- For the filling, you will need to cook the ingredients well in a pan and ensure that the vegetables have browned on the outside.
- To make the salad, toss the ingredients together. Place the tortilla and add a layer of sauce, followed by the beans and the filling at the center. Before you roll it, you will need to place the salad on top of the filling.
- Pre-heat the Instant Vortex smart oven for around 5 minutes at 200 Fahrenheit. Open the fry basket and keep the burritos inside. Close the basket properly. Let the Air
- Fryer remain at 200 Fahrenheit for another 15 minutes or so. Halfway through, remove the basket and turn all the burritos over in order to get a uniform cook.

735. Broccoli & Cheese Egg Ramekins

Preparation Time: 15 minutes
Cooking Time: 25 minutes
Servings: 4

Ingredients:

- 1 lb. broccoli
- 4 eggs, beaten
- 1 cup cheddar cheese, shredded
- 1 cup heavy cream
- ½ tsp ground nutmeg
- 1 tsp ginger powder
- Salt and black pepper to taste

Directions:

- In boiling water, steam the broccoli for 5 minutes. Drain and place in a bowl to cool. Mix in the eggs, heavy cream, nutmeg, ginger, salt, and pepper. Divide the mixture between greased ramekins and sprinkle the cheddar cheese on top. Place in a baking tray and cook in your Instant Vortex for 10 minutes at 360 F on Bake function. Serve.

736. Zucchini Parmesan Crisps

Preparation Time: 15 minutes
Cooking Time: 11 minutes
Servings: 4

Ingredients:

- 4 small zucchinis, cut lengthwise
- ½ cup Parmesan cheese, grated
- ½ cup breadcrumbs
- ¼ cup melted butter
- ¼ cup chopped parsley
- 4 garlic cloves, minced
- Salt and black pepper to taste

Directions:

- Preheat Instant Vortex on Air Fry function to 350 F. In a bowl, mix breadcrumbs, Parmesan cheese, garlic, parsley, salt, and pepper. Stir in butter. Place the zucchinis cut-side up in a baking tray.
- Spread the cheese mixture onto the zucchini evenly. Cook for 13 minutes. Increase the temperature to 370 F and cook for 3 more minutes for extra crunchiness. Serve hot.

737. Asian-Inspired Broccoli

Preparation Time: 15 minutes
Cooking Time: 10 minutes
Servings: 2

Ingredients:

- 12 ounces (340 g) broccoli florets
- 2 tablespoons Asian hot chili oil
- 1 teaspoon ground Sichuan peppercorns (or black pepper)
- 2 garlic cloves, finely chopped
- 1 (2-inch) piece fresh ginger, peeled and finely chopped
- Kosher salt and freshly ground black pepper

Directions:

- Toss the broccoli florets with the chili oil, Sichuan peppercorns, garlic, ginger, salt, and pepper in a mixing bowl until thoroughly coated.
- Transfer the broccoli florets to the air fryer basket.
- Put the air fryer basket on the baking pan and slide into Rack Position 2, select Air Fry, set temperature to 375°F (190°C), and set time to 10 minutes.
- Stir the broccoli florets halfway through the cooking time.
- When cooking is complete, the broccoli florets should be lightly browned and tender. Remove the broccoli from the oven and serve on a plate.

738. Spicy Sweet Potato Fries

Preparation Time: 15 minutes
Cooking Time: 22 minutes
Servings: 4

Ingredients:

- 2 tbsp. sweet potato fry seasoning mix
- 2 tbsp. olive oil
- 2 sweet potatoes
- Seasoning Mix:
- 2 tbsp. salt
- 1 tbsp. cayenne pepper
- 1 tbsp. dried oregano

- 1 tbsp. fennel
- 2 tbsp. coriander

Directions:

- Preparing the ingredients. Slice both ends off sweet potatoes and peel. Slice lengthwise in half and again crosswise to make four pieces from each potato.
- Slice each potato piece into 2-3 slices, then slice into fries.
- Grind together all of seasoning mix ingredients and mix in the salt.
- Ensure the Instant Vortex air fryer oven is preheated to 350 degrees.
- Toss potato pieces in olive oil, sprinkling with seasoning mix and tossing well to coat thoroughly.
- Air Frying. Add fries to air fryer rack/basket. Set temperature to 350°F, and set time to 27 minutes. Select START/STOP to begin.
- Take out the basket and turn fries. Turn off air fryer oven and let cook 10-12 minutes till fries are golden.

739. Garlic Toast with Cheese

Preparation Time: 15 minutes
Cooking Time: 12 minutes
Servings: 3

Ingredients:

- ¾ cup grated cheese
- 2 tsp. of oregano seasoning
- Some red chili flakes to sprinkle on top
- Take some French bread and cut it into slices
- 1 tbsp. olive oil (Optional)
- 2 tbsp. softened butter
- 4-5 flakes crushed garlic
- A pinch of salt to taste
- ½ tsp. black pepper powder

Directions:

- Take a clean and dry container. Place all the ingredients mentioned under the heading "Garlic Butter" into it and mix properly to obtain garlic butter. On each slice of the French bread, spread some of this garlic butter. Sprinkle some cheese on top of the layer of butter. Pour some oil if wanted.
- Sprinkle some chili flakes and some oregano.
- Pre heat the Instant Vortex smart oven at 240 Fahrenheit for around 5 minutes. Open the fry basket and place the bread in it making sure that no two slices touch each other. Close the basket and continue to cook the bread at 160 degrees for another 10 minutes to toast the bread well.

740. Vegetable Fried Mix Chips

Preparation Time: 15 minutes
Cooking Time: 20 minutes
Servings: 4

Ingredients:

- 1 large eggplant
- 4 potatoes
- 3 zucchinis
- ½ cup cornstarch
- ½ cup olive oil
- Salt to season

Directions:

- Preheat Instant Vortex on Air Fry function to 390 F. Cut the eggplant and zucchini in long 3-inch strips. Peel and cut the potatoes into 3-inch strips; set aside.
- In a bowl, stir in cornstarch, ½ cup of water, salt, pepper, oil, eggplant, zucchini, and potatoes. Place one-third of the veggie strips in the basket and fit in the baking tray; cook for 12 minutes, shaking once.
- Once ready, transfer them to a serving platter. Repeat the cooking process for the remaining veggie strips. Serve warm.

741. Classic Baked Potatoes

Preparation Time: 15 minutes
Cooking Time: 15 minutes
Servings: 4

Ingredients:

- 1 lb. potatoes

- 2 garlic cloves, minced
- Salt and black pepper to taste
- 1 tsp rosemary
- 1 tsp butter, melted

Directions:

- Preheat Air fryer oven to 360 F on Air Fry function. Prick the potatoes with a fork. Place into frying basket and press Start. Cook for 25 minutes. Cut the potatoes in half and top with butter and rosemary. Season with salt and pepper and serve.

742. Garlicky Veggie Bake

Preparation Time: 15 minutes
Cooking Time: 10 minutes
Servings: 3

Ingredients:

- 3 turnips, sliced
- 1 large red onion, cut into rings
- 1 large zucchini, sliced
- Salt and black pepper to taste
- 2 cloves garlic, crushed
- 1 bay leaf, cut in 6 pieces
- 1 tbsp olive oil

Directions:

- Place the turnips, onion, and zucchini in a bowl. Toss with olive oil, salt, and pepper.
- Preheat Instant Vortex on Air Fry function to 380 F. Place the veggies into a baking pan. Slip the bay leaves in the different parts of the slices and tuck the garlic cloves in between the slices. Cook for 15 minutes. Serve warm with as a side to a meat dish or salad.

743. Amazing Macadamia Delight

Preparation Time: 15 minutes
Cooking Time: 12 minutes
Servings: 6

Ingredients:

- 3 cups macadamia nuts
- 3 tbsp liquid smoke

- Salt to taste
- 2 tbsp molasses

Directions:

- Preheat Instant Vortex on Bake function to 360 F. In a bowl, add salt, liquid, molasses, and cashews and toss to coat. Place the cashews in baking tray and press Start. Cook for 10 minutes, shaking the basket every 5 minutes. Serve.

744. Stuffed Eggplant Baskets

Preparation Time: 15 minutes
Cooking Time: 12 minutes
Servings: 3

Ingredients:

- 1 tsp. cumin powder
- Salt and pepper to taste
- 3 tbsp. grated cheese
- 1 tsp. red chili flakes
- ½ tsp. oregano
- 6 eggplants
- ½ tsp. salt
- ½ tsp. pepper powder
- 1 medium onion finely chopped
- 1 green chili finely chopped
- 1 ½ tbsp. chopped coriander leaves
- 1 tsp. fenugreek
- 1 tsp. dried mango powder
- ½ tsp. basil
- ½ tsp. parsley

Directions:

- Take all the ingredients under the heading "Filling" and mix them together in a bowl.
- Remove the stem of the eggplant. Cut off the caps. Remove a little of the flesh as well. Sprinkle some salt and pepper on the inside of the capsicums.
- Leave them aside for some time.
- Now fill the eggplant with the filling prepared but leave a small space at the top. Sprinkle grated cheese and also add the seasoning.

- Pre heat the Instant Vortex smart oven at 140 degrees Fahrenheit for 5 minutes. Put the capsicums in the fry basket and close it. Let them cook at the same temperature for another 20 minutes. Turn them over in between to prevent over cooking.

745. Cayenne Tahini Kale

Preparation Time: 15 minutes
Cooking Time: 13 minutes
Servings: 4

Ingredients:

Dressing:

- ¼ cup tahini
- ¼ cup fresh lemon juice
- 2 tablespoons olive oil
- 1 teaspoon sesame seeds
- ½ teaspoon garlic powder
- ¼ teaspoon cayenne pepper

Kale:

- 4 cups packed torn kale leaves (stems and ribs removed and leaves torn into palm-size pieces)
- Kosher salt and freshly ground black pepper, to taste

Directions:

- Make the dressing: Whisk together the tahini, lemon juice, olive oil, sesame seeds, garlic powder, and cayenne pepper in a large bowl until well mixed.
- Add the kale and massage the dressing thoroughly all over the leaves. Sprinkle the salt and pepper to season.
- Place the kale in the air fryer basket in a single layer.
- Put the air fryer basket on the baking pan and slide into Rack Position 2, select Air Fry, set temperature to 350°F (180°C), and set time to 15 minutes.
- When cooking is complete, the leaves should be slightly wilted and crispy. Remove from the oven and serve on a plate.

746. Crispy Indian Wrap

Preparation Time: 20 minutes
Cooking Time: 8 minutes
Servings: 4

Ingredients:

- Cilantro Chutney
- 2¾ cups diced potato, cooked until tender
- 2 teaspoons oil (coconut, sunflower, or safflower)
- 3 large garlic cloves, minced or pressed
- 1½ tablespoons fresh lime juice
- 1½ teaspoons cumin powder
- 1 teaspoon onion granules
- 1 teaspoon coriander powder
- ½ teaspoon sea salt
- ½ teaspoon turmeric
- ¼ teaspoon cayenne powder
- 4 large flour tortillas, preferably whole grain or sprouted
- 1 cup cooked garbanzo beans (canned are fine), rinsed and drained
- ½ cup finely chopped cabbage
- ¼ cup minced red onion or scallion

Directions:

- Cooking oil spray (sunflower, safflower, or refined coconut)
- Make the Cilantro Chutney and set aside.
- In a large bowl, mash the potatoes well, using a potato masher or large fork. Add the oil, garlic, lime, cumin, onion, coriander, salt, turmeric, and cayenne. Stir very well, until thoroughly combined. Set aside.
- Lay the tortillas out flat on the counter. In the middle of each, evenly distribute the potato filling. Add some of the garbanzo beans, cabbage, and red onion to each, on top of the potatoes.
- Spray the air fryer basket with oil and set aside. Enclose the Indian wraps by folding the bottom of the tortillas up and over the filling, then folding the sides in—and finally rolling the bottom up to form, essentially, an enclosed burrito.
- Place the wraps in the air fryer basket, seam side down. They can touch each other a little

bit, but if they're too crowded, you'll need to cook them in batches. Fry for 5 minutes. Spray with oil again, flip over, and cook an additional 2 or 3 minutes, until nicely browned and crisp. Serve topped with the Cilantro Chutney.

747. Easy Peasy Pizza

Preparation Time: 5 minutes
Cooking Time: 9 minutes
Servings: 1

Ingredients:

♦ Cooking oil spray (coconut, sunflower, or safflower)

♦ 1 flour tortilla, preferably sprouted or whole grain

♦ ¼ cup vegan pizza or marinara sauce

♦ 1/3 cup grated vegan mozzarella cheese or Cheesy Sauce

♦ Toppings of your choice

Directions:

▪ Spray the air fryer basket with oil. Place the tortilla in the air fryer basket. If the tortilla is a little bigger than the base, no probs! Simply fold the edges up a bit to form a semblance of a "crust."

▪ Pour the sauce in the center, and evenly distribute it around the tortilla "crust" (I like to use the back of a spoon for this purpose).

▪ Sprinkle evenly with vegan cheese, and add your toppings. Bake for 9 minutes, or until nicely browned. Remove carefully, cut into four pieces, and enjoy.

748. Eggplant Parmigiana

Preparation Time: 15 minutes
Cooking Time: 40 minutes
Servings: 4

Ingredients:

♦ 1 medium eggplant (about 1 pound), sliced into ½-inch-thick rounds

♦ 2 tablespoons tamari or shoyu

♦ 3 tablespoons nondairy milk, plain and unsweetened

♦ 1 cup chickpea flour (see Substitution Tip)

♦ 1 tablespoon dried basil

♦ 1 tablespoon dried oregano

♦ 2 teaspoons garlic granules

♦ 2 teaspoons onion granules

♦ ½ teaspoon sea salt

♦ ½ teaspoon freshly ground black pepper

♦ Cooking oil spray (sunflower, safflower, or refined coconut)

♦ Vegan marinara sauce (your choice)

♦ Shredded vegan cheese (preferably mozzarella; see Ingredient Tip)

Directions:

▪ Place the eggplant slices in a large bowl, and pour the tamari and milk over the top. Turn the pieces over to coat them as evenly as possible with the liquids. Set aside.

▪ Make the coating: In a medium bowl, combine the flour, basil, oregano, garlic, onion, salt, and pepper and stir well. Set aside.

▪ Spray the air fryer basket with oil and set aside.

▪ Stir the eggplant slices again and transfer them to a plate (stacking is fine). Do not discard the liquid in the bowl.

▪ Bread the eggplant by tossing an eggplant round in the flour mixture. Then, dip in the liquid again. Double up on the coating by placing the eggplant again in the flour mixture, making sure that all sides are nicely breaded. Place in the air fryer basket.

▪ Repeat with enough eggplant rounds to make a (mostly) single layer in the air fryer basket. (You'll need to cook it in batches, so that you don't have too much overlap and it cooks perfectly.)

▪ Spray the tops of the eggplant with enough oil so that you no longer see dry patches in the coating. Fry for 8 minutes. Remove the air fryer basket and spray the tops again. Turn each piece over, again taking care not to overlap the rounds too much. Spray the tops with oil, again making sure that no dry patches remain. Fry for another 8 minutes, or until nicely browned and crisp.

- Repeat steps 5 to 7 one more time, or until all of the eggplant is crisp and browned.

- Finally, place half of the eggplant in a 6-inch round, 2-inch-deep baking pan and top with marinara sauce and a sprinkle of vegan cheese. Fry for 3 minutes, or until the sauce is hot and cheese is melted (be careful not to overcook, or the eggplant edges will burn). Serve immediately, plain or over pasta. Otherwise, you can store the eggplant in the fridge for several days and then make a fresh batch whenever the mood strikes by repeating this step!

749. Luscious Lazy Lasagna

Preparation Time: 15 minutes
Cooking Time: 15 minutes
Servings: 4

Ingredients:

- 8 ounces lasagna noodles, preferably bean-based, but any kind will do
- 1 tablespoon extra-virgin olive oil
- 2 cups crumbled extra-firm tofu, drained and water squeezed out
- 2 cups loosely packed fresh spinach
- 2 tablespoons nutritional yeast
- 2 tablespoons fresh lemon juice
- 1 teaspoon onion granules
- 1 teaspoon sea salt
- 1/8 teaspoon freshly ground black pepper
- 4 large garlic cloves, minced or pressed
- 2 cups vegan pasta sauce, your choice
- ½ cup shredded vegan cheese (preferably mozzarella)

Directions:

- Cook the noodles until a little firmer than al dente (they'll get a little softer after you air-fry them in the lasagna). Drain and set aside.

- While the noodles are cooking, make the filling. In a large pan over medium-high heat, add the olive oil, tofu, and spinach. Stir-fry for a minute, then add the nutritional yeast, lemon juice, onion, salt, pepper, and garlic.

Stir well and cook just until the spinach is nicely wilted. Remove from heat.

- To make half a batch (one 6-inch round, 2-inch-deep baking pan) of lasagna: Spread a thin layer of pasta sauce in the baking pan. Layer 2 or 3 lasagna noodles on top of the sauce. Top with a little more sauce and some of the tofu mixture. Place another 2 or 3 noodles on top, and add another layer of sauce and then another layer of tofu. Finish with a layer of noodles, and then a final layer of sauce. Sprinkle about half of the vegan cheese on top (omit if you prefer; see the Ingredient Tip from the Eggplant Parmigiana).

- Place the pan in the air fryer and bake for 15 minutes, or until the noodles are browning around the edges and the cheese is melted. Cut and serve.

- If making the entire recipe now, repeat steps 3 and 4.

750. Pasta with Creamy Cauliflower Sauce

Preparation Time: 10 minutes
Cooking Time: 18 minutes
Servings: 4

Ingredients:

- 4 cups cauliflower florets
- Cooking oil spray (sunflower,
- safflower, or refined coconut)
- 1 medium onion, chopped
- 8 ounces pasta, your choice (about 4 cups cooked; use gluten-free pasta if desired)
- Fresh chives or scallion tops, for garnish
- ½ cup raw cashew pieces (see Ingredient Tip)
- 1½ cups water
- 1 tablespoon nutritional yeast
- 2 large garlic cloves, peeled
- 2 tablespoons fresh lemon juice
- 1½ teaspoons sea salt
- ¼ teaspoon freshly ground black pepper

Directions:

- Place the cauliflower in the air fryer basket, spritz the tops with oil spray, and roast for 8 minutes. Remove the air fryer basket, stir, and add the onion. Spritz with oil again and roast for another 10 minutes, or until the cauliflower is browned and the onions are tender.

- While the vegetables are roasting in the air fryer, cook the pasta according to the package directions and mince the chives or scallions. Set aside.

- In a blender jar, place the roasted cauliflower and onions along with the cashews, water, nutritional yeast, garlic, lemon, salt, and pepper. Blend well, until very smooth and creamy. Serve a generous portion of the sauce on top of the warm pasta, and top with the minced chives or scallions. The sauce will store, refrigerated in an airtight container, for about a week.

751. Lemony Lentils with "Fried" Onions

Preparation Time: 10 minutes
Cooking Time: 30 minutes
Servings: 4

Ingredients:

- 1 cup red lentils
- 4 cups water
- Cooking oil spray (coconut, sunflower, or safflower)
- 1 medium-size onion, peeled and cut into ¼-inch-thick rings
- Sea salt
- ½ cup kale, stems removed, thinly sliced
- 3 large garlic cloves, pressed or minced
- 2 tablespoons fresh lemon juice
- 2 teaspoons nutritional yeast
- 1 teaspoon sea salt
- 1 teaspoon lemon zest (see Ingredient Tip)
- ¾ teaspoon freshly ground black pepper

Directions:

- In a medium-large pot, bring the lentils and water to a boil over medium-high heat. Reduce the heat to low and simmer, uncovered, for about 30 minutes (or until the lentils have dissolved completely), making sure to stir every 5 minutes or so as they cook (so that the lentils don't stick to the bottom of the pot).

- While the lentils are cooking, get the rest of your dish together. Spray the air fryer basket with oil and place the onion rings inside, separating them as much as possible. Spray them with the oil and sprinkle with a little salt. Fry for 5 minutes. Remove the air fryer basket, shake or stir, spray again with oil, and fry for another 5 minutes. (Note: You're aiming for all of the onion slices to be crisp and well browned, so if some of the pieces begin to do that, transfer them from the air fryer basket to a plate.)

- Remove the air fryer basket, spray the onions again with oil, and fry for a final 5 minutes or until all the pieces are crisp and browned.

- To finish the lentils: Add the kale to the hot lentils, and stir very well, as the heat from the lentils will steam the thinly sliced greens. Stir in the garlic, lemon juice, nutritional yeast, salt, zest, and pepper. Stir very well and then distribute evenly in bowls. Top with the crisp onion rings and serve.

752. Balsamic Artichokes

Preparation Time: 11 minutes
Cooking Time: 8 minutes
Servings: 4

Ingredients:

- 2 tsp of balsamic vinegar
- Black pepper and salt
- 1/4 cup of olive oil
- 1 tsp of oregano
- 4 big trimmed artichokes
- 2 tbsp of lemon juice
- 2 cloves of garlic

Directions:

- Sprinkle the artichokes with pepper and salt.
- Brush oil over the artichokes and add lemon juice.
- Place the artichokes on the Air fryer .

- Set the Air fryer at Air fryer/Grill, timer at 7 minutes at 3600F.
- Mix garlic, lemon juice, pepper, vinegar, oil in a bowl.
- Add oregano and salt.
- Mix well.
- Serve the artichokes with balsamic vinaigrette.

753. Cheesy Artichokes

Preparation Time: 20 minutes
Cooking Time: 20minutes
Servings: 5

Ingredients:

- 1 tsp of onion powder
- 1/2 cup of chicken stock
- 14 ounces of artichoke hearts
- 8 ounces of mozzarella
- 1/2 cup of mayonnaise
- 8 ounces of cream cheese
- 10 ounces of spinach
- 3 cloves of garlic
- 16 ounces of grated parmesan cheese
- 1/2 cup of sour cream

Directions:

- Mix cream cheese, onion powder, chicken stock, and artichokes in a bowl.
- Add sour cream, mayonnaise, spinach to the bowl.
- Transfer the mixture to the Air fryer pan
- Set the Air fryer to Air fryer/Grill.
- Set timer to 6 minutes at 3500F.
- Serve immediately

754. Beet Salad with Parsley Dressing

Preparation Time: 15 minutes
Cooking Time: 30 minutes
Servings: 4

Ingredients:

- Black pepper and salt
- 1 clove of garlic
- 2 tbsp of balsamic vinegar
- 4 beets
- 2 tbsp of capers
- 1 bunch of chopped parsley
- 1 tbsp of olive oil

Directions:

- Place beets on the Air fryer pan.
- Set the Air fryer to air fry function.
- Set timer and temperature to 15 minutes and 3600F.
- In another bowl, mix pepper, garlic, capers, salt, and olive oil. Mix well
- Remove the beets from the Air fryer and place it on a flat surface.
- Peel and put it in the salad bowl
- Serve with vinegar.

755. Blue Cheese Salad and Beets

Preparation Time: 10 minutes
Cooking Time: 30 minutes
Servings: 5

Ingredients:

- 1 tbsp of olive oil
- Black pepper and salt
- 6 beets
- 1/4 cup of blue cheese

Directions:

- Set the beets on the Air fryer pan.
- Set the Air fryer to air fry function.
- Set timer to 15 minutes.
- Cook at 3500F
- Transfer it to a plate.
- Add pepper, blue cheese, oil, and salt.
- Serve immediately

756. Broccoli Salad

Preparation Time: 15 minutes
Cooking Time: 20 minutes
Servings: 4

Ingredients:

- 6 cloves of garlic
- 1 head of broccoli
- Black pepper and salt
- 1 tbsp of Chinese rice wine vinegar
- 1 tbsp of peanut oil

Directions:

- Mix oil, salt, broccoli, and pepper.
- Place the mixture on the Air fryer pan.
- Set the Air fryer to air fry function.
- Cook for 9 minutes at 3500F.
- Place the broccoli in the salad bowl and add peanuts oil, rice vinegar, and garlic.
- Serve immediately.

757. Brussels Sprout with Tomatoes Mix

Preparation Time: 10 minutes
Cooking Time: 20 minutes
Servings: 3

Ingredients:

- 6 halved cherry tomatoes
- 1 tbsp of olive oil
- 1 pound of Brussel sprouts
- Black pepper and salt
- 1/4 cup of chopped green onions

Directions:

- Sprinkle pepper and salt on the Brussels sprout.
- Place it on the Air fryer pan.
- Set the Air fryer to air fry function.
- Cook for 10 minutes at 3500F.
- Place the cooked sprout in a bowl, add pepper, green onion, salt, olive oil, and cherry tomatoes.
- Mix well and serve immediately

758. Cheesy Brussels Sprout

Preparation Time: 1 hour
Cooking Time: 20 minutes
Servings: 3

Ingredients:

- 1 lemon juice
- 2 tbsp of butter
- 1 pound of Brussel sprout
- 3 tbsp of grated parmesan
- Black pepper and salt

Directions:

- Place the Brussel sprout on the Air fryer pan.
- Set the Air fryer to air fry function.
- Cook for 8 minutes at 3500F.
- Heat butter in a pan over medium heat, add pepper, lemon juice, and salt.
- Add Brussel sprout and parmesan.
- Serve immediately.

759. Spicy Cabbage

Preparation Time: 15 minutes
Cooking Time: 20 minutes
Servings: 5

Ingredients:

- 1 grated carrot
- 1/2 tsp of cayenne pepper
- 1/4 cup of apple cider vinegar
- 1 cabbage
- 1 tsp of red pepper flakes
- 1 tbsp of sesame seed oil
- 1/4 cups of apple juice

Directions:

- Put carrot, cayenne, cabbage, and oil on the Air fryer pan.
- Add vinegar, pepper flakes, and apple juice.
- Set the Air fryer to air fry function.
- Cook for 8 minutes at 3500F
- Serve immediately

760. Sweet Baby Carrots

Preparation Time: 10 minutes
Cooking Time: 25 minutes
Servings: 4

Ingredients:

- 1 tbsp of brown sugar

- 2 cups of baby carrots
- 1/2 tbsp. of melted butter
- Black pepper and salt

Directions:

- Mix butter, sugar, pepper, carrot, and salt in a bowl.
- Transfer the mix to the Air fryer pan
- Set the Air fryer to air fry function.
- Cook for 10 minutes at 3500F
- Serve immediately

761. Zucchini Mix and Herbed Eggplant

Preparation Time: 20 minutes
Cooking Time: 20 minutes
Servings: 3

Ingredients:

- 1 tsp of dried thyme
- 3 tbsp of olive oil
- 1 eggplant
- 2 tbsp of lemon juice
- 1 tsp of dried oregano
- 3 cubed zucchinis
- Black pepper and salt

Directions:

- Place the eggplants on the Air fryer pan, add thyme, zucchinis, olive oil, salt.
- Add pepper, oregano, and lemon juice.
- Set the Air fryer to air fry function.
- Cook for 8 minutes at 3600F
- Serve immediately

762. Potato and Crispy Leek Soup

Preparation Time: 15 minutes
Cooking Time: 31 minutes
Servings: 6

Ingredients:

- 2 tablespoons extra-virgin olive oil, divided
- 4 leeks, cleaned and thinly sliced, divided
- 4 garlic cloves, minced

- 5 Yukon Gold potatoes, peeled and diced
- 3 thyme sprigs, stems removed
- 2 bay leaves
- 5 cups vegetable broth
- ¾ cup white wine
- 1½ teaspoons dried oregano
- 1 teaspoon sea salt
- ½ teaspoon freshly ground black pepper
- 1½ cups light cream
- ½ cup grated Cheddar cheese

Directions

- Select Sear/Sauté and set to Medium High. Select Start/Stop to begin. Allow the pot to preheat for 5 minutes.
- Put 1 tablespoon of oil and three-quarters of the sliced leeks in the pot. Cook until soft, about 5 minutes. Add the garlic and cook for 1 minute more.
- Add the potatoes, thyme, bay leaves, vegetable broth, white wine, oregano, salt, and black pepper to the pot. Assemble the Pressure Lid, making sure the pressure release valve is in the Seal position.
- Select Pressure and set to High. Set the time to 10 minutes, then select Start/Stop to begin.
- When pressure cooking is complete, quick release the pressure by moving the pressure release valve to the Vent position. Carefully remove the lid when the unit has finished releasing pressure.
- Remove and discard the bay leaves. Add the cream and use a potato masher to mash the soup to your desired consistency. Evenly top with the cheese.
- In a small bowl, toss the remaining sliced leeks with the remaining 1 tablespoon of oil. Place the Reversible Rack in the pot in the higher position. Place a sheet of aluminum foil on top of the rack and arrange the leeks on top.
- Close the Crisping Lid. Select Broil and set the time to 5 minutes. Select Start/Stop to begin.

- When cooking is complete, check to see if the leeks have reached your desired crispiness. Remove the rack from the pot and serve the crispy leeks over the soup.

TIP: I like a little texture in this soup, but if you prefer a thinner or smoother texture, transfer the soup to a high-speed blender in step 6 instead of mashing with a potato masher.

763. Chickpea, Spinach, and Sweet Potato Stew

Preparation Time: 15 minutes
Cooking Time: 23 minutes
Servings: 6

Ingredients:

- 1 tablespoon extra-virgin olive oil
- 1 yellow onion, diced
- 4 garlic cloves, minced
- 4 sweet potatoes, peeled and diced
- 4 cups vegetable broth
- 1 (15-ounce) can fire-roasted diced tomatoes, undrained
- 2 (15-ounce) cans chickpeas, drained
- 1½ teaspoons ground cumin
- 1 teaspoon ground coriander
- ½ teaspoon paprika
- ½ teaspoon sea salt
- ½ teaspoon freshly ground black pepper
- 4 cups baby spinach

Directions:

- Select Sear/Sauté and set to Medium High. Select Start/Stop to begin. Allow the pot to preheat for 5 minutes.

- Combine the oil, onion, and garlic in the pot. Cook, stirring occasionally, for 5 minutes.

- Add the sweet potatoes, vegetable broth, tomatoes, chickpeas, cumin, coriander, paprika, salt, and black pepper to the pot. Assemble the Pressure Lid, making sure the pressure release valve is in the Seal position.

- Select Pressure and set to High. Set the time to 8 minutes, then select Start/Stop to begin.

- When pressure cooking is complete, quick release the pressure by moving the pressure release valve to the Vent position. Carefully remove the lid when the unit has finished releasing pressure.

- Add the spinach to the pot and stir until wilted. Serve.

TIP: If you would prefer to assemble this recipe before you go into the office so there's a nice warm bowl of stew waiting for you when you get home, instead of using Pressure, select Slow Cook and set to Low for 6 to 7 hours.

764. Mushroom and Gruyère Tarts

Preparation Time: 15 minutes
Cooking Time: 31 minutes
Servings: 4

Ingredients:

- 2 tablespoons extra-virgin olive oil, divided
- 1 small white onion, sliced
- 5 ounces shiitake mushrooms, sliced
- ¼ teaspoon sea salt
- ¼ teaspoon freshly ground black pepper
- ¼ cup dry white wine
- 1 sheet puff pastry, thawed
- 1 cup shredded Gruyère cheese
- 1 tablespoon thinly sliced fresh chives

Directions:

- Select Sear/Sauté and set to High. Select Start/Stop to begin. Allow the pot to preheat for 5 minutes.

- Combine 1 tablespoon of oil, the onion, and the mushrooms in the pot. Cook, stirring occasionally, for 5 minutes, or until the vegetables are browned and tender. Season with the salt and black pepper, then add the wine and cook until it has evaporated, about 2 minutes. Transfer the vegetables to a bowl and set aside.

- Unfold the puff pastry and cut it into 4 squares. Using a fork, pierce the dough and brush both sides with the remaining 1 tablespoon of oil.

- Evenly divide half the cheese among the puff pastry squares, leaving a ½-inch border around the edges. Divide the mushroom and

302

onion mixture among the pastry squares, then divide the remaining cheese among them.

- Place the Cook & Crisp Basket in the pot. Close the Crisping Lid. Preheat the unit by selecting Air Crisp, setting the temperature to 400°F, and setting the time to 5 minutes.

- Once preheated, place 1 tart in the Air Fryer Basket.

- Close the Crisping Lid. Select Air Crisp, set the temperature to 360°F, and set the time to 6 minutes. Select Start/Stop to begin.

- After 6 minutes, check for your desired browning. Remove the tart from the basket and transfer to a plate.

- Repeat steps 6 through 8 with the remaining tarts.

- Serve garnished with the chives.

TIP: These tarts make for a tasty appetizer or a light meal. When served as a main, pair them with a mixed green salad dressed with mustard vinaigrette.

765. Stuffed Portobello Mushrooms

Preparation Time: 15 minutes
Cooking Time: 28 minutes
Servings: 4

Ingredients:

- 4 large portobello mushrooms, stems and gills removed
- 2 tablespoons extra-virgin olive oil
- ½ cup cooked quinoa
- 1 tomato, seeded and diced
- 1 bell pepper, seeded and diced
- ¼ cup Kalamata olives, pitted and chopped
- ½ cup crumbled feta cheese
- Juice of 1 lemon
- ½ teaspoon sea salt
- ½ teaspoon freshly ground black pepper
- Minced fresh parsley, for garnish

Directions:

- Place the Cook & Crisp Basket in the pot. Close the Crisping Lid. Preheat the unit by selecting Air Crisp, setting the temperature to

375°F, and setting the time to 5 minutes. Press Start/Stop to begin.

- Coat the mushrooms with the oil. Open the Crisping Lid and arrange the mushrooms, open-side up, in a single layer in the preheated Cook & Crisp Basket.

- Close the Crisping Lid. Select Air Crisp, set the temperature to 375°F, and set the time to 20 minutes. Select Start/Stop to begin.

- In a medium mixing bowl, combine the quinoa, tomato, bell pepper, olives, feta cheese, lemon juice, salt, and black pepper.

- Open the Crisping Lid and spoon the quinoa mixture evenly into the 4 mushrooms. Close the lid. Select Air Crisp, set the temperature to 350°F, and set the time to 8 minutes. Press Start/Stop to begin.

- Garnish with fresh parsley and serve immediately.

766. Mushroom Club Sandwich

Preparation Time: 15 minutes
Cooking Time: 10 minutes
Servings: 2

Ingredients:

- ¼ tbsp. Worcestershire sauce
- ½ tsp. olive oil
- ½ flake garlic crushed
- ¼ cup chopped onion
- ¼ tbsp. red chili sauce
- ½ cup water
- 2 slices of white bread
- 1 tbsp. softened butter
- 1 cup minced mushroom
- 1 small capsicum

Directions:

- Take the slices of bread and remove the edges. Now cut the slices horizontally.

- Cook the ingredients for the sauce and wait till it thickens. Now, add the mushroom to the sauce and stir till it obtains the flavors. Roast the capsicum and peel the skin off. Cut the capsicum into slices. Apply the sauce on the slices.

- Pre-heat the Air fryer oven for 5 minutes at 300 Fahrenheit. Open the basket of the Fryer and place the prepared Classic Sandwiches in it such that no two Classic Sandwiches are touching each other. Now keep the fryer at 250 degrees for around 15 minutes. Turn the Classic Sandwiches in between the cooking process to cook both slices. Serve the Classic Sandwiches with tomato ketchup or mint sauce.

767. Panko Green Beans

Preparation Time: 10 minutes
Cooking Time: 15 Minutes
Servings: 4

Ingredients:

- ½ cup flour
- 2 eggs
- 1 cup panko bread crumbs
- ½ cup grated Parmesan cheese
- 1 teaspoon cayenne pepper
- Salt and black pepper, to taste
- 1½ pounds (680 g) green beans

Directions:

- In a bowl, place the flour. In a separate bowl, lightly beat the eggs. In a separate shallow bowl, thoroughly combine the bread crumbs, cheese, cayenne pepper, salt, and pepper.
- Dip the green beans in the flour, then in the beaten eggs, finally in the bread crumb mixture to coat well. Transfer the green beans to the air fryer basket.
- Put the air fryer basket on the baking pan and slide into Rack Position 2, select Air Fry, set temperature to 400°F (205°C), and set time to 15 minutes.
- Stir the green beans halfway through the cooking time.
- When cooking is complete, remove from the oven to a bowl and serve.

768. Roasted Vegetables Salad

Preparation Time: 10 minutes
Cooking Time: 85 Minutes
Servings: 5

Ingredients:

- 3 eggplants
- 1 tbsp of olive oil
- 3 medium zucchini
- 1 tbsp of olive oil
- 4 large tomatoes, cut them in eighths
- 4 cups of one shaped pasta
- 2 peppers of any color
- 1 cup of sliced tomatoes cut into small cubes
- 2 teaspoon of salt substitute
- 8 tbsp of grated parmesan cheese
- ½ cup of Italian dressing
- Leaves of fresh basil

Directions:

- Preparing the Ingredients. Wash your eggplant and slice it off then discard the green end. Make sure not to peel.
- Slice your eggplant into 1/2 inch of thick rounds. 1/2 inch)
- Pour 1tbsp of olive oil on the eggplant round.
- Air Frying. Put the eggplants in the basket of the Instant Vortex air fryer oven and then toss it in the air fryer oven. Cook the eggplants for 40 minutes. Set the heat to 360 ° F
- Meanwhile, wash your zucchini and slice it then discard the green end. But do not peel it.
- Slice the Zucchini into thick rounds of ½ inch each. Toss your ingredients
- Add 1 tbsp of olive oil.
- Air Frying. Cook the zucchini for 25 minutes on a heat of 360° F and when the time is off set it aside.
- Wash and cut the tomatoes.
- Air Frying. Arrange your tomatoes in the basket of the Instant Vortex air fryer oven. Set the timer to 30 minutes. Set the heat to 350° F
- When the time is off, cook your pasta according to the pasta guiding directions, empty it into a colander. Run the cold water

on it and wash it and drain the pasta and put it aside.

- Meanwhile, wash and chop your peppers and place it in a bow

- Wash and thinly slice your cherry tomatoes and add it to the bowl. Add your roasted veggies.

- Add the pasta, a pinch of salt, the topping dressing, add the basil and the parm and toss everything together. (It is better to mix with your hands). Set the ingredients together in the refrigerator, and let it chill

- Serve your salad and enjoy it!

769. Veggie & Garlic Bake

Preparation Time: 10 minutes
Cooking Time: 20 Minutes
Servings: 4

Ingredients:

- 1 lb turnips, sliced
- 1 large red onion, cut into rings
- 1 large zucchini, sliced
- Salt and black pepper to taste
- 2 cloves garlic, crushed
- 1 bay leaf, cut in 6 pieces
- 1 tbsp olive oil

Directions:

- Place turnips, onion, and zucchini in a bowl. Toss with olive oil and season with salt and pepper. Preheat Instant Vortex on AirFry function to 330 F. Place the veggies into a baking pan.

- Slip the bay leaves in the different parts of the slices and tuck the garlic cloves in between the slices. Press Start and cook for 15 minutes. Serve warm with as a side to a meat dish or salad.

770. Vegan Meatloaf

Preparation Time: 10 minutes
Cooking Time: 65 Minutes
Servings: 8

Ingredients:

- Nonstick cooking spray
- 3 1/3 cups chickpeas, cooked
- 1 onion, chopped fine
- 2 stalks celery, chopped
- 2 carrots, chopped fine
- 2 cloves garlic diced fine
- 2 cups panko bread crumbs
- ½ cup almond milk, unsweetened
- 3 tbsp. vegan Worcestershire sauce
- 3 tbsp. soy sauce, divided
- 2 tbsp. olive oil
- 2 tbsp. flax seeds, ground
- ¼ cup + 2 tbsp. tomato paste
- 1 tsp liquid smoke
- ¼ tsp pepper
- 2 tbsp. maple syrup
- 2 tbsp. apple cider vinegar
- 1 tsp paprika

Directions:

- Place rack in position Lightly spray a 9-inch loaf pan with cooking spray.

- Place chickpeas, onion, celery, carrots, cloves, bread crumbs, milk, Worcestershire, 2 tablespoons soy sauce, oil, flax seeds, 2 tablespoons tomato paste, liquid smoke, and pepper in a food processor, you may need to do this in batches. Pulse until ingredients are combined but don't over blend. Transfer each batch to a large bowl, then mix together.

- Set oven to bake on 375°F for 35 minutes.

- Press mixture into the prepared pan. After the oven has preheated 5 minutes, add loaf pan to the oven and bake 30 minutes.

- In a small bowl, whisk together remaining tomato paste and soy sauce, along with the syrup, vinegar, and paprika until smooth.

- When the timer goes off, remove the loaf from the oven. Spoon glaze over top and bake another 20-25 minutes. Let cool 10 minutes before slicing and serving.

771. Cauliflower Bites

Preparation Time: 15 minutes
Cooking Time: 18 Minutes
Servings: 4

Ingredients:

- 1 Head Cauliflower, cut into small florets
- Tsps Garlic Powder
- Pinch of Salt and Pepper
- 1 Tbsp Butter, melted
- 1/2 Cup Chili Sauce
- Olive Oil

Directions:

- Preparing the Ingredients. Place cauliflower into a bowl and pour oil over florets to lightly cover.
- Season florets with salt, pepper, and the garlic powder and toss well.
- Air Frying. Place florets into the Instant Vortex air fryer oven at 350 degrees for 14 minutes.
- Remove cauliflower from the Air fryer oven.
- Combine the melted butter with the chili sauce
- Pour over the florets so that they are well coated.
- Return to the Instant Vortex air fryer oven and cook for additional 3 to 4 minutes
- Serve as a side or with ranch or cheese dip as a snack.

772. Roasted Bell Peppers With Garlic

Preparation Time: 10 minutes
Cooking Time: 22 Minutes
Servings: 4

Ingredients:

- 1 green bell pepper, sliced into 1-inch strips
- 1 red bell pepper, sliced into 1-inch strips
- 1 orange bell pepper, sliced into 1-inch strips
- 1 yellow bell pepper, sliced into 1-inch strips
- 2 tablespoons olive oil, divided
- ½ teaspoon dried marjoram
- Pinch salt
- Freshly ground black pepper, to taste
- 1 head garlic

Directions:

- Toss the bell peppers with 1 tablespoon of olive oil in a large bowl until well coated. Season with the marjoram, salt, and pepper. Toss again and set aside.
- Cut off the top of a head of garlic. Place the garlic cloves on a large square of aluminum foil. Drizzle the top with the remaining 1 tablespoon of olive oil and wrap the garlic cloves in foil.
- Transfer the garlic to the air fryer basket.
- Put the air fryer basket on the baking pan and slide into Rack Position 2, select Roast, set temperature to 330°F (166°C) and set time to 15 minutes.
- After 15 minutes, remove from the oven and add the bell peppers. Return to the oven and set time to 7 minutes.
- When cooking is complete or until the garlic is soft and the bell peppers are tender.
- Transfer the cooked bell peppers to a plate. Remove the garlic and unwrap the foil. Let the garlic rest for a few minutes. Once cooled, squeeze the roasted garlic cloves out of their skins and add them to the plate of bell peppers. Stir well and serve immediately.

773. Vegan Beetroot Chips

Preparation Time: 1 hour
Cooking Time: 9 Minutes
Servings: 2

Ingredients:

- 4 cups golden beetroot slices
- 2 tbsp olive oil
- 1 tbsp yeast flakes
- 1 tsp vegan seasoning
- Salt to taste

Directions:

- In a bowl, add the oil, beetroot slices, vegan seasoning, and yeast and mix well. Dump the coated chips in the basket.
- Set the heat to 370 F and press Start.
- Cook on AirFry function for14-16 minutes, shaking once halfway through. Serve.

774. Cheesy Cabbage Wedges

Preparation Time: 15 minutes
Cooking Time: 25 Minutes
Servings: 4

Ingredients:

- ½ head cabbage, cut into wedges
- 2 cups Parmesan cheese, chopped
- 4 tbsp melted butter
- Salt and black pepper to taste
- ½ cup blue cheese sauce

Directions:

- Brush the cabbage wedges with butter and coat with mozzarella cheese.
- Place the coated wedges in the greased basket and fit in the baking tray; cook for 20 minutes at 380 F on Air Fry setting.
- Serve with blue cheese sauce.

775. Okra Flat Cakes

Preparation Time: 20 minutes
Cooking Time: 65 Minutes
Servings: 8

Ingredients:

- 2 or 3 green chilies finely chopped
- 1 ½ tbsp. lemon juice
- Salt and pepper to taste
- 2 tbsp. garam masala
- 2 cups sliced okra
- 3 tsp. ginger finely chopped
- 1-2 tbsp. fresh coriander leaves

Directions:

- Mix the ingredients in a clean bowl and add water to it. Make sure that the paste is not too watery but is enough to apply on the okra.
- Pre heat the Air fryer oven at 160 degrees Fahrenheit for 5 minutes.
- Place the French Cuisine Galettes in the fry basket and let them cook for another 25 minutes at the same temperature. Keep rolling them over to get a uniform cook.
- Serve either with mint sauce or ketchup.

776. Black Gram French Cuisine Galette

Preparation Time: 1 hour
Cooking Time: 30 Minutes
Servings: 6-8

Ingredients:

- 2 or 3 green chilies finely chopped
- 1 ½ tbsp. lemon juice
- Salt and pepper to taste
- 2 cup black gram
- 2 medium potatoes boiled and mashed
- 1 ½ cup coarsely crushed peanuts
- 3 tsp. ginger finely chopped
- 1-2 tbsp. fresh coriander leaves

Directions:

- Mix the ingredients in a clean bowl.
- Mold this mixture into round and flat French Cuisine Galettes.
- Wet the French Cuisine Galettes slightly with water.
- Pre heat the Air fryer oven at 160 degrees Fahrenheit for 5 minutes. Place the French Cuisine Galettes in the fry basket and let them cook for another 25 minutes at the same temperature. Keep rolling them over to get a uniform cook.
- Serve either with mint sauce or ketchup.

777. Cayenne Spicy Green Beans

Preparation Time: 10 minutes
Cooking Time: 20 Minutes
Servings: 4

Ingredients:

- 1 cup panko breadcrumbs
- 2 whole eggs, beaten
- ½ cup Parmesan cheese, grated
- ½ cup flour
- 1 tsp cayenne pepper
- 1 ½ pounds green beans
- Salt to taste

Directions:

- In a bowl, mix panko breadcrumbs, Parmesan cheese, cayenne pepper, salt, and pepper.
- Roll the green beans in flour and dip in eggs. Dredge beans in the parmesan-panko mix.
- Place the prepared beans in the greased cooking basket and fit in the baking tray; cook for 15 minutes on Air Fry function at 350 F, shaking once.
- Serve and enjoy!

778. Gherkins Flat Cakes

Preparation Time: 20 minutes
Cooking Time: 30 Minutes
Servings: 4

Ingredients:

- 2 or 3 green chilies finely chopped
- 1 ½ tbsp. lemon juice
- Salt and pepper to taste
- 2 tbsp. garam masala
- 2 cups sliced gherkins
- 3 tsp. ginger finely chopped
- 1-2 tbsp. fresh coriander leaves

Directions:

- Mix the ingredients in a clean bowl and add water to it. Make sure that the paste is not too watery but is enough to apply on the gherkin.
- Pre heat the Air fryer oven at 160 degrees Fahrenheit for 5 minutes. Place the French Cuisine Galettes in the fry basket and let them cook for another 25 minutes at the same temperature. Keep rolling them over to get a uniform cook.
- Serve either with mint sauce or ketchup.

779. Cabbage Flat Cakes

Preparation Time: 15 minutes
Cooking Time: 30 Minutes
Servings: 4

Ingredients:

- 2 or 3 green chilies finely chopped
- 1 ½ tbsp. lemon juice
- Salt and pepper to taste
- 2 tbsp. garam masala
- 2 cups halved cabbage leaves
- 3 tsp. ginger finely chopped
- 1-2 tbsp. fresh coriander leaves

Directions:

- Mix the ingredients in a clean bowl and add water to it. Make sure that the paste is not too watery but is enough to apply on the cabbage.
- Pre heat the Air fryer oven at 160 degrees Fahrenheit for 5 minutes. Place the French Cuisine Galettes in the fry basket and let them cook for another 25 minutes at the same temperature. Keep rolling them over to get a uniform cook.
- Serve either with mint sauce or ketchup.

780. Asian-inspired Broccoli

Preparation Time: 10 minutes
Cooking Time: 10 Minutes
Servings: 2

Ingredients:

- 12 ounces (340 g) broccoli florets
- 2 tablespoons Asian hot chili oil
- 1 teaspoon ground Sichuan peppercorns (or black pepper)
- 2 garlic cloves, finely chopped
- 1 (2-inch) piece fresh ginger, peeled and finely chopped
- Kosher salt and freshly ground black pepper

Directions:

- Toss the broccoli florets with the chili oil, Sichuan peppercorns, garlic, ginger, salt, and pepper in a mixing bowl until thoroughly coated.
- Transfer the broccoli florets to the air fryer basket.
- Put the air fryer basket on the baking pan and slide into Rack Position 2, select Air Fry, set temperature to 375°F (190°C), and set time to 10 minutes.
- Stir the broccoli florets halfway through the cooking time.

- When cooking is complete, the broccoli florets should be lightly browned and tender. Remove the broccoli from the oven and serve on a plate.

781. Mint French Cuisine Galette

Preparation Time: 45 minutes
Cooking Time: 30 Minutes
Servings: 6

Ingredients:

- 1-2 tbsp. fresh coriander leaves
- 2 or 3 green chilies finely chopped
- 1 ½ tbsp. lemon juice
- Salt and pepper to taste
- 2 cups mint leaves (Sliced fine)
- 2 medium potatoes boiled and mashed
- 1 ½ cup coarsely crushed peanuts
- 3 tsp. ginger finely chopped

Directions:

- Mix the sliced mint leaves with the rest of the ingredients in a clean bowl.
- Mold this mixture into round and flat French Cuisine Galettes.
- Wet the French Cuisine Galettes slightly with water. Coat each French Cuisine Galette with the crushed peanuts.
- Pre heat the Air fryer oven at 160 degrees Fahrenheit for 5 minutes. Place the French Cuisine Galettes in the fry basket and let them cook for another 25 minutes at the same temperature. Keep rolling them over to get a uniform cook.
- Serve either with mint sauce or ketchup.

782. Stuffed Portobello Mushrooms With Vegetables

Preparation Time: 15 minutes
Cooking Time: 8 Minutes
Servings: 4

Ingredients:

- 4 portobello mushrooms, stem removed
- 1 tablespoon olive oil
- 1 tomato, diced
- ½ green bell pepper, diced
- ½ small red onion, diced
- ½ teaspoon garlic powder
- Salt and black pepper, to taste
- ½ cup grated Mozzarella cheese

Directions:

- Using a spoon to scoop out the gills of the mushrooms and discard them. Brush the mushrooms with the olive oil.
- In a mixing bowl, stir together the remaining ingredients except the Mozzarella cheese. Using a spoon to stuff each mushroom with the filling and scatter the Mozzarella cheese on top.
- Arrange the mushrooms in the air fryer basket.
- Put the air fryer basket on the baking pan and slide into Rack Position 2, select Roast, set temperature to 330°F (166°C) and set time to 8 minutes.
- When cooking is complete, the cheese should be melted.
- Serve warm.

783. Cottage Cheese Gnocchi's

Preparation Time: 15 minutes
Cooking Time: 8 Minutes
Servings: 2-3

Ingredients:

- 2 tsp. ginger-garlic paste
- 2 tsp. soya sauce
- 2 tsp. vinegar
- 1 ½ cup all-purpose flour
- ½ tsp. salt
- 5 tbsp. water
- 2 cups grated cottage cheese
- 2 tbsp. oil

Directions:

- Squeeze the dough and cover it with plastic wrap and set aside. Next, cook the ingredients for the filling and try to ensure that the cottage cheese is covered well with the sauce.

- Roll the dough and place the filling in the center. Now, wrap the dough to cover the filling and pinch the edges together.

- Pre heat the Air fryer oven at 200° F for 5 minutes. Place the gnocchi's in the fry basket and close it. Let them cook at the same temperature for another 20 minutes. Recommended sides are chili sauce or ketchup.

784. Cottage Cheese French Cuisine Galette

Preparation Time: 15 minutes
Cooking Time: 30 Minutes
Servings: 4

Ingredients:

- 1-2 tbsp. fresh coriander leaves
- 2 or 3 green chilies finely chopped
- 1 ½ tbsp. lemon juice
- Salt and pepper to taste
- 2 tbsp. garam masala
- 2 cups grated cottage cheese
- 1 ½ cup coarsely crushed peanuts
- 3 tsp. ginger finely chopped

Directions:

- Mix the ingredients in a clean bowl.

- Mold this mixture into round and flat French Cuisine Galettes.

- Wet the French Cuisine Galettes slightly with water. Coat each French Cuisine Galette with the crushed peanuts.

- Pre heat the Air fryer oven at 160 degrees Fahrenheit for 5 minutes. Place the French Cuisine Galettes in the fry basket and let them cook for another 25 minutes at the same temperature. Keep rolling them over to get a uniform cook. Serve either with mint sauce or ketchup.

785. Green Beans with Shallot

Preparation Time: 10 minutes
Cooking Time: 10 minutes
Servings: 4

Ingredients:

- 1½ pounds French green beans, stems removed and blanched
- 1 tablespoon salt
- ½ pound shallots, peeled
- ½ teaspoon ground white pepper
- 2 tablespoons olive oil

Directions:

- Coat the vegetables with the rest of the ingredients in a bowl. Transfer to the air fryer basket.

- Press "Power Button" turn the dial to select "air fry".

- Push "Temp" to set the temperature at 400°F.

- Press "Timer" to set the cooking time to 10 minutes. Cook making sure the green beans achieve a light brown color.

- Serve hot.

786. Black Bean and Tomato Chili

Preparation Time: 15 minutes
Cooking Time: 23 minutes
Servings: 6

Ingredients:

- 1 tablespoon olive oil
- 1 medium onion, diced
- 3 garlic cloves, minced
- 1 cup vegetable broth
- 3 cans black beans, drained and rinsed
- 2 cans diced tomatoes
- 2 chipotle peppers, chopped
- 2 teaspoons cumin
- 2 teaspoons chili powder
- 1 teaspoon dried oregano
- ½ teaspoon salt

Directions:

- Over a medium heat, fry the garlic and onions in the olive oil for 3 minutes.

- Add the remaining ingredients, stirring constantly and scraping the bottom to prevent sticking.

- Take a dish and place the mixture inside. Put a sheet of aluminum foil on top.
- Press "Power Button" turn the dial to select "bake".
- Push "Temp" to set the temperature at 400°F.
- Press "Timer" to set the cooking time to 20 minutes.
- When ready, plate up and serve immediately.

787. Potatoes with Zucchinis

Preparation Time: 10 minutes
Cooking Time: 45 minutes
Servings: 4

Ingredients:

- 2 potatoes, peeled and cubed
- 4 carrots, cut into chunks
- 1 head broccoli, cut into florets
- 4 zucchinis, sliced thickly
- Salt and ground black pepper, to taste
- ¼ cup olive oil
- 1 tablespoon dry onion powder

Directions:

- In a baking dish, add all the ingredients and combine well.
- Press "Power Button" turn the dial to select "bake".
- Push "Temp" to set the temperature at 400°F.
- Press "Timer" to set the cooking time to 45 minutes. Cook ensuring the vegetables are soft and the sides have browned before serving.

788. Cauliflower Faux Rice

Preparation Time: 15 minutes
Cooking Time: 40 minutes
Servings: 8

Ingredients:

- 1 large head cauliflower, rinsed and drained, cut into florets
- ½ lemon, juiced

- 2 garlic cloves, minced
- 2 (8-ounce / 227-g) cans mushrooms
- 1 (8-ounce / 227-g) can water chestnuts
- ¾ cup peas
- 1 egg, beaten
- 4 tablespoons soy sauce
- 1 tablespoon peanut oil
- 1 tablespoon sesame oil
- 1 tablespoon minced fresh ginger
- Cooking spray

Directions:

- Mix the peanut oil, soy sauce, sesame oil, minced ginger, lemon juice, and minced garlic to combine well.
- In a food processor, pulse the florets in small batches to break them down to resemble rice grains. Drain the chestnuts and roughly chop them. Pour into the basket.
- Press "Power Button" turn the dial to select "air fry".
- Push "Temp" to set the temperature at 350°F.
- Press "Timer" to set the cooking time to 20 minutes. Add the mushrooms and the peas to the air fryer oven and continue to air fry for another 15 minutes.
- Lightly spritz a frying pan with cooking spray. Prepare an omelet with the beaten egg, ensuring it is firm. Lay on a cutting board and slice it up. When the cauliflower is ready, throw in the omelet and select Bake, and cook for an additional 5 minutes. Serve hot.

789. Spicy Cauliflower Roast

Preparation Time: 15 minutes
Cooking Time: 20 minutes
Servings: 4

Ingredients:

Cauliflower:

- 5 cups cauliflower florets
- 3 tablespoons vegetable oil
- ½ teaspoon ground cumin
- ½ teaspoon ground coriander

- ♦ ½ teaspoon kosher salt

Sauce:

- ♦ ½ cup Greek yogurt or sour cream
- ♦ ¼ cup chopped fresh cilantro
- ♦ 1 jalapeño, coarsely chopped
- ♦ 4 cloves garlic, peeled
- ♦ ½ teaspoon kosher salt
- ♦ 2 tablespoons water

Directions:

- ▪ In a large bowl, combine the cauliflower, oil, cumin, coriander, and salt. Toss to coat.
- ▪ Press "Power Button" turn the dial to select "broil".
- ▪ Push "Temp" to set the temperature at 400°F.
- ▪ Press "Timer" to set the cooking time to 20 minutes.
- ▪ Put the cauliflower in the air fryer basket. Cook for 20 minutes, stirring halfway through the cooking time.
- ▪ Meanwhile, in a blender, combine the yogurt, cilantro, jalapeño, garlic, and salt. Blend, adding the water as needed to keep the blades moving and to thin the sauce.
- ▪ At the end of cooking time, transfer the cauliflower to a large serving bowl. Pour the sauce over and toss gently to coat. Serve immediately.

790. Mediterranean Air Fried Veggies

Preparation Time: 10 minutes
Cooking Time: 6 minutes
Servings: 4

Ingredients:

- ♦ 1 large zucchini, sliced
- ♦ 1 cup cherry tomatoes, halved
- ♦ 1 parsnip, sliced
- ♦ 1 green pepper, sliced
- ♦ 1 carrot, sliced
- ♦ 1 teaspoon mixed herbs
- ♦ 1 teaspoon mustard
- ♦ 1 teaspoon garlic purée
- ♦ 6 tablespoons olive oil

- ♦ Salt and ground black pepper, to taste

Directions:

- ▪ Preheat the air fryer oven to 400°F (204°C).
- ▪ Combine all the ingredients in a bowl, making sure to coat the vegetables well.
- ▪ Press "Power Button" turn the dial to select "air fry".
- ▪ Push "Temp" to set the temperature at 400°F.
- ▪ Press "Timer" to set the cooking time to 6 minutes and air fry, ensuring the vegetables are tender and browned.
- ▪ Serve immediately.

791. Cayenne Tahini Kale

Preparation Time: 5 minutes
Cooking Time: 15 minutes
Servings: 3

Ingredients:

Dressing:

- ♦ ¼ cup tahini
- ♦ ¼ cup fresh lemon juice
- ♦ 2 tablespoons olive oil
- ♦ 1 teaspoon sesame seeds
- ♦ ½ teaspoon garlic powder
- ♦ ¼ teaspoon cayenne pepper

Kale:

- ♦ 4 cups packed torn kale leaves
- ♦ Kosher salt
- ♦ Black pepper, freshly ground

Directions:

- ▪ Make the dressing: Whisk together the tahini, lemon juice, olive oil, sesame seeds, cayenne pepper and garlic powder in a large bowl until well mixed.
- ▪ Add the kale and massage the dressing thoroughly all over the leaves. Sprinkle the salt and pepper to season.
- ▪ Press "Power Button" turn the dial to select "air fry".

- Push "Temp" to set the temperature at 350°F.
- Press "Timer" to set the cooking time to 15 minutes.
- Place the kale in the air fryer basket in a single layer and air fry until the leaves are slightly wilted and crispy.
- Remove from the basket and serve on a plate.

792. Cauliflower, Chickpea, and Avocado Mash

Preparation Time: 10 minutes
Cooking Time: 25 minutes
Servings: 4

Ingredients:

- 1 medium head cauliflower, cut into florets
- 1 can chickpeas, drained and rinsed
- 1 tablespoon extra-virgin olive oil
- 2 tablespoons lemon juice
- Salt and ground black pepper, to taste
- 4 flatbreads, toasted
- 2 ripe avocados, mashed

Directions:

- In a bowl, mix the chickpeas, cauliflower, lemon juice and olive oil. Sprinkle salt and pepper as desired.
- Put inside the air fryer basket.
- Press "Power Button" turn the dial to select "air fry".
- Push "Temp" to set the temperature at 425°F.
- Press "Timer" to set the cooking time to 25 minutes.
- Spread on top of the flatbread along with the mashed avocado. Sprinkle with more pepper and salt and serve.

CASSEROLES, FRITTATA AND QUICHE

793. Cheesy Chicken Divan

Preparation Time: 5 minutes
Cooking Time: 2 minutes
Servings: 4

Ingredients:

- 4 chicken breasts
- Salt and ground black pepper, to taste
- 1 head broccoli, cut into florets
- 1/2 cup cream of mushroom soup
- 1 cup shredded Cheddar cheese
- 1/2 cup croutons
- Cooking spray

Directions:

- Spritz the air fry basket with cooking spray.
- Put the chicken breasts in the air fry basket and sprinkle with salt and ground black pepper.
- Place the basket on the air fry position.
- Select Air Fry. Set temperature to 390°F (199°C) and set time to 14 minutes. Flip the breasts halfway through the cooking time.
- When cooking is complete, the breasts should be well browned and tender.
- Remove the breasts from the air fryer grill and allow to cool for a few minutes on a plate, then cut the breasts into bite-size pieces.
- Combine the chicken, broccoli, mushroom soup, and Cheddar cheese in a large bowl. Stir to mix well.
- Spritz a baking pan with cooking spray. Pour the chicken mixture into the pan. Spread the croutons over the mixture.
- Place the pan on the bake position.
- Select Bake. Set time to 10 minutes.

- When cooking is complete, the croutons should be lightly browned and the mixture should be set.
- Remove the baking pan from the air fryer grill and serve immediately.

794. Cheesy-Creamy Broccoli Casserole

Preparation Time: 5 minutes
Cooking Time: 30 minutes
Servings: 4

Ingredients:

- 4 cups broccoli florets
- ¼ cup heavy whipping cream
- 1/2 cup sharp Cheddar cheese, shredded
- ¼ cup ranch dressing
- Kosher salt and ground black pepper, to taste

Directions:

- Combine all the ingredients in a large bowl. Toss to coat well broccoli well.
- Pour the mixture into a baking pan.
- Place the pan on the bake position.
- Select Bake, set temperature to 375°F (190°C) and set time to 30 minutes.
- When cooking is complete, the broccoli should be tender.
- Remove the baking pan from the air fryer grill and serve immediately.

795. Cheesy Chorizo, Corn, and Potato Frittata

Preparation Time: 8 minutes
Cooking Time: 12 minutes
Servings: 4

Ingredients:

- 2 tablespoons olive oil
- 1 chorizo, sliced
- 4 eggs
- 1/2 cup corn
- 1 large potato, boiled and cubed
- 1 tablespoon chopped parsley
- 1/2 cup feta cheese, crumbled

- Salt and ground black pepper, to taste

Directions:

- Heat the olive oil in a nonstick skillet over medium heat until shimmering.

- Add the chorizo and cook for 4 minutes or until golden brown.

- Whisk the eggs in a bowl, then sprinkle with salt and ground black pepper.

- Mix the remaining ingredients in the egg mixture, then pour the chorizo and its fat into a baking pan. Pour in the egg mixture.

- Place the pan on the bake position.

- Select Bake, set temperature to 330°F (166°C) and set time to 8 minutes. Stir the mixture halfway through.

- When cooking is complete, the eggs should be set.

- Serve immediately.

796. Taco Beef and Green Chile Casserole

Preparation Time: 10 minutes
Cooking Time: 15 minutes
Servings: 4

Ingredients:

- 1 pound (454 g) 85% lean ground beef
- 1 tablespoon taco seasoning
- 1 (7-ounce / 198-g) can diced mild green chiles
- 1/2 cup milk
- 2 large eggs
- 1 cup shredded Mexican cheese blend
- 2 tablespoons all-purpose flour
- 1/2 teaspoon kosher salt
- Cooking spray

Directions:

- Spritz a baking pan with cooking spray.

- Toss the ground beef with taco seasoning in a large bowl to mix well. Pour the seasoned ground beef in the prepared baking pan.

- Combing the remaining ingredients in a medium bowl. Whisk to mix well, then pour the mixture over the ground beef.

- Place the pan on the bake position.

- Select Bake, set temperature to 350°F (180°C) and set time to 15 minutes.

- When cooking is complete, a toothpick inserted in the center should come out clean.

- Remove the casserole from the air fryer grill and allow to cool for 5 minutes, then slice to serve.

797. Golden Asparagus Frittata

Preparation Time: 5 minutes
Cooking Time: 25 minutes
Servings: 4

Ingredients:

- 1 cup asparagus spears, cut into 1-inch pieces
- 1 teaspoon vegetable oil
- 1 tablespoon milk
- 6 eggs, beaten
- 2 ounces (57 g) goat cheese, crumbled
- 1 tablespoon minced chives, optional
- Kosher salt and pepper, to taste

Directions:

- Add the asparagus spears to a small bowl and drizzle with the vegetable oil. Toss until well coated and transfer to the air fry basket.

- Place the basket on the air fry position.

- Select Air Fry. Set temperature to 400°F (205°C) and set time to 5 minutes. Flip the asparagus halfway through.

- When cooking is complete, the asparagus should be tender and slightly wilted.

- Remove the asparagus from the air fryer grill to a baking pan.

- Stir together the milk and eggs in a medium bowl. Pour the mixture over the asparagus in the pan. Sprinkle with the goat cheese and the chives (if using) over the eggs. Season with salt and pepper.

- Place the pan on the bake position.

- Select Bake, set temperature to 320°F (160°C) and set time to 20 minutes.

- When cooking is complete, the top should be golden and the eggs should be set.

- Transfer to a serving dish. Slice and serve.

798. Corn and Bell Pepper Casserole

Preparation Time: 10 minutes
Cooking Time: 20 minutes
Servings: 4

Ingredients:

- 1 cup corn kernels
- ¼ cup bell pepper, finely chopped
- 1/2 cup low-fat milk
- 1 large egg, beaten
- 1/2 cup yellow cornmeal
- 1/2 cup all-purpose flour
- 1/2 teaspoon baking powder
- 2 tablespoons melted unsalted butter
- 1 tablespoon granulated sugar
- Pinch of cayenne pepper
- ¼ teaspoon kosher salt
- Cooking spray

Directions:

- Spritz a baking pan with cooking spray.
- Combine all the ingredients in a large bowl. Stir to mix well. Pour the mixture into the baking pan.
- Place the pan on the bake position.
- Select Bake, set temperature to 330ºF (166ºC) and set time to 20 minutes.
- When cooking is complete, the casserole should be lightly browned and set.
- Remove the baking pan from the air fryer grill and serve immediately.

799. Creamy-Mustard Pork Gratin

Preparation Time: 15 minutes
Cooking Time: 21 minutes
Servings: 4

Ingredients:

- 2 tablespoons olive oil
- 2 pounds (907 g) pork tenderloin, cut into serving-size pieces
- 1 teaspoon dried marjoram
- ¼ teaspoon chili powder
- 1 teaspoon coarse sea salt
- 1/2 teaspoon freshly ground black pepper
- 1 cup Ricotta cheese
- 11/2 cups chicken broth
- 1 tablespoon mustard
- Cooking spray

Directions:

- Spritz a baking pan with cooking spray.
- Heat the olive oil in a nonstick skillet over medium-high heat until shimmering.
- Add the pork and sauté for 6 minutes or until lightly browned.
- Transfer the pork to the prepared baking pan and sprinkle with marjoram, salt, chili powder, and ground black pepper.
- Combine the remaining ingredients in a large bowl. Stir to mix well. Pour the mixture over the pork in the pan.
- Place the pan on the bake position.
- Select Bake, set temperature to 350ºF (180ºC) and set time to 15 minutes. Stir the mixture halfway through.
- When cooking is complete, the mixture should be frothy and the cheese should be melted.
- Serve immediately.

800. Broccoli, Carrot, and Tomato Quiche

Preparation Time: 6 minutes
Cooking Time: 14 minutes
Servings: 4

Ingredients:

- 4 eggs
- 1 teaspoon dried thyme
- 1 cup whole milk
- 1 steamed carrots, diced
- 2 cups steamed broccoli florets
- 2 medium tomatoes, diced
- ¼ cup crumbled feta cheese
- 1 cup grated Cheddar cheese
- 1 teaspoon chopped parsley
- Salt and ground black pepper, to taste

- Cooking spray

Directions:

- Spritz a baking pan with cooking spray.

- Whisk together the eggs, salt, thyme, and ground black pepper in a bowl and fold in the milk while mixing.

- Put the broccoli, carrots, and tomatoes in the prepared baking pan, then spread with 1/2 cup Cheddar cheese and feta cheese. Pour the egg mixture over, then scatter with remaining Cheddar on top.

- Place the pan on the bake position.

- Select Bake, set temperature to 350°F (180°C) and set time to 14 minutes.

- When cooking is complete, the egg should be set and the quiche should be puffed.

- Remove the quiche from the air fryer grill and top with chopped parsley, then slice to serve.

801. Herbed Cheddar Cheese Frittata

Preparation Time: 10 minutes
Cooking Time: 20 minutes
Servings: 4

Ingredients:

- 1/2 cup shredded Cheddar cheese
- 1/2 cup half-and-half
- 4 large eggs
- 2 tablespoons chopped scallion greens
- 2 tablespoons chopped fresh parsley
- 1/2 teaspoon kosher salt
- 1/2 teaspoon ground black pepper
- Cooking spray

Directions:

- Spritz a baking pan with cooking spray.

- Whisk together all the ingredients in a large bowl, then pour the mixture into the prepared baking pan.

- Place the pan on the bake position.

- Select Bake, set temperature to 300°F (150°C) and set time to 20 minutes. Stir the mixture halfway through.

- When cooking is complete, the eggs should be set.

- Serve immediately.

802. Cauliflower, Okra, and Pepper Casserole

Preparation Time: 8 minutes
Cooking Time: 12 minutes
Servings: 4

Ingredients:

- 1 head cauliflower, cut into florets
- 1 cup okra, chopped
- 1 yellow bell pepper, chopped
- 2 eggs, beaten
- 1/2 cup chopped onion
- 1 tablespoon soy sauce
- 2 tablespoons olive oil
- Salt and ground black pepper, to taste

Directions:

- Spritz a baking pan with cooking spray.

- Put the cauliflower in a food processor and pulse to rice the cauliflower.

- Pour the cauliflower rice in the baking pan and add the remaining ingredients. Stir to mix well.

- Place the pan on the bake position.

- Select Bake, set temperature to 380°F (193°C) and set time to 12 minutes.

- When cooking is complete, the eggs should be set.

- Remove the baking pan from the air fryer grill and serve immediately.

-

803. Sumptuous Chicken and Vegetable Casserole

Preparation Time: 15 minutes
Cooking Time: 15 minutes
Servings: 4

Ingredients:

- ♦ 4 boneless and skinless chicken breasts, cut into cubes
- ♦ 2 carrots, sliced
- ♦ 1 yellow bell pepper, cut into strips
- ♦ 1 red bell pepper, cut into strips
- ♦ 15 ounces (425 g) broccoli florets
- ♦ 1 cup snow peas
- ♦ 1 scallion, sliced
- ♦ Cooking spray
- ♦ Sauce:
- ♦ 1 teaspoon Sriracha
- ♦ 3 tablespoons soy sauce
- ♦ 2 tablespoons oyster sauce
- ♦ 1 tablespoon rice wine vinegar
- ♦ 1 teaspoon cornstarch
- ♦ 1 tablespoon grated ginger
- ♦ 2 garlic cloves, minced
- ♦ 1 teaspoon sesame oil
- ♦ 1 tablespoon brown sugar

Directions:

- ▪ Spritz a baking pan with cooking spray.
- ▪ Combine the chicken, bell peppers, and carrot in a large bowl. Stir to mix well.
- ▪ Combine the ingredients for the sauce in a separate bowl. Stir to mix well.
- ▪ Pour the chicken mixture into the baking pan, then pour the sauce over. Stir to coat well.
- ▪ Place the pan on the bake position.
- ▪ Select Bake, set temperature to 370ºF (188ºC) and set time to 13 minutes. Add the broccoli and snow peas to the pan halfway through.
- ▪ When cooking is complete, the vegetables should be tender.
- ▪ Remove the pan from the air fryer grill and sprinkle with sliced scallion before serving.

804. Easy Chickpea and Spinach Casserole

Preparation Time: 10 minutes
Cooking Time: 22 minutes
Servings: 4

Ingredients:

- ♦ 2 tablespoons olive oil
- ♦ 2 garlic cloves, minced
- ♦ 1 tablespoon ginger, minced
- ♦ 1 onion, chopped
- ♦ 1 chili pepper, minced
- ♦ Salt and ground black pepper, to taste
- ♦ 1 pound (454 g) spinach
- ♦ 1 can coconut milk
- ♦ 1/2 cup dried tomatoes, chopped
- ♦ 1 (14-ounce / 397-g) can chickpeas, drained

Directions:

- ▪ Heat the olive oil in a saucepan over medium heat. Sauté the ginger and garlic in the olive oil for 1 minute, or until fragrant.
- ▪ Add the chili pepper, onion, salt and pepper to the saucepan. Sauté for 3 minutes.
- ▪ Mix in the spinach and sauté for 3 to 4 minutes or until the vegetables become soft. Remove from heat.
- ▪ Pour the vegetable mixture into a baking pan. Stir in chickpeas, dried tomatoes and coconut milk until well blended.
- ▪ Place the pan on the bake position.
- ▪ Select Bake, set temperature to 370ºF (188ºC) and set time to 15 minutes.
- ▪ When cooking is complete, transfer the casserole to a serving dish. Let cool for 5 minutes before serving.

805. Classic Mediterranean Quiche

Preparation Time: 10 minutes
Cooking Time: 30 minutes
Servings: 4

Ingredients:

- ♦ 4 eggs
- ♦ ¼ cup chopped Kalamata olives
- ♦ 1/2 cup chopped tomatoes
- ♦ ¼ cup chopped onion
- ♦ 1/2 cup milk
- ♦ 1 cup crumbled feta cheese
- ♦ 1/2 tablespoon chopped oregano

- 1/2 tablespoon chopped basil
- Salt and ground black pepper, to taste
- Cooking spray

Directions:

- Spritz a baking pan with cooking spray.
- Whisk the eggs with remaining ingredients in a large bowl. Stir to mix well.
- Pour the mixture into the prepared baking pan.
- Place the pan on the bake position.
- Select Bake, set temperature to 340°F (171°C) and set time to 30 minutes.
- When cooking is complete, the eggs should be set and a toothpick inserted in the center should come out clean.
- Serve immediately.

806. Cheesy Mushrooms and Spinach Frittata

Preparation Time: 7 minutes
Cooking Time: 8 minutes
Servings: 2

Ingredients:

- 1 cup chopped mushrooms
- 2 cups spinach, chopped
- 4 eggs, lightly beaten
- 3 ounces (85 g) feta cheese, crumbled
- 2 tablespoons heavy cream
- A handful of fresh parsley, chopped
- Salt and ground black pepper, to taste
- Cooking spray

Directions:

- Spritz a baking pan with cooking spray.
- Whisk together all the ingredients in a large bowl. Stir to mix well.
- Pour the mixture in the prepared baking pan.
- Place the pan on the bake position.
- Select Bake, set temperature to 350°F (180°C) and set time to 8 minutes. Stir the mixture halfway through.

- When cooking is complete, the eggs should be set.
- Serve immediately.

WRAPS AND SANDWICHES

807.　Crunchy Chicken Egg Rolls

Preparation Time: 10 minutes
Cooking Time: 24 minutes
Servings: 4

Ingredients:

- 1 pound (454 g) ground chicken
- 2 teaspoons olive oil
- 2 garlic cloves, minced
- 1 teaspoon grated fresh ginger
- 2 cups white cabbage, shredded
- 1 onion, chopped
- ¼ cup soy sauce
- 8 egg roll wrappers
- 1 egg, beaten
- Cooking spray

Directions:

- Spritz the air fry basket with cooking spray.

- Heat olive oil in a saucepan over medium heat. Sauté the garlic and ginger in the olive oil for 1 minute, or until fragrant. Add the ground chicken to the saucepan. Sauté for 5 minutes, or until the chicken is cooked through. Add the cabbage, onion and soy sauce and sauté for 5 to 6 minutes, or until the vegetables become soft. Remove the saucepan from the heat.

- Unfold the egg roll wrappers on a clean work surface. Divide the chicken mixture among the wrappers and brush the edges of the wrappers with the beaten egg. Tightly roll up the egg rolls, enclosing the filling. Arrange the rolls in the basket.

- Place the basket on the air fry position.

- Select Air Fry, set temperature to 370°F (188°C) and set time to 12 minutes. Flip the rolls halfway through the cooking time.

- When cooked, the rolls will be crispy and golden brown.

- Transfer to a platter and let cool for 5 minutes before serving.

808.　Panko-Crusted Avocado and Slaw Tacos

Preparation Time: 15 minutes
Cooking Time: 6 minutes
Servings: 4

Ingredients:

- ¼ cup all-purpose flour
- ¼ teaspoon salt, plus more as needed
- ¼ teaspoon ground black pepper
- 2 large egg whites
- 1¼ cups panko bread crumbs
- 2 tablespoons olive oil
- 2 avocados, peeled and halved, cut into 1/2-inch-thick slices
- 1/2 small red cabbage, thinly sliced
- 1 deseeded jalapeño, thinly sliced
- 2 green onions, thinly sliced
- 1/2 cup cilantro leaves
- ¼ cup mayonnaise
- Juice and zest of 1 lime
- 4 corn tortillas, warmed
- 1/2 cup sour cream
- Cooking spray

Directions:

- Spritz the air fry basket with cooking spray.

- Pour the flour in a large bowl and sprinkle with salt and black pepper, then stir to mix well.

- Whisk the egg whites in a separate bowl. Combine the panko with olive oil on a shallow dish.

- Dredge the avocado slices in the bowl of flour, then into the egg to coat. Shake the excess off, then roll the slices over the panko.

- Arrange the avocado slices in a single layer in the basket and spritz the cooking spray.

- Place the basket on the air fry position.

- Select Air Fry, set temperature to 400°F (205°C) and set time to 6 minutes. Flip the slices halfway through with tongs.

- When cooking is complete, the avocado slices should be tender and lightly browned.

- Combine the cabbage, onions, jalapeño, cilantro leaves, lime juice, mayo, and zest, and a touch of salt in a separate large bowl. Toss to mix well.

- Unfold the tortillas on a clean work surface, then spread with cabbage slaw and air fried avocados. Top with sour cream and serve.

809. Golden Cabbage and Mushroom Spring Rolls

Preparation Time: 20 minutes
Cooking Time: 14 minutes
Servings: 14

Ingredients:

- 2 tablespoons vegetable oil
- 4 cups sliced Napa cabbage
- 5 ounces (142 g) shiitake mushrooms, diced
- 3 carrots, cut into thin matchsticks
- 1 tablespoon minced fresh ginger
- 1 tablespoon minced garlic
- 1 bunch scallions, white and light green parts only, sliced
- 2 tablespoons soy sauce
- 1 (4-ounce / 113-g) package cellophane noodles
- ¼ teaspoon cornstarch
- 1 (12-ounce / 340-g) package frozen spring roll wrappers, thawed
- Cooking spray

Directions:

- Heat the olive oil in a nonstick skillet over medium-high heat until shimmering.

- Add the cabbage, carrots, and mushrooms and sauté for 3 minutes or until tender.

- Add the garlic, scallions, and ginger and sauté for 1 minutes or until fragrant.

- Mix in the soy sauce and turn off the heat. Discard any liquid remains in the skillet and allow to cool for a few minutes.

- Bring a pot of water to a boil, then turn off the heat and pour in the noodles. Let sit for 10 minutes or until the noodles are al dente.

- Transfer 1 cup of the noodles in the skillet and toss with the cooked vegetables. Reserve the remaining noodles for other use.

- Dissolve the cornstarch in a small dish of water, then place the wrappers on a clean work surface. Dab the edges of the wrappers with cornstarch.

- Scoop up 3 tablespoons of filling in the center of each wrapper, then fold the corner in front of you over the filling. Tuck the wrapper under the filling, then fold the corners on both sides into the center. Keep rolling to seal the wrapper. Repeat with remaining wrappers.

- Spritz the air fry basket with cooking spray. Arrange the wrappers in the basket and spritz with cooking spray.

- Place the basket on the air fry position.

- Select Air Fry, set temperature to 400°F (205°C) and set time to 10 minutes. Flip the wrappers halfway through the cooking time.

- When cooking is complete, the wrappers will be golden brown.

- Serve immediately.

810. Cheesy Philly Steaks

Preparation Time: 20 minutes
Cooking Time: 20 minutes
Servings: 2

Ingredients:

- 12 ounces (340 g) boneless rib-eye steak, sliced thinly
- 1/2 teaspoon Worcestershire sauce
- 1/2 teaspoon soy sauce
- Kosher salt and ground black pepper, to taste
- 1/2 green bell pepper, stemmed, deseeded, and thinly sliced
- 1/2 small onion, halved and thinly sliced
- 1 tablespoon vegetable oil
- 2 soft hoagie rolls, split three-fourths of the way through
- 1 tablespoon butter, softened
- 2 slices provolone cheese, halved

Directions:

- Combine the steak, soy sauce, salt, ground black pepper, and Worcestershire sauce in a large bowl. Toss to coat well. Set aside.
- Combine the bell pepper, onion, vegetable oil, salt, and ground black pepper in a separate bowl. Toss to coat the vegetables well.
- Pour the steak and vegetables in the air fry basket.
- Place the basket on the air fry position.
- Select Air Fry, set temperature to 400°F (205°C) and set time to 15 minutes.
- When cooked, the steak will be browned and vegetables will be tender. Transfer them on a plate. Set aside.
- Brush the hoagie rolls with butter and place in the basket.
- Select Toast and set time to 3 minutes. Place the basket on the toast position. When done, the rolls should be lightly browned.
- Transfer the rolls to a clean work surface and divide the steak and vegetable mix in between the rolls. Spread with cheese. Place the stuffed rolls back in the basket.
- Place the basket on the air fry position.
- Select Air Fry and set time to 2 minutes. When done, the cheese should be melted.
- Serve immediately.

811. Cheesy Chicken Wraps

Preparation Time: 30 minutes
Cooking Time: 5 minutes
Servings: 12

Ingredients:

- 2 large-sized chicken breasts, cooked and shredded
- 2 spring onions, chopped
- 10 ounces (284 g) Ricotta cheese
- 1 tablespoon rice vinegar
- 1 tablespoon molasses
- 1 teaspoon grated fresh ginger
- ¼ cup soy sauce
- 1/3 teaspoon sea salt

- ¼ teaspoon ground black pepper, or more to taste
- 48 wonton wrappers
- Cooking spray

Directions:

- Spritz the air fry basket with cooking spray.
- Combine all the ingredients, except for the wrappers in a large bowl. Toss to mix well.
- Unfold the wrappers on a clean work surface, then divide and spoon the mixture in the middle of the wrappers.
- Dab a little water on the edges of the wrappers, then fold the edge close to you over the filling. Tuck the edge under the filling and roll up to seal.
- Arrange the wraps in the basket.
- Place the basket on the air fry position.
- Select Air Fry, set temperature to 375°F (190°C) and set time to 5 minutes. Flip the wraps halfway through the cooking time.
- When cooking is complete, the wraps should be lightly browned.
- Serve immediately.

812. Golden Avocado and Tomato Egg Rolls

Preparation Time: 10 minutes
Cooking Time: 5 minutes
Servings: 5

Ingredients:

- 10 egg roll wrappers
- 3 avocados, peeled and pitted
- 1 tomato, diced
- Salt and ground black pepper, to taste
- Cooking spray

Directions:

- Spritz the air fry basket with cooking spray.
- Put the avocados and tomato in a food processor. Sprinkle with salt and ground black pepper. Pulse to mix and coarsely mash until smooth.

- Unfold the wrappers on a clean work surface, then divide the mixture in the center of each wrapper. Roll the wrapper up and press to seal.
- Transfer the rolls to the basket and spritz with cooking spray.
- Place the basket on the air fry position.
- Select Air Fry, set temperature to 350°F (180°C) and set time to 5 minutes. Flip the rolls halfway through the cooking time.
- When cooked, the rolls should be golden brown.
- Serve immediately.

813.　Korean Beef and Onion Tacos

Preparation Time: 1 hour 15 minutes
Cooking Time: 12 minutes
Servings: 6

Ingredients:

- 2 tablespoons gochujang
- 1 tablespoon soy sauce
- 2 tablespoons sesame seeds
- 2 teaspoons minced fresh ginger
- 2 cloves garlic, minced
- 2 tablespoons toasted sesame oil
- 2 teaspoons sugar
- 1/2 teaspoon kosher salt
- 11/2 pounds (680 g) thinly sliced beef chuck
- 1 medium red onion, sliced
- 6 corn tortillas, warmed
- ¼ cup chopped fresh cilantro
- 1/2 cup kimchi
- 1/2 cup chopped green onions

Directions:

- Combine the ginger, garlic, gochujang, sesame seeds, soy sauce, sesame oil, salt, and sugar in a large bowl. Stir to mix well.
- Dunk the beef chunk in the large bowl. Press to submerge, then wrap the bowl in plastic and refrigerate to marinate for at least 1 hour.
- Remove the beef chunk from the marinade and transfer to the air fry basket. Add the onion to the basket.

- Place the basket on the air fry position.
- Select Air Fry, set temperature to 400°F (205°C) and set time to 12 minutes. Stir the mixture halfway through the cooking time.
- When cooked, the beef will be well browned.
- Unfold the tortillas on a clean work surface, then divide the fried beef and onion on the tortillas. Spread the green onions, kimchi, and cilantro on top.
1. Serve immediately.

814.　Crispy Pea and Potato Samosas

Preparation Time: 30 minutes
Cooking Time: 22 minutes
Servings: 16

Ingredients:

Dough:

- 4 cups all-purpose flour, plus more for flouring the work surface
- ¼ cup plain yogurt
- 1/2 cup cold unsalted butter, cut into cubes
- 2 teaspoons kosher salt
- 1 cup ice water

Filling:

- 2 tablespoons vegetable oil
- 1 onion, diced
- 11/2 teaspoons coriander
- 11/2 teaspoons cumin
- 1 clove garlic, minced
- 1 teaspoon turmeric
- 1 teaspoon kosher salt
- 1/2 cup peas, thawed if frozen
- 2 cups mashed potatoes
- 2 tablespoons yogurt
- Cooking spray

Chutney:

- 1 cup mint leaves, lightly packed
- 2 cups cilantro leaves, lightly packed
- 1 green chile pepper, deseeded and minced
- 1/2 cup minced onion
- Juice of 1 lime
- 1 teaspoon granulated sugar
- 1 teaspoon kosher salt

♦ 2 tablespoons vegetable oil

Directions:

- Put the flour, butter, salt, and yogurt in a food processor. Pulse to combine until grainy. Pour in the water and pulse until a smooth and firm dough forms.

- Transfer the dough on a clean and lightly floured working surface. Knead the dough and shape it into a ball. Cut in half and flatten the halves into 2 discs. Wrap them in plastic and let sit in refrigerator until ready to use.

- Meanwhile, make the filling: Heat the vegetable oil in a saucepan over medium heat.

- Add the onion and sauté for 5 minutes or until lightly browned.

- Add the coriander, garlic, cumin, salt, and turmeric and sauté for 2 minutes or until fragrant.

- Add the potatoes, peas, and yogurt and stir to combine well. Turn off the heat and allow to cool.

- Meanwhile, combine the ingredients for the chutney in a food processor. Pulse to mix well until glossy. Pour the chutney in a bowl and refrigerate until ready to use.

- Make the samosas: Remove the dough discs from the refrigerator and cut each disc into 8 parts. Shape each part into a ball, then roll the ball into a 6-inch circle. Cut the circle in half and roll each half into a cone.

- Scoop up 2 tablespoons of the filling into the cone, press the edges of the cone to seal and form into a triangle. Repeat with remaining dough and filling.

- Spritz the air fry basket with cooking spray. Arrange the samosas in the basket and spritz with cooking spray.

- Place the basket on the air fry position.

- Select Air Fry, set temperature to 360°F (182°C) and set time to 15 minutes. Flip the samosas halfway through the cooking time.

- When cooked, the samosas will be golden brown and crispy.

- Serve the samosas with the chutney.

815. Cheesy Sweet Potato and Bean Burritos

Preparation Time: 15 minutes
Cooking Time: 30 minutes
Servings: 6

Ingredients:

♦ 2 sweet potatoes, peeled and cut into a small dice
♦ 1 tablespoon vegetable oil
♦ Kosher salt and ground black pepper, to taste
♦ 6 large flour tortillas
♦ 1 (16-ounce / 454-g) can refried black beans, divided
♦ 1 1/2 cups baby spinach, divided
♦ 6 eggs, scrambled
♦ ¾ cup grated Cheddar cheese, divided
♦ ¼ cup salsa
♦ ¼ cup sour cream
♦ Cooking spray

Directions:

- Put the sweet potatoes in a large bowl, then drizzle with vegetable oil and sprinkle with salt and black pepper. Toss to coat well.

- Place the potatoes in the air fry basket.

- Place the basket on the air fry position.

- Select Air Fry, set temperature to 400°F (205°C) and set time to 10 minutes. Flip the potatoes halfway through the cooking time.

- When done, the potatoes should be lightly browned. Remove the potatoes from the air fryer grill.

- Unfold the tortillas on a clean work surface. Divide the air fried sweet potatoes, black beans, spinach, scrambled eggs, and cheese on top of the tortillas.

- Fold the long side of the tortillas over the filling, then fold in the shorter side to wrap the filling to make the burritos.

- Wrap the burritos in the aluminum foil and put in the basket.

- Place the basket on the air fry position.

- Select Air Fry, set temperature to 350°F (180°C) and set time to 20 minutes. Flip the burritos halfway through the cooking time.
- Remove the burritos from the air fryer grill and spread with sour cream and salsa. Serve immediately.

816. Golden Chicken and Yogurt Taquitos

Preparation Time: 15 minutes
Cooking Time: 12 minutes
Servings: 4

Ingredients:

- 1 cup cooked chicken, shredded
- ¼ cup Greek yogurt
- ¼ cup salsa
- 1 cup shredded Mozzarella cheese
- Salt and ground black pepper, to taste
- 4 flour tortillas
- Cooking spray

Directions:

- Spritz the air fry basket with cooking spray.
- Combine all the ingredients, except for the tortillas, in a large bowl. Stir to mix well.
- Make the taquitos: Unfold the tortillas on a clean work surface, then scoop up 2 tablespoons of the chicken mixture in the middle of each tortilla. Roll the tortillas up to wrap the filling.
- Arrange the taquitos in the basket and spritz with cooking spray.
- Place the basket on the air fry position.
- Select Air Fry, set temperature to 380°F (193°C) and set time to 12 minutes. Flip the taquitos halfway through the cooking time.
- When cooked, the taquitos should be golden brown and the cheese should be melted.
- Serve immediately.

Protein 10.8g

817. Crunchy Shrimp and Zucchini Potstickers

Preparation Time: 35 minutes

Cooking Time: 5 minutes
Servings: 10

Ingredients:

- 1/2 pound (227 g) peeled and deveined shrimp, finely chopped
- 1 medium zucchini, coarsely grated
- 1 tablespoon fish sauce
- 1 tablespoon green curry paste
- 2 scallions, thinly sliced
- ¼ cup basil, chopped
- 30 round dumpling wrappers
- Cooking spray

Directions:

- Combine the zucchini, chopped shrimp, curry paste, fish sauce, basil, and scallions in a large bowl. Stir to mix well.
- Unfold the dumpling wrappers on a clean work surface, dab a little water around the edges of each wrapper, then scoop up 1 teaspoon of filling in the middle of each wrapper.
- Make the potstickers: Fold the wrappers in half and press the edges to seal.
- Spritz the air fry basket with cooking spray.
- Transfer the potstickers to the basket and spritz with cooking spray.
- Place the basket on the air fry position.
- Select Air Fry, set temperature to 350°F (180°C) and set time to 5 minutes. Flip the potstickers halfway through the cooking time.
- When cooking is complete, the potstickers should be crunchy and lightly browned.
- Serve immediately.

818. Cod Tacos with Salsa

Preparation Time: 5 minutes
Cooking Time: 15 minutes
Servings: 4

Ingredients:

- 2 eggs
- 1¼ cups Mexican beer

- 11/2 cups coconut flour
- 11/2 cups almond flour
- 1/2 tablespoon chili powder
- 1 tablespoon cumin
- Salt, to taste
- 1 pound (454 g) cod fillet, slice into large pieces
- 4 toasted corn tortillas
- 4 large lettuce leaves, chopped
- ¼ cup salsa
- Cooking spray

Directions:

- Spritz the air fry basket with cooking spray.

- Break the eggs in a bowl, then pour in the beer. Whisk to combine well.

- Combine the almond flour, coconut flour, cumin, chili powder, and salt in a separate bowl. Stir to mix well.

- Dunk the cod pieces in the egg mixture, then shake the excess off and dredge into the flour mixture to coat well. Arrange the cod in the basket.

- Place the basket on the air fry position.

- Select Air Fry, set temperature to 375°F (190°C) and set time to 15 minutes. Flip the cod halfway through the cooking time.

- When cooking is complete, the cod should be golden brown.

- Unwrap the toasted tortillas on a large plate, then divide the cod and lettuce leaves on top. Baste with salsa and wrap to serve.

819.   Golden Spring Rolls

Preparation Time: 10 minutes
Cooking Time: 18 minutes
Servings: 4

Ingredients:

- 4 spring roll wrappers
- 1/2 cup cooked vermicelli noodles
- 1 teaspoon sesame oil
- 1 tablespoon freshly minced ginger
- 1 tablespoon soy sauce
- 1 clove garlic, minced
- 1/2 red bell pepper, deseeded and chopped

- 1/2 cup chopped carrot
- 1/2 cup chopped mushrooms
- ¼ cup chopped scallions
- Cooking spray

Directions:

- Spritz the air fry basket with cooking spray and set aside.

- Heat the sesame oil in a saucepan on medium heat. Sauté the garlic and ginger in the sesame oil for 1 minute, or until fragrant. Add soy sauce, carrot, red bell pepper, mushrooms and scallions. Sauté for 5 minutes or until the vegetables become tender. Mix in vermicelli noodles. Turn off the heat and remove them from the saucepan. Allow to cool for 10 minutes.

- Lay out one spring roll wrapper with a corner pointed toward you. Scoop the noodle mixture on spring roll wrapper and fold corner up over the mixture. Fold left and right corners toward the center and continue to roll to make firmly sealed rolls.

- Arrange the spring rolls in the basket and spritz with cooking spray.

- Place the basket on the air fry position.

- Select Air Fry, set temperature to 340°F (171°C) and set time to 12 minutes. Flip the spring rolls halfway through the cooking time.

- When done, the spring rolls will be golden brown and crispy.

- Serve warm.

820.   Creamy-Cheesy Wontons

Preparation Time: 5 minutes
Cooking Time: 6 minutes
Servings: 4

Ingredients:

- 2 ounces (57 g) cream cheese, softened
- 1 tablespoon sugar
- 16 square wonton wrappers
- Cooking spray

Directions:

- Spritz the air fry basket with cooking spray.

- In a mixing bowl, stir together the sugar and cream cheese until well mixed. Prepare a small bowl of water alongside.

- On a clean work surface, lay the wonton wrappers. Scoop ¼ teaspoon of cream cheese in the center of each wonton wrapper. Dab the water over the wrapper edges. Fold each wonton wrapper diagonally in half over the filling to form a triangle.

- Arrange the wontons in the basket. Spritz the wontons with cooking spray.

- Place the basket on the air fry position.

- Select Air Fry, set temperature to 350°F (180°C) and set time to 6 minutes. Flip the wontons halfway through the cooking time.

- When cooking is complete, the wontons will be golden brown and crispy.

- Divide the wontons among four plates. Let rest for 5 minutes before serving.

821. Golden Chicken Empanadas

Preparation Time: 25 minutes
Cooking Time: 12 minutes
Servings: 12

Ingredients:

- 1 cup boneless, skinless rotisserie chicken breast meat, chopped finely
- ¼ cup salsa verde
- 2/3 cup shredded Cheddar cheese
- 1 teaspoon ground cumin
- 1 teaspoon ground black pepper
- 2 purchased refrigerated pie crusts, from a minimum 14.1-ounce (400 g) box
- 1 large egg
- 2 tablespoons water
- Cooking spray

Directions:

- Spritz the air fry basket with cooking spray. Set aside.

- Combine the chicken meat, Cheddar, salsa verde, cumin, and black pepper in a large bowl. Stir to mix well. Set aside.

- Unfold the pie crusts on a clean work surface, then use a large cookie cutter to cut out 31/2-inch circles as much as possible.

- Roll the remaining crusts to a ball and flatten into a circle which has the same thickness of the original crust. Cut out more 31/2-inch circles until you have 12 circles in total.

- Make the empanadas: Divide the chicken mixture in the middle of each circle, about 11/2 tablespoons each. Dab the edges of the circle with water. Fold the circle in half over the filling to shape like a half-moon and press to seal, or you can press with a fork.

- Whisk the egg with water in a small bowl.

- Arrange the empanadas in the basket and spritz with cooking spray. Brush with whisked egg.

- Place the basket on the air fry position.

- Select Air Fry, set temperature to 350°F (180°C) and set time to 12 minutes. Flip the empanadas halfway through the cooking time.

- When cooking is complete, the empanadas will be golden and crispy.

- Serve immediately.

822. Fast Cheesy Bacon and Egg Wraps

Preparation Time: 15 minutes
Cooking Time: 10 minutes
Servings: 3

Ingredients:

- 3 corn tortillas
- 3 slices bacon, cut into strips
- 2 scrambled eggs
- 3 tablespoons salsa
- 1 cup grated Pepper Jack cheese
- 3 tablespoons cream cheese, divided
- Cooking spray

Directions:

- Spritz the air fry basket with cooking spray.

- Unfold the tortillas on a clean work surface, divide the bacon and eggs in the middle of the tortillas, and then spread with scatter and salsa with cheeses. Fold the tortillas over.

- Arrange the tortillas in the basket.

- Place the basket on the air fry position.

- Select Air Fry, set temperature to 390°F (199°C) and set time to 10 minutes. Flip the tortillas halfway through the cooking time.

- When cooking is complete, the cheeses will be melted and the tortillas will be lightly browned.

- Serve immediately.

823.   Beef and Seeds Burgers

Preparation Time: 15 minutes
Cooking Time: 10 minutes
Servings: 4

Ingredients:

- 1 teaspoon cumin seeds
- 1 teaspoon mustard seeds
- 1 teaspoon coriander seeds
- 1 teaspoon dried minced garlic
- 1 teaspoon dried red pepper flakes
- 1 teaspoon kosher salt
- 2 teaspoons ground black pepper
- 1 pound (454 g) 85% lean ground beef
- 2 tablespoons Worcestershire sauce
- 4 hamburger buns
- Mayonnaise, for serving
- Cooking spray

Directions:

- Spritz the air fry basket with cooking spray.

- Put the garlic, seeds, salt, red pepper flakes, and ground black pepper in a food processor. Pulse to coarsely ground the mixture.

- Put the ground beef in a large bowl. Pour in the seed mixture and drizzle with Worcestershire sauce. Stir to mix well.

- Divide the mixture into four parts and shape each part into a ball, then bash each ball into a patty. Arrange the patties in the basket.

- Place the basket on the air fry position.

- Select Air Fry, set temperature to 350°F (180°C) and set time to 10 minutes. Flip the

patties with tongs halfway through the cooking time.

- When cooked, the patties will be well browned.

- Assemble the buns with the patties, then drizzle the mayo over the patties to make the burgers. Serve immediately.

824.   Thai Pork Burgers

Preparation Time: 10 minutes
Cooking Time: 14 minutes
Servings: 6

Ingredients:

- 1 pound (454 g) ground pork
- 1 tablespoon Thai curry paste
- 11/2 tablespoons fish sauce
- ¼ cup thinly sliced scallions, white and green parts
- 2 tablespoons minced peeled fresh ginger
- 1 tablespoon light brown sugar
- 1 teaspoon ground black pepper
- 6 slider buns, split open lengthwise, warmed
- Cooking spray

Directions:

- Spritz the air fry basket with cooking spray.

- Combine all the ingredients, except for the buns in a large bowl. Stir to mix well.

- Divide and shape the mixture into six balls, then bash the balls into six 3-inch-diameter patties.

- Arrange the patties in the basket and spritz with cooking spray.

- Place the basket on the air fry position.

- Select Air Fry, set temperature to 375°F (190°C) and set time to 14 minutes. Flip the patties halfway through the cooking time.

- When cooked, the patties should be well browned.

- Assemble the buns with patties to make the sliders and serve immediately.

825.   Golden Cabbage and Pork Gyoza

Preparation Time: 10 minutes
Cooking Time: 10 minutes
Servings: 48

Ingredients:

- 1 pound (454 g) ground pork
- 1 head Napa cabbage (about 1 pound / 454 g), sliced thinly and minced
- 1/2 cup minced scallions
- 1 teaspoon minced fresh chives
- 1 teaspoon soy sauce
- 1 teaspoon minced fresh ginger
- 1 tablespoon minced garlic
- 1 teaspoon granulated sugar
- 2 teaspoons kosher salt
- 48 to 50 wonton or dumpling wrappers
- Cooking spray

Directions:

- Spritz the air fry basket with cooking spray. Set aside.
- Make the filling: Combine all the ingredients, except for the wrappers in a large bowl. Stir to mix well.
- Unfold a wrapper on a clean work surface, then dab the edges with a little water. Scoop up 2 teaspoons of the filling mixture in the center.
- Make the gyoza: Fold the wrapper over to filling and press the edges to seal. Pleat the edges if desired. Repeat with remaining wrappers and fillings.
- Arrange the gyozas in the basket and spritz with cooking spray.
- Place the basket on the air fry position.
- Select Air Fry, set temperature to 360°F (182°C) and set time to 10 minutes. Flip the gyozas halfway through the cooking time.
- When cooked, the gyozas will be golden brown.
- Serve immediately.

826.   Golden Cheesy Potato Taquitos

Preparation Time: *5 minutes*
Cooking Time: *6 minutes*

Servings: 12

Ingredients:

- 2 cups mashed potatoes
- ½ cup shredded Mexican cheese
- 12 corn tortillas
- Cooking spray

Directions:

- Line a baking pan with parchment paper.
- In a bowl, combine the cheese and potatoes until well mixed. Microwave the tortillas on high heat for 30 seconds, or until softened. Add some water to another bowl and set alongside.
- On a clean work surface, lay the tortillas. Scoop 3 tablespoons of the potato mixture in the center of each tortilla. Roll up tightly and secure with toothpicks if necessary.
- Arrange the filled tortillas, seam side down, in the prepared baking pan. Spritz the tortillas with cooking spray.
- Place the pan into the air fryer grill.
- Select Air Fry, set temperature to 400°F (205°C) and set time to 6 minutes. Flip the tortillas halfway through the cooking time.
- When cooked, the tortillas should be crispy and golden brown.
- Serve hot.

827.   Spinach and Ricotta Pockets

Preparation Time: 20 minutes
Cooking Time: 10 minutes
Servings: 8

Ingredients:

- 2 large eggs, divided
- 1 tablespoon water
- 1 cup baby spinach, roughly chopped
- ¼ cup sun-dried tomatoes, finely chopped
- 1 cup ricotta cheese
- 1 cup basil, chopped
- ¼ teaspoon red pepper flakes
- ¼ teaspoon kosher salt
- 2 refrigerated rolled pie crusts

- ◆ 2 tablespoons sesame seeds

Directions:

- ■ Spritz the air fry basket with cooking spray.
- ■ Whisk an egg with water in a small bowl.
- ■ Combine the tomatoes, spinach, the other egg, basil, ricotta cheese, salt, and red pepper flakes in a large bowl. Whisk to mix well.
- ■ Unfold the pie crusts on a clean work surface and slice each crust into 4 wedges. Scoop up 3 tablespoons of the spinach mixture on each crust and leave ½ inch space from edges.
- ■ Fold the crust wedges in half to wrap the filling and press the edges with a fork to seal.
- ■ Arrange the wraps in the basket and spritz with cooking spray. Sprinkle with sesame seeds.
- ■ Place the basket on the air fry position.
- ■ Select Air Fry, set temperature to 380°F (193°C) and set time to 10 minutes. Flip the wraps halfway through the cooking time.
- ■ When cooked, the wraps will be crispy and golden.
- ■ Serve immediately.

828.   Fast Turkey, Leek, and Pepper Burger

Preparation Time: 10 minutes
Cooking Time: 20 minutes
Servings: 4

Ingredients:

- ◆ 1 cup leftover turkey, cut into bite-sized chunks
- ◆ 1 leek, sliced
- ◆ 1 Serrano pepper, deveined and chopped
- ◆ 2 bell peppers, deveined and chopped
- ◆ 2 tablespoons Tabasco sauce
- ◆ ½ cup sour cream
- ◆ 1 heaping tablespoon fresh cilantro, chopped
- ◆ 1 teaspoon hot paprika
- ◆ ¾ teaspoon kosher salt
- ◆ ½ teaspoon ground black pepper
- ◆ 4 hamburger buns
- ◆ Cooking spray

Directions:

- ■ Spritz a baking pan with cooking spray.
- ■ Mix all the ingredients, except for the buns, in a large bowl. Toss to combine well.
- ■ Pour the mixture in the baking pan.
- ■ Place the pan on the bake position.
- ■ Select Bake, set temperature to 385°F (196°C) and set time to 20 minutes.
- ■ When done, the turkey will be well browned and the leek will be tender.
- ■ Assemble the hamburger buns with the turkey mixture and serve immediately.

829.   Cheesy Vegetable Wraps

Preparation Time: 15 minutes
Cooking Time: 9 minutes
Servings: 4

Ingredients:

- ◆ 8 ounces (227 g) green beans
- ◆ 2 portobello mushroom caps, sliced
- ◆ 1 large red pepper, sliced
- ◆ 2 tablespoons olive oil, divided
- ◆ ¼ teaspoon salt
- ◆ 1 (15-ounce / 425-g) can chickpeas, drained
- ◆ 3 tablespoons lemon juice
- ◆ ¼ teaspoon ground black pepper
- ◆ 4 (6-inch) whole-grain wraps
- ◆ 4 ounces (113 g) fresh herb or garlic goat cheese, crumbled
- ◆ 1 lemon, cut into wedges

Directions:

- ■ Add the mushrooms, red pepper, green beans to a large bowl. Drizzle with 1 tablespoon olive oil and season with salt. Toss until well coated.
- ■ Transfer the vegetable mixture to a baking pan.
- ■ Slide the pan into the air fryer grill.
- ■ Select Air Fry, set temperature to 400°F (205°C) and set time to 9 minutes. Stir the vegetable mixture three times during cooking.

- When cooked, the vegetables should be tender.
- Meanwhile, mash the chickpeas with lemon juice, pepper and the remaining 1 tablespoon oil until well blended
- Unfold the wraps on a clean work surface. Spoon the chickpea mash on the wraps and spread all over.
- Divide the cooked veggies among wraps. Sprinkle 1 ounce crumbled goat cheese on top of each wrap. Fold to wrap. Squeeze the lemon wedges on top and serve.

830. Golden Prawn and Cabbage Egg Rolls

Preparation Time: 20 minutes
Cooking Time: 18 minutes
Servings: 4

Ingredients:

- 2 tablespoons olive oil
- 1 carrot, cut into strips
- 1-inch piece fresh ginger, grated
- 1 tablespoon minced garlic
- 2 tablespoons soy sauce
- ¼ cup chicken broth
- 1 tablespoon sugar
- 1 cup shredded Napa cabbage
- 1 tablespoon sesame oil
- 8 cooked prawns, minced
- 8 egg roll wrappers
- 1 egg, beaten
- Cooking spray

Directions:

- Spritz the air fry basket with cooking spray. Set aside.
- Heat the olive oil in a nonstick skillet over medium heat until shimmering.
- Add the carrot, garlic, and ginger and sauté for 2 minutes or until fragrant.
- Pour in the soy sauce, sugar, and broth. Bring to a boil. Keep stirring.
- Add the cabbage and simmer for 4 minutes or until the cabbage is tender.

- Turn off the heat and mix in the sesame oil. Let sit for 15 minutes.
- Use a strainer to remove the vegetables from the liquid, then combine with the minced prawns.
- Unfold the egg roll wrappers on a clean work surface, then divide the prawn mixture in the center of wrappers.
- Dab the edges of a wrapper with the beaten egg, then fold a corner over the filling and tuck the corner under the filling. Fold the left and right corner into the center. Roll the wrapper up and press to seal. Repeat with remaining wrappers.
- Arrange the wrappers in the basket and spritz with cooking spray.
- Place the basket on the air fry position.
- Select Air Fry, set temperature to 370°F (188°C) and set time to 12 minutes. Flip the wrappers halfway through the cooking time.
- When cooking is complete, the wrappers should be golden.
- Serve immediately.

831. Panko-Crusted Tilapia Tacos

Preparation Time: 20 minutes
Cooking Time: 5 minutes
Servings: 4

Ingredients:

- 2 tablespoons milk
- 1/3 cup mayonnaise
- ¼ teaspoon garlic powder
- 1 teaspoon chili powder
- 1½ cups panko bread crumbs
- ½ teaspoon salt
- 4 teaspoons canola oil
- 1 pound (454 g) skinless tilapia fillets, cut into 3-inch-long and 1-inch-wide strips
- 4 small flour tortillas
- Lemon wedges, for topping
- Cooking spray

Directions:

- Spritz the air fry basket with cooking spray.

- Combine the milk, garlic powder, mayo, and chili powder in a bowl. Stir to mix well. Combine the panko with salt and canola oil in a separate bowl. Stir to mix well.

- Dredge the tilapia strips in the milk mixture first, then dunk the strips in the panko mixture to coat well. Shake the excess off.

- Arrange the tilapia strips in the basket.

- Place the basket on the air fry position.

- Select Air Fry, set temperature to 400°F (205°C) and set time to 5 minutes. Flip the strips halfway through the cooking time.

- When cooking is complete, the strips will be opaque on all sides and the panko will be golden brown.

- Unfold the tortillas on a large plate, then divide the tilapia strips over the tortillas. Squeeze the lemon wedges on top before serving.

832. Beef and Pepper Fajitas with Cheese

Preparation Time: 15 minutes
Cooking Time: 10 minutes
Servings: 4

Ingredients:

- 1 pound (454 g) beef sirloin steak, cut into strips
- 2 shallots, sliced
- 1 orange bell pepper, sliced
- 1 red bell pepper, sliced
- 2 garlic cloves, minced
- 2 tablespoons Cajun seasoning
- 1 tablespoon paprika
- Salt and ground black pepper, to taste
- 4 corn tortillas
- ½ cup shredded Cheddar cheese
- Cooking spray

Directions:

- Spritz the air fry basket with cooking spray.

- Combine all the ingredients, except for the tortillas and cheese, in a large bowl. Toss to coat well.

- Pour the beef and vegetables in the basket and spritz with cooking spray.

- Place the basket on the air fry position.

- Select Air Fry, set temperature to 360°F (182°C) and set time to 10 minutes. Stir the beef and vegetables halfway through the cooking time.

- When cooking is complete, the meat will be browned and the vegetables will be soft and lightly wilted.

- Unfold the tortillas on a clean work surface and spread the cooked beef and vegetables on top. Scatter with cheese and fold to serve.

833. Crispy Creamy- Cheesy Crab Wontons

Preparation Time: 10 minutes
Cooking Time: 10 minutes
Servings: 8

Ingredients:

- 24 wonton wrappers, thawed if frozen
- Cooking spray

Filling:

- 5 ounces (142 g) lump crabmeat, drained and patted dry
- 4 ounces (113 g) cream cheese, at room temperature
- 2 scallions, sliced
- 1½ teaspoons toasted sesame oil
- 1 teaspoon Worcestershire sauce
- Kosher salt and ground black pepper, to taste

Directions:

- Spritz the air fry basket with cooking spray.

- In a medium-size bowl, place all the ingredients for the filling and stir until well mixed. Prepare a small bowl of water alongside.

- On a clean work surface, lay the wonton wrappers. Scoop 1 teaspoon of the filling in the center of each wrapper. Wet the edges with a touch of water. Fold each wonton wrapper diagonally in half over the filling to form a triangle.

- Arrange the wontons in the basket. Spritz the wontons with cooking spray.
- Place the basket on the air fry position.
- Select Air Fry, set temperature to 350°F (180°C) and set time to 10 minutes. Flip the wontons halfway through the cooking time.
- When cooking is complete, the wontons will be crispy and golden brown.
- Serve immediately.

834. Mexican Spicy Chicken Burgers

Preparation Time: 15 minutes
Cooking Time: 20 minutes
Servings: 6

Ingredients:

- 4 skinless and boneless chicken breasts
- 1 small head of cauliflower, sliced into florets
- 1 jalapeño pepper
- 3 tablespoons smoked paprika
- 1 tablespoon thyme
- 1 tablespoon oregano
- 1 tablespoon mustard powder
- 1 teaspoon cayenne pepper
- 1 egg
- Salt and ground black pepper, to taste
- 2 tomatoes, sliced
- 2 lettuce leaves, chopped
- 6 to 8 brioche buns, sliced lengthwise
- ¾ cup taco sauce
- Cooking spray

Directions:

- Spritz the air fry basket with cooking spray. Set aside.
- In a blender, add the cauliflower florets, paprika, jalapeño pepper, cayenne pepper, oregano, mustard powder and thyme and blend until the mixture has a texture similar to bread crumbs.
- Transfer ¾ of the cauliflower mixture to a medium bowl and set aside. Beat the egg in a different bowl and set aside.
- Add the chicken breasts to the blender with remaining cauliflower mixture. Sprinkle with

salt and pepper. Blend until finely chopped and well mixed.

- Remove the mixture from the blender and form into 6 to 8 patties. One by one, dredge each patty in the reserved cauliflower mixture, then into the egg. Dip them in the cauliflower mixture again for additional coating.
- Place the coated patties into the basket and spritz with cooking spray.
- Place the basket on the air fry position.
- Select Air Fry, set temperature to 350°F (180°C) and set time to 20 minutes. Flip the patties halfway through the cooking time.
- When cooking is complete, the patties should be golden and crispy.
- Transfer the patties to a clean work surface and assemble with the buns, tomato slices, chopped lettuce leaves and taco sauce to make burgers. Serve and enjoy.

835. Bulgogi Burgers with Korean mayo

Preparation Time: 15 minutes
Cooking Time: 10 minutes
Servings: 4

Ingredients:

Burgers:

- 1 pound (454 g) 85% lean ground beef
- 2 tablespoons gochujang
- ¼ cup chopped scallions
- 2 teaspoons minced garlic
- 2 teaspoons minced fresh ginger
- 1 tablespoon soy sauce
- 1 tablespoon toasted sesame oil
- 2 teaspoons sugar
- ½ teaspoon kosher salt
- 4 hamburger buns
- Cooking spray

Korean Mayo:

- 1 tablespoon gochujang
- ¼ cup mayonnaise
- 2 teaspoons sesame seeds
- ¼ cup chopped scallions

- ♦ 1 tablespoon toasted sesame oil

Directions:

- Combine the ingredients for the burgers, except for the buns, in a large bowl. Stir to mix well, then wrap the bowl in plastic and refrigerate to marinate for at least an hour.

- Spritz the air fry basket with cooking spray.

- Divide the meat mixture into four portions and form into four balls. Bash the balls into patties.

- Arrange the patties in the basket and spritz with cooking spray.

- Place the basket on the air fry position.

- Select Air Fry, set temperature to 350°F (180°C) and set time to 10 minutes. Flip the patties halfway through the cooking time.

- Meanwhile, combine the ingredients for the Korean mayo in a small bowl. Stir to mix well.

- When cooking is complete, the patties should be golden brown.

- Remove the patties from the air fryer grill and assemble with the buns, then spread the Korean mayo over the patties to make the burgers. Serve immediately.

BREAD & PIZZA

836. Air Fryer Grill Pizza Sandwiches

Preparation Time: 5 minutes
Cooking Time: 5 minutes
Servings: 1

Ingredients:

♦ 1 French bread sandwich roll, sliced
♦ 5 tsp. pizza sauce
♦ 15-20 slices pepperoni
♦ 1 cup mozzarella cheese, shredded

Directions:

▪ Preheat the Air Fryer Grill to 2500C or 4820F.
▪ Spread pizza sauce on the bread.
▪ Add toppings, cheese, and pepperoni on each slice of bread.
▪ Toast it until the cheese melts.

837. Veg Pizza

Preparation Time: 10 minutes
Cooking Time: 10 minutes
Servings: 2

Ingredients:

♦ 1 cup tomatoes, sliced
♦ Capsicum, sliced
♦ 4 baby corns
♦ 1-2 tsp. pizza sauce
♦ 1 cup mozzarella cheese
♦ 1 cups all-purpose flour
♦ 1.5 tsp. oregano seasoning
♦ Salt
♦ 1.5 tsp. yeast
♦ 2-3 tsp. oil
♦ 1.5 cup of water

Directions:

▪ Make pizza dough with all-purpose flour adding oil, salt, yeast, and water.

▪ Spread the remaining ingredients on the pizza base made of dough.
▪ Preheat the Air Fryer Grill and bake for 10 minutes.

838. Air Fryer Grill-baked Grilled Cheese

Preparation Time: 5 minutes
Cooking Time: 5 minutes
Servings: 1

Ingredients:

♦ 2 slices bread
♦ 1-2 tsp. mayonnaise
♦ 2-3 tsp. cheddar cheese
♦ Fresh spinach

Directions:

▪ Preheat the Air Fryer Grill to 2000C or 4000F.
▪ Spread mayonnaise and cheese on the bread.
▪ Bake for 5-7 minutes. Add the spinach.

839. Hot Ham and Cheese Sandwich

Preparation Time: 10 minutes
Cooking Time: 5 minutes
Servings: 2

Ingredients:

♦ 2-4 sandwich bread
♦ Olive oil
♦ 1/4 tsp. oregano & basil
♦ 4 ounces ham, sliced
♦ 4 ounces cheese, sliced

Directions:

▪ Preheat the Air Fryer Grill to 2000C or 4000F.
▪ Apply olive oil and sprinkle oregano on both sides of bread slices.
▪ Put the ham, spread cheese over one bread slice, and place the other on the sheet.
▪ Bake for 10 minutes.

840. Garlic Bread

Preparation Time: 5 minutes
Cooking Time: 15 minutes
Servings: 4

Ingredients:

- 4 pieces baguette, cut in half
- Mint leaves, chopped
- 2-3 tsp. butter
- 2-3 garlic cloves, minced

Directions:

- Mix butter, mint, and garlic.
- Spread mixture on every slice.
- Bake at 200C or 400F in the Air Fryer Grill for 5-6 minutes

841. Cheese Chili Toast

Preparation Time: 5 minutes
Cooking Time: 5 minutes
Servings: 2

Ingredients:

- 2-4 slices bread
- Capsicum, chopped
- Salt & pepper
- 1-2 Chilies
- 20gm cheese, grated
- 10gm cream
- Oil

Directions:

- Place the bread on the baking pan.
- Make a mixture of oil, capsicums, peppers, salt, and chilies.
- Apply the mixture on bread and grated cheese
- Bake at 180 degrees or 350°F or 177°C for 5-7 minutes in the Air Fryer Grill. You're all set.

842. Chicken Focaccia Bread Sandwiches

Preparation Time: 5 minutes
Cooking Time: 10 minutes
Servings: 6

Ingredients:

- Flatbread or Focaccia, halved
- 2 cups chicken, sliced
- Fresh basil leaves
- 1 cup sweet pepper, roasted

Directions:

- Roast the chicken at 1770C or 3500F in the Air Fryer Grill for 25 to 30 minutes.
- Spread mayonnaise on the bread and put the remaining ingredients on top.

843. Pepperoni Pizza

Preparation Time: 10 Minutes
Cooking Time: 20 Minutes
Servings: 8

Ingredients:

- Pepperoni, sliced
- 1 cup pizza sauce
- 1 cup mozzarella cheese
- Readymade pizza dough
- Parmesan cheese, grated

Directions:

- Arrange toppings on pizza dough.
- Preheat the Air Fryer Grill to 1770C or 3500F.
- Bake for 25 minutes.

844. Cheese Pizza

Preparation Time: 10 Minutes
Cooking Time: 10 Minutes
Servings: 4

Ingredients:

- Readymade pizza base
- 2-3 tsp. tomato ketchup
- 100gm cheese, shredded
- Salt & pepper
- 2 ounces mushroom
- Capsicum, onions, tomatoes

Directions:

- Preheat the Air Fryer Grill to 250₀C or 482₀F.
- Spread ketchup on the pizza base and then toppings and cheese.
- Bake for 10-12 minutes.

845. Basil Pizza

Preparation Time: 10 minutes
Cooking Time: 7 minutes
Servings: 2

Ingredients:

- 1 pizza dough
- 1/2 tablespoon olive oil
- 1 cup pizza sauce
- 11/2 cups part-skim mozzarella cheese, shredded
- 11/2 cups part-skim provolone cheese, shredded
- 10 fresh basil leaves

Directions:

- Place the water tray in the bottom of Smokeless Electric Grill.
- Place about 2 cups of lukewarm water into the water tray.
- Place the drip pan over water tray and then arrange the heating element.
- Now, place the grilling pan over heating element.
- Plugin the Smokeless Electric Grill and press the 'Power' button to turn it on.
- Then press 'Fan" button.
- Set the temperature settings according to manufacturer's directions.
- Cover the grill with lid and let it preheat.
- With your hands, stretch the dough into the size that will fit into the grilling pan.
- After preheating, remove the lid and grease the grilling pan.
- Place the dough over the grilling pan.
- cover with the lid and cook for about 2-3 minutes
- Remove the lid and with a heat-safe spatula, flip the dough.

- Cover with the lid and cook for about 2 minutes.
- Remove the lid and flip the crust.
- Immediately, spread the pizza sauce over the crust and sprinkle with both kinds of cheese.
- Cover with the lid and cook for about 1 minute.
- Remove the lid and cook for about 1 minute or until the cheese is melted.
- Remove from the grill and immediately top the pizza with basil leaves.
- Cut into desired sized wedges and serve.

846. Personal Mozzarella Pizza Crust

Preparation Time: 5 Minutes
Cooking Time: 10 Minutes
Servings: 1

Ingredients:

- 1/2 cup shredded whole-milk mozzarella cheese
- Two tablespoons blanched finely ground almond flour
- One tablespoon full-fat cream cheese
- One large egg white

Directions:

- Place mozzarella, almond flour, and cream cheese in a medium microwave-safe bowl. Microwave for 30 seconds. Stir until an even ball of dough is made. Add egg white, then stirring until soft round dough forms.
- Press into a 6" round pizza crust.
- Cut a piece of parchment to suit your air fryer basket and place crust on parchment.
- Regulate the temperature to 350°F and set the timer for 10 minutes.
- Flip after 5 minutes. During this time, put any desired toppings on the crust. Continue cooking until golden. Serve immediately.

847. Crustless Three-Meat Pizza

Preparation Time: 5 Minutes
Cooking Time: 5 Minutes
Servings: 1

Ingredients:

- 1/2 cup shredded mozzarella cheese
- Seven slices pepperoni
- ¼ cup cooked ground sausage
- Two slices sugar-free bacon, cooked and crumbled
- One tablespoon grated Parmesan cheese

Directions:

- Cover the bottom of a 6" cake pan with mozzarella. Place pepperoni, sausage, and bacon on top of the cheese and sprinkle with Parmesan. Place pan into the air fryer basket.
- Regulate the temperature to 400°F and set the timer for 5 minutes.
- Remove when the cheese is bubbling and golden. Serve warm with pizza sauce for dipping.

848. Low-Carb Pizza Crust

Preparation Time: 10 Minutes
Cooking Time: 20 Minutes
Servings: 4

Ingredients:

- 1 tbsp. full-fat cream cheese
- 1/2 cup whole-milk mozzarella cheese, shredded
- 2 tbsp. flour
- 1 egg white

Directions:

- Prepare the cream cheese, mozzarella, and flour in a microwaveable bowl and heat in the microwave for half a minute. Mix well to create a smooth consistency. Add in the egg white and stir to form a soft ball of dough.
- With slightly wet hands, press the dough into a pizza crust about six inches in diameter.
- Arrange sheet of parchment paper in the bottom of your fryer and lay the crust on top. Cook for ten minutes at 350degreesF, turning the crust over halfway through the cooking time.

- Top the pizza base with the toppings of your choice and enjoy!

849. Salmon Burgers

Preparation Time: 20 minutes
Cooking Time: 22 minutes
Servings: 6

Ingredients:

- large russet potatoes, peeled and cubed
- 1 (6-oz.) cooked salmon fillet
- 1 egg
- ¾ cup frozen vegetables (of your choice), parboiled and drained
- tablespoons fresh parsley, chopped
- 1 teaspoon fresh dill, chopped
- Salt and ground black pepper, as required
- 1 cup breadcrumbs
- ¼ cup olive oil

Directions:

- In a pan of the boiling water, cook the potatoes for about 10 minutes.
- Drain the potatoes well.
- Move the potatoes into a bowl and mash with a potato masher.
- Set aside to cool completely.
- In another bowl, add the salmon and flake with a fork.
- Add the cooked potatoes, egg, parboiled vegetables, parsley, dill, salt, and black pepper and mix until well combined.
- Make 6 equal-sized patties from the mixture.
- Coat patties with breadcrumb evenly and then drizzle with the oil evenly.
- When the unit beeps to show that it is preheated, open the lid.
- Organize the patties in "Air Fry Basket" and put it in the oven.
- Flip the patties once halfway through.
- Serve hot.

850. Banana Bread

Preparation Time: 10 Minutes

Cooking Time: 1 hour
Servings: 12

Ingredients:

- 2 cups all-purpose flour
- 2 1/3 cups mashed bananas
- 1 teaspoon baking soda
- ¾ cup brown sugar
- ¼ teaspoon salt
- ½ cup butter, unsalted
- 2 eggs

Directions:

- Turn on the oven, set the temperature to 350 degrees F, and then select the oven cooking Directions.
- Meanwhile, take a large bowl, place flour in it, add salt and baking soda and then stir until mixed.
- Place cream in a separate bowl, add butter, and then beat in sugar until creamy.
- Whisk in eggs and mashed banana and then stir in the flour mixture until smooth.
- Take a 9-by-5 inches loaf pan, grease it with oil, spoon the batter in it and then bake for 1 hour until firm and then top turn golden brown.
- When done, let the bread cool in its pan for 10 minutes, then take it out and cool the bread completely.
- Cut the bread into slices and then serve.

851. Mushroom Pita Pizzas

Preparation Time: 10 minutes
Cooking Time: 5 minutes
Servings: 4

Ingredients:

- (3-inch) pitas - 1 tablespoon olive oil
- ¾ cup pizza sauce
- 1 (4-ounce) jar sliced mushrooms, drained
- ½ teaspoon dried basil
- green onions, minced
- 1 cup grated mozzarella or provolone cheese
- 1 cup sliced grape tomatoes

Directions:

- Put each piece of pita with oil and top with the pizza sauce. Put the mushrooms and sprinkle with basil and green onions. Put with the grated cheese.
- Bake for 5 to 10 minutes or until the cheese is melted and starts to brown. Put with the grape tomatoes.

852. Bread Pudding

Preparation Time: 10 minutes
Cooking Time: 32 Minutes
Servings: 4

Ingredients:

- 1/2 lb. white bread; cubed
- 3/4 cup milk
- 3/4 cup water
- tsp. cinnamon powder
- 1 cup flour
- 3/5 cup brown sugar
- tsp. cornstarch
- 1/2 cup apple; peeled; cored and roughly chopped.
- 1 tbsp. honey
- 1 tsp. vanilla extract
- oz. soft butter

Directions:

- In a bowl; mix bread with apple, milk with water, honey, cinnamon, vanilla and cornstarch and whisk well.
- Mix flour with sugar and butter and stir until you obtain a crumbled mixture.
- Press half of the crumble mix on the bottom of your air fryer; add bread and apple mix, add the rest of the crumble and cook everything at 350 °F, for 22 minutes. Divide bread pudding on plates and serve.

853. Shrimp Sandwiches

Preparation Time: 10 minutes
Cooking Time: 15 Minutes
Servings: 4

Ingredients:

- ◆ 1 ¼ cups cheddar; shredded
- ◆ 2 tbsp. green onions; chopped.
- ◆ whole wheat bread slices
- ◆ oz. canned tiny shrimp; drained
- ◆ tbsp. mayonnaise
- ◆ 2 tbsp. butter; soft

Directions:

- ▪ In a bowl; mix shrimp with cheese, green onion and mayo and stir well.
- ▪ Spread this on part of the bread slices; top with the other bread slices, cut into halves diagonally and spread butter on top.
- ▪ Place sandwiches in your air fryer and cook at 350 °F, for 5 minutes. Divide shrimp sandwiches on plates and serve them for breakfast.

854.   Bread Rolls

Preparation Time: 10 minutes
Cooking Time: 22 Minutes
Servings: 4

Ingredients:

- ◆ potatoes; boiled; peeled and mashed
- ◆ 1/2 tsp. turmeric powder
- ◆ curry leaf springs
- ◆ 1/2 tsp. mustard seeds
- ◆ bread slices; white parts only
- ◆ 1 coriander bunch; chopped.
- ◆ green chilies; chopped
- ◆ Small yellow onions; chopped.
- ◆ 2 tbsp. olive oil
- ◆ Salt and black pepper to the taste

Directions:

- ▪ Heat up a pan with 1 tsp. oil; add mustard seeds, onions, curry leaves and turmeric, stir and cook for a few seconds.
- ▪ Add mashed potatoes, salt, pepper, coriander and chilies, stir well; take off heat and cool it down.
- ▪ Divide potatoes mix into 8 parts and shape ovals using your wet hands.

- ▪ Wet bread slices with water; press in order to drain excess water and keep one slice in your palm.
- ▪ Add a potato oval over bread slice and wrap it around it.
- ▪ Do the same with the rest of the potato mix and bread.
- ▪ Heat up your air fryer at 400 degrees F; add the rest of the oil, add bread rolls; cook them for 12 minutes. Divide bread rolls on plates and serve for breakfast.

855.   Bacon and Garlic Pizzas

Preparation Time: 10 minutes
Cooking Time: 10 minutes
Servings: 4

Ingredients:

- ◆ dinner rolls, frozen
- ◆ garlic cloves minced
- ◆ ½ teaspoon oregano dried
- ◆ ½ teaspoon garlic powder
- ◆ 1 cup tomato sauce
- ◆ bacon slices, cooked and chopped
- ◆ 1 and ¼ cups cheddar cheese, grated
- ◆ Cooking spray

Directions:

- ▪ Place dinner rolls on a working surface and press them to obtain 4 ovals.
- ▪ Spray each oval with cooking spray, transfer them to your air fryer and cook them at 370 degrees F for 2 minutes.
- ▪ Spread tomato sauce on each oval, divide garlic, sprinkle oregano and garlic powder and top with bacon and cheese.
- ▪ Return pizzas to your heated air fryer and cook them at 370 degrees F for 8 minutes more.
- ▪ Serve them warm for lunch.
- ▪ Enjoy!

856.   Cauliflower Pizza Crust

Preparation Time: 26 minutes
Cooking Time: 20 minutes
Servings: 2

Ingredients:

- 1 (12-oz.) Steamer bag cauliflower
- 1 large egg.
- ½ cup shredded sharp cheddar cheese.
- tbsp. Blanched finely ground almond flour
- 1 tsp. Italian blend seasoning

Directions:

- Cook the cauliflower according to the directions on the package. Take it out of the bag and place it on a cheesecloth or paper towel to remove excess water. Place the cauliflower in a large bowl.

- Cut a piece of parchment to fit in the fryer basket. Press cauliflower into a 6-inch round circle. Place in the fryer basket. Set the temperature to 360 ° F and set the timer for 11 minutes. After 7 minutes, turn the pizza dough over.

- Add your favorite garnish to the pizza. Place back in the fryer basket and cook an additional 4 minutes or until fully cooked and golden. Serve immediately.

857.   Shrimp and Grilled Cheese Sandwiches

Preparation Time: 10 minutes
Cooking Time: 5 minutes
Servings: 4

Ingredients:

- 1¼ cups shredded Colby, Cheddar, or Havarti cheese
- 1 (6-ounce) can tiny shrimp, drained
- tablespoons mayonnaise
- tablespoons minced green onion
- slices whole-grain or whole-wheat bread
- tablespoons softened butter

Directions:

- Mix the cheese, shrimp, mayonnaise, and green onion in a medium bowl.

- Put this combination on two of the slices of bread.

- Place with the other slices of bread to make two sandwiches.

- Cook in the oven for 5 to 7 minutes

- Until the bread is browned and crisp and the cheese is melted.

- Chop in half and serve warm.

858.   French Toast from Heaven!

Preparation Time: 5 minutes
Cooking Time: 20 minutes
Servings: 3

Ingredients:

- slices of preferred bread
- ¾ cup of milk
- eggs
- 1 tsp. pure vanilla extract
- 1 tbsp. ground cinnamon

Directions:

- Start by preheating your air fryer toast oven at 320 degrees F.

- Mix all the ingredients except the bread in a medium bowl until well mixed.

- Dunk each slice of bread into the egg mix, gently shake the excess off and place it in a greased pan.

- Cook in the fryer, each side for 3 minutes, and repeat for the remaining slices.

- To serve, drizzle with maple syrup.

859.   Prosciutto Sandwich

Preparation Time: 10 minutes
Cooking Time: 5 minutes
Servings: 1

Ingredients:

- bread slices
- mozzarella slices
- 2 tomato slices
- 2 prosciutto slices
- 2 basil leaves
- 1 teaspoon olive oil
- A pinch of salt and black pepper

Directions:

- Arrange mozzarella and prosciutto on a bread slice.
- Season with salt and pepper, place in your air fryer and cook at 400 degrees F for 5 minutes.
- Drizzle oil over prosciutto, add tomato and basil, cover with the other bread slice, cut sandwich in half and serve. Enjoy!

860.   Ham and Cheese sandwich

Preparation Time: 15 minutes
Cooking Time: 20 minutes
Servings: 2

Ingredients:

- eggs
- slices of bread of choice
- slices turkey
- slices ham
- tbsp. half and half cream
- tsp. melted butter
- slices Swiss cheese
- ¼ tsp. pure vanilla extract
- Powdered sugar and raspberry jam for serving

Directions:

- Combine the eggs, vanilla, and cream in a bowl and set aside.
- Make a sandwich with the bread layered with cheese slice, turkey, ham, cheese slice, and the top slice of bread to make two sandwiches. Gently press on the sandwiches to somewhat flatten them.
- Set your air fryer toast oven to 350 degrees F.
- Spread out kitchen aluminum foil, cut it about the same size as the sandwich, and spread the melted butter on the foil's surface.
- Dip the sandwich in the egg mixture and let it soak for about 20 seconds on each side. Repeat this for the other sandwich. Place the soaked sandwiches on the prepared foil sheets, then place them on the basket in your fryer.

- Cook for 12 minutes, then flip the sandwiches and brush with the remaining butter and cook for another 5 minutes or until well browned.
- Place the cooked sandwiched on a plate and top with the powdered sugar, and serve with a small raspberry jam bowl.

861.   Margherita Pizza

Preparation Time: 30 minutes
Cooking Time: 18 Minutes
Servings: 4

Ingredients:

- 1 whole-wheat pizza crust
- 1/2 cup mozzarella cheese, grated
- 1/2 cup can tomatoes
- 2 tbsp olive oil
- 3 Roma tomatoes, sliced
- 10 basil leaves

Directions:

- Fit the Air fryer oven with the rack in position
- Roll out whole wheat pizza crust using a rolling pin. Make sure the crust is ½-inch thick.
- Sprinkle olive oil on top of pizza crust.
- Spread can tomatoes over pizza crust.
- Arrange sliced tomatoes and basil on pizza crust. Sprinkle grated cheese on top.
- Place pizza on top of the oven rack and set to bake at 425 F for 23 minutes.
- Slice and serve.

862.   Lemon-raspberry Muffins

Preparation Time: 15 minutes
Cooking Time: 15 Minutes
Servings: 6

Ingredients:

- 2 cups almond flour
- ¾ cup Swerve
- 1¼ teaspoons baking powder
- 1/3 teaspoon ground allspice

- 1/3 teaspoon ground anise star
- ½ teaspoon grated lemon zest
- ¼ teaspoon salt
- 2 eggs
- 1 cup sour cream
- ½ cup coconut oil
- ½ cup raspberries

Directions:

- Line a muffin pan with 6 paper liners.

- In a mixing bowl, mix the almond flour, Swerve, baking powder, allspice, anise, lemon zest, and salt.

- In another mixing bowl, beat the eggs, sour cream, and coconut oil until well mixed. Add the egg mixture to the flour mixture and stir to combine. Mix in the raspberries.

- Scrape the batter into the prepared muffin cups, filling each about three-quarters full.

- Put the muffin pan into Rack Position 1, select Convection Bake, set temperature to 345°F (174°C), and set time to 15 minutes.

- When cooking is complete, the tops should be golden and a toothpick inserted in the middle should come out clean.

- Allow the muffins to cool for 10 minutes in the muffin pan before removing and serving.

863. Almond Pecan Cookies

Preparation Time: 10 minutes
Cooking Time: 20 Minutes
Servings: 16

Ingredients:

- 1/2 cup butter
- 1 tsp vanilla
- 2 tsp gelatin
- 2/3 cup Swerve
- 1 cup pecans
- 1/3 cup coconut flour
- 1 cup almond flour

Directions:

- Fit the Air fryer oven with the rack in position

- Add butter, vanilla, gelatin, swerve, coconut flour, and almond flour into the food processor and process until crumbs form.

- Add pecans and process until chopped.

- Make cookies from prepared mixture and place onto a parchment-lined baking pan.

- Set to bake at 350 F for 25 minutes. After 5 minutes place the baking pan in the preheated oven.

- Serve and enjoy.

864. Cinnamon Cheesecake Bars

Preparation Time: 20 minutes
Cooking Time: 30 Minutes
Servings: 12

Ingredients:

- Nonstick cooking spray
- 16 oz. cream cheese, soft
- 1 tsp vanilla
- 1 ¼ cups sugar, divided
- 2 tubes refrigerated crescent rolls
- 1 tsp cinnamon
- ¼ cup butter

Directions:

- Place the rack in position Spray the bottom of an 8x11-inch pan with cooking spray.

- In a medium bowl, beat cream cheese, vanilla, and ¾ cup sugar until smooth.

- Roll out one can of crescent rolls on the bottom of prepared pan, sealing the perforations and pressing partway up the sides.

- Spread cream cheese mixture evenly over crescents.

- Roll out second can of crescents over the top of cheese mixture, sealing the perforations.

- In a small bowl, stir together cinnamon and remaining sugar. Melt the butter.

- Set oven to bake on 375°F for 35 minutes.

- Sprinkle the cinnamon sugar over the top of the crescents and drizzle with melted butter.

- After the oven has preheated for 5 minutes, place the pan in the oven and bake 30 minutes until the top is golden brown.
- Cool completely. Cover and refrigerate at least 2 hours before slicing and serving.

865. Brownies

Preparation Time: 20 minutes
Cooking Time: 30 Minutes
Servings: 15

Ingredients:

- ½ cup condensed milk
- 1 tbsp. unsalted butter
- 2 tbsp. water
- ½ cup chopped nuts
- 3 tbsp. melted dark chocolate
- 1 cup all-purpose flour

Directions:

- Add the ingredients together and whisk till you get a smooth mixture.
- Prepare a tin by greasing it with butter. Transfer the mixture into the tin.
- Preheat the fryer to 300 Fahrenheit for five minutes. You will need to place the tin in the basket and cover it. Check whether the brownies have been cooked using a knife or a toothpick and remove the tray. When the brownies have cooled, cut them and serve with a dollop of ice cream.

866. Almond Butter Cookies

Preparation Time: 20 minutes
Cooking Time: 12 Minutes
Servings: 12

Ingredients:

- 1 teaspoon vanilla extract
- 1 cup almond butter, soft
- 1 egg
- 2 tablespoons erythritol

Directions:

- In a bowl, mix all the ingredients and whisk really well.

- Spread this on a cookie sheet that fits the air fryer lined with parchment paper, introduce in the fryer and cook at 350 degrees F and bake for 12 minutes.
- Cool down and serve.

867. Choco Cookies

Preparation Time: 10 minutes
Cooking Time: 8 Minutes
Servings: 8

Ingredients:

- 3 egg whites
- 3/4 cup cocoa powder, unsweetened
- 1 3/4 cup confectioner sugar
- 1 1/2 tsp vanilla

Directions:

- Fit the Air fryer oven with the rack in position
- In a mixing bowl, whip egg whites until fluffy soft peaks. Slowly add in cocoa, sugar, and vanilla.
- Drop teaspoonful onto parchment-lined baking pan into 32 small cookies.
- Set to bake at 350 F for 8 minutes. After 5 minutes place the baking pan in the preheated oven.
- Serve and enjoy.

868. Chocolate Pudding

Preparation Time: 5 minutes
Cooking Time: 20 Minutes
Servings: 6

Ingredients:

- 24 ounces cream cheese, soft
- 2 tablespoons almond meal
- ¼ cup erythritol
- 3 eggs, whisked
- 1 tablespoon vanilla extract
- ½ cup heavy cream
- 12 ounces dark chocolate, melted

Directions:

- In a bowl mix all the ingredients and whisk well.
- Divide this into 6 ramekins, put them in your air fryer and cook at 320 degrees F for 20 minutes.
- Keep in the fridge for 1 hour before serving.

869. Tasty Pumpkin Cookies

Preparation Time: 15 minutes
Cooking Time: 25 Minutes
Servings: 27

Ingredients:

- 1 egg
- 2 cups almond flour
- 1/2 tsp baking powder
- 1 tsp vanilla
- 1/2 cup butter
- 1 tsp liquid stevia
- 1/2 tsp pumpkin pie spice
- 1/2 cup pumpkin puree

Directions:

- Fit the Air fryer oven with the rack in position
- In a large bowl, add all ingredients and mix until well combined.
- Make cookies from mixture and place onto a parchment-lined baking pan.
- Set to bake at 300 F for 30 minutes. After 5 minutes place the baking dish in the preheated oven.
- Serve and enjoy.

870. Crustless Pizza

Preparation Time: 20 minutes
Cooking Time: 15 Minutes
Servings: 1

Ingredients:

- 2 slices sugar-free bacon; cooked and crumbled
- 7 slices pepperoni
- ½ cup shredded mozzarella cheese
- ¼ cup cooked ground sausage

- 2 tbsp. low-carb, sugar-free pizza sauce, for dipping
- 1 tbsp. grated Parmesan cheese

Directions:

- Cover the bottom of a 6-inch cake pan with mozzarella. Place pepperoni, sausage and bacon on top of cheese and sprinkle with Parmesan
- Place pan into the air fryer basket. Adjust the temperature to 400 Degrees F and set the timer for 5 minutes.
- Remove when cheese is bubbling and golden. Serve warm with pizza sauce for dipping.

871. Lemon-Butter Shortbread

Preparation Time: 10 minutes
Cooking Time: 36 to 40 minutes
Servings: 4

Ingredients:

- 1 tablespoon grated lemon zest
- 1 cup granulated sugar
- 1 pound (454 g) unsalted butter, at room temperature
- 1/4 teaspoon fine salt
- 4 cups all-purpose flour
- 1/3 cup cornstarch
- Cooking spray

Directions:

- Add the lemon zest and sugar to a stand mixer fitted with the paddle attachment and beat on medium speed for 1 to 2 minutes. Let stand for about 5 minutes. Fold in the butter and salt and blend until fluffy.
- Mix together the flour and cornstarch in a large bowl. Add to the butter mixture and mix to combine.
- Spritz the sheet pan with cooking spray and spread a piece of parchment paper onto the pan. Scrape the dough into the pan until even and smooth.
- Select Bake, set temperature to 325°F (160°C), and set time to 36 minutes. Select Start to begin preheating.

- Once the unit has preheated, place the pan in the oven.

- After 20 minutes, check the shortbread, rotating the pan if it is not browning evenly. Continue cooking for another 16 minutes until lightly browned.

- When done, remove the pan from the oven. Slice and allow to cool for 5 minutes before serving.

872. Vanilla Chocolate Chip Cookies

Preparation Time: 10 minutes
Cooking Time: 22 minutes
Servings: 30

Ingredients:

- 1/3 cup (80g) organic brown sugar
- 1/3 cup (80g) organic cane sugar
- 4 ounces (112g) cashew-based vegan butter
- ½ cup coconut cream
- 1 teaspoon vanilla extract
- 2 tablespoons ground flaxseed
- 1 teaspoon baking powder
- 1 teaspoon baking soda
- Pinch of salt
- 2¼ cups (220g) almond flour
- ½ cup (90g) dairy-free dark chocolate chips

Directions:

- Line a baking sheet with parchment paper.

- Mix together the brown sugar, cane sugar, and butter in a medium bowl or the bowl of a stand mixer. Cream together with a mixer.

- Fold in the coconut cream, vanilla, flaxseed, baking powder, baking soda, and salt. Stir well.

- Add the almond flour, a little at a time, mixing after each addition until fully incorporated. Stir in the chocolate chips with a spatula.

- Scoop the dough onto the prepared baking sheet.

- Select Bake, set temperature to 325°F (160°C), and set the time to 22 minutes. Select Start to begin preheating.

- Once the unit has preheated, place the baking sheet in the oven.

- Bake until the cookies are golden brown.

- When cooking is complete, transfer the baking sheet onto a wire rack to cool completely before serving.

873. Fudge Pie

Preparation Time: 15 minutes
Cooking Time: 26 minutes
Servings: 8

Ingredients:

- 1½ cups sugar
- ½ cup self-rising flour
- 1/3 cup unsweetened cocoa powder
- 3 large eggs, beaten
- 12 tablespoons (1½ sticks) butter, melted
- 1½ teaspoons vanilla extract
- 1 (9-inch) unbaked pie crust
- ¼ cup confectioners' sugar (optional)

Directions:

- Thoroughly combine the sugar, flour, and cocoa powder in a medium bowl. Add the beaten eggs and butter and whisk to combine. Stir in the vanilla.

- Pour the prepared filling into the pie crust and transfer to a perforated pan.

- Select Bake, set temperature to 350°F (180°C), and set time to 26 minutes. Select Start to begin preheating.

- Once the oven has preheated, slide the pan into the oven.

- When cooking is complete, the pie should be set.

- Allow the pie to cool for 5 minutes. Sprinkle with the confectioners' sugar, if desired. Serve warm.

874. Pumpkin Pudding and Vanilla Wafers

Preparation Time: 10 minutes
Cooking Time: 15 minutes
Servings: 4

Ingredients:

- 1 cup canned no-salt-added pumpkin purée (not pumpkin pie filling)
- ¼ cup packed brown sugar
- 3 tablespoons all-purpose flour
- 1 egg, whisked
- 2 tablespoons milk
- 1 tablespoon unsalted butter, melted
- 1 teaspoon pure vanilla extract
- 4 low-fat vanilla wafers, crumbled
- Cooking spray

Directions:

- Coat a baking pan with cooking spray. Set aside.
- Mix the pumpkin purée, brown sugar, flour, whisked egg, milk, melted butter, and vanilla in a medium bowl and whisk to combine. Transfer the mixture to the baking pan.
- Select Bake, set temperature to 350°F (180°C), and set time to 15 minutes. Select Start to begin preheating.
- Once the oven has preheated, slide the pan into the oven.
- When cooking is complete, the pudding should be set.
- Remove the pudding from the oven to a wire rack to cool.
- Divide the pudding into four bowls and serve with the vanilla wafers sprinkled on top.

875. Coconut Cookies with Pecans

Preparation Time: 10 minutes
Cooking Time: 25 minutes
Servings: 10

Ingredients:

- 1½ cups coconut flour
- 1½ cups extra-fine almond flour
- ½ teaspoon baking powder
- 1/3 teaspoon baking soda
- 3 eggs plus an egg yolk, beaten
- ¾ cup coconut oil, at room temperature
- 1 cup unsalted pecan nuts, roughly chopped
- ¾ cup monk fruit
- ¼ teaspoon freshly grated nutmeg
- 1/3 teaspoon ground cloves
- ½ teaspoon pure vanilla extract
- ½ teaspoon pure coconut extract
- 1/8 teaspoon fine sea salt

Directions:

- Line a perforated pan with parchment paper.
- Mix the coconut flour, almond flour, baking powder, and baking soda in a large mixing bowl.
- In another mixing bowl, stir together the eggs and coconut oil. Add the wet mixture to the dry mixture.
- Mix in the remaining ingredients and stir until a soft dough form.
- Drop about 2 tablespoons of dough on the parchment paper for each cookie and flatten each biscuit until it's 1 inch thick.
- Select Bake, set temperature to 370°F (188°C), and set time to 25 minutes. Select Start to begin preheating.
- Once the oven has preheated, slide the pan into the oven.
- When cooking is complete, the cookies should be golden and firm to the touch.
- Remove from the oven to a plate. Let the cookies cool to room temperature and serve.

876. Gooey White Chocolate Cookies

Preparation Time: 5 minutes
Cooking Time: 11 minutes
Serving 10

Ingredients:

- 8 ounces (227 g) unsweetened white chocolate
- 2 eggs, well beaten
- 3/4 cup butter, at room temperature
- 1 2/3 cups almond flour
- ½ cup coconut flour
- ¾ cup granulated Swerve
- 2 tablespoons coconut oil
- 1/3 teaspoon grated nutmeg
- 1/3 teaspoon ground allspice

- ♦ 1/3 teaspoon ground anise star
- ♦ ¼ teaspoon fine sea salt

Directions:

- Line a baking sheet with parchment paper.
- Combine all the ingredients in a mixing bowl and knead for about 3 to 4 minutes, or until a soft dough form. Transfer to the refrigerator to chill for 20 minutes.
- Make the cookies: Roll the dough into 1-inch balls and transfer to the parchment-lined baking sheet, spacing 2 inches apart. Flatten each with the back of a spoon.
- Select Bake, set temperature to 350°F (180°C), and set time to 11 minutes. Select Start to begin preheating.
- Once the oven has preheated, slide the baking sheet into the oven.
- When cooking is complete, the cookies should be golden and firm to the touch.
- Transfer to a wire rack and let the cookies cool completely. Serve immediately.

877. Black and White Brownies

Preparation Time: 10 minutes
Cooking Time: 20 minutes
Servings: 1

Ingredients:

- ♦ 1 egg
- ♦ ¼ cup brown sugar
- ♦ 2 tablespoons white sugar
- ♦ 2 tablespoons safflower oil
- ♦ 1 teaspoon vanilla
- ♦ 1/3 cup all-purpose flour
- ♦ ¼ cup cocoa powder
- ♦ ¼ cup white chocolate chips
- ♦ Nonstick cooking spray

Directions:

- Spritz a baking pan with nonstick cooking spray.
- Whisk together the egg, brown sugar, and white sugar in a medium bowl. Mix in the safflower oil and vanilla and stir to combine.

- Add the flour and cocoa powder and stir just until incorporated. Fold in the white chocolate chips.
- Scrape the batter into the prepared baking pan.
- Select Bake, set temperature to 340°F (171°C), and set time to 20 minutes. Select Start to begin preheating.
- Once the oven has preheated, slide the pan into the oven.
- When done, the brownie should spring back when touched lightly with your fingers.
- Transfer to a wire rack and let cool for 30 minutes before slicing to serve.

878. Peanut Butter-Chocolate Bread Pudding

Preparation Time: 10 minutes
Cooking Time: 10 minutes
Servings: 8

Ingredients:

- ♦ 1 egg
- ♦ 1 egg yolk
- ♦ 3/4 cup chocolate milk
- ♦ 3 tablespoons brown sugar
- ♦ 3 tablespoons peanut butter
- ♦ 2 tablespoons cocoa powder
- ♦ 1 teaspoon vanilla
- ♦ 5 slices firm white bread, cubed
- ♦ Nonstick cooking spray

Directions:

- Spritz a baking pan with nonstick cooking spray.
- Whisk together the egg, egg yolk, chocolate milk, brown sugar, peanut butter, cocoa powder, and vanilla until well combined.
- Fold in the bread cubes and stir to mix well. Allow the bread soak for 10 minutes.
- When ready, transfer the egg mixture to the prepared baking pan.
- Select Bake, set temperature to 330°F (166°C), and set time to 10 minutes. Select Start to begin preheating.

- Once the oven has preheated, slide the pan into the oven.
- When done, the pudding should be just firm to the touch.
- Serve at room temperature.

879. Soda Bread

Preparation Time: 15 minutes
Cooking Time: 30 minutes
Servings: 10

Ingredients:

- 3 cups whole-wheat flour
- 1 tablespoon sugar
- 2 teaspoon caraway seeds
- 1 teaspoon baking soda
- 1 teaspoon sea salt
- ¼ cup chilled butter, cubed into small pieces
- 1 large egg, beaten
- 1½ cups buttermilk

Directions:

- In a large bowl, mix together the flour, sugar, caraway seeds, baking soda and salt and mix well.
- With a pastry cutter, cut in the butter flour until coarse crumbs like mixture is formed.
- Make a well in the center of flour mixture.
- In the well, add the egg, followed by the buttermilk and with a spatula, mix until well combined.
- With floured hand, shape the dough into a ball.
- Place the dough onto a floured surface and lightly knead it.
- Shape the dough into a 6-inch ball.
- With a serrated knife, score an X on the top of the dough.
- Press "Power Button" of Air Fry Oven and turn the dial to select the "Air Crisp" mode.
- Press the Time button and again turn the dial to set the cooking time to 30 minutes.
- Now push the Temp button and rotate the dial to set the temperature at 350 degrees F.

- Press "Start/Pause" button to start.
- When the unit beeps to show that it is preheated, open the lid.
- Arrange the dough in lightly greased "Air Fry Basket" and insert in the oven.
- Place the pan onto a wire rack to cool for about 10 minutes.
- Carefully, invert the bread onto wire rack to cool completely before slicing.
- Cut the bread into desired-sized slices and serve.

880. Baguette Bread

Preparation Time: 15 minutes
Cooking Time: 20 minutes
Servings: 8

Ingredients:

- ¾ cup warm water
- ¾ teaspoon quick yeast
- ½ teaspoon demerara sugar
- 1 cup bread flour
- ½ cup whole-wheat flour
- ½ cup oat flour
- 1¼ teaspoons salt

Directions:

- In a large bowl, place the water and sprinkle with yeast and sugar.
- Set aside for 5 minutes or until foamy.
- Add the bread flour and salt mix until a stiff dough form.
- Put the dough onto a floured surface and with your hands, knead until smooth and elastic.
- Now, shape the dough into a ball.
- Place the dough into a slightly oiled bowl and turn to coat well.
- With a plastic wrap, cover the bowl and place in a warm place for about 1 hour or until doubled in size.
- With your hands, punch down the dough and form into a long slender loaf.

- Place the loaf onto a lightly greased baking sheet and set aside in warm place, uncovered, for about 30 minutes.
- Press "Power Button" of Air Fry Oven and turn the dial to select the "Air Bake" mode.
- Press the Time button and again turn the dial to set the cooking time to 20 minutes.
- Now push the Temp button and rotate the dial to set the temperature at 450 degrees F.
- Press "Start/Pause" button to start.
- When the unit beeps to show that it is preheated, open the lid.
- Carefully, arrange the dough onto the "Wire Rack" and insert in the oven.
- Carefully, invert the bread onto wire rack to cool completely before slicing.
- Cut the bread into desired-sized slices and serve.

881. Yogurt Bread

Preparation Time: 20 minutes
Cooking Time: 40 minutes
Servings: 10

Ingredients:

- 1½ cups warm water, divided
- 1½ teaspoons active dry yeast
- 1 teaspoon sugar
- 3 cups all-purpose flour
- 1 cup plain Greek yogurt
- 2 teaspoons kosher salt

Directions:

- Add ½ cup of the warm water, yeast and sugar in the bowl of a stand mixer, fitted with the dough hook attachment and mix well.
- Set aside for about 5 minutes.
- Add the flour, yogurt, and salt and mix on medium-low speed until the dough comes together.
- Then, mix on medium speed for 5 minutes.
- Place the dough into a bowl.

- With a plastic wrap, cover the bowl and place in a warm place for about 2-3 hours or until doubled in size.
- Transfer the dough onto a lightly floured surface and shape into a smooth ball.
- Place the dough onto a greased parchment paper-lined rack.
- With a kitchen towel, cover the dough and let rest for 15 minutes.
- With a very sharp knife, cut a 4x½-inch deep cut down the center of the dough.
- Press "Power Button" of Air Fry Oven and turn the dial to select the "Air Roast" mode.
- Press the Time button and again turn the dial to set the cooking time to 40 minutes.
- Now push the Temp button and rotate the dial to set the temperature at 325 degrees F.
- Press "Start/Pause" button to start.
- When the unit beeps to show that it is preheated, open the lid.
- Carefully, arrange the dough onto the "Wire Rack" and insert in the oven.
- Carefully, invert the bread onto wire rack to cool completely before slicing.
- Cut the bread into desired-sized slices and serve.

882. Sunflower Seed Bread

Preparation Time: 15 minutes
Cooking Time: 18 minutes
Servings: 6

Ingredients:

- 2/3 cup whole-wheat flour
- 2/3 cup plain flour
- 1/3 cup sunflower seeds
- ½ sachet instant yeast
- 1 teaspoon salt
- 2/3-1 cup lukewarm water

Directions:

- In a bowl, mix together the flours, sunflower seeds, yeast, and salt.

- Slowly, add in the water, stirring continuously until a soft dough ball form.
- Now, move the dough onto a lightly floured surface and knead for about 5 minutes using your hands.
- Make a ball from the dough and place into a bowl.
- With a plastic wrap, cover the bowl and place at a warm place for about 30 minutes.
- Grease a cake pan.
- Coat the top of dough with water and place into the prepared cake pan.
- Press "Power Button" of Air Fry Oven and turn the dial to select the "Air Crisp" mode.
- Press the Time button and again turn the dial to set the cooking time to 18 minutes.
- Now push the Temp button and rotate the dial to set the temperature at 390 degrees F.
- Press "Start/Pause" button to start.
- When the unit beeps to show that it is preheated, open the lid.
- Arrange the pan in "Air Fry Basket" and insert in the oven.
- Place the pan onto a wire rack to cool for about 10 minutes.
- Carefully, invert the bread onto wire rack to cool completely before slicing.
- Cut the bread into desired-sized slices and serve.

883. Date Bread

Preparation Time: 15 minutes
Cooking Time: 22 minutes
Servings: 10

Ingredients:

- 2½ cup dates, pitted and chopped
- ¼ cup butter
- 1 cup hot water
- 1½ cups flour
- ½ cup brown sugar
- 1 teaspoon baking powder
- 1 teaspoon baking soda
- ½ teaspoon salt

- 1 egg

Directions:

- In a large bowl, add the dates, butter and top with the hot water.
- Set aside for about 5 minutes.
- In another bowl, mix together the flour, brown sugar, baking powder, baking soda, and salt.
- In the same bowl of dates, mix well the flour mixture, and egg.
- Grease a baking pan.
- Place the mixture into the prepared pan.
- Press "Power Button" of Air Fry Oven and turn the dial to select the "Air Crisp" mode.
- Press the Time button and again turn the dial to set the cooking time to 22 minutes.
- Now push the Temp button and rotate the dial to set the temperature at 340 degrees F.
- Press "Start/Pause" button to start.
- When the unit beeps to show that it is preheated, open the lid.
- Arrange the pan in "Air Fry Basket" and insert in the oven.
- Place the pan onto a wire rack to cool for about 10 minutes.
- Carefully, invert the bread onto wire rack to cool completely before slicing.
- Cut the bread into desired-sized slices and serve.

884. Date & Walnut Bread

Preparation Time: 15 minutes
Cooking Time: 35 minutes
Servings: 5

Ingredients:

- 1 cup dates, pitted and sliced
- ¾ cup walnuts, chopped
- 1 tablespoon instant coffee powder
- 1 tablespoon hot water
- 1¼ cups plain flour
- ¼ teaspoon salt
- ½ teaspoon baking powder

- ♦ ½ teaspoon baking soda
- ♦ ½ cup condensed milk
- ♦ ½ cup butter, softened
- ♦ ½ teaspoon vanilla essence

Directions:

- In a large bowl, add the dates, butter and top with the hot water.
- Set aside for about 30 minutes.
- Drain well and set aside.
- In a small bowl, add the coffee powder and hot water and mix well.
- In a large bowl, mix together the flour, baking powder, baking soda and salt.
- In another large bowl, add the condensed milk and butter and beat until smooth.
- Add the flour mixture, coffee mixture and vanilla essence and mix until well combined.
- Fold in dates and ½ cup of walnut.
- Line a baking pan with a lightly greased parchment paper.
- Place the mixture into the prepared pan and sprinkle with the remaining walnuts.
- Press "Power Button" of Air Fry Oven and turn the dial to select the "Air Crisp" mode.
- Press the Time button and again turn the dial to set the cooking time to 35 minutes.
- Now push the Temp button and rotate the dial to set the temperature at 320 degrees F.
- Press "Start/Pause" button to start.
- When the unit beeps to show that it is preheated, open the lid.
- Arrange the pan in "Air Fry Basket" and insert in the oven.
- Place the pan onto a wire rack to cool for about 10 minutes.
- Carefully, invert the bread onto wire rack to cool completely before slicing.
- Cut the bread into desired-sized slices and serve.

885.   Brown Sugar Banana Bread

Preparation Time: 15 minutes
Cooking Time: 30 minutes

Servings: 4

Ingredients:

- ♦ 1 egg
- ♦ 1 ripe banana, peeled and mashed
- ♦ ¼ cup milk
- ♦ 2 tablespoons canola oil
- ♦ 2 tablespoons brown sugar
- ♦ ¾ cup plain flour
- ♦ ½ teaspoon baking soda

Directions:

- Line a very small baking pan with a greased parchment paper.
- In a small bowl, add the egg and banana and beat well.
- Add the milk, oil and sugar and beat until well combined.
- Add the flour and baking soda and mix until just combined.
- Place the mixture into prepared pan.
- Press "Power Button" of Air Fry Oven and turn the dial to select the "Air Crisp" mode.
- Press the Time button and again turn the dial to set the cooking time to 30 minutes.
- Now push the Temp button and rotate the dial to set the temperature at 320 degrees F.
- Press "Start/Pause" button to start.
- When the unit beeps to show that it is preheated, open the lid.
- Arrange the pan in "Air Fry Basket" and insert in the oven.
- Place the pan onto a wire rack to cool for about 10 minutes.
- Carefully, invert the bread onto wire rack to cool completely before slicing.
- Cut the bread into desired-sized slices and serve.

886.   Cinnamon Banana Bread

Preparation Time: 15 minutes
Cooking Time: 20 minutes
Servings: 8

Ingredients:

- 1 1/3 cups flour
- 2/3 cup sugar
- 1 teaspoon baking soda
- 1 teaspoon baking powder
- 1 teaspoon ground cinnamon
- 1 teaspoon salt
- ½ cup milk
- ½ cup olive oil
- 3 bananas, peeled and sliced

Directions:

- In the bowl of a stand mixer, add all the ingredients and mix well.
- Grease a loaf pan.
- Place the mixture into the prepared pan.
- Press "Power Button" of Air Fry Oven and turn the dial to select the "Air Crisp" mode.
- Press the Time button and again turn the dial to set the cooking time to 20 minutes.
- Now push the Temp button and rotate the dial to set the temperature at 330 degrees F.
- Press "Start/Pause" button to start.
- When the unit beeps to show that it is preheated, open the lid.
- Arrange the pan in "Air Fry Basket" and insert in the oven.
- Place the pan onto a wire rack to cool for about 10 minutes.
- Carefully, invert the bread onto wire rack to cool completely before slicing.
- Cut the bread into desired-sized slices and serve.

887.   Banana & Walnut Bread

Preparation Time: 15 minutes
Cooking Time: 25 minutes
Servings: 10

Ingredients:

- 1½ cups self-rising flour
- ¼ teaspoon bicarbonate of soda
- 5 tablespoons plus 1 teaspoon butter
- 2/3 cup plus ½ tablespoon caster sugar
- 2 medium eggs

- 3½ oz. walnuts, chopped
- 2 cups bananas, peeled and mashed

Directions:

- In a bowl, mix together the flour and bicarbonate of soda.
- In another bowl, add the butter, and sugar and beat until pale and fluffy.
- Add the eggs, one at a time along with a little flour and mix well.
- Stir in the remaining flour and walnuts.
- Add the bananas and mix until well combined.
- Grease a loaf pan.
- Place the mixture into the prepared pan.
- Press "Power Button" of Air Fry Oven and turn the dial to select the "Air Crisp" mode.
- Press the Time button and again turn the dial to set the cooking time to 10 minutes.
- Now push the Temp button and rotate the dial to set the temperature at 355 degrees F.
- Press "Start/Pause" button to start.
- When the unit beeps to show that it is preheated, open the lid.
- Arrange the pan in "Air Fry Basket" and insert in the oven.
- After 10 minutes of cooking, set the temperature at 338 degrees F for 15minutes.
- Place the pan onto a wire rack to cool for about 10 minutes.
- Carefully, invert the bread onto wire rack to cool completely before slicing.
- Cut the bread into desired-sized slices and serve.

888.   Banana & Raisin Bread

Preparation Time: 15 minutes
Cooking Time: 40 minutes
Servings: 6

Ingredients:

- 1½ cups cake flour
- 1 teaspoon baking soda
- ½ teaspoon ground cinnamon

- Salt, to taste
- ½ cup vegetable oil
- 2 eggs
- ½ cup sugar
- ½ teaspoon vanilla extract
- 3 medium bananas, peeled and mashed
- ½ cup raisins, chopped finely

Directions:

- In a large bowl, mix together the flour, baking soda, cinnamon, and salt.
- In another bowl, beat well eggs and oil.
- Add the sugar, vanilla extract, and bananas and beat until well combined.
- Add the flour mixture and stir until just combined.
- Place the mixture into a lightly greased baking pan and sprinkle with raisins.
- With a piece of foil, cover the pan loosely.
- Press "Power Button" of Air Fry Oven and turn the dial to select the "Air Bake" mode.
- Press the Time button and again turn the dial to set the cooking time to 30 minutes.
- Now push the Temp button and rotate the dial to set the temperature at 300 degrees F.
- Press "Start/Pause" button to start.
- When the unit beeps to show that it is preheated, open the lid.
- Arrange the pan in "Air Fry Basket" and insert in the oven.
- After 30 minutes of cooking, set the temperature to 285 degrees F for 10 minutes.
- Place the pan onto a wire rack to cool for about 10 minutes.
- Carefully, invert the bread onto wire rack to cool completely before slicing.
- Cut the bread into desired-sized slices and serve.

889. Pub Burgers

Preparation Time: 30 minutes
Cooking Time: 30 minutes
Servings: 8

Ingredients:

- 2-pound ground beef
- 3 green onions, chopped
- 1 tbsp. ketchup
- 8 slices American cheese
- 8 Burger Buns, split
- 1/2 tsp. salt
- 1/4 tsp. pepper
- 10 ¾-ounce can chicken gumbo soup partially drained
- 10 ¾-ounce tomato soup
- 2 tbsp. mustard

Directions:

- Select Sauté on normal.
- Cook ground beef until no longer pink.
- Put in the rest of the ingredients except for cheese and bun to Air fryer.
- Cook on High Pressure with Manual mode for 7 minutes.
- Spoon beef mixture onto buns.
- Add cheese slices to serve.

890. Buffalo Chicken Sliders

Preparation Time: 15 minutes
Cooking Time: 15-20 minutes
Servings: 6-12

Ingredients:

- 2.5 pounds boneless, chicken breast cut into large pieces
- 4 tbsp. butter
- 3 green onions, diced
- 1/2 cup ranch dressing
- 12 sweet Hawaiian rolls
- 1/2 cup chicken broth
- 3/4 cup Frank's Buffalo Sauce
- 1 tbsp. dry ranch dressing mix
- 2 garlic cloves, minced
- 8 oz. cheddar cheese, shredded

Directions:

- Add chicken pieces, butter, dry ranch dressing mix, chicken broth, hot sauce, and garlic cloves to the Air fryer.
- Pressure Cook for 15 minutes.
- Shred chicken with forks.
- Let the chicken soak in the prepared sauce for a couple of minutes.
- Fill each roll with buffalo chicken, cheese, ranch, and green onions and serve.

891. Bacon Pizza

Preparation Time: 10 minutes
Cooking Time: 20 minutes
Servings: 4

Ingredients:

- Flour, for dusting
- Nonstick baking spray with flour
- 4 frozen large whole-wheat dinner rolls, thawed
- 5 cloves garlic, minced
- ¾ cup pizza sauce
- ½ teaspoon dried oregano
- ½ teaspoon garlic salt
- 8 slices precooked bacon, cut into 1-inch pieces
- 1¼ cups shredded Cheddar cheese

Directions:

- Set to 360 Bake. On a lightly floured surface, press out each dinner roll to a 5-by-3-inch oval.
- Spray four 6-by-4-inch pieces of heavy-duty foil with nonstick spray and place one crust on each piece.
- Bake, two at a time, for 2 minutes or until the crusts are set, but not browned.
- Meanwhile, in a small bowl, combine the garlic, pizza sauce, oregano, and garlic salt. When the pizza crusts are set, spread each with some of the sauce. Top with the bacon pieces and Cheddar cheese.
- Bake, two at a time, for another 8 minutes or until the crust is browned and the cheese is melted and starting to brown.

Nutrition:

Calories:312
Fat: 10.5g
Fiber: 5.9g
Carbs: 40.1g
Protein: 10.5 g

892. Mexican Style Pizza

Preparation Time: 10 minutes
Cooking Time: 10 minutes
Servings: 4

Ingredients:

- ¾ cup refried beans (from a 16-ounce can)
- ½ cup salsa
- 10 frozen precooked beef meatballs, thawed and sliced
- 1 jalapeño pepper, sliced
- 4 whole-wheat pita breads
- 1 cup shredded pepper Jack cheese
- ½ cup shredded Colby cheese
- 1/3 cup sour cream

Directions:

- Set to 370 Bake. In a medium bowl, combine the refried beans, salsa, meatballs, and jalapeño pepper.
- Preheat the air fryer for 3 to 4 minutes or until hot.
- Top the pitas with the refried bean mixture and sprinkle with the cheeses.
- Bake for 7 to 9 minutes or until the pizza is crisp and the cheese is melted and starts to brown.
- Top each pizza with a dollop of sour cream and serve warm.

893. Paprika Sweet Potato Chips

Preparation Time: 15 minutes
Cooking Time: 40 minutes
Servings: 4

Ingredients:

- 31-ounces of sweet potatoes, peeled and cut into chips
- ½ teaspoon salt

- ♦ 2 tablespoons olive oil
- ♦ ½ tablespoon paprika

Directions:

- Toss all the ingredients together in a bowl.
- Place in a pan inside your air fryer and cook for 40-minutes at 300°Fahrenheit.

894. Cheddar Muffins

Preparation Time: 15 minutes
Cooking Time: 15 minutes
Servings: 8

Ingredients:

- ♦ 2 cups All-purpose flour
- ♦ 1 ½ cup milk
- ♦ ½ tsp. baking powder
- ♦ ½ tsp. baking soda
- ♦ 2 tbsp. butter
- ♦ 2 cups melted cheddar
- ♦ 1 tbsp. sugar
- ♦ 2 tsp. vinegar
- ♦ Muffin cups

Directions:

- Combine the ingredients except milk to create a crumbly blend.
- Add this milk to the blend and make a batter and pour into the muffin cups.
- Preheat the fryer to 300 F and cook 15 minutes.
- Check whether they are done using a toothpick.

Nutrition:

Calories:185
Fat: 2.5g
Fiber: 1.9g
Carbs: 13.5g
Protein: 1.8g

895. Kale Chips

Preparation Time: 15 minutes
Cooking Time: 6-10 minutes
Servings: 3-4

Ingredients:

- ♦ 6 cups packed kale leaves, de-stemmed.
- ♦ 1 tbsp extra-virgin olive oil
- ♦ 1 tsp soy sauce, low in sodium
- ♦ 1 tsp black sesame seeds
- ♦ 1/2 tsp dried garlic, minced
- ♦ Poppy seeds (optional)

Directions:

- Wash and dry kale leaves.
- Toss with olive oil and soy sauce in a bowl ensuring the leaves are covered equally.
- Place piece of kale leaves in air fryer basket and cook at 188°C for 6 minutes or until fresh.
- Shake basket partially through cooking.
- Place kale leaves on a level sheet and sprinkle with sesame seeds, poppy seeds, and garlic.

896. Mediterranean Turkey Burgers

Preparation Time: 30 minutes
Cooking Time: 16-18 minutes
Servings: 4

Ingredients:

- ♦ 1 lb. ground turkey
- ♦ ½ cup breadcrumbs
- ♦ ¼ cup Parmesan cheese, grated
- ♦ 1 egg, beaten
- ♦ 1 tbsp minced garlic
- ♦ 1 tbsp olive oil
- ♦ 1 tsp horseradish sauce
- ♦ 4 tbsp Greek yogurt
- ♦ 4 buns, halved
- ♦ 4 tomato slices

Directions:

- Preheat air fryer to 380 F. Grease the air fryer basket with cooking spray.
- In a bowl, combine ground turkey, breadcrumbs, Parmesan cheese, egg, garlic, salt, and black pepper. Mix well. Form balls and flatten to make patties. Brush them with olive oil and place in the air fryer.

- Air Fry for 16-18 minutes, flipping once halfway through until nice and golden. Mix the yogurt with horseradish sauce. Assemble the burgers by spreading the yogurt mixture, then the patties, and finally top with fresh tomato slices. Serve immediately.

897. Spiced Mixed Nuts

Preparation Time: 15 minutes
Cooking Time: 10 minutes
Servings: 6

Ingredients:

- ½ cup pecans
- ½ cup walnuts
- ½ cup almonds
- A pinch of cayenne pepper
- 2 tbsp sugar
- 2 tbsp egg whites
- 2 tsp ground cinnamon
- Cooking spray

Directions:

- Add cayenne pepper, sugar, and cinnamon to a bowl and mix well; set aside.
- In another bowl, mix pecans, walnuts, almonds, and egg whites. Add in the spice mixture and stir.
- Grease a baking dish with cooking spray. Pour in the nuts and place in the fryer.
- Bake for 6 minutes. After, stir the nuts using a wooden vessel and cook further for 4 minutes.
- Pour the nuts in the bowl and let cool before serving.

898. Tomato Quick Bread

Preparation Time: 15 minutes
Cooking Time: 25-30 minutes
Servings: 6

Ingredients:

- 1 and ½ cups flour
- 1 teaspoon cinnamon powder
- 1 teaspoon baking powder
- 1 teaspoon baking soda

- ¾ cup maple syrup
- 1 cup tomatoes chopped
- ½ cup olive oil
- 2 tablespoon apple cider vinegar

Directions:

- In a bowl, mix flour with baking powder, baking soda, cinnamon and maple syrup and stir well. In another bowl, mix tomatoes with olive oil and vinegar and stir well.
- Combine the 2 mixtures, stir well, pour into a greased round pan that fits your air fryer, introduce in the fryer and cook at 360 degrees F for 30 minutes.
- Leave cake to cool down, slice and serve. Enjoy!

899. Beef Jerky

Preparation Time: 30 minutes
Cooking Time: 60 minutes
Servings: 4

Ingredients:

- 1 cup beer
- 1/2 cup tamari sauce
- 1 teaspoon liquid smoke
- 2 garlic cloves, minced
- Sea salt and ground black pepper
- 1 teaspoon ancho chili powder
- 2 tablespoons honey
- 3/4-pound flank steak, slice into strips

Directions:

- Place all ingredients in a ceramic dish; let it marinate for 3 hours in the refrigerator.
- Slice the beef into thin strips Marinate the beef in the refrigerator overnight.
- Now, discard the marinade and hang the meat in the cooking basket by using skewers.
- Air fry at 190 degrees f degrees for 1 hour. Store it in an airtight container for up to 2 weeks.

900. Hawaiian Pork Sliders

Preparation Time: 15 minutes
Cooking Time: 15 minutes

Servings: 8

Ingredients:

- Olive oil
- ½ cup crushed pineapple, drained
- 1-pound lean ground pork
- 1 teaspoon Worcestershire sauce
- ½ teaspoon garlic powder
- ½ teaspoon salt
- ½ teaspoon freshly ground black pepper
- Pinch of cayenne pepper
- 8 whole-wheat slider buns

Directions:

- Set to 370 F. Spray a fryer basket lightly with olive oil.
- In a large bowl, mix together the pineapple, pork, Worcestershire sauce, garlic powder, salt, and pepper.
- Form the mixture into 8 patties.
- Place the patties in the fryer basket in a single layer and spray lightly with olive oil. You may need to cook them in batches.
- Air fry for 7 minutes. Flip the patties over, lightly spray with olive oil, and cook until the patties reach an internal temperature of at least 145°F, an additional 5 to 8 minutes.
- Place the cooked patties on the slider buns and serve.

901. Hoisin Turkey Burgers

Preparation Time: 40 minutes
Cooking Time: 20 minutes
Servings: 4

Ingredients:

- Olive oil
- 1-pound lean ground turkey
- ¼ cup whole-wheat bread crumbs
- ¼ cup hoisin sauce
- 2 tablespoons soy sauce
- 4 whole-wheat buns

Directions:

- Set to 360 F. Spray a fryer basket lightly with olive oil.
- In a large bowl, mix together the turkey, bread crumbs, hoisin sauce, and soy sauce.
- Form the mixture into 4 equal patties. Cover with plastic wrap and refrigerate the patties for 30 minutes.
- Place the patties in the fryer basket in a single layer. Spray the patties lightly with olive oil.
- Air fry for 10 minutes. Flip the patties over, lightly spray with olive oil, and cook until golden brown, an additional 5 to 10 minutes.
- Place the patties on buns and top with your choice of low-calorie burger toppings like sliced tomatoes, onions, and cabbage slaw.

902. Pepperoni Chips

Preparation Time: 5 minutes
Cooking Time: 8- 10 minutes
Servings: 5

Ingredients:

- 6 oz pepperoni slices

Directions:

- Place one batch of pepperoni slices in the air fryer basket.
- Cook for 8 minutes at 360 F.
- Cook remaining pepperoni slices using same steps.
- Serve and enjoy.

903. Caramel Popcorn

Preparation Time: 10 minutes
Cooking Time: 5-10 minutes
Servings: 8

Ingredients:

- 8 cups of popcorn
- 1 butter tablet
- 1 cup of sugar
- 1/3 cup whipped cream

Directions:

- Put a quantity of corn in a pan in put it into the air fryer. Drizzle with a little olive oil.

- Set the temperature at 2400F for 5 minutes.

- When the popcorn is ready, put it in a large bowl and set aside while preparing the sauce.

- Mix butter, sugar and cream and heat over medium heat, stirring constantly. In a few minutes the sauce should be boiling, continue boiling until the mixture reaches the soft ball stage 2400F.

- Remove mixture from heat and pour over popcorn, stirring until all popcorn is well coated. Be sure to serve it right away.

DESSERT, CAKE, COOKIE

904. Grilled Curried Fruit

Preparation Time: 10 minutes
Cooking Time: 5 minutes
Servings: 6 to 8

Ingredients:

- 2 peaches
- 2 firm pears
- 2 plums
- 2 tablespoons melted butter
- 1 tablespoon honey
- 2 to 3 teaspoons curry powder

Directions:

- Cut the peaches in half, remove the pits, and cut each half in half again. Cut the pears in half, core them, and remove the stem. Cut each half in half again. Do the same with the plums.

- Spread a large sheet of heavy-duty foil on your work surface. Arrange the fruit on the foil and drizzle with the butter and honey. Sprinkle with the curry powder.

- Wrap the fruit in the foil, making sure to leave some air space in the packet.

- Put the foil package in the basket and grill for 5 to 8 minutes, shaking the basket once during the cooking time, until the fruit is soft and tender.

905. Apple Peach Cranberry Crisp

Preparation Time: 10 minutes
Cooking Time: 12 minutes
Servings: 8

Ingredients:

- 1 apple, peeled and chopped
- 2 peaches, peeled and chopped
- 1/3 cup dried cranberries
- 2 tablespoons honey
- 1/3 cup brown sugar
- ¼ cup flour
- ½ cup oatmeal
- 3 tablespoons softened butter

Directions:

- In a 6-by-6-by-2-inch pan, combine the apple, peaches, cranberries, and honey, and mix well.

- In a medium bowl, combine the brown sugar, flour, oatmeal, and butter, and mix until crumbly. Sprinkle this mixture over the fruit in the pan.

- Bake for 10 to 12 minutes or until the fruit is bubbly and the topping is golden brown. Serve warm.

906. Orange Cornmeal Cake

Preparation Time: 7 minutes
Cooking Time: 23 minutes
Servings: 8

Ingredients:

- Nonstick baking spray with flour
- 1¼ cups all-purpose flour
- 1/3 cup yellow cornmeal
- ¾ cup white sugar
- 1 teaspoon baking soda
- ¼ cup safflower oil
- 1¼ cups orange juice, divided
- 1 teaspoon vanilla
- ¼ cup powdered sugar

Directions:

- Spray a 6-by-6-by-2-inch baking pan with nonstick spray and set aside.

- In a medium bowl, combine the flour, cornmeal, sugar, baking soda, safflower oil, 1 cup of the orange juice, and vanilla, and mix well.

- Pour the batter into the baking pan and place in the air fryer. Bake for 23 minutes or until a toothpick inserted in the center of the cake comes out clean.

- Remove the cake from the basket and place on a cooling rack. Using a toothpick, make about 20 holes in the cake.

- In a small bowl, combine remaining ¼ cup of orange juice and the powdered sugar and stir well. Drizzle this mixture over the hot cake slowly so the cake absorbs it.

- Cool completely, then cut into wedges to serve.

907.　Black Forest Hand Pies

Preparation Time: 10 minutes
Cooking Time: 15 minutes
Servings: 6

Ingredients:

- 3 tablespoons milk or dark chocolate chips
- 2 tablespoons thick, hot fudge sauce
- 2 tablespoons chopped dried cherries
- 1 (10-by-15-inch) sheet puff pastry, thawed
- 1 egg white, beaten
- 2 tablespoons sugar
- ½ teaspoon cinnamon

Directions:

- In a small bowl, combine the chocolate chips, fudge sauce, and dried cherries.

- Roll out the puff pastry on a floured surface. Cut into 6 squares with a sharp knife.

- Divide the chocolate chip mixture onto the center of each puff pastry square. Fold the squares in half to make triangles. Firmly press the edges with the tines of a fork to seal.

- Brush the triangles on all sides sparingly with the beaten egg white. Sprinkle the tops with sugar and cinnamon.

- Place in the air fryer basket and bake for 15 minutes or until the triangles are golden brown. The filling will be hot, so cool for at least 20 minutes before serving.

908.　Marble Cheesecake

Preparation Time: 10 minutes
Cooking Time: 20 minutes
Servings: 8

Ingredients:

- 1 cup graham cracker crumbs
- 3 tablespoons softened butter
- 1 1/2 (8-ounce) packages cream cheese, softened
- 1/3 cup sugar
- 2 eggs, beaten
- 1 tablespoon flour
- 1 teaspoon vanilla
- ¼ cup chocolate syrup

Directions:

- For the crust, combine the graham cracker crumbs and butter in a small bowl and mix well. Press into the bottom of a 6-by-6-by-2-inch baking pan and put in the freezer to set.

- For the filling, combine the cream cheese and sugar in a medium bowl and mix well. Beat in the eggs, one at a time. Add the flour and vanilla.

- Remove 2/3 cup of the filling to a small bowl and stir in the chocolate syrup until combined.

- Pour the vanilla filling into the pan with the crust. Drop the chocolate filling over the vanilla filling by the spoonful. With a clean butter knife stir the fillings in a zigzag pattern to marbleize them.

- Bake for 20 minutes or until the cheesecake is just set.

- Cool on a wire rack for 1 hour, then chill in the refrigerator until the cheesecake is firm.

909.　Chocolate Peanut Butter Molten Cupcakes

Preparation Time: 10 minutes
Cooking Time: 13 minutes
Servings: 8

Ingredients:

- Nonstick baking spray with flour
- 1 1/3 cups chocolate cake mix (from 15-ounce box)
- 1 egg
- 1 egg yolk

361

- ¼ cup safflower oil
- ¼ cup hot water
- 1/3 cup sour cream
- 3 tablespoons peanut butter
- 1 tablespoon powdered sugar

Directions:

- Double up 16 foil muffin cups to make 8 cups. Spray each lightly with nonstick spray; set aside.

- In a medium bowl, combine the cake mix, egg, egg yolk, safflower oil, water, and sour cream, and beat until combined.

- In a small bowl, combine the peanut butter and powdered sugar and mix well. Form this mixture into 8 balls.

- Spoon about ¼ cup of the chocolate batter into each muffin cup and top with a peanut butter ball. Spoon remaining batter on top of the peanut butter balls to cover them.

- Arrange the cups in the air fryer basket, leaving some space between each. Bake for 10 to 13 minutes or until the tops look dry and set.

- Let the cupcakes cool for about 10 minutes, then serve warm.

910. Chocolate Peanut Butter Bread Pudding

Preparation Time: 10 minutes
Cooking Time: 12 minutes
Servings: 8

Ingredients:

- Nonstick baking spray with flour
- 1 egg
- 1 egg yolk
- ¾ cup chocolate milk
- 2 tablespoons cocoa powder
- 3 tablespoons brown sugar
- 3 tablespoons peanut butter
- 1 teaspoon vanilla
- 5 slices firm white bread, cubed

Directions:

- Spray a 6-by-6-by-2-inch baking pan with nonstick spray.

- In a medium bowl, combine the egg, egg yolk, chocolate milk, cocoa, brown sugar, peanut butter, and vanilla, and mix until combined. Stir in the bread cubes and let soak for 10 minutes.

- Spoon this mixture into the prepared pan. Bake for 10 to 12 minutes or until the pudding is firm to the touch.

911. Big Chocolate Chip Cookie

Preparation Time: 7 minutes
Cooking Time: 9 minutes
Servings: 8

Ingredients:

- Nonstick baking spray with flour
- 3 tablespoons softened butter
- 1/3 cup plus 1 tablespoon brown sugar
- 1 egg yolk
- 1/2 cup flour
- 2 tablespoons ground white chocolate
- ¼ teaspoon baking soda
- ½ teaspoon vanilla
- ¾ cup chocolate chips

Directions:

- In medium bowl, beat the butter and brown sugar together until fluffy. Stir in the egg yolk.

- Add the flour, white chocolate, baking soda, and vanilla, and mix well. Stir in the chocolate chips.

- Line a 6-by-6-by-2-inch baking pan with parchment paper. Spray the parchment paper with nonstick baking spray with flour.

- Spread the batter into the prepared pan, leaving a ½-inch border on all sides.

- Bake for about 9 minutes or until the cookie is light brown and just barely set.

- Remove the pan from the air fryer and let cool for 10 minutes. Remove the cookie from the pan, remove the parchment paper, and let cool on a wire rack.

912. Frosted Peanut Butter Cookie

Preparation Time: 10 minutes
Cooking Time: 10 minutes
Servings: 4

Ingredients:

- 3 tablespoons butter, at room temperature
- 1/3 cup plus 1 tablespoon brown sugar
- 1 egg yolk
- ⅔ cup flour
- 5 tablespoons peanut butter, divided
- ¼ teaspoon baking soda
- 1 teaspoon vanilla
- ½ cup semisweet chocolate chips

Directions:

- In a medium bowl, beat the butter and brown sugar together until fluffy. Stir in the egg yolk.
- Add the flour, 3 tablespoons of the peanut butter, the baking soda, and vanilla, and mix well.
- Line a 6-by-6-by-2-inch baking pan with parchment paper.
- Spread the batter into the prepared pan, leaving a ½-inch border on all sides.
- Bake for 7 to 10 minutes or until the cookie is light brown and just barely set.
- Remove the pan from the air fryer and let cool for 10 minutes. Remove the cookie from the pan, remove the parchment paper, and let cool on a wire rack.
- In a small heatproof cup, combine the chocolate chips with the remaining 2 tablespoons of peanut butter. Bake for 1 to 2 minutes or until the chips are melted. Stir to combine and spread on the cookie.

913.   Ranch Kale Chips

Preparation Time: 5 minutes
Cooking Time: 4 hours
Servings: 2

Ingredients:

- 2 tablespoon Extra Virgin Olive Oil
- 2 tablespoon ranch seasoning
- 1 bunch kale

Directions:

- Place the kale in a large bowl.
- Drizzle the olive oil over the kale and toss in the kale until all the pieces are coated in oil.
- Sprinkle the ranch seasoning over the kale and toss in the kale well to coat with the seasoning.
- Arrange the kale in a single layer on three Air Flow racks. Place the racks on the lower, middle and upper shelves of the Power Air Fryer oven.
- Press the power button then the dehydrator button (4 hour cook time) and increase the cooking temperature to 125°F.

914.   Vanilla Bean Meringues

Preparation Time: 10 minutes
Cooking Time: 3 ½ hours
Servings: 4

Ingredients:

- 4 extra large egg whites
- 1½ cup sugar
- 1 teaspoon salt
- Seeds from 1 vanilla bean

Directions:

- Combine the sugar and salt in a bowl.
- Beat the egg whites on medium speed in a separate bowl until very frothy and soft peaks begin to form.
- Add the sugar mixture little by little to the egg whites and beat until medium peaks form.
- Add the vanilla extract and seeds to the egg whites, increase the speed of the mixer to high and beat until stiff peaks form.
- Transfer the egg whites to a star or rosette tipped piping bag and place small mounds on three Air Flow racks lined with parchment paper. Place the racks on the lower, middle and upper shelves of the Power AirFryer oven.
- Press the power button, then the dehydrator button and raise the cooking temperature to 170°F and set cooking time to 3 ½ hours.

915. Pignoli Cookies

Preparation Time: 30-45 minutes
Cooking Time: 30 minutes
Servings: 36

Ingredients:

- 2 cup pine nuts
- 4 large egg whites
- 1 cup confectioners' sugar
- 1/2 cup sugar
- 10-ounce almond paste

Directions:

- Whisk together the almond paste and sugar in a bowl until just combined.
- Pat 2 egg whites into the almond mixture.
- Gradually add the confectioner's sugar to the almond mixture and mix well to make a dough.
- Beat the remaining two egg whites in a separate bowl until the whites are foamy.
- Dip your fingers in the flour to prevent the dough from sticking to your fingers. Shape the dough into 1 inch. balls, dip the balls in the egg whites and cover each ball with the pine nuts.
- Place the balls on two parchment-lined Air Flow Racks and flatten each ball lightly.
- Position the racks on the bottom and center shelves of the appliance.
- Press the power button, reduce the cooking temperature to 325°F and raise the cooking time to 18 minutes. Turn racks midway through cook time (9 minutes).

916. Jam Filled Buttermilk Scones

Preparation Time: 30-45 minutes
Cooking Time: 30 minutes
Servings: 8

Ingredients:

- 2¼ cup flour
- 1 teaspoon salt
- 1/4 cup sugar
- 2 teaspoon Baking Powder
- 12 tablespoon butter
- 2 large eggs
- 1/3 cup buttermilk
- 1 teaspoon Vanilla Extract
- 1/2 cup strawberry jams
- 2 tablespoon demerara sugar

Directions:

- Mix baking powder, flour, sugar and salt in a container.
- Grate the butter into the bowl using the larger holes on a box grater.
- Mix the ingredients in the bowl.
- Whisk the patted eggs, vanilla, and buttermilk into the bowl, to complete the dough.
- Split the dough in half, form each half of the dough into a disk, cover the disks in plastic wrap and place in the refrigerator for 60 minutes.
- Place a disc in a new sheet of plastic wrap. Roll the disc to ½ inch thickness.
- Spread the jam on the disk leaving a ½ in. scab around the edges.
- Roll the other disc in another sheet of plastic wrap to ½ inch thickness.
- Place the second disc over the first disc and gently press the discs to seal the edges.
- Cut the dough into eight wedges.
- Place shims on two parchment-lined Air Flow racks. Generously brush the wedges with the buttermilk and sprinkle with the demerara sugar. Place the racks on the bottom and center shelves of the appliance.
- Press the power button and increase cook temperature to 375 ° F and cook time to 18 minutes. Rotate the racks after 10 minutes.

917. Mini Chocolate Peanut Butter Cupcakes

Preparation Time: 30 minutes
Cooking Time: 15 minutes
Servings: 48

Ingredients:

- 2/3 cup flour

- 1 cup vegetable oil
- 1/2 cup whole milk
- 1 cup sugar
- 2 cup confectioners' sugar
- 1/4 cup water
- 1/2 teaspoon salt
- 1 tablespoon whole milk
- 1 large egg
- 3/2 teaspoon Vanilla Extract
- 1/3 cup cocoa
- 1 stick unsalted butter
- 1/2 teaspoon baking soda
- Chocolate pearls
- Peanut Butter Frosting
- 1 teaspoon Baking Powder

Directions:

- Combine the egg, ½ cup milk, vegetable oil, and vanilla in a bowl and beat to combine.
- Bring together the baking powder, baking soda, flour, sugar, cocoa and salt with the egg mixture and whisk.
- Gradually add the boiling water to the mixture and toss very well.
- Pour or pour batter into foil cupcake liners until about two-thirds of each is full.
- Place cupcake liners on two Air Flow racks. Position the racks on the bottom and middle shelves of the appliance.
- Press the power button (15-minute cook time) and decrease cook temperature to 350°F. Turn racks halfway through cook time (7 ½ minutes).
- Let the cupcakes cool for 30 minutes.
- Bring together the peanut butter and butter in a bowl. Add the confectioners' sugar and 1 tablespoon milk slowly until frosting is creamy.
- Top cupcakes with frosting and chocolate pearls.

918.   Veggie Chips

Preparation Time: 30 minutes
Cooking Time: 10 hours
Servings: 2

Ingredients:

- 2 medium-sized sweet potatoes, skinned & finely chopped
- 3 large parsnips, peeled & thinly chopped
- 3 medium-sized beets, skinned & thinly chopped

Directions:

- Place the sliced vegetables on the Air Flow racks. Do not overlap.
- Press the Dehydrate button. Raise the temperature to 115oF.
- Set the timer for 10 hours to start the cook cycle.
- You may need to add extra time to add crispiness.
- Optional- salt to taste.

919.   Cheddar Biscuits

Preparation Time: 40 minutes
Cooking Time: 15 minutes
Servings: 16

Ingredients:

- 3/4 cup buttermilk
- 1/2 teaspoon seafood seasoning
- 1/2 cup scallions, chopped
- 1/4 teaspoon Cayenne powder
- 2 cup flour
- 1 stick butter
- 2 teaspoon Baking Powder
- 3/2 cup cheddar, shredded

Directions:

- In a bowl, combine the flour and butter until it is the size of a pea.
- Add the remaining ingredients and whisk.
- Divide into 16 balls and place in an Air Flow Rack.
- Press the baking button. Reduce the timer to 15 minutes to start the cook cycle.
- Serve.

920.   Maryland Crab Cakes

Preparation Time: 20 minutes
Cooking Time: 20 minutes
Servings: 12

Ingredients:

- 1 teaspoon salt
- 1 cup cracker crumbs
- 1-pound Lump crab meat
- 1 pinch salt and pepper to season
- 2 tablespoon fresh parsley, chopped
- 1 teaspoon seafood seasoning
- 1/2 teaspoon ground black pepper
- 1/4 cup scallions, finely chopped
- 1 tablespoon sweet chili sauce
- 1 teaspoon garlic, minced
- 1 cup mayonnaise
- 1 tablespoon sweet pickle relish
- 1/4 cup Celery, diced
- 1 tablespoon Lemon juice
- 1 tablespoon Thai chili sauce

Directions:

- In a large bowl, bring together all the breadcrumb ingredients except the crabmeat and cookie crumbs.
- Gently mix the crab meat and 1/4 cup of the cracker crumbs.
- Spread the remaining crumbs out on a work surface.
- Form 12 equal-sized balls with crab mixture.
- Place the balls on top of the crumbs to coat evenly and press gently to make a patty.
- Place in a refrigerator for 20 minutes.
- Place the crab cakes on the Air Flow racks.
- Press the Steaks / Chops button. Reduce timer to 20 minutes to begin cook cycle.
- While the crab cakes are cooking, prepare the dipping sauce: combine all the ingredients and season with salt and pepper.
- Serve hot crab cakes with dipping sauce.

921. Banana Bundt Cake with Cream Cheese Icing

Preparation Time: 10 minutes

Cooking Time: 40 minutes
Servings: 8

Ingredients:

- 1 cup all-purpose flour
- 1 teaspoon baking powder
- 2 teaspoons vanilla extract
- 1/3 cup vegetable oil
- 1 egg
- 1/2 teaspoon cinnamon
- 1/2 teaspoon baking soda
- 2 bananas, peeled
- 2 oz. cream cheese, softened
- 2 tablespoons heavy cream
- 2 tablespoons butter, softened
- 3/4 cup sugar
- 1 cup powdered sugar
- 1/2 teaspoon salt

Directions:

- In a bowl, mash the bananas then mix in the egg.
- Next add the oil, sugar, and 1 teaspoon vanilla extract. Mix well.
- Gently sift the flour, baking soda, and cinnamon into the bowl with the banana.
- Pour the mixture into a Bundt pan.
- Choose the bake function in your air fryer oven.
- Bake for 14 minutes at 32o°F.
- Rotate the pan and continue baking for 16 minutes.
- Let rest for 10 minutes.
- Put butter and cream cheese in a microwavable bowl.
- Microwave for 8 seconds until butter is melted.
- Stir and cook for another 8 seconds.
- Add powdered sugar and the remaining 1 teaspoon vanilla extract.
- Add cream and whisk until you get your preferred consistency. More cream creates a thicker consistency.

922. Luscious Triple Berry Cobbler

Preparation Time: 10 minutes
Cooking Time: 22 minutes
Servings: 6

Ingredients:

- 3 tablespoons melted butter
- 1/4 cup flour
- 1/2 cup quick oats
- 1/2 cup raspberries or blackberries
- 1/2 cup strawberries
- 1 cup blueberries
- 2-1/8 cups of white sugar, divided
- 1 teaspoon lemon juice
- 1/4 cup brown sugar
- 1 teaspoon vanilla

Directions:

- Combine berries, 1/8 cup white sugar, and lemon juice in a large mixing bowl.
- In a separate bowl, mix flour, vanilla, oats, melted butter, brown sugar, and the other 1/8 cup of white sugar.
- Mix well.
- Coat pan with non-stick cooking spray.
- Put the oats mixture in first.
- Then add the berries.
- Choose the bake function in your air fryer oven.
- Bake for 12 minutes at 390°F.

923. Chocolate Raspberry Lava Cake

Preparation Time: 35 minutes
Cooking Time: 15 minutes
Servings: 3

Ingredients:

- 1 large egg
- 3 tablespoons all-purpose flour
- 3 tablespoons white sugar
- 6 tablespoons unsalted butter
- 1 large egg yolk
- A pinch of salt
- 1/2 teaspoon vanilla extract
- 4 oz. semi-sweet chocolate bar, broker into smaller pieces
- Fresh raspberries

Directions:

- Combine butter and chocolate in a microwavable bowl.
- Microwave for 1 minute, stirring every few seconds until melted. Set aside.
- Grease 3 ramekins that are 6 oz. each. Set aside.
- In a large bowl, combine the chocolate, flour, and salt. Mix well.
- Fill each ramekin halfway.
- Choose the air fry function.
- Air fry for 8-10 minutes at 370°F.

924. Crumbly Air Fryer Carrot Cake

Preparation Time
Cooking Time: 50 minutes
Servings: 6

Ingredients:

- 2/3 cup all-purpose flour
- 2 tablespoons dark brown sugar
- 1/2 cup buttermilk
- 1 teaspoon baking powder
- 1/4 teaspoon baking soda
- 3 tablespoons canola oil
- 2 teaspoons pumpkin pie spice
- 1/3 cup white whole wheat flour
- 1/3 cup walnuts, chopped and toasted
- 1/4 cup dried cranberries
- 1 large egg, lightly beaten
- 1 cup shredded carrots
- 1 teaspoon vanilla extract
- 1/3 cup white sugar plus another 2 more tablespoons
- 1/4 teaspoon salt
- 1 teaspoon orange zest, grated

Directions:

- Preheat air fryer to 350°F.

- Grease a 6-inch round baking pan and lightly dust with flour. Set aside.
- Whisk together orange zest, buttermilk, vanilla, brown sugar, white sugar, oil, and egg in a large bowl.
- In a separate bowl, combine flours, baking soda, salt, 1 teaspoon pumpkin spice, and baking powder.
- Slowly add the egg mixture to the dry ingredients.
- Add dried cranberries and carrots.
- Pour batter into baking pan.
- Combine the remaining 2 tablespoons white sugar, 1 teaspoon pumpkin spice, and walnuts in a small bowl.
- Sprinkle this mixture over the batter evenly.
- Choose the air fry function in your air fryer oven.
- Air fry for 35 minutes or until the toothpick comes out clean when checked.

925. Keto-Friendly Chocolate Cake

Preparation Time: 2 hours
Cooking Time: 15 minutes
Servings: 6

Ingredients:

- 2 large eggs
- 1/3 cup unsweetened cocoa powder
- 1 teaspoon baking powder
- 1-1/2 cups almond flour
- 1/3 cup unsweetened almond milk
- 1 teaspoon vanilla extract
- 1/2 cup powdered swerve
- 1/4 teaspoon salt

Directions:

- Mix all the ingredients in a large bowl.
- Grease baking tin and pour in the batter.
- Air fry for 10 minutes at 350°F.

926. Air Fryer Pandan Cake

Preparation Time: 2 hours
Cooking Time: 35 minutes

Servings: 2

Ingredients:

- 4-1/2 tablespoons plain flour
- 2 egg whites
- 2 egg yolks
- 1/4 tablespoon baking powder
- 2-1/3 tablespoon sugar
- 1 tablespoon coconut milk
- 1 teaspoon pandan essence or extract
- 1-1/3 teaspoon olive oil

Directions:

- Sift the flour and baking powder in a bowl and set aside.
- Preheat air fryer to 302°F.
- Using a hand mixer, mix the egg white with half the sugar to make the meringue.
- Add olive oil and mix.
- Next add coconut milk, pandan essence, and flour.
- Add 1/3 of the meringue to the flour mixture. Fold with a spatula.
- Add the rest of the meringue and stir gently.
- Pour mixture to a baking pan or tray.
- Cover with foil and poke small holes on it with a toothpick.
- Choose the air fry function in your air fryer oven.
- Bake for 25 minutes.
- Remove foil and bake for 5 more minutes.

927. 3-Ingredient Chocolate Mug Cake

Preparation Time: 2 minutes
Cooking Time: 16 minutes
Servings: 1

Ingredients:

- 1 tablespoon water
- 2 tablespoons unsweetened applesauce
- 6 tablespoons chocolate cake mix

Directions:

- Whisk all ingredients until smooth.
- Pour batter into an 8-oz. mug that can withstand high heat.
- Choose the air fry function in your air fryer oven.
- Air fry for 13 minutes or until cooked.

Nutrition:

Calories per serving: 98;
Protein: 3.28g;
Carbs: 15.32g;
Fat: 3.26g
Sugar: 2.86g

928.   Zesty Orange Drizzle Cake

Preparation Time: 20 minutes
Cooking Time: 1 hour 2 minutes
Servings: 6

Ingredients:

- 1 cup all-purpose flour
- 4 egg yolks
- 1/4 cup vegetable oil
- 1-1/2 teaspoon baking powder
- 1/4 cup water
- 1/3 cup plus sugar for the batter
- 1/3 cup sugar for egg white mixture
- 1/2 teaspoon kosher salt
- 4 egg whites
- 1 can chilled condensed milk
- 1 teaspoon vinegar
- 3 tablespoons orange juice plus more for frosting
- Orange zest

Directions:

- Mix egg yolks and sugar until fluffy.
- Add orange juice, water, and oil.
- Sift baking soda, flour, and salt on top of the egg mixture.
- Add zest and mix well.
- Whisk the egg whites, sugar, and vinegar in a separate bowl until stiff.

- Slowly fold the egg white mixture into the batter until well combined.
- Line pan with parchment paper.
- Choose the bake function in your air fryer oven.
- Bake for 42 minutes at 310°F.
- To make the frosting, combine condensed milk, orange juice, and orange zest in a bowl.
- Mix using a hand mixer for 4 minutes.

929.   Banana Fluffy Cake

Preparation Time: 30 minutes
Cooking Time: 20 minutes
Servings: 3

Ingredients:

- 1-1/2 tablespoons castor sugar
- 2 tablespoons rice flour
- 1 banana mashed
- 1 banana sliced
- 1 large egg, white and yolk separated

Directions:

- Preheat air fryer to 356°F.
- Whisk the egg white until foamy.
- Add sugar until soft peaks.
- Add egg yolk, flour, then the mashed banana.
- Put batter into paper cups or lined muffin trays and top with a sliced banana.
- Choose the air fry function.
- Air fry for 8 minutes.

930.   Durian Burnt Cheesecake

Preparation Time: 20 minutes
Cooking Time: 23 minutes
Servings: 1

Ingredients:

- 9 oz. chilled cream cheese
- 8 fl. cream
- 2 large eggs
- 5 tablespoons caster sugar
- 3-1/2 tablespoons cake flour
- 1 cup durian flesh

Directions:

- Preheat air fryer to 392°F.
- Line a 6-inch round baking tin.
- Combine all ingredients in a food processor until smooth.
- Gently pour into a lined baking tin.
- Choose bake function.
- Bake for 23 minutes.

931. Air Fryer Lemon Berry Cakes

Preparation Time: 10 minutes
Cooking Time: 30 minutes
Servings: 4

Ingredients:

- 2 eggs
- 1 cup fresh blueberries
- 2 tablespoons lemon juice
- 3/4 cup sugar
- 1 tablespoon olive oil
- 6 oz. strawberry or raspberry yogurt
- 1-1/2 teaspoon sea salt
- 1-1/2 cup all-purpose flour
- 2 teaspoons baking powder
- 1/2 cup milk

Directions:

- Combine all wet ingredients in a large bowl.
- Slowly incorporate the dry ingredients until runny.
- Fold in the berries.
- Grease Bundt pans.
- Pour batter into pans.
- Choose the bake function.
- Bake for 25 minutes at 400°F.

932. Air Fryer Blueberry Swirl Cake

Preparation Time: 20 minutes
Cooking Time: 40 minutes
Servings: 8

Ingredients:

- 1/3 cup vegetable oil

- 1 box yellow cake mix
- Non-stick cooking spray
- 2 eggs
- 1/2 cup butter, room temperature
- 21 oz. blueberry pie filling

Directions:

- Combine the cake mix, butter, and vegetable oil in a large bowl.
- Pour batter into greased baking pan.
- Add the blueberry pie filling on top and create swirls.
- Choose the bake function.
- Bake for 15 minutes at 320°F.

933. Air Fryer Apple Cake

Preparation Time: 20 minutes
Cooking Time: 20 minutes
Servings: 8

Ingredients:

- 1 cup all-purpose flours
- 3 eggs
- 1 cup brown sugar
- 1 cup apples, peeled and diced

Directions:

- Combine eggs and sugar in a bowl until smooth.
- Add flour and mix.
- Add the apples making sure that all they are evenly coated with the batter.
- Pour batter into a greased pan.
- Choose the air fry function.
- Air fry for 12-15 minutes at 320°F.

934. Toothsome Nutella Cake

Preparation Time: 20 minutes
Cooking Time: 18 minutes
Servings: 2

Ingredients:

- 1-1/2 cup Nutella
- 1/2 cup Nutella for frosting

- ◆ 4 eggs
- ◆ 1/2 cup all-purpose flour

Directions:

- Mix Nutella, eggs, and flour in a large bowl until smooth.
- Grease pan with oil or spray with non-stick oil.
- Pour batter into pan.
- Choose the air fry function.
- Set temperature to°F.
- Air fry for 13 minutes or until the center is fully cooked.

935. Air Fryer Pumpkin Cake

Preparation Time: 10 minutes
Cooking Time: 20 minutes
Servings: 10

Ingredients:

- ◆ 1 tablespoon pumpkin pie spice
- ◆ 12 oz. evaporated milk
- ◆ 3 large room temperature eggs
- ◆ 1 cup walnuts, diced
- ◆ 1 package yellow cake mix
- ◆ 1 cup granulated sugar
- ◆ 15 oz. pumpkin puree
- ◆ 3/4 cup melted unsalted butter
- ◆ 8 tablespoons room temperature butter for frosting
- ◆ 1 teaspoon ground cinnamon
- ◆ 8 oz. room temperature cream cheese
- ◆ 1 cup powdered sugar
- ◆ 2 tablespoons vanilla extract

Directions:

- Combine pumpkin puree, eggs, sugar, milk, ground cinnamon, and pumpkin spice in a large bowl.
- Next add the cake mix, diced walnuts, and melted unsalted butter. Mix well.
- Pour batter on greased pan or skillet.
- Choose the bake function.
- Bake for 15 minutes at 320°F.

- In a separate bowl create frosting by combining cream cheese, butter, sugar, vanilla extract, and walnuts.

936. Mini Berry Cheese Cakes

Preparation Time: 10 minutes
Cooking Time: 3 hours 20 minutes
Servings: 8

Ingredients:

- ◆ 1/2 cup plus 2 teaspoons granulated sugar
- ◆ 1-1/2 cups graham cracker crumbs
- ◆ 8 oz. cream cheese, room temperature
- ◆ 1/4 cup melted butter
- ◆ 1/2 cup sour cream
- ◆ 8 oz. fresh blackberries
- ◆ 1 egg
- ◆ 1/2 teaspoon vanilla extract
- ◆ 1 teaspoon lemon juice

Directions:

- Mix butter, sugar, and graham crumbs.
- Scoop and push graham mixture to the bottom of each muffin liner.
- In a separate bowl, combine cream cheese, sour cream, sugar, vanilla, egg, and lemon juice until smooth.
- Add the cream cheese mixture on top of graham crumbs until the muffin liner is almost filled.
- Choose the air fry function.
- Air fry for 15 minutes at 320°F or until the center is set.
- Let cakes cool and refrigerate for 3-4 hours.

937. Copycat Recipe Starbucks Coffee Cake

Preparation Time: 10 minutes
Cooking Time: 32 minutes
Servings: 6

Ingredients:

- ◆ 1 teaspoon ground cinnamon plus 1 teaspoon for topping
- ◆ 1/3 cup half and half or light cream

- 1 cup room temperature butter plus ½ cup for topping
- 1 teaspoon salt
- 3/4 cup brown sugar plus 1 cup for topping
- 1/2 cup white sugar
- 1 teaspoon baking powder
- 2 eggs
- 2 cups flour plus 1 cup for topping
- 1 teaspoon vanilla
- 1/2 cup pecan, diced

Directions:

- Combine 1 cup butter, ¾ cup brown sugar, and white sugar in a bowl until creamy.
- Add baking powder, eggs, flour, vanilla, salt, and half & half. Mix well.
- Coat pan with olive oil and pour the batter in.
- In a separate bowl, combine 1 cup brown sugar, 1 cup flour, ½ cup butter, and 1 teaspoon cinnamon.
- Fold in the pecans.
- Spread the pecan mixture over the batter.
- Choose the air fry function.
- Set temperature for 320°F.
- Air fry for 12 minutes or until the toothpick comes out clean.

938. Heavenly Chocolate-Cherry Dump Cake

Preparation Time: 5 minutes
Cooking Time: 17 minutes
Servings: 6

Ingredients:

- 1 package Devil's Food Cake mix
- 1 container chocolate frosting
- 2 large eggs
- 1/2 cup chocolate chips
- 1 teaspoon vanilla
- 21 oz. canned cherry

Directions:

- Combine cherries, cake mix, eggs, chocolate chips, and vanilla in a large mixing bowl.

- Pour batter on a greased pan.
- Choose the air fry function.
- Set temperature to 320°F.
- Air fry for 12 minutes or until the toothpick comes out clean when the center is poked.

939. Sweetened Plantains

Preparation Time: 5 Minutes
Cooking Time: 8 Minutes
Servings: 4

Ingredients:

- 2 ripe plantains, sliced
- 2 teaspoons avocado oil
- Salt to taste
- Maple syrup

Directions:

- Toss the plantains in oil.
- Season with salt.
- Cook in the air fryer basket at 400 degrees F for 10 minutes, shaking after 5 minutes.
- Drizzle with maple syrup before serving.

940. Roasted Bananas

Preparation Time: 5 Minutes
Cooking Time: 5 Minutes
Servings: 2

Ingredients:

- 2 cups bananas, cubed
- 1 teaspoon avocado oil
- 1 tablespoon maple syrup
- 1 teaspoon brown sugar
- 1 cup almond milk

Directions:

- Coat the banana cubes with oil and maple syrup.
- Sprinkle with brown sugar.
- Cook at 375 F in the air fryer for 5 minutes.
- Drizzle milk on top of the bananas before serving.

941. Pear Crisp

Preparation Time: 10 Minutes
Cooking Time: 25 Minutes
Servings: 2

Ingredients:

- 1 cup flour
- 1 stick vegan butter
- 1 tablespoon cinnamon
- ½ cup sugar
- 2pears, cubed

Directions:

- Mix flour and butter to form crumbly texture.
- Add cinnamon and sugar.
- Put the pears in the air fryer.
- Pour and spread the mixture on top of the pears.
- Cook at 350 degrees F for 25 minutes.

942. Easy Pears Dessert

Preparation Time: 10 Minutes
Cooking Time: 25 Minutes
Servings: 12

Ingredients:

- 6 big pears, cored and chopped
- ½ cup raisins
- 1 teaspoon ginger powder
- ¼ cup coconut sugar
- 1 teaspoon lemon zest, grated

Directions:

- In a container that fits your air fryer, mix pears with raisins, ginger, sugar and lemon zest, stir, introduce in the fryer and cook at 350 degrees F for 25 minutes.
- Divide into bowls and serve cold.
- Enjoy!

943. Vanilla Strawberry Mix

Preparation Time: 10 Minutes
Cooking Time: 20 Minutes
Servings: 10

Ingredients:

- 2 tablespoons lemon juice
- 2 pounds strawberries
- 4 cups coconut sugar
- 1 teaspoon cinnamon powder
- 1 teaspoon vanilla extract

Directions:

- In a pot that fits your air fryer, mix strawberries with coconut sugar, lemon juice, cinnamon and vanilla, stir gently, introduce in the fryer and cook at 350 degrees F for 20 minutes
- Divide into bowls and serve cold.
- Enjoy!

944. Sweet Bananas and Sauce

Preparation Time: 10 Minutes
Cooking Time: 20 Minutes
Servings: 4

Ingredients:

- Juice of ½ lemon
- 3tablespoons agave nectar
- 1 tablespoon coconut oil
- 4bananas, peeled and sliced diagonally
- ½ teaspoon cardamom seeds

Directions:

- Arrange bananas in a pan that fits your air fryer, add agave nectar, lemon juice, oil and cardamom, introduce in the fryer and cook at 360 degrees F for 20 minutes
- Divide bananas and sauce between plates and serve.
- Enjoy!

945. Cinnamon Apples and Mandarin Sauce

Preparation Time: 10 Minutes
Cooking Time: 20 Minutes
Servings: 4

Ingredients:

- 4 apples, cored, peeled and cored
- 2 cups mandarin juice

- ¼ cup maple syrup
- 2 teaspoons cinnamon powder
- 1 tablespoon ginger, grated

Directions:

- In a pot that fits your air fryer, mix apples with mandarin juice, maple syrup, cinnamon and ginger, introduce in the fryer and cook at 365 degrees F for 20 minutes
- Divide apples mix between plates and serve warm.
- Enjoy!

946. Chocolate Vanilla Bars

Preparation Time: 10 Minutes
Cooking Time: 7 Minutes
Servings: 12

Ingredients:

- 1 cup sugar free and vegan chocolate chips
- 2 tablespoons coconut butter
- 2/3 cup coconut cream
- Tablespoons stevia
- ¼ teaspoon vanilla extract

Directions:

- Put the cream in a bowl, add stevia, butter and chocolate chips and stir
- Leave aside for 5 minutes, stir well and mix the vanilla.
- Transfer the mix into a lined baking sheet, introduce in your air fryer and cook at 356 degrees F for 7 minutes.
- Leave the mix aside to cool down, slice and serve.
- Enjoy!

947. Raspberry Bars

Preparation Time: 10 Minutes
Cooking Time: 6 Minutes
Servings: 12

Ingredients:

- ½ cup coconut butter, melted
- ½ cup coconut oil

- ½ cup raspberries, dried
- ¼ cup swerve
- ½ cup coconut, shredded

Directions:

- In your food processor, blend dried berries very well.
- In a bowl that fits your air fryer, mix oil with butter, swerve, coconut and raspberries, toss well, introduce in the fryer and cook at 320 degrees F for 6 minutes.
- Spread this on a lined baking sheet, keep in the fridge for an hour, slice and serve.
- Enjoy!

948. Cocoa Berries Cream

Preparation Time: 10 Minutes
Cooking Time: 10 Minutes
Servings: 4

Ingredients:

- 3 tablespoons cocoa powder
- 14 ounces coconut cream
- 1 cup blackberries
- 1 cup raspberries
- 2 tablespoons stevia

Directions:

- In a bowl, whisk cocoa powder with stevia and cream and stir.
- Add raspberries and blackberries, toss gently, transfer to a pan that fits your air fryer, introduce in the fryer and cook at 350 degrees F for 10 minutes.
- Divide into bowls and serve cold.
- Enjoy!

949. Cocoa Pudding

Preparation Time: 10 Minutes
Cooking Time: 20 Minutes
Servings: 2

Ingredients:

- 2 tablespoons water
- ½ tablespoon agar

- 4 tablespoons stevia
- 4 tablespoons cocoa powder
- 2 cups coconut milk, hot

Directions:

- In a bowl, mix milk with stevia and cocoa powder and stir well.
- In a bowl, mix agar with water, stir well, add to the cocoa mix, stir and transfer to a pudding pan that fits your air fryer.
- Introduce in the fryer and cook at 356 degrees F for 20 minutes.
- Serve the pudding cold.
- Enjoy!

950.   Blueberry Coconut Crackers

Preparation Time: 10 Minutes
Cooking Time: 30 Minutes
Servings: 12

Ingredients:

- ½ cup coconut butter
- ½ cup coconut oil, melted
- 1 cup blueberries
- 3 tablespoons coconut sugar

Directions:

- In a pot that fits your air fryer, mix coconut butter with coconut oil, raspberries and sugar, toss, introduce in the fryer and cook at 367 degrees F for 30 minutes
- Spread on a lined baking sheet, keep in the fridge for a few hours, slice crackers and serve.
- Enjoy!

951.   Sweet Vanilla Rhubarb

Preparation Time: 10 Minutes
Cooking Time: 10 Minutes
Servings: 4

Ingredients:

- 5 cups rhubarb, chopped
- 2 tablespoons coconut butter, melted
- 1/3 cup water

- 1 tablespoon stevia
- 1 teaspoon vanilla extract

Directions:

- Put rhubarb, ghee, water, stevia and vanilla extract in a pan that fits your air fryer, introduce in the fryer and cook at 365 degrees F for 10 minutes
- Divide into small bowls and serve cold.
- Enjoy!

952.   Pineapple Pudding

Preparation Time: 10 Minutes
Cooking Time: 5 Minutes
Servings: 8

Ingredients:

- 1 tablespoon avocado oil
- 1 cup rice
- 14ounces milk
- Sugar to the taste
- 8ounces canned pineapple, chopped

Directions:

- In your air fryer, mix oil, milk and rice, stir, cover and cook on High for 3 minutes.
- Add sugar and pineapple, stir, cover and cook on High for 2 minutes more.
- Divide into dessert bowls and serve.

953.   Coconut Pancake

Preparation Time: 10 Minutes
Cooking Time: 20 Minutes
Servings: 4

Ingredients:

- 2 cups self-rising flour
- 2 tablespoons sugar
- 2 eggs
- 1 and ½ cups coconut milk
- A drizzle of olive oil

Directions:

- In a bowl, mix eggs with sugar, milk and flour and whisk until you obtain a batter.

- Grease your air fryer with the oil, add the batter, spread into the pot, cover and cook on Low for 20 minutes.
- Slice pancake, divide between plates and serve cold.

954. Cinnamon Rolls

Preparation Time: 2 Hours
Cooking Time: 15 Minutes
Servings: 8

Ingredients:

- 1-pound vegan bread dough
- ¾ cup coconut sugar
- 1 and ½ tablespoons cinnamon powder
- 2 tablespoons vegetable oil

Directions:

- Roll dough on a floured working surface, shape a rectangle and brush with the oil.
- In a bowl, mix cinnamon with sugar, stir, sprinkle this over dough, roll into a log, seal well and cut into 8 pieces.
- Leave rolls to rise for 2 hours, place them in your air fryer's basket, cook at 350 degrees F for 5 minutes, flip them, cook for 4 minutes more and transfer to a platter.
- Enjoy!

955. Cherries and Rhubarb Bowls

Preparation Time: 10 Minutes
Cooking Time: 35 Minutes
Servings: 4

Ingredients:

- 2 cups cherries, pitted and halved
- 1 cup rhubarb, sliced
- 1 cup apple juice
- 2 tablespoons sugar
- ½ cup raisins.

Directions:

- In a pot that fits your air fryer, combine the cherries with the rhubarb and the other ingredients, toss, cook at 330 degrees F for 35 minutes, divide into bowls, cool down and serve.

956. Pumpkin Bowls

Preparation Time: 10 Minutes
Cooking Time: 15 Minutes
Servings: 4

Ingredients:

- 2 cups pumpkin flesh, cubed
- 1 cup heavy cream
- 1 teaspoon cinnamon powder
- 3 tablespoons sugar
- 1 teaspoon nutmeg, ground

Directions:

- In a pot that fits your air fryer, combine the pumpkin with the cream and the other ingredients, introduce in the fryer and cook at 360 degrees F for 15 minutes.
- Divide into bowls and serve.

957. Buttery Fennel and Garlic

Preparation Time: 10 Minutes
Cooking Time: 5 Minutes
Servings: 4

Ingredients:

- ½ stick butter
- 2 garlic cloves, sliced
- ½ teaspoon salt
- 1 and ½ pounds fennel bulbs, cut into wedges
- ¼ teaspoon ground black pepper
- ½ teaspoon cayenne
- ¼ teaspoon dried dill weed
- 1/3 cup dry white wine
- 2/3 cup stock

Directions:

- Set your Deluxe to Sauté mode and add butter, let it heat up
- Add garlic and cook for 30 seconds
- Add rest of the ingredients
- Lock lid & cook on LOW pressure for 3 minutes

- Remove lid and serve
- Enjoy!

958. Simple Poached Pears

Preparation Time: 5 Minutes
Cooking Time: 10 Minutes
Servings: 6

Ingredients:

- 6 firm pears, peeled
- 4 garlic cloves, minced
- 1 stick cinnamon
- 1 fresh ginger, minced
- 1 bottle of dry red wine
- 1 bay leaf
- Mixed Italian herbs as needed
- 1 and 1/3 cups stevia

Directions:

- Peel the pears leaving the stems attached
- Pour wine into your Deluxe
- Add cinnamon, cloves, and ginger, bay leaf, and stevia, stir gently
- Add pears to the pot
- Close the lid
- Cook for 9 minutes on HIGH
- Quickly release the pressure
- Take the pears out using a tong, keep them on the side
- Set Sauté mode, make the mixture into half
- Drizzle the mixture with pears
- Serve and enjoy!

959. Cheesy Cauliflower Steak

Preparation Time: 10 Minutes
Cooking Time: 30 Minutes
Servings: 4

Ingredients:

- 1 tablespoon mustard
- 1 head cauliflower
- 1 teaspoon avocado mayonnaise
- ½ cup parmesan cheese, grated
- ¼ cup butter, cut into small pieces

Directions:

- Set your Deluxe to Sauté mode and add butter and cauliflower
- Sauté for 3 minutes
- Add remaining ingredients and stir
- Lock lid and then cook on HIGH pressure for about 25-30 minutes
- Release pressure naturally over 10 minutes
- Serve and enjoy!

960. Garlic and Mushroom Munchies

Preparation Time: 10 Minutes
Cooking Time: 8 Minutes
Servings: 4

Ingredients:

- ¼ cup vegetable stock
- 2 tablespoons extra virgin olive oil
- 1 tablespoon Dijon mustard
- 1 teaspoon dried thyme
- 1 teaspoon of sea salt
- ½ teaspoon dried rosemary
- ¼ teaspoon fresh ground black pepper
- 2 pounds cremini mushrooms, cleaned
- 6 garlic cloves, minced
- ¼ cup fresh parsley, chopped

Directions:

- Take a small bowl and whisk in vegetable stock, mustard, olive oil, salt, thyme, pepper and rosemary
- Add mushrooms, garlic and stock mix to your Deluxe
- Close lid and cook on SLOW COOK Mode (LOW) for 8 hours
- Open the lid and stir in parsley
- Serve and enjoy!

961. Warm Glazed Up Carrots

Preparation Time: 5 Minutes
Cooking Time: 5 Minutes
Servings: 4

Ingredients:

- ◆ 2 pounds carrots
- ◆ Pepper as needed
- ◆ 1 cup of water
- ◆ 1 tablespoon coconut butter

Directions:

- Wash carrots thoroughly & peel then, slice the carrots
- Add carrots, water to the Deluxe
- Lock pressure lid & cook for 4 minutes on HIGH pressure
- Release pressure naturally
- Strain carrots and strain carrots
- Mix with coconut butter, enjoy with a bit of pepper

962. Decadent Lemon Mousse

Preparation Time: 10 Minutes
Cooking Time: 12 Minutes
Servings: 2

Ingredients:

- ◆ 1-2 ounces cream cheese, soft
- ◆ ½ teaspoon lemon liquid stevia
- ◆ ½ cup heavy cream
- ◆ 1/8 cup fresh lemon juice
- ◆ 2 pinch salt

Directions:

- In a bowl add heavy cream, cream cheese, stevia, lemon juice and salt
- Pour the mixture into a ramekin and transfer to Deluxe
- Close the lid
- Set Bake/Roast mode
- Bake for 12 minutes to 350-degree F
- Check the doneness it before remove from the Deluxe
- Serve and enjoy!

963. Pumpkin Carrot Pudding

Preparation Time: 10 Minutes
Cooking Time: 20 Minutes
Servings: 2

Ingredients:

- ◆ 2 cups pumpkin, pureed
- ◆ 2 cups carrots, shredded
- ◆ 2 whole eggs
- ◆ 1 tablespoon granulated Erythritol
- ◆ 1 teaspoon ground nutmeg
- ◆ 1 tablespoon extra-virgin olive oil
- ◆ ½ sweet onion, finely chopped
- ◆ 1 cup heavy whip cream
- ◆ ½ cup cream cheese, soft
- ◆ ¼ cup pumpkin seeds, garnish
- ◆ ¼ cup water
- ◆ ½ teaspoon salt

Directions:

- Add oil to your Deluxe and whisk in pumpkin, carrots, heavy cream, cream cheese, eggs, erythritol, onion, nutmeg, water and salt
- Stir gently and close the lid
- Cook for 10 minutes on HIGH
- Release pressure naturally over 10 minutes
- Top with the pumpkin seeds
- Serve and enjoy!

964. Awesome Poached Pears

Preparation Time: 5 Minutes
Cooking Time: 10 Minutes
Servings: 6

Ingredients:

- ◆ 6 firm pears, peeled
- ◆ 4 garlic cloves, minced
- ◆ 1 stick cinnamon
- ◆ 1 fresh ginger, minced
- ◆ 1 bottle of dry red wine
- ◆ 1 bay leaf
- ◆ Mixed Italian herbs as needed
- ◆ 1 and 1/3 cups stevia

Directions:

- Peel the pears leaving the stems attached
- Pour wine into your Deluxe

- Add cinnamon, cloves, ginger, bay leaf and stevia, stir gently
- Add pears to the pot
- Close the lid
- Cook for 9 minutes on HIGH
- Quickly release the pressure
- Take the pears out using a tong, keep them on the side
- Set Sauté mode, make the mixture into half
- Drizzle the mixture with pears
- Serve and enjoy!

965. Spiced Baked Apple and Homemade Apple Spice

Preparation Time: 5 Minutes
Cooking Time: 10 Minutes
Servings: 4

Ingredients:

- 4 smalls to medium-sized apples
- 2 tablespoons coconut oil
- 2 tablespoons sugar
- 2 tablespoons ground cinnamon
- 2 teaspoons ground nutmeg
- 1 ½ teaspoons allspice

Directions:

- Homemade Apple Spice:
- In a medium bowl, mix cinnamon, nutmeg, and allspice.
- Pour into a small air-tight container.
- Shake well to make sure the spice is well mixed.
- Wash, peel, and slice the apples into rounds. Place them in a bowl.
- Melt the coconut oil in a small saucepan on the stove.
- Drizzle melted coconut oil over the sliced apples.
- Sprinkle the apples with homemade apple spice and sugar.
- Use a spoon to stir the apples to make sure the spice and coconut oil covers all the apple slices.

- Use non-stick cooking spray to spray the cake pan.
- Preheat the Air Fryer to 350°F or 180°Celsius (C). Use the Air Fry setting and set the Preheat for 3 minutes.
- Place the apple slices in the cake pan.
- Place the cake pan in the preheated Air Fryer.
- Set the Air Fryer for 10 minutes and use the Air Fry setting to start baking the apple slices.
- At 5 minutes, pause the Air Fryer, open the Air Fryer draw to check and turn the apple slices.
- Start the Air Fryer to cook the apples for the last 5 minutes.
- After 10 minutes, the Air Fryer will switch off. The apples should be cooked through.
- Once the apples are cooked, remove the Air Fryer drawer and place it on the cooling rack or mat.
- Remove the cake pan from the air fryer, use oven gloves.
- Divide into portions and serve.

966. Sugar Dough Dippers

Preparation Time: 17 Minutes
Cooking Time: 8 Minutes
Servings: 4

Ingredients:

- 1 teaspoon white sugar
- 2 cups all-purpose flour
- ¼ teaspoon baking soda
- ½ teaspoon baking powder
- 1 flat teaspoon salt
- 4 tablespoons butter
- 1/2 cup buttermilk
- 2 tablespoons whole fresh milk

Directions:

- In a bowl, sieve together 1 ½ cups of flour, salt, baking soda, and baking powder.
- Put 1 tablespoon of the butter aside.
- Use the rest of the butter to rub into the flour mix to make a crumbling mixture.

- Pour the buttermilk into the flour mixture, stir with a cake spatula until the mixture turns into dough. Do not over mix, you want it to be a nice manageable dough texture.

- Clean a working surface and sprinkle some flour over it. This is where you are going to cut out the biscuits from the dough.

- Manipulate the dough into a round shape that is at least ½ inch thick.

- Use a round cookie-cutter that is not too large, cut out 10 round dough shapes.

- Use non-stick cooking spray to spray the Air Fryer drawer.

- Line the Air Fryer drawer with Air Fryer parchment paper.

- Preheat the Air Fryer to 400°F. Use the Air Fry setting and set the Preheat for 3 minutes.

- Melt the last block of butter in a small saucepan on the stovetop.

- Brush the cookies with the melted butter.

- Place the cookies in the Air Fryer. Do not crowd and only use one layer to fill the Air Fryer drawer.

- Set the Air Fryer for 8 minutes and use the Air Fry setting to start cooking the dessert.

- After 8 minutes, the Air Fryer will switch off. The dough balls should be golden brown and cooked through.

- Once the dough dippers are cooked, remove the Air Fryer drawer and place it on the cooling rack or mat.

- Remove the dough dippers by using the spatula or food tongs.

- Divide into portions and serve.

967. Churro Donuts

Preparation Time: 35 Minutes
Cooking Time: 55 Minutes
Servings: 12

Ingredients:

- 1/4 teaspoon salt
- 1/4 cup, plus 2 Tbsp. unsalted butter, divided
- 1/2 cup all-purpose flour
- 1/3 cup white sugar
- 2 teaspoons cinnamon
- 4 ounces baking chocolate (bittersweet is the best)
- 2 large fresh eggs (do not use eggs from the fridge)
- 2 tablespoons heavy cream
- 1/2 cup fresh water
- 2 tablespoons vanilla yogurt

Directions:

- On the stovetop at MEDIUM heat, bring the water to a boil in a saucepan.

- When the water is boiling, add ¼ cup butter and salt.

- Add flour and take the heat down one notch on the stove.

- Use a wooden spoon or whisk, mix the flour and water mix into a dough.

- The mixture will start to smooth out in about 30 seconds.

- Stir the mixture until the dough starts to get a bit stiff. It will start to come away from the sides of the saucepan. This process takes about 3 minutes, you will know when it is ready because it forms a film at the bottom of the pan.

- Pour the mixture into a heatproof, clean bowl when it is ready.

- Keep stirring the mixture for about 1 to 2 minutes, or until the mixture has cooled down a bit.

- If the mixture is no longer piping hot, add the eggs and stir vigorously.

- When the mixture is completely smooth pour it into a piping bag.

- The mixture needs to set in the refrigerator for at least 30 minutes.

- Spray the bottom of the Air Fryer drawer with non-stick cooking spray.

- Place Air Fryer parchment paper on the bottom of the Air Fryer.

- Preheat the Air Fryer to 380°F. Use the Air Fry setting and set the Preheat for 3 minutes.

- After 30 minutes, take the churro mixture from the fridge.

- Pipe 6, 3-inch long churro donuts onto the parchment paper in the Air Fryer drawer.
- Set the Air Fryer for 10 minutes and use the Air Fry setting to start cooking the churros.
- At 5 minutes, pause the Air Fryer, open the Air Fryer draw to check the churros.
- Turn the churros over and start the Air Fryer to cook the churros for the last 5 minutes.
- After 10 minutes, the Air Fryer will switch off. The churros should be golden brown and cooked through.
- Repeat steps #16 to #20 until all the churros have been cooked.
- While the churros are cooking, mix the cinnamon and sugar.
- Melt the chocolate either in the microwave or on the stovetop.
- Mix the melted chocolate with the cream, continue heating until the mixture is smooth and thick.
- Remove the chocolate mixture from the microwave or stove and add the yogurt.
- Remove the churros from the Air Fryer by using the spatula or food tongs.
- Pour the last of the melted butter over the browned churros and sprinkle them with cinnamon and sugar.
- Serve warm churros with the chocolate sauce.

968. Plum Apple Crumble

Preparation Time: 10 to 15 Minutes
Cooking Time: 20 Minutes
Servings: 6 to 7

Ingredients:

- 2 ½ ounces caster sugar
- 1/3 cup oats
- 2/3 cup flour
- 1/2 stick butter, chilled
- 1 tablespoon cold water
- 1 tablespoon honey
- 1/2 teaspoon ground mace
- 1/4-pound plums, pitted and chopped
- 1/4-pound apples, cored and chopped

- 1 tablespoon lemon juice
- 1/2 teaspoon vanilla paste
- 1 cup cranberries

Directions:

- Place your air fryer on a flat kitchen surface; plug it and turn it on. Set temperature to 390 degrees F and let it preheat for 4-5 minutes.
- Take out the cake pan and gently coat it using a cooking oil or spray.
- In a bowl of medium size, thoroughly mix the plums, apples, lemon juice, sugar, honey, and mace. Add the fruit mixture to the bottom of a cake pan.
- In a bowl of medium size, thoroughly mix the remaining ingredients and top with the fruit mix.
- Push the air-frying basket in the air fryer. Cook for 20 minutes.
- Slide out the basket; serve warm!

969. Creamy Banana Puffs

Preparation Time: 10 to 15 Minutes
Cooking Time: 10 Minutes
Servings: 8

Ingredients:

- 4 ounces instant vanilla pudding
- 4 ounces cream cheese, softened
- 1 package (8-ounce) crescent dinner rolls, refrigerated
- 1 cup milk
- 2 bananas, sliced
- 1 egg, lightly beaten

Directions:

- Place your air fryer on a flat kitchen surface; plug it and turn it on. Set temperature to 355 degrees F and let it preheat for 4-5 minutes.
- Unroll crescent dinner rolls and make 8 squares.
- In a bowl of medium size, thoroughly mix the pudding and milk; whisk in the cream cheese.

- Add the mixture in the pastry squares. Top with the slices of banana. Fold them over the filling, pressing the edges to seal. Brush each pastry puff with the whisked egg.
- Add them to the basket. Push the air-frying basket in the air fryer. Cook for 10 minutes.
- Slide out the basket; serve warm!

970. Fiesta Pastries

Preparation Time: 15 Minutes
Cooking Time: 20 Minutes
Servings: 8

Ingredients:

- ½ of apple, peeled, cored, and chopped
- One teaspoon fresh orange zest, grated finely
- 7.05-ounce prepared frozen puff pastry, cut into 16 squares
- ½ tablespoon white sugar
- ½ teaspoon ground cinnamon

Directions:

- Preheat the Air fryer to 390 $_0$ F and grease an Air fryer basket.
- Mix all ingredients in a bowl except puff pastry.
- Arrange about one teaspoon of this mixture in the center of each square.
- Fold each square into a triangle and slightly press the edges with a fork.
- Arrange the pastries in the Air fryer basket and cook for about 10 minutes.
- Dish out and serve immediately.

971. Classic Buttermilk Biscuits

Preparation Time: 15 Minutes
Cooking Time: 8 Minutes
Servings: 4

Ingredients:

- ½ cup cake flour
- 1¼ cups all-purpose flour
- ¾ teaspoon baking powder
- ¼ cup + 2 tablespoons butter, cut into cubes
- ¾ cup buttermilk

Directions:

- Preheat the Air fryer to 400 $_0$ F and grease a pie pan lightly.
- Sift together flours, baking soda, baking powder, sugar, and salt in a large bowl.
- Add cold butter and mix until a coarse crumb is formed.
- Stir in the buttermilk slowly and mix until a dough is formed.
- Press the dough into ½ inch thickness onto a floured surface and cut out circles with a 1¾-inch round cookie cutter.
- Arrange the biscuits in a pie pan in a single layer and brush butter on them.
- Transfer into the Air fryer and cook for about 8 minutes until golden brown.

972. Coconut-Coated White Chocolate Cookies

Preparation Time: 15 Minutes
Cooking Time: 12 Minutes
Servings: 8

Ingredients:

- 3½-ounce butter
- One small egg
- 5-ounce self-rising flour
- 1¼-ounce white chocolate, chopped
- Three tablespoons desiccated coconut

Directions:

- Preheat the Air fryer to 355 $_0$ F and grease a baking sheet lightly.
- Mix sugar and butter in a large bowl and beat till fluffy.
- Whisk in the egg, vanilla extract, flour, and chocolate and mix until well combined.
- Place coconut in a shallow dish and make small balls from the mixture.
- Roll the balls into coconut evenly and arrange them onto the baking sheet.
- Press each ball into a cookie-like shape and transfer it into the air fryer.

- Cook for about 8 minutes and set the Air fryer to 320 o F.
- Cook for about 4 minutes and dish out to serve.

973. Tasty Lemony Biscuits

Preparation Time: 15 Minutes
Cooking Time: 5 Minutes
Servings: 10

Ingredients:

- 8½ ounce self-rising flour
- 3½-ounce cold butter
- One small egg
- One teaspoon fresh lemon zest, grated finely

Directions:

- Preheat the Air fryer to 355 o F and grease a baking sheet lightly.
- Mix flour and sugar in a large bowl.
- Add cold butter and mix until a coarse crumb is formed.
- Stir in the egg, lemon zest, and lemon juice and mix until a dough is formed.
- Press the dough into ½ inch thickness onto a floured surface and cut dough into medium-sized biscuits.
- Position the biscuits on a baking sheet in a single layer and transfer it into the air fryer.
- Cook for 5 minutes until golden brown and serve with tea.

974. Basic Butter Cookies

Preparation Time: 10 Minutes
Cooking Time: 10 Minutes
Servings: 8

Ingredients:

- 4-ounce unsalted butter
- 1 cup all-purpose flour
- ¼ teaspoon baking powder
- 1¼-ounce icing sugar

Directions:

- Preheat the Air fryer to 340 o F and grease a baking sheet lightly.
- Mix butter, icing sugar, flour, and baking powder in a large bowl
- Blend well until a dough is formed and transfer into the piping bag fitted with a fluted nozzle.
- Pipe the dough onto a baking sheet and arrange the baking sheet in the air fryer.
- Cook for about 10 minutes and wait until golden brown and serve with tea.

975. Perfect Apple Pie

Preparation Time: 15 Minutes
Cooking Time: 30 Minutes
Servings: 6

Ingredients:

- One frozen pie crust, thawed
- One large apple, peeled, cored, and chopped
- One tablespoon butter, chopped
- One egg, beaten

Directions:

- Preheat the Air fryer to 320 o F and grease a pie pan lightly.
- Cut two crusts, first about 1/8-inch larger than pie pan and second, a little smaller than first one.
- Arrange the large crust at the bottom of the pie pan.
- Mix apple, two tablespoons of sugar, cinnamon, lemon juice, and vanilla extract in a large bowl
- Put the apple mixture evenly over the bottom crust and top with butter.
- Arrange the second crust on top and seal the edges.
- Cut four slits in the top crust carefully and brush with egg.
- Sprinkle with sugar and arrange the pie pan in the Air fryer basket.
- Cook for about 30 minutes and dish out to serve.

976. Crispy Fruit Tacos

Preparation Time: 5 Minutes
Cooking Time: 5 Minutes
Servings: 2

Ingredients:

- Two soft shell tortillas
- Four tablespoons strawberry jelly
- ¼ cup blueberries
- ¼ cup raspberries

Directions:

- Preheat the Air fryer to 300 $_0$ F and grease an Air fryer basket.
- Put two tablespoons of strawberry jelly over each tortilla and top with blueberries and raspberries.
- Sprinkle with powdered sugar and transfer into the Air fryer basket.
- Cook for about 5 minutes until crispy and serve.

977. Healthy Fruit Muffins

Preparation Time: 10 Minutes
Cooking Time: 10 Minutes
Servings: 6

Ingredients:

- 1 cup milk
- One pack Oreo biscuits, crushed
- ¾ teaspoon baking powder
- One banana, peeled and chopped
- One apple, peeled, cored, and chopped

Directions:

- Preheat the Air fryer to 320 $_0$ F and grease six muffin cups lightly.
- Mix milk, biscuits, cocoa powder, baking soda, and baking powder in a bowl until a smooth mixture is formed.
- Divide this mixture into the prepared muffin cups and transfer it into the air fryer basket.
- Cook for about 10 minutes and remove from Air fryer.

- Mix banana, apple, honey, lemon juice, and cinnamon in a bowl.
- Scoop out some portion from the center of muffins and fill with the fruit mixture.
- Refrigerate for 2 hours and serve chilled.

978. Chocolate Lover's Muffins

Preparation Time: 10 Minutes
Cooking Time: 10 Minutes
Servings: 8

Ingredients:

- 1½ cups all-purpose flour
- Two teaspoons baking powder
- One egg
- 1 cup yogurt
- ½ cup mini chocolate chips

Directions:

- Preheat the Air fryer to 355 $_0$ F and grease eight muffin cups lightly.
- Mix flour, baking powder, sugar, and salt in a bowl
- Whisk egg, oil, yogurt, and vanilla extract in another bowl.
- Combine the flour and egg mixtures and mix until a smooth mixture is formed.
- Fold in the chocolate chips and divide this mixture into the prepared muffin cups.
- Transfer into the Air fryer basket and cook for about 10 minutes.
- Refrigerate for 2 hours and serve chilled.

979. Delicate Pear Pouch

Preparation Time: 10 Minutes
Cooking Time: 15 Minutes
Servings: 4

Ingredients:

- Two small pears, peeled, cored, and halved
- 2 cups prepared vanilla custard
- Four puff pastry sheets
- One egg, beaten lightly

Directions:

- Preheat the Air fryer to 330 ₒ F and grease an Air fryer basket.
- Place a spoonful of vanilla custard and a pear half in the center of each pastry sheet.
- Blend sugar and cinnamon in a bowl, then sprinkle on the pear halves.
- Pinch the corners of sheets together to shape into a pouch and transfer into the Air fryer basket.
- Cook for about 15 minutes and top with whipped cream.
- Dish out and serve with the remaining custard.

980.   Red Velvet Cupcakes

Preparation Time: 15 Minutes
Cooking Time: 12 Minutes
Servings: 12

Ingredients:

- 2 cups refined flour
- ¾ cup peanut butter
- Three eggs
- 1 cup butter
- 1 cup cream cheese

Directions:

- Preheat the Air fryer to 340 ₒ F and grease 12 silicon cups lightly.
- For cupcakes:
- Mix all the fixings in a large bowl until well combined.
- Transfer the mixture into silicone cups and place them in the air fryer basket.
- Cook for about 12 minutes and dish out.
- For Frosting:
- Mix all the fixings in a large bowl until well combined.
- Top each cupcake evenly with frosting and serve.

981.   Apple Dumplings

Preparation Time: 10 Minutes
Cooking Time: 25 Minutes
Servings: 2

Ingredients:

- Two sheets puff pastry
- Two small apples, peeled and cored
- Two tablespoons raisins
- Two tablespoons butter, melted
- One tablespoon brown sugar

Directions:

- Preheat the Air fryer to 355 ₒ F and grease an Air fryer basket.
- Mix sugar and raisins in a bowl and fill each apple core with it.
- Place the apple in the center of each pastry sheet and fold to cover the apple completely.
- Seal the edges and transfer the dumplings into the Air fryer basket.
- Cook for about 25 minutes and dish out in a platter.

982.   Heavenly Tasty Lava Cake

Preparation Time: 10 Minutes
Cooking Time: 3 Minutes
Servings: 6

Ingredients:

- 2/3 cup unsalted butter
- Two eggs
- 2/3 cup all-purpose flour
- 1 cup chocolate chips, melted
- 1/3 cup fresh raspberries

Directions:

- Preheat the Air fryer to 355 ₒ F and grease six ramekins lightly.
- Mix sugar, butter, eggs, chocolate mixture, flour, and salt in a bowl until well combined.
- Fold in the melted chocolate chips and divide this mixture into the prepared ramekins.
- Transfer into the Air fryer basket and cook for about 3 minutes.
- Garnish with raspberries and serve immediately.

983.   Vegan Donuts

Preparation Time: 10 Minutes
Cooking Time: 15 Minutes
Servings: 4

Ingredients:

- 8 ounces whole wheat flour
- Two tablespoons coconut sugar
- One tablespoon flax meal mixed with two tablespoons water
- Two and ½ tablespoons vegetable oil
- One teaspoon baking powder

Directions:

- In a bowl, mix one tablespoon oil with sugar, baking powder, and flour and stir.
- In a second bowl, mix the flax meal with one and ½ tablespoons oil and milk and stir well.
- Combine the two mixtures, stir, shape donuts from this mix, place them in your air fryer's basket and cook using 360 degrees F for 15 minutes.
- Serve them warm.
- Enjoy!

984. Cinnamon Rice with Coconut

Preparation Time: 10 Minutes
Cooking Time: 35 Minutes
Servings: 4

Ingredients:

- Three and ½ cups of water
- 1 cup of coconut sugar
- 2 cups white rice, washed and rinsed
- Two cinnamon sticks
- ½ cup coconut, shredded

Directions:

- In your air fryer, mix water with coconut sugar, rice, cinnamon, and coconut, stir, cover, and cook at 365 degrees F for 35 minutes.
- Divide pudding into cups and serve cold.
- Enjoy!

985. Pineapple and Apricots

Preparation Time: 10 Minutes
Cooking Time: 12 Minutes
Servings: 10

Ingredients:

- 6 cups canned pineapple chunks, drained
- 4 cups canned apricots, halved and drained
- 3 cups natural applesauce
- 2 cups canned mandarin oranges, drained
- Two tablespoons stevia

Directions:

- Put pineapples, apricots, applesauce, oranges, cinnamon, and stevia in a pan that fits your air fryer, introduce in the fryer, and cook at 360 degrees F for 12 minutes.
- Divide into small bowls and serve cold.
- Enjoy!

986. Air-Fried Smores

Preparation Time: 5 Minutes
Cooking Time: 5 Minutes
Servings: 4

Ingredients:

- Whole graham crackers (4)
- Marshmallows (2)
- Chocolate - such as Hershey's (4 pieces)

Directions:

- Tear the graham crackers in half to make eight squares. Cut the marshmallows in half crosswise with a pair of scissors.
- Place the marshmallows cut side down on four graham squares. Place marshmallow side up in the Air Fryer basket, cook at 390° Fahrenheit for four to five minutes or wait until golden.
- Remove them from the fryer and place a piece Break all graham crackers in half to create eight squares—cut marshmallows in half crosswise with a pair of scissors.
- Place the marshmallows, cut side down, on four graham squares of chocolate and graham square on top of each toasted marshmallow and serve.

987. Banana Smores

Preparation Time: 5 Minutes
Cooking Time: 5 Minutes
Servings: 4

Ingredients:

- Bananas (4)
- Mini-peanut butter chips (3 tbsp.)
- Graham cracker cereal (3 tbsp.)
- Mini-chocolate chips - semi-sweet (3 tbsp.)

Directions:

- Heat the Air Fryer in advance at 400° Fahrenheit.
- Slice the un-peeled bananas lengthwise along the inside of the curve. Don't slice through the bottom of the peel. Open slightly - forming a pocket.
- Fill each pocket with chocolate chips, peanut butter chips, and marshmallows. Poke the cereal into the filling.
- Arrange the stuffed bananas in the fryer basket, keeping them upright with the filling facing up.
- Air-fry until the peel has blackened and the chocolate and marshmallows have toasted (6 minutes).
- Chill for 1-2 minutes. Spoon out the filling to serve.

988. Cherry Pie

Preparation Time: 5 Minutes
Cooking Time: 25 Minutes
Servings: 8

Ingredients:

- Cherry pie filling (21 oz. can)
- Milk (1 tbsp.)
- Refrigerated pie crusts (2)
- Egg yolk (1)

Directions:

- Warm the fryer at 310° Fahrenheit.
- Poke holes into the crust after placing it on a pie plate. Allow the excess to hang over the edges. Place in the Air Fryer for five (5) minutes
- Transfer the basket with the pie plate onto the countertop.
- Fill it with the cherries. Remove the excess crust.
- Cut the remaining crust into ¾-inch strips - weaving a lattice across the pie.
- Make an egg wash using the milk and egg. Brush the pie—Air-fry for 15 minutes. Serve with a scoop of ice cream.

989. Fluffy Peanut Butter Marshmallow Turnovers

Preparation Time: 5 Minutes
Cooking Time: 15 Minutes
Servings: 4

Ingredients:

- Filo pastry (4 defrosted sheets)
- Chunky peanut butter (4 tbsp.)
- Melted butter (2 oz.)
- Marshmallow fluff (4 tsp.)
- Sea salt (1 pinch)

Directions:

- Custom the temperature of the Air Fryer at 360° Fahrenheit.
- Use the melted butter to brush one sheet of the filo. Put the second sheet on top and brush it also with butter. Continue the process until you have completed all four sheets.
- Cut the layers into four—12-inch x 3-inch strips.
- Place one teaspoon of the marshmallow fluff on the underside and one tablespoon of the peanut butter.
- Fold the tip over the filo strip to form a triangle, making sure the filling is completely wrapped.
- Seal the ends by means of a slight amount of butter. Place the completed turnovers into the Air Fryer for three to five minutes.

- When done, they will be fluffy and golden brown.
- Add a touch of sea salt for the sweet/salty combo.

990.   Funnel Cake Bites

Preparation Time: 5 Minutes
Cooking Time: 15 Minutes
Servings: 8

Ingredients:

- Greek yogurt (1 cup)
- Self-rising flour (1 cup - divided)
- For Dusting: Powdered sugar
- Optional: Vanilla bean paste (1 tbsp.)

Directions:

- Heat the Air Fryer at 375° Fahrenheit.
- Combine the yogurt, ¾ of the flour, and vanilla if using.
- Roll out the dough using the remainder of the flour.
- Slice it into 32 squares and place in the Air Fryer (8 at a time).
- Set the timer for 4 minutes. Flip then over and continue to air-fry for another 3 to 4 minutes until ready.
- Lightly dust with the sugar as desired and serve.

991.   Healthy Pop-Tarts

Preparation Time: 25 Minutes
Cooking Time: 50 Minutes
Servings: 6

Ingredients:

- Strawberries (.33 cup or 8 oz. - quartered)
- Granulated sugar (.25 cup)
- Refrigerated pie crusts (14.1 oz. pkg. Use 1)
- Powdered sugar (.t cup/2 oz.)
- Lemon juice (1.5 tsp. /1 lemon)

Directions:

- Stir the strawberries and granulated sugar in a medium-sized microwavable bowl. Let the mixture stand for 15 minutes, stirring occasionally—microwave on high until shiny and reduced, about 10 minutes, stirring halfway through cooking. Cool completely, about 30 minutes.
- Roll the pie crust and cut it into a 12-inch circle on a lightly floured surface. Cut the dough into 12 rectangles (2.5 x 3-inch), rerolling scraps, as needed.
- Spoon about two teaspoons strawberry mixture into the center of six of the dough rectangles, leaving a .5-inch border. Brush the edges of filled dough rectangles with water, top with remaining dough rectangles, pressing edges with a fork to seal. Coat tarts well with a cooking oil spray.
- Place three tarts in a single layer in the Air Fryer basket, and cook at 350° Fahrenheit or until it's golden brown (10 min.). Repeat with remaining tarts.
- Place on a wire rack to cool wholly, about 30 minutes.
- Whisk the powdered sugar and lemon juice in a small bowl until smooth. Spoon the glaze over cooled tarts.
- If you want, add a few candy sprinkles.

992.   Plain Cheesecake

Preparation Time: 5 Minutes
Cooking Time: 25 Minutes
Servings: 15

Ingredients:

- Unsalted butter (2 tbsp.)
- Honey graham cracker crumbs (1 cup)
- Cream cheese (1 lb.)
- Large eggs (2)
- Vanilla extract (.5 tsp.)

Directions:

- Set the Air Fryer to reach 350° Fahrenheit.
- Cut a hole in the center of a piece of parchment paper and place it into the baking dish.

- Combine the graham cracker crust and the butter. Press the mixture into the baking pan. Air-fry for four minutes

- Blend the sugar and cream cheese with a mixer, adding one egg at a time until the mixture is creamy. Pour in the vanilla and stir well.

- Pour the cheese mixture into the top of the crust and place it back into the Air Fryer for 15 minutes lowering the heat to 310° Fahrenheit.

- Place in the fridge for about three hours before serving.

993. Yogurt Pineapple Sticks

Preparation Time: 5 Minutes
Cooking Time: 25 Minutes
Servings: 4

Ingredients:

- Pineapple (half of 1)
- Desiccated coconut (.25 cup)

The Dip:

- Fresh mint (1 small sprig)
- Vanilla yogurt (1 cup)

Directions:

- Warm the Air Fryer to reach 392° Fahrenheit.

- Slice the pineapple into stick segments. Dip the chunks of pineapple into the coconut. Arrange the sticks of pineapple into the cooker basket and air-fry for ten minutes.

- Dice the mint into fine pieces and mix in with the yogurt.

- Empty the dip into a serving dish. Arrange the baked sticks around the dip to serve.

994. Low Carb Snickerdoodle Cookies

Preparation Time: 5 Minutes
Cooking Time: 25 Minutes
Servings: 16

Ingredients:

- 2 cups superfine almond flour
- ½ tsp. baking soda

- ¾ cup erythritol sweetener
- 1 tsp. ground cinnamon
- 2 tbsp. erythritol

Directions:

- Switch on the oven to 350 degrees.

- Combine all the fixings until you form a stiff dough.

- Then roll the cookie dough into 16 equal-sized balls, about 1 ½ inches wide.

- Blend the sweetener and cinnamon in a small bowl to create the coating.

- Then roll the balls generously in the cinnamon coating.

- Place the covered cookie balls on a cookie sheet covered in parchment paper. Then gently smash with a flat round surface.

- Bake for 15 minutes, then cool before serving.

995. Low Carb Peanut Butter Cookies

Preparation Time: 5 Minutes
Cooking Time: 25 Minutes
Servings: 27

Ingredients:

- Two large eggs
- ½ cup erythritol
- One ¼ cup creamy peanut butter
- ¾ cup peanuts
- ¼ tsp. Salt

Directions:

- Crush the peanuts and set aside. Preheat the oven to 350 degrees and use a cookie sheet covered with parchment paper.

- Combine eggs, sweetener, salt, and creamy peanut butter in a blender or food processor. Manage until smooth and clean offsides when mixture sticks.

- Toss in crushed peanuts and join with other ingredients. Leave some crunch for texture.

- Scoop the dough into spheres and place them on a baking sheet.

- Press the dough using a fork to create a crosshatch top. Wipe fork with water before using it again.
- Bake for 20 minutes or wait until golden brown and crunchy.

996. Fried Oreos

Preparation Time: 10 Minutes
Cooking Time: 12 Minutes
Servings: 4

Ingredients:

- One can of refrigerated crescent rolls
- 8 Oreo cookies
- 1/2 cup milk
- 1/4 cup powdered sugar

Directions:

- Separate each crescent roll and flatten it with your hand.
- Dunk an Oreo in the milk quickly, then place it in the center of the crescent roll.
- Fold the crescent roll over the Oreo and press to close.
- Preheat your fryer to 375 degrees.
- Cook the Oreos for 12 minutes, flipping once at the halfway point.
- Dust the cookies with powdered sugar before serving.

997. Strawberry Cheesecake Chimichangas

Preparation Time: 15 Minutes
Cooking Time: 10 Minutes
Servings: 6

Ingredients:

- 6 (8-inch) soft flour tortillas
- 8 ounces cream cheese
- Two tablespoons sour cream
- One teaspoon vanilla extract
- 3/4 cups strawberries

Directions:

- Allow the cream cheese to soften and slice your strawberries into thin slices.
- Beat together cream cheese, vanilla, sugar, and sour cream.
- Fold the strawberries into the mixture.
- Spread the filling on the bottom 1/3 of each tortilla.
- Fold the bottom and top of the tortilla in, then roll it up from the sides.
- Cook at 340 for about 8 minutes or until the tortillas become crisp.
- Allow cooling a few minutes before serving.

998. Monkey Bread

Preparation Time: 7 Minutes
Cooking Time: 7 Minutes
Servings: 4

Ingredients:

- 1 cup self-rising flour
- 1 cup non-fat Greek yogurt
- One teaspoon sugar
- 1/2 teaspoon cinnamon

Directions:

- Mix the flour and yogurt until it forms a dough.
- Roll the dough and form a circle, then cut it into fourths.
- Flatten each quarter and cut it into eight pieces.
- Roll the pieces into balls.
- Combine cinnamon and sugar into a bag and shake well to mix.
- Add eight balls to the bag and shake to cover.
- Preheat the fryer to 375 degrees.
- Put the balls in a loaf pan that fits your basket.
- Cook in your fryer for 7 minutes.

999. Fried Banana Smores

Preparation Time: 5 Minutes
Cooking Time: 7 Minutes
Servings: 4

Ingredients:

- Four bananas
- Three tablespoons mini semi-sweet chocolate chips
- Three tablespoons mini peanut butter chips
- Three tablespoons mini marshmallows
- Three tablespoons graham cracker cereal

Directions:

- Preheat the fryer to 400 degrees.
- Cut the bananas lengthwise on the inside of the curve, being careful not to cut all the way through.
- Fill the banana with chocolate chips, peanut butter chips, and marshmallows.
- Press graham cracker pieces into any open areas.
- Put the bananas in the fryer, leaning on each other to keep them upright.
- Cook for 7 minutes and let cool slightly before serving.

1000. Quick Chocolate Mug Cake

Preparation Time: 2 Minutes
Cooking Time: 10 Minutes
Servings: 1

Ingredients:

- 1/4 cup self-rising flour
- Five tablespoons caster sugar
- One tablespoon cocoa powder
- Three tablespoons whole milk
- Three teaspoons coconut oil

Directions:

- Preheat the fryer to 400 degrees.
- Mix all of the ingredients in a coffee mug.
- Bake in the fryer for 10 minutes.
- Be careful when removing the mug. It will be hot.

1001. Mini Molten Lava Cakes

Preparation Time: 10 Minutes
Cooking Time: 10 Minutes

Servings: 4

Ingredients:

- Four ramekins
- 3 1/2 tablespoons self-rising flour
- 3 1/2 ounces unsalted butter
- 3 1/2 ounces dark chocolate pieces
- Two eggs

Directions:

- Spray the ramekins and set them aside.
- Thaw the chocolate and butter in a dish for thirty 30 at a time, mixing after each time.
- Beat the eggs and mix in the sugar.
- Stir egg and chocolate mixtures together, then add flour and mix well.
- Preheat your fryer to 375 degrees.
- Fill each ramekin with the batter about 3/4 of the way.
- Bake in your fryer for 10 minutes, then serve warm.

1002. Blueberry Apple Crumble

Preparation Time: 10 Minutes
Cooking Time: 15 Minutes
Servings: 2

Ingredients:

- One red apple
- 1/2 cup frozen blueberries
- 1/4 cup plus one tablespoon brown rice flour
- Two ramekins
- 1/2 teaspoon ground cinnamon

Directions:

- Finely dice the red apples.
- Mix the fruit in one bowl and all other ingredients in another.
- Preheat fryer to 350 degrees.
- Put the fruit in ramekins and sprinkle the flour mixture over it.
- Bake in the fryer for 15 minutes.

CONVERSION CHART FOR THE KITCHEN

VOLUME MEASUREMENT CONVERSIONS

Cups	Tablespoons	Teaspoons	Milliliters
		1 tsp	5 ml
1/16 cup	1 tbsp	3 tsp	15 ml
1/8 cup	2 tbsp	6 tsp	30 ml
1/4 cup	4 tbsp	12 tsp	60 ml
1/3 cup	5 1/3 tbsp	16 tsp	80 ml
1/2 cup	8 tbsp	24 tsp	120 ml
2/3 cup	10 2/3 tbsp	32 tsp	160 ml
3/4 cup	12 tbsp	36 tsp	180 ml
1 cup	16 tbsp	48 tsp	240 ml

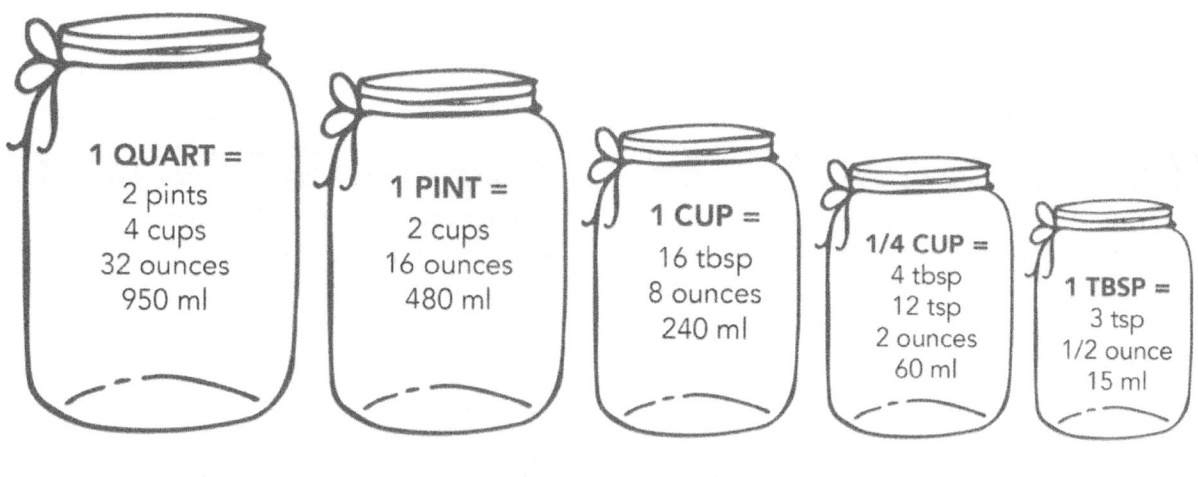

1 QUART =
2 pints
4 cups
32 ounces
950 ml

1 PINT =
2 cups
16 ounces
480 ml

1 CUP =
16 tbsp
8 ounces
240 ml

1/4 CUP =
4 tbsp
12 tsp
2 ounces
60 ml

1 TBSP =
3 tsp
1/2 ounce
15 ml

COOKING TEMPERATURE CONVERSIONS

Celcius/Centigrade	F= (C x 1.8) + 32
Fahrenheit	C= (F-32) x 0.5556

BAKING INGREDIENT CONVERSION

BUTTER

Cups	Grams
1/4 cup	57 grams
1/3 cup	76 grams
1/2 cup	113 grams
1 cup	227 grams

PACKED BROWN SUGAR

Cups	Grams	Ounces
1/4 cup	55 grams	1.9 oz
1/3 cup	73 grams	2.58 oz
1/2 cup	110 grams	3.88 oz
1 cup	220 grams	7.75 oz

ALL-PURPOSE FLOUR \ CONFECTIONER'S SUGAR

Cups	Grams	Ounces
1/8 cup	16 grams	.563 oz
1/4 cup	32 grams	1.13 oz
1/3 cup	43 grams	1.5 oz
1/2 cup	64 grams	2.25 oz
2/3 cup	85 grams	3 oz
3/4 cup	96 grams	3.38 oz
1 cup	128 grams	4.5 oz

GRANULATED SUGAR

Cups	Grams	Ounces
2 tbsp	25 grams	.89 oz
1/4 cup	50 grams	1.78 oz
1/3 cup	67 grams	2.37 oz
1/2 cup	100 grams	3.55 oz
2/3 cup	134 grams	4.73 oz
3/4 cup	150 grams	5.3 oz
1 cup	201 grams	7.1 oz

Made in the USA
Monee, IL
13 December 2021